FAMOUS EUROPEAN AIRCRAFT

SEPECAT Jaguar

JAMES JACKSON

SEPECAT Jaguar

A Development and Operational History

James Jackson

First published in 2025 by
Hikoki Publications Ltd
An imprint of Crécy Publishing Ltd
1a Ringway Trading Est
Shadowmoss Rd
Manchester
M22 5LH
England

www.crecy.co.uk

ISBN 9 781800 353299

Printed in Türkiye by Ozlem Print

MIX
Paper | Supporting responsible forestry
FSC® C176481
FSC www.fsc.org

COVER SEPECAT Jaguar GR.1A XZ112 diving during a photographic sortie in 1991 when No. 54(F) Squadron celebrated its 75th birthday with this colourful scheme featuring the squadron's blue and yellow chequerboard identification markings. ***Geoffrey Lee/BAE Systems***

BACK COVER MAIN Jaguar GR.3A XX766 of No. 16(R) Squadron flying a training sortie in 2002 carrying practice bomb carriers on the outer underwing hardpoints. ***Terry Panopalis Collection***

BACK COVER LOWER 1 Jaguar Marine prototype M05 is prepared for launch from the aircraft carrier *Clemenceau* during October 1971. The aircraft is loaded with six dummy bombs and a centreline fuel tank. ***Terry Panopalis Collection***

BACK COVER LOWER 2 Jaguar A4 during integration trials of the Aérospatiale AS.30L laser-guided air-to-surface missile and the Thomson-CSF ATLIS laser target designation pod. ***Blue Envoy Collection***

BACK COVER LOWER 3 Jaguar International OS204 of the Royal Air Force of Oman on a sortie in April 2006. ***Terry Panopalis Collection***

PAGE TWO Jaguar E19 of Escadron de Chasse 2/7 'Argonne' taking off from Base Aérienne BA 113 Saint Dizier-Robinson on training sortie in 1977. EC 2/7 was the Armeé de l'Air's Jaguar operational training unit. The artwork on the tail fin denotes this aircraft as belonging to Escadrille SPA 48 'Tête de Coq' (Rooster's Head). ***Author's Collection***

PAGE THREE Jaguar A27 of Escadron de Chasse EC 1/7 'Provence', Escadrille SPA 77 'Croix de Jerusalem' being flown in 1975 by Commandant Pelisson. ***Author's Collection***

ABOVE Jaguar GR.1A XX745 was assigned to No. 16(R) Squadron, the RAF's Jaguar Operational Conversion Unit, during the 1990s. The aircraft is painted in air defence grey with toned down markings and is carrying CBLS pods for practice bombs on the outboard hardpoints and two fuel tanks inboard. ***Terry Panopalis Collection***

Contents

A pair of Jaguars are escorting a Breguet Br.1150 Atlantique maritime patrol aircraft during a naval cooperation exercise. The ship they are overflying is the Landing Ship Dock *Orage*. *Author's Collection*

Acknowledgements

A book relies on the work and support of many people beyond that of the author. Firstly, I would like to thank my family, friends and work colleagues for all their support and encouragement throughout. I would like to give special thanks to Chris Gibson for all his kind assistance in the supply of information and images and for his invaluable editorial advice.

The research for this book has relied on primary sources to a large extent. Thanks must go to the staff of the National Archives at Kew, London. I also wish to thank Tony Wilson at the North West Heritage Group at Warton and Dave Forster and Erik Baigar, who provided very interesting background knowledge on avionics. I would also like to give a special mention to the Secret Projects Forum (*www.secretprojects.co.uk*) run by Paul Martell-Mead, which is an invaluable resource on an eclectic mix of aviation and defence projects and which is a productive hub and meeting place for aviation researchers from around the world.

The book would be incomplete without images. Special thanks go to Terry Panopalis for providing these from his seemingly inexhaustible archive and Julian Temple, BAE Systems' Heritage Archivist, for all his assistance. The French aviation historian Phillipe Ricco was generous in providing some very interesting photographs. Paul Chapman and Tony Buttler have also kindly dug through their personal archives to provide images. It has once again been a pleasure to work with Luca Landino, who wonderfully brought three of the Jaguar drawing board projects into life as three-dimensional digital artworks.

I must also thank those involved in the production of the book. Neil Lewis kindly edited the text and provided his reassuring guidance and support. It has been a pleasure to work with Jeremy Pratt, Jordan Bradley and Alistair Plumb at Crécy Publishing in bringing *SEPECAT Jaguar: A Development and Operational History* to fruition.

James Jackson, Morecambe, 2025

No. II(AC) Squadron was RAF Germany's specialist tactical reconnaissance unit flying the Jaguar, including XZ111, seen here on a training sortie during the early 1980s. ***MoD via Terry Panopalis Collection***

Introduction

The SEPECAT Jaguar was one of the most capable ground-attack fighter aircraft of its generation. The Jaguar was the result of two decades of collaboration between France and the United Kingdom and gave the Armée de l'Air and the Royal Air Force a potent strike platform that served for thirty years before its retirement in the early 2000s in both air forces. Today, the Jaguar is still in front-line service with the Indian Air Force and was also acquired by the air forces of Ecuador, Oman and Nigeria. The Jaguar is most often remembered for its contribution to Operation Desert Storm over the skies of Kuwait and Iraq in 1990, but its combat career included lesser-known conflicts in Mauritania, Chad and Bosnia. Having entered service fifty years ago, the Jaguar is undeniably old enough to qualify as a 'classic' aircraft. It was unmistakable with its thin but 'lumpy' fuselage, high-mounted swept wing, stalky undercarriage and its twin jet exhausts shaded by large anhedral tailplanes.

Although often overshadowed by its contemporaries in terms of performance, equipment and saleability, the Jaguar communities of pilots and groundcrew around the world formed a tight-knit esprit de corps who knew that the aircraft could be demanding and would catch out an unwary pilot, but they were happy to fly it to the maximum of its designed performance. Jokes by the pilots like 'it only takes off due to the curvature of the earth' highlighted its main Achilles heel, but the pilots knew that the Jaguar was dependable and rugged and in combat the type proved its worth alongside the best of the competition of its era. Its charm outweighed any shortcomings and engendered a fierce loyalty from its pilots and the groundcrews who maintained the aircraft.

The Jaguar was an aircraft of contrasts from the very beginning; a fighter born out of the need for a supersonic trainer; a product of Anglo-French collaboration in aviation technology but perceived – rightly or wrongly – as being neglected by its Gallic parent; the Adour engine that proved dependable and remains in production today but which never gave the Jaguar enough power; an aircraft with one of the world's first digital weapon systems but without radar; a low-attitude attacker that found itself fighting as a medium-level dive-bomber. It was an aircraft whose limelight was often taken by the

One of the early production two-seat Jaguar International OB conversion trainers on a test flight before delivery in 1977 to the Sultan of Oman's Air Force. ***Terry Panopalis Collection***

Jaguar GR.1A XZ362 of No. 41(F) Squadron, RAF, equipped for the reconnaissance role with a recce pod under the fuselage and a Phimat chaff dispenser pod on the outer starboard wing hardpoint. ***Terry Panopalis Collection***

Hawker Siddeley Harrier capable of vertical take-off and landing and Dassault's extensive Mirage family of fighters.

In service, the Jaguar proved to be an adaptable aircraft, fulfilling the roles of ground attack, tactical nuclear bomber, reconnaissance, advanced flying training and being upgraded to become a precision strike platform and an anti-ship strike aircraft. The Jaguar also went to sea, the Jaguar M being developed to provide France's Marine Nationale with a modern strike aircraft. Sadly, a mixture of cost and several technical issues prevented this version from entering service.

This book is the history of the Jaguar from its very beginnings in 1962 as a potential training platform to the current day. Starting with the French ECAT (avion école combat et d'appui tactique) requirement, the background history on both sides of the Channel is discussed before heading to the technical development of the Jaguar and the formation of the SEPECAT (Société Européenne de Production de l'avion Ecole de Combat et d'Appui Tactique) company in 1966. The flight testing programme is also explored in depth, revealing how complicated and cutting edge the Jaguar was. Service use by all six operators of the Jaguar is examined in depth, including the technical developments and upgrades made over the years. The political background to the export deals for the Jaguar International, including those that did not come to fruition for one reason or another, are also explained. The Active Control Technology research aircraft conversion to conduct research into fly-by-wire flight control systems is also examined, as are several proposed developments – such as the Big Wing Jaguar – that remained on the drawing board.

Originally this book was to have been part of a series on Famous British Aircraft, but given the Jaguar's Anglo-French heritage it is only fitting that it sits within a Famous European Aircraft series to mark its success as a collaborative venture.

Note on Units

The Jaguar was a product of the French aviation industry and a British aviation industry converting to metric measurements, and was naturally measured in metric units of measurement. For consistency of the intended readership, all data is provided in imperial units with conversion to metric units. Speeds are given in knots (kt) and Mach numbers (where relevant), weights are given in pounds (lb) and kilograms (kg). Range figures using nautical miles (nm) have been used throughout. Where possible aircraft weights quoted in the main text will be the all-up weight (AUW), which includes the weight of the aircraft's structure, engines, fuel, oil, crew and payload. Exceptions to this are noted in the text.

Note on Designations

All aircraft serving with the British armed forces are given an official designation outlining their role and a Mark number denoting major differences between variants. For example, the Jaguar was given the 'GR' prefix for the Ground attack Reconnaissance role, rendered as GR.Mk.1. In the main text the designations are presented in a shortened form, for example, GR.1.

CHAPTER ONE

ECAT to Jaguar

The SEPECAT Jaguar had an unlikely family history for a tactical fighter. Its roots stretched back to light fighter prototypes of the mid-1950s and two-seat training aircraft. But the background was more complicated than that, melding two disparate sets of requirements for the air forces of two nations. During the early 1960s, the Armeé de l'Air (AdlA) wanted a basic subsonic tactical ground-attack fighter that could also be built as a two-seat advanced trainer. At the same time, the Royal Air Force (RAF) had its sights set on a supersonic advanced trainer capable of speeds up to Mach 2 and equipped with variable-geometry wings.

International collaboration in the aviation sector was increasing as governments sought to reduce the financial burden of research and development (R&D) and to spread the production costs across a larger production run. France became the United Kingdom's preferred partner and both air forces quickly saw the similarities between their requirements and political encouragement provided the necessary impetus to find enough common ground on which to build a unified design. Even so, the end result was perhaps not what either partner really wanted at the time; indeed the subsequent career of the Jaguar with both users reflected this dichotomy until the end of its service life four decades later.The aviation industries on either side of the English Channel produced several advanced designs but the United Kingdom's decision to give the French the leadership of the programme saw Britain's manufacturers efforts ending in vain. The Breguet Br.121

The SEPECAT Jaguar's origins were French, intended as a subsonic lightweight tactical fighter, but collaboration with the United Kingdom saw it emerge as a more sophisticated supersonic aircraft. This aircraft is A92 of the Escadron de Chasse 2/11 'Vosges' in the late 1970s. ***Author's Collection***

emerged as a sound basis for further development in partnership to create what became the Jaguar. The engine was also developed collaboratively. Even the way of doing business together was new, as both nations set up a new joint company – SEPECAT – to manage the programme. Within a short space of time, the Jaguar was further developed as the RAF's emphasis switched to finding a new ground-attack fighter and the French Marine Nationale sought a new attack aircraft for its aircraft carriers.

ECAT

The AdlA had introduced the supersonic delta-winged Dassault Mirage IIIC interceptor into service during 1959 and its larger derivative, the Mirage IVA nuclear bomber, in 1964. Flying training at this time was conducted using Lockheed T-33 Shooting Stars obtained from the USA during the 1950s and the Fouga CM.170R Magisters – the world's first twin-engined jet-powered basic trainer – which had entered service in 1956. The student pilots faced a large step up from these relatively basic subsonic trainers to the Mirage IIIB operational conversion trainer, which in addition was expensive to operate. The planned Mirage IIIV vertical/short take-off and landing (V/STOL) tactical strike fighter was expensive and the AdlA realised that a cheaper fighter would be needed to operate alongside it. The desire for a light tactical fighter had existed since 1953 and had been subsumed within North Atlantic Treaty Organisation (NATO) requirement NBMR.2 a year later, although its outcome – the Fiat G.91 – had been politically unacceptable for purchase by the French. By 1959, the AdlA's attention had switched to equally abortive V/STOL concepts. In 1962 the Service Technique de l'Aéronautique (STAé – Technical Department of Aeronautics), which defined the AdlA's technical requirements and evaluated proposals from industry, began working on the Ecole/Appui (ECAP) requirement for a trainer with a ground-attack capability. The planned in-service date for ECAP was 1968.

Within two years, however, ECAP was superseded by the Ecole de Combat et Appui Tactique (ECAT) requirement, which altered the priority to a light tactical strike fighter that could be developed into a trainer. ECAT was intended for the AdlA and the Marine Nationale's air arm, the Aéronavale, and was released to the aviation industry in January 1964. The performance requirements included a maximum speed of Mach 0.9 at sea level, a range of 269nm (500km) at 450kt, rapid acceleration from 450kt to Mach 0.9 as well as being capable of sustaining 3.5g turns at maximum speed. Flight handling was especially important for a training aircraft and the requirements called for excellent low-altitude manoeuvrability and excellent handling, even in rough weather conditions, and no aerodynamic disturbances at high speed. ECAT also called for good take-off performance, with the tactical fighter to be capable of getting airborne within 2,625ft (800m) from an unprepared strip. Turnaround time between sorties, including rearming and refuelling, was not to exceed 15 minutes.

Armament would be two fixed 30mm DEFA (Direction des Études et Fabrications d'Armement) cannon with 100 rounds of ammunition each and five external hardpoints rated to carry the Nord AS.30 air-to-surface missile (ASM), Matra/Hawker Siddeley Dynamics AS.37 Martel anti-radar missile or 880lb (400kg) bombs, napalm tanks and rocket pods. Two oblique cameras or one panoramic version would be fitted in the nose for photographic reconnaissance. Avionics would include a simple gyroscopic gunsight, missile control equipment, Doppler radar and a twin gyro platform for navigation as well as Tactical Air Navigation (TACAN) and a bearing and distance indicator.

The emphasis of the programme was on the fighter, but the need for the trainer version was more urgent and was required in service first – by 1970. Within two months of the release of ECAT, the British and French had agreed to co-operate on the programme and the requirements were altered to accommodate the RAF's needs.

ECAT contenders

At least five designs were seriously considered and evaluated: the Breguet Br.121, Dassault MD.911 Cavalier, Nord 3600 Harpon, Potez CM.173 Super Magister and the Sud Aviation SA.125.

Breguet Aviation seemed well placed to offer a winning design. In 1953 it had begun work on the Br.1100 single-seat light tactical strike fighter. Powered by a pair of reheated Turbomeca Gabizo turbojets, a prototype was flown on 31 March 1957. Unfortunately, greater than expected drag around the rear fuselage prevented the attainment of supersonic speed. The closely related Br.1001 Taon was redesigned for a single unreheated Bristol Siddeley Orpheus 3 turbojet to meet NBMR.2. The two prototypes – 01 completed to French standards and 02 to NATO standard – made their maiden flights on 25 July 1957 and 18 January 1958 respectively. On 25 April 1958 prototype 01 broke the speed record for a 540nm (1,000km) closed circuit at 564.6kt. Despite its good performance, the NATO assessment favoured the Fiat G.91 and the Breguet aircraft were quickly shelved. Breguet, however, continued to refine the basic design; the Br.1003 of 1957 with a larger wing and a more powerful Orpheus 12 engine and the navalised Br.1003M for the Aéronavale, but neither were built. The Br.1005 was proposed in November 1958 with an enlarged wing with reduced 25° leading edge sweep and the armament was modified with a ventral retractable rocket pack that could be replaced by a photo-reconnaissance pack.

ECAT Designs						
	Breguet Br.121	Dassault MD.911 Cavalier	Dassault MD.912 Cavalier II	Nord 3600 Harpon	Potez CM.173 Super Magister	Potez P.92
Span	26ft 11in (8.2m)	28ft 2.5in (8.6m)	26ft 11in (8.2m)	–	37ft 1in (11.3m)	–
Length	53ft 2in (16.2m)	45ft 3in (13.79m)	40ft 0in (12.2m)	–	33ft 5.5in (10.2m)	46ft 7in (14.2m)
Wing area	–	–	215.1ft² (20m²)	344.1ft² (27m²)	186ft² (17.3m²)	–
Gross weight	15,430lb (7,000kg)	13,645lb (6,190kg)	16,005lb (7,260kg)	22,490lb (10,200kg) with Orpheus, 27,480lb (12,465kg) with Tourmalet	7,450lb (3,380kg)	–
Powerplant	Two Tourmalet 6,750lbf (30kN)	Two GE J85 4,050lbf (18kN)	Two RB.172-45R 4,750lbf (27kN) reheated	Two Tourmalet, RB.172-49R, M45 or Orpheus 803	Two Marboré VI 1,080lbf (4.8kN)	Two Tourmalet, RB.172-45R or M45
Maximum speed/height	Mach 1.8	Mach 1.5	Mach 1.6 at 36,090ft (11,000m)	Mach 0.96 with Orpheus, Mach 2.08 with M45 at 36,090ft (11,000m)	Mach 0.82	Mach 0.97 clean, Mach 0.92-0.95 with one AS.37 Martel missile
Armament	Two 30mm DEFA cannon, five hardpoints for bombs and rockets	Two 30mm DEFA cannon, five hardpoints for bombs and rockets	One 30mm DEFA cannon, seven hardpoints for bombs and rockets	Two 30mm DEFA cannon, five hardpoints for bombs and rockets	Two 12.7mm machine guns, four hardpoints for bombs and rockets	Seven hardpoints for bombs and rockets

The starting point for the Jaguar, the Breguet Br.1001 Taon. ***Author's Collection***

For its ECAT submission, Breguet dusted off the Br.1000 series and further refined it as the Br.121. The wings were enlarged and the fuselage was redesigned for two 6,750lbf (30kN) thrust Turbomeca T-260 Tourmalet turbofans that offered a maximum speed of Mach 1.8 at altitude. The gross weight was estimated to be 15,430lb (7,000kg). Using the Br.1000 airframe offered a rugged design that would be easy to maintain. The versatility of the basic design was demonstrated by the five versions that were offered:

- Br.121A – single-seat tactical strike aircraft
- Br.121B – two-seat tactical strike aircraft
- Br.121C – private-venture single-seat interceptor to capitalise on the supersonic performance
- Br.121E – two-seat training aircraft
- Br.121P – single-seat reconnaissance aircraft

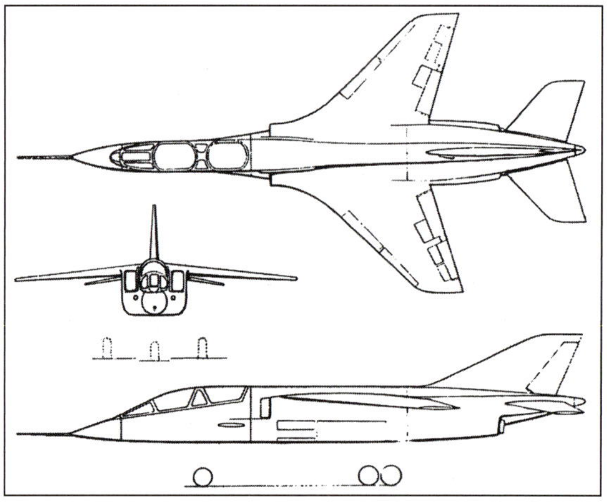

The Breguet Br.121 differs in detail from the Jaguar, notably the arrangement of the intakes, the tandem undercarriage mainwheel configuration and the location of 30mm DEFA cannon in the lower fuselage. ***Author's Collection***

The armament was a pair of 30mm DEFA cannon and three or five external hardpoints, one on the fuselage centreline and the remainder under the wings. The armament of the Br.121C included two Matra R.530 air-to-air missiles (AAMs). The Br.121F could carry up to four cameras in the nose. The Br.121 could take off from within 1,970ft (600m) from an unprepared strip and had sufficient range to carry a weapons load weighing 1,320lb (600kg) over 270nm (500km) with a ferry range of 2,700nm (5,000km) with external fuel tanks.

Dassault Aviation announced its MD.911 Cavalier programme on 9 March 1964 and declared their intention to have a prototype flying for the following year's Paris Air Show. Dassault and Nord Aviation agreed to co-operate on 14 May; both would offer their own submissions but agreed that if either company won the contract the production would be shared. The Cavalier was offered in single-seat attack and two-seat trainer versions. Originally designed with a low-mounted wing and a T-tail, the design evolved during 1965 with a shoulder-mounted wing with leading edge root extensions above the engine intakes and the horizontal tailplanes were moved to the lower fuselage. Unusually for a French design, the engines were to be sourced from America – a pair of 4,050lbf (18kN) General Electric J85 turbojets, which provided a maximum speed of

Mach 1.5. Gross weight was estimated at 13,645lb (6,190kg). The armament was two 30mm DEFA cannon and five external hardpoints, including the capability to carry an AS.37 Martel ASM on the centreline station. A full-scale mock-up was built but no prototype would ever appear at the Paris Air Show.

Dassault refined the strike version into the MD.912 Cavalier II powered by two 4,725lbf (21kN) Rolls-Royce RB.172-45R engines with two additional underwing hardpoints. The Cavalier III reverted to the J85s and had modified leading edge root extensions, but its inferior range compared to the Cavalier I saw it being abandoned. Dassault also designed the MD.921 with a variable-geometry (VG) wing along with the navalised MD.922.

Nord Aviation designed the 3600 Harpon. Nord's designers made use of a modular fuselage that could be easily adapted for the training role. The two engines – either a pair of Tourmalet, RB.172-45 or -49R, Orpheus 803 or SNECMA M45 Mars – were enclosed by removable panels to ensure easy maintenance and which allowed easy future upgrading with different engines. The aircraft's systems were specially designed to achieve the required 15-minute turnaround time between sorties. Nord studied a number of wing layouts, including 45° and 50° swept wings, before settling on a low-mounted cropped delta. Leading edge root extensions below the intakes shielded them from debris on take-off and gun gas ingestion during strafing attacks. Armament was a pair of 30mm DEFA cannon and external hardpoints, including a Martel on the centreline. Gross weight was the highest of the ECAT designs at 22,490lb (10,200kg).

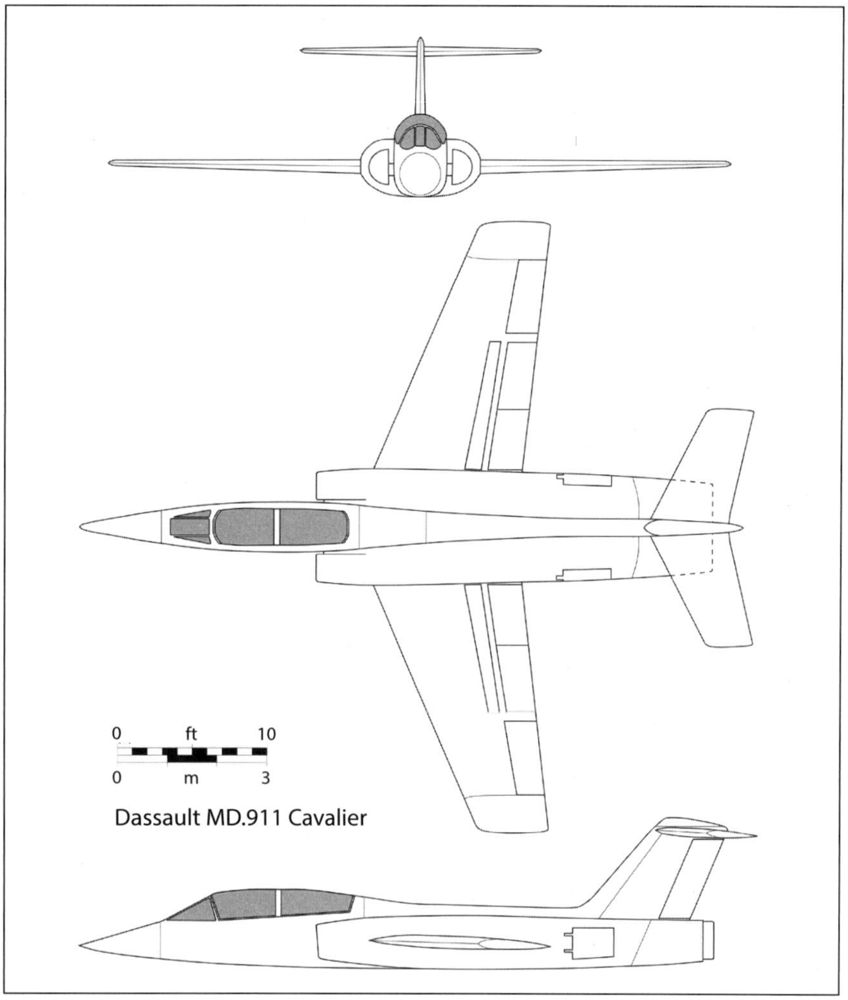

The original MD.911 Cavalier was a relatively basic design that went through many iterations, but which lost out to the Br.121. ***Author***

Potez had acquired Fouga in 1958 and were keen to update the Magister to maintain their position supplying the AdlA with trainers. The upgraded CM.173 Super Magister featured 1,080lbf (4.8kN) Turbomeca Marboré VI turbojets, integral wing fuel tanks and improved electrics and avionics. The prototype made its maiden flight on 8 June 1964 but no production order was received. The P.94 was a further development with a pair of 1,190lbf (5.3kN) Super Marboré VI and fitted with the longer-stroke undercarriage of the navalised CM.175 Zéphyr. No fixed armament was offered but the underwing hardpoints could accommodate gun pods, rocket pods, bombs or anti-tank missiles. The CM.173 was rebranded as the P.94A in August 1965 to act as the prototype for the production standard P.94B. No order was received and licence production discussions with South Africa in 1966 failed to obtain an agreement.

Potez also offered a new design, the unusual P.92 with a low swept wing and tailplanes with two Tourmalet, M45 or RB.172 engines mounted in separate nacelles above the rear fuselage just ahead of the

One of the ECAT requirements was the carriage of a single AS.37 Martel ASM, which is depicted hanging from the ventral pylon of the two-seat Br.121B tactical strike aircraft. ***Breguet via Author's Collection***

RIGHT The Potez CM.173 was an updated Magister. The prototype F-ZWWL was flown but achieved no sales success. *Philippe Ricco*

BELOW The Potez P.92 was an unusual design with a bulbous lower fuselage faired into the wing roots that contained the twin-wheel main undercarriage and the 30mm DEFA cannon. The wing has leading-edge slats and the small rectangles at the wing root are spoiler airbrakes. This is the single-seat version; the two-seater would sacrifice a fuselage fuel tank. *Author*

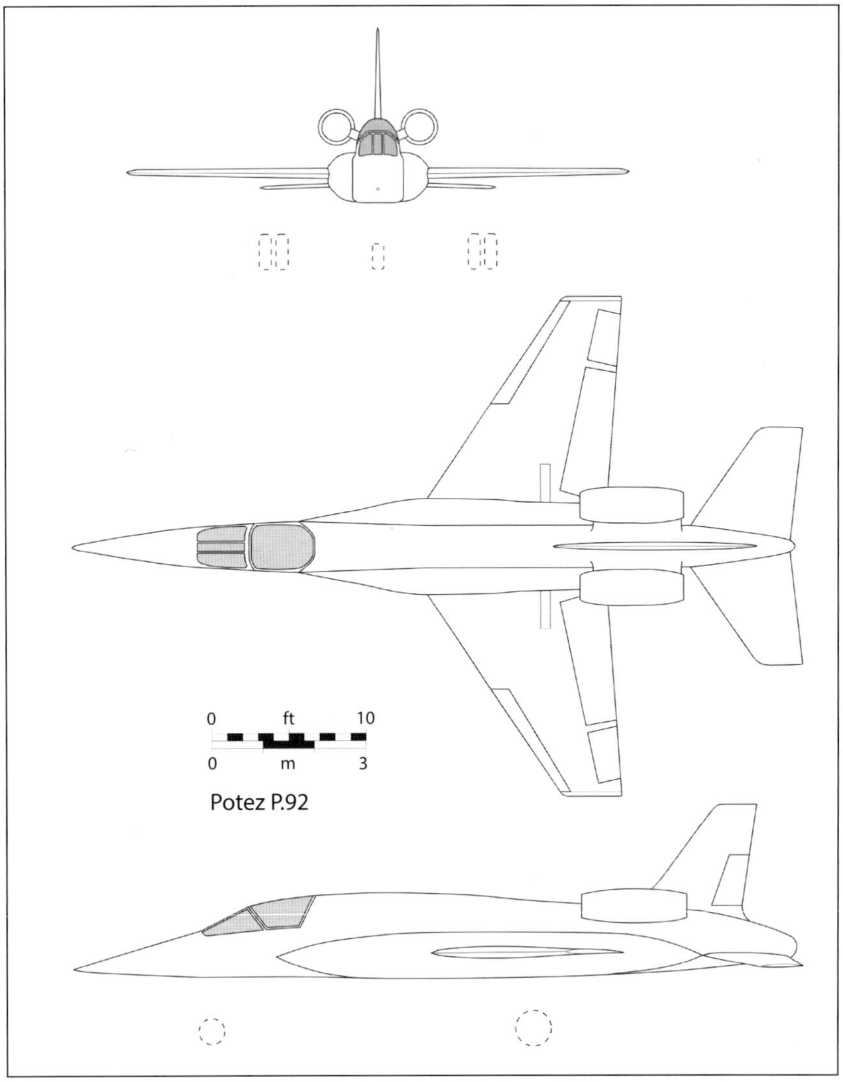

vertical tail fin (a similar arrangement to the later Republic A-10A Thunderbolt II attack aircraft). Seven external hardpoints were provided, including a single Martel on the centreline pylon. Sud Aviation offered a twin-engined aircraft, the SA.125, but little is known about this design.

AST.362

By 1960 the RAF had recognised the need for an advanced trainer with supersonic performance on which to train student pilots before they were posted to an Operational Conversion Unit (OCU) to prepare them for joining a front-line squadron. The arrival of the English Electric Lightning into Fighter Command service in 1960 had required Flying Training Command to seek new aircraft to cope with the increased demands on pilots' flying abilities. Two trainers with transonic performance were in service by 1962, the Hawker Hunter T.7 and the Folland Gnat T.1, but training needs continued to grow in complexity. The future replacements for the Hunter, English Electric Canberra, de Havilland Sea Vixen and Blackburn Buccaneer were all to be sophisticated supersonic aircraft, in particular the British Aircraft Corporation (BAC) TSR.2 being designed for automatic terrain-following flight and the V/STOL Hawker Siddeley P.1154. An advanced trainer to bridge the gap between these advanced aircraft and the subsonic Percival Jet Provost T.4, on which the student earned their wings, was required for the 1970s.

The Air Staff wanted an advanced trainer that could give students experience of steep climbing attitudes and supersonic terrain-following flight so that they were adequately prepared for the operational training at the OCU by honing their reaction times. The Northrop T-38A Talon supersonic advanced trainer, which had entered service with the United States Air Force in 1961, was influential in indicating the kind of capability that the RAF was looking for.

In December 1961 the Air Ministry began drafting AST.362 for a Variable Geometry Pilot Training Aircraft for advanced and operational conversion training. At this time the VG wing was the aircraft designers' favoured method of obtaining docile and safe handling at low speeds for take-off and landing, while retaining optimal low drag for sustained supersonic performance. To obtain high lift for low-speed flight, the leading edge sweep would be reduced and for supersonic flight at altitude the wings would be swept back to increase the leading edge sweep and decrease the wing area. The required speed with the wings in the forward position was 400kt between sea level and 10,000ft (3,050m) and Mach 0.75 between 10,000–30,000ft (3,050–9,145m). Enough internal fuel was required for two 50-minute sorties. With the wings swept back the speed would be Mach 0.95 at sea level and Mach 1.2 at 40,000ft (12,190m), with enough fuel for 50 minutes.

By June 1962 these performance limits had been increased; Mach 0.9 at sea level and Mach 1.2 at the tropopause with 60 minutes' endurance with the wings extended and Mach 0.93 and Mach 2.0 respectively with 45 minutes' endurance with full sweep. The aircraft had to be capable of operating from a 6,000ft (1,830m) runway in the wet and able to sustain a 1.5g turn (later increased to 1.75g) at 48,000ft (14,630m). A fatigue life of 6,000 flight hours was required. Originally even VTOL capability was desired, despite the additional technical complication that this would add.

The inclusion of a secondary armed counter-insurgency role had the immediate effect of requiring AST.362's classification to be increased to 'Secret'. The armament requirements covered 1,000lb (454kg) retarded bombs, 28lb (12kg) practice bombs and a nuclear weapon simulator. Two 30mm ADEN cannon would also be fitted (Armament Development Enfield; the Armament Development Establishment being the weapon's designers and the Royal Small Arms Factory at Enfield being the manufacturer). The cockpit was to be equipped to represent the latest front-line types with advanced avionics such as head-up displays (HUD), an Inertial Navigation System (INS), TACAN and an Instrument Landing System (ILS). In addition, the naval trainer would have precision radar approach equipment.

Cost was another key factor and AST.362 sought value for money by remaining viable in the training role into the 1980s. The rear cockpit would be used not only by the flying instructors but also trainee navigators to teach crew co-operation. It was argued that by the early 1970s live armament and radar training would be less commonplace as cheaper simulators took over these roles. Even so, the estimated cost of £200 per flying hour was far greater than the Gnat at £84 or the Hunter's £90. The annual running costs for a fleet of AST.362 aircraft would be £4.74 million compared to £1.26 million for the Gnat. As development of the TSR.2 and P.1154 became bogged down in technical, fiscal and inter-service political issues during 1963, AST.362 was deferred with a revised in-service date of 1975. The Royal Navy would require 45 aircraft. On top of the estimated R&D costs of £47 million, the unit cost was £460,000, so buying 150 aircraft could cost up to £92.5 million. While some offset could be gained from selling surplus Gnats and Hunters on the export market, it was estimated that the total expenditure, including running costs, between 1966 and 1980 could total £116 million.

AST.362 contenders

Folland Aircraft Limited at Hamble, which had been part of the Hawker Siddeley Aviation group since 1959, was eager to promote a successor to the Gnat and had begun design work while AST.362 was being formulated. Until this time, most of the VG wing studies in Britain had been conducted by Vickers at Weybridge, building on work begun by Barnes Wallis for his Swallow intercontinental airliner project. When Vickers merged with English Electric to form BAC in 1960 this expertise was dispersed across the industry. Maurice Brennan left Weybridge, where he had been working on the OR.346 studies for a VG research aircraft intended to result in a two-seat naval strike aircraft, to take up position as Chief Engineer at Folland. Hawker Siddeley's Technical Director, Stuart Davies, suggested to Brennan that he should apply his knowledge of VG wings into further developing the Gnat.

The first result of this effort was the single-engined Fo.146 trainer proposed in October 1960 with a VG wing. By January 1962 the Fo.146 had been optimised for the light strike role, powered by two Rolls-Royce RB.153 turbofans. At the time of Brennan's arrival Folland had been working on the Gnat Mk.5, an advanced supersonic development with a new 5% thickness/chord (t/c) ratio wing. The Gnat Mk.5 was planned in two variants; a single-seat light fighter equipped with Ferranti AI.23 AIRPASS radar and as a two-seat trainer. Powered by two reheated RB.153R turbofans, the maximum speed was estimated to be Mach 2.4 with a time to 50,000ft (15,240m) of three minutes and a maximum ceiling of 60,000ft (18,290m).

Brennan fitted a VG wing to create the Fo.147. The wings could be swept between 0° and 25° at low speeds and were fitted with slotted trailing edge flaps to give the same low-speed performance as the Gnat. Sweeping the wings backwards to 60–70° would allow speeds up to Mach 2.2 – the brochure optimistically claimed that speeds up to Mach 3 might be possible with further development. The wing sweep mechanism consisted of

AST362 Designs							
	Fo.147	Fo.148	HS.1170B	HS.1173	P.45 EAG.3410 & EAG.3411	P.45 EAG.3408 & EAG3409	P.45 EAG.3397 MP.2 & MP.3
Span	36ft 6in (11.13m) forward, 18ft 0in (5.49m) swept	35ft 0in (10.67m) forward	25ft 0in (7.62m)	25ft 0in (7.62m)	36ft 7in (11.15m) forward, 20ft 2in (6.15m) swept	24ft 4.5in (7.45m)	36ft 7in (11.15m) forward, 20ft 2in (6.15m) swept
Length	51ft 0in (15.54m)	47ft 0in (14.33m)	50ft 0in (15.24m)	35ft 0in (13.72m)	45ft 2in (13.77m)	45ft 4.5in (13.83m) EAG3408, 45ft 0in (13.71m) EAG.3409	48ft 11in (14.92m) MP.2, 49ft 0in (14.93m) MP.3
Wing area	186ft^2 (17.3m^2) forward, 195ft^2 (18.1m^2) swept	–	200ft^2 (18.6m^2)	210ft^2 (19.5m^2)	160ft^2) (14.8m^2) (forward, 138.5ft^2 (12.8m^2) swept	305ft^2 (17.3m^2)	160ft^2 (14.8m^2) forward, 138.5ft^2 (12.8m^2) swept
All-up weight	18,500lb (8,392kg)	16,500lb (7,848kg)	20,850lb (9,458kg)	20,250lb (9,185kg)	19,700lb (8,935kg) EAG.3410, 18,830lb (8,541kg) EAG.3411	18,830lb (8,541kg) EAG.3409	18,560lb (8,418kg) MP.2, 19,950lb (9,049kg) MP.3
Powerplant	Two RB.153 reheated	One RB.153-64, 11,750lbf (52.2kN) reheated	One BS.94/5, 19,000lbf (84.8kN) with PCB	One RB.72-57AR, 13,000lbf (57.8kN) reheated	Two scaled RB.172054 EAG3410, scaled RB.172-54R EAG.3411	Two scaled RB.172-54 EAG3408, scaled RB.172-54R EAG.3409	One RB.168-1R Spey MP.2, RB.168-1 Spey MP.3
Max Speed/ height	Mach 2.2	Mach 2.05	Mach 1.7 at 36,000ft (10,970m)	Mach 2.4 at 36,000ft (10,970m)	Mach 2.2 at 36,000ft (10,970m)	Mach 2.2 at 36,000ft (10,970m)	Mach 2.2 at 36,000ft (10,970m)
Armament	None	Two hardpoints for Bullpup ASMs or Red Top AAMs	Five hardpoints for bombs and rockets	Two 30mm ADEN cannon, five hardpoints for bombs and rockets	Two 30mm ADEN cannon, five hardpoints for bombs and rockets EAG.3410	Two 30mm ADEN cannon, five hardpoints for bombs and rockets EAG.3409	Two 30mm ADEN cannon, one hardpoint for AS.37 Martel MP.3

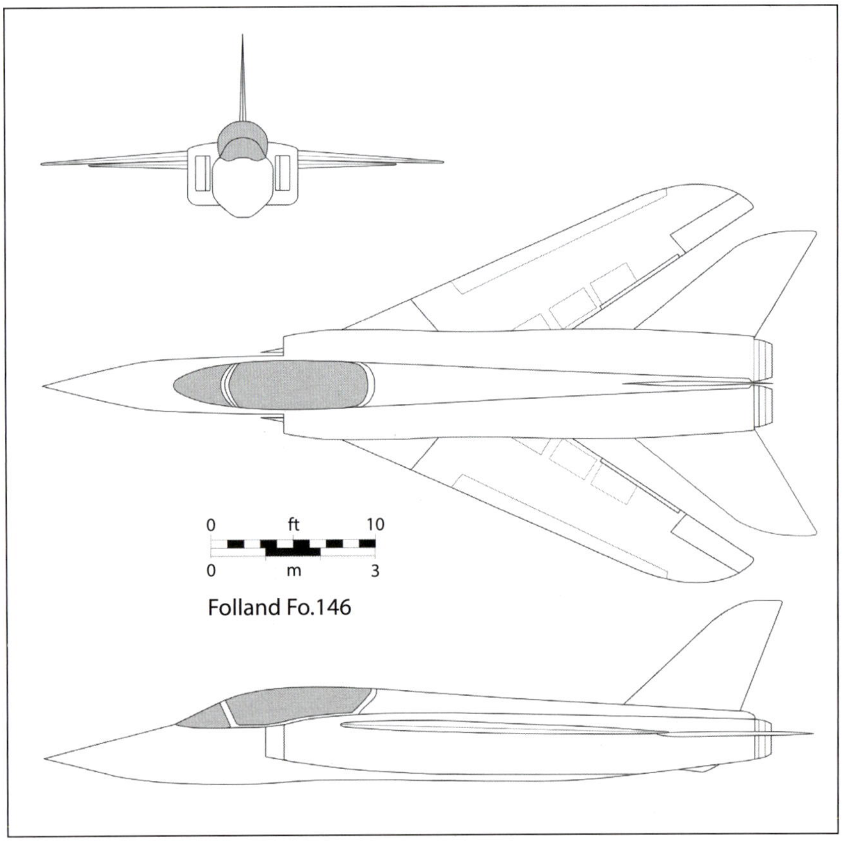

The Folland Fo.146 incorporated design work from the Gnat Mk.5 and variable-geometry wings due to Maurice Brennan's influence as Folland's newly appointed Chief Engineer. ***Author***

three tracks in the fuselage and ball-screws driven by duplicated hydraulic motors. As the sweep decreased the leading edge of the wing moved down the track along the fuselage. The Mk.5's horizontal tailplanes were replaced by a retractable, rotating, all-moving foreplane beneath the forward fuselage for trimming combined with all-moving wing tip elevons. A second design option retained a conventional set of all-moving tail surfaces. The estimated all-up weight (AUW) for the tailless design was 18,500lb (8,390kg). The Fo.147 was pitched as an advanced trainer capable of flying simulated operational flight profiles, but it was proposed that weapons training would use the dedicated two-seat fighter variant equipped with radar and carrying a payload of up 2,500lb (1,133kg) of AAMs, ASMs, rocket pods or bombs.

The Fo.148 was a design closer to its Gnat origins and appeared in May 1962. The wing sweep mechanism was similar in concept to the Fo.147's but used an aerodynamically cleaner 'pivot and shoe' arrangement that removed the moving parts ahead of the wing. The wing had full-span leading edge flaps and slotted trailing edge flaps. The Fo.148 was offered in three versions: the Stage One primary trainer with fixed wings and powered by an unreheated RB.153; Stage Two Gnat replacement with VG wings; Stage Three offered full equipment including Ferranti radar (either AI.23 or the related Blue Parrot for the strike role), INS and two fuselage hardpoints for AGM-12 Bullpup ASMs or Red Top infrared (IR)-homing AAMs. It would be powered by a reheated RB.153-61 fitted with a thrust reverser to

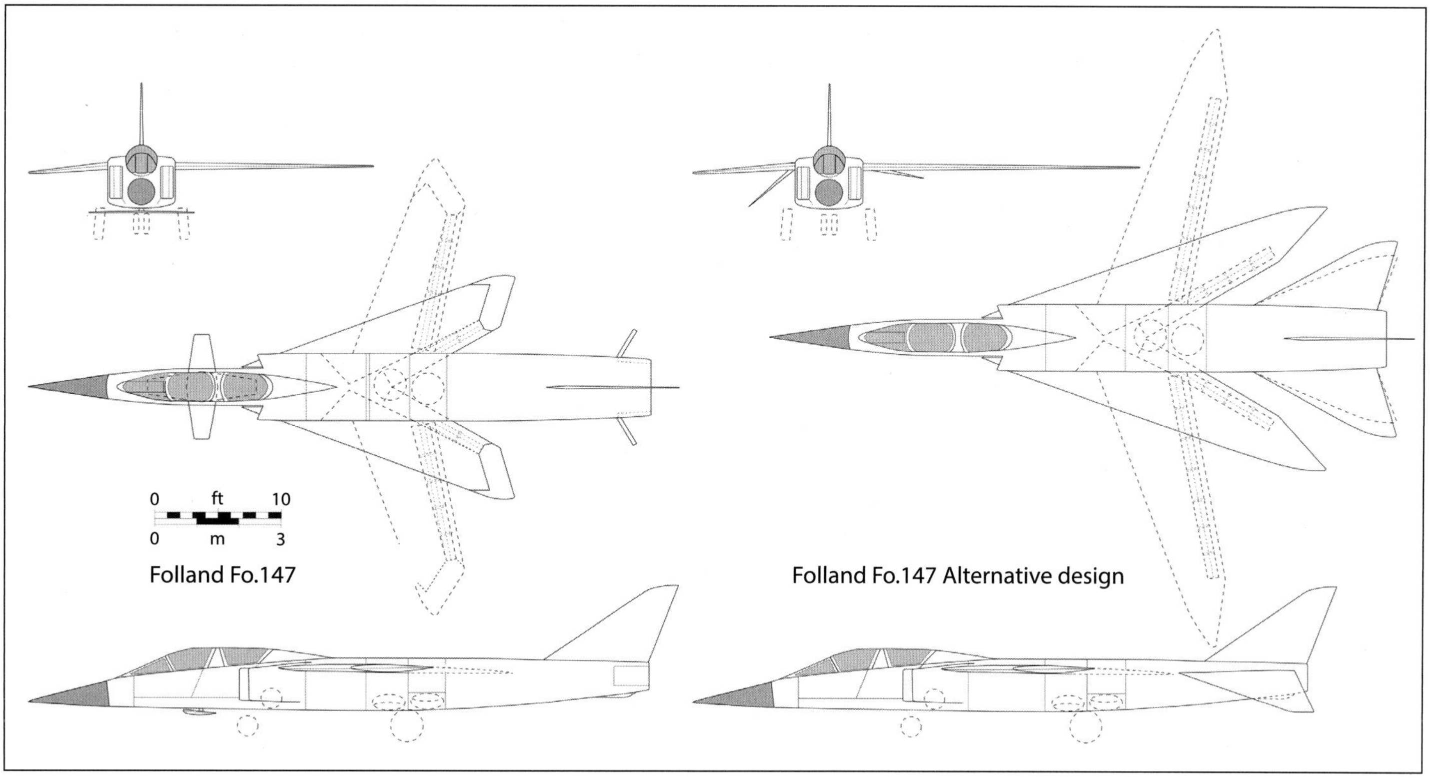

The Folland Fo.147 was studied in two variants. The main design had a retractable foreplane under the forward fuselage and tip ailerons. The alternative design used tailerons that required longer-span wings that were relocated to compensate for changes to the centre of gravity. Both were very ambitious designs, blurring the line between advanced trainer and front-line fighter. *Author*

reduce the landing run. The estimated radius for training missions was 330nm (610km). Folland claimed that a prototype could be ready in 1963 or 1964. The Fo.148 looked like a capable design, but as AST.362 took shape no official interest was received and therefore Folland's last 'Fo'-designated design remained on the drawing board and Hawker Siddeley discontinued use of the Folland name the following year.

The Hawker Siddeley Group began working informally on AST.362 studies during late 1963. The now-subsumed Folland design office at Hamble proposed the HS.1170B developed from the HS.1170 subsonic V/STOL fighter designed by the former Hawker design office at Kingston upon Thames. The HS.1170 had been a joint project with the West German company Focke-Wulf to meet the Luftwaffe's VAK.191 requirement for a nuclear-armed strike fighter. The HS.1170B had a fixed wing with 40° leading edge sweep, leading-edge slats, full-span slotted flaps and ailerons. The fuselage was enlarged with a tandem cockpit and had a bicycle undercarriage layout with the main units retracting into the fuselage with outriggers under the wings. The 13,500lbf (60kN) Bristol Siddeley BS.94/5 turbofan had 'mild' plenum chamber burning to provide an augmented thrust of 19,000lbf (84.4kN) to enable the aircraft to reach Mach 1.1 at sea level and Mach 1.7 at 36,000ft (10,970m). Alongside this design, Hamble proposed the private venture HS.1171, returning to the VG wing formula with two Rolls-Royce RB.172 turbofans.

Not to be outdone, Kingston designed their own private venture. They began with the SGA.153, which had an estimated weight of 13,000lb (5,900kg) and one or two Rolls-Royce turbofans for a maximum speed of Mach 1.8. The armament included two ADEN cannon and Hawker hoped that it might be attractive as a light fighter. The SGA.153 was scaled up as the HS.1173 as Kingston's main submission. This was a conventional fixed-wing aircraft with single and two-seat variants. The fuselage had no load-bearing structure beneath the cockpit to save weight and featured a large dorsal spine housing the fuel tanks. The fuel capacity totalled 580gal (2,637L) – the single-seater had 700gal (3,183L) – to provide a good supersonic range without the need for external drop tanks, leaving the four underwing hardpoints free for weapons. Two ADEN cannon were mounted beneath the intakes. The wing had a 'dogtooth' leading edge with two-part slats, double-slotted trailing edge flaps and spoilers that augmented the ailerons at high speeds. Powered by a reheated

A model of the alternative conventional Fo.147 design. *Tony Buttler*

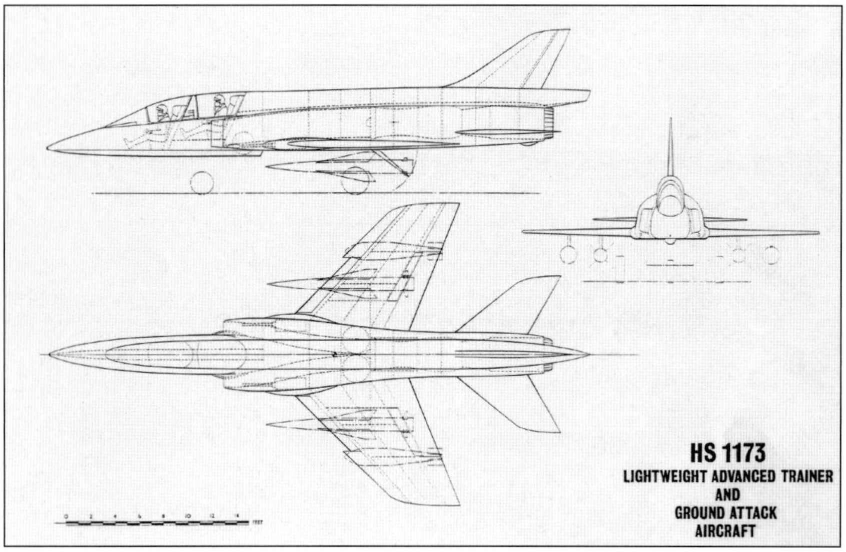

Hawker Siddeley's Kingston design team pitched the HS.1173 as a private venture. The fat dorsal spine contained more than half of the internal fuel. The ventral spine beneath the cockpit was an unusual feature that contained the flying control rods as there was no load-carrying structure beneath the cockpit floor to save weight. ***Tony Buttler***

13,000lbf (57.8kN) RB.172-57AR fed by two-shock intakes, the aircraft could reach Mach 1.4 at sea level and Mach 2.4 at 36,000ft (10,970m) in reheat. The gross weight was estimated at 20,500lb (9,185kg). In truth, Kingston had their eyes focused on the single-seater as a Hunter replacement rather than AST.362, but without any official interest the project was abandoned in March 1965.

With the demise of OR.346 by the end of 1962, BAC moved their VG wing design team from Weybridge to join the former English Electric team at Warton in Lancashire. This team was tasked with formulating BAC's submission and the P.45 was the result. A great deal of research was undertaken and several designs were studied. The initial starting point was the EAG.3397 with a VG wing. (Note that the EAG numbers are technical drawings and can refer either to a specific drawing or a block of drawings, rather than to a particular project. These numbers are issued sequentially). The trainer version, MP.2, was to be powered by a single Rolls-Royce RB.168-1R Spey turbofan, the single-seat MP.3 would be armed with two 30mm ADEN cannon packs and a ventral hardpoint for one AS.37 Martel ASM, and the Spey was unreheated.

Studies EAG.3408 and EAG.3409 had a fixed delta wing of very similar planform to the TSR.2 – then still under development – with 58° leading edge sweep and part-span blown flaps for high lift at low speeds as well as anhedral on the wing tips. The single-seat EAG.3408 would be powered by two unreheated RB.172 turbofans. The armament configuration was unusual, with the ADEN cannon moved to fixed pods near the wing tips, and the wings had both underwing and overwing hardpoints. The latter was an attempt to reduce drag when carrying external stores; this feature was also applied to the Lightning F.6 around this time and would later reappear on the Jaguar. The two-seat EAG.3409 was similar but had scaled RB.172-54R engines with reheat, and the fuselage had a more distinctive humped profile for the stepped tandem seating for the student and instructor compared with the EAG.3397 MP.2.

The definitive P.45 design, the EAG.3411, reverted to the VG wing but was otherwise similar to EAG.3409. The single-seat EAG.3410 was likewise a VG-winged version of the EAG.3408. The VG wing pivoted around vertical pins in the fuselage and could be altered between 25 and 68° sweep. The wing root was sealed

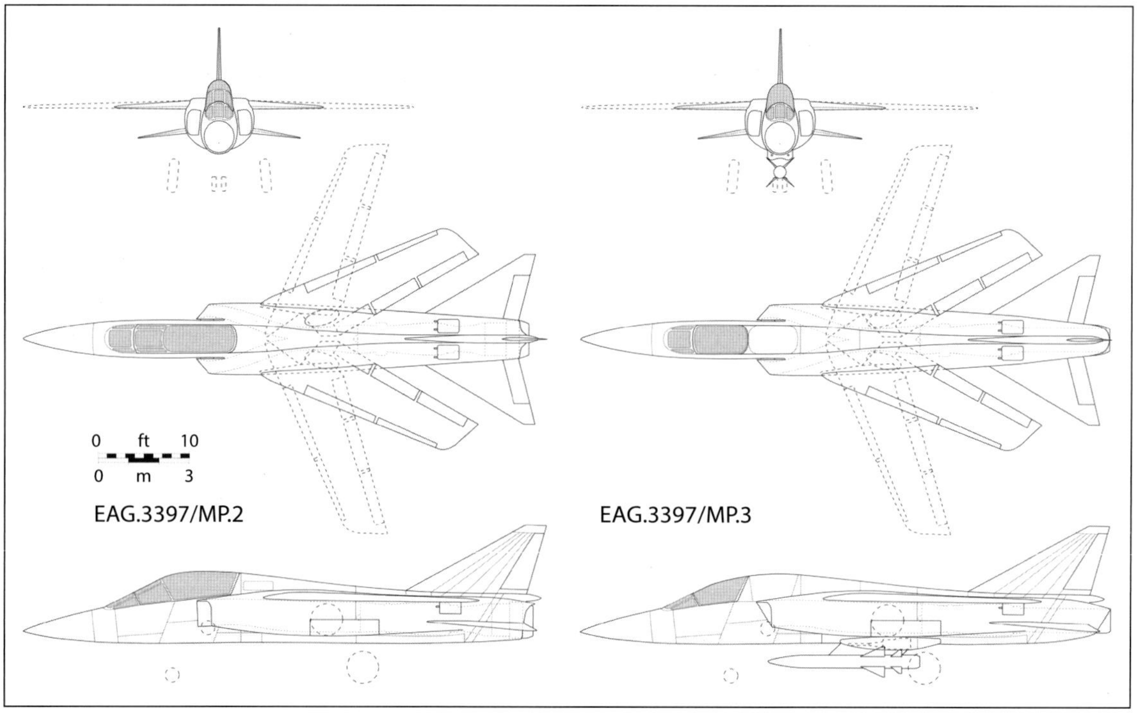

The BAC design team at Warton began its P.45 series with the single-engined, variable-geometry EAG.3397 design. The single-seat MP.3 version gained two ventral cannon packs and a pylon for a single AS.37 Martel ASM. ***Author***

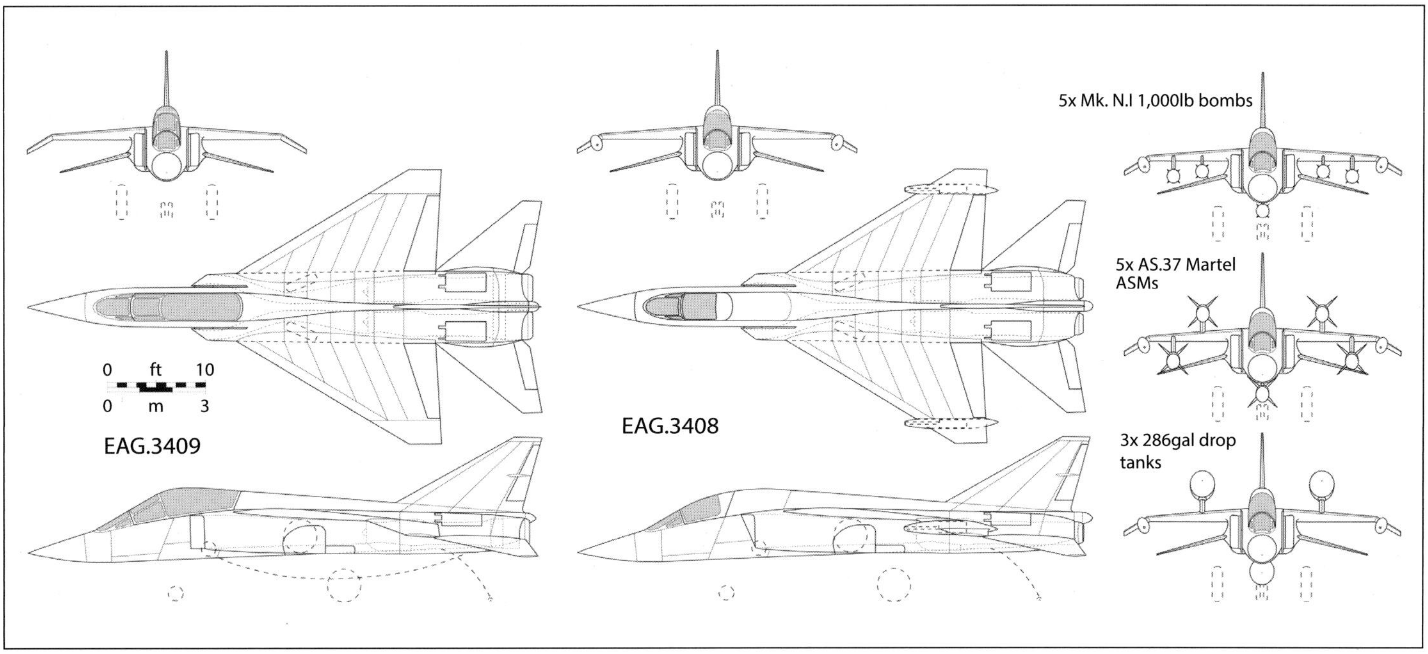

The two-seat P.45 EAG.3409 and the single-seat EAG.3408 looked like mini-TSR.2s with a very similar wing planform. The EAG.3408 had several unusual features with the 30mm cannon mounted in pods near the wing tips, and the wings had a mix of underwing and overwing pylons. Similar overwing pylons would appear on the Jaguar. *Author*

by two overlapping hinged metal doors closing upwards and inwards with rubber edges forward and inflatable rubber tubes on the aft edges. At low angles of sweep the wing took advantage of its leading-edge slats and full-span Fowler flaps for good take-off and landing performance. A simple fixed ramp intake was used as reheat would only be used during take-off and supersonic flight.

BAC emphasised the low cost and highlighted that it could be immediately placed into development as a VG wing research aircraft. BAC had been very keen since the late 1950s to get such a testbed into the air,

The favoured P.45 design to fulfil AST.362 was EAG.3411 powered by two scaled RB.172-54Rs. The single-seat strike variant EAG.3410 had non-reheated RB.172s with a revised intake boundary layer splitter and a smaller-diameter rear fuselage. A ventral weapons pack carried two 30mm ADEN cannon. Having a variable geometry wing complicated the choices for external weapons, so ventral and dorsal pylons were planned. *Author*

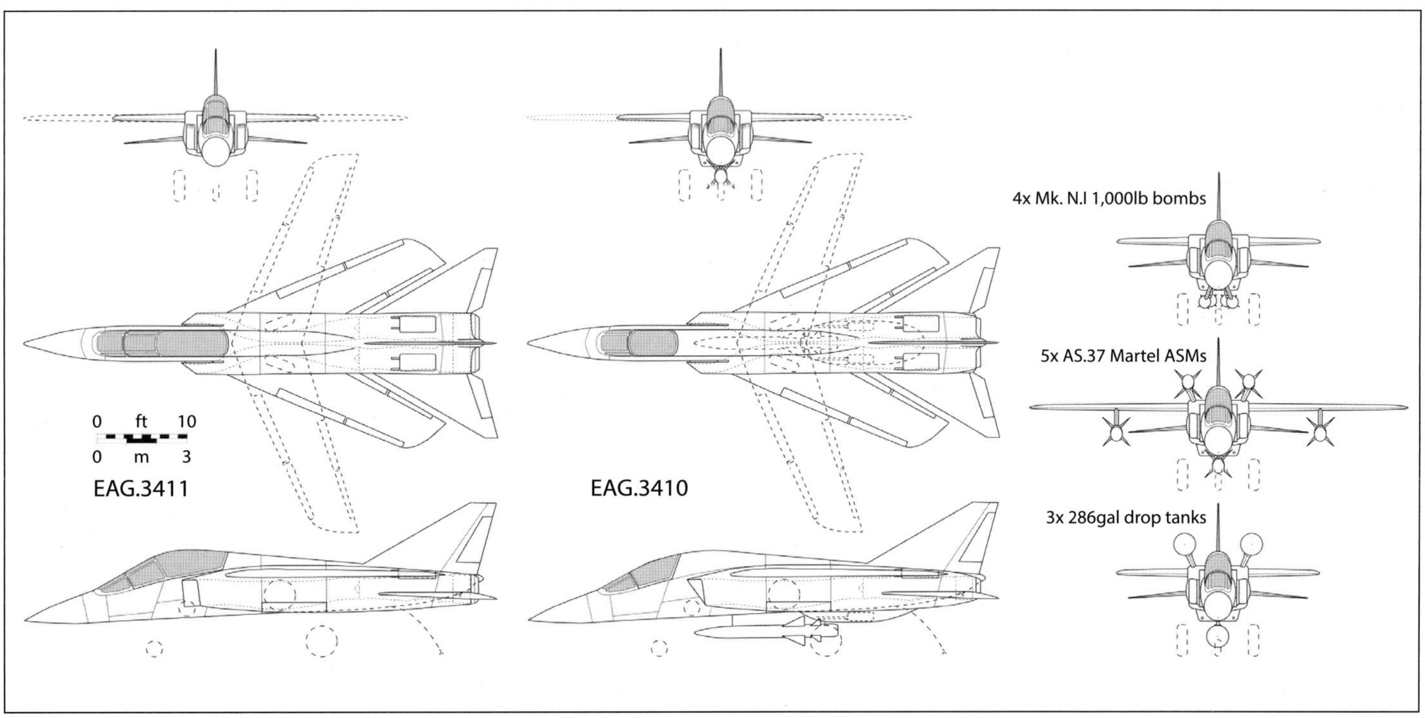

but without success due to lack of Treasury support. BAC estimated that from an Instruction to Proceed in early 1965 the first flight would take place 39 months later, with service release for the trainer by the end of 1970 and early 1972 for the strike version. BAC foresaw the P.45 being a multi-role aircraft suitable as an interceptor for overseas use, light strike and reconnaissance. Two ADEN pods could be fitted on ventral hardpoints, a centreline hardpoint could accommodate an AS.30 ASM and there were two underwing hardpoints for use when the wings were extended at minimum speed. BAC proposed fitting the light fighter with a 76cm (30in) diameter radar to work with a pulse-doppler guided version of the European HM.45 AAM (a Swiss licence-built Hughes GAR-11 Falcon). While the RAF's views on what made a good fighter differed from BAC's, with an estimated £15 million R&D cost the RAF became interested in the strike role. There was early export interest too. In November 1964 the Dutch Air Attaché, Colonel Fucquin de Grave, made enquiries about the P.45 while studying potential replacements for its Lockheed F-104G Starfighters. With hindsight, a BAC report written the following month on the P.45's export potential was highly optimistic at foreseeing a 25% market penetration of 1,000 aircraft by 1975.

Collaboration

International collaboration in the aviation sector was increasing as governments sought to reduce the burden of R&D and production costs. In addition, European manufacturers increasingly saw collaboration as a way to compete against the American and Soviet aviation industries and their exports. Although the UK made overtures to – and received proposals from – West Germany, Italy, the Netherlands and Australia on a range of aviation and military projects, it was France that became the preferred industrial partner during this period. The AdlA first showed interest in AST.362 as the basis of a collaborative project in December 1963 when the RAF's Deputy Chief of the Air Staff (DCAS), Air Marshal Sir Christopher Hartley, visited Paris to discuss potential VTOL strike aircraft requirements (the French declining an invitation to collaborate on P.1154 or TSR.2). Further meetings of officials took place in Paris on the 20th and in London on 16 January 1964. Air Marshal Hartley was informed by the Air Ministry and the Ministry of Aviation (MoA) that an Anglo-French programme was possible if the necessary initial political steps could be taken.

AST.362 was put on hold while the political and Service discussions began to take shape. A further meeting in Paris on 6 February firmed up the requirements with Group Captain Hugh Eccles of the Operational Requirements branch and his French counterpart, Colonel Besset, agreeing a feasible basis on which to collaborate. In April, informal talks between the British Minister of Defence, Peter Thorneycroft, and his French counterpart, Minister of the Armed Forces Pierre Messmer, began to explore collaboration on a political level.

At this time the future of AST.362 looked uncertain. The Air Ministry was trying to fund the development of TSR.2, P.1154 and the Hawker Siddeley HS.681 tactical transport with little hope of AST.362 emerging from last place in the funding queue to allow work to begin. Group Captain Eccles commented that if a collaborative project proved impossible then that would 'automatically terminate the project', at least in the short term until a postulated VG-winged Lightning replacement entered service after 1975. Fallback plans included retaining the Gnat in service until 1980 or converting more surplus Hunter F.6 fighters into T.7 trainers.

There were certainly technical differences to overcome. ECAT called for operation from grass strips, which meant low-pressure tyres but resisted any form of thrust vectoring or VTOL capability, which the MoA felt would be essential to meet the take-off and landing requirements unless a VG wing was used. To meet the fuel load and low approach speed requirements, a thicker wing profile was favourable for sufficient internal space for wing tanks and full-span flaps and leading-edge slats, whereas the supersonic speeds of AST.362 favoured a thinner wing. The French wanted a lower AUW, which the MoA felt was bound to increase as the design matured, and French studies calculated that an aircraft designed to meet AST.362 would be 40–50% more expensive than ECAT. There were few off-the-shelf options; an assessment by the Assistant Chief of the Air Staff (Operational Requirements) – ACAS(OR) – Air Vice-Marshal Reginald Emson, identified the T-38A Talon as the only available comparable aircraft, but it was neither cheap nor politically desirable to purchase. The RAF asked its scientific team to assess the difference in cost of developing an Anglo-French trainer or running the Gnats until 1980 before designing a replacement. The resulting report in September 1964 was non-committal, taking the long-term view that both options would cost about the same. The AdlA put the trainer second on their priority list but it was actually required in service first; given their pressing need for an advanced trainer, they wanted ECAT operational by 1970, five years sooner than AST.362's target date.

Despite these issues, in March the Air Staffs of both nations agreed a provisional requirement. The aircraft would be a dual-role trainer/strike aircraft for the RAF, Royal Navy and the AdlA. Even though the French favoured the strike version and the British the trainer, there was enough commonality around which to develop a single airframe, which would save money and hopefully prove attractive to potential export nations. This was a

Had collaboration with France broken down it is likely that the P.45 would have been developed into the RAF's future attack aircraft. This what-if BAC Tempest GR.1 is in No. II(AC) Squadron markings of the late 1970s.
Luca Landino

novel process for the AdlA too; for the first time they were integrated into a development programme from the beginning and able to provide input into the design process as the end user. The draft requirement was issued to the industries of both nations and detailed technical discussions began in May.

Hawker Siddeley and BAC proceeded with finalising their designs, submitting the HS.1170B and the P.45 during the summer of 1964, the MoA assessment report by A T Jarret and K W Clark being issued on 24 September. Each design utilised identical airframes and engines for the trainer and strike versions, although the latter had more advanced avionics. Both designs had five external hardpoints for weapons and a maximum speed of around Mach 0.7 with a full external load. Jarret and Clark liked that the P.45's VG wing gave the ability for the instructor to vary the handling characteristics of the aircraft to expand the training syllabus as the student pilot progressed towards operational capability. The VG wing was deemed to offer superior performance and flexibility compared to the thrust vectoring on the HS.1170B, which was expensive and lacked any engine-out safety. The report estimated that either trainer could be in service by 1970, with the strike HS.1170B following in 1971 and the strike P.45 a year later. Both designs seemed evenly balanced but the P.45 was marginally the favoured choice.

In hindsight, the provision of a VG wing for such a small aircraft with relatively low performance seems difficult to justify given the additional weight burden of the sweep mechanism and the additional cost it would have incurred – both the MoA and BAC estimated that the research effort for the wings alone would have cost £6 million. AST.362, in specifying such advanced features as VG wings and potential V/STOL capability, was needlessly complicating the requirements for an advanced trainer. Neither design was anything like the T-38A Talon that the Air Staff had been using as a template back in 1961. The Air Staff resolutely stuck to its preference for VG wings, although the Chief of the Air Staff, Air Chief Marshal Sir S Charles Elworthy, was becoming sceptical about their necessity.

On 24 July Air Vice-Marshal Emson was briefed in Paris on the various ECAT designs but progress was slow. At another meeting in Paris on 25 September the French set a deadline that if Britain did not decide to collaborate within five days they would begin ECAT as a national programme. Faced with this ultimatum, the impasse was broken; within days the Operational Requirements Committee asked the Weapons Development Committee to approve the initiation of the project study costing £25,000. By the autumn, negotiations on weight limits were nearing agreement and AST.362 was rewritten to comply with the joint specifications, being endorsed on 5 November as

This early model shows the evolution of the Br.121 into something closer to the eventual Jaguar. Note the radar nose. The AS.30 ASM shown under the wing alongside paired bomb carriers would not be carried in service. ***Author's Collection***

NAST.362 (Naval and Air Staff Target) and reissued the following July (the Air Staff and Admiralty had formally merged into the Ministry of Defence [MoD] earlier that year). The revised requirements removed the need to carry the nuclear weapon simulator and the Red Top AAM IR acquisition round for weapons training.

The Winner is?

The ECAT selection was decided in January 1965; the Br.121 was the winning design. Dassault continued to refine its various Cavalier studies during the first quarter of 1965 but thereafter abandoned its efforts.

The French Ministries were increasingly impatient with the delays caused by British indecision and were ready to go it alone. Political discussions finally resumed on 5 February 1965 when ACAS(OR) Emson and the MoA's Director-General of Scientific Research/Air, Rhys Probert, met with their counterparts General Maurin (equivalent to DCAS) and General Violette of the Direction Technique des Constructions Aéronautique (DTCA). Emson and Probert had a lot of explaining to do given the cancellation of the P.1154 and the AW.681 just three days earlier in favour of buying American aircraft. Maurin and Violette were suspicious but conceded that the British government had no alternative; they were resolute that France would press ahead with ECAT if the UK dropped out. While they accepted the supersonic requirements, they remained sceptical of the utility of the VG wing – Emson and Probert still had hopes of convincing them that it was the ideal aerodynamic solution.

Given the recent cancellations, the MoA were keen to get Hawker Siddeley and Bristol Siddeley on to the programme – they also had doubts about BAC's management given the problems with TSR.2 and Concorde – but Emson felt that reopening the partnership discussions would be detrimental and both companies remained excluded. The Treasury harboured serious misgivings about the need for a new trainer and referred to co-operation with the French as 'hazardous in the extreme'. Finally they gave grudging approval, but only if TSR.2 was cancelled, leading an exasperated Emson to lament to DCAS Air Marshal Hartley, 'Is it possible to drive home the point that with every day that passes, French confidence in our willingness to co-operate with them is shrinking?' Ultimately TSR.2 would meet its demise, but by the end of the month both governments had formally agreed to collaborate on ECAT and other VG-winged combat aircraft studies.

On 18 February it was announced that Rolls-Royce and Turbomeca would jointly produce the engine for ECAT. The STAé had rejected the competing Bristol Siddeley-SNECMA development of the M45 Mars. The resulting turbofan would be a combination of the front section of the T.260 Tourmalet with the middle and rear sections of the RB.172-45R. In London, the Weapons Development Committee endorsed a commitment of £1.5 million to cover the UK's share of the development costs. On 26 March the VG wing was ruled out as uneconomical and unlikely to be ready by 1970. This dashed any hopes that the P.45 might be selected and was a blow to the Air Staff and BAC, who had made strenuous efforts to justify the VG wing. The Air Staff conceded that the VG wing was only essential if the P.45 was further developed into a fighter, but future fighter procurement policy was still undecided. Threatening to go it alone on NAST.362 also risked collapsing the negotiations under way on other VG wing projects and helicopter development, therefore the UK abandoned its national efforts in the hope of obtaining a cheaper solution from France. BAC's Managing Director of the Preston Division, Frederick Page, wrote to the MoA to contest the decision and pitch his team as the best contender to be the British industrial partner – unknown to Page, the MoA had already decided that. BAC's Executive Director, Sir George Edwards, agreed that Breguet should lead on ECAT with BAC providing input into the design and hopefully wresting lead status on the other VG-winged combat aircraft studies. BAC also knew that the programme could be profitable with a solid home market and potential export sales with minimal R&D costs compared with more advanced projects. The President of Breguet, General (retired) Henri Ziegler, had been enmeshed into military aviation committees during his military career and had the support of the Ministerial Delegation for Armament (DMA), which had been founded by President de Gaulle in 1961 to oversee defence production and planning. Henri Ziegler had also been the head of the airline Air France when it purchased the Vickers Viscount and so was acquainted with the ex-Vickers personalities of BAC, which helped enormously to get the project off the ground and did much to smooth Breguet's relations with BAC.

The Memorandum of Understanding (MoU) entitled *Collaboration in the Aeronautical Field* was signed in London by Secretary of State for Defence Denis Healey, Minister of Aviation Roy Jenkins and Minister of the Armed Forces Pierre Messmer on 17 May. The MoU covered the collaborative development of ECAT, a VG wing combat aircraft, Airborne Early Warning aircraft and helicopters (the AEW aircraft would later be abandoned but the helicopter collaboration would result in the Sud Aviation SA.321 Gazelle, SA.330 Puma and Westland

An artist's depiction of the Jaguar B trainer for the RAF and the Jaguar A fighter for the AdlA. *SEPECAT via Author's Collection*

WG.13 Lynx). Breguet would lead on ECAT in partnership with BAC, with Rolls-Royce and Turbomeca developing the turbofan. The MoU outlined the production plan for 300 aircraft split between 75 trainers and 75 single-seat strike aircraft for the AdlA and 150 trainers for the RAF. The MoU covered Stage I of the ECAT programme, the construction of the prototypes (the Stage 0 preliminary study phase had already been completed). Four prototypes would be built at an estimated cost of £8.68 million (120 million French Francs – FF) with the prototype Adour engines costing £10 million (138.2 million FF). The costs would be shared equally.

The VG wing combat aircraft became the Anglo-French Variable Geometry Aircraft (AFVG), with BAC as the prime contractor working together with Dassault and its engine being developed by Bristol Siddeley and SNECMA. The AFVG was to be a strike aircraft to complement the RAF's General Dynamics F-111Ks then on order and included interceptor and carrier-based versions. The MoU stipulated the formation of a Management Committee to oversee each of the four projects, comprising four representatives from each nation. These committees would oversee development, approve the technical specifications, work out the detailed financial arrangements and management property and rights.

Br.121 becomes Jaguar

Following the signing of the MoU, on 26 May a team from BAC, the MoD and MoA arrived at Breguet's headquarters at Vélizy-Villacoublay to evaluate how the Br.121 could meet the joint requirements. ECAT had originally been a reasonably basic aircraft but the RAF wanted an aircraft that offered more potential with better avionics and supersonic performance. BAC were also keen to push these aspects to improve its export potential. The AdlA felt that the changes went against their requirements but the increased potential on offer was undeniably attractive and agreement was reached.

A name for the aircraft was required ahead of the official launch of the programme at the Paris Salon de l'Aéronautique in June. The process proved to be exceedingly straightforward. Henri Ziegler, telephoned George Edwards to propose the name Jaguar – an aggressive feline that was spelt the same in both languages. By the end of the day Edwards had managed to obtain agreement from his company and the car manufacturer Jaguar Cars Limited to use the name, completely bypassing the MoA and RAF. Edwards had wisely avoided the interminable rounds of ministerial and RAF brainstorming sessions and ballots that most military aircraft went through to

This early artwork of the proposed Jaguar B advanced trainer for the RAF shows the original-style intakes and is depicted in Flying Training Command colours – silver overall with dayglo nose and tail panels. ***Author's Collection***

acquire a name. The sub-variants received single-letter suffixes to denote their role:

- Jaguar A (Appui/support) – single-seat attack for the AdlA
- Jaguar B (Biplace/two-seat) – two-seat trainer for the RAF
- Jaguar E (Ecole/school) – two-seat trainer for the AdlA
- Jaguar K – reserved for export models but never used
- Jaguar M (Marine) – single-seat attack for the Aéronavale
- Jaguar S (Strike) – single-seat attack for the RAF

BAC's design team at Warton led by Ivan Yates began making design changes. Cockpit mock-ups were assembled at Warton and evaluated during mid-September by representatives from the RAF, Royal Navy, Breguet and the AdlA. BAC designed an improved two-seat cockpit with the nose droop increased and the rear seat raised by 15in (38cm) to give an improved forward view of 8.5° below the horizontal datum (AST.362 had originally specified 11°). Further single-seat and two-seat cockpit mock-ups were built at Villacoublay as Breguet was responsible for cockpit design. Evaluations lasted well into 1966 as equipment changes required rechecking of fittings and available space.

This display model from circa 1967 shows off the lines of the Jaguar. The engine intakes and radar radome are the main differences from the aircraft as built. ***Terry Panopalis Collection***

Breguet's design team received two personnel seconded from the Ecole du Personnel Navigant d'Essais et de Réception (Test and Reception Flight Personnel School – EPNER) in September, to provide input from experienced test pilots. The UK and France had their own official design requirements to which all military aircraft were constructed – Av.P.970 and Règlements Air respectively. The MoD decided to use the Règlements Air to ease the transition, although translating its 500 pages of technical text took a while to achieve. The Jaguar was Britain's first aircraft to be completely designed and manufactured using metric units. The first four prototypes and the static test airframe were built with a mix of ISO metric and ISO inch threaded fasteners. After some heated debate it was agreed that ISO inch fasteners would be used on the subsequent prototypes and production aircraft (in return BAC agreed that Concorde would be all metric).

BAC was given responsibility for designing a new wing with a lower t/c ratio with a symmetrical aerofoil to attain Mach 1.3 in a 1.5g turn at high altitude, as required by AST.362. The wing had extensive high-lift devices that consisted of leading-edge slats and full-span, double-slotted trailing edge extension flaps. Breguet's use of spoilers for lateral control rather than traditional ailerons was retained. The wing had 40° quarter-chord wing sweep with 3° anhedral. The fuselage was lengthened with a 7.8in (20cm) plug and reshaped as the internal arrangements were adjusted and to maintain the fuselage area curve required for transonic performance. The fuselage of the two-seat version was 2ft 11in (90cm) longer. Both the vertical and horizontal tail surfaces were enlarged and their t/c ratio reduced. The empennage and rear fuselage were also strengthened to withstand greater aerodynamic loads when rolling at supersonic speeds. The transonic rate of roll at Mach 0.9 was to be at least 150°/sec.

Structurally, most of the airframe was of high-strength aluminium alloy with some titanium alloy parts in the engine bays, and stainless steel was used in high-stress points such as the tailplane spigot housing and fin and pylon attachment points (there had been some debate with Breguet, who advocated using honeycomb structures, of which they had extensive experience). The Jaguar was BAC's first production military aircraft to use new bonding techniques to mate chemically milled skin panels to an adhesive-bonded aluminium core. The airframe was stressed to 8.6g with a design maximum of 12g and the fatigue life was calculated at 3,000 hours for the single-seat variants and 6,000 for two-seaters. One part of the

TSR.2 programme was salvaged, an aerodynamically compensated 'bulb' pitot static tube to measure airspeed, which was fitted to the nose cone.

The fuel capacity had to meet varying radius of action and speed requirements. The Jaguar A and M were to have a radius of 270nm (500km) at 450kt with five minutes of low-level combat manoeuvring at Mach 0.9 while carrying a Martel ASM. In contrast, the Jaguar S was required to achieve a hi-lo-hi sortie of 615nm (1,138km) at Mach 0.8 while flying at optimum cruising altitude with ten minutes low-level combat at 420kt carrying two 1,000lb (454kg) bombs. The Jaguar S hi-lo-lo-hi profile with the same bombload was 160nm (296km) at Mach 0.75 at optimum altitude, with 200nm (370km) flown at 420kt at 200ft (61m) and five minutes of low-altitude manoeuvring at Mach 0.9. The trainers also had different sortie profiles; an hour-long high altitude sortie with ten minutes at Mach 1.5 for the Jaguar E; an hour-long low-altitude sortie at Mach 0.6 with 20 minutes at Mach 0.9 for the Jaguar B.

The fuel system transferred fuel around the wing and fuselage tanks to maintain the limits of acceptable centres of gravity for all the various load configurations. Although originally only intended for the Jaguar M, the provision of an in-flight refuelling probe was soon adopted across the single-seat variants. A range of fixed and retractable probes were studied by Breguet. There was sufficient space in the nose for a retractable probe and this solution was chosen. The drawback was that when extended the probe affected the airflow into the starboard engine intake, causing some asymmetric thrust issues. The lack of space in the nose in the trainer versions saw them later receiving a fixed probe in the nose cone replacing the pitot tube.

The AdlA insisted on retaining the 15-minute turnaround time between sorties. Features such as an integrated access ladder (later made inoperable on the GR.1), quick removal of equipment via access doors and plug-in type equipment as well as access to the engines without stepladders were retained. The lack of an integral auxiliary power unit was seen as a drawback as the aircraft could not self-start its engines or keep its systems on standby when operating from semi-prepared strips. This was overcome by the addition of a ground-based trolley to supply air and power.

British-built aircraft would receive 30mm ADEN Mk.4 cannon, while French Jaguars would use the 30mm DEFA 553 – both were revolver cannon developed from the German Mauser 213C at the end of the Second World War. Due to the different munitions and stores used by each nation (the French requiring the provision to carry several types of US-supplied bombs) different pylons and ejector release units had to be fitted as a common pylon design proved to be inefficient. Both nations would use the Matra/Hawker Siddeley Dynamics Martel then under development as an anti-radar missile with passive homing and TV guidance for precision strike (only the anti-radar version was used on the Jaguar).

There was a study in early 1966 to fit the Jaguar with wing tip launch rails for AIM-9 Sidewinder IR-homing AAMs but this was abandoned due to lack of interest at that time. A 1970 BAC study judged that retrofitting them would cause structural and flutter issues. Guns would provide the sole self-defence capability against enemy aircraft, with the possibility of using unguided rocket pods for engaging helicopters.Both air forces wanted the capability to carry tactical nuclear weapons; the 25kT AN 52 for the AdlA and the 0.5–10kT WE.177A and 200kT WE.177C for the RAF. The integration of these weapons was conducted separately by both nations to avoid any leakage of nuclear secrets. Indeed the Foreign Office was concerned that developing a nuclear-capable aircraft might give the erroneous impression that the UK was assisting France's nuclear capability.

This close-up of Jaguar A154 shows the 'L'-shaped retractable refuelling probe that stowed neatly in the nose, the lower door closing following the probe's extension to reduce drag. ***Author's Collection***

A production Jaguar A displaying its 30mm DEFA 553 revolver cannon and ammunition. Under the wings are six 880lb (400kg) bombs on triple ejector racks and on the centreline is a 264gal (1,200L) fuel tank. ***Author's Collection***

Breguet was responsible for the design of the cockpit. This is the instrument panel of the single-seat Jaguar A. ***Author's Collection***

The front cockpit of the two-seat Jaguar E trainer. ***Author's Collection***

The avionics – including the instruments, navigational equipment, weapons control and radios – were different between the French and British versions. A Thomson-CSF TAV-38 laser rangefinder was fitted to the Jaguar M to improve bombing accuracy and was also added to the Jaguar A. The Jaguar E would have a gunsight in the forward cockpit and a head-down display (HDD) for the instructor, whereas the Jaguar B would have HUDs in both cockpits. The RAF saw the HUD as essential for improving navigational accuracy and weapons effectiveness. The Jaguar A would have a passive radar warning receiver (RWR) against X-band radars over the forward arc but the RAF wanted a miniaturised version of the electronic countermeasures (ECM) system that had been in development for the TSR.2, which covered the S, X, C and J-bands. This proved to be too challenging and expensive, so BAC opted for the French RWR, but adding aft aerials to provide all-round coverage as an interim fit.

The Jaguar A was designed for two internal cameras for reconnaissance, the Jaguar S only having space for one. The ejection seats were also different, French aircraft receiving the ballistic Martin-Baker Mk.4 JAM while British aircraft had the improved Martin-Baker Mk.9B seat with a rocket providing zero-zero capability, so that it could be safely fired on the ground at low speed (this seat was later fitted to French aircraft as the FJ9).

The AdlA wanted armour plating in order to provide the Jaguar A pilot with a measure of protection, but the Royal Aircraft Establishment (RAE) argued that the marginal improvement in survivability did not outweigh the resulting weight penalty and recommended against fitting armour to the Jaguar S.

The design changes caused an alarming weight increase. By November 1965 the estimated AUW had grown from 20,379lb (9,244kg) to 21,660lb (9,825kg). Of this increase, 1,038lb (470kg) was attributable to the redesign of the wings and fuselage to meet the supersonic requirements and 198lb (90kg) to correct the underestimated weights of the rear fuselage and engines. By June 1966 the weight had risen to 22,145lb (10,045kg), again mostly due to adjusted figures for the engines and increased fuel load. A Weight Reduction

The Jaguar's empennage with its anhedral tailplanes was distinctive. The small upwards-pointing tube at the base of the rudder is the fuel dump vent; the braking parachute was housed in the tail cone below. The ventral fins were added during prototype flight testing to aid stability. The knight's head art on the fin of E7 is the insignia of Escadrille SPA 15 'Casque de Bayard' (Bayard's Helmet), belonging to the Escadron de Chasse 1/7 'Provence'. ***Author's Collection***

Committee was formed to investigate ways to substitute lighter materials and equipment. The recommendations to remove the arrester hook fittings and reduce the vertical rate of descent limits for the undercarriage were rejected by the Marine Nationale's representative due to the greater stresses that the Jaguar M would encounter (the standard undercarriage was rated for 11.8ft/sec (4m/sec) rate of descent). It proved difficult to save weight but uprating the Adour's thrust by 10% offset some of the increase. With the design phase nearly complete the situation stabilised and on 3 December the provisional specification was issued and the design was frozen.

SEPECAT

Further progress during March 1966 saw the specification for the prototypes being finalised, the joint technical requirements agreed and funding approval from the French government. The DTCA – the French equivalent of the MoA – was made responsible for authorising the contracts for Jaguar aircraft and the AFVG engine as the executive agency, with the MoA being the executive agency for the Adour and the AFVG aircraft contracts (during 1967 the new Ministry of Technology [Mintech] replaced the MoA).

Alongside the formation of a Management Committee for each of the four projects, the DTCA insisted on the formation of joint companies to oversee development and production. These companies would receive the contracts and would insulate the partners from direct governmental interference and provide some protection in the event that one side attempted to withdraw from the collaboration. The joint company to be formed by Breguet and BAC was initially called the Société Européenne de Construction de l'Avion Jaguar (SECJAG) before settling on Société Européenne de Production de l'Avion Ecole de Combat et Appui Tactique (SEPECAT) shortly before the company was founded on 10 May. Breguet and BAC each held a 50% stake, the company having a capital of 100,000 FF divided into 1,000 shares.

ABOVE LEFT The French company Messier was responsible for the design and manufacturer of the undercarriage. It was specially designed as a twin-wheel unit for use on soft and rough ground and was rated for a 11.8ft/sec (4m/sec) rate of descent. ***Author's Collection***

ABOVE RIGHT SEPECAT exhibited a full-scale mock-up at the Paris Salon de l'Aéronautique in June 1967. The design shows strong similarity to the Br.121 but is close to the final Jaguar design. The main different is the outward-sloping lips of the engine intakes. ***Author's Collection***

The mock-up Jaguar A on display at Le Bourget in June 1967 was given fictitious AdlA markings as A142. ***Philippe Ricco***

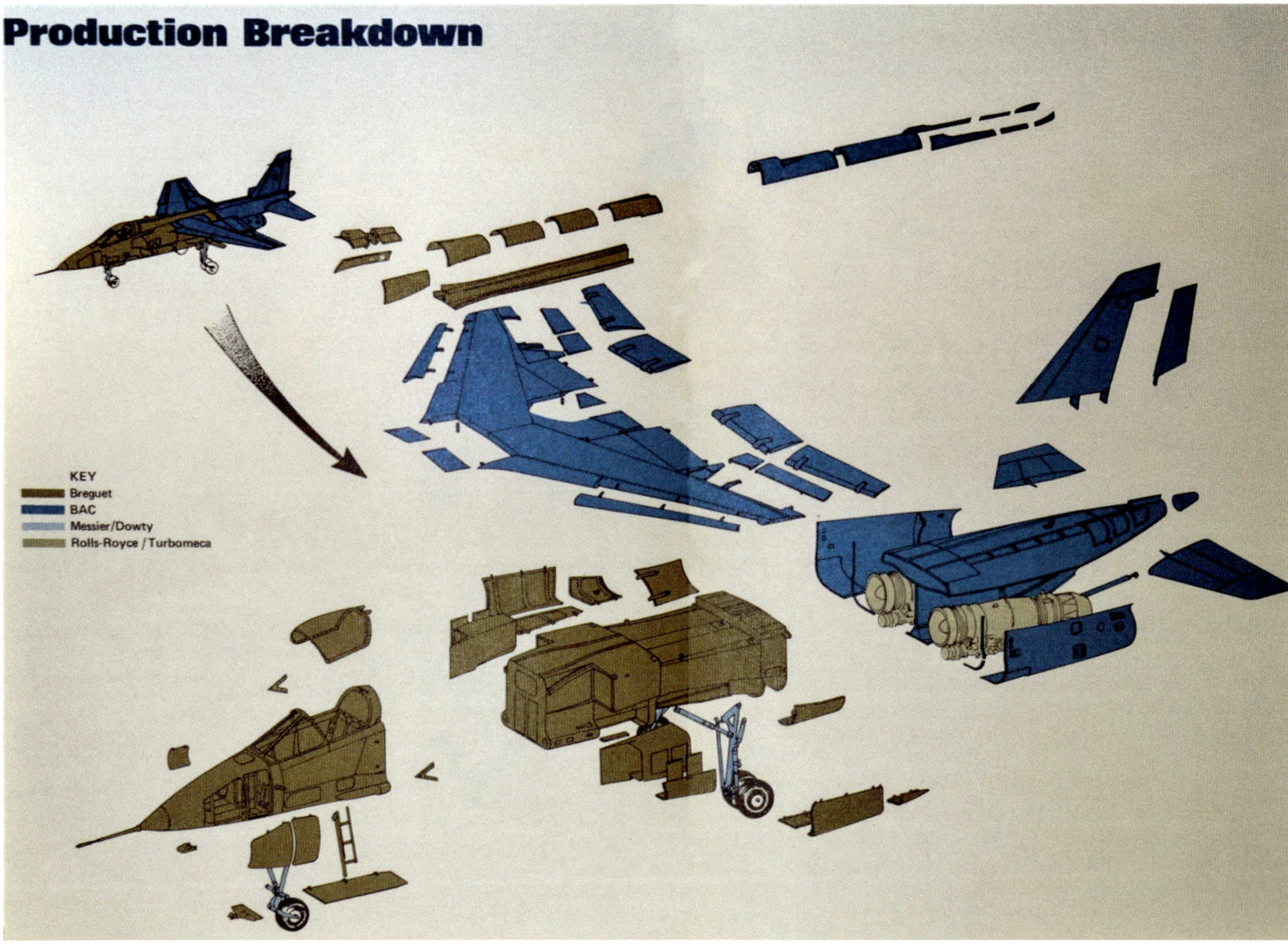

The workshare division: the dark blue airframe sections were the responsibility of BAC, the brown sections were those of Breguet/ Dassault. *SEPECAT via Paul Chapman*

The Board of Directors was made up of Henri Ziegler, Raoul Vivant and Paul Jaillard from Breguet with Frederick Page, Allen Greenwood and Harry Baxendale of BAC. Breguet's Technical Director Georges Ricard was appointed head of design, Jean Etienne Barge became head of production with Baxendale as head of finance and Greenwood responsible for export sales. SEPECAT had no permanent staff of its own, they were all seconded from the partners. Former test pilot and BAC executive Jeffrey Quill and Paul-Emile Jaillard (who was President of SEPECAT during 1971–73) immediately set up a sales/ publicity committee to ensure that SEPECAT had a coherent publicity campaign that projected stability.BAC was responsible for manufacturing the wings, tail surfaces and rear fuselage and would assemble all aircraft destined for the RAF at Warton. Breguet would build the front and centre fuselage sections and assemble all French airframes at Toulouse-Colomiers. BAC appointed Ivan Yates as Project Manager, B O Heath as head of the Technical Team and T O Williams as Production Manager. The production of components was also split to avoid duplication of work. The French company Messier was responsible for the undercarriage. The flying control system was designed by Fairey Hydraulics using twin electro-hydraulic actuators for the control surfaces and an advanced damping and feel feedback system.

The French government announced in June 1967 that Dassault Aviation would merge with Breguet and in December 1971 both were unified as Avions Marcel Dassault-Breguet Aviation (AMD-BA). This would not change the workshare agreement but it would put the Jaguar in direct internal competition with Dassault's Mirage series of fighters. Potential expansion of SEPECAT to involve West German or Belgian industry was also investigated during 1967 (for more details see Chapter 9).

Support costs were assisted by the introduction of FRUGAL (France et Royaume-Uni, Gestion d'une Association Logistique – France and United Kingdom, Management of a Logistical Partnership). This was an integrated supply support agreement to provide a spares holding for all the items common to at least one sub-variant. Each partner produced specific parts that were supplied to both air forces via their usual depots and maintenance units. Both nations opted to keep a minimum stock of spares from their opposite partner's suppliers sufficient to cover six months of peacetime consumption to guard against any disruption of supply. Both nations paid for their own share of the stocks but the larger production runs reduced the procurement costs. FRUGAL was not opened to potential export users, they had to buy their spares directly from SEPECAT.

By mid-1966 metal had been cut for the prototypes but on 6 May both governments briefly paused the programme to reassess the spiralling costs. Zeigler knew that Jaguar was key for his company to remain competitive in the military aircraft business and he pressed the DMA to continue supporting the programme. Satisfied by SEPECAT's revised cost estimates, both governments approved the opening of Stage I contract negotiations on 27 July. To save development time, it was planned to go directly from the prototype stage to series production, thereby eliminating any pre-series production aircraft – this was novel to the French Ministries, but less so in Britain.

Adour

Rolls-Royce Turbomeca Limited (RRTM) was formed on 22 June 1966 to develop and manufacture the Jaguar's engine. RRTM's capital was £100 divided into 100 shares, Rolls-Royce and Turbomeca each holding a 50% stake. Although the original intention was a 50/50 workload split, Rolls-Royce took a 60% stake in the R&D phase due to it taking on the development of the afterburner.

Design work had begun in early 1965 to combine the T-260 Tourmalet and the RB.172, both of which had been selected for many of the ECAT and AST.362 designs. The result was essentially a combination of the Tourmalet's front compressor section with scaled-down combustion and turbine RB.172-45R sections, emerging as essentially a new design with improved performance. Designated RT.172 by Rolls-Royce, the name Adour was bestowed in 1965 – a river in south-west France flowing from the Pyrenees to the Bay of Biscay and similar sounding to the River Adur in Sussex. The Adour was designed entirely using metric units. Originally with a dry thrust rating of 4,200lbf (18.6kN) and 6,300lbf (28kN) reheated, the engine was upgraded as the Jaguar grew in weight.

Production was divided with Turbomeca manufacturing the high-pressure (HP) and low-pressure (LP) compressors and shafts, casing and the external pipework; SNECMA was responsible for building the afterburner section. Rolls-Royce produced the combustion chamber, HP and LP turbines and shafts, main shaft bearings, compressor outlet and the bypass duct and mixer. Two assembly lines were set up at Derby and Tarnos. British companies were responsible for the majority of the engine accessories.

The RT.172 Adour installation is revealed as prototype A03 undergoes servicing. There was some limited room for physical growth of the engine, to accommodate increased-diameter afterburners and exhausts for example, but the Adour's relatively limited thrust would always remain a problem. ***Philippe Ricco***

GR.1 XX756 became Ground Instruction Airframe 8899M at No. 2 School of Technical Training at RAF Cosford in 1986. With its engine cowlings and both RT.172 Adour Mk.102 turbofans removed, the ease of access to the engine bay is revealed. An Adour could be changed within four hours. ***Terry Panopalis Collection***

The Adour was a turbofan with two coaxial shafts forming two bodies; the LP body with a two-stage compressor fan connected to a single-stage turbine and the HP body with a five-stage axial compressor connected to a single-stage turbine. The engine had an annular combustion chamber. Coupling an afterburner to a turbofan was more difficult compared with a turbojet due to the separate hot and cold air streams essential to the concept of the turbofan. Following bench tests the original individual flow mixers were replaced by an annular bypass duct nozzle to mix the cold and hot gas streams, which improved fuel consumption. The reheat burner assembly was also redesigned.

Extensive development testing in Derby's altitude chamber was undertaken to ensure reliable ignition and satisfactory combustion. The reheat ignition used the catalyst system derived for the RB.168-25R Spey as fitted to British-assembled McDonnell Douglas F-4 Phantoms. The catalyst was a 2in (5cm) diameter platinum-rhodium gauze located downstream of the turbine section, which spontaneously ignited the fuel sprayed on to it, with radial and circumferential channels propagating the flame across the burners. A second catalyst was added to the Adour Mk.102 to ensure more reliable ignition and provide improved thrust control.

Although the Jaguar prototypes suffered from the Adour's teething problems – there being no flying testbed to prove the engine beforehand – the basic design proved reliable once development was completed. It is still available for production at the time of writing and almost 3,000 have been produced in a range of variants, both with and without reheat. Arguably the Adour was a greater financial success for the aviation industries of both nations than the Jaguar.

Co-operation got off to a rocky start, with Turbomeca refusing to send staff to Derby for talks and technical visits, even when they were struggling with cracks in the LP compressor during initial testing in early 1966. Co-operation improved following the formation of RRTM and a visit by the Jaguar Management Committee to Derby in November 1971 greatly impressed the French members, which overcame their initial animosity towards Rolls-Royce.

Bench tests of the prototype engine began in mid-February 1967 but during development the weight grew. This led to some disagreement about the best means to maintain the brochure weight of 1,559lb (707kg). RRTM hoped to increase the use of magnesium but the Management Committee refused to sanction its use apart from on the external wheelcase and the oil pump cover due to the fire risk. Early Jaguar flights revealed that the fuel consumption was 10% greater than estimated; several quick fixes reduced this to around 6%. The initial development contract was issued on a fixed price basis and RRTM suffered a financial loss as a result.

Disruption was caused when Rolls-Royce Limited collapsed into bankruptcy in 1971 due to the cost overruns on the RB.211 high-bypass turbofan programme. This resulted in contract renegotiations and settlements, as well as concerns regarding slippage of deliveries (the fuel drop tank production contracts held by Rolls-Royce (Composites) Ltd were also affected). The company was rescued by the government and reformed as Rolls-Royce (1971) Ltd, which on 28 July 1972 became the new British shareholder and Turbomeca received £6.45 million from the MoD's Procurement Executive to settle the outstanding contractual debts. On the same day an order for a further 280 Rolls-Royce and 220 Turbomeca-assembled engines was signed to ensure sufficient engines for the 186 Jaguars then on firm order. By March 1978, 960 Adours had been delivered, 488 from Derby and 472 from Tarnos.

Change of plan: Jaguar S

The single-seat Jaguar S emerged in early 1966 as a means of filling the gap created by the cancellation of the P.1154 and TSR.2 and provided a cheaper ground-attack aircraft than the F-4M Phantom FGR.2 then on order. Issue 2 of NAST.362 was endorsed on 19 May 1966 to cover its development. Conversely, the Labour government's Defence Review in February 1966 had cancelled the CVA-01 aircraft carrier programme and the UK's defence posture was reoriented to focus on NATO commitments in Europe. This resulted in the downsizing of the carrier fleet during the 1970s, removing the Royal Navy's need for a new advanced trainer (and its tentative plans to acquire the Jaguar M and AFVG) and resulting in them withdrawing from NAST.362 (which reverted to AST.362).

The planned force of 96 Jaguar S would equip five squadrons; three based in the UK and two in West Germany, assigned to the Supreme Allied Commander Europe as part of the UK's NATO commitment. They would be used for short-range interdiction, close support and battlefield reconnaissance, and would enable the Phantoms to replace the ageing Lightning in the interceptor role. The Jaguar would complement the AFVG intended for medium-range tactical strike and reconnaissance and the Hawker Siddeley Harrier GR.1, which would provide 'intimate' close support to the Army. The 130 Jaguar B trainers would provide 79 aircraft for the OCU plus 47 attrition reserves, covering the wastage losses for 15 years of use. A proposal to use a small number of French Jaguar E to form the OCU until the Jaguar B was ready for production was rejected.

The MoU was amended on 9 January 1968 to include the Jaguar S and the carrier-based Jaguar M. The development of these two additional variants was estimated to increase the R&D costs by around £13 million, the Jaguar S airframe modifications costing £2.3 million plus £2.5 million for the equipment. The

In 1967 SEPECAT began marketing the Jaguar and a suitably exciting promotional image featuring one of the early models was presented in a mock low-level attack run in RAF colours. *SEPECAT via Author's Collection*

decision in 1970 to install the improved Adour Mk.102 with fully modulated reheat control added another £3.5 million and by 1972 the unit cost was £1.2 million, the Jaguar B costing £20,000 less.

The amendment also covered Stage IV, the launch of initial production. The production run was expanded to 400 aircraft, France insisting that Britain should increase its overall order to 200 aircraft to maintain parity within the production plan. The AdlA would still receive 75 Jaguar A and 75 Jaguar E with 40 Jaguar M and ten Jaguar E added for the Aéronavale; the RAF order was revised to 130 Jaguar B and 96 Jaguar S. The Jaguar A and E were estimated to enter service in January 1971 with the RAF's S and B following in January and July 1972 respectively and the Aéronavale's Jaguar M in January 1973. The estimated cost of Stage IV production was £204 million (2,012 million FF). The first two production orders covered 25 Jaguar A, 25 Jaguar E, 15 Jaguar S and 15 Jaguar B.

On both sides of the Channel the Jaguar quickly fell from favour as a trainer. The AdlA became increasingly dissatisfied with the Jaguar E and they issued new requirements that replicated those of ECAT. The AdlA and Luftwaffe released a call for proposals with a new

The first prototype E01 revealed the final design of the two-seat trainer variant on its roll-out at Breguet's factory at Vélizy-Villacoublay on 17 April 1968. *SEPECAT via Author's Collection*

Radius calculations						
Load	Take-off weight	Fuel load	Take-off ground run	Combat radius lo-lo	Combat radius hi-lo-lo-hi	Combat radius hi-lo-hi
One Martel	23,350lb (10,590kg)	6,900lb (3,130kg)	2,200ft (670m)	270nm (500km)	480nm (890km)	585nm (1,080km)
Two 1,000lb (454kg) bombs, one 230gal tank	26,870lb (12,188kg)	8,660lb (3,928kg)	3,280ft (1,000m)	295nm (550km)	505nm (935km)	615nm (1,140km)
One Martel, two 230gal tanks	27,910lb (12,660kg)	10,420lb (4,725kg)	3,100ft (945m)	365nm (675km)	630nm (1,165km)	735nm (1,360km)
Eight 1,000lb (454kg) bombs	31,400lb (14,242kg)	6,900lb (3,130kg)	4,400ft (1,340m)	140nm (260km)	165nm (305km) 1	85nm (340km)

collaborative programme on 22 July 1969. Dassault was ahead of the game, having already sought a partnership with Dornier during 1968 following rejection of the Cavalier. By the summer of 1970 the Alpha Jet programme was making good progress.

The RAF had also realised that the AST.362 supersonic trainer was too ambitious and expensive to operate. The Air Force Board in July 1970 agreed to remove the Jaguar from the pre-OCU training pattern and replace it with a subsonic advanced trainer. The Steering Committee on Flying Training now had six years' experience of training pilots for the Lightning – experience missing when AST.362 was originally written – to confirm that subsonic trainers were up to the task. To some government officials this sudden shift was a surprise given that the Jaguar B trainer requirement had featured in the Defence Debates in the House of Commons as late as December 1969. BAC and Hawker Siddeley Aviation were less surprised, having begun private venture studies in 1968 into a new generation of subsonic trainers that could double as light strike aircraft for the export market. An outline AST.397 was circulated in September 1970. Within two years the Hawker Siddeley HS.1182 Hawk, powered by an unreheated Adour, was in development and within a decade the Hawk and Alpha Jet were direct competitors for export sales.Buying a cheaper subsonic trainer saved enough money to fund four additional Jaguar S squadrons (three UK-based and five in Germany, the ninth squadron was never formed). The Defence and Overseas Policy Committee approved the change on 1 September 1970 and the production plan was amended to 165 Jaguar S and 35 Jaguar B trainers (a plan to buy just 15 Jaguar B was rejected because Mintech wanted to maintain the minimum order of 200 aircraft and because of the Jaguar OCU's requirements). A similar shift occurred in the AdlA's order, the split changing to 160 Jaguar A and 40 Jaguar E. The third production order placed in early 1971 covered 34 Jaguar A, 15 Jaguar E, 68 Jaguar S and 20 Jaguar B; the British share costing £40 million at July 1970 prices.

The provisional technical specification was issued in October 1968 and the partial mock-up was inspected at Warton on 20 March 1969 by officials from the MoD, Mintech and the Institute of Aviation Medicine. The estimated take-off weights were 27,851lb (12,630kg) in the close support role and 30,135lb (13,670kg) for tactical strike, carrying two 1,150lb (520kg) retarded bombs. It was initially thought that a modified undercarriage would be required to cope with the additional weight but following further investigation the standard undercarriage was deemed adequate for the load.

The maximum speed at sea level was limited to Mach 1.1 following a dive from 39,370ft (12,000m). The take-off distance clearing a 50ft (15m) obstacle had to be within 5,820ft (1,775m) – roughly the performance of the Jaguar prototypes with an added margin of 720ft (220m). The Air Staff wanted the capability to lift 4,000lb (1,815kg) of weapons from a semi-prepared strip. The landing distance clearing a 50ft obstacle had to be within 3,770ft (1,150m) – a margin of 210ft (65m) over the prototypes. The provision of 90psi tyres for the mainwheels and 40psi for the nosewheel allowed operation from grass strips. The radius of action was to be at least 530nm (980km). SEPECAT did not offer a guaranteed ferry range but Mintech estimated that full internal fuel plus three 264gal (1,200L) drop tanks would attain 1,900nm (3,518km).

The fixed armament consisted of two 30mm ADEN Mk.4 cannon with 150 rounds of ammunition per gun – only the starboard gun was fitted in the Jaguar B to save weight and internal space (at one point relying on external gun pods was considered). The ADEN Mk.4 had a rate of fire of 1,200 1,400rpm and a muzzle velocity of 2,345ft/sec (715m/sec). The Jaguar S was cleared to carry the WE.177 tactical nuclear bomb, the R&D cost for the necessary modifications being £1.43 million. The other weapons specified for the Jaguar S included:

- 1,000lb (454kg) freefall and retarded bombs
- Napalm tanks (developed to meet NASR.1209)
- 600lb (272lg) Hunting BL.755 cluster bombs with anti-tank bomblets (developed to meet NASR.1197)
- Matra Type 155 rocket pods containing 18 2.75in (68mm) SNEB rocket projectiles
- Mark 60B LEPUS flare bombs
- Carrier Bomb Light Series (CBLS) No. 100 Mk.1 for two 28lb (13kg) or four 4lb (1.8kg) practice bombs

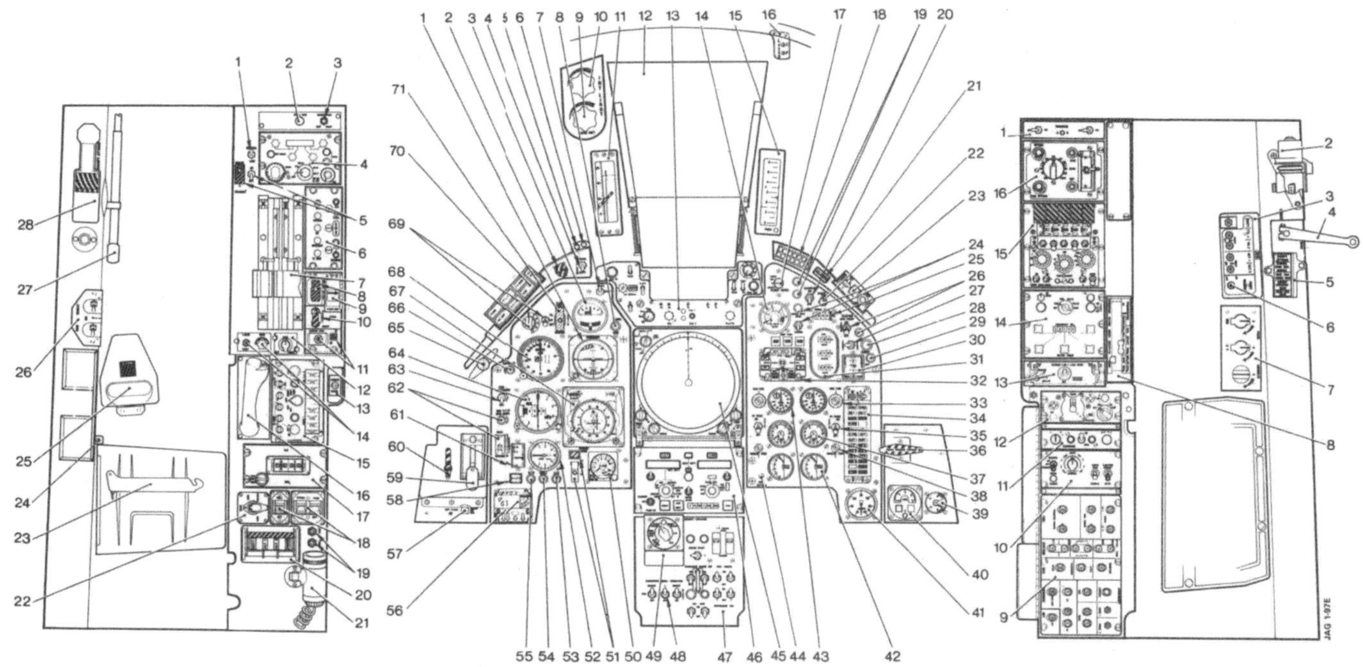

Left Console and Side Panel
1 Mute Sensitivity Switch
2 Stall Warning Button/Indicator
3 Rudder Test Switch
4 V/UHF Controller
5 Standby UHF Switches
6 CCS Controller
7 Throttle Box
8 Slat Override Switch
9 Flap Selector
10 Pitch Trim Switch and Indicator
11 Rudder Trim Switch and Indicator
12 Internal Lights Dimmer
13 Seat Raise/Lower Switch
14 Land/Taxi Lights Switch and NCU Dimmer
15 IFF/SSR Controller
16 Hand Controller and Laser Commit Switch
17 ILS Controller
18 Autostabiliser Switches
19 Roll and Yaw Trim Circuit Breakers
20 Crash Switch
21 Wander Lamp
22 Master Armament Safety Switch
23 PEC Cover Stowage
24 Stall Warning Incidence Selector Switch
25 Internal Ladder Winding Handle (Inoperative)
26 PTR Selector Switches
27 Arrester Hook Handle
28 Canopy Jettison Handle

Front Panel
1 Attitude Indicator
2 Clear Aircraft Jettison Button
3 Turn and Slip Indicator
4 Late Arm Switch
5 Low Altitude Warning Light
6 Head Up Gear Not Down Warning Light
7 F1/F4 Refuel Isolation Switch
8 Laser Test Push Button
9 Incidence Indicator Lighting Dimmer
10 Integral Lighting Dimmer
11 Incidence Indicator
12 HUD
13 HUD Control Panel
14 Fuel Flowmeter
15 Accelerometer
16 Laser Indicator Lights
17 Air Refueling Selector
18 Passive Warning Recorded
19 Air-to-Air Refuelling Lights
20 HUD Camera Master Switch
21 Attention Getter
22 Fuel Guage Test Button
23 Special Weapon Control Panel
24 Fuel Crossfeed Switch and Indicator
25 Fuel Detotalicer
26 EHP Switch and Indicator
27 Cont/Serve Switch
28 Telebrief Indicator
29 IFF Failure Light
30 Hydraulic Pressure Guage
31 Fuel Contents Guage
32 Fuel Transfer Panel and Drop Tank Indicators
33 Engine Fire Warning Button/Indicator (2)
34 CWP
35 Hydraulic Bypass Switches (2)
36 Brakes Selector Handle
36 TGT Indicators (2)
38 Reheat Fire Warning Indicator
39 Voltmeter
40 Oxygen Contents Guage
41 Cabin Altimeter
42 Nozzle Area Indicators (2)
43 Percentage RPM Indicators
44 Max Rating Switch
45 Projected Map Display
46 Navigation Model Control Panel
47 Engine Switch Panel
48 External Lights Switches
49 HSI Mode Switch
50 Radar Altimeter
51 Rudder Gearing Switch and Indicator
52 VSI
53 Airbrake Indicator Light
54 Arrester Hook Indicator Light
55 Nosewheel Steering Indicator
56 Slat/Flap/Landing Gear Position Indicator
57 Anti-Dazzle Lights Switch
58 Combat Slats Button/Indicator
59 Landing Gear Selector
60 Landing Gear Emergency Selector
61 Pitch Trim Indicator
62 Diff Tailplane Switch and Indicator
63 Fuel Jettison Switch
64 Altimeter
65 Brake Parachute Handle
66 ILS Marker Light
67 HSI
68 CSI
69 Laser Controls
70 Weapon Aiming Mode Selector Panel
71 AJAX Switch

Right Console and Side Wall
1 Two-Channel Switch Panel
2 Standby Compass
3 Electrical Generation System Controls
4 Canopy Locking Handle
5 Safety Pin Stowage
6 Pitot Heaters Switch
7 Internal Lights Panel
8 Cabin Air/Demisting Controls
9 Circuit Breaker Panel
10 Air Conditioning Panel
11 Compass Control Panel
12 TACAN Controller
13 Cockpit Voice Recorded
14 HF Controller
15 Conventional Weapon Control Panel
16 Special Weapon Fuze Control Unit or Reconnaissance Control Panel

A cockpit layout diagram for the Jaguar GR.1. ***Crown Copyright via Author***

Jaguar S avionics

It had been intended to fit the analogue Ferranti FE541 navigation/attack system into the Phantom FGR.2, Harrier GR.1 and the Jaguar S and B. Elliott Automation Space and Advanced Military Systems Limited (EASAMS) had tendered a digital system for the Jaguar, but the potential technical problems and development delays prevented its selection for the initial production Jaguars. Then Ferranti encountered problems installing the FE541 into the Phantom, which raised concerns regarding integrating it into the Jaguar. In May 1967 Mintech proposed cancelling Ferranti's contract in favour of using EASAMS' digital system. Ferranti protested and demanded a chance to tender a digital system, but after discussions with the RAF it was decided to deny Ferranti this opportunity to avoid any further delays. At the same time, Marconi offered its AD570 Doppler and AD670 digital computer for the Jaguar A unsuccessfully in competition with Electronique Marcel Dassault (the electronics arm of Dassault).

A BAC study in July estimated that the changes would increase development costs by £1.14 million and delay entry into service to 1973 but it recommended the EASAMS system due to its greater potential and Breguet raised no objections. Another favourable factor was that a digital system would prove more attractive to export customers. Mintech also wanted to ensure that EASAMS remained competitive in the field of inertial navigation systems to avoid a Ferranti monopoly (in September 1968 GEC and English Electric merged bringing Elliott and Marconi together as Marconi-Elliott Avionic Systems

The Jaguar production line at Warton was in full flow when this photograph was taken in late 1974. The aircraft in the foreground is S52, serial XX755, which made its first flight on 12 March 1975. Sadly, its service life was short, being lost in a mid-air collision with GR.1 XX749 on 10 December 1979. ***Terry Panopalis Collection***

Limited). EASAMS submitted a fixed-price £2.1 million quotation for the development costs. Development included flight trials aboard the company's Douglas DC-3 Dakota as well as RAE-operated de Havilland Comet and Canberra testbeds. The first Jaguar S prototype S06 would initially fly without the full system installed. BAC stopped all work relating to the Ferranti system in September.

The Navigation/Weapon Aiming Sub-System (NAVWASS) was based on the E.3 inertial platform, which had been developed for the Hawker Siddeley Nimrod MR.1 maritime patrol aircraft, married to a 920M digital computer (which had a basic store of 8,192 words) and a Type B moving map display. The upgraded E.3R had a rotating platform to reduce the effect of gyro drift, but this inadvertently caused problems as the readouts were transmitted over slip rings and any interruption caused by these rings moving would cause a system failure. The system interfaced with the HUD developed by Smiths Industries Limited and Specto Avionics. Eight navigational waypoints could be fed into the system and it could handle range and bearing offsets. The 'black boxes' used a new form of hollow cold wall construction to pass the cooling air through, with further cooling provided by a metal grid overlaid on the multilayer printed circuit boards.

Other navigation equipment included CILS 75/76 ILS (officially designated as Airborne Radio Installation ARI.18227/1), AN/ARN-91 TACAN, AN/APN-198 radar altimeter (designated ARI.23232), a C2J gyro magnetic compass and an E2B standby compass. One problem was that cockpit space was at a premium and the NAVWASS control panel had to fit in the space planned for the original Ferranti analogue system and was located behind the control stick. The ergonomic issues would lead to a loss of accuracy and effectiveness.

The Air Staff wanted to fit a modern sensor to feed target range data into the fire-control system. BAC looked at the feasibility of fitting a radar and confirmed that an extended nose would provide sufficient space. Ferranti had proposed a lightweight J-band set that might fit and a development of the AFVG's terrain-following radar was another possibility. These sets would have a range of 3nm

(5.5km) against a 161ft^2 (15m^2)-sized target but lacked any aerial search or lock-on capabilities for air combat. Developing either of these radars, or using the current Radar Ranging Mk.4, would cost up to £2 million. None of the then-current French radars would fit and the new Texas Instruments terrain-following radar offered little air-to-air capability (this radar eventually equipped the AFVG's successor, the Panavia Tornado).

At this time the French were looking to integrate a laser rangefinder into the Pilot Attack Sight for their Jaguar A and M. The Radar Research Establishment, in its assessment of the options, favoured a radar, arguing that development of a laser rangefinder would take longer and cost the same for less additional capability than a radar offered. The Air Staff chose to ignore this advice and selected the laser rangefinder. It would be another decade before BAC would revisit the idea of fitting a radar.

The Ferranti Laser Ranger and Marked-Target Seeker (LRMTS, designated ARI.23231) was fitted in the nose. It was developed under Air Staff Requirement ASR.861, which was approved in March 1970, and was also retrofitted into the Harrier. It worked by directing a pulse of IR energy from a stabilised YAG laser at the target, calculating the range from measuring the time it took the scattered return energy to arrive back at the seeker. Continuous range updating was possible. Nearer the target, the target marker was switched on and the target seeker automatically acquired and tracked the target from the scattered return energy. The effective range was greater than 4.8nm (9km) in good weather conditions. The targeting information was displayed on the HUD. The LRMTS had no ability to guide laser-guided bombs. If a technical fault occurred, a revisionary attack mode used the radar altimeter and barometric/inertial height navigation modes within NAVWASS. The Jaguar B lacked the LRMTS so weapons training used the revisionary modes. The estimated cost of development and airframe modifications was £48 million.

A reconnaissance pod was developed under ASR.850 to complement the fixed F.95 camera in the aircraft (which was later deleted to save weight and space). The pod would equip the Jaguars assigned to two specialist reconnaissance squadrons, supplementing the Phantom FGR.2s to make up a shortfall in NATO reconnaissance capabilities. It was optimised for medium-level photography with five F.95 cameras – one facing ahead and four in a fan for horizon-to-horizon coverage – along with a medium-altitude F.126 camera and an IR linescanner. The Jaguar lacked any spare electrical generation capacity to fit night-capable cameras.

Initially it had been planned to design a smaller-diameter pod. A proposal to use the Harrier's pod was rejected as it only contained cameras and lacked the flexibility for all-weather use. The Phantom's pod contained a linescanner and sideways-looking radar but was too large. As a result the MoD agreed to collaborate with France on their larger pod. When uncertainties surrounding the carrier-based Jaguar M caused the French to withdraw from the project, the MoD decided to continue development. It was estimated that development would cost £1.5 million, with production of 28 pods plus spares, tooling and the associated cameras and linescanner equipment bringing the total to £3.25 million. Approval to proceed was obtained in October 1971, but the cost of only 24 pods had increased to £4.78 million.

The development of the Improved F.95 Mk.10 camera was also approved to ensure the necessary low-altitude, horizon-to-horizon coverage with improved resolution. Flight trials of the linescanner began in March 1970 in converted Canberra WK163 and continued until 1977. The Army withdrew its requirement for medium-altitude reconnaissance coverage, but the transfer of the Phantom to the air defence role provided the necessary rationale to fill the gap until the Tornado entered service in the early 1980s.

The provision of an accident data recorder that would record flight parameters, store the information and withstand a crash impact had been part of AST.362. The Air Staff argued whether such equipment was necessary given the weight and space required, but after much discussion the provision was approved. This decision would prove very beneficial for the flight test programme. With the design of the airframe frozen and the various systems and avionics being firmed up, efforts now turned to building the prototypes and making the Jaguar a reality.

This reconnaissance pod under construction reveals the camera installations: the ports for the forward-facing and port low oblique Vinten F.95 Mk 10 cameras; the aperture for the rear drum for the F.126 camera and, aft of that, the space for the EMI/Hawker Siddeley Dynamics infrared linescanner. ***Terry Panopalis Collection***

CHAPTER TWO

Development

Following the signing of Memorandum of Understanding (MoU) in May 1965 by the British and French governments to collaborate on the development of the Jaguar, Breguet Aviation and the British Aircraft Corporation (BAC) began finalising its design and preparing to build the prototypes. The flight testing programme was a joint effort between both countries and encompassed eight prototype aircraft. The joint company Société Européenne de Production de l'Avion Ecole de Combat et Appui Tactique (SEPECAT) was responsible for the development and production programmes. Breguet and BAC test pilots would fly the prototypes alongside colleagues from the national aeronautical test organisations, the Armeé de l'Air (AdlA) and the Royal Air Force (RAF).

The trials programme followed several stages. First was initial flight testing before expanding the flight envelope as well as performance and handling checks. Every possible underwing load, including asymmetric loadouts, had to be tested for drag and handling effects. The prototypes were not just going through aerodynamic testing, they were also the platforms for engine and avionics development. Service trials had to be carried out before release to service could be granted; these included checking out the navigation/attack systems in weapon accuracy trials as well as combat evaluation. Testing reliability and maintainability was equally important to ensure that availability in the field matched the manufacturer's claims. More than a decade was spent testing. Several issues with the airframe and

Jaguar prototypes E01, E02 and A03 flying in formation in 1969. Each of the French prototypes was assigned an identifying code letter: E01 'B', E02 'C', A03 'D', A04 'E' and M05 'J'. *SEPECAT via Author's Collection*

RT.172 Adour engines were uncovered that required rectification. Some of these shortcomings would never be fully addressed, but the Jaguar was further modified and upgraded throughout its service life. In this chapter the flight test programme is described as the Jaguar made its journey off the drawing board and became flying hardware.

Prototypes

Originally four prototypes and a static fatigue test airframe were ordered, but the addition of the Jaguar M and Jaguar S saw an additional four prototypes being ordered on 9 February 1968. The prototypes were contracted under French ministerial procedures. The original contract stipulated a first flight before 1 March 1968, with the prototypes being offered for acceptance no later than 31 October 1969. This timescale slipped as development of the airframe and the Adour encountered problems. The assembly of the first prototype began in January 1968. SEPECAT stood to gain 3 million French Francs (FF) in technical bonuses if targets to better the specified minimum requirements for take-off distance, radius of action and supersonic performance were reached.

Rolls-Royce Turbomeca Limited (RRTM) were tasked with providing 15 flight-ready RT.172 Adour engines for the prototypes in time for the specified trials period. The Adour had only undergone bench testing – the first flight of the Jaguar prototype E01 would be the first flight of the engine too.

Breguet's Chief Test Pilot Bernard Witt was nominated as the Project Manager for the test flight programme. Other Breguet test pilots involved included Jacques Desmazures and Jacques Jesberger, a former Aéronavale and Centre d'Essais en Vol (CEV – Flight Test Centre) test pilot, who was responsible for flying the Jaguar M. Dassault's Chief Test Pilot, Jean Marie Saget, joined the programme later, conducting the first spinning tests. BAC's flight test team would ultimately involve Paul Millett as the Project Test Pilot (from 1970 he was the Warton Division's Chief Test Pilot) along with Chief Test Pilot Jimmy Dell, Tim Ferguson, John Cockburn, Eric Bucklow, Dave Eagles, Jerry Lee (appointed Jaguar Project Pilot in 1975) and Peter Ginger during the 1970s. Between 1971 and 1974, Kenneth Peter Orme was posted to the Aeroplane and Armament Experimental Establishment (A&AEE) and was nominated as the Jaguar Project Pilot (he retired from the RAF in 1981, joining BAe's test pilot team and continuing to fly the Jaguar).

Several national research organisations were involved in the flight testing programme. In the United Kingdom, the Royal Aircraft Establishment (RAE) was

Prototypes			
Prototype	**Registraton/Serial**	**First Flown**	**Fate**
E01	F-ZWRB	08/09/1968	Crashed 26/03/1970
E02	F-ZWRC	11/02/1969	Preserved at the Conservatoire de l'Air et de l'Espace d'Aquitaine, Bordeaux
A03	F-ZWRD	29/03/1969	Writen off 14/02/1972
A04	F-ZWRE	27/05/1969	Preserved at the Musee Aeroscopia, Toulouse-Blagnac
M05	F-ZWRJ	14/11/1969	Preserved at the Musee de Traditon de l' Aeronautque Navale, Rochefort
S06	XW560	18/08/1969	Destroyed 11/08/1972, nose secton preserved at the Boscombe Down Aviaton Collecton.
S07	XW563	12/06/1970	Preserved at Norwich County Hall, Norfolk
S08	XW566	30/08/1971	Preserved at the Farnborough Air Sciences Trust, Farnborough

The first prototype, E01, after its roll-out in April 1968. Note the original engine intakes with the prominent boundary air splitter plate and the shorter nosewheel leg door. Less obvious is the shorter tail fin. *SEPECAT via Paul Chapman*

responsible for aerospace research and development and operated Farnborough and Thurleigh as its main flight test centres. The RAE was overseen by the Ministry of Aviation (MoA) and its successor, the Ministry of Technology (Mintech). The A&AEE at Boscombe Down was responsible for military flight testing and evaluation; it reported to the Ministry of Defence (MoD), which in the early 1970s took over responsibility for military procurement within its Procurement Executive – MoD(PE).

In March 1969, Mintech and BAC agreed that an RAF squadron leader with experience of test flying would be assigned to Warton as an Operational Requirements Liaison Officer. They would participate in the development flying and would ensure that the latest developments in operational and flying training were being fed into the development programme and that the aircraft and its systems were meeting the requirements. Lacking any executive authority, they were to give input and provide feedback to the MoD while avoiding any infringements on Mintech's areas of responsibility.

In France, the Office Nationale d'Etude et de Recherches Aéronautiques (ONERA – National Agency for Aerospace Studies and Research) fulfilled largely the same role as the RAE. The CEV was the Defence Ministry's military flight testing organisation, with the airfield at Melun Villaroche one of its major sites. The Centre d'Expériences Aériennes Militaires (CEAM – Centre for Military Aerial Experimentation) based at Base Aérienne (BA) 118 Mont de Marsan was the equivalent to the A&AEE. CEAM pilots Commandant Gautier, Commandant Gillou and engineering officer Capitane Rolland were involved in the test flying.

CEAM was deeply involved in testing several items of the Jaguar's avionics and systems: the fire control system aboard Mirage IIIE No. 03; the Instrument Landing System and indicator on a Gloster Meteor NF.11; the electrical circuit aboard English Electric Canberra; the Doppler radar and the AJAX artificial feel system on Mirage IIIB No. 235; the CSF 131 gunsight aboard Mirage IIIB No. 202; and the oxygen system aboard Mirage IIIB No. 232. In total, nearly 200 hours of flight testing was carried out between January 1969 and April 1970. As the personnel of the test establishments of both nations got to know each other better, with agreement on methods of testing and common standards, the development process became smoother. Much of the flight testing was carried out jointly in parallel, which saved time and cost.

1960s: First flights

The first Jaguar prototype, the two-seat E01, was rolled out at Breguet's factory at Vélizy-Villacoublay on 17 April 1968. Ground tests and taxi runs were performed by Bernard Witt. The first flight was scheduled for 15 June but was delayed by the outbreak of unrest in Paris that month. The aircraft was dismantled and transported to Breguet's facility at BA 125 Istres-Le Tubé, which would become the home of the flight test programme as Villacoublay was too close to Orly airport to allow safe airspace for test flying. Istres was home to the EPNER test pilots' school – the Ecole du Personnel Navigant d'Essais et de Réception (Test and Reception Flight Personnel School) – and was one of the main flight test centres in France, used by Dassault and other French companies.

E01 gets airborne for the first time at Base Aérienne 125 Istres-Le Tubé with Breguet's Chief Test Pilot Bernard Witt at the controls on 8 September 1968. *SEPECAT via Author's Collection*

E01 climbs out on its maiden flight. ***SEPECAT via Author's Collection***

The delay enabled one of the main fuselage frames to be replaced by a stronger design. Following reassembly, the preliminary taxying trials were completed by 5 August. These revealed that some minor modifications were required that delayed the first flight by a few weeks, preventing E01's planned appearance at the Society of British Aircraft Constructors (SBAC) Show at Farnborough.

Witt finally conducted the maiden flight on 8 September. It lasted 25 minutes and the aircraft attained an altitude of 18,000ft (5,490m). The aircraft was flown supersonically during its third flight. E01 was assigned to tests covering aerodynamics, handling, flutter and general systems behaviour. Witt and BAC Chief Test Pilot Jimmy Dell shared the flying programme, Dell making his first flight on 15 October. E01 carried out 20 flights between 8 September and 19 October, mostly by Witt, but some by Dell, including one supersonic sortie.

The aircraft was then laid up for three weeks for servicing and modifications, including the replacement of the de-rated prototype Adours with fully rated engines. The time was used to rectify some of the issues revealed during the early test flights; modifications were made to the main undercarriage doors to solve a locking problem and the rudder was coupled to the lateral control spoilers through the autostabilisation system to counter the yawing effect produced when the spoilers were deflected. Four further flights were flown between 30 November and 17 December before modifications were made to the engine test equipment. E01 returned to flight on 8 January and completed five flights by the 20th. Problems with leaking wing fuel tanks meant that the aircraft had to fly with them empty.

Lateral control was provided by differential tailplane (+/-10° movement) and the variable coupling of the rudder with the wing spoilers. Artificial feel in pitch was provided by the AJAX system, which had originally been designed for the Breguet Br.1150 Atlantic maritime patrol aircraft and had been flight tested by the CEV on a Mirage IIIB. AJAX was a variable force gradient spring roller/cam device. It took some time to get the artificial feel right and the pitch damper was not used for these early flights. Artificial feel for yaw was provided by a spring in the control linkage and the differential tailplane selector. Artificial feel for roll using the spoilers also used a spring. The roll gearing was arranged to minimise sideslip in rolling manoeuvres.

Then followed the five flights of the First Reception Trials Programme by the various official evaluating establishments between 21 and 25 January 1969. These flights assessed the handling qualities. Two flights were flown by the CEV, two by A&AEE pilot Flight Lieutenant R S Hargreaves and one by the CEAM's Commandant Guillou. Guillou's flight (the aircraft's 34th) lasted 70 minutes and focused on operational aspects. The programme totalled five hours 50 minutes.

It was concluded that the aircraft was generally very pleasant to fly within the restricted envelope then being assessed. Longitudinal control was excellent even without the pitch damper and during transonic deceleration. Deficiencies were found in the standard of lateral control, especially at low speeds. There were recommendations to reduce the spoiler forces and effectiveness, especially when rolling and when flaps were deployed, as well as improving the effectiveness of the airbrakes and to reduce the nose-up trim when they were extended. The CEV pilot argued that handling with the high-lift devices extended was unacceptable but Hargreaves disagreed, feeling that the trim changes were acceptable given the light stick forces. Guillou commented on the great sensitivity to sideslip, the slow rolling speed and hypersensitivity in the roll with the flaps extended. Engine operation was satisfactory but thrust control was difficult due to the throttle box and the engines' response to the throttle movement. There were also numerous critiques of the cockpit layout and instrumentation.

E01 then underwent six weeks of engineering work. Wing fences were fitted to restrict span-wise airflow and the anti-spin strakes on the nose and the anti-spin parachute were removed. The take-off weight was 21,208lb (9,620kg). A meeting of the various stakeholders was held at Istres on 11 February to discuss the progress. At this early stage of flight testing the pilots felt that the aircraft performed well in the transonic region but suffered from high levels of buffeting at high approach speeds and extending the airbrakes and flaps caused a large pitching moment.

Dell made ten flights in E01 and E02 during early 1969 and he, along with Witt, converted fellow BAC test pilot Paul Millett to the type in March. Millett made his first solo in E01 on 29 March and soon after became the lead British project pilot.

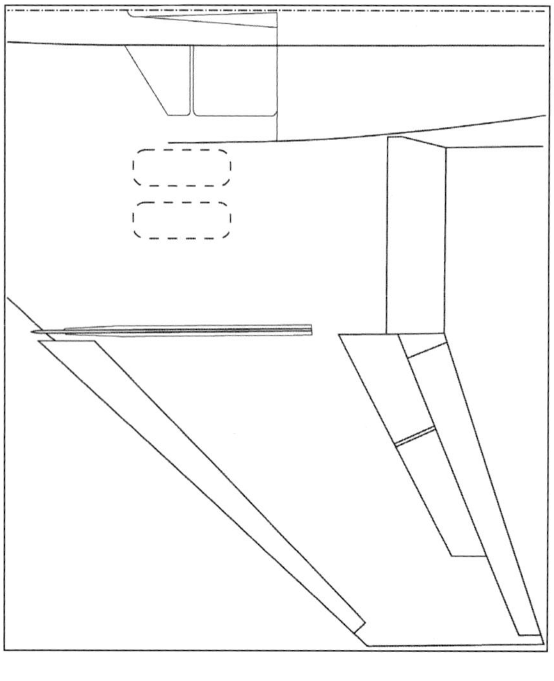

A diagram of E01's wing fence arrangement. The fence was 72.6in (1,845mm) long and was positioned 83.3in (2,117mm) from the aircraft's centreline. ***Author***

Some examples of the flight test sorties conducted during the spring of 1969 reveal the breadth of work undertaken. Bernard Witt took E01 up for its 35th flight on 18 March, consisting of trials of the differential tailplane/spoiler lateral control in all configurations at different altitudes up to 37,000ft (11,280m) and including low-speed handling. Witt found that the rate of roll was satisfactory with less pronounced sideslip oscillations. Rolling was regular and continuous in turns, but roll effectiveness was still excessive with full flap selected on approach, although sideslip was reduced. The flaps had been modified with the maximum deflection increased from 39° to 42°, but this caused buffeting, probably due to the increase in lift. Witt noted that work was needed on improving the airflow over the tailplane to benefit from this increased lift. The newly installed, and faster-responding, two-speed tailplane trim improved the longitudinal control.

Two days later, Witt took the aircraft aloft for an 80-minute flight for differential tailplane tests in clean configuration between 350–450kt at 35,000ft (10,670m). He also explored the lift boundaries and low-speed handling in all configurations as well as looping in full cold power (without reheat). E01 then had its wing fences removed and on 24 March Witt made further differential tailplane tests at 30,000ft (9,145m) to compare the results. He then carried out further test points covering transonic performance, lift boundaries, stalls with 40° flap and low-speed handling with and without the yaw damper activated. The results proved that the fences were no longer necessary given the improvement gained from linking the spoilers to the differential tailplane.

On Flight No. 41 on 27 March, Bernard Witt and Paul Millett – on his second familiarisation flight – went aloft to measure the rate of roll with the wing fences reinstalled. Measurements were taken at 350, 400 and 480kt along with a climb to 38,000ft (11,580m) and low-speed handling tests at 20,000ft (6,100m). Three circuits and overshoots were completed before landing. Millett, in his report, confirmed the very satisfactory view from the rear seat in flight, on the ground and during take-off, approach and landing.

BAC's Director of Flight Operations (and former Chief Test Pilot) Roland Beamont was in the back seat for E01's 44th flight on 1 April with Jimmy Dell in the front cockpit. The test points for this sortie included optimisation of the rudder autostabiliser gain settings and the differential tailplane in partial and 360° rolls. Beamont was there to make independent observations. From the rear seat, the runway was blocked from view between 400 and 200ft (120–60m) on the approach due to the windscreen's arch, but there was an excellent view for sighting ground attacks. Beamont described the aircraft as an 'extremely likeable aeroplane with no vices within the flight envelope experienced'. He found

E01 is prepared for a flight at Istres. This view shows well the original Adour afterburner nozzle configuration and the braking parachute compartment in the tail cone. *SEPECAT via Paul Chapman*

an excellent team spirit at Istres under Witt's leadership.

A flight test programme meeting was held at Vélizy on 24 April 1969. By this time E01 had amassed 57 flights and had been used for work on lateral control, refining the yaw damper and investigations into banking hypersensitivity with the flaps deflected – which was solved by reducing the deflection of the inner flaps. Initial flights carrying underwing fuel tanks were also flown. Following its 57th flight on 18 April, E01 was grounded to fix the fuel leaks from the wing tanks and to replace one of the Adours for overhaul. Repairing the wing tanks required the wing to be removed, the opportunity being taken to carry out three weeks of servicing and modifications.

By June the trials had progressed to manoeuvring and rolling tests at various leading-edge slat settings. Paul Millett took E01 up for Flight No. 76 on 13 June for just over an hour to investigate roll entry manoeuvres at 5,000ft (1,525m) at speeds of 350–520kt and the manoeuvre boundaries at 20,000ft at 320kt with the slats set at 0°, 6° and 9°. Simulated single-engine flying was carried out between 250 and 200kt along with a simulated single-engine approach, overshoot and landing. Millett reported that the automatic differential tailplane control worked well and that the aircraft's lateral and directional behaviour was now better than that of E02. Later the same day, Millett repeated the trial, this time at 30,000ft at Mach 0.9, along with stable flights under same conditions for comparison. Millett also flew ground-attack manoeuvres at 400–450kt, carried out reheat lighting checks and made several simulated single-engine landing approaches.

E01 was flown by Roland Beamont on a test flight at Warton on 3 March 1970, which included general handling tests with a ventral tank fitted, engine handling, rolling under 'g', 'bonker' firings – small explosive detonators attached to induce flutter vibrations to see how well they dampened out – and an assessment of the roll damper.

E01's flying career was brought to an unexpected end on 26 March. The aircraft was on approach to Istres when the starboard engine suffered a catastrophic fire. The pilot, Commandant Brossier, shut down the engine and selected the fire suppression system, but he also accidentally shut down the good engine and the resulting loss of the second hydraulic system caused the flying controls to lock solid. Neglecting to select manual emergency power, Brossier had no choice but to eject. The lessons learned led to the installation of an automated emergency power system that would activate in the event of double engine failure to maintain hydraulic power. The loss of E01 slowed down the development programme significantly.

The second two-seater prototype was E02. Bernard Witt made the first flight on 11 February 1969, being aloft for 80 minutes. The aircraft was assigned to engine and flight performance testing, including spinning and flutter investigations. For the Adour development programme, the aircraft was based at Warton from September 1971. On the first flight, Witt climbed the aircraft to 10,000ft (3,050m) at 350kt and then carried out 4g manoeuvres at 450kt before ascending to 35,000ft with acceleration to Mach 0.92, to enable a supersonic dive at Mach 1.02. Rolls were made at 20,000ft before Witt explored the low-speed handling (at this stage, E02 lacked wing fences). A Morane Saulnier MS.760B Paris II chase plane filmed the low-speed manoeuvres.

The second Jaguar E prototype, E02, taxying with Bernard Witt in the forward cockpit in early 1969. ***SEPECAT via Paul Chapman***

Final checks before E02 taxies out for its first flight at Istres on 11 February 1969 with Bernard Witt at the controls. ***SEPECAT via Author's Collection***

E02 had received its wing fences by the time of Flight No. 7 on 8 March. Witt took the aircraft up for a sortie lasting 50 minutes. He made a reheated climb to 20,000–30,000ft (6,100–9,145m), reaching Mach 1.1 at that altitude. Witt then carried out a relight of the starboard engine and performed an Immelmann turn from 3,500ft (1,065m). Witt noted that the Adours did not achieve their expected thrust, either at cold or reheat settings, and the reheat failed to operate above 31,000ft (9,450m).

For Flight No. 13 on 18 March, Jimmy Dell made a 45-minute sortie for aft centre-of-gravity manoeuvring checks, pulling 5g at a speed of 500kt at 3,000ft (915m) and then 3.5g at 400kt and 25,000ft (7,620m). Dell caried out a relight of the port engine, throttle 'slam' accelerations at Mach 0.8 at 20,000ft, followed by more manoeuvre checks at 300kt at 20,000ft. He then carried out engine relight checks and performed an Immelmann at 450kt and 3,000ft. Dell noted that the fitting of a restrictor in the reheat pipe had improved the performance; E02 reaching Mach 1.18 at 32,000ft (9,750m) and climbing to 36,000ft (10,970m) at Mach 1.06.

The test programme progressed to flutter checks. Ground tests had been conducted using E02 with empty fuel tanks, then full-load trials as well as tests with and without external stores on the underwing hardpoints. BAC's calculations had focused on subsonic speeds while Dassault dealt with the transonic region between Mach 0.9 and Mach 1.4. The most critical vibration couplings were those on the horizontal stabiliser, with a high risk of explosive flutter in transonic flight at low altitude. The existing mass balance was retained for the airborne trials using bonkers. On 29 March Dell performed Flight No. 16, lasting an hour at a weight of 22,820lb (10,350kg) with bonker firings at Mach 0.85 at 17,000ft (5,180m), with the pilot noting that he felt a very slight disturbance. He then made a maximum-reheat climb from 25,000ft up to the reheat extinction altitude. Following this, the port afterburner failed and Dell carried out level flight checks and stick force/g checks at 10,000ft.

The next flight two days later was much more relaxed, Dell flying in formation with E01 and A03 for a photoshoot with a Mirage IIIB and Dassault Mystère 20

E02 showing the Jaguar's clean lines when unencumbered by pylons and aerials and other military equipment. Today, E02 is on display at the Conservatoire de l'Air et de l'Espace d'Aquitaine, Bordeaux. *SEPECAT via Author's Collection*

as camera ships before carrying out reheat lighting checks. A meeting at Warton on 3 April reviewed the flutter studies, especially the effect caused by carrying and jettisoning external stores, and E01 later joined the flutter investigations.

Relighting the afterburners proved to be a serious problem. The 20th flight on 17 April was curtailed early when Dell encountered problems during the climbing and relighting checks. Dell took E02 aloft on 16 May for Flight No. 22, carrying out relight checks on the port engine but it failed to relight. After Dell shut down the engine there was a fire in the combustion area, which was quickly extinguished. Four days later Dell was still encountering problems during fuel flow checks and a practise demonstration for the forthcoming Paris Air Show. Later that day Dell tried again but this time the starboard afterburner failed. E02 had been fitted with prototype engines Nos. 22 and 23 since its initial run-up tests on 22 February. Following the flight the engineers discovered cracking on the exhaust cone of engine No. 23 and it was replaced by engine No. 25. On the very next flight engine No. 22 suffered a regulator failure and was swapped with No. 18. Following a sortie on 17 April the engineers found cracks on the exhaust cone of after just one flight and it was replaced by No. 26. This engine immediately suffered reheat ignition and surging problems during ground running. At that point a crack was discovered in the air intake and E02 was grounded for repairs.

A change of pilots brought no better luck. Paul Millett took E02 up for a refamiliarisation flight on 31 May, including reheat relighting and low-speed handling at 20,000ft, but only one engine would relight. Two days later Millett flew Flight No. 29 involving fuel consumption checks at 34,000ft (10,360m), reheat lighting checks and Dutch rolls – a combined yawing and rolling movement – and rolling manoeuvres at Mach 0.8, both with and without the yaw autostabilisation engaged. The autostabiliser improved the damping of the Dutch roll, decreased the yawing and any excursions in steady rolling manoeuvres.

Millett displayed E02 at Le Bourget at the Paris Salon de l'Aéronautique during 5–8 June. Following this interlude, test flying resumed. On 23 October BAC test pilot Tim Ferguson had his first familiarisation flight, flying with Witt. On 28 November Millett and Witt flew a lateral handling sortie – this was the 100th Jaguar flight and Millett's 30th.

The first single-seat Jaguar prototype, A03, flew supersonically on its first flight on 29 March 1969 at Istres, with Witt at the controls for the 70-minute trip. The first flight had been delayed by problems with

The first Jaguar A prototype, A03, spools up as it prepares to depart on its maiden flight at BA 125 Istres on 29 March 1969. Bernard Witt was again the pilot. *SEPECAT via Author's Collection*

reassembling the elevator servo-controls and incorporation of modifications arising from experience gained during E01's flight trials. There were also problems sourcing flight-cleared Adours for the aircraft. A03 was assigned to the development of the navigation/attack system as well as store clearance carriage trials and weapons firing. Bernard Witt flew the first sorties, including one on 23 April, which studied the problems affecting the air conditioning system and the modified airbrakes.

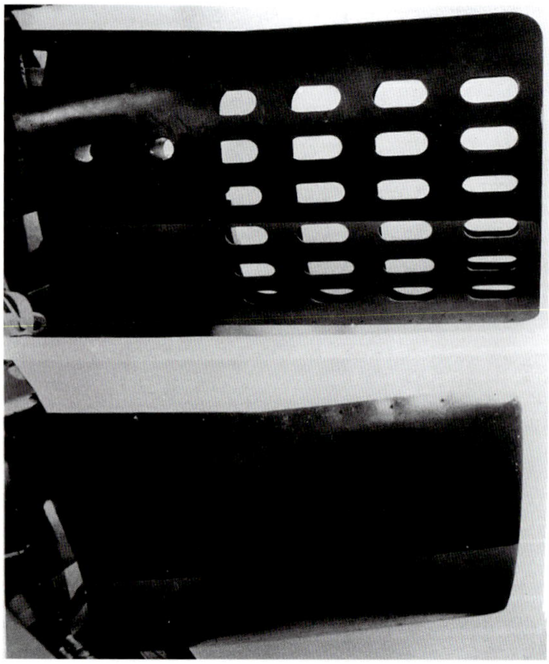

The original plain airbrakes (pictured at the bottom) produced high levels of buffeting and pitching at high approach speeds and were modified to a perforated design. *Author's Collection*

Witt flew two sorties on 8 May, the aircraft's 5th and 6th flights, the latter of which ended with an incident. Witt had been aloft for 35 minutes, carrying out reheat and relighting tests at 20,000ft before heading back to Istres. During his approach the port engine stalled and Witt touched down 2,400ft (730m) short of the runway, in the undershoot area. Witt made a gentle touchdown at 120kt and hoped that the aircraft would reach the main runway on its mainwheels, but as the speed dropped below 110kt the nose wheel came into contact with the ground and collapsed. Witt felt no shocks or bumps from the main undercarriage, however, which attested to its strength for rough field landings.

The second single-seat prototype, A04, made its first flight on 27 May at Istres, flown by Jimmy Dell. A04 was assigned to flight handling tests for the single-seater, stores clearance and weapons firing. The next day Dell began the programme of engine handling and flight envelope expansion, taking the aircraft up for over an hour, carrying out handling tests at 10,000ft and checking the effectiveness of the roll dampers at 350kt – which he discovered were unserviceable. Dell then climbed to 40,000ft (12,190m), before diving to 30,000ft, attaining Mach 1.1 before using the airbrakes to decelerate to Mach 0.9. Following this a ten-minute photographic sortie was flown alongside a Mirage IIIB. After the flight, Dell commented on the differences

A03 gets airborne. The main nosewheel undercarriage door was later shortened while the section attached to the nose leg was lengthened to cure vibrations in flight. *SEPECAT via Author's Collection*

Jaguar A04 was assigned to flight handling tests, stores clearance and weapons firing. At the time of this photograph the 30mm DEFA cannon ports had not been installed. *Author's Collection*

from the two-seat Jaguar E; the handling had been improved (especially at low speeds) and the transonic performance was similar, as was the deceleration from the airbrakes.

Dell flew A04 again on the 29th for handling checks at 10,000ft and 30,000ft at Mach 0.85 as well as decelerations at 20,000ft and checks of the manoeuvring limits at 320kt. During a single-engine approach with 20° flap at 170kt, a fire warning annunciator for the port engine came on. Dell performed a single-engine landing, selecting reheat on the starboard engine to enable him to hop over the runway lip and barrier. The application of asymmetric power caused the port wing to drop but Dell corrected it and landed safely. Flight No. 5 on 2 June involved Dell flying handling checks at 36,000ft (10,970m) and rolling manoeuvres during a descent from 34,000ft with lateral and longitudinal jerking of the control stick and Dutch rolls. The reheat lighting was also checked. Turns at Mach 0.86 were made at 36,000ft, the starboard wing dropping sharply at a 5° angle of incidence (the angle of the wing in relation to the airflow, also known as angle of attack – AoA). Applying the leading edge combat slat delayed – and reduced the sharpness of – the drop up to 7° AoA.

Following the flight the groundcrew replaced the port Adour with engine No. 22. Dell performed a 45-minute flight test on 4 June, including fuel consumption and reheat lighting checks. Later that day Dell set off on a ferry flight from Istres to the CEV at Melun Villaroche. A Dassault Super Mystère B2 fighter accompanied A04, Dell finding that he had to throttle well back during the climb at 350kt to enable his escort to maintain formation. Some problems with the fuel feed system were encountered, but the emergency transfer system worked and the flight continued. On approaching Melun Villaroche, Dell extended the airbrakes on approach and the Super Mystère rapidly overtook him, proving the efficiency of the Jaguar's airbrakes. The visit to Melun Villaroche was to enable a safe demonstration work-up for the 1969 Paris Salon. The following day Dell flew two practise demonstrations with E01 and E02 before heading to Le Bourget airport. By this stage A04 had only made ten flights. Dell demonstrated the aircraft on the 7th and 8th. After a three-day stopover, Dell flew back to Istres, again having to throttle back in the climb so that his Super Mystère escort could keep up. Dell landed in light rain without any problems.

Following the jaunt to Paris, test and demonstration flying continued. Dell flew a test sortie on 21 June with a maximum power climb to 38,000ft (11,580m) at 450kt, performing a Dutch roll at 36,000ft and checking the manoeuvre limits at that altitude with the slats extended at 9°, which gave significant improvement. Another Dutch roll was flown at 20,000ft, followed by a practice demonstration but problems remained with the fuel feed system.

A04's 16th flight was another ferry to Melun Villaroche on the 23rd with an escorting Super Mystère. Fuel feed problems were encountered again, as was a storm with heavy rain. Dell found that he had no

The first prototype Jaguar S, S06, was completed at Warton. It was assigned to navigation/attack system development as well as weapon trials. ***BAE Systems via Author's Collection***

S06 received the serial XW560 and was externally little different from the Jaguar A. ***BAE Systems via Author's Collection***

visibility on landing, advising the technicians that the windscreen needed a rain dispersal system or a water repellent coating. Dell took the Jaguar across the English Channel the following day, the ferry flight from Melun Villaroche to the Central Flying School (CFS) at RAF Little Rissington taking 50 minutes. An RAF Hunter F.6 flew as escort. Dell encountered two snags; the compass proved to be erratic and the brake parachute failed to deploy properly on landing. On the 26th Dell flew his demonstration at Little Rissington to mark the CFS's 57th anniversary; the audience included Queen Elizabeth II, Prince Philip the Duke of Edinburgh, Prince Charles and the Queen Mother. The next day A04 was flown directly back to Istres in 75 minutes. Escorted by a Hunter F.6 again, Dell climbed at maximum dry power, but unlike the Super Mystère the Hunter had some power in hand – not surprising given that the Hunter's Rolls-Royce Avon produced a maximum thrust of 11,250lbf (50.04kN) compared with 9,200lbf (40.92kN) combined from both Adours in dry thrust.

The naval prototype, M05, made its first flight on 14 November 1969 at Melun Villaroche with Jacques Jesberger at the controls. Further details of M05's experimental flying career are discussed in Chapter 8.

The first British-built prototype, the single-seat S06 (serial XW560), was rolled out at Warton on 18 August 1969. Following ground checks and taxi trials, Jimmy Dell performed the maiden flight on 12 October, including some time at supersonic speed during the 55-minute sortie. On landing, he was greeted by Managing Director Freddie Page, Roland Beamont and Project Director Ivan Yates. S06 was assigned to navigation/attack system development, as well as weapon trials and in-flight refuelling tests. Early ground gunnery trials revealed that the structure of the gun bay was insufficiently strong to absorb the recoil forces. S06 received reinforcement modifications on one side only ahead of its first flight to avoid causing delays but sufficient to allow the armament trials to go ahead.

The second Jaguar S prototype, S07 (XW563), was the first to be fitted with the full Navigation/Weapon Aiming Sub-System (NAVWASS) and was the first aircraft in Europe to fly with a digital inertial navigation system. The maiden flight took place on 12 June 1970 at Warton with Jimmy Dell at the controls. S07 was assigned to avionics trials and stores carriage, including Matra R.550 Magic air-to-air missile (AAM) trials. S06 and S07 flew a joint sortie on 23 December 1970, flown by Paul Millett and John Cockburn from Warton. This flight brought the combined flying hours of the two British prototypes to 155 hours in 200 flights.

The sole two-seat Jaguar B prototype, B08 (XW566), flew on 30 August 1971 with Paul Millett at the controls; the flight lasted 46 minutes and included two minutes

S07 was the first Jaguar S with the full NAVWASS system, although it initially lacked the LRMTS, and carried out armament clearance trials. The inner wing hardpoints are equipped with a tandem beam for two 1,000lb (454kg) bombs with a pair of Matra rocket pods on the outer hardpoints. ***Philippe Ricco***

supersonic. The aircraft was assigned to flight trials specific to the two-seat cockpit, as well as avionics development. B08 was built with 80% production parts, effectively being the only pre-production aircraft.

Teething troubles

By mid-February 1972 the prototypes had amassed 1,674 flights totalling 1,700 flying hours. Several of the early production aircraft joined the flight test effort and several challenges remained to be overcome. Some significant changes were necessary; two ventral fins and an enlarged vertical tail fin were required to improve stability and the engine intakes were redesigned.

During the early summer of 1973 it was confirmed that all the Jaguars suffered from defective lateral flight handling at low altitude when flying at speeds between 400–450kt with an AoA greater than 8° and a load factor higher than 3g. The cause was a combination of mechanical and thermal stresses caused by the aircraft's acceleration that led to relative distortion of the fuselage and unwanted deflection of the rudder that caused sideslipping. A means had to be found to fix the aircraft already built using mechanical and electrical fixes in the directional control circuits. The mechanical solution was developed by Dassault but this method could not correct the thermal distortion. The electrical solution used sensors to measure the structural distortion, signalling the autostabiliser to apply the required rudder deflection to compensate.

Until the tests could be completed a flight restriction to a load factor of 3g below 985ft (300m) and 10° diving angle was applied by SEPECAT. The RAF found this unacceptable as it would render its early production aircraft non-operational and they pressed the CEV to expediate the trials. The AdlA were monitoring the situation but did not impose any flight restrictions and wanted to see which solution worked before implementing anything.

Jaguars B08, S2 and B1 were used to test the electrical solution and E1 tested the mechanical system. Early results were not encouraging; the mechanical modification seemed to overcompensate and the RAF worried about the reliability of the electrical system. BAC also developed a spoiler/rudder coupling to reduce the load on the spoilers and transferred the rudder trim from the port-side cockpit console to the control column to allow the pilot to trim the aircraft quicker. This was trialled on S2 and A04. The RAF pursued the electrical solution and BAC's modifications, but France had to pay towards the costs under the terms of the MoU and this caused some ill feeling as they had selected the mechanical solution. Although the development programme was a binational affair, both partners often disagreed on how best to rectify issues and in some cases were duplicating each other's work.

Fatigue cracking on the lower wing skin was observed on the fatigue test rig on 5 November 1973 and then appeared on the early British production aircraft S2. This was solved by making a stress-relieving cut-out. An identical crack on the upper skin of the fatigue test frame occurred on 26 February 1974 after 3,358 hours, equating to the Jaguar S's 2,000-hour safe flying life. The same solution was applied successfully. Cracking on the wing trailing edges was noted on British and French aircraft after relatively few flying hours in early 1973. The cracks appeared on aircraft that had been carrying four, two or even no external stores at all. Aerostructures specialists from both nations investigated the problem and devised a structural modification that added 5lb (2.4kg) of weight to the aircraft.

The RAF's Jaguars were fitted with fatigue meters, so the MoD(PE) became quite relaxed about the fatigue life limits, but the AdlA had decided not to fit them and therefore any structural issues caused them more worry. For one fatigue issue BAC proposed using a simple reinforcement plate with adhesive bonding augmented by interference fit bolts. This was supported by the RAE but SEPECAT's Technical Director Marcel Berjon rejected this solution given problems that he had encountered with the Br.1150 Atlantic. The RAE was not concerned due to the different materials used on the Atlantic, but the STAé backed Berjon and there was an impasse until agreement could be reached.

Jaguar S2 also suffered wing spoiler attachment point failures during the lateral instability trials. The spoilers were replaced but failed again after eight hours. Testing on B08 discovered that the problem was caused in the transonic region when turbulence on the upper part of the spoilers could cause an uncommanded deployment that went unnoticed by the pilot. The decision was made to strengthen the attachment points and the Dassault engineers abandoned coupling the spoilers with the rudder. B08 was also used for main undercarriage bay stress tests during 1977–78.

Another serious issue was the violent and uncontrolled departure from flight at high AoA. The airflow over the canopy and inner wing sections caused fin masking to occur and carrying external stores exacerbated this. The roll autostabiliser lost effectiveness over 13° AoA, the spoilers lost their effectiveness above 12° and above 400kt the tailplane differential gearing offered little roll control (rolling due to sideslip was more frequent than compared with other aircraft). The airflow separation reduced the natural Dutch roll damping to zero, as AoA increased the damping accelerated the roll rate, leading to a rapid divergence.

There was disagreement in early 1974 about the warning system to be fitted to guard against a departure. The AdlA wanted to use Dassault's system that gave a 'compulsive warning' when the never-exceed AoA limit was reached, as they believed that any 'worst value' control law would be exceeded by front-line squadron pilots in certain situations, for example when in clean configuration. The A&AEE and MoD(PE) wanted to use a Ferranti system with nominal warnings at a 14° operational limit, a 17° never exceed limit and when the rate of change exceeded 3°/sec. The RAF was unconcerned about the 3° difference between the clean and external load configurations in operational conditions because they felt that any pilot using more than 17° AoA would find themselves in a disadvantageous tactical position anyway.

Both partners agreed to disagree and fitted their own chosen systems, although they agreed on the need for a stick shaker to back up the audio warning (in the case of the Jaguar S to be fitted from production aircraft S136 and retrofitted to previous aircraft). Sufficient improvement had been made by early 1974 to achieve clearance for stores release at 5g/14° incidence (normal operational limit) and 6g/17° (never exceed limit).

The Jaguar's stall was not conventional; airflow separation on the outboard wing sections began around 9° AoA, and as the angle increased the inboard vortex flow patterns offset the outboard loss of lift from the separated flow – the Jaguar could never reach maximum lift. There was also a lack of stall warning; pre-stall buffet began around 9°, but beyond 14° the buffet did not increase, even if the AoA increased to 30°, and a stall warner was added. Wing rock was not a reliable stall warning as it was a Dutch roll motion; as AoA increased so did the possibility of violent divergence occurring within two seconds. Recovery was difficult, if not impossible below 10,000ft, due to the full spin along with engine surging or flameout. Therefore pilots were advised to avoid rapid rolling at high AoA and if wing rock was encountered the AoA should be relaxed immediately.

The Jaguar underwent further changes as requirements were raised or dropped. Some of these were jointly funded through SEPECAT for both users and others were self-funded national projects. The Jaguar A and S would receive several new items; anti-glare lights, a hand-powered emergency hydraulic pump (the Jaguar A also received an electric backup pump), roll damper and automatic slats. The Jaguar S gained inertially activated crash switches and reverted to the original longer control column (including additional flight testing to re-balance the pitch control) – it was discovered that when shorter pilots raised the ejection seat to keep their eyes level with the Head-Up-Display (HUD) that the shorter control column did not allow enough lateral movement between the thighs; the need to keep a pilot's eyes level with the HUD was a lesson that was factored into future cockpit design requirements. The Jaguar A also received AIM-9 Sidewinder and Matra R.550 Magic AAMs, a blind flying screen, cockpit fire extinguisher, anti collision lights, PTR for the Adour Mk.102 engines and a flaps down warning system. To offset these gains the hot-air windscreen rain dispersal was removed, the RAF dropped their requirements for napalm tanks, AS.37 Martel air-to-surface missile (ASM) and the internal F.95 camera; the AdlA dropped their requirements for napalm tanks, AS.30 ASM and AVTAG fuelling.

E01, E02 and A03 in formation in 1969. Two of these prototypes had short lives; A01 crashed on 26 March 1970 and A03 was written off following a heavy landing on 14 February 1972. ***SEPECAT via Author's Collection***

CEAM carried out exhaustive maintenance assessments – known as a VAMOM – on prototypes A04 and S07 using AdlA mechanics with representatives from SEPECAT, RRTM and the major subcontractors such as Microturbo, Dunlop and Messier in attendance. The VAMOM on A04 consisted of 285 maintenance operations and resulted in 270 modification requests. This effort evolved into a continual process of assessment and refinement. By July 1971, 387 of the 469 modifications requested had been implemented into the production aircraft.

There were also other future requirements under discussion, including crash barrier and airfield arrester gear compatibility tests and hot weather trials (especially relevant for the export market and RAF use in the Middle East) and a target-towing capability. The AdlA was also looking to add an engine surge warning alarm, the TAV-38 laser rangefinder and an electronic countermeasures (ECM) pod.

SEPECAT was reluctant to pick up all the costs and felt that the national governments should pay. The Jaguar Management Committee, however, felt that the cost should be shared and reminded SEPECAT that had the aircraft actually been delivered, the company would have been liable under the contract guarantee to remedy the defects that the modifications had been designed to overcome. In return, the Committee felt that late delivery penalties should not be applied to SEPECAT because it had been the Ministries who had insisted on the modifications being made before delivery, despite the delays that entailed.

The desire to get the Jaguar into service without delay prompted co-operation using production aircraft on a short-term basis to avoid duplication of effort. For example, some airframes at Warton were used for ground resonance tests and measurements for the AdlA.

A strike at BAC lasting 13 weeks during 1972 lost the company 300,000 man-hours, which severely impacted production (the Breguet line being reliant on UK-produced parts) and delayed NAVWASS and reconnaissance pod development. Warton was affected again by industrial action during late 1973. During January–March 1974 the coal miners' strike in the UK led to the Energy Crisis, which imposed electricity consumption restrictions and a three-day working week. BAC was restricted to 65% of normal electricity consumption but managed to secure a waiver from the working day restrictions. Even so, production at BAC all the airframe and engine suppliers and sub-contractors were affected. In the spring of 1977 it was Dassault's turn to be affected by industrial action, delaying the delivery of four aircraft – by this time the rate of production had been decreased from 2.25 to 1.5 airframes per month to keep production going until July 1981.The economic impacts of inflation had also made themselves felt; the UK's estimated development costs of £66.3 million in December 1970 rose to £70.6 million by July 1971 (including £1 million due to the reconnaissance pod), but still leaving £3.9 million unspent from the contingency fund. By May 1977 the UK's production costs were £307.5 million for 200 aircraft, 488 engines plus the various modification costs.

Adour problems

One fundamental problem with the Adour was its lack of power. As early as 1965, the RAF had approached RRTM with a recommendation to increase the dry thrust by 15%, but the cost implications had caused the AdlA to object. To counter increasing airframe weight, a 10% thrust increase was provided in the Mk.101 engine; 5,115lbf (22.8kN) dry thrust and 7,305lbf (32.5kN) reheated. By the summer of 1971 flight testing had shown a clear need for additional thrust due to the poor thrust/weight ratio. Manoeuvring at low altitudes when carrying external stores at weights around 28,000lb (12,700kg) required the use of reheat, which reduced range. The single-engine approach was the most critical aspect due to the disparity between the maximum dry thrust and minimum reheated thrust, and the safety margins were unacceptable. This was highlighted by Bernard Witt's accident in A03 in May 1969 at Istres and another undershoot soon after with another prototype that luckily resulted in no damage.

RRTM was provided with £750,000 to study the problem. The solution was part throttle reheat (PTR) to allow the selection of minimum reheat at 80–100% of dry thrust rpm for smoother and quicker application of reheat. It was also proposed to fit a second platinum-rhodium catalyst in the afterburner for better control of fuel ignition and burning. This solution was agreed in December, but the AdlA was reluctant to fully endorse the catalyst solution until it was proven in trials, early production Jaguar A and E aircraft receiving interim single-catalyst engines.

The Adour Mk.102 with double catalysts was tested on E02. The first of 40 Phase I flights was carried out on 16 September 1971 (E02's 193rd flight) by Rolls-Royce test pilot Graham Andrews and observer D Wilkinson with very satisfactory results. Phase II comprised 27 flights, then Phase III trials by A&AEE and CEV pilots. The performance of the engine at dry thrust was similar to the Mk.101. Modulating the thrust from maximum to minimum reheat caused some pop surges at speeds below 300kt at altitudes above 20,000ft, as did cancelling the reheat at altitudes above 10,000ft. On one occasion the pilot inadvertently reselected minimum reheat three seconds after cancellation following take-off and suffered a serious engine stall.

Ultimately, pop surging was recognised as being fairly harmless to the engine and was accepted as a foible of the engine by the RAF. The AdlA, however, was less satisfied. The CEV encountered engine surging during gun and missile firing at lower speeds than those indicated by Dassault's tests and the starboard engine surged at speeds around 40kt lower than the port engine. Random 'silent surges', of which the pilot was often unaware until serious engine damage was caused by the rising temperature, remained a serious concern to both air forces.

RRTM devised four modifications to improve the situation; Modification Mod. 144 added a speed switch to stop surging when the throttle was slammed into reheat for rapid acceleration; Mod. 171 introduced a revised pressure ratio control unit to solve surging on reheat selection; Mod. 175 added an optimised amplifier to solve the reheat cancellation surges; a modified Flow Control Unit improved the fuel flow to limit surging in dry power (engine surge performance with PTR above 10,000ft was never officially cleared – even into the early 1990s). BAC also trialled a revised gun shroud on early production aircraft S3 (serial XX110) and B2 (XX841) to provide better protection for the intake from gun gas ingestion.

The Adour suffered from other serious problems and incidents destroyed two of the Jaguar prototypes and grounded a third. Vibration trials during early 1972 did not go well, which dented the RAF's confidence. They reasoned that if prototype engines fettled in the manufacturer's workshops had issues, then mass production service engines would fare even worse. RRTM was running 200 hours of service cycle endurance tests on a test rig using a production engine when the high-pressure (HP) drum compressor suffered a failure, then the HP drum's third stage failed on prototype engine No. 21 aboard prototype S06 in August 1972, destroying the aircraft.

The investigation focused on the titanium used in the manufacture. RRTM offered a service life of 250 hours, with an inspection at 150 hours, and highlighted that Adours supplied to Japan for the Mitsubishi T-2A had exceeded 250 hours without any issues. In contrast, the AdlA found that their early production engines were only lasting 60–95 hours. A total of £2 million was set aside for modification work and the grade of titanium used was altered from IM 684 to IM 685. A service life of 1,000 hours was the ultimate goal, with

Adour designs						
	RT.172-15	RT.172-16	RT.172-23	RT.172-17	RT.172-18	RT.172-19
Dry thrust	5,400lbf (24.02kN)	5,440lbf (24.19kN)	5,450lbf (24.24kN)	5,545lbf (24.66kN)	5,760lbf (25.62kN)	6,080lbf (27.04kN)
Reheat thrust	7,640lbf (33.98kN)	8,400lbf (37.36kN)	7,900lbf (35.14kN)	8,810lbf (39.18kN)	9,075lbf (40.36kN)	9,500lbf (42.25kN)
Weight	1,665lb (755kg)	–	–	1,678lb (761kg)	–	1,750lb (793kg)
Bench hours	1,020	–	–	2,000	–	3,000
Cost	£3.135m	–	–	£9.65m	–	£22.1m

500 hours guaranteed from the start of the modified drum's production. Production was hampered by problems forging the IM 685 alloy in France and production issues at Turbomeca, especially with electron beam welding.

The need for more thrust remained. In May 1972 the Marine Nationale stated that they wanted 6,360lbf (28.3kN) of dry thrust for the Jaguar M to ensure a safe engine-out landing, although they would accept a minimum of 5,500lbf (24.4kN). The MoD was calling for 20% additional dry thrust. RRTM concluded that such an upgrade would result in a larger and more expensive engine that would not be ready for production before 1975. The MoD accepted that a small increase in power and an improved exhaust nozzle would be sufficient and would also benefit the HS.1182 Hawk basic flying trainer then under development.

RRTM offered two minimum change engines, the RT.172-15 and -23, while investigating longer-term 'major change' developments. Six variants were studied, providing a range of improvements of 17–31% in dry thrust and 10–37% in reheated thrust compared with the Mk.101/Mk.102 engines – which themselves were 11% and 6% greater than the original specification respectively. The proposals had new low-pressure (LP) and HP turbine rotors with improved cooling, the RT.172-18 and -19 gaining a larger-diameter LP compressor and the -18 receiving skewed blades for the HP compressor. Most of the designs also benefited from a new chuted fuel/air mixer, a revised fuel feed system and a hotter afterburner. All but the RT.172-15 had a larger jet pipe, the Jaguar having space for an increase of 3in (7.6cm) in diameter and 9in (22.8cm) in length without modification. The MoD(PE) considered the RT.172-16 to be the most attractive choice.

By early 1974 RRTM was offering the RT.172-26 and -30 but there was no funding available to pursue these options. The AdlA were focused on improving the current Mk.102's level of performance. The RAF decided in 1977 to go ahead with the Mk.104, which offered a performance similar to the RT.172-26 and allowed the upgrade of existing Mk.102 engines. The Mk.104 had a redesigned LP compressor and an improved flame-tube in the afterburner. The dry thrust was increased by 2.8% to 5,450lbf (24.2kN) and reheated thrust by 9.5% to 8,280lbf (36.8kN). The AdlA decided not to adopt the Mk.104 to avoid the additional costs and the increase in fuel consumption, but this decision would impose performance limits on the Jaguar A throughout its life.

The intakes were modified. The RAE issued a report in August 1969 on wind tunnel tests it had undertaken at Bedford to determine the optimum size and form of the intakes. It was found that reducing the entry area from the prototypes' 2.84ft^2 (0.264m^2) intake would reduce the amount of spillage drag by 15–20% to improve performance between Mach 0.8 and 1.8. The 10° wedge compression surface was also removed to alter the configuration into a pitot intake. As a result the intakes of the prototypes were rebuilt during overhauls during the early 1970s.

During the late 1970s the Adour was still beset by teething issues. Early Mk.102 engines had erratic

A wind tunnel model of the single-seat Jaguar during tests to refine the engine intakes. ***Author's Collection***

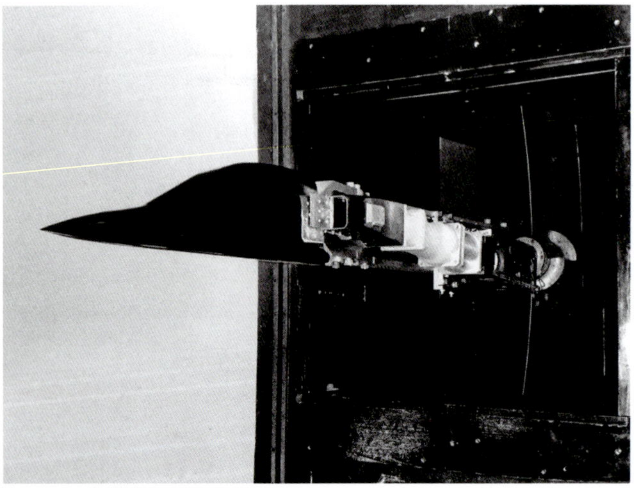

A model of the two-seat Jaguar in the wind tunnel during tests to refine the drag created by the intakes. ***Author's Collection***

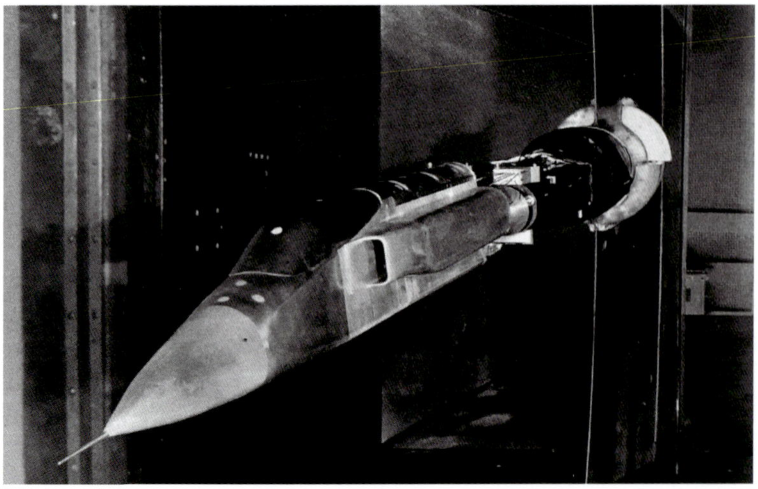

performance due to the build-up of carbon in the flame tube. A modified flame tube was fitted but then a series of flameouts were encountered. It was found that the glowing hot carbon deposits had been masking undiscovered uneven fuel flow issues. These were corrected by altering the settings of the fuel control unit. Surging on selecting reheat remained a problem and the Mk.102 engines were modified with a quicker nozzle response and improved burner spray patterns to alleviate the issue. The uprated Mk.104 operated closer to the surge line, especially in hot conditions.Several Mk.102 engines experienced cracking of the second-stage LP compressor disc at the retaining pin holes, and stator vane cracking in the first-stage LP compressor with no obvious cause was observed during strain gauge testing.The Management Committee was very concerned and pressed RRTM to investigate. A new LP compressor blade was designed to reduce vibration and extend service life. High rates of wear in the HP compressor stators were discovered in 1975, the inner ring seal being replaced using electron beam welding to permit a stator life of 1,500 hours with an intermediate check at 750 hours (a further modification in the mid-1980s removed the need for this check).

During rig investigations into a HP turbine blade failure, an LP turbine disc failed due to resonance. No resonance had occurred during rig tests or on production engines. RRTM carried out further testing with production engines to determine the cause but a second LP turbine disc failed on a test engine with strengthened turbine blades. No build error was found but further investigations were required. In June 1978 an uncontained failure of a second-stage LP turbine disc during a ground test destroyed Jaguar GR.1 XX761 and the exhaust detuner attached to it. The fatigue failure had been caused by an aerodynamic vibration in the disc that was excited by a critical mix of HP nozzle guide vanes. A thicker disc was introduced and engines with the critical mixes of guide vanes were removed.

The RT.172 Adour required a lot of development to improve its reliability and thrust rating. Developed alongside the Jaguar airframe, any delays and faults impacted the entire flight test programme. This aircraft is the second production Jaguar A. *Author's Collection*

By mid-1976 the RAF was experiencing a high number of cracks in the exhaust mixer cone, which RRTM put down to the higher thrust demands required by the RAF compared with the AdlA's operational flight profiles. The solution was to use stitch welding rather than spot welding for the cone fairings.

1970s: Testing the Jaguar E & A

Following the loss of E01 on 26 March 1970, E02 was the remaining Jaguar E prototype. On 10 May 1971, Paul Millett and Jacques Jesberger flew a handling test and aft CG trial. The aircraft then joined the Adour test programme, Millett making the ferry flight from BA 120 Cazaux, near Biscarrosse, to Warton on 9 September.

CEAM was responsible for technical testing with emphasis on operational aspects for the AdlA. Several early production aircraft were assigned for testing, including A2, being towed out of a hardened aircraft shelter at BA116 Luxeuil in 1972. *Author's Collection*

Jaguar A2 was fully equipped and the muzzle of the port 30mm DEFA cannon can just be seen inside the gunport. The early production aircraft had the original intake with the boundary layer splitter plate. ***Author's Collection***

The aircraft was fitted with Mk.102 engines and flew its first test sortie at Boscombe Down on 31 December, but on return cracks were discovered in the main undercarriage attachment points. This led to E02, A03 and A04 being grounded for repairs.

E02 did not fly again until 24 March 1972, by which time it had received production standard engines with PTR. Phase III PTR tests resumed at Boscombe Down, including a flight by Roland Beamont and Paul Millett on 2 August. In May 1973, E02 completed the PTR control trials and testing of a fuel collector box venting modification, which in the event proved too expensive for production. During May and June the aircraft was laid up and refitted with the new pitot air intakes and equipment for spinning trials. There was a delay in returning to flight due to leaking wing fuel tanks. Flights finally resumed on 10 August. Fixes for the continuing fuel tank leaks took place during September and October.

E02 replaced B08 in the high-incidence/AoA and spinning trials programme from December 1973. These flights were dogged by several issues and delays. During a sortie on 21 January 1974, the aircraft unexpectedly departed into a fully developed spin with deployment of the anti-spin parachute being required to effect recovery. The AdlA initially blamed the BAC pilot, Tim Ferguson, for poor procedure but this was soon discovered not to be the case. The spinning procedure previously developed with Jaguar M05 had been applied, the controls being released at the departure point to take up the pre-trimmed condition. The two-seater's dual flight control circuit seemed to allow the inertia effects to cause a large lateral control movement and a more violent oscillatory spin than that encountered on the single-seaters.

BAC and the RAF stressed that due to the risks involved, further flights to determine the control loss characteristics and develop spin avoidance techniques should take precedence over the planned trials. Later the same month, Jaguar B XX136 suffered a flick roll at 19° incidence at 15,000ft (4,570m) during an A&AEE test flight. The roll was so violent that the pilot, Flight Lieutenant Peter Orme, was not sure in which direction the roll was.

Following the installation of a modified anti-spin parachute, the departure trials recommenced with E02 on 14 March. The recovery procedure was amended to positively return the controls to the optimum position at the point of departure. Although the French Ministries continued to complain about the lengthy duration of the trials (partly due to continuing fuel leaks and lack of support equipment), the MoD refused to transfer E02 back to France, having little confidence that the CEV test team would complete the tests safely and accurately. Tim Ferguson flew over 100 spinning sorties in the aircraft, being awarded the Derry and Richards Memorial Medal and the RP Alston Memorial Medal in 1976 in recognition of his work. These sorties

Prototype A03 following its landing mishap on 14 February 1972. ***Philippe Ricco***

Eight multicoloured dummy 1,100lb (500kg) bombs are hanging from the five hardpoints aboard A04 for bomb release trials. *SEPECAT via Terry Panopalis Collection*

confirmed that the two-seater had worse spinning characteristics than the single-seater. Following the end of its test life, E02 was airfreighted back to France on 29 May 1980 as an instructional airframe.

Following repairs after Bernard Witt's short landing in May 1969, prototype A03 returned to flight. Following experience from static gunnery trials, the structure of A03's gun bays were reinforced to absorb the recoil forces of the cannon to allow the armament trials to go ahead. The aircraft was badly damaged at Istres on 14 February 1972 when returning from an engine evaluation flight. This disrupted its planned work on flight refuelling, gun firing, performance demonstrations and stalling/spinning trials. Misfortune struck again a few months later when an engine fire led to the aircraft being written off and used for ground tests and as a spares source for the remaining prototypes.

During the summer of 1970, Commandant Guillou of the CEAM made his first flight in prototype A04. He noted the progress that had been made in reducing roll sensitivity with the flaps extended, but the transverse yaw and roll damping was still unacceptable. In addition, a CEAM report in September 1970 called for major improvements to the throttles and engine controls, which were rated as being unacceptable even for an experimental aircraft. On 20 November Commandant Gautier of CEAM flew A04 for further assessment.

A04 was handed over to the joint A&AEE and CEV team at Istres in early December 1971 for official initial release trials – termed Reception in France and CA Release, Controller Air Release, in Britain – the point at which a set of defined performance and capability parameters were released to enable Service pilots to operate the aircraft. The trials were completed by the end of January and CA Release in the clean configuration soon followed. A04 then undertook French pylon and stores clearance work and also trialled an improved pitch control.

The aircraft also took part in aerial refuelling trials, with some of these sorties being flown by Paul Millett. Following initial air-to-air refuelling trials with the AdlA's Boeing C 135F Stratotankers, it was decided to modify the probe on both the Jaguar A and S to maintain commonality. The first in-flight refuelling sortie to prove the compatibility with the RAF's Handley Page Victor K.2 tanker was flown on 1 October 1971, which indicated that the original probe may have been acceptable for the RAF, at least in the interim.

A04 was laid up on 15 March 1973 due to wing root fuel tank leaks. Following repair, it arrived at CEV in May for handling trials with various stores configurations including bombs, fuel tanks and rockets. As an indication of how large this task was, no fewer than 350 load configurations had to be tested throughout the programme for the French and British aircraft. The CEV trials were completed by the end of July and the aircraft returned to SEPECAT. It carried out simulated 880lb (400kg) bomb and nuclear weapon drops as well as

The first production Jaguar E, E1. This aircraft began its service career with the CEAM. ***Author's Collection***

jettisoning full and empty fuel tanks. The poor results of the asymmetric stores release trials led to SEPECAT prohibiting such releases in service, which concerned the AdlA.

Following more asymmetric trials, A04 progressed to rocket pod carriage and release trials. In January 1974, trials with rigid slats – which had been added in response to the slat fatigue problem – revealed no improvement in the flying qualities.

Following the cancellation of the Jaguar Marine programme, the naval prototype M05 was reassigned to spinning trials. Wind tunnel tests conducted at Lille University had explored the likely types of spin to be encountered and any potentially erratic behaviour. The aircraft was fitted with recording equipment and the jet pipes were modified for oil injection so that the aircraft's gyrations could be recorded on camera from the resulting smoke trails. Two electro-hydraulic pumps and three batteries were fitted to enable recovery to the airfield should a double engine flameout occur and the engines fail to relight. M05 had its check flight following the modifications on 4 July 1973.

Progress was slow; 30° AoA was only achieved at the end of the month and the spinning trials did not properly begin until September. Wind tunnel tests were used to study the phase immediately before entering the spin to assess the hazards for the test pilots. Paul Millett returned to Istres and flew the aircraft during 20–22 November, the minimum altitude for the spin test being 40,000ft. He found that the spin was highly oscillatory in all axes and – disconcertingly – smoke would issue from the intakes and flow forwards past the cockpit canopy when the aircraft slid backwards in the spin. Test pilots Peter Orme from the A&AEE (who had taken a French test pilots course and was fluent in the language) and Nick Warner were also involved in the spinning trials, along with Bernard Witt and Jean-Marie Saget.

M05 was delivered to CEV on 10 January 1974 for induced stall trials in clean configuration, followed by similar trials by the A&AEE. It then took part in a SEPECAT high AoA study with different load configurations. Orme flew M05 11 times between 13 June and 15 July at Istres. His first flight in M05 was a telemetry test with a simulated dead-stick landing. The next day he flew high AoA departures, which resulted in a multi-turn spin and double engine flameout. Luckily he managed to recover the aircraft and relight both engines for a safe landing. One flight was a recovery from a vertical manoeuvre; pulling into a vertical climb at Mach 0.9 at 35,000ft, cancelling the reheat and maintaining the vertical climb until the airspeed fell to zero, tumbling over and falling back down. At 40,000ft both engines entered a silent surge and began to overheat. Throttling back to idle made no difference so Orme had to shut them down. Finally the apex was reached and the nose pitched down. A gentle roll to the right and gravity accelerating the aircraft in the dive brought the aircraft back to normal flight and the engines were restarted.

Orme's final flight was M05's 400th flight and proved exciting when the aircraft unintentionally entered a linear spin, which was similar to a 'falling leaf' manoeuvre, for up to ten seconds – something that the Jaguar had never done before. For his contributions to the test programme, Orme was awarded the Air Force Cross in 1975 and the AdlA's Silver Flight Safety Medal for his actions during a flight training incident. Jacques Jesberger became reacquainted with M05 in 1975 for load carrying trials, which he flew in collaboration with Bernard Witt. M05 made its final flight on 12 December 1975.

The first production Jaguar E, E1, joined the test programme at Istres following its formal acceptance by the AdlA in December 1971. The aircraft was used for ground tests to measure pitch control and test sorties included trials of a new fuel feeder vent design and DEFA cannon firing tests at the CEV. E1 also carried out radio trials and five aerial refuelling flights in June 1973 using a new nose refuelling probe, the pilots commenting that the Jaguar E was more sensitive during the drogue hook-up compared with the Jaguar A.

During July and August E1 flew rudder compensation trials in connection with the fuselage flexing issue and the stresses on the spoilers were measured. New Adour Mk.102 engines were fitted in September before another series of aerial refuelling and performance trials, including handling and stall warning, which were completed in January 1974. E1 was then laid up for modifications before beginning trials with rigid slats in February to validate the tests flown with A04 and to settle the engineers' worries that vortices coming off the slats might lead to handling issues. These were followed by radio tests at the CEV before beginning armament tests specific to the Jaguar E.

Jaguar E2 was flown to CEAM at Mont-de-Marsan by Commandant Gautier and Captaine Rolland and handed over on 4 May 1972 for the trials programme. CEAM nicknamed E2 'Matou' (Tomcat). Test maintenance operations were carried out such as changing the wheels after landing. Engine starting in cold temperatures during the winter of 1972–73 was also carried out, which required several adjustments to the starter system. The use of a braking parachute without a bag was tested successfully, which saved appreciable time when repacking the parachute following a landing.

The first production Jaguar A, A1, joined the test programme in the summer of 1972. Navigation tests ended in late March 1973 and were followed by radar altimeter tests, and weapon trials, including freefall and retarded bomb releases, at Cazaux to prove the fire control system. Following an appearance at Le Bourget for the Paris Air Show, little flying was undertaken due to equipment failures and a lack of spares. During a period of maintenance in the winter of 1973–74 a serious contamination of the hydraulic circuit required most of the hydraulic equipment to be replaced. This delayed the resumption of systems and armament trials until May 1974.

Production Jaguar A2 joined E2 at CEAM for operational trials. In 1972 it visited BA 116 Luxeuil, the home of 4éme Escadre de Chasse. The third aircraft, A3, was initially assigned to nuclear weapon carriage and AN 52 bomb drop trials. These finished in July 1973 and

Prototype A04 flying over BA 118 Mont de Marsan during its assignment to CEAM, based at the airfield. Note the unusual split AdlA/RAF roundel and it appears that the ground crew have added their own artwork too! ***Author's Collection***

Trials of the emergency landing arrester hook were undertaken, as well as tests that involved deliberately running into runway crash barriers to see if they caused any damage to the airframe. Jaguar A1 was used for this task. ***Philippe Ricco***

the aircraft then went to CEAM for further nuclear-related trials. During January 1974 modifications were made to upgrade the equipment and prepare for R.550 Magic AAM tests. Within a month the aircraft was carrying out gun-firing flights to determine the trajectory of the cartridge cases, which had been hitting the tail fin of the ventral fuel tank when it was fitted. A3 then headed to the CEV to determine the flight envelope for the production configuration.

In 1971 the decision was made to switch to the new DEFA 553 cannon. Ground tests were completed, but flight tests were delayed to the end of 1971 due to the more pressing need for Adour development. Frustratingly for the AdlA, the DEFA 553 caused the same engine surging effects from ingesting the gun gases and airframe vibrations as the older DEFA 552. The modified gun support structure had to balance the conflicting demands of maximum strength and minimal weight and the result was a compromise; firing both cannon resulted in severe vibration in the cockpit, which affected aiming. Jaguar A4 was also used for TAV-38 laser rangefinder system trials.

1970s: Testing the Jaguar S & B

The first prototype Jaguar S, S06, carried on its trials programme. BAC Chief Test Pilot Jimmy Dell's long test flying career of over 5,000 flying hours ended on 24 October 1970 when he flew a flutter test in S06 before retiring from test flying. John Cockburn joined the team five days later and undertook a familiarisation flight. He went on to fly engine handling, performance and tail fin bonker firing flutter trials. Another newcomer to the team was Dave Eagles, who made his first Jaguar familiarisation flight on 18 February 1971. The first RAF pilot to fly the Jaguar was Squadron Leader Neil Hayward, in S06 at Warton on 22 December 1970.

On 23 February, Paul Millett flew S06 direct from Warton to Istres, covering the 738nm (1,366km) in 85 minutes, which included 25 minutes at low level on arrival to accomplish a test point. CEAM flew the aircraft during the three days at Istres, including checks on the roll damper. On 17 March the aircraft made its 200th flight, Millett being at the controls for the 36-minute test flight. Two days later S06 participated in the A&AEE's 50th Anniversary celebrations at Boscombe Down, with Princess Anne in attendance.

By early spring 1971 the British portion of the test programme was well under way, with S06 and S07

The second production Jaguar E, E2, with CEAM at Mont de Marsan. The aircraft carried the code 118-AC on the port side and 118-AA to starboard. ***Author's Collection***

Jaguar S07 XW563 during trials carrying two underwing fuel tanks and two 1,000lb (454kg) bombs on the ventral hardpoint. Every combination of underwing stores had to be aerodynamically checked in all phases of flight, including stores jettison. *BAE Systems via Author's Collection*

clocking up 263 flying hours in 261 sorties. The Duke of Edinburgh visited Warton on 30 June and inspected the Jaguar final assembly line, being accompanied by Sir George Edwards, Freddie Page, Ivan Yates and Paul Millett, who also flew a display in S06. The aircraft went to the A&AEE in mid-July 1972, before going to the Paris Air Show. During the month Millett flew handling checks, fuel tank jettisons and releases of four 1,000lb (454kg) bombs.

S06 met an unexpected demise. It was destroyed on the ground on 11 August due to an uncontained engine failure, when the third-stage of the HP compressor drum suffered a fatigue failure. The debris flung out ruptured a fuel tank and the ensuing fire consumed the aircraft, Millett just managing to escape the inferno.

While prototype S07 was at Warton, a team of 20 RAF engineers performed 200 engineering tasks on the airframe over a ten-day period, practically stripping the aircraft down and reassembling it during their maintenance assessment. Following its reassembly, test flying resumed. The aircraft flew its 200th flight on 17 March 1971 and on 13 July Paul Millett, Tim Ferguson and John Cockburn flew a combined seven sorties in one day, a record at that time.

Much of early 1972 was spent on NAVWASS development work before heading to Boscombe Down in the summer. NAVWASS was achieving an accuracy of 2–4nm (3.7–7.4km) after an hour's flying time – including high-g turns – by the summer. The main problem was that it took 36 minutes to warm up after a cold soak at temperatures down to -3°C. A team of Elliott engineers based at Warton kept writing and debugging the NAVWASS software until it worked perfectly. S07 underwent flutter trials at the A&AEE to obtain production clearance for the weapon pylons and the fuel drop tanks. Flight trials with the tandem beam to carry a pair of bombs on the inner underwing pylons took longer to obtain clearance.

Much of 1973 was spent on flutter and weapon firing flights, fuel tank jettison trials and use of the CBLS with practice bombs for aiming accuracy trials. On 26 July 1973, test pilot Eric Bucklow performed his first solo flight on the Jaguar with a supersonic performance and engine-handling test. At end of July,

S06 XW560 breaks from the camera ship during a test sortie. *BAE Systems via Terry Panopalis Collection*

A single 1,000lb (454kg) bomb has just been released from the inboard underwing hardpoint from S07. *Terry Panopalis Collection*

S07 was fitted with a rudder damper to cure the flutter caused by the fairing for the Marconi radar warning receiver (RWR), which had been added to the vertical fin above the rudder, and test flights were flown during August. The aircraft was laid up in mid-October for modifications for the Special Weapon Tests for the WE.177 nuclear bomb, emerging the following January. Paul Millett flew one of these WE.177 handling test sorties on 21 March 1974.

Further NAVWASS and radio tests followed, but the bulk of the test flying into 1975 was dedicated to obtaining WE.177 clearance. S07 was also used for toss bombing trials with dummy 1,000lb bombs during January–February 1975 at the A&AEE. Handed back to BAC in February 1975, S07 was finally put into storage at Boscombe Down in June 1977. It then was then passed to RAF Brüggen as a static weapons loading trainer with the maintenance serial 8563M applied.

The BAC test pilots noted that B08 seemed to suffer from a persistent buffeting, which had not been apparent on E02, although the first production aircraft E1 shared the problem to a lesser extent. To discover the cause, 25 flights were made with aerodynamic refinements, tufting and vortex generators during late 1971. Some improvement was noted but the buffet was still marginally unacceptable in the landing approach and cruise configurations. The buffet was eventually diagnosed as being caused by the fuselage's fundamental bending mode being excited by vibrations in flight.

Paul Millett flew flap performance tests in January 1972, one of these also involving BAC production test pilot Peter Ginger. Roland Beamont flew B08 with Millett on 19 June – B08's 64th flight – to make an assessment from the rear seat prior to the aircraft being used on the Indian Air Force evaluation. Beamont found the stability and control to be good, despite the heavy longitudinal control stick force and the slightly oversensitive lateral control in turbulence with the roll autostabilisation disabled. The cockpit environment was judged to be good and he was especially impressed by the accuracy of NAVWASS in poor weather (the fifth dummy attack was aborted, however, due to a drift of over 1 mile (1.6km)). The aircraft had excellent stability even in cloud and turbulence, but the heavy rain hampered visibility of the ground targets from the rear seat. Beamont flew another rear assessment during a weapons aiming test flown by John Cockburn on 16 February 1973. Having been employed as a test pilot with Ferranti before joining BAC, Cockburn became the key test pilot for NAVWASS.

On 20 June Paul Millett flew Squadron Leader John Preece, the Jaguar Operational Requirements Liaison Officer, in the back seat to get a taste of the Jaguar's capabilities. Tests were made during 1973 on the fuel system (including a collector box vent modification that was not entirely satisfactory, but cheaper, than the modification trialled on E01), the air conditioning and the hydraulics system. Eric Bucklow began assisting the flight test programme in the back seat in March. Beamont and

Ferguson made an assessment flight of the production standard roll stabiliser at Warton on 4 April.

After a lay-up period during August, the aircraft was delivered by Squadron Leader Preece and test pilot Jerry Lee to the A&AEE at Boscombe down on 12 September to complete the two-seater prototype acceptance trials. Following its stay with the A&AEE, B08 flew across the Channel to the CEV to perform the same task. B08 then returned to complete the NAVWASS trials. Another lay-up period ended in January 1974, during which B08 received additional instrumentation and structural adjustments. The aircraft undertook fuel circuit and braking and heat qualification tests prior to another lay-up to receive the new pitot intakes.

From the summer of 1975, trials focused on clearing the Lepus flare (two being carried on the centreline fuselage hardpoint and one on each outboard wing pylon) and other items, such a three 264gal (1,200L) drop tank configuration for ferry flights ahead of the planned series of winter trials in Canada. Then B08 returned to clearing the CBLS and bomb configurations for CA Release of the Jaguar T.2 as entry into RAF service beckoned.

The RAF's first production Jaguar S, S1 (serial XX108), made its maiden flight from Warton on 12 October 1972, with Deputy Chief Test Pilot Tim Ferguson at the controls for the 71-minute flight, with a portion flown supersonically. The first task was to take up the arrester hook trials that S06 had been unable to start before it was destroyed. These were undertaken at the A&AEE in early May 1973. S1 was then used for handling checks and proving the release conditions with external stores. Following modifications, the aircraft returned to the A&AEE on 25 January 1974 for a bombing accuracy programme, followed by load release and flight quality testing in new configurations of external stores.

Jaguar S2 (XX109) was the first aircraft to have the full avionics fit and the Laser Ranger and Marked-Target Seeker (LRMTS). Chief Test Pilot Paul Millett took it aloft on 16 November from Warton, going supersonic during the flight, which lasted 75 minutes. The second prototype LRMTS, coded X2, was fitted to the avionics rig at Warton in September 1972 for validation before being fitted to S2 for flight trials in early 1973. LRMTS flight trials using Canberra B.2/8 WJ643 since March 1971 had proved mostly satisfactory.

Following a check of the arrester hook as part of the trials involving S1, the aircraft went to the A&AEE for handling trials with external stores in April 1973. The aircraft was laid up for modifications to the LRMTS and addition of the RWR in October. Flight tests were carried out with the long control column, as well lateral control tests and trials with wing fences and vortex generators in an attempt to increase the high AoA limits. Leading-edge slat strengthening tests were also flown. Unserviceability while with the A&AEE saw S2 returned to Warton in early 1974 for rectification work before resuming LRMTS development trials. S2 was then used by the A&AEE for symmetrical and asymmetrical underwing loads as well as fuselage bending compensation and coupling trials.

Jaguar S3 (XX110) began ground ADEN cannon firing trials on 26 March 1973, which revealed an issue with the NAVWASS system. This was subsequently rectified and in-flight gunnery trials began. No issues were found when firing one gun but there were still structural problems when firing both guns, with high vibration in the cockpit and nosewheel bay areas. Some structural stiffening was applied, but the problem was never fully resolved and during the Gulf War in 1991 the pilots still encountered severe cockpit vibrations when firing both guns. High-Mach flights to prove the new intake splitters fitted in early June were carried out; the modifications were satisfactory and Paul Millett attained Mach 1.4 in a dive on 20 June. Gunnery trials continued well into 1974 to expand the firing limitations, including firing at supersonic speeds on 15 May. The pilots criticised some aspects of the aiming display, which led to modifications. A new gun silencer was tested and fitted from production aircraft S70 onwards.

During 13 May–24 June 1974, joint A&AEE/RAF air-to-ground trials were flown to reduce the computation error that was occurring under positive pitching conditions, resulting in too large an angle being displayed on the HUD. A total of 12 sorties were flown, but success was mixed due to poor weather and resulted in computations that were accurate in elevation but with some azimuth error remaining. The pilots also found that the aircraft weaved in certain configurations, which made azimuth

Aerial refuelling clearance trials with the RAF's Handley Page Victor tanker fleet were carried out using S07, which has made contact with the drogue streamed out by Victor K.1A XH618 of No. 57 Squadron. *Blue Envoy Collection*

The first production T.2 trainer, XX136, in September 1974 while undertaking trials with the A&AEE. The aircraft had a short life, getting into an unrecoverable flat spin and crashing in Dorset on 22 November 1974, both crew ejected safely. ***Terry Panopalis Collection***

tracking difficult. Despite this, it was agreed that CA Release could be given for air-to-ground firing, subject to minor improvements.

The first production two-seat Jaguar B, B1 (XX136), first flew on 28 March 1973, flown by John Cockburn and Reg Stock. The aircraft went to the A&AEE on 23 May for handling trials for CA Release and was also used for long control column and lateral control tests. It then took part in spoiler/rudder interconnection trials, this being BAC's preferred solution to reduce the load on the spoilers to reduce the fatigue risk. On 12 February 1974 the aircraft returned to Warton to be fitted with reinforced spoilers and modifications to the AJAX and NAVWASS systems.

On 22 November, while carrying out a clearance trial at high AoA carrying a centreline 264gal (1,200L) fuel tank and two 1,000lb bombs inboard, the aircraft departed and entered a violent spin that could not be recovered. Jaguar project pilot Flight Lieutenant Cruickshank and the Officer Commanding A&AEE 'A' Squadron, Wing Commander Clive Rustin, ejected at 9,000ft (2,740m) and the aircraft crashed. Cruickshank suffered back injuries on ejection and was in hospital for a prolonged period. Luckily the A&AEE were able to retrieve the magnetic recording tape from the recorders and apply the results into the ongoing AoA trials successfully.The avionics were also progressing. A dummy reconnaissance pod was completed in 1972 for aircraft loading trials. The EMI IR linescanner was flight tested from April 1972 aboard a Canberra operated by the Royal Radar Establishment. Some design and reliability problems were encountered with the ARI.18220/3 Plessey PTR377 UHF/VHF radio transceiver and the ARI.23143 PTR175 was fitted as an interim replacement (the PTR175 was a British development of the American Collins ARC-52 and lacked the PTR377's data transmission capability). The PTR 377 never gave satisfactory service, however, and was replaced from 1981 by the Marconi AD120 VHF and Magnavox ARC 164 UHF transceivers (the installation being designated ARI.23315/4).

E02 was displayed at the 28th Salon de l'Aéronautique at Le Bourget, Paris, in June 1969. The code '208' was the show number assigned by the organisers. *Author's Collection*

Shows

The prototypes also had to represent the Jaguar at the two premier European air shows, the Salon de l'Aéronautique at Le Bourget, Paris, and the SBAC Show at Farnborough. At the 28th Salon at Le Bourget in June 1969, all four of the French prototypes then extant marked the Jaguar's debut. The British debut of Concorde and Jaguar at Farnborough followed in September 1970. S06 was flown by Jimmy Dell and Paul Millett and was accompanied by E01, A03 and M05. On 9 September, Paul Millett suffered engine trouble during his display in S06, causing him to abort the flight. M05 was selected as the backup aircraft to fill the display slot but an engine malfunction resulted in an aborted take-off run and M05 remained grounded for the remainder of the show.

At Paris in 1971, S06 was flown by Tim Ferguson and A04 by Paul Millett, while also in attendance were E02, A03 and M05. B08 was flown by Tim Ferguson and Paul Millett with Roy Kenward during 8–10 September at Farnborough 1972, being joined by S07 and early production Jaguar E3.

At the 30th Salon in 1973, S06 and S07 were joined by a production Jaguar A. A04 was displayed with eight dummy bombs (pairs on the ventral and inner wing hardpoints with singles outboard), as was S07 (tandem bombs on the ventral and inner wing hardpoints with singles outboard).

At Farnborough in 1974, B1 XX136 was flown by John Cockburn and Jerry Lee, making runway-length inverted passes and rolling during slow passes with the undercarriage and flaps extended and conducting short landings. The first production Jaguar S1 was also shown and the flying display included early GR.1s XX114, XX726, XX728, XX729 and T.2s XX138 and XX146.

A typical wet Farnborough week in 1971 with Jaguar A03 loaded with a dummy AS.37 Martel anti radar missile. *Terry Panopalis Collection*

A04 made an appearance at the 1973 Paris Salon de l'Aéronautique carrying eight dummy 1,100lb (500kg) bombs, twin carriers on the ventral and inboard pylons and singles outboard. ***Author's Collection***

The 1975 Paris Air Show featured T.2 XX841 flown by Tim Ferguson and John Cockburn; its delivery to the RAF was delayed so that it could appear. Production Jaguars A20 and E21 were also on display. By now the prototypes were old news and production aircraft dominated the line-ups. For example, Farnborough 1976 hosted T.2 XX915 and GR.1s XZ358, XZ362 and XZ363. From that point on Jaguars were represented in smaller numbers, often in Jaguar International guise, before disappearing at Farnborough in 1986.

Anything the Jaguar A can do ... S07 was also flown at Le Bourget in 1973 with eight dummy 1,000lb (454kg) bombs, in the same configuration as A04 except that the ventral bombs were carried in tandem. ***Author's Collection***

WSAM

The Chief of the Air Staff, Marshal of the Royal Air Force Sir Denis Spotswood, approved the Weapon System Accuracy Measurement (WSAM) trials in the summer of 1972 to lead the way for an Initial Operational Capability in March 1974, followed by Full Operational Capability by the end of that year. Being a national programme, the MoD had to foot the £200,000 bill itself. The trials would consist of 200 sorties totalling 275 flying hours, including weapons release over the Larkhill and West Freugh bombing ranges. The WSAM trials were be flown by the A&AEE from the autumn of 1973 in partnership with the RAF's Central Trials and Tactics Organisation (CTTO). Following WSAM were the Intensive Flying Trials and the Operational Capability Trials by the CTTO, as well as operational turnaround and role-changing tests.

The Engineering Development and Investigation Team at RAF Lossiemouth also undertook engineering and servicing trials, which gave rise to a large number of modifications, many of which had to be retrospectively installed into early production aircraft (the Jaguar Modifications Committee approved 818 modifications, 590 for the AdlA's Jaguars and 626 for the RAF's). In France much of the modification work was undertaken by industry, whereas in the UK it was the RAF's maintenance units that had to undertake this work.

Jaguars S3 (XX110), S5 (XX112) and S6 (XX113) were assigned to the WSAM trials. BAC test pilot Jerry Lee delivered S5 to Boscombe Down on 17 September 1973. John Lumsden, one of the No. 1 Jaguar Conversion Team Course pilots, was assigned to represent the RAF. Poor weather and the Energy Crisis hampered initial progress but thereafter things improved and the trials lasted around 18 months in total. Lumsden flew 87 sorties in the GR.1 and he dropped 52 practice bombs, eight dummy BL.755 cluster bombs and 60 dummy 1,000lb bombs. The ballistics data gained was invaluable in honing the system and obtaining service clearance. The NAVWASS hand controller and HUD were also fine-tuned.

The CTTO led the tactical trials, which fed back into WSAM to make a combined package. This experience would lead to dedicated Operational Evaluation Units being set up for future RAF combat aircraft to ease their introduction into service. XX110 was returned in November but the other two aircraft were retained for LRMTS development.

A&AEE dispatched GR.1 S17 (XX720) for tropical trials in the United States, first visiting Nellis Air Force Base (AFB) in Nevada during 12 July to 24 August 1974. The aircraft was fitted with the Adour Mk.102 equipped with a JP103 double catalyst in the afterburner. The aim of the trial was to test engine handling in high air and ground temperatures. The static thrust was also measured on the test stand at Edwards AFB. Satisfactory performance was demonstrated during the 45 flights operating with peak temperatures of 41°C and no problem was foreseen in extending the CA Release to cover ground ambient temperatures up to 45°C. The only caveat was that reheat propagation might be delayed when using AVTAG fuel.

S07 at the Paris Air Show with a pair of dummy 1,000lb (454kg) bombs on the centreline and two fuel tanks under the wings. ***Terry Panopalis Collection***

XX720 transferred to Eglin AFB in Florida in September to fly in the hot and humid conditions up to 35°C. One problem that was encountered was overheating of the inertial platform during ground running – the ambient air was used to keep the platform cool (the platform itself ran at 73°C inside a nitrogen-filled cannister kept at 55°C with outside air blown over the external casing on the ground and from the air conditioning system in the air). The A&AEE recommended that in ambient ground temperatures between 35 and 40°C the aircraft should take off within 40 minutes of selecting gyro alignment. In service the Jaguar's air conditioning was often found to be ineffective, and the pilot had to choose between cooling the avionics or the cockpit but never both at the same time.

XX720 flew to Canadian Forces Base Cold Lake on 15 September for cold weather trials, which began on 28 October. Few slushy, snowy or icy conditions were initially encountered and so the trials were extended after Christmas in the hope of obtaining colder temperatures. The aircraft and avionics were subjected to cold soaking and open air servicing. The lowest cold soak was -35°C, while swings up to -60°C were obtained by rolling the aircraft outside from heated hangars. The aircraft was subjected to blowing snow with wind gusts up to 42kt and up to 6in (15cm) of snow fall. A total of 16 flights were undertaken, with a dozen of these following a cold soaking. Generally few problems were encountered. The result was an extension of the

As service release neared the RAF began gearing up. Seen here at Warton is a mix of prototype Jaguar S and early production GR.1 and T.2 aircraft. ***Blue Envoy Collection***

CA Release to temperatures down to -10°C (later relaxed to -15°C) with -25°C possible with certain minor modifications to the engine control system, throttles, ejection seat, oxygen control panel and cockpit canopy. XX720 returned to Boscombe Down via Winnipeg, Ottawa, Goose Bay, St Johns and Lajes in the Azores on 13 February 1975.

In another related icing trial, a Jaguar was flown behind the RAE's Canberra B.2 WV787, which was fitted with an icing spray rake under the tail, to check the effectiveness of the de-icing systems.

In March 1975 the A&AEE used XX720 for flight refuelling trials, which concentrated on the ferrying external fuel tank configurations and normally used the Victor K.2 tanker's wing refuelling pod stations, although the centreline station was also checked out. The Jaguar's probe could be extended and retracted between 270 and 300kt (it could remain extended up to 350kt) below 28,000ft (8,534m), this altitude limit was imposed to prevent engine surging.

GR.1 S41 (XX744) was delivered to the A&AEE for Nuclear Biological and Chemical clearance tests, radio trials and electromagnetic compatibility clearance tests in 1975 following electromagnetic interference problems in two incidents during September 1974; Jaguar pilots flying past the radio transmitters at Rampisham near Weymouth in Dorset and Daventry had reported autostabiliser and engine control interference.

Jaguar T.2 B19 (XX831) was issued to the A&AEE for a short loan period and carried out 17 engine flameout test flights in early 1975. Trials on grass runways had been completed by October 1977. Take-offs had been demonstrated at a maximum weight of 30,865lb (14,000kg) and landings at 24,250lb (11,000kg). Trials using the same grass runway showed that it could withstand 35 take-offs and that use was only limited by the deterioration of the grass. The RAF would only use grass runways in wartime but taxying practice on grass was authorised in peacetime.

Further developments

After the Jaguar entered front-line service the development tasks did not cease. There were still issues to be resolved and new problems emerging as the pilots and ground crews got to grips with the aircraft and future improvements were investigated. The first two production GR.1s were retained as instrumented aircraft for stores configuration clearances, high AoA trials, LRMTS and reconnaissance pod clearances until the end of 1976. Test pilot Peter Ginger would fly many of these tests, making his last test flight on XX109 on 2 February 1979.

XX109 flew bomb release trials at West Freugh as late as 1979 and made its final flight on 29 July 1986 with BAe's Jaguar Project Pilot Derek Reeh at the controls for a structural stress test flight of the F4 fuselage fuel tank. XX109 had accumulated 853 flying hours in 791 test sorties over 14 years and had contributed to the development of NAVWASS, LRMTS, the reconnaissance pod, the Adour as well as laser-guided bomb handling and jettison, handling and flutter tests for the Phimat chaff and AN/ALQ-101(V)10 ECM pods and AIM-9L Sidewinder jettison and live firing trials.

The AdlA began missile firing envelope trials with the Martel and Magic, with the first live Martel firing on 9 March 1977. AIM-9 Sidewinder firing trials for the RAF began in November 1980. A fuel dipping system for the Adour was developed, momentarily reducing the fuel flow to the engines so that ingesting the missile exhaust plume into the intakes would not cause surging. The system was proved on E02 in March 1978 before further trials were flown on A3. Trials to marry the Thomson-CSF ATLIS laser rangefinder pod to the Aérospatiale AS.30L ASM were delayed until 1980. In early 1978 the AdlA stated that they wanted a heading and altitude hold system to ease the pilot's workload, allowing the pilot to conduct in-cockpit operations, such as NAVWASS waypoint updates, more safely. The RAF considered modifying the autostabiliser system to provide a similar capability and Smiths Ltd drew up a technical proposal. Both nations investigated whether a common development programme was possible, but the idea was never taken further.

The A&AEE continued work on the AoA limits and by March 1978 had completed tests of their system, demonstrating up to 20° AoA without departures or incidents; the CA Release limit was set at 17° to provide a margin of safety. BAe proposed fitting a high-authority autostabiliser to allow safe handling up to 17° AoA. BAe offered a simplex system while Smiths offered a comprehensive triplex system in the pitch and yaw circuits, but the estimated £12–14 million cost and eight-year development time counted against its adoption. Automatic combat flap deployment was investigated using GR.1 XX108 at Warton during 1978 in a joint programme with the AdlA, but this was later dropped.

The second production GR.1, XX109, received a set of carbon fibre engine bay doors in 1983. The use of carbon fibre saved weight, an important consideration given the Adour's low thrust. ***Terry Panopalis Collection***

A considerable amount of structural research into carbon fibre composites was taking place across the aviation industry at this time and some of this work was being fed into Jaguar. The key advantage of using composite materials was reducing weight. Initial research during 1970–71 looked at producing a wing spoiler and a tail fin. A collaboration with Grumman Aerospace led to BAe designing composite engine bay doors (and the necessary manufacturing tooling), which were test flown on a Jaguar in 1979. Grumman produced the port door with BAe finishing the port door and building the starboard door. BAe invested £3 million into a composite manufacturing facility at its Preston Strand Road site and this facility was used to produce 30 sets of Jaguar underwing panels, spine panels and curved fuel tank access panels under an MoD contract. The next step was the manufacture of a complete wing and it was hoped to feed this work into the P.97 Super Jaguar and Big Wing Jaguar studies then under way. Discussions took place in 1976 with Hawker Siddeley Chadderton on a possible joint venture covering three wings. Similar work had been carried out in France and STAé was very interested in potential applications to the Jaguar. Following the award of a contract to BAe Warton in 1977 one wing was built as a demonstrator for static and fatigue load testing – no funds were available for a flight test programme – and was 14% lighter than the standard wing and had very high structural efficiency.

CHAPTER THREE

Taming the Beast – Training

Ahead of the delivery of its first SEPECAT Jaguars in the spring of 1973, the Royal Air Force had to prepare the pilots and groundcrews who would operate it. When the Air Staff began its planning in July 1968, the two-seat Jaguar B (Biplace) trainer made up the majority of the production order and was planned to equip an Operational Conversion Unit (OCU) based at RAF Lossiemouth with others serving as advanced flying trainers with Flying Training Command at RAF Valley and with the Central Flying School (CFS). In July 1970 the Air Force Board changed the emphasis to the single-seat Jaguar S (Strike) and the flying training role was dropped, other than use by the Jaguar OCU. No. 226 OCU would go on to train all the RAF's Jaguar pilots and many others from overseas as well.

Planning

As detailed planning began in 1972, it was clear that trained manpower would be at a premium as the build-up of Jaguars coincided with the reassignment of RAF Germany's (RAFG) McDonnell Douglas F-4M Phantom FGR.2 squadrons to the air defence role. The Vice Chief of the Air Staff (VCAS), Air Chief Marshal Sir Denis Smallwood, suggested adopting the training pattern that had been implemented a couple of years earlier for the Hawker Siddeley Harrier GR.1. The initial training staff of instructors would form the Jaguar Conversion Team (JCT). They would convert the first 24 pilots for the initial two squadrons by June 1974, then the JCT would be expanded into an OCU. The planned Aircraft Establishment of 36 aircraft was around a quarter of the total force and gave a utilisation rate of 252 hours annually.

The first production Jaguar T.2, XX136, on a test flight with the A&AEE in September 1974. ***BAE Systems via Author's Collection***

The first two squadrons would remain at Lossiemouth to undertake Intensive Flying Trials during their operational work-up. Once they were ready, they would replace the two Coltishall-based English Electric Lightning squadrons and OCU. This would prove the aircraft in service before the first RAFG squadron formed in 1975 and would keep the Phantom force intact in Germany until the Jaguar was ready to take over.

The RAF began forecasting its pilot needs and discovered a shortfall of experienced ground-attack pilots. At that time, there were 40 pilots in the backlog of pre-OCU students who had completed basic flying training and were deemed suitable for streaming on to fast jets. Looking ahead, pilots would initially be drawn from the Phantom FGR.2 and Harrier GR.1 squadrons before 'first tourists' – pilots on their first operational tour following completion of training – were brought into the process (at one point it had been envisioned having 55% first tourists in the aircrew establishment).

There were sufficient Hawker Hunter FGA.9s to form an additional squadron to provide cost-effective operational training to utilise the backlog of pre-OCU students and also be a ground attack shadow squadron within No. 38 Group. No. 45 Squadron formed at RAF West Raynham on 1 August 1972, disbanding in July 1976 at RAF Wittering when its role was taken over by the Tactical Weapons Unit (TWU).

Pilots posted to the Jaguar OCU would first complete the TWU course. This reduced the pilot wastage rate and the amount of tactical weapons training that the OCU needed to carry out. Although the Jaguar had originally been designed as a trainer, it was foreseen that the conversion task would be complicated. First tourists would find the supersonic Jaguar a large step up from the Hunter. From experience with the Phantom and Harrier OCUs, it was known that modern navigation/attack systems doubled the conversion training time compared with previous generations of aircraft. A syllabus of 73 hours was planned, comprising 20 hours dual and 53 hours solo in basic and advanced squadron training. Reconnaissance role training required teaching the bare fundamentals of recce, but the pilots also had to be able to defend themselves and fulfil the ground-attack role. In addition, postgraduate courses were required for more than 20 instructors annually in the Pilot Attack Instructor, Instrument Rating Examiner and Reconnaissance Instructor categories.

Lossiemouth was a Royal Navy airfield for the Fleet Air Arm until its closure in 1969. It was decided to base the OCU at Lossiemouth (originally the home of the TWU, RAF Brawdy in Wales, had been proposed) to make use of the air-to-ground Tain range for weapons practice. Having excellent facilities and only 15 minutes flying time away, Tain was ideal for honing the NAVWASS system and the pilots in their operational role. Each student on the full OCU course would expend 420 rounds of 30mm ammunition, 50 4lb (1.8kg) retarded and 20 28lb (13kg) freefall practice bombs and 30 inert SNEB rockets. The Staff Instructors course would see each student expending 2,160 30mm rounds, 52 4lb and 20 28lb practice bombs and 72 inert rockets. On the front-line squadrons it was forecast that each pilot would annually use 2,900 30mm rounds, 80 4lb and 80 28lb practice bombs and 100 inert and 20 live rockets during weapons training.

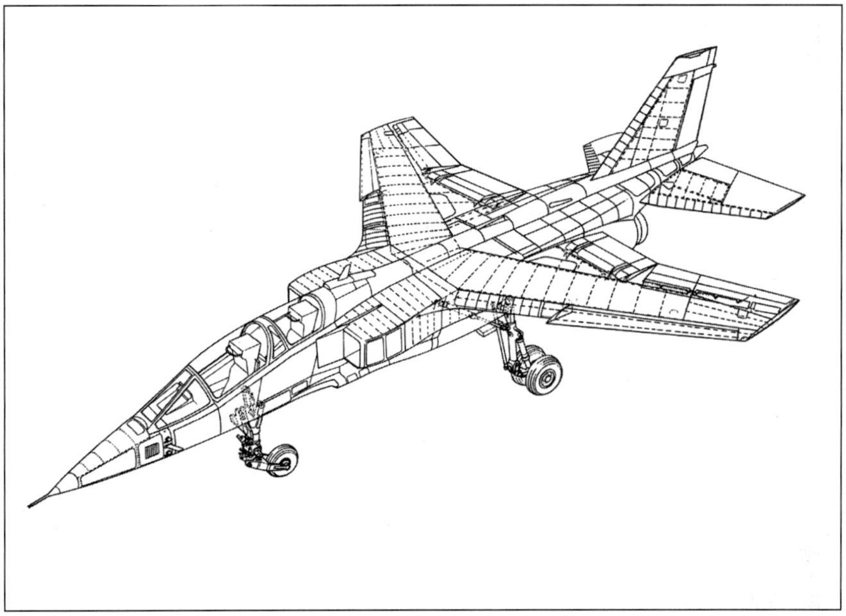

An isometric technical drawing of the two-seat Jaguar B, which was very similar externally to the Armeé de l'Air's Jaguar E. *SEPECAT via Paul Chapman*

Full-mission simulators were installed at Lossiemouth, Coltishall and Brüggen. These were housed in special buildings containing four rooms for the simulator cockpit, the control and instruction room, computer room and the model room. Simulators were not like those of today. They had fully representative cockpits and motion simulation using hydraulic rams to simulate taxying, high-speed turbulence, acceleration and deceleration. The outside world was replicated with a wide-angle projection on to a screen relaying the image from an adjacent room in which a camera was moved over a scale model landscape. Sound was also provided for realism. The sorties were video recorded for analysis and debriefing. The simulators were sufficiently capable for a pilot to fly a full mission and were especially useful for training techniques for handling emergencies such as loss of hydraulic power or combat damage.

JCT

The JCT was formed at Lossiemouth on 1 July 1973 under the command of Wing Commander John R Walker with a strength of ten pilots, two engineering officers and an adjutant. The plan was that the JCT would form the OCU on 24 June 1974, although this date slipped back to 1 October. The immediate task was for the members of the JCT to complete the industrial courses before beginning conversion flying. The JCT would train

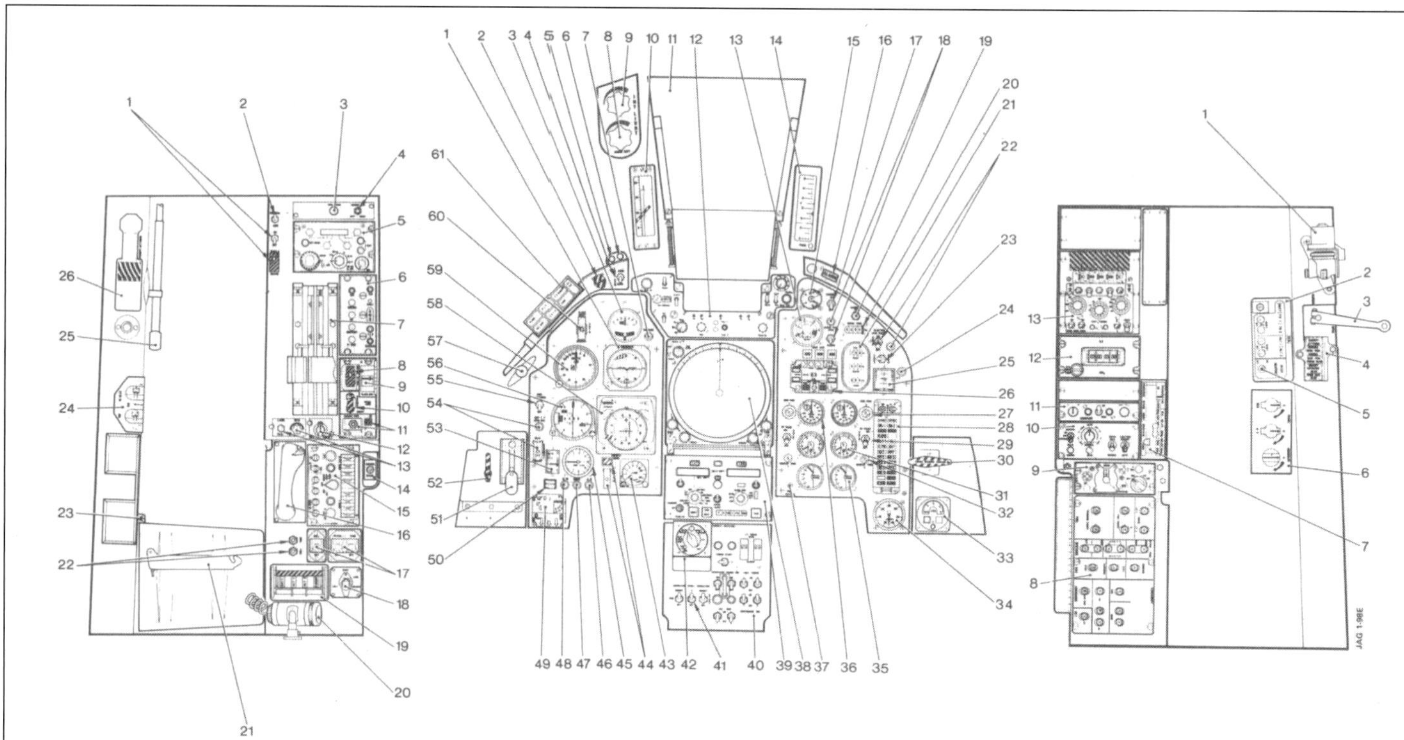

Left Console and Side Panel
1 Standby UHF Switches
2 Mute Sensitivity Switches
3 Stall Warning Button/Indicator
4 Rudder Test Switch
5 V/UHF Controller
6 CCS Controller
7 Throttle Box
8 Slat Override Switch
9 Flap Selector
10 Pitch Trim Switch and Indicator
11 Rudder Trim Switch and Indicator
12 Internal Lights Dimmer
13 Land/Taxi Lights Switch and NCU Dimmer
14 Seat Raise/Lower Switch
15 IFF/SSR Controller
16 Hand Controller
17 Autostabiliser Switches
18 Master Armament Safety Switch
19 Crash Switch
20 Wander Lamp
21 PEC Cover Stowage
22 Roll and Yaw Trim Circuit Breakers
23 Stall Warning Incidence Selector Switch
24 PTR Selector Switches
25 Arrester Hook Handle
26 Canopy Jettison Handle

Front Panel
1 Attitude Indicator
2 Clear Aircraft Jettison Button
3 Turn and Slip Indicator
4 Late Arm Switch
5 Low Altitude Warning Light
6 Head Up Gear Not Down Warning Light
7 ILS Marker Lamp
8 Incidence Indicator Lighting Dimmer
9 Integral Lighting Dimmer
10 Incidence Indicator
11 HUD
12 HUD Control Panel
13 Fuel Flowmeter
14 Accelerometer
15 Voltmeter
16 Attention Getter
17 HUD Camera Master Switch
18 Fuel Crossfeed Switch and Indicator
19 Fuel Guage Test Button
20 Fuel Detotaliser
21 Fuel Contents Guage
22 EHP Switch and Indicator
23 Cont/Serve Switch
24 IFF Failure Light
25 Hydraulic Pressure Guage
26 Fuel Transfer Panel and Drop Tank Indicators
27 Engine Fire Warning Button/Indicator (2)
28 CWP
29 Hydraulic Bypass Switches (2)
30 Brakes Selector Handle
31 TGT Indicators (2)
32 Reheat Fire Warning Indicator
33 Oxygen Contents Guage
34 Cabin Altimeter
35 Nozzle Area Indicators (2)
36 Percentage RPM Indicators
37 Max Rating Switch
38 Projected Map Display
39 Navigation Model Control Panel
40 Engine Switch Panel
41 External Lights Switches
42 HSI Mode Switch
43 Radar Altimeter
44 Rudder Gearing Switch and Indicator
45 VSI
46 Airbrake Indicator Light
47 Arrester Hook Indicator Light
48 Nosewheel Steering Indicator
49 Slat/Flap/Landing Gear Position Indicator
50 Combat Slats Button/Indicator
51 Landing Gear Selector
52 Landing Gear Emergency Selector
53 Pitch Trim Indicator
54 Diff Tailplane Switch and Indicator
55 Fuel Jettison Switch
56 Altimeter
57 Brake Parachute Handle
58 HSI
59 CSI
60 AJAX Switch
61 Weapon Aiming Mode Selector Panel

Right Console and Side Wall
1 Standby Compass
2 Electrical Generation System Controls
3 Canopy Locking Handle
4 Safety Pin Stowage
5 Pitot Heaters Switch
6 Internal Lights Panel
7 Cabin Air/Demisting Controls
8 Circuit Breaker Panel
9 TACAN Controller
10 Air Conditioning Panel
11 Compass Control Panel
12 ILS Controller
13 Conventional Weapon Control Panel

A cockpit layout diagram of the Jaguar T.2's front cockpit for the student pilot. ***Crown Copyright via Author***

three courses for No. 6 and No. 54(F) Squadrons, with Course No. 2 due to start on 14 January 1974. Construction work at Lossiemouth was behind schedule with the hangar accommodation unready and the first simulator building was not ready for use until July 1974.

Wing Commander Walker and his ten pilots arrived at the British Aircraft Corporation's (BAC) Warton site on 2 July to begin the three-week ground school course. Following this they headed to Rolls-Royce's headquarters at Derby for three days' training on the Adour. During August the pilots split into three groups for visits to Smiths Industries Limited for training on the head-up display (HUD). Eight of the pilots attended an aeromedical course at RAF North Luffenham during 14–17 August (the remaining three pilots attending on 12 September). In between these courses the pilots were kept busy preparing lectures for the ground school, as the ground instructors would not arrive until early 1974.

At Warton on 3 September, Wing Commander Walker, Squadron Leader Hayward and Squadron Leader Fowler were converted on to the Jaguar by test pilots Paul Millett, John Cockburn and Tim Ferguson. Three days later the Chief of Air Staff of the Indian Air Force, Air Chief Marshal O P Mehra, visited the unit, accompanied by the Air Officer Commanding No. 38 Group, Air Vice Marshal Frederick Hazlewood. Wing Commander Walker gave a

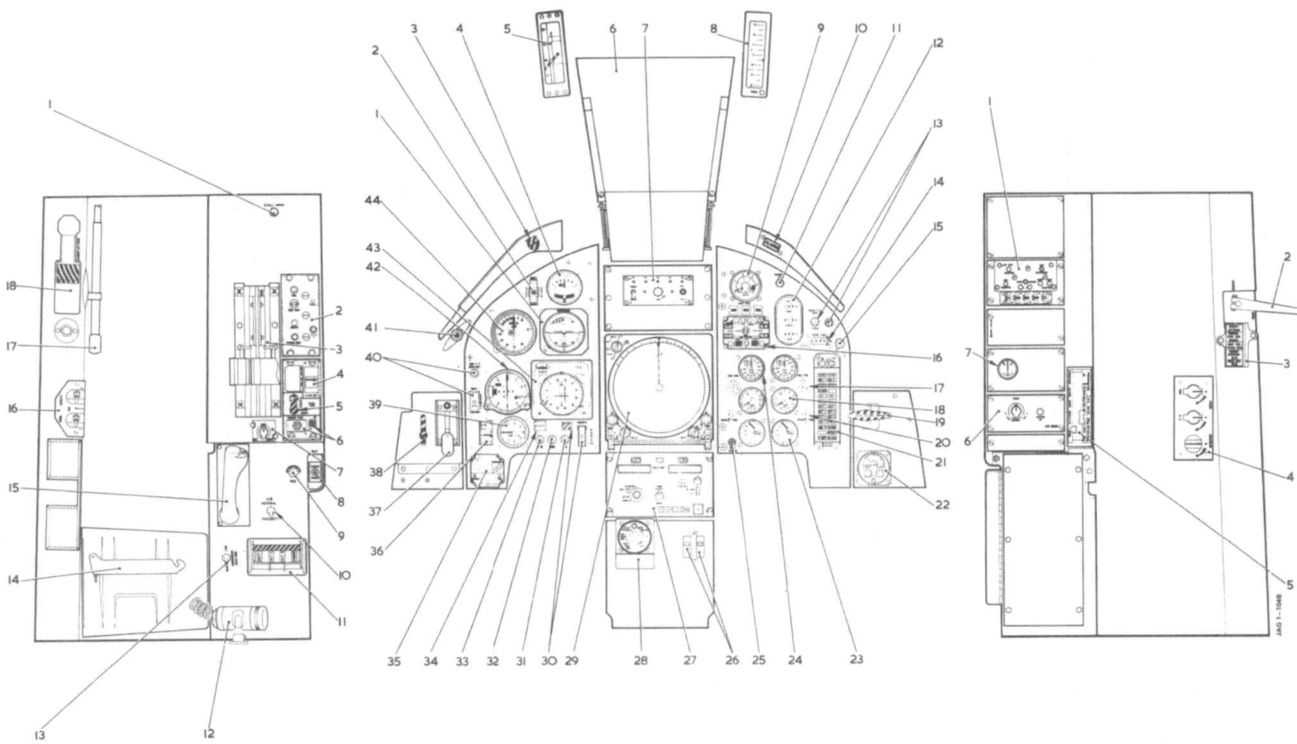

Left Console and Side Panel
1 Stall Warning Indicator
2 CCS Controller
3 Throttle Box
4 Flap Selector
5 Pitch Trim Normal/Emergency Selector
6 Rudder Trim Switch and Indicator
7 Internal Lights Dimmer
8 Seat Raise/Lower Switch
9 NCU Dimmer
10 Airbrake Priority Switch
11 Crash Switch
12 Wander Lamp
13 Armament Override Switch
14 PEC Cover Stowage
15 Hand Controller
16 PTR Selector Switches
17 Arrester Hook Handle
18 Canopy Jettison Handle

Front Panel
1 Attitude Indicator
2 AJAX Switch
3 Clear Aircraft Jettison Button
4 Turn and Slip Indicator
5 Incidence Indicator
6 HUD
7 HUD Control Panel
8 Accelerometer
9 Voltmeter
10 Attention Getter
11 Fuel Guage Test Button
12 Fuel Contents Guage
13 Fuel Crossfeed Switch and Indicator
14 Fuel Detotaliser
15 IFF Failure Light
16 Fuel Transfer Panel and Drop Tank Indicators
17 Engine Fire Warning Button/Indicator (2)
18 TGT Indicators (2)
19 Brakes Selector Handle
20 Reheat Fire Warning Indicator
21 CWP
22 Oxygen Contents Guage
25 Nozzle Area Indicators (2)
24 Percentage RPM Indicators
25 Max Rating Indicator
26 LP Cocks Switches
27 Navigation Model Control Panel
28 HSI Mode Switch
29 Projected Map Display
30 Rudder Gearing Switch and Indicator
31 Airbrake Indicator Light
32 Arrester Hook Indicator Light
33 Nosewheel Steering Indicator Light
34 Combat Slats Button/Indicator
35 Slat/Flap/Landing Gear Position Indicator
36 Pitch Trim Indicator
37 Landing Gear Selector
38 Landing Gear Emergency Selector
39 VSI
40 Diff Tailplane Switch and Indicator
41 Brake Parachute Handle
42 Altimeter
43 HSI
44 CSI

Right Console and Side Wall
1 Armament Monitor Panel
2 Canopy Locking Handle
3 Safety Pin Stowage
4 Internal Lights Panel
5 Cabin Air/Demisting Controls
6 Air Conditioning Panel
7 Compass Annunciator

A cockpit layout diagram of the Jaguar T.2's rear cockpit for the instructor. *Crown Copyright via Autho*

presentation and Millett flew an impressive display in T.2 XX137. By the 13th the JCT had three GR.1s (XX111, XX114 and XX115) but the first T.2, XX137, was delayed due to technical problems.

Walker, Hayward and Fowler returned to Lossiemouth on the 13th with their conversion completed and 17 sorties under their belts. They flew a total of 38 hours ten minutes during the month and were impressed by the accuracy of NAVWASS and the good handling in the circuit at low speeds and in high-speed, low-altitude flight. The other JCT pilots received five hours' refresher training in the Hunter before converting to the Jaguar from 2 October. Frequent attack sorties were flown over Tain, although at this stage the aircraft had no pylons nor ability to release weapons. Conversion was converted by the end of the month

T.2 XX136 was displayed by BAC at the Society of British Aircraft Constructors Show at Farnborough in September 1974. Originally planned as the main variant for the RAF as an advanced trainer, the T.2 was relegated to conversion training, the order being cut from 130 to just 35. *Author's Collection*

XX136 was flown at Farnborough by BAC test pilots John Cockburn and Jerry Lee, the displays including inverted passes along the runway and rolls during slow passes with the undercarriage and flaps extended. *Author's Collection*

and work focused on preparing the course for the first batch of students. On 30 October, Air Officer Commanding Strike Command, Air Chief Marshal Sir Andrew Humphrey, was given two flights in T.2 XX137 so that he could experience the Jaguar's performance at first hand from the rear and front seats.

Two days later the long-awaited pylons began to arrive; GR.1 XX117 having the inboard pylons fitted and making four sorties carrying Carrier Bomb Light Series (CBLS) with 4lb retarded practice bombs on the same day. Flight Lieutenant B A Horton from the Aeroplane and Armament Experimental Establishment's (A&AEE) Handling Squadron was the JCT's first student, arriving for conversion on 1 November.

Hangar No. 3 was finally completed on the 12th and what would become No. 1 Squadron of the OCU could now move in. Night flying checks were completed and Instrument Rating Tests were flown but poor weather and a lack of spares hampered progress, the unit resorting to weekend flying to maintain the schedule.

A shortened three-day ground school was run in early December for staff officers from the MoD, Strike Command and No. 38 Group. Air Vice Marshal Hazlewood also returned for a two-flight experience with Wing Commander Walker. The JCT was pleased with the results of the retarded bombing sorties it flew that month. On the 16th a first was achieved when GR.1 XX115 was flown with inboard external fuel tanks. The next day, the seventh GR.1 arrived – by this time the JCT should have had 17 aircraft but they only had nine due to production delays. The Station Commander at Lossiemouth, Group Captain M M J Robinson, began his conversion the same day.

January 1974 saw the formation of No. 3 Squadron, the Simulator and Ground school. The ground instructors arrived and began the task of completing the lectures; the Officer Commanding, Squadron Leader Trowern, received a short conversion on to the Jaguar. The ten students of Course No. 1 arrived on the same day as the instructors did, so things must have been hectic. The ten students were joined in class by five staff officers.

On 1 February the first aircraft fitted with the fuselage distortion modification and the long control column were delivered – GR.1s XX121 and XX122. GR.1 XX721 arrived on the 28th, which was the first JCT aircraft with automatic slats. Progress was smooth, with Course No. 1 progressing ahead of schedule. An evaluation team from the Belgian Air Force visited on 26–27 February to discuss the aircraft and its operation.

Course No. 2 arrived on 15 March to begin the fortnight-long ground school. Seven days later Course No. 1 graduated and formed the nucleus of No. 54(F) Squadron on the 29th – the same day that No. 2 Course began their conversion flying. Supporting the sales drive continued to be a part of the JCT's remit and at the end of the month BAC's Chief Sales Director Glen Hobday visited to discuss the Jaguar's progress.

Lossiemouth held a Jaguar Press Day on 5 June with General Giraud and the head of the Armeé de l'Air's (AdlA) tactical air forces attending, as well as representatives from BAC. The closeness of Anglo-French co-operation was emphasised, especially on the subject of support and supply. The press party were briefed on the OCU and NAVWASS and were shown a static Jaguar with panels removed to reveal the insides and two more aircraft loaded with various stores. The flying programme included a low-level attack on the airfield, a solo demonstration and a short landing.

BAC redesigned the Jaguar's two-seat cockpit in 1965, increasing the nose droop and raising the rear seat by 15in (38cm) to give an improved forward view of 8.5° below the horizon. ***Author's Collection***

OCU

No. 226 OCU was reformed at Lossiemouth out of the JCT on 1 October 1974. Not until 1977 would the OCU gain its torch and quiver unit badge markings. Its aircraft were adorned with a Lumsden tartan flash on the tail fin from 1980 to further aid identification. No. 226 had been a fighter OCU since its formation in August 1946, having stood down as the Lightning OCU at Coltishall on 30 September. On 2 October, a flight of OCU T.2s flew to Base Aérienne 113 Saint-Dizier-Robinson, the home of the AdlA's first Jaguar unit, the 7ème Escadre de Chasse, on a goodwill visit.

Just two days after its official formation, No. 226 OCU visited Base Aérienne 113 Saint-Dizier-Robinson and the Armeé de l'Air's first Jaguar unit, 7eme Escadre de Chasse, on 2 October 1974. XX142 crashed into the Moray Firth after loss of control while flying inverted on 22 June 1979, with both pilots sadly killed. ***Author's Collection***

T.2 XX141 remained with the OCU from the formation of the JCT until the 1990s. Here it awaits its next training sortie at Lossiemouth. ***Terry Panopalis Collection***

The average student pilot arriving fresh from flying training on the BAe Hawk T.1 found the Jaguar with its complex avionics and demanding handling characteristics to be a daunting – but welcome – prospect. The syllabus was comprised of a series of phases, the early ones concentrating on a particular facet of flying the Jaguar before proceeding to consolidate the knowledge gained.

The ground school lasted two weeks, introducing the aircraft's systems to ensure that the students could operate them in both normal and emergency situations. Classroom studies were followed by the simulator to learn the cockpit layout and pre-flight checks before starting to 'fly' in the simulator. The aim was to get the student into the position of being able to go solo after three dual sorties.

Pilots who completed their first solo flight at No. 226 OCU were awarded this certificate to mark the occasion. ***Author's Collection***

BRITISH AIRCRAFT CORPORATION
DASSAULT-BREGUET AVIATION

jaguar

This certificate is to mark the first solo flight in an Anglo/French JAGUAR

By..

On..

Officer Commanding Jaguar Operational Conversion Unit RAF Lossiemouth

The conversion flying phase involved introducing the student to the Jaguar's characteristics. Students were taught to avoid low speeds as much as possible; the rapid rise of lift-induced drag, coupled with low excess power, led to rapid speed decay when manoeuvring and the possibility of exceeding the angle of attack (AoA) limits. The instrument flying phase demonstrated the full potential of the head-up display (HUD) and the student had to demonstrate the ability to use all the instruments on the panel, even though the HUD was the main flight instrument. One consequence of the French-designed cockpit, however, was that the standard RAF blind flying panel was absent, which could confuse the unwary pilot looking inside the cockpit during an emergency.

The formation phase taught the importance of tactical formations. Students had to be competent to fly as wingman and to lead in an emergency. Starting off in pairs, the phase progressed to a four aircraft card formation (two pairs in trail). The low-level flying phase taught the student how to get the best out of the NAVWASS, HUD, Projected Map Display (PMD) and the horizontal situation indicator in low-altitude flight. Low-level navigation training emphasised the importance of pre-flight planning. Steering information from NAVWASS was presented in the HUD but accurate navigation depended on the inertial platform, the position shown on the PMD being cross-checked with visual references (such as landmarks) any errors corrected by inputting an updated fix. Even with NAVWASS, a hand-held 1:50,000 scale map was still necessary to obtain a precise target location.

The weapons phase consisted of 16 sorties, including level and shallow-dive bombing using 6lb (3kg) retarded practice bombs to mimic the delivery profiles of 1,000lb retarded bombs and BL.755 cluster bombs. Sorties also included gun strafing and toss/loft bombing using 28lb freefall practice bombs. Training was given in using the fixed sight as a reversionary mode in case of system failure. Students were taught how to use the Continuously Computed Impact Point (CCIP) mode – which removed the need to fly to absolutely accurate parameters – by combining the altitude, velocity and weapon ballistics with slant range information obtained

A T.2 of No. 226 OCU over the wild terrain of northern Scotland on a training sortie in 1981. Each of the CBLS on the outboard hardpoints is carrying a pair of 28lb (13kg) practice bombs. *USAF*

from the Laser Ranger and Marked-Target Seeker (LRMTS) or the radar altimeter. The pilot positioned the bombs fall line over the target's position in the HUD and released the bombs when the CCIP marker at the base of the bombs fall line was over the target. Engaging targets of opportunity used another mode with automatic weapons release when the CCIP marker reached the computed target position. The Simulated Attack Profile phase put all the knowledge into practice to organise an attack, fly as wingman to a staff pilot and lead one sortie. The tactical manoeuvring phase taught the basics of controlling other aircraft in fast-moving air threat environments. The first step was to refresh the student's basic fighter manoeuvre skills at medium altitude in 2 v 1 scenarios. Once the student had mastered this at a safe altitude, the sorties moved to low level with a variety of stores configurations, building up to a full war load. All the sorties were flown dual in a T.2 so that the instructor could provide instant feedback in addition to the detailed debrief. The operational phase demonstrated a routine squadron training sortie. The result was a pilot ready for the front-line squadron environment.

This No. 226 OCU T.2 on display on a rainy day in 1984 is surrounded by an array of weaponry. Although lacking the LRMTS, the T.2 was fully combat capable in the ground-attack role with bombs and rockets. The inclusion of a pair of Paveway II LGBs and a dummy AGM-84 Harpoon anti-ship missile was somewhat optimistic, presumably in an attempt to attract export Jaguar International customers. *Blue Envoy Collection*

Lossiemouth was modernised with hardened aircraft shelters to improve defence and survivability. Had the Cold War turned hot, nine of the OCU's GR.1s would have augmented RAF Germany's Jaguar squadrons, with eight of them allocated a WE.177 nuclear bomb. The remainder of the OCU's Jaguars would have become makeshift UK air defence fighters. *Blue Envoy Collection*

Getting to grips with the Jaguar took time. Among its fleet, the OCU had eight early production GR.1s and four T.2s that lacked fuselage flexing compensation. The A&AEE recommended acceleration limits of +5g when flown clean and +3g when carrying stores until the aircraft were modified. The OCU staff felt that the limits were unnecessary and overcautious, claiming that they had never encountered the problem. The OCU also found the initial 20kt crosswind limit imposed by BAC restrictive. From their experience, they advocated expanding the limit to 30kt in the dry and 25kt in the wet, with or without a braking parachute. BAC found that the Jaguar's crosswind handling was indeed considerably better than forecast and the limits were relaxed.The first overseas pilots to convert on to the Jaguar during 1975 were Captain Ed Cubleigh of the United States Air Force (USAF) and Captain Odd Sandvik of the Royal Norwegian Air Force. The OCU also undertook flight demonstrations with the T.2 for visiting dignitaries and potential customers on behalf of BAC's marketing campaign. One of the OCU's T.2s was loaned to BAC during Farnborough Week in 1974 so that pilots from Saudi Arabia and Major General Bordersen of the Danish Air Force could fly it.

On 23 September 1977, nine of the OCU's GR.1s were declared to SACEUR – the Supreme Allied Commander Europe. In wartime they would augment RAFG's Jaguar force. Originally 20 OCU aircraft had

The OCU's Jaguars gained the Lumsden tartan flash on the tail fin from 1980 to aid identification. XX144 also carries the badge of No. 16(R) Squadron following the issuing of the nameplate to the OCU in November 1991. *Terry Panopalis Collection*

Jaguar GR.1A XZ385 and a T.2 from Lossiemouth cavorting about the skies. Note that the inverted XZ385 is venting fuel. *Blue Envoy Collection*

been provisioned for and the excess war reserve weapons stock was handed to the Harrier squadrons to increase their wartime rate of effort for no additional cost to the MoD.

A symposium of Jaguar operators was held in early 1979 and the training aspects were discussed. The topic of providing more junior pilots with access to tactical leadership training was raised and recommended as something that the TWU should provide. The OCU was by now teaching aerodynamic braking and the loft/toss bombing manoeuvre training had been changed to reflect operational delivery profiles, while the instructors were investigating teaching laser-guided bomb delivery. It was recommended to include air-to-air gunnery in future Qualified Weapons Instructor (QWI) courses. There were several complaints too; it was felt that OCU staff needed to spend more time on the front-line squadrons, the range facilities needed extending to reflect operational weapons delivery and laser-ranging clearances and the availability of live weapons was inadequate.

The OCU had to move out of No. 3 hangar in 1980 to make way for two incoming Hawker Siddeley Buccaneer S.2 squadrons and was relocated into refurbished huts and concrete arch hangars. At this point the OCU's two squadrons were reformed as two flights within a combined unit. A request to the MoD for a shadow squadron numberplate as a new identity was refused as the OCU had no war role as an independent unit.

The OCU settled into its role of training replacement pilots and offering refresher courses as well as postgraduate courses for QWIs, Instrument Examiner Rating examiners and Tactics instructors. Three courses would run simultaneously with staggered phases to allow at least one cohort to fly at all times regardless of the weather conditions. There were also ground school and flying courses for Jaguar pilots from the Fuerza Aérea Ecuatoriana (Ecuadorian Air Force), Sultan of Oman's Air Force and Indian Air Force. Being a non-front-line combat unit, the OCU was not subject to the Tactical Evaluation (TACEVAL) combat readiness and capability evaluation under wartime conditions, but the co-located Buccaneer and Avro Shackleton Airborne Early Warning (AEW) squadrons were and this disrupted flying training. This led to the OCU decamping during exercise periods to Coltishall or Brüggen to continue training, albeit in unfamiliar surroundings for the students.

No. 16 Squadron has had the nickname 'The Saints' since its formation at Saint-Omer in France on 10 February 1915. Hence when No. 226 OCU became No. 16(R) Squadron, its Jaguars often sported the recognisable stick figure of Leslie Charteris' The Saint character. *SDASM Archives*

GR.1A XX116 received its distinctive paint all-black scheme as 'The Saint' in 1993as the OCU's display aircraft. It was flown at airshows by Flight Lieutenant Andy Cubin for three seasons. *Terry Panopalis Collection*

The OCU acted as an agent for the CFS in the Standardisation and Evaluation role for the Jaguar Force. This entailed visiting the front-line squadrons at regular intervals to check the quality of the flying and use of weaponry, checking that standards were being maintained consistently across the squadrons, observing squadron operations and gathering feedback and suggestions for future improvements for the OCU. The OCU also provided the Jaguar display pilot, who would fly a low-level aerobatic routine at air shows and open days.

During the summer of 1986, thoughts at the MoD turned to rationalising the Jaguar Force to save money by moving the OCU to Coltishall and reducing the number of operational Jaguars. Reducing the Jaguar fleet by 12 aircraft (an entire squadron) would have allowed sufficient space for the OCU to move in and would have reduced the OCU's output to six long courses, three short courses and two QWI courses per year. Against this, the provision of additional domestic accommodation at Coltishall and moving the simulator would entail total moving costs of between £2.6 million and £8.8 million. Interestingly, Coltishall was noted to have poorer weather and that would entail up to 15% extra flying time for the pilots to complete the entire training syllabus. The plan was postponed.

ABOVE Jaguar T.2A XX832 was issued to No. 16(R) Squadron in May 1995, following four years of storage at Shawbury, and is seen here the following October on a training sortie. The aircraft survived a mid-air collision with GR.1A XX745 in July 2000 and today resides at Chino in California in private ownership. *P Foster via Terry Panopalis Collection*

LEFT 'The Saint' gets airborne. When flown clean without any underwing stores the Jaguar was surprisingly sprightly and agile. *Terry Panopalis Collection*

RAF Coltishall was granted the Freedom of the City of Norwich in 1967 and in 2002 GR.3A XX766 of No. 16(R) Squadron was suitably adorned to celebrate the airfield's link with the city. *Terry Panopalis Collection*

In early March 2005 GR.3 received this tail art to celebrate No. 16 Squadron's 90th birthday. The squadron disbanded a few days later on the 11th. *D Hedge via Terry Panopalis Collection*

On 1 November 1991 the OCU was finally assigned a shadow squadron numberplate, taking up the identity of No. 16 (Reserve) Squadron. Plans to move from Lossiemouth to Coltishall were revived in 1993 but was again postponed. Not until July 2000 did No. 16(R) Squadron move, but its stay at Coltishall was brief as the OCU was disbanded on 11 March 2005 as the Jaguar Force began to wind down. The reduced training requirements were met by a flight attached to No. 41(F) Squadron, until that squadron was itself disbanded a year later. Flight Lieutenant Matt D'Aubyn was the last RAF Jaguar pilot to be trained and was among the last of the pilots to fly the Jaguar in British skies in July 2006. A total of 1,038 pilots were trained by the OCU, of which 841 were first tourists.

ETPS & RAE

The Empire Test Pilots' School (ETPS) was another user of the Jaguar. With a need for modern two-seat aircraft on which to train test pilots, the MoD agreed in July 1973 to fund two aircraft. The choice was between the Harrier T.2, costing £2.59 million, or the Jaguar T.2 for £2.98 million. The ETPS felt that it would be a shame not to have V/STOL capabilities given the syllabus they flew and that many of its students from overseas air forces were from nations who were actively looking to buy or develop V/STOL aircraft. The forthcoming development of the Sea Harrier FRS.1 would also need suitably qualified test pilots. The additional V/STOL conversion time that the students would require was a drawback, however. The Jaguar was more flexible and had a superior digital navigation/attack system that could be reprogrammed for test exercises. The decision went in favour of the Jaguar.

Two aircraft were acquired, T.2s XX915 and XX916 being delivered in July and December 1976. The pair were averaging 189 sorties and 212 flying hours annually by 1978. XX915 was flown by Nigerian, Canadian and Turkish pilots and was borrowed for an Indian Air Force evaluation in March 1978. Both aircraft were lost in accidents; XX916 to a bird strike on 24 July 1981 and XX915 to an engine fire on 17 January 1984.

They were replaced by aircraft transferred from the RAF, T.2As XX145 and XX830. XX145 was briefly used for Thermal Imaging Airborne Laser Designator (TIALD) pod trials at Farnborough in the 1990s before being retired by the ETPS by mid-2006. XX830 was transferred in 1986 and was retired in 1996. Other short-term loans were T.2As XX846 in February 1989, XX842 during 1989–90 and XX841 during 1990–92.

The Royal Aircraft Establishment (RAE) put forward a proposal in 1979 to buy four Jaguar T.2s, along with a

T.2 XX915 was one of the first two Jaguars operated by the ETPS. It crashed due to an engine fire on 17 January 1984. ***MoD via Terry Panopalis Collection***

The tenth production T.2, XX145, was assigned to the ETPS in the early 1980s and was not withdrawn from service until 2006. It is now on display at the Boscombe Down Aviation Collection at Old Sarum, Wiltshire. Behind the Jaguar is one of the North American Harvards used as camera ships by the RAE. ***Terry Panopalis Collection***

spare interchangeable wing, to support its research and development programmes throughout the 1980s. The cost was estimated at £17.7 million. Some of the planned research programmes were linked to Air Staff Target AST.403 for a Jaguar successor and weapon projects like the AST.1227 advanced anti-armour weapon as well as supporting industry research and trialling equipment for future upgrades for the Jaguar, Harrier and Tornado. The programmes the RAE had lined up included: the Store Carriage and Release Aerodynamic Programme (SCRAEP); Store Carriage and Release Improved Manoeuvrability Programme (SCRIMP) – part of BAe's Active Control Technology fly-by-wire flight control system effort; Demonstration and Evaluation of Ground Attack Systems 1-Seat (DEGAS-1); Demonstration and Evaluation of Ground Attack Systems 2-Seat (DEGAS-2); Demonstration and Evaluation of Fighter Operational Equipments (DEFOE), focusing on avionics and sensors.

In addition, the RAE foresaw use on supersonic sorties, handling trials, air combat practice and continuation training (which at that time was reliant on ageing Hunters and de Havilland Sea Vixens) covering 250–275 training sorties per year (nearly a hundred more than the TWU at Brawdy flew annually). In the event, only one Jaguar T.2 was acquired and ZB615 was the last British-operated Jaguar to be built, making its maiden flight at Warton on 23 September 1982. It would be operated by the RAE and its various successor organisations (DRA/DERA/QinetiQ) until November 2005.

Other Jaguars were also operated by the RAE on short-term loans. The venerable prototype B08 XW566 was still working on several projects, mostly at Warton, until its final flight on 17 June 1985 (the airframe was then used for electromagnetic compatibility and lightning strike testing). On loan from the RAF and A&AEE from August 1980 was GR.1 XX979, and GR.1 XX765 was converted for the Active Control Technology research programme during the early 1980s (see Chapter 11). XX833 was assigned to the RAE in February 1989 following its upgrade to T.2A standard and was later transferred to the DRA Experimental Flying Squadron. T.2A XX835 was transferred in September 1986 and was later upgraded to T.2B standard and operated at Farnborough until 1995. T.2A XX846 was loaned between November 1987 and August 1988 and XX842 was shared with the ETPS during 1989–90.

T.2A ZB615 was the last Jaguar built at Warton for British use and was acquired for the RAE. It was being flown on trials work for the Institute of Aviation Medicine when this photograph was taken in October 1988. ***Terry Panopalis Collection***

The final Jaguar airworthy in UK skies was XX833, by then based at Boscombe Down with the Aircraft Test and Evaluation Centre. The final flights came on 20 December 2007; Squadron Leader Andy Blythe and Wing Commander Paul Shakespeare flying a tour of places forever linked to the Jaguar in the morning – Coltishall, Marham (where the ex-Jaguar engineers now were), Coningsby and Warton – and in the afternoon a final low-level flight around Wales, including a flypast of St Athan. XX833 had flown 4,700 sorties totalling over 5,335 flying hours. Modifications for trials work had included specialist instrumentation, a recording and telemetry system, a Head Tracker System to feed steering and target information into the FIN1064 computer and used in conjunction with the Helmet Mounted Display and Integrated Panoramic Night Vision Goggles to provide a helmet-mounted sight capability. XX833 had also been used to test the Jaguar 96/97 updates. During its time at Boscombe Down XX833 had endured five bird strikes, a lightning strike and had consumed nine engines during 864 sorties – a fitting testament to how hard XX833 was flown, retiring just seven months shy of forty years after the Jaguar first took to the skies over Villacoublay.

The ETPS operated T.2 XX830 between 1986 and 1996. It is seen here in August 1989 in the attractive 'Raspberry Ripple' colour scheme used by the RAE and ETPS and carrying suitably titled fuel tanks. ***Terry Panopalis Collection***

The prototype Jaguar B, B08 XW566, was still earning a living with the RAE in 1985 as a testbed. ***Terry Panopalis Collection***

CHAPTER FOUR

Cold War Warrior – RAF service

The Royal Air Force took delivery of its first SEPECAT Jaguar on 30 May 1973. The type would serve as one of the RAF's key ground attack and strike aircraft for the next 34 years. This chapter looks at the first two decades of service during the years of the Cold War. Replacing the McDonnell Douglas F-4M Phantom FGR.2 with RAF Germany (RAFG), the Jaguar became the RAF's main interdiction and counter-air platform based in the Federal Republic of Germany and in the United Kingdom. In addition to these roles, the Jaguar would also perform tactical nuclear strike and serve with two dedicated tactical reconnaissance squadrons. The pilots had to get to grips with their new mount, which could quickly catch out an unwary pilot. The accident rate was high during the first decade of operation, a reflection of the dangers of flying fast at low altitude. The Jaguar was upgraded during this period with improved avionics and more powerful engines to rectify remove some of its shortcomings. As the Cold War drew to an end, the Jaguar had formed part of the North Atlantic Treaty Organisation's (NATO) deterrent against potential aggression from the Soviet Union and its Warsaw Pact allies successfully.

The Jaguar's main role was to interdict ground targets, including air bases, air defences and armoured formations. GR.1 XZ384 of No. 20 Squadron stationed at RAF Brüggen is carrying a full load of eight dummy 1,000lb (454kg) bombs over the snowy landscape of north-western Europe. ***Terry Panopalis Collection***

Flying Officer R J Corbet of No. 54(F) Squadron at the controls of GR.1 XX766. *Blue Envoy Collection*

Planning

The Air Staff began planning the Jaguar's introduction into service as early as July 1968. At that time it was forecast that the single-seat Jaguar S (Strike) would enter service in 1972 with five ground attack squadrons at Coltishall and RAF Gütersloh in West Germany. In July 1970 the Air Force Board authorised a force of nine squadrons. The first three squadrons would form with RAFG in the strike/attack role, followed by two UK-based strike squadrons with Air Support Command, which would also receive a dedicated reconnaissance squadron before the final two RAFG squadrons were formed for reconnaissance and strike/attack. RAFG would then have 72 Jaguars, with the strike/attack squadrons at RAF Brüggen and the reconnaissance squadron at RAF Laarbruch (the ninth squadron, which had earlier been earmarked for the Far East Air Force, was abandoned as part of the 1974 Defence Review). The operational roles envisioned for the Jaguar were:

- Counter-air operations
- Close air support
- Reconnaissance (visual, photographic and infrared)
- Strike (nuclear and conventional weapons)

Normal operational sorties would penetrate enemy defences at heights not exceeding 250ft (76m) by day and 1,000ft (305m) at night. The basic element would be a combat pair, although larger formations would be flown. Close air support sorties could be either independent or under the control of forward air controllers (FAC) – who were equipped with laser designators from 1980. In the strike role, the nuclear weapon would be carried on the centreline pylon with two fuel tanks inboard and electronic countermeasures (ECM) pods outboard under the wings. The provision of two cannon gave a self-defence capability against enemy aircraft but it was accepted that the Jaguar had no air defence capability.

Tactical reconnaissance aircraft usually operated singly with the reconnaissance pod fitted on the centreline and ECM pods outboard. The two specialist reconnaissance squadrons had a secondary attack role. The UK-based squadrons maintained a readiness to deploy 75% of their aircraft within 72 hours. With the provision for aerial refuelling and external fuel tanks, range was not considered to be a problem and sufficient oxygen was carried aboard for up to 15 hours' flying time. Maintaining aerial refuelling proficiency in the UK-based squadrons was deemed important for the reinforcement role. RAFG strike squadrons maintained a nuclear-armed quick reaction alert (QRA) at 15-minute readiness on a 24-hour basis, 365 days a year. For attack squadrons, 50% of their aircraft had to

The impressive array of weapons that the Jaguar GR.1 could carry. At the back are 1,000lb (454kg) HE bombs, then BL.755 cluster bombs and between them practice bombs. Eight Matra rocket pods and their 2.75in (68mm) SNEB rocket projectiles flank two AIM-9G Sidewinders and an AS.37 Martel anti-radar missile (never carried operationally in the RAF). At the front are the two 30mm ADEN cannon and ammunition. ***Blue Envoy Collection***

be combat ready within six hours and 70% within 12 hours. The estimated wartime weapons expenditure for an attack squadron carrying out 202 sorties over six days was 60,600 rounds of 30mm ammunition, 970 BL.755 cluster bombs, 243 1,000lb (454kg) bombs, 8,730 2.75in (68mm) SNEB rockets and 485 Lepus flares (the recce squadrons only had stockpiles of 30mm ammunition and BL.755).

Operational turnaround including refuelling and rearming was completed within 30 minutes, with each squadron simultaneously turning around four aircraft. Reconfiguring an aircraft from the strike role to the attack role was planned to take only 15 minutes, or 30 minutes to change from reconnaissance to attack.

Jaguar GR.1

The RAF assigned the role designation GR.1 (GR for Ground Attack, Reconnaissance) to the Jaguar S and the Jaguar B was designated T.2 (T for Trainer). The first production order covered 30 aircraft; 15 Jaguar GR.1 (construction number S1–15) and 15 T.2 (B1–15). The second order covered 81 aircraft; 61 GR.1 (S16–76) and 20 T.2 (B16–35). The third covered 45 GR.1 (S77–121) and the fourth 44 GR.1 (S122–165). The MoD assigned each airframe a serial number (a full list of serials and construction numbers can be found in Appendix 2).

The RAF's first production aircraft, GR.1 serial XX108, made its maiden flight from Warton on 12 October 1972, with British Aircraft Corporation (BAC) Deputy Chief Test Pilot Tim Ferguson at the controls. XX109 was the first aircraft to have the definitive Laser Ranger and Marked-Target Seeker (LRMTS) and full avionics fit. Chief Test Pilot Paul Millett made its maiden flight on 16 November. The first two-seat Jaguar B, T.2 XX136, first flew on 28 March 1973 at Warton with test pilots John Cockburn and Reg Stock at the controls. Of the initial seven production aircraft, all but XX111 were temporarily retained for the development programme.

Under the provisional Plan R it was hoped to have a surplus of 30 Jaguars by mid-1975 so that the early production aircraft could be upgraded to the latest standard without affecting front-line squadron strength. Due to production delays this did not happen, also delaying the modifications and increasing the scope of the work required. The first delivery was GR.1 XX111 on 30 May 1973 to RAF Lossiemouth for the Jaguar Conversion Team (JCT).

The first of the second production batch, GR.1 XX719, made its maiden flight on 31 January 1974. The workers at BAC's Samlesbury factory, where the wings were built, got a chance to see the Jaguar up close when Chief Production Test Pilot Peter Ginger landed GR.1 XX724 on the short runway there on 1 May 1974. The first of the third production batch, GR.1 XX955, made its maiden flight on 18 September 1975 (the 99th and 100th Warton-built Jaguars XX834 and XX835 were flown together on 25 February 1975 by John Cockburn and Dave Eagles). The first aircraft of the fourth batch, GR.1 XZ355, flew on 10 June 1976, with the final GR.1, XZ400, flying on 29 June 1979 (BAC had been merged with Hawker Siddeley and nationalised to form British Aerospace [BAe] in 1977).

By October 1978 the Warton production line had ceased to produce aircraft for the RAF. BAe funded 20 aircraft sets for export production in the hope of securing an Indian Air Force deal but also found itself funding a batch of ten Jaguar A sets for the French. The Air Staff attempted to support the production line in July 1978 with proposals for another 20 aircraft to maintain the force strength to 1986 or six additional T.2s fitted with radar warning receiver (RWR) equipment, but these ideas went no further.

The Initial Controller Air Release (CA release) was obtained on 30 August 1973 and covered all aircraft completed to the build standard issued by BAC on 23 February 1973 for use by day and night over land and sea. Amendment lists were issued as trials progressed for clearances for specific modifications, equipment or weapons. The engine was the Rolls-Royce Turbomeca Adour Mk.102 with JP102 single catalyst or JP103 double catalyst in the afterburner, rated at 5,115lbf (22.75kN) dry thrust and 7,305lbf (32.5kN) reheated.

The maximum take-off weight was 31,745lb (14,400kg), the maximum normal landing weight was 21,165lb (9,600kg) with an overload limit of 29,760lb (13,500kg). For an emergency single-engine landing the maximum weight was 22,045lb (10,000kg) using partial throttle reheat (PTR) to obtain the required 180kt approach speed. The wheels and brakes were rated up to a maximum speed of 195kt, brake parachute deployment was at 150kt (185kt in an emergency).

The normal speed limit when flown clean was Mach 0.95 with a never exceed limit of Mach 1.0 at low level, Mach 1.25 above 20,000ft (6,100m) and Mach 1.3 at 45,000ft (13,715m) with a never exceed speed of Mach 1.4. With external stores, the low-altitude speed limit was Mach 0.85 with a never exceed speed of Mach 0.9, and at 45,000ft those limits increased to Mach 0.9 and 0.95 respectively.

Prolonged flights with heavy asymmetric stores were not permitted in normal flight. The airbrakes were cleared throughout the full speed range, except when 264gal (1,200L) fuel tanks were carried on the inboard pylons, when the limit was Mach 0.9. The normal acceleration limits in clean condition were -2g to +7.25g (3g to +8g never exceed) up to Mach 0.9 at a weight of 22,710lb (10,300kg); at higher weights these limits were -2g to +6.75g. Carrying external stores further reduced these limits to -1g to +5.25g normal (-2g to +6g never exceed).

Toss bombing of 1,000lb bombs involved approaching the target at Mach 0.9 at 250–500ft (76–150m) and making a 4g pull-up with a 1g climb at 35°. Releasing the bomb at 400–500kt tossed it forwards by around 4.4nm (8km). Clearances for the 30mm ADEN cannon involved a lengthy list of modifications for 120 aircraft. By November 1974 there had been three cases of yaw autostabiliser system failure, including in one case a hardover during a 60° banked turn. All three pilots had recovered successfully, but it had the potential to cause a serious accident in low-altitude flight. In addition, the yaw autostabiliser was critical to modification Mod. 703 to cure the fuselage flexing problem. The Aeroplane & Armament Experimental Establishment (A&AEE) utilised prototype B08 to examine simulated failures. HF radio interference caused some of the problems, which was gradually filtered out, but sticking relays and rogue computers were also responsible. The rate of failure was reduced to become comparable with other RAF front-line aircraft.

The use of motorways as emergency airstrips had been pioneered in Switzerland and Sweden and NATO became interested in the concept. BAC made a series of trials on 26–27 April 1975 using GR.1 XX109 on a short stretch of the unopened M55 motorway near Blackpool, just up the road from Warton. This was partly in response to MoD interest and partly to demonstrate the Jaguar's short-field capability in competition with the Harrier's VTOL ability. Test pilot Tim Ferguson landed the aircraft on to the motorway carrying just a centreline fuel tank, the aircraft being turned around on the carriageway before being refuelled and armed with four dummy BL.755 bombs before taking off. Landing required a

BAC test pilot Tim Ferguson gets GR.1 XX109 airborne off the M55 motorway with a load of dummy BL.755 cluster bombs that had been loaded while the aircraft was refuelled on the motorway. ***BAE Systems via Blue Envoy Collection***

Tim Ferguson applies the braking parachute to bring XX109 to a halt on the M55. Using the parachute enabled the landing to be accomplished in just over 1,200ft (365m). ***Terry Panopalis Collection***

Entente Cordiale. Squadron Leader P J Day shakes hands with his French counterpart as No. 14 Squadron arrives for an exchange visit to fellow Jaguar operator Escadron EC 3/7 'Languedoc' at BA 113 Saint-Dizier-Robinson on 10 August 1978. ***Author's Collection***

steep approach with a high AoA and took just over 1,200ft (365m) using the braking parachute; take-off was achieved in 1,500–1,800ft (460–550m). Ferguson commented that, 'Landing the Jaguar on a motorway presents no problems beyond the capability of a squadron pilot, providing he has done a few practice short landings.' The RAF made no attempt to replicate this trial in the UK, although it would in West Germany a couple of years later.

Rough surface trials at the A&AEE at Boscombe Down used a landing strip that crossed a runway and two taxiways with various 'lumps' added in between to make a rough alternating soil and tarmac surface. Tests were also made on a simulated damaged runway repaired with Class 60 trackways. The Jaguar's specially designed undercarriage performed very well and test pilot Jerry Lee described travelling over the trackways as being like 'driving a well-sprung limousine over a cattle grid'. Trials on grass included operations with full internal fuel and two 1,000lb bombs with wheel and parachute braking, turning and high-speed taxying. A public demonstration of the Jaguar's capability was given at the 1975 Society of British Aircraft Constructors Show at Farnborough, when Peter Ginger displayed GR.1 XX108 operating entirely from the grass rather than using the runway, a feat repeated by Jerry Lee and Chris Yeo at the Paris Air Show in 1979.

Coltishall Wing

Coltishall, near Norwich in Norfolk, was formally earmarked for the Jaguar in November 1971. The Jaguar replaced the Lightnings stationed there since the early 1960s; the station's motto 'Aggressive in Defence' reflected Coltishall's long heritage as a fighter station. Coltishall was home to three Jaguar squadrons, Nos. 6, 41(F) and 54(F). They were part of RAF Strike Command's No. 38 Group until 17 November 1983 when it was absorbed into No. 1 Group, which commanded Strike Command's UK-based combat air assets. The squadrons made use of nearby ranges at Holbeach, Wainfleet, Theddlethorpe and Cowden. For 33 years Coltishall was the heart of the Jaguar Force and many pilots and groundcrew who served there fondly remember the esprit de corps that enabled some remarkable achievements in peacetime and in combat.

No. 54(F) Squadron had been formed on 15 May 1916 as part of the Royal Flying Corps and had

No. 54(F) Squadron's Jaguars lined up at Coltishall. ***MoD via Tony Panopalis Collection***

T.2 XX847 of No. 41(F) Squadron taxying at Coltishall. All RAF Jaguars were completed with wrap-around disruptive camouflage of Dark Sea Grey (British Standard Colour BS381C-638) and Dark Green (BS381C-641). *Terry Panopalis Collection*

converted on to the Phantom FGR.2 in 1969. Earmarked for conversion to the Jaguar, the initial JCT graduates formed a Jaguar element at Lossiemouth on 21 March 1974. The squadron ceased Phantom operations at RAF Coningsby on 22 April and reformed the following day as a Jaguar unit. Once the squadron was fully converted, it moved to Coltishall on 8 August under the command of Wing Commander Terry Carlton and was declared combat ready in early 1975.

No. 6 Squadron was the fifth oldest in the RAF, forming on 31 January 1914. Unusually, it had a continuous period of service from that date, through both world wars with 45 years based abroad, before returning to the UK in 1969 to become the first Phantom FGR.2 unit, based at Coningsby. It disbanded on 30 September 1974, reforming a day later at Lossiemouth out of the initial cadre of JCT students under the command of Wing Commander R J Quarterman. Conversion flying began in early October and the squadron moved to Coltishall the following month. One of the flight commanders was Peter Orme, an Empire Test Pilots' School (ETPS) trained test pilot who had completed a tour with the A&AEE as the Jaguar Project Pilot.

No. 41(F) Squadron had been formed in April 1916 and had several incarnations, converting to the Phantom FGR.2 at Coningsby on 1 April 1972. Its first Jaguar, GR.1 XZ113, arrived on 27 April 1976 and on 1 April 1977 it became the third Jaguar Coltishall squadron. Its specialist reconnaissance role is covered detail later in this chapter.

The work-up of Nos. 54(F) and 6 Squadrons was often interrupted by visiting staff and VIPs wanting to see and discuss the RAF's latest aircraft, as well as evaluation teams from prospective export buyers wanting to see the aircraft in action. Even so, No. 54 got off to a rapid start, taking part in NATO Exercise Bold Guard, involving British, German and Dutch forces in September 1974 and making a deployment to Karup in Denmark later that autumn. Training was intensive in the low flying areas around the UK. Simulated Attack Profiles were flown at 250ft (76m) – even as low as 100ft (30m) in parts of the Scottish and Welsh routes – at speeds of 360–420kt with a high-altitude ingress or exit. They were also bounced by other Jaguars for air combat manoeuvring training.

Training by 1980 had settled down to an annual routine of: an Annual Practice Camp (APC) at Decimomannu in Sardinia; one major NATO exercise; a ten-day NATO squadron exchange; four No. 38 Group exercises; one NATO Mallet Blow exercise using the RAF Spadeadam Electronic Warfare Training Facility and RAF Otterburn bombing ranges. The Tactical Evaluation (TACEVAL) was a strenuous combat readiness evaluation under wartime conditions for all NATO units. A Part One TACEVAL was a no-notice, one-day event that would see the airbase put on a war footing when the assessors arrived, including preparation of ground and NBC – Nuclear, Biological and Chemical – defences. The conclusion of the assessment was usually a mass take-off of all available aircraft. A full four-day Part Two TACEVAL was a scheduled exercise to operate

GR.1 XX766 of No. 54(F) Squadron against a mountainous backdrop, illustrating the typical terrain encountered during deployments to Bardufoss in northern Norway. *Blue Envoy Collection*

under wartime conditions with a deployment to a forward airfield and flying of wartime roles.

The squadrons were declared to SACEUR's (the Supreme Allied Commander Europe) Strategic Reserve (Air) for counter-air interdiction and close air support operations. Nos. 54(F) and 6 Squadrons would deploy to the Royal Danish Air Force's Flyvestation Tirstrup in the NATO Northern Region or RAF Wildenrath near the German–Dutch border in the Central Region or Villafranca in northern Italy near Verona in the Southern Region. No. 41(F) Squadron had wartime forward airfield deployments earmarked for Norway and made regular winter deployments to Bodø and Andøya, before being reassigned in 1980 to NATO's Allied Command Europe (ACE) Mobile Force, with a wartime deployment to Bardufoss in northern Norway, some 90nm (160km) north of the Arctic Circle.

Tirstrup was a very basic airfield, basically a runway and dispersals but with no living accommodation except tents and no covered servicing facilities, apart from some buried shipping containers to provide some workspace and storage. Eventually Tirstrup was modernised as part of NATO's hardening programme with Hardened Aircraft Shelters (HAS) and a bunker for BL.755 storage (an oversight in the design of the latter meant that the doors were too small for the RAF's standard loading trolley, so the bombs had to be placed on to a special smaller trolley, wheeled outside, transferred on to the standard trolley and then wheeled to the aircraft – a ludicrous solution in wartime). Bardufoss had a 'Rock Hangar' that the Germans had burrowed into the mountain side using prisoner of war labour during the Second World War, which had seven stalls for aircraft.

The squadrons would have to deploy at 72 hours' notice with necessary ground support. The wartime effort would be six days at intensive rate (24 sorties per aircraft for 70% of the deployed aircraft), 30 days at sustained rate (35 sorties per aircraft for 100% of the aircraft) and 30 days quiet rate (12 sorties per aircraft). A squadron-strength deployment would usually require around 35 Lockheed C-130K Hercules C.1 movements to transport all the support equipment. Three tactical fly-away packs containing the necessary servicing equipment and consumables were acquired, each being capable of supporting twelve aircraft for six days at intensive rates of effort.

The squadrons could also be deployed under the United Kingdom Mobile Force (Air), which included all three Coltishall squadrons, a squadron of Hawker Siddeley Andover C.1 light tactical transports, one Westland Wessex HC.2 and two Sud Aviation SA.330 Puma HC.1 tactical transport helicopter squadrons.

During March and April 1975, No. 54(F) Squadron flew the first phase of the Jaguar Night Operational Trial – codenamed Topcat – which had been organised by the Central Tactics and Trials Organisation (CTTO). Topcat covered low-altitude navigation, formation flying, toss bombing manoeuvres at night and checks on the adequacy of the cockpit lighting and instrumentation. A total of 75 sorties were flown over Yorkshire, Lincolnshire and the Wash at a minimum height of 1,000ft – later relaxed to 500ft (150m). A new NAVWASS tape programme was used to record up to 16 parameters. This data was downloaded following landing and ready within 30 minutes for the debriefing.

The pilots noted errors at the first NAVWASS waypoint update on 53 sorties. Even with visual fixes on landmarks (the chance of seeing an unlit landmark was about 50%), the mean error at the first fix was 1nm (1.8km), increasing to 1.6nm (2.9km) by the third fix, but Topcat had proved inconclusive whether a visual fix to update the position would be successful. The pilots found that the cockpit workload increased the faster they flew – managing 530kt at 500ft over the sea – and argued that two pilots in a Jaguar T.2 would be able fly with greater confidence and accuracy at night. Much of the cockpit lighting and instruments were rated as unsatisfactory and some of the issues were hazardous for safe flying. Adhesive reflective strips had been added to the aircraft for formation flying but these were often not visible, although the exhaust glow in minimum reheat was visible 6–7nm (11–14km) away.

Toss manoeuvre trials using Lepus flares were made at the Wainfleet Range, aiming at a simulated target 14,150ft (4,310m) away. The closest the 50 Lepus and eight Super Lepus flares got was within 4,950ft (1,510m).

Banking away over mountains, GR.1 XX723 reveals the tandem beam on the ventral hardpoint and is carrying two CBLS for practice bombs on the outer wing pylons. *Blue Envoy Collection*

This formation of No. 226 OCU Jaguars at low level over the sea carrying practice 1,000lb (454kg) bombs illustrates well the typical attack profile that Jaguar pilots flew. *Blue Envoy Collection*

A vic consisting of one Jaguar from No. 20 Squadron leading a pair from the UK-based No. 54(F) Squadron, including XX723. *Blue Envoy Collection*

A second phase of trials covering navigation over darkened terrain and co-ordinated attacks under Lepus flare illumination took place at Canadian Forces Base (CFB) Cold Lake in September 1976.

No. 6 Squadron deployed to Decimomannu in January 1975 for its first APC, dropping live bombs in level and diving attacks up to an angle of 40° and achieving good serviceability away from home (at this stage the ADEN cannon had not been cleared for use). Decimomannu was used by many NATO air forces for weapons training at the nearby ranges at Capo Frasca. By the following year, the cannon was cleared for use and the next APC included gunnery practice.

No. 54(F) Squadron visited Escadron de Chasse 3/7 'Languedoc' at Base Aérienne 113 Saint-Dizier in April 1975. The French squadron had formed during the same month as No. 54, so both units were at a similar stage of maturity with the Jaguar. No. 6 Squadron hosted a detachment of Lockheed F-104G Starfighters from the Federal German Navy's Marinefliegergeschwader 2 in April 1976. In return, half of the squadron went on exchange to Büchel in May 1977 as the guests of another F-104G unit, the Luftwaffe's Jagdbombergeschwader 33. Other regular detachments were made to Cyprus and Malta as well as three-week long deployment to Tirstrup. During their stay at Tirstrup, the pilots would participate in NATO exercises; Cold Fire with FAC sorties in support of 1 Brigade and Belgian Corps troops in northern Germany, Botany Bay Tactical Air Support for Maritime Operations (TASMO) in co-operation with the Royal Danish Navy and the Highwood counter-air exercise by simulating incoming Soviet attacks against their home, Coltishall, and the nearby early warning radar station at RAF Neatishead.

A four-day Part Two TACEVAL would often see Nos. 6 and 54(F) Squadrons deploy to Tirstrup for interdiction and FAC sorties into northern Germany and TASMO in the Baltic Sea; the first of these took place in February 1976. TASMO sorties could go as far east in the Baltic Sea as the Danish island of Bornholm. Overwater sorties relied on NAVWASS being operational but the pilots obtained some good results, one of which was the first spotting of a Soviet Project 775 *Ropucha*-class Landing Ship Tank by a No. 6 Squadron Jaguar.

The 1980s continued in much the same vein; a constant cycle of exercises and deployments and training. By 1987 the training load had increased to: two squadron-strength NATO exercises; cross-training flights with the RAFG involving two aircraft per month; up to two squadron-strength deployments to the Northern Region; a one-month exchange with the Armeé de l'Air (AdlA); the NATO Squadron Exchange Programme; servicing flights to Denmark for binational groundcrew training; NATO Tactical Leadership

Programme involving two aircraft per squadron; Air Combat Manoeuvring Instrumentation flights; APC at Decimomannu; Red Flag and Maple Flag air combat exercises held at Nellis Air Force Base (AFB) in Nevada and CFB Cold Lake respectively.

No. 6 Squadron first attended Red Flag in 1978. Flying from Norfolk to Nevada and Alberta involved transatlantic flights that were supported by Handley Page Victor – and later BAC VC10 and Lockheed Tristar – aerial refuelling tankers. As only UK-based pilots were tanker qualified, the Coltishall squadrons were given the task of ferrying Jaguars across the Atlantic whenever RAFG squadrons took part in Red Flag and Maple Flag.

Options for rationalising the Jaguar Force were studied in the summer of 1986 to save running costs and manpower from April 1988. A series of options were drawn up: reducing the Aircraft Establishment (AE) by four, six or 12 aircraft (the latter resulting in one squadron being disbanded) and either concentrating the Jaguar Force at Lossiemouth (with Coltishall closing) or moving the OCU to Coltishall. Closing Coltishall was rejected, but the costs and operational drawbacks of moving the OCU from Lossiemouth caused this plan to be postponed. The proposal to cut a full squadron would have affected the viability of the Strategic Reserve (Air) deployment and was also dropped.

As development of the Air Staff Target AST.403 Jaguar replacement slowed, it became clear that the type would remain in front-line service for another decade. In August 1987 the Air Staff released an Operational Policy Statement for the Jaguar Force into the 1990s. The Jaguar Force would number 68 GR.1A and 20 T.2A and would retain the Regional Reinforcement Squadron roles operating from Tirstrup and Bardufoss, with No. 226 OCU contributing four GR.1As as reinforcements for Tirstrup, the remaining aircraft being used for local UK air defence.

This Jaguar of No. 54(F) Squadron has just released a pair of retarded 1,000lb (454kg) bombs from medium altitude. *Blue Envoy Collection*

All UK-based squadrons were trained in air-to-air refuelling for their strategic deployment roles. This also enabled transatlantic flights for Exercise Red Flag And Maple Flag air combat exercises in the USA and Canada. This pair of No. 54 Jaguars are hooked up to Handley Page Victor K.2 XM715 of No. 55 Squadron. *Blue Envoy Collection*

RAF Germany

The station motto of RAF Brüggen 'To Seek and Strike' and the famous sign at the entrance gates 'The task of this station in peace is to train for war – don't you forget it' were very apt for the home of the RAFG's Jaguar Wing. Brüggen was opened in 1953 as a purpose-built airfield for the RAF, located 27 miles (43km) west of Düsseldorf near the Dutch–German border. It was one of RAFG's 'Clutch Airfields' on which were based its force of interdiction, close air support and air defence aircraft.The introduction of the Jaguar coincided with the redevelopment of the airfield with dispersed HAS for the aircraft and hardened facilities for command operations and pilot briefing for better protection from conventional and nuclear strikes, as well as chemical and biological threats, following lessons learned from the 1967 Arab–Israeli Six-Day War. Each squadron had its own area comprising nine two-aircraft HAS that were protected by barbed wire and guard posts. Visual camouflage came from attempts to 'tone down' the runways, buildings and vehicles. Initially, the HAS areas were expected to be used only during exercises and wartime but they were soon in everyday use.

No. 14 Squadron had been formed in February 1915, being briefly disbanded during 1945–46 before reforming in the British Zone of Occupation in Germany at RAF Wahn as a fighter-bomber squadron before reforming out of No. 88 Squadron as an English Electric Canberra B(I).8 interdiction unit at Wildenrath. In July 1970 it moved to Brüggen and converted to the Phantom FGR.2. No. 14 was the first RAFG Jaguar squadron to form, under the command of Wing Commander Anthony Mumford. Jaguar T.2 XX836 arrived on 7 April 1975 and the squadron was declared operational on 9 July.

No. 17 Squadron had also been formed in February 1915. It reformed at Wahn as a reconnaissance squadron with the Canberra PR.7 in June 1956, moving to Brüggen in October 1970 and converting to the Phantom FGR.2. Jaguar conversion began in June 1975

The RAFG Jaguar Wing. A formation comprising all five squadrons. From front to rear: XZ391 of No. II(AC) with a reconnaissance pod, XZ374 of No. 14, XX768 of No. 17, XX960 from No. 20 and XZ391 of No. 31 Squadron. *Blue Envoy Collection*

ABOVE Out with the old and in with the new. Changing of the guard in No. 14 Squadron in mid-1975 as the Jaguar supplants the McDonnell Douglas Phantom FGR2. XX762 was destroyed when it crashed into Beinn a'Chleigh mountain in Argyle on 23 November 1979. Flight Lieutenant Alan Graham Proctor ejected but sadly died from head trauma and hypothermia before he could be rescued. *Blue Envoy Collection*

LEFT GR.1 XX761 of No. 14 Squadron flying over Brüggen. A CBLS pod is mounted on the ventral hardpoint. *Terry Panopalis Collection*

GR.1 XZ356 of No. 17 Squadron overflying a dam in southern Germany. ***Author's Collection***

No. 31 Squadron received its first Jaguars in January 1976. XX968 is seen parked outside its HAS in June 1980, the nearby trees providing some natural cover and camouflage. ***Terry Panopalis Collection***

under the command of Wing Commander Roy Humphreyson. The first aircraft, T.2 XX840, arrived in June and conversion was completed by February 1976.

No. 31 Squadron was formed in October 1915 and became another of RAFG's reconnaissance squadrons with the Canberra PR.7 in March 1956 at Laarbruch. It converted to the Phantom FGR.2 at Brüggen in July 1971. The squadron reformed on the Jaguar in January 1976 and was declared operational on 1 July.

No. 20 Squadron was unique among the Jaguar squadrons in having been a Harrier unit before conversion. Formed in September 1915, it had reformed at Wildenrath on the Harrier GR.1 in December 1970. The squadron began forming a Jaguar element at Brüggen in January 1977 before being officially reformed on 1 March. The first Jaguar to be received was GR.1 XZ374 on 4 February.

No. II(AC) Squadron was based at Laarbruch and operated in the reconnaissance role. It could trace its history back to 13 May 1912, when it was formed out of the Army's Royal Engineer's 2 (Aeroplane) Company as part of the new Royal Flying Corps. The squadron was equipped with the Phantom FGR.2 in December 1970. Conversion on to the Jaguar began in July 1976 and was declared operational on 1 October. The first Jaguar received at Laarbruch on 26 February 1976 was GR.1 XZ101 and the remaining 11 GR.1s and one T.2 arrived

Jaguar XX959 of No. 20 Squadron gets airborne for a practise bombing sortie in June 1981 with CBLS practise bomb pods on the outboard hardpoints. ***Terry Panopalis Collection***

over the following two months. The Jaguar took over the recce role from the Phantom on 1 October 1976. Its specialist role is covered in more detail later in this chapter.

The Jaguar Wing would operate in the counter-air interdiction role. The weapon of choice against airfields was the freefall 1,000lb bomb, a 30° diving attack being recommended to obtain a bomb angle of impact of 45° to crater runways – 16 aircraft carrying six bombs were required to achieve a 41% probability of closing a runway. It was accepted that modern hardened facilities were invulnerable to all but a direct hit, but unhardened airfields could be attacked effectively by retarded bombs and BL.755 cluster bombs.

Battlefield interdiction to support NATO armies would involve sorties by 105 Jaguars and 48 Harriers to hit targets like amphibious bridging equipment and pontoon bridges across rivers and waterways – a Jaguar with six 1,000lb bombs could sink two pontoon sections. Against surface-to-air missile (SAM) or anti-aircraft artillery (AAA) sites the BL.755 or Variable Timing (VT)-fused 1,000lb bombs were the most effective options. The use of Lepus flares for target illumination for visual acquisition was necessary in night attacks; in a pairs formation, one aircraft would carry four flares, the other four bombs to attack two targets.

For the close support role, the BL.755 cluster bomb was designed for anti-armour use with its 147 bomblets scattering over an area of 550 × 130ft (167 × 40m). The bomblets could penetrate up to 9.8in (250mm) of armour plating (this was later improved with a new bomblet) and exploded into over 2,000 fragments, which could penetrate unarmoured vehicles. VT-fused bombs or BL.755 were effective weapons against infantry, more so than gun strafing attacks. Nuclear strikes are described later in this chapter.

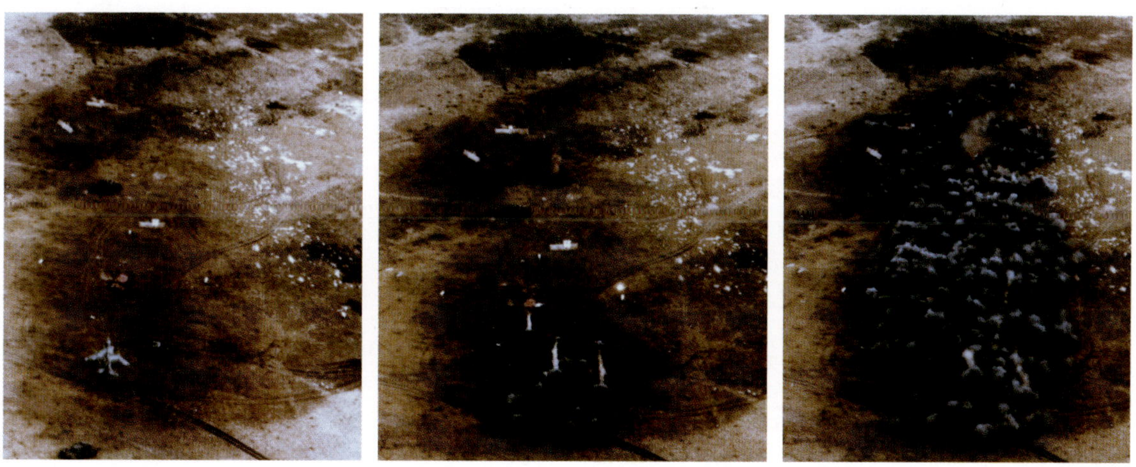

This set of photographs of a release of four live BL.755 cluster bombs from a Jaguar over derelict tank targets at the Kirkcudbright ranges shows how the retarded petals open to slow the bombs, allowing the submunitions to disperse over the target. ***Blue Envoy Collection***

This map shows the Cold War situation facing the RAFG. The Jaguar Force was located close to the German-Dutch border, well back from the potential frontline, but their Option Alpha air interdiction targets were in heavily defended areas in East Germany and northern Czechoslovakia. ***Author***

The likely geographical area of Jaguar wartime operations in East Germany was over the plain bounded to the north by the Baltic Sea and the Thüringer Walde and Erzgebirge mountains to the south. Apart from the Harz mountains in the south-west, most of the terrain did not rise above 500ft and was covered by woods, marshes, lakes and rivers. There were numerous low-altitude flying hazards such as electricity pylons, radio transmitter masts and industrial chimneys. Fog was especially likely from November until mid-March and there was a likelihood of 40 days of snow coverage on the ground – providing additional ambient light at night but tending to mask targets on the ground. There would be up to 15 hours of darkness a day in the winter months, compared with fewer than six in the summer. The minimum ideal conditions for daytime and night-time penetration sorties would occur 97% and 75% of the time throughout the year.

The airspace over East Germany was well defended by Soviet and East German forces. The ageing S-75 Dvina (NATO designation SA-2 *Guideline*) SAM system was being withdrawn, but there were still 22 sites in operation, together with 29 known S-125 Neva (SA-3 *Goa*) sites. The Jaguar would be operating towards the lower ceiling limits of these systems and would fly below the engagement envelope of the 2K11 Krug (SA-4 *Ganef*) mobile system issued to army regiments and located over 19 miles (30km) behind the Forward Edge of the Battle Area (FEBA). The newer mobile 2K12 Kub (SA-6 *Gainful*) was dangerous, especially during high loft bombing manoeuvres and its low-to-medium altitude companion, the 9K33 Osa (SA-8 *Gecko*), was equally formidable. They would be located some 3–19 miles (5–30km) behind the FEBA. The mobile 9K31 Strela-1 (SA-9 *Gaskin*) was an infrared (IR)-homing missile that was deployed at regimental level on the FEBA and up to 5km (3 miles) behind the front, being especially dangerous during egress from the target area. In addition, Soviet infantry were equipped with shoulder-fired 9K32 Strela-2 (SA-7 *Grail*) and 9K310 Igla-1 (SA-16 *Gimlet*) IR-homing missiles, although their effectiveness was not considered to be good. Backing up these SAM systems were thousands of AAA sites with calibres ranging from 23mm to 100mm; the most dangerous being the self-propelled ZSU-23-4 Shilka with four 23mm cannon with radar tracking, which could fire on the move. RAF planners hoped that its small ammunition supply – lasting only 33 seconds – and the 3,000-round barrel life would reduce its effectiveness. Jaguar pilots were advised to keep below 200ft (60m) at speeds up to 480kt. Until the mid-1980s Warsaw Pact air forces had few fighters equipped with look-down shoot-down radar capability, although fighters like the Mikoyan-Gurevich MiG-23 *Flogger* had superior thrust/weight and wing loading ratios that favoured them in aerial combat. Little training against targets flying below 1,000ft had been observed by Western intelligence and although combat air patrols against low-flying threats had been introduced by 1980, it was judged that these preparations would be ineffective against the low-flying Jaguars. By the late 1980s the MiG-29 *Fulcrum* had the capability to pick out low-flying targets with its radar and passive IR sensor. Ultimately, it was unwise to underestimate the dangers given the hundreds of Warsaw Pact aircraft operating in a relatively small area of airspace.

The advice given to Jaguar pilots was to keep low and accelerate to as high a speed as possible to put distance between them and the attacker. Given the lack of any self-defence air-to-air missile (AAM) capability at that time, it was suggested to release a 1,000lb retarded bomb when the attacking fighter got within missile firing range. The bomb would detonate 1,350ft (410m) behind the Jaguar and hopefully cause the attacker to break off or overshoot – although this would not work against a co-ordinated attack by several fighters.

The Jaguar made an early impression on General John Vogt Jr, the Commander of Allied Air Forces Central Europe and United States Air Forces Europe. Following a flight in a Jaguar he described it as 'a doggone good close-support airplane; good low-altitude medium battlefield support airplane or a battlefield interdiction weapon; carries a lot of ordnance; highly manoeuvrable; good acceleration and performance down in the area where it was designed to fight'. Despite not having an all-weather capability, he praised the Jaguar as 'a very fine weapons delivery platform, with good accuracies, good manoeuvrability, and good performance. It will add immeasurably to our capability in Allied Forces.'

Nos. 14 and 17 Squadrons were declared combat capable to SACEUR in the nuclear laydown/ground burst mode on 1 January and 1 February 1976 respectively, and on 1 July were declared combat ready using the fully automatic loft/air burst mode. No. 31 Squadron's declaration to SACEUR was delayed by three months due to manpower shortages and led to a knock-on delay in No. 20 Squadron achieving its operational status. The former Officer Commanding of No. 226 OCU, John Walker (now a group captain), was posted as Brüggen's Station Commander between February 1976 and January 1978.

RAF Brüggen was the first of RAFG's airfields to receive HAS for its aircraft. A GR.1 of No. 14 Squadron is seen outside of one of the newly completed HAS in 1975. ***Crown Copyright via Terry Panopalis***

Wartime preparation was the order of the day. Pilots were cleared to fly down to 500ft over Germany and 250ft (76m) over designated low-flying areas with a minimum visibility limit of 2.7nm (5km), although pilots often flew in worse conditions. The peacetime ratio of 1.25 pilots per aircraft proved insufficient to maintain a viable strike force, so from mid-1977 this was increased to 1.5 pilots per aircraft, a total of 18 per squadron.

The Brüggen Wing had pre-planned attack operations in case of the outbreak of a no-notice war. For example, Option Alpha was a counter-air mission against airfields in East Germany and Option Zulu was a close air support/interdiction against Soviet armour crossing the Inner German Border (IGB).

In peacetime, the readiness state required 60% of the aircraft to be loaded with BL.755 bombs and ready

Although this pair of Jaguars, XX743 and XZ396, belong to No. 226 OCU at Lossiemouth, this image illustrates the typical interior of a HAS in which the aircraft would be maintained and brought to readiness in wartime. ***Author's Collection***

Soaking up the French sun. No. 54(F) Squadron had only been declared combat ready shortly before they visited BA 113 Saint-Dizier-Robinson and its resident Jaguar unit Escadron de Chasse 3/7 'Languedoc'. The rear aircraft is an early production GR.1 lacking the LRMTS in the nose. ***Author's Collection***

for operations within six hours, and all aircraft to be ready within 12 hours. Initially the Jaguars were loaded with live BL.755s every Friday afternoon in case war broke out over the weekend. Eventually the wear and tear on the bomb attachment lugs saw the live BL.755 being left on the trolley beside the aircraft in the HAS in readiness for loading.

The RAFG's war reserve provision of fuel drop tanks allowed for 60% of war sorties using two tanks and 25% with one tank. However, the Central Region tasking indicated that all sorties would require two tanks so the war reserve was expanded from 1,068 to 1,288 tanks in 1978, which also covered the wartime reinforcements from No. 226 OCU and the future increase of the squadron AE from 12 to 15 aircraft.

No. 17 Squadron took part in live bombing trials at Garvie Island in Scotland using 1,000lb retarded bombs on 25–26 May 1977, being joined by No. 226 OCU on 31 May–1 June. The objective was to evaluate a video tape recording system for scoring the hits. A mix of level and 5° dive releases using the Continuously Computed Impact Point and revisionary targeting modes achieved CEPs of 140ft (42m) and 100ft (30m) respectively. No. 14 Squadron made an exchange visit to fellow Jaguar operator Escadron de Chasse 3/7 'Languedoc' at Saint-Dizier with a mixed flight of GR.1s and T.2s on 10 August 1978.

The RAF's newest tactical nuclear aircraft alongside one of its V-Force predecessors, the Avro Vulcan. The Jaguar is XZ389 of No. 20 Squadron at the Queen's Silver Jubilee Review held at Finningley during 29–30 July 1977. ***Terry Panopalis Collection***

A GR.1 of No. 14 Squadron taxying at during the exchange visit to Saint-Dizier on 10 August 1978. A CBLS is fitted on the centreline hardpoint. *Author's Collection*

No. 17 Squadron was the first to take part in Exercise Red Flag at Nellis AFB in 1978. The preparations included a two-week work-up at Lossiemouth with the minimum flying height reduced to 100ft (30.5m) using an audio height warner set at 80ft (24m). A new fighter evasion tactic was devised; if an enemy fighter closed within gun range, the pilot would jink by rolling 90° of bank and pushing to -1 or -2g. This proved very successful during Red Flag, although the manoeuvre caused the aircraft's batteries to leak acid, so they had to be modified. Adour Mk.102E engines were also fitted in an attempt to boost performance in the hot conditions. The provision of a chaff dispenser required the inventiveness of Brüggen's No. 431 Maintenance Unit, who devised the 'Johhny Walker Get You Home Gun' – a six-shot chaff dispenser fitted in place of the braking parachute, with release using the brake parachute handle in the cockpit. Electronic warfare was even more basic – radio jamming by one of the flight commanders loudly singing on the radio frequency during combat. The Jaguar performed well despite these improvisations and lessons were learned for future upgrades.

RAFG units won the Salmond Trophy bombing competition in 1975, 1976 and 1977 thanks to the efforts

RAFG squadrons attended Exercise Red Flag air combat exercises at Nellis AFB in Nevada. XZ356 of No. 17 Squadron is seen an early 1980s Red Flag deployment with a single CBLS for practice bombs. In the background a pair of McDonnell Douglas F-15A Eagle fighters of the USAF are getting airborne. *Author's Collection*

RIGHT Another No. 17 Squadron Jaguar at Nellis for Red Flag was XX768 sporting an unusual store on the outer starboard hardpoint, possibly an Air Combat Manoeuvring Instrumentation pod. An AN/ALQ-101(V10) ECM pod is carried on the port side. *Author's Collection*

BELOW A mixed formation of No. II(AC) Squadron Jaguars and Phantoms, the Jaguar in the foreground is XZ108, which was delivered to the squadron on 9 June 1976. *Terry Panopalis Collection*

A Jaguar GR.1 of No. 31 Squadron coming into land on a section of newly completed autobahn in West Germany to practise dispersed operations. *Crown Copyright via Terry Panopalis*

of No. 14 Squadron and in 1977 Nos 14, 17, II (AC) and 31 Squadrons took the first four places. Visiting USAF Vought A-7D Corsair IIs of the 23rd Tactical Fighter Wing won the trophies at the Strike Command Tactical Bombing Competition as invited guests in 1977, the Corsairs returning to win the overall trophy again in 1978, although the Jaguars won the individual bombing and strafing competitions. The Corsair's success highlighted the Jaguar's shortcomings. The A-7 had air-to-ground radar and utilised Doppler radar and inertial navigation for navigational waypoint fixes. It had a larger 1:1 display HUD stabilised on the outside world, whereas the Jaguar's smaller HUD was a 5:1 display with a fixed horizon line and only showed 1/5th of the true angle of climb or dive (for example a 5° instrument descent was 25° in reality), which hampered accurate aiming and could be dangerous in certain situations. In addition, NAVWASS was unreliable; 25% of the Jaguars in the 1977 competition suffered an inflight failure that forced the pilots to resort to map and stopwatch navigation. A bombing accuracy problem was revealed during the 1976 Tactical Bombing Competition. The targets had been located on an upward slope of around 3° and despite the pilots compensating for the incorrect radar altimeter input (the height of the terrain beneath the aircraft and the target differed due to the sloping ground), their bombs impacted 350ft (106m) beyond the targets. The primary height data input into NAVWASS was the radar altimeter, the 920M air data computer also providing barometric information and the vertical velocity from the E3R inertial platform. The A&AEE discovered that using the LRMTS to provide

The No. II(AC) Squadron flightline at Laarbruch in 1978. *USAF*

the slant range and depression angle was the most accurate method for terrain variations within 15ft (5m). Wind error, especially over uneven hilly terrain, was also important when dropping retarded bombs; an updraught slowing a bomb by 0.46 seconds would result in a 70ft (21m) miss error.

On 27 September 1977 Jaguars participated in an exercise to assess the feasibility of operating off autobahn strips in wartime. The Luftwaffe had extensive plans to operate from the autobahn network and 22 strips had by that time been included within newly constructed sections. The RAFG was considering joining these operations and they were invited to participate in the trials on the new Bremen–Bremerhaven section of autobahn before it opened to the public. Three waves of four Jaguars were flown from Brüggen, making a series of overshoots and touch-and-goes before landing. After being refuelled, they took off for a full training sortie and returned to land at Brüggen.

While it was recognised that such strips might pose logistical and command and control problems, the fact that RAFG's airfields would be overcrowded (up to 70 Jaguars at Brüggen and 70 Tornados and Jaguars at Laarbruch) made the scheme attractive. There were also studies under way to use civil and disused airfields as satellite airfields in wartime.

Squadron training by 1980 consisted of: the APC at Decimomannu; one ten-day NATO squadron exchange; four RAFG exercises; a NATO Mallet Blow exercise; and one annual TACEVAL. Brüggen became the first NATO base to be awarded 'Excellent' grades across the board for a TACEVAL in 1978. The Jaguars participated in the major air defence Exercise Elder Forest 80 during 14–15 April 1980, which involved eight NATO air forces and tested the UK's air defences, reinforced by Tactical Weapons Unit Hunters and Hawks and USAF Northrop F-5Es and McDonnell Douglas F-15A Eagles. The attacking 'Red Force' comprised RAFG Phantoms and Jaguars alongside Saab Drakens, General Dynamics F-111As, Canadair NF-5 Freedom Fighters, North American F-100 Super Sabres, F-104G Starfighters, Dassault Mirages and US-based Boeing B-52 Stratofortress bombers.

A No. 14 Squadron GR.1 is prepared for another sortie inside its HAS. The groundcrew are wearing NBC protective gear. The threat of chemical attack on airfields by the Warsaw Pact was taken seriously and exercises were often held in simulated NBC conditions. The pilot would remain inside the cockpit during the turnaround, relying on the Jaguar's own NBC pack to filter the incoming air. *Crown Copyright via Terry Panopalis*

A pair of No. 17 Squadron Jaguars being readied for an Exercise Red Flag mission at Nellis AFB in January 1984. The foremost aircraft is XZ385. *Terry Panopalis Collection*

Out with the old and in with the new, reprise. The Panavia Tornado GR.1 replaced the Jaguars in the strike and reconnaissance roles with RAFG during the 1980s. *Blue Envoy Collection*

Training by 1987 included NATO exercises Mallet Blow, Crimson Falcon and Ample Gain (the latter involving swapping ground crews to support flying operations), two Lone Ranger deployment flights per pilot, Red Flag and Maple Flag and ultra-low level training in the UK and Canada. On top of this were MAXEVALs and MINEVALs; a MAXEVAL was a TACEVAL rehearsal, while MINEVALs were conducted at the behest of a station commander to prepare for the MAXEVAL and to remedy any deficiencies noted prior to the TACEVAL.

All this training to wartime conditions came at a cost; over nine years seven pilots were killed in 21 crashes (six flights into ground, five due to loss of control, six to engine failure or fire, three in mid-air collisions, one bird strike) – plus another was accidentally shot down by an AIM-9 Sidewinder AAM fired from a Phantom FGR.2 during a practice interception.

The Jaguar ended up being an interim aircraft for RAFG, serving for a decade before being replaced by the more capable Panavia Tornado GR.1. This decision had been reached during the summer of 1980, when it was decided to maintain the UK-based Buccaneers in the maritime role until the early 1990s and replace the RAFG's Jaguars instead. The first squadron to transition to the Tornado was No. 20 on 24 June 1984, thus earning the distinction of being the only RAF squadron to have operated the Harrier, Jaguar and Tornado. No. 31 converted between 13 June and 1 November 1984. No 17 received its first Tornado on 16 August 1984 and its transition was completed on 1 March 1985. No. 14 flew its last Jaguar sortie on 14 October 1985, by which time conversion on to the Tornado was well under way and completed on 1 November. The last Jaguar left Brüggen on 21 October, flying to RAF Shawbury for storage. More than 120 Jaguars had passed through Brüggen over the years.

No. II(AC) Squadron was the final Jaguar squadron due to the delayed entry into service of the reconnaissance Tornado GR.1A variant. In July 1986 the squadron took part in NATO exercise TAM 86 at Kleine Brogel. The last operational RAFG Jaguar sortie was flown on 16 December 1988 by the Officer Commanding, Wing Commander Threadgould.

Many Jaguars went into storage at Shawbury and still had plenty of fatigue life left, some having accrued as few as 1,500 flying hours. A total of 66 Jaguars were issued as maintenance ground instructional airframes to No. 1 and No. 2 School of Technical Training at RAF Halton and RAF Cosford – the latter later coming under the control of the Defence College of Aeronautical Engineering and today the Defence College of Technical Training – and the Aircraft Maintenance Instruction Flight at Cranwell.

Maintenance numbers			
Maintenance Number	Serial	Constructon Number	Inital Locaton
8563M	XW563	07	Brüggen
8600M	XX761	S58	Lossiemouth
8815M	XX118	S11	No. 1 SoTT Halton
8816M	XX734	S31	Coltshall
8821M	XX115	S8	DCAE Cosford
8895M	XX746	S43	No. 2 SoTT Cosford
8896M	XX821	S70	No. 2 SoTT Cosford
8897M	XX969	S91	No. 2 SoTT Cosford
8898M	XX119	S12	DCAE Cosford
8899M	XX756	S53	No. 2 SoTT Cosford
8900M	XZ368	S135	No. 2 SoTT Cosford
8901M	XZ383	S148	No. 2 SoTT Cosford
8902M	XX739	S36	No. 1 SoTT Halton
8903M	XX747	S44	No. 1 SoTT Halton
8904M	XX966	S88	No. 1 SoTT Halton
8905M	XX975	S97	No. 1 SoTT Halton
8906M	XX976	S98	No. 1 SoTT Halton
8907M	XZ371	S138	No. 2 SoTT Cosford
8908M	XZ382	S147	No. 1 SoTT Halton
8918M	XX109	S2	Coltshall
8923M	XX819	S68	No. 2 SoTT Cosford
8937M	XX751	S48	No. 2 SoTT Cosford
8945M	XX818	S67	No. 1 SoTT Halton
8946M	XZ389	S154	No. 1 SoTT Halton
8947M	XX726	S23	No. 1 SoTT Halton
8948M	XX757	S54	No. 1 SoTT Halton
8949M	XX743	S40	No. 1 SoTT Halton
8950M	XX956	S78	No. 1 SoTT Halton
8951M	XX727	S24	No. 2 SoTT Cosford
8952M	XX730	S27	No. 2 SoTT Cosford
8953M	XX959	S81	No. 2 SoTT Cosford
8954M	XZ384	S149	No. 2 SoTT Cosford
8955M	XX110	S3	No. 2 SoTT Cosford
8978M	XX837	B25	No. 1 SoTT Halton
9003M	XZ390	S155	No. 2 SoTT Cosford
9004M	XZ370	S137	No. 2 SoTT Cosford
9005M	XZ374	S141	No. 2 SoTT Cosford
9006M	XX967	S89	No. 2 SoTT Cosford
9007M	XX968	S90	No. 2 SoTT Cosford
9008M	XX140	B5	No. 2 SoTT Cosford
9009M	XX763	S60	No. 4 SoTT St Athan
9010M	XX764	S61	No. 4 SoTT St Athan
9019M	XX824	S73	No. 1 SoTT Halton
9020M	XX825	S74	No. 1 SoTT Halton
9021M	XX826	S75	No. 2 SoTT Cosford
9022M	XX958	S80	No. 2 SoTT Cosford
9023M	XX844	B32	No. 2 SoTT Cosford
9087M	XX753	S50	RAF Exhibiton Flight
9110M	XX736	S33	Coltshall

Nuclear role

The Jaguar holds a unique place in RAF history, being the only single-seat, nuclear-armed aircraft that it has operated to date. The Operational Requirements Committee endorsed the decision to proceed with an operational nuclear capability in August 1972. BAC Chief Test Pilot Paul Millett flew the first 'special weapon'-handling flight in prototype S07 (XW563) on 21 March 1974.

The strike role Jaguars were assigned to SACEUR to support the Flexible Response Policy – the ultimate response being the release of nuclear weapons. Pilots had to achieve the navigation and bombing accuracy standards laid down by SACEUR; a maximum miss distance of 500ft (150m) for a laydown attack and 2,000ft (610m) for a toss manoeuvre. The nuclear role was constantly trained and practised. During some TACEVALs a pilot would be selected to rehearse a 'selective release' procedure, flying the mission profile (without a live weapon). Brüggen also practised launching the entire Jaguar Wing and within a few years this was accomplished in complete radio silence.

The GR.1 was cleared to carry one WE.177 bomb on a Mk.103 Special Weapon Carrier on the ventral pylon with a Mk.115 Explosive Release Unit (not all GR.1s had WE.177 wiring, for example those of the reconnaissance-focused squadrons). NAVWASS would have its specific nuclear weapons flight programme inserted, which had a variety of HUD symbology and WE.177-specific ballistic information for pre-computed toss and laydown profiles. The delivery method was preset on the ground and could not be changed in flight – although a manual reversionary mode was available by setting the depression angle and releasing the bomb after the aircraft symbol and the target overlapped in the HUD.

Two variants of the WE.177 could be carried. The WE.177A had a cover identity as the HE 600lb MC bomb and the WE.177C was the HE 950lb MC No. 2, implying to the casual observer that these were conventional weapons. The WE.177A was a variable-yield 0.5–10kT (kilotons) weapon, originally issued to the Royal Navy but later transferred to RAF stocks. Only one yield was selected for use on the Jaguar but the fusing system gave low- or high-airburst options. The 190kT WE.177C only had a low-airburst capability. Both could be delivered in the retarded laydown mode. Given the size of some Warsaw Pact airfields and the provision of hardened facilities, the RAF estimated that to destroy one airfield up to four WE.177As might be needed, or a single WE.177C.

There were fewer weapons assigned than aircraft because it was calculated that some aircraft would be lost in the conventional phase of the war before the release of tactical nuclear weapons was authorised. Planners sought to hold back enough aircraft during the conventional phase to ensure that the stock of nuclear weapons could be delivered by the surviving aircraft. The UK-based Nos. 6 and 54(F) Squadrons and No. 226 OCU were each allocated eight WE.177s for their 12 aircraft in 1975 (some 10% of the planned WE.177 stockpile) and by 1978 the Brüggen Wing would carry 21% of the RAF's WE.177s. By 1985 only the UK-based squadrons and the OCU were allocated nuclear weapons (around 10% of the stockpile), reflecting the switch to the Tornado as the main nuclear strike force. The WE.177 was withdrawn from RAF use in 1998.

Following the granting of operational clearance from 1 December 1975, Brüggen maintained a nuclear-armed QRA. At any one time five aircraft were at armed readiness with the pilots on standby. Each squadron would man two of the 'Q' aircraft every four weeks. Each of the four squadrons had an assigned target, with a fifth target shared between the Wing. Declarations to SACEUR were dependent on the number of available 'strike-wired' Jaguars capable of carrying WE.177. For example, in August 1980 the Air Staff had to wrestle with the notional and real availability figures; on the 28th the RAF possessed 78 strike-wired GR.1s, 56 of which were at Brüggen and the rest in the UK. Under NATO declarations the expected number at Brüggen was 60, with a minimum of 48. In addition to this, NATO expected 69 Jaguars at Brüggen for post-alert attack (the minimum was 57, including nine from the OCU). There were – depending on whether the UK-based aircraft were counted or not – either 59 or 102 available attack Jaguars.

A typical nuclear sortie would be as follows. The WE.177 would be loaded on to the aircraft inside the HAS. Prior to the arrival of the weapon convoy, the HAS would be declared a secure 'Follow On Area' and the RAF Police guards protecting it would be issued with live ammunition. The policemen had a photograph of the pilot assigned to the HAS for identification. The allocated pilot would be issued with a Strike Enabling Facility Key and would proceed to the HAS with another accompanying pilot to ensure that the 'two-man rule' was maintained. Once identified and admitted inside, the pilot would formally accept the weapon from the Weapon Load Supervising Officer (WLSO), witnessed by the policemen. The two pilots together would check that the weapon release switches were wire locked and safe before setting the yield, burst height and delivery method on the control panel. Then the weapon would be armed with the Strike Enabling Facility Key.

If this was a training exercise, the WE.177 would be handed back to the WLSO and unloaded, being replaced by a CBLS with practice bombs and the pilot would fly the exercise mission to the Nordhorn range. If it was the real thing, the pilot would wait in the cockpit at readiness until the release message was received. The station hooter would sound and one door of each HAS would be opened. This was one of the precautions put in place by the Nuclear Weapons Safety Committee to provide an effective physical barrier that could not be overcome by an unskilled member of the groundcrew acting as an accomplice to the pilot and so prevent an unauthorised take-off.

The Combat Operations Centre would broadcast the call signs, individual release codes for each mission and the R-Hour for release. Each pilot would then open his sealed envelope, verifying the code and matching it with the policemen's code. Then the policemen would let the groundcrew open the other door. The aircraft would

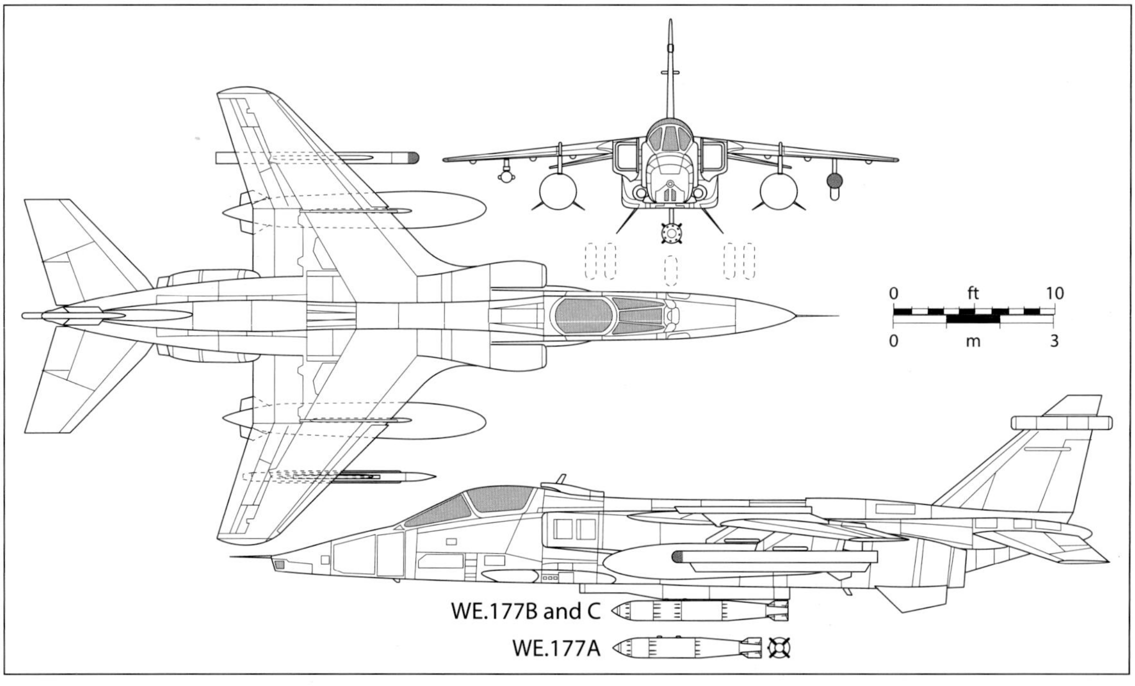

This general arrangement drawing shows the nuclear strike loadout in the 1980s with a WE.177A or WE.177C nuclear bomb on the centreline, two 264gal (1,200L) fuel drop tanks inboard, an AN/ ALQ-101(V)10 ECM pod on the outer port hardpoint and a Phimat chaff pod on the starboard side. The higher-yield WE.177C bomb was larger. ***Chris Gibson***

perform a mass take-off, the runway being divided along the centreline with two squadrons using each half.

The aircraft would hold over friendly territory before heading to their F-Point near the IGB. From the F-Point they would head to their targets beyond the IGB. The cockpit was equipped with a Master Safety Switch. Should the aircraft have to divert, the pilot remained responsible for the weapon and had to be able to establish a protected No-Lone Zone around the aircraft to ensure that no one person was ever left alone with the weapon.

Mission planning was governed by deconfliction requirements with the aircraft required to cross the IGB at specific times and places, which meant that sorties could not take the best routes to avoid defended areas. The sole consideration was getting to the target at the right Time on Target within three seconds accuracy.

The planners deemed that the major risk during the penetration would be the flash from other nuclear explosions, which could at best impair the pilot's vision, or at worst permanently blind him. Famously the V-Force bomber pilots and co-pilots were issued with eye patches and flash blinds so that they could endure four nuclear flashes before flying blind. The CTTO hopefully estimated that; 'provided the eyelids are working normally, the blink is fast enough to prevent permanent damage by day. At night there is a greater chance of retinal damage'. It was estimated a pilot might be dazzled for 3–80 seconds depending on whether he was looking at an explosion some 16nm (30km) away in his peripheral vision or directly at a nearby one. Despite these prosaic estimates, Jaguar pilots were issued with an eye patch to save at least one eye.

Assuming arrival at target area intact, the Initial Point was also dictated by the tasking authority, so again might offer a suboptimal run-in to the target. Weapons release was automatic for whichever delivery mode had been preselected. SACEUR, however, could order last-minute reassignment of targets or changes to the delivery mode prior to R-Hour. In this case, given that it took 30 minutes to update NAVWASS, it was more likely that the pilot would have to use the manual reversionary mode.Following release it was not thought that the blast overpressure or radiation from the explosion would damage the airframe or the pilot, but the heat generated was a hazard with potential damage to metal components, charring inside the cockpit and burns to the pilot. The best plan was to escape from the blast zone as fast as possible, remaining tail-on to the burst.

Recon role

The GR.1s assigned to the reconnaissance role had an additional reconnaissance pod control panel in the cockpit and the necessary wiring to interface the pod carried on the centreline pylon. The EMI-designed pod contained a forward-facing Vinten F95 Mk 7 camera with a 6in (152mm) lens and four Vinten F95 Mk 10 cameras for 194° horizon-to-horizon coverage: two high oblique cameras with 3in (76mm) lenses and two low obliques with 1.5in (38mm) lenses. The forward-looking and low oblique cameras were mounted on the front drum unit with the high obliques on the rear drum unit; the drums rotated 180° to enable the cameras to look out through optically accurate glass panels. The oblique cameras had 250ft (76m) of film for 1,250 frames (usually around 960 useable exposures), the forward-facing camera having 200ft (60m) for 1,000 frames. The rear drum could be replaced by a vertically mounted F126 survey camera with a 6in lens for medium-altitude photography and 250ft of film for 318 frames. The cameras had image movement compensation and automatic exposure control; they were usually loaded with black and white film, although natural colour and infrared false colour (for spotting camouflage) films were available.

This Jaguar is carrying an EMI reconnaissance pod. The port for the forward low oblique Vinten F.95 Mk 10 cameras and the aft aperture for the EMI/ Hawker Siddeley Dynamics infrared linescanner are evident in this view. *Author's Collection*

At the rear of the pod was an EMI/Hawker Siddeley Dynamics Type 401 infrared linescanner (IRLS), which had a 120° field of view and could be offset by 30° to port or starboard to give 180° coverage, although it worked best when the target was vertically below. The IRLS had a five-channel IR-detector that scanned the ground below the aircraft and was roll-stabilised up to 55° for image continuity when the aircraft banked. It recorded the heat signatures received from the ground on to 300ft (91m) of film, which was sufficient to cover a 29nm (53km)-long strip of terrain 170ft (52m) wide when flying at 50ft (15m), or a 590nm (1,090km) by 3,460ft (1,055m) strip from 1,000ft. Given that it relied on sufficient background contrast to show targets of interest, it was best used at low altitude with a resolution of 12in (30cm) from 200ft (60m), although bridges, river craft, aircraft and buildings were still

No. II(AC) Squadron was RAFG's specialist Jaguar reconnaissance unit, with a secondary attack role. XZ111 is carrying the recce pod on the centreline along with two underwing fuel tanks. ***Author's Collection***

This drawing shows the typical loadout for the tactical reconnaissance role in the 1980s with the recce pod on the centreline, two 264gal (1,200L) fuel drop tanks and the AN/ALQ-101(V)10 and Phimat ECM and chaff pods. ***Chris Gibson***

visible up to an altitude of 800ft (245m).The pod also contained an air-conditioning system and the Data Converter Unit, which annotated the camera and IRLS films with navigational and timestamp data from NAVWASS. The pod was 19ft (5.8m) long, 25.5in (65cm) in diameter and weighed 1,234lb (560kg). When fitted, the Jaguar was limited to manoeuvres not exceeding 12° of AoA and 4.5g. Pod production began in May 1974 but the early production linescanners were not ready until 1976 and technical issues delayed full operational capability until 1977–78.

If the briefed target had been photographed successfully, the pilot would radio back the Essential Elements of Information required for the specific target

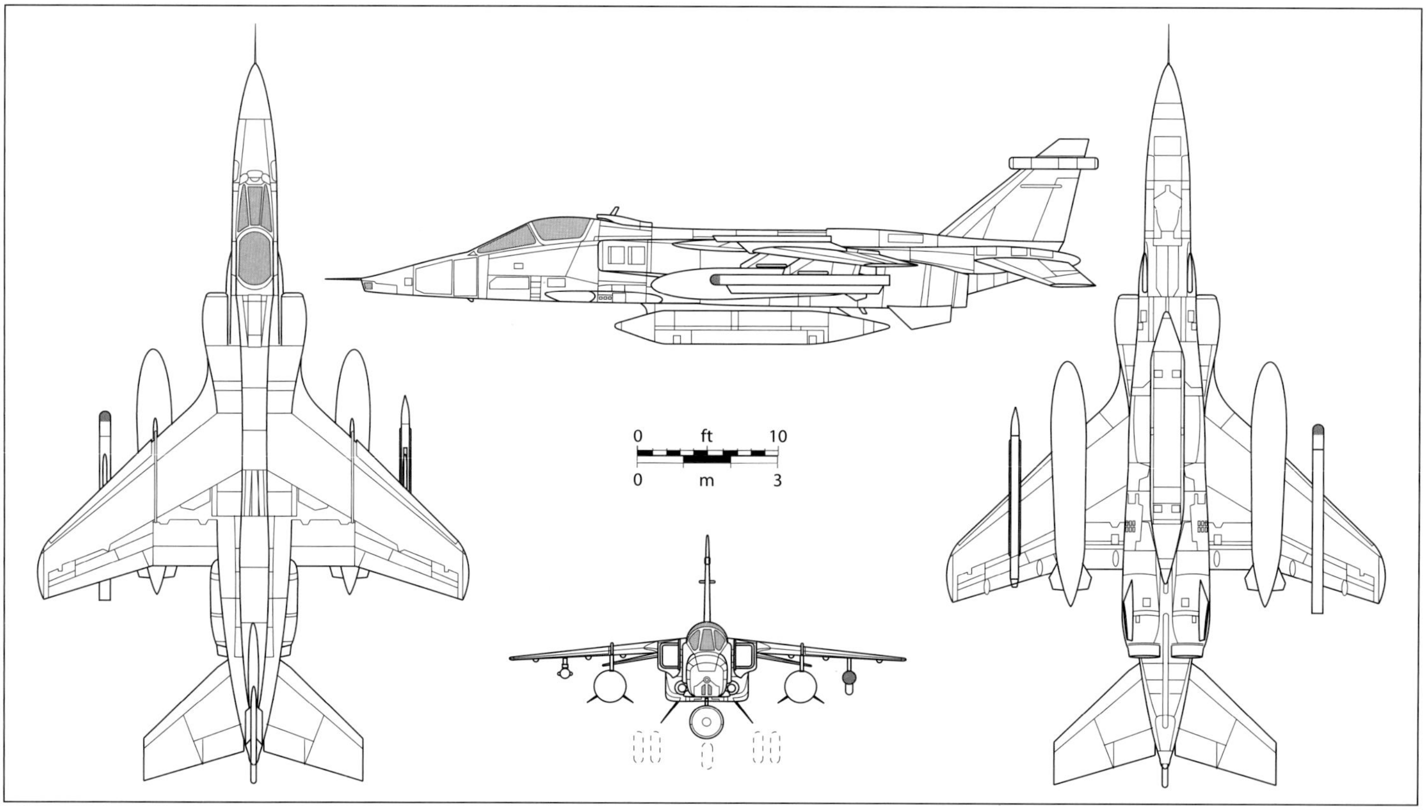

to the Reconnaissance Information Centre (RIC). Visual reconnaissance by the pilot was an important backup in case the pod suffered a technical malfunction and provided intelligence interpretation; a tape cassette voice recorder was also provided for this purpose. The pilot had an event marking button on the throttle, pressing this whenever a target of interest was spotted would place a special mark and the NAVWASS data stamp on the camera and/or IRLS film for later evaluation.On return to the airfield, the film magazines would be removed by the Air Camera Fitters and taken by motorbike to the RIC for processing. The RIC consisted of a number of Portakabin-type structures – a Mobile Air Reconnaissance Exploitation Laboratory (MAREL) – housing all the necessary developing equipment and staffed by around 60 personnel (at Laarbruch the RIC was inside one of the HAS and at Bardufoss it would be inside the 'Rock Hangar'). The mobile Air Transportable Reconnaissance Exploitation Laboratory (ATREL) comprised up to 14 lorry-based cabins which housed all the processing, printing and photo interpretation equipment required for tactical deployments. As No. II(AC) Squadron's key task was producing imagery for the Army, a Ground Liaison Officer (GLO) was assigned from the Intelligence Corps.

In wartime, there were no pre-planned operations for No. 41(F) Squadron's Bardufoss deployment. Missions would be immediate taskings from the Joint Norwegian Operations Centre at Reitan. Missions would likely be line-searches or pinpoint locations and tasks such as keeping the few possible coastal areas suitable for seaborne invasion – places like Porsanger Fjord, Alta Flord or Tromsø – under observation, or observing the enemy's main overland thrusts via the Finnmark Plain into north-eastern Norway via Sweden.

No. II(AC) Squadron had four wartime pre-planned Reconnaissance Programmes (RECPROMs): RECPROM 1 border surveillance along the western edge of the IGB to detect incursions; RECPROM 2 route reconnaissance west of the IGB to identify the progress of any invasion; RECPROM 3 route reconnaissance of main lines of communication east of the IGB to locate assembly areas, reserve forces and static installations; RECPROM 4 reconnaissance of aviation and air defence installations. There would also be immediate taskings to accommodate; if no specific Time on Target was given, there were set time limits of 30 minutes for a single target or 20 minutes per target for multiple targets.

Following the sortie, the Mission Report had to be submitted within 45 minutes of engine shut down. Film processing in the RIC was divided between two machines in case of faults. The 70mm film from the F95 cameras was developed using Type 11 developing machines that could process up to 180ft (55m) of film a minute. The negatives were passed to the photo-interpreters (PIs) for analysis using stereoscopes to provide a 3D image with a six-strand light table. Any individual frames of interest were quickly printed. The PIs completed their initial analysis within 15 minutes and the full report took another 30 minutes.The pilot would complete the visual observation report before seeing the films. The Essential Elements of Information required for each target varied according to the specific category of target. There were 19 target categories: airfields, missile systems, electronics, military installations, storage and repair facilities, military activity on the ground, ferries and river crossings, shipping, route reconnaissance, terrain reconnaissance, coastlines, bridges, water control facilities, ports, railway facilities, industrial installations, electrical power generation, urban areas and specific structures. The more mobile a target was, the higher its priority for coverage was (static installations, for example, could be covered by satellites).

Contact! Jaguar XZ360 of No. 41(F) Squadron receiving fuel on a reconnaissance sortie, carrying a very weathered recce pod. ***P Foster via Terry Panopalis Collection***

Initially, there were no reconnaissance pods at No. 226 OCU and recce training was conducted at squadron level. Around 25% of the first intake were first tourists, but the majority had previous recce experience on the Phantom FGR.2, Hunter FR.10 or Canberra PR.9. First tourists received a basic flight syllabus to train them for the specialist recce task, taking six months to reach limited combat-ready status with another 250 flying hours required to achieve full combat status. The squadrons had a secondary attack role so the pilots received training in the relevant delivery profiles for BL.755, freefall and retarded bombs, rockets and cannon strafing.

A No. 54(F) Squadron Jaguar flying over the flat rural landscape of Norfolk. *Author's Collection*

A typical routine recce training mission would consist of three static targets and a line-search, for example a route reconnaissance. The routing and best approaches to the targets were calculated, together with the fuel requirements. The objective was to capture the required images in a single low-level, high-speed pass. All pilots would reconnoitre the same targets, with a communal debrief to compare results.

Given the number of NATO installations, No. II(AC) had a rich list of targets in north-western Europe to practise on, whereas No. 41(F) in the UK needed to be more inventive when trying to find mobile targets to spot. To compensate, a pair of Jaguars would deploy regularly to Laarbruch for Exercise Hawkeye to brush up their skills. Both squadrons attended Red Flag, No. II(AC) being the first to go, making its debut in 1980. The squadrons performed well at TACEVAL too, No. II(AC) being the first Jaguar unit to attain four Grade 1 results in its annual assessment.

No. II(AC) Squadron suffered several accidents in its early years of Jaguar operations. GR.1 XZ102 was lost on 14 December 1976 following an uncontrolled roll immediately after take-off, due to the tailplane powered feedback control unit having not been connected. The pilot, Flight Lieutenant William Langworthy, ejected safely. On 25 February 1977, Flight Lieutenant Douglas Graham Stein was killed flying GR.1 XZ120 when he lost contact with his formation in cloud on a bombing sortie to the Nordhorn ranges and crashed into the North Sea. The cause was not confirmed but the investigators speculated that disorientation while flying through the clouds was likely. During a deployment to Goose Bay, GR1s XZ105 and XZ110 collided during the break to land on 16 June 1983. Both pilots ejected safely but both aircraft were destroyed.

Flying the Jaguar

Pilots enjoyed flying the Jaguar. The aircraft was impressively smooth and stable in low-level, high-speed flight, even in turbulent conditions, and had good range and load-carrying capability. But pilots also described it as 'Jekyll and Hyde' aircraft as it had a dark side that could become apparent very quickly.

Exceeding the AoA limits could result in a severe departure at very short notice.

When flown in clean condition, the Jaguar could, surprisingly, hold its own in air combat, but once loaded with underwing stores, that performance rapidly fell away. The CTTO's tactics manual advised pilots to avoid any deliberate engagements; discretion was the better part of valour. A clean Jaguar had a low thrust/weight ratio of 0.59:1 using reheat, which when loaded with full external tanks and four bombs fell to 0.43:1, resulting in poor sustained turning performance. Using reheat in combat was inevitable, which reduced range and increased the dangers from IR-homing AAMs. The maximum sustained rate of turn at sea level with 50% internal fuel and maximum reheat was 9°/sec, but only 6°/sec when loaded with a drop tank and four BL.755 (in contrast, the CTTO noted that the MiG-21 *Fishbed* sustained 13°/sec). The maximum instantaneous turn pulling 8g above Mach 0.7 was 18°/sec when flown clean. The high wing loading did not help; 85lb/in^2 (5.9kg/cm^2) clean with two-thirds internal fuel or 95lb/in^2 (6.6kg/cm^2) with empty drop tanks and four 1,000lb bombs.

Cockpit ergonomics had been carefully considered by BAC and Breguet and the HUD and the PMD proved very popular with pilots. The engine instruments were analogue dials, the fuel flow gauges being colour coded. Digital fuel contents gauges were fitted and although the complex fuel control panel allowed detailed monitoring of the fuel transfer process, it added to the pilot's workload. Changing Identification Friend or Foe (IFF) codes required the pilot to put his head inside the cockpit and turn his head, which could cause disorientation. There were more problematic ergonomic issues relating to the NAVWASS system, which will be looked at in more detail later in this chapter.

A dramatic four-ship formation flying over The Needles at low level. The weathering on the nose caps of the fuel tanks and dummy bombs indicates the level of wear and tear encountered during low-level flying in all weathers. ***Blue Envoy Collection***

Every Jaguar squadron had access to at least one T.2 for continuation training. This one is T.2 XX829 of No. 6 Squadron in June 1984. ***Terry Panopalis Collection***

Maintaining the Jaguar

RAF St Athan was the Major Servicing Unit (MSU) for the Jaguar and RAF Abingdon the major maintenance and modification centre. An Aircraft Engineering Development and Integration Team was set up at Coltishall. A lot of design effort had gone into making the Jaguar an easy to maintain aircraft. Rearming and refuelling could be accomplished in 20 minutes. Initially, serviceability gave some cause for concern, with a 10% Aircraft on Ground rate, but this improved to 5% and was often better than other front-line RAF aircraft. Its reliability rate was, on average, 600 faults per 1,000 flying hours, compared to 1,300 faults for the Tornado.

Provision of engine spares were problematic during the rapid expansion of the Jaguar Force and hydraulic pumps and anti-collision lights were also particular issues. A glut of spares following the withdrawal of RAFG's Jaguars in the 1980s eased the supply situation, but convincing the accountants to release more funding when those stocks ran down in the 1990s was a challenge.

The weapons system was tested every six months due to the lack of any Built-In Test Equipment. The origin of fuel leaks was often difficult to trace and the collector tanks behind the cockpit were accessible only via the nose wheel bay. The Adour could be changed within four hours and the provision of engine test facilities removed the need for post-installation flight tests. Being a comparatively simple aircraft, most faults did not present safety-critical issues and the Jaguar was never grounded due to technical issues within its first decade of service.

The Jaguar demonstrated its reliability during Operation Granby in 1990 by sustaining 100% availability with an adverse operational effect rate of only three per 100 sorties. Serviceability of Special Trial Fits, such as chaff launchers and specific avionics, was more problematic as spares, funds and clearances were always harder to obtain. Deployments were supported by Fly Away Packs to provide an array of tools and consumables and the Air-Portable Avionic Workshop, a portable cabin fitted with test equipment. Two C-130 Hercules loaded with support equipment and groundcrew would usually accompany the Jaguars on overseas deployments.

The groundcrews were kept busy with repairs too. Between 1977 and 1983 there were 95 accidents, including bird strikes, fires and mid-air collisions, resulting in 30 write-offs and 14 fatalities. By 2001, 69 Jaguars had been written off in various accidents.

The Jaguar was vulnerable to battle damage as the designers had given insufficient thought to systems redundancy. For example, there were two hydraulic systems but the pipes for both circuits were often located next to each other and there was no manual reversion, so loss of hydraulic fluid resulted in a serious hazard. The fuel system lacked self-sealing tanks or fire suppression. The CTTO bemoaned the lack of cockpit armour, although earlier analysis by the Royal Aircraft Establishment (RAE) had judged armour to be ineffective.

Bird strikes caused far more structural damage compared with other RAF combat aircraft, the groundcrews christening the Jaguar 'the Bacofoil Bomber' for its thin skin. The loss of T.2 XX147 on 26

Turnaround time to switch a Jaguar from the reconnaissance role to that of attack was to be 30 minutes. GR.1 XZ101 of No. II(AC) Squadron is parked with a recce pod and two 264gal (1,200L) fuel tanks for its next sortie. The large vent in the rear of the HAS in the background allowed the aircraft inside to run its engines. ***Terry Panopalis Collection***

March 1979 to a bird strike led to an inquiry into possible improvements. By that time, bird strikes had already caused 18 accidents and another six would occur before the end of the year. The possible solutions were to strengthen the canopy and quarterlights, reinforce the forward fuselage, fit a deflector plate to prevent bird ingress through the gap between the canopy and the top of the windscreen and a stronger blast screen between the two cockpits in the T.2. Adding plating to the fuselage was not cost-effective and the stronger blast screen was abandoned after static trials showed that it could shatter, or even worse, detach and fall into the rear pilot's lap.

A new canopy was expensive and progress stalled, meanwhile T.2s XX828 and XX916 were lost on 1 June and 24 July 1981 to bird strikes, the latter being a fatal accident as navigator Flight Lieutenant S Sparkes drowned following his ejection. The T.2's larger canopy was more at risk from impacts and the intakes often ingested the resulting Perspex fragments. Finally, a new 12.7mm thick stretched acrylic canopy capable of withstanding a 1lb (46g) bird hitting at 450kt was approved for the T.2 and fitted from 1984 alongside stronger quarterlights and deflector plates. A multiple detonating cord was fitted to shatter the thicker canopy in the event of ejection.

There were fatigue life concerns. The fatigue test wing specimen in France suffered a wing centreline joint failure at the equivalent of 2,300 flying hours of low-level, high-speed operation in March 1979. The RAF was concerned and released a spare wing to BAe for full-scale fatigue testing and a wing strengthening programme – (Modifications Mod. 889 and 1041) adding steel plates to the rear spar – and the addition of operational load monitoring equipment was implemented. The monitoring equipment paid early dividends, leading to improvements to the tail fin attachments, and the AdlA was also convinced to introduce similar equipment (it had earlier decided not to fit fatigue meters).

A ground collision on 28 July 1982 involving GR.1 XX382 and an F-104G Starfighter led to Mod. 1097 to fit high-intensity strobe lights, although the amount of wiring required and consequent high man-hour cost meant that installation work was delayed to 1986. An AR5 NBC system was added (the filters were fitted into the body of the ejection seat to save space), making the Jaguar the first single-seat aircraft able to carry out full operations in an NBC environment.

The Adour was still temperamental. GR.1 XX760 was lost on 13 September 1982 due to a fatigue failure of the combustion chamber outer casing due to high stresses caused by the natural frequency resonance of an air offtake pipe. Rolls-Royce estimated a fatigue life of 1,000 hours but the crack propagation rate was possibly as short as seven flights. Support brackets for the offtake pipe were added to alter the natural vibration frequency and checks were imposed every 25 flying hours until a stronger casing was introduced a few years later.

Armourers loading a 1,000lb Paveway II LGB under simulated NBC conditions during a TACEVAL in 1980. ***Crown Copyright via Terry Panopalis***

In November 1982, inspections of the first-stage low-pressure (LP) stator vanes every 25 flying hours were imposed to detect fatigue until Turbomeca could deliver revised vanes. Increased second-stage LP stator failures were encountered in 1983, due to aerodynamic excitation caused by the compressor casing support struts downstream of the stator. The solution was to use a plasma spray to restore the worn vane roots.

Pilots reported that on shutting down an engine, they sometimes accidentally closed the low-pressure (LP) fuel cock of the other engine. To avoid this, Mod. 980 was issued in February 1979 to interchange the LP cocks with the hydraulic bypass switches. Pilots soon complained about the time it took to implement the change and the safety hazard posed by flying both standards of aircraft at the same time. Therefore the modification was suspended the following December and later cancelled. The folly of this was shown when GR.1 XX957 was lost on 21 October 1981 after it was struck by lightning just after take-off, causing the port engine to surge. The pilot accidentally shut off the starboard LP fuel cock when shutting down the port engine, forcing him to eject.

Plastic Jaguars

The RAF owned two plastic Jaguars. Specialised Mouldings Limited, based in Huntingdon, was contracted in 1974 by the Inspectorate of Recruitment to provide a full-size model (FSM) for the Exhibition Flight as a representative modern combat aircraft that could be taken to air shows and other public events. Delivered in 1975, the model had a steel frame and scaffolding boards for the wings that were covered

From the early 1980s AIM-9G Sidewinders were cleared for use on the GR.1A. Dedicated overwing rails to free up the outboard pylons for ECM and chaff pods were not fitted until the 1990s. This Jaguar is XX970 of No. 6 Squadron. ***Author's Collection***

with glass fibre-reinforced plastic. The result was a very believable model that was painted in the colours of No. 54(F) Squadron with the fake serials 'XX732', 'XX718' and 'XX725' during its life with the Flight. In 2000 it was donated to the Sultan of Oman's Air Force Museum. Another FSM was built in 1976, being painted in No. 14 and No. 41(F) Squadron colours during its life along with the fake serials 'XX755', 'XX824' and 'XZ363'.

Specialised Mouldings saw a business opportunity and offered to build a fleet of FSMs as airfield decoys. The use of dummy aircraft had begun during the Second World War and even as late as the 1970s remained useful in fooling ground-attack pilots. Retired airframes, such as Lightnings, were retained on airfields in West Germany alongside crude shape decoys made in the local station workshops. Decoys did not need to be accurate representations of the real thing, often a shape or a shadow would be enough to distract a pilot's attention away from real targets. Decoys might also confuse saboteurs and intelligence analysts, although to fool the latter, the decoys needed to be closely representative of the real thing in both visual appearance and IR signature and would also need dummy ground equipment. While decoys would be useful in a conventional war, in a nuclear exchange they would be useless. Given the costs involved, the Air Staff politely refused Specialised Mouldings' proposal and continued to rely on hulked Lightnings.

GR.1A upgrade

Under the Anglo-French Memorandum of Understanding (MoU), all modifications had to be approved by the Jaguar Modifications Committee and the Adour Engines Modification Committee. Each nation had the right to make its own modifications, but approval was only likely if the advantages of diverging from the common standards were considered to be sufficiently beneficial. The amount of negotiation required proved to be a drawback to keeping the Jaguar updated.The MoU had a cut-off date for these arrangements, the 'defini perfectible' – the point at which the Jaguar was deemed to be perfected. At that point all future modifications would be handled on a national basis. Shortly before the Gulf War in 1990 the MoD(PE) – the Ministry of Defence's Procurement Executive – unilaterally declared that 'defini perfectible' status had been achieved. The RAF had not been consulted beforehand and found itself having to deal with the consequences, as did the AdlA. But the advantage was quicker decision-making on future upgrades and from 1990 the Jaguar underwent a decade of continual improvement.

The Adour was upgraded as the Mk.104, which was fitted between 1978 and 1984. Rolls-Royce Turbomeca Limited was keen to promote the private venture RT.172-58 (built for export as the Mk.811) but the MoD felt that it was too expensive. GR.1 XZ358 was fitted with the RT.172-26 (Mk.104) in 1976, being displayed at the Farnborough and Paris Air Shows for the next few years. The Mk.104 was rated at 5,260lbf (23.9kN) dry thrust and 8,600lbf (38.2kN) reheated.

At the request of the Air Staff, BAe carried out a feasibility study in 1979 on fitting rocket-assisted take-off (RATO) to improve take-off performance. A pair of Cuckoo IV rocket motors (as used in the Skylark sounding rocket) would be fitted beneath the rear fuselage just under the tail pipes to shorten the take-off run from 4,820ft (1,470m) to 1,840ft (560m) when laden with 8,000lb (3,630kg) of bombs. Compared to spending over £100 million on the Mk.104, the estimated £5 million cost for RATO seemed an exceptionally cheap wartime solution. This option was not taken forward.

The provision of AAMs had been discussed when the Jaguar had been designed, but the RAF had decided not to carry the AIM-9 Sidewinder due to its lack of head-on engagement capability. But by 1979 Jaguar pilots were calling for them, not to go chasing enemy aircraft but as a means to reduce the options open to enemy fighters and maintain their own confidence. Given the poor turning performance due to the low thrust/weight ratio and high wing loading, the chances of bringing the pair of ADEN cannon to bear on to a fighter target seemed unlikely. The increasing threat from the new generation of Warsaw Pact fighters such as the MiG-29 *Fulcrum* and Sukhoi Su-27 *Flanker* increased the demand for a self-defence capability. Experiences from the Red Flag and Maple Flag air combat exercises reinforced the need, as did the lessons from the Falklands campaign in 1982. This led to the Jaguar being cleared for the AIM-9G Sidewinder on the outer underwing hardpoints.

BAC designed an overwing pylon for AAMs as a private venture for the Jaguar International, costing

£2.3 million, with testing including three live firings of the Matra R.550 Magic during 1975–76. Given that the outer underwing pylons would often be occupied by AN/ALQ-101(V)10 ECM and Phimat chaff pods, the overwing pylons were retrofitted to the GR.1A in the early 1990s.

During the late 1970s the Jaguar was cleared to carry the American1,000lb Paveway II laser-guided bomb (LGB). The AN/AVQ-23E PAVE SPIKE laser designator was fitted to the Buccaneer S.2B and co-operative trial sorties with the Buccaneers designating and the Jaguars releasing the Paveways were flown. BAe's Jaguar Project Pilot, Derek Reeh, began carriage and release trials for the 2,000lb (907kg) Paveway III in 1986.

It had been foreseen that in wartime British weapons might be of short supply or unavailable, so several American weapons were cleared for carriage and release, although no ballistic data was provided for the weapon-aiming computer. These included the Mk.82 Snakeye retarded bomb and the Mk.20 Rockeye cluster bomb.

Although during its development NAVWASS had been praised for its accuracy, operational use had revealed its limitations. As early as August 1977 Ferranti had been contracted to carry out a feasibility study on replacing the 920M computer.

A number of ergonomic defects were noted that affected accuracy due to the pilot inadvertently making data entry errors. These errors tended to transfer to the HUD display, which if the pilot did not cross-check against the other instruments, could lead to problems and cause accidents. Data input relied on the Navigation Control Unit, mounted low in the cockpit near the control column, and a hand controller. The procedure required eight steps on the panel for each digit entered; entering at least 13 digits for a latitude and longitude required 104 actions, taking ten minutes on the ground and doing them while flying was considerably more difficult. Shorter pilots often had to unlock their shoulder harness to enable them to lean forwards to reach the panel, reducing their forward vision and risking an inadvertent forward movement of the control column, which the Institute of Aviation Medicine (IAM) felt may have been a factor in at least two fatal crashes. Something had to be done to improve safety and the result was Air Staff Requirement ASR.1009 for an NAVWASS Avionics Update. This built upon two years of studies and proposals from Marconi

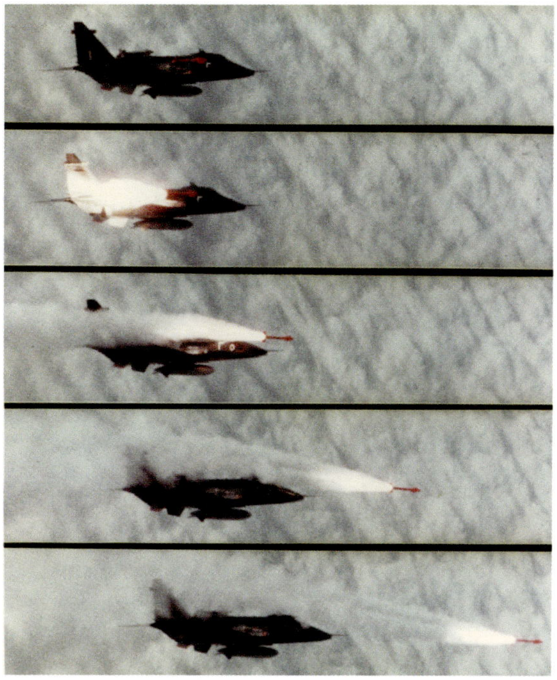

One of the test firings of a Matra R.550 Magic AAM from the overwing missile rail developed by BAe. Note how the exhaust plume clears the wing and intakes to avoid rocket exhaust gas ingestion. *Terry Panopalis Collection*

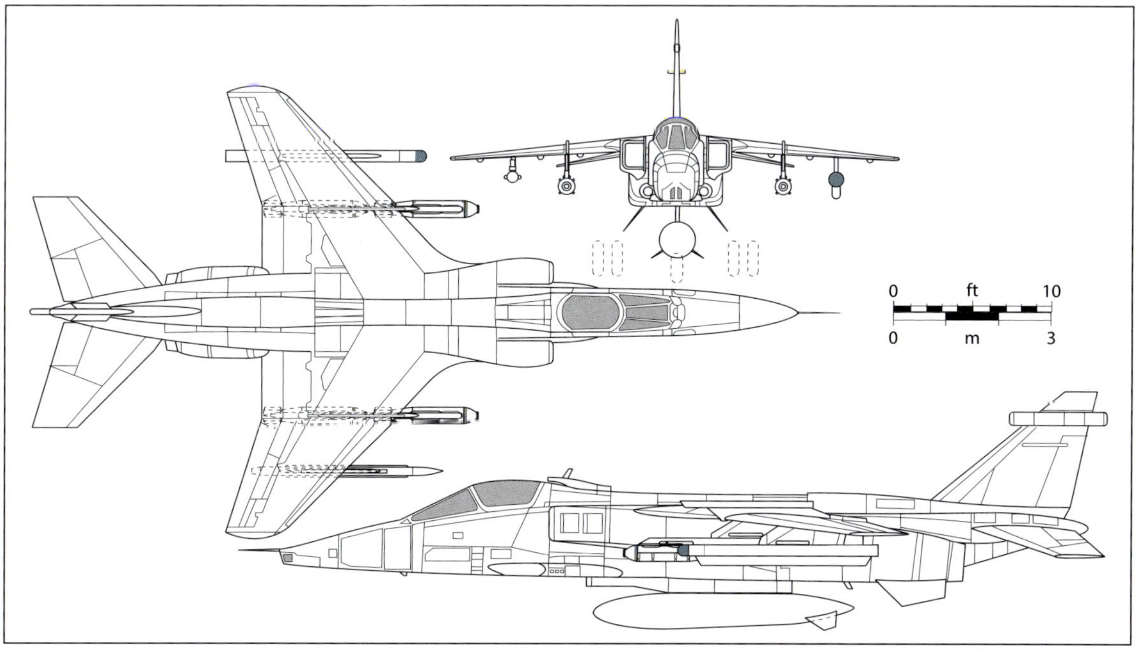

The typical GR.1A loadout for the battlefield interdiction role in the 1980s with four BL.755 cluster bombs inboard, an AN/ALQ-101(V)10 ECM pod to port, a Phimat chaff pod to starboard and a centreline 264gal (1,200L) fuel drop tank. *Chris Gibson*

This No. 226 OCU Jaguar illustrates well the GR.1A of the late 1980s with its ECM and chaff pods along with two 1,000lb (454kg) practice bombs and a drop tank. *Author's Collection*

and Ferranti. The IAM carried out an ergonomic appraisal and issued recommendations to reduce the mental workload, possibility of operator error and the time required looking inside the cockpit. Input from BAe's Senior Avionics Development Test Pilot John Cockburn, who had flown most of the NAVWASS trials, was also invaluable (he had been a test pilot at Ferranti before joining BAC in 1966). The IAM recommended moving the Navigation Control Unit to the cockpit coaming along with a coaming-mounted keyboard, which Ferranti implemented.

The 920M computer was replaced by the FIN 1064, which offered improved accuracy and reliability. It had a larger 64kb word memory for programmes plus two 1,024 16-bit word capacity data pools; one for input/output flight data and calculations and the other to store mission data. Automatic mode attack selection was possible by designating the target point in the flight plan to an appropriate attack mode. The additional computer power enabled the provision of warnings if the aircraft was approaching the ground at a near critical speed and pre-flight inertial alignment was accomplished faster. The compact computer enabled one unit to replace the original system's five units, saving space and 110lb (50kg) of weight. An attitude monitor was fitted that warned the pilot of any discrepancy between the HUD and cockpit instruments.

The opportunity was taken to replace the PMD with the Ferranti Combined Map and Electronic Display (COMED), which projected a topographical map on to a CRT display and could cover an area of 750nm^2 (1,390km^2) with input from the inertial system and other electro-optical sensors. The pilot could superimpose geographical reference points, terrain features, navigational tracks, targets and enemy defensive areas imported from Ferranti's Portable Data Store System (PODS), which used the Autoplan briefing aid system. In March 1981 a representative of Ferranti visited Brüggen and Gütersloh to investigate the mission planning process. He noted that in wartime pilots would fly up to five sorties from the HAS without leaving it (in fact, due to potential NBC contamination he would not even leave the cockpit between sorties), so the PODS data loading had to be done by a qualified airman. COMED was selected by the Indian Air Force for its Jaguars and licence-built in America by Bendix for the McDonnell Douglas F/A-18A Hornet.

Flight tests of the avionics began on 31 July 1981 with GR.1 XX108. BAe's Senior Experimental Test Pilot and Jaguar Project Pilot, Chris Yeo, flew the trials, commenting after the initial 75-minute flight that, 'I have never flown an aircraft with such an accurate navigation system. It will be a great bonus to RAF pilots and will ease their workload.' Peter Orme, who had joined BAe from the RAF in 1981, took over the trials programme from 1982. The tests were successful and approval to proceed with the upgrade came in 1983. A plan to sell some of the active Jaguar fleet to fund the upgrade thankfully foundered, but the number of upgraded aircraft was cut back. A total of 90 GR.1s were upgraded at Abingdon and St Athan during 1985–87, being redesignated as GR.1A on completion, along with 20 T.2s, which became the T.2A.

No. 38 Group was tasked with assigning two Qualified Weapon Instructors (QWIs) to introduce the upgraded GR.1A and T.2A into operational service, No. 226 OCU being the first unit that would receive the aircraft. The Coltishall Development Team was composed of Squadron Leader D G Needham and Flight Lieutenant M J Metcalf. They undertook all the validation flights of navigational and weapon-aiming performance and recommended any necessary software changes. They also produced a ground school and conversion flying syllabus, training the initial batch of OCU instructors and the Abingdon air test pilot so that he could take over responsibility for air testing the upgraded aircraft from the team. The Team also made amendments to the Jaguar QWI manual and liaised with the A&AEE and the RAF Handling Squadron at Boscombe Down.

Electronic warfare

The Marconi RWR (designated Airborne Radio Installation ARI.18223) was cleared for service in 1977. Shortcomings soon became apparent; its frequency coverage of 2.5–18.0GHz missed newer radar and SAM guidance signals in the 0.8–1.1GHz range. The display only gave the quadrant in which an emission was detected, rather than the relative angle of the threat, which more modern receivers did, and there was no indication of the range of the threat. It provided a nine-level threat priority system that alerted the pilot to the most dangerous threats – generally SAM fire-control radars were rated higher than AAA fire-control radars. The control panel was located low down in the cockpit on the starboard console; the pilot could not see the threat warning or operate the switches without changing hands on the control column and looking into the cockpit. The panel was moved on to the cockpit coaming as part of the GR.1A/T.2A upgrade.

Originally the RAF had wanted a miniaturised version of the ECM system being developed for TSR.2. This had proved too challenging and expensive, so ASR.853 was raised in 1970 for a radar jammer pod for Jaguar and the Tornado to reduce their vulnerability to air, land and ship-based defensive weapons systems by degrading their fire control radars. Marconi Space & Defence Systems began development of the BG.725 system in 1972. It used spot noise emissions tuned to the frequency of the hostile radar to deny range and angle bearings. Two jamming transmitters offered a 60° cone of coverage forward and aft and were able to jam two threats simultaneously in both frequency bands covered (4.9–9.5 and 9–16.5GHz). It was estimated that on a daylight penetration at 200ft (61m) it would reduce the attrition of a single aircraft by around 20% and a formation of eight by 50%.

During the 1974 Defence Review it was agreed to use BG.725 on the Tornado (entering service as Skyshadow) and buy American ECM pods for the Jaguar to save money. The RAF already had a stock of 72 Westinghouse AN/ALQ-101(V)8 pods for the Blackburn Buccaneer, but these were insufficient to equip the Jaguar as well. Three suitable systems were identified: the Westinghouse AN/ALQ-119 using repeater and switched noise techniques; AN/ALQ-119 with Compass Tie programme modifications including the AN/ALR-46 RWR, computer derived threat logic and response spot noise jamming; and the Westinghouse AN/ALQ-131 response spot noise and repeater jammer. There was a growing realisation that some operations would be flown at medium altitudes, including pop up for weapons delivery, and the American pods offered better protection in these scenarios. Buying up to 397 BG.725 pods (145 for Jaguar and 252 for the Tornado), including research and spares, would have cost £149 million. In comparison, 433 ALQ-119 pods would cost £45 million (or £83 million including the Compass Tie features), or 397 ALQ-131 pods would cost £87 million.

The recommendation was to buy the ALQ-131, but Anglo-American talks broke down over technology sharing and interest shifted to systems like AN/ALQ-178 Rapport III internal ECM and RWR or the AN/ALQ-136 and ALQ-162 jammers, which would fit in the internal space freed up by the FIN 1064 upgrade. Marconi designed an installation for their new Zeus digital system featuring an RWR and a jammer developed from Northrop Defence Systems components, and they also proposed a 'mini BG.725' with the low-band noise jammer removed. The Nott Defence Review by Margaret Thatcher's newly elected Conservative government in 1980 deferred the fitting of ECM to Jaguar to save money.

The Air Staff eventually decided to equip the Jaguar with the improved ALQ-101(V)10 pod, which had been ordered for the Buccaneer. The (V)10 had a capability approaching that of the ALQ-119 and covered three

Jaguar XZ117 was upgraded to GR.1A standard in January 1987 and is seen here a year later in March 1988 carrying a reconnaissance pod. It had been with No. 41(F) Squadron since May 1976, passing to No. 51(F) Squadron in May 1991. Today it is a ground instructional airframe at Cosford. ***P Foster via Terry Panopalis Collection***

A pair of GR.1As of No. 41(F) Squadron, with XZ107 sporting makeshift winter camouflage in the foreground, about to refuel from a VC10 tanker during a deployment to Bardufoss in March 1988. *Terry Panopalis Collection*

frequency bands: low (2.6–5.5GHz) (deleted on Jaguar), mid (4.85–9.7GHz) and high (8.9–16.5GHz). The pod used noise, repeater and range/velocity gate pull-off jamming but could not counter newer 9K33 Osa (SA-8 *Gecko*), 2K12 Kub (SA-6 *Gainful*) and S-300P (SA-10 *Grumble*) SAM systems. The Jaguar, being a single-seat aircraft, only used the three automatic operational modes out of the seven modes available.

Given the limits on carrying asymmetric stores, the ECM pod was balanced by a Phimat chaff dispenser pod on the opposite outboard pylon. This led to a reconfiguration of the other pylons; the fuel tank on the centreline with tandem beams on the inner underwing pylons to carry four bombs. If additional fuel was a necessity, then two underwing drop tanks could be carried with a pair of centreline bombs.During the late 1970s ASTs 612 and 613 were raised for podded chaff and infrared countermeasures (IRCM) for the RAF's combat aircraft, but budgetary constraints forced the Jaguar's removal from these ASTs. An informal engineering fix by RAFG utilising the tail braking parachute compartment to store chaff was only a stopgap. Following the Falklands War, trials revealed that the Tractor AN/ALE-40(N) chaff dispenser gave adequate chaff and IRCM protection – although the CTTO noted that flares would be ineffective if reheat was on – and that a single Philips-Matra Phimat chaff dispenser pod gave sufficient protection for the Harrier GR.3.In early 1983 it was decided to fit the Jaguar with ALE-40 for IRCM and Phimat for chaff. Two ALE-40 were mounted in scabbed fairings beneath the engines, which slightly increased drag and caused a slight reduction in directional stability. They were usually loaded with 15 2 × 1in (5cm × 2.5cm) PW218 flares but could also carry either 30 1 × 1in (2.5 × 2.5cm) Chemring CH5084 Broadband chaff cartridges or PW118 flares. The Phimat pod was carried on one of the outboard underwing pylons, holding 240 packets of Chemring Broadband aluminised glass fibre chaff that covered the 7.5–17.5GHz range, with four frequency bands covered in each packet (the 231lb [105kg] Phimat pod was used as a counter-balance for ALQ-101, which required a 359lb (163kg) counterweight to be added).

CHAPTER FIVE

Jaguar on the front line – France

In the spring of 1973 the Armeé de l'Air (AdlA) began to form its first front-line units on the SEPECAT Jaguar, thus fulfilling the need for a light tactical strike fighter that it had outlined in the Ecole de Combat et Appui Tactique requirement a decade earlier. The Jaguar's service until 2005 would be the most active of any of the type's operators. The rugged aircraft found itself assigned to support France's interests in the Francophone ex-colonies of West and Central Africa. The Jaguar would take the AdlA into combat for the first time since the Algerian War of the early 1960s in Mauritania; several deployments to Chad followed, seeing action against Colonel Gaddafi's Libyan forces. Then followed Operation Desert Storm to liberate Kuwait following Iraq's invasion in 1990 and peacekeeping duties over the Balkans during the remainder of the 1990s. Although the French Jaguars never received the extensive avionic, engine and weaponry upgrades as those of the Royal Air Force, they proved to be effective and dependable aircraft in combat.

The start of a new era. A brand new early production Jaguar A of Escadron de Chasse EC 1/7 'Provence' on the apron at Base Aérienne 113 Saint-Dizier-Robinson in October 1972. *Author's Collection*

Jaguar A20 of EC 1/7 was displayed at the 1975 Paris Salon, exhibiting the array of Matra ordnance that the Jaguar was capable of utilising, including bombs, rocket projectiles and the AS.37 anti-radar missile. ***Blue Envoy Collection***

Jaguar A & E

The AdlA had ordered 160 single-seat Jaguar A (Appui/support) and 40 Jaguar E (Ecole/school) two-seat trainers. The first production Jaguar E (construction number E1) made its maiden flight at Toulouse-Colomiers on 2 November 1971 and was formally accepted by the AdlA the following month. The first production Jaguar A, A1, flew on 20 April 1972 and was delivered the following month (a full list of serials and construction numbers can be found in Appendix 3). With the early aircraft supporting the development flying programme to obtain service clearances, the first deliveries to front-line units did not occur until 1973; nine Jaguar E trainers were available for conversion flying by the end of that year.

The Jaguar had several operational missions: ground attack; precision attacks using laser-guided weapons; tactical nuclear strike; anti-radar attack; electronic warfare and reconnaissance. The nuclear strike and anti-radar missions were designed to support the Force de Frappe, France's strategic nuclear deterrent, by clearing the way for the Dassault Mirage IVA bombers on their way eastwards to attack their targets in Western Russia.

The CT 51 radar-jamming pod was carried in the air defence suppression role to counter S-band and L-band radars. The 881lb (400kg) pod was carried on an inboard pylon. It was relegated to training use by the late 1980s. This Jaguar is A14 during the CT 51 clearance trials. ***Phillipe Ricco***

The Jaguar A had less-sophisticated avionics compared with the British Jaguar S. The navigation/attack avionics included an air-data computer, SFIM 153-6 twin-gyro inertial platform, Decca RDN 72 Doppler radar for measuring ground drift (licence-built by Electronique Marcel Dassault), Crouzet Type 90 navigation computer, Thomson-CSF Type 31 weapon-aiming computer with an Electronique Marcel Dassault fire-control computer and a Thomson-CSF 121-196 attack sight/head-up display (HUD) optimised for the air-to-ground role as well as the usual VHF Omni-directional Range (VOR)/Instrument Landing System (ILS) and Tactical Air Navigation (TACAN). Self-defence equipment consisted of a Thomson-CSF DRAX radar warning receiver with 120° forward coverage with continuous wave and track-while-scan modes and Identification Friend or Foe (IFF).

An Omera 40 panoramic strike camera was fitted in the nose for reconnaissance. In addition, Jaguars assigned to the reconnaissance role carried an RP 36P camera pod on the centreline hardpoint. The pod contained three cameras for medium- and low-altitude photography.

The Jaguar E lacked the Doppler radar, weapon-aiming computer and the HUD, instead having a gunsight in the forward cockpit with a head-down display for the instructor in the rear cockpit.

Following the Gulf War, a stand-alone GPS receiver was fitted to some aircraft, which enabled the pilot to manually input navigational waypoint fixes to update the navigation computer. Production aircraft from A81 onwards were fitted with an under-nose Thomson-CSF TAV-38 laser rangefinder with a range up to 5.4nm (10km) for use in clear weather conditions and from A131 onwards the Thomson-CSF ATLIS (Automatic Tracking Laser Illumination System) laser designation pod could be carried on the centreline hardpoint. The cockpit was provided with a small CRT display for the ATLIS imagery to the right of the HUD.

The capability to carry a CT 51 radar jammer pod was introduced from aircraft A80 onwards; the 880lb (400kg) pod was carried on an inboard underwing pylon. The CT 51 could jam S-band and L-band radars but it lacked transmitting power and was relegated to training use by the late 1980s. The facility to jettison the CT 51 pod was made inoperable due to their cost and the risks of an inadvertent release by the pilot. It took more than a year to convince the staff officers that given the Adour's low thrust on take-off, an engine failure would be a choice between losing the pod or the entire aircraft and possibly the pilot. This led to the reinstatement of the jettison facility.

It has been alleged that Dassault applied political pressure on the AdlA not to upgrade the Jaguar. Whether or not this is true, the aircraft certainly received very few upgrades, most likely because of other financial and operational considerations preventing such work taking place. Unlike the RAF, the AdlA decided to retain the original RT.172 Adour Mk.102 engine rated at 5,115lbf (23.4kN) dry thrust and 7,305lbf (32.5kN) reheated. This decision would impose performance limits on the aircraft throughout its life – a common joke by AdlA pilots was that the Jaguar only managed to take off because of the curvature of the earth's surface! The Jaguar A had a retractable aerial refuelling probe in the nose and several Jaguar Es received a fixed probe on the nose cone.

The AS.37 Martel was a collaborative venture between Matra and Hawker Siddeley Dynamics. Jaguar A154 is launching a test missile in the mid-1990s. The Martel was retired from French service in 1998. *Author's Collection*

The Jaguar A's fixed armament comprised two 30mm DEFA 553 cannon with 150 rounds of ammunition (only one was fitted in the Jaguar E). It was a French development of the German Mauser 213 revolver gun by the Direction des Études et Fabrications d'Armement. The rate of fire was 1,300rpm and the nitro-chrome steel barrel had a life of 5,000 rounds. The electric control provided three settings: continuous fire (not normally used), 0.5 seconds and one second maximum continuous burst. A gun camera was fitted to record any hits for post-flight debriefing.

The four underwing and one ventral hardpoint pylons were developed by Alkan and were equipped with a pyrotechnic ejector and two crutches to hold

For the tactical nuclear strike role a 25Kt AN 52 bomb would be carried on the centreline pylon. The store seen here is an inert CEP 52 practice version. *Author's Collection*

Jaguar A4 was used for integration trials of the Aérospatiale AS.30L laser-guided ASM with the Thomson-CSF ATLIS laser target designation pod. The size of the AS.30L, designed to destroy hardened structures and ships, is evident here. ***Blue Envoy Collection***

An AS.30L test round blasts away from Jaguar A4. The missile was powered by a two-stage solid-fuel rocket motor. The booster section exhausted through two large nozzles located near the rear edges of the main fins – as seen here – while the sustainer exhausted through the rear centreline nozzle. ***Phillipe Ricco***

the bombs in place as well as the necessary wiring and fuzing units. Adapters were fitted for use with rocket launcher pods. Alkan also offered its Type F1 universal adapter, which could carry two 1,100lb (500kg) or three 550lb (250kg) bombs. The payload options included:

- Freefall and retarded high-explosive bombs weighing between 550lb (250kg) and 2,205lb (1,000kg) – later including Matra BGL-150, BGL-400 and BGL-1000 laser-guided bombs (LGBs) and the Arcole penetrating bomb.
- 2.75in (68mm) Matra F1 rocket pods firing SNEB rockets or Thomson Brandt 3.9in (100mm) rocket pods.
- Matra/Thomson Brandt BLG 66 Belouga cluster bombs; entered service in 1979; dispensed 151 66mm fragmentation and anti-tank grenades. Two release settings covered an area of 131 × 393ft (40 × 120m) or 196 × 787ft (60 × 240m). The bomb and the grenades had retarding parachutes.
- Aérospatiale AS.30L laser-guided air-to-surface missile (ASM); its hardened steel-covered 530lb (240kg) warhead was designed to penetrate concrete up to 6ft 6in (2m) thick. Guidance was via the ATLIS designation pod coupled with gyro midcourse updating; it could cover 6nm (11km) in 20 seconds. Usually one missile was carried under the starboard wing, balanced by a fuel tank to port with the ATLIS pod on the centreline.
- One AS.37 Martel anti-radar ASM on the centreline pylon.
- Up to 18 Thomson Brandt BAP-100 anti-runway rocket-powered bombs or BAT-120 parachute-retarded, anti-armour bombs.
- One AN 52 tactical nuclear bomb with a yield of 25kT (kilotons); from aircraft A16 onwards.
- Matra R.550 Magic infrared (IR)-homing air-to-air missiles (AAMs) on the outboard pylons

The ATLIS laser designator was a private-venture development by the American Martin-Marietta company. With official sanction, Thomson-CSF had negotiated a technology transfer deal that allowed them to further develop the system, with Martin-Marietta receiving half of any sales income in return. In July 1976 two pilots from the Centre d'Essais en Vol

(CEV – Flight Test Centre) and the Centre d'Expériences Aériennes Militaires (Centre for Military Aerial Experimentation – CEAM) visited the company's facility at Orlando, Florida, to evaluate the system and the feasibility of single-pilot operation in a fighter. Both pilots agreed that it would be possible to carry out the laser designation task while flying the Jaguar, but warned that it required a heavy workload. The pilot had to bring the nose of his aircraft towards the target, locate the target in the 4.3in (11cm) black and white monitor located on the starboard coaming, centring the target in the monitor using a small joystick. Then the pilot would release the laser-guided weapon, turning away while the pod automatically tracked the target while flying at 500–800ft (150–240m) at 450kt.

Jaguar A4 was used for the initial trial installation and the first flight took place at the Calamar range on 11 October 1976. Tests were flown in various weather conditions and the CEV pilot managed to lock on to two nearby Dassault Mystère IV fighters, indicating that an air-to-air mode may have been possible. The integration of LGBs caused some difficulties because they required stabilised tracking for over 40 seconds compared with half that time for the AS.30L. A United States Air Force (USAF) and two RAF pilots also evaluated the system. A total of 44 test flights were flown by seven pilots and 700 passes were made against a wide variety of targets.

The AdlA decided to proceed with the purchase and operational training of Jaguar pilots began in the summer of 1985. Matra had begun LGB development in 1978 and production began in the mid-1980s. The ATLIS and AS.30L pairing provided a stand-off precision attack capability that the RAF's Jaguars lacked throughout their service life. Thomson-CSF and Martin-Marietta went on to develop the smaller and lighter ATLIS II with a digital databus interface.

From 1978 a series of self-protection aids appeared on the outer underwing pylons; Matra Phimat chaff or Bofors BOZ-103 chaff/infrared countermeasures (IRCM) pods, Barracuda and Barax I- and J-Band radar jammer pods and later the improved TMV-015 Barem and DB-3163 Remora I- and J-Band pods. An 18-cartridge Lacroix LC530 flare dispenser was fitted in the tail cone from 1984 following combat experience in Mauritania and Chad and these were later accompanied by 56-cartridge Alkan 5020/5021 conformal IRCM and chaff launchers fixed to the sides of the fuselage under the wing roots.

There was a proposal to convert some Jaguars into Suppression of Enemy Air Defences (SEAD) aircraft, but the cost saw this proposal scaled back. Instead one squadron received the Thomson-CSF Basilisk jamming pod (developed from the Caiman pod fitted to the Mirage F1) optimised against search radars from 1991.

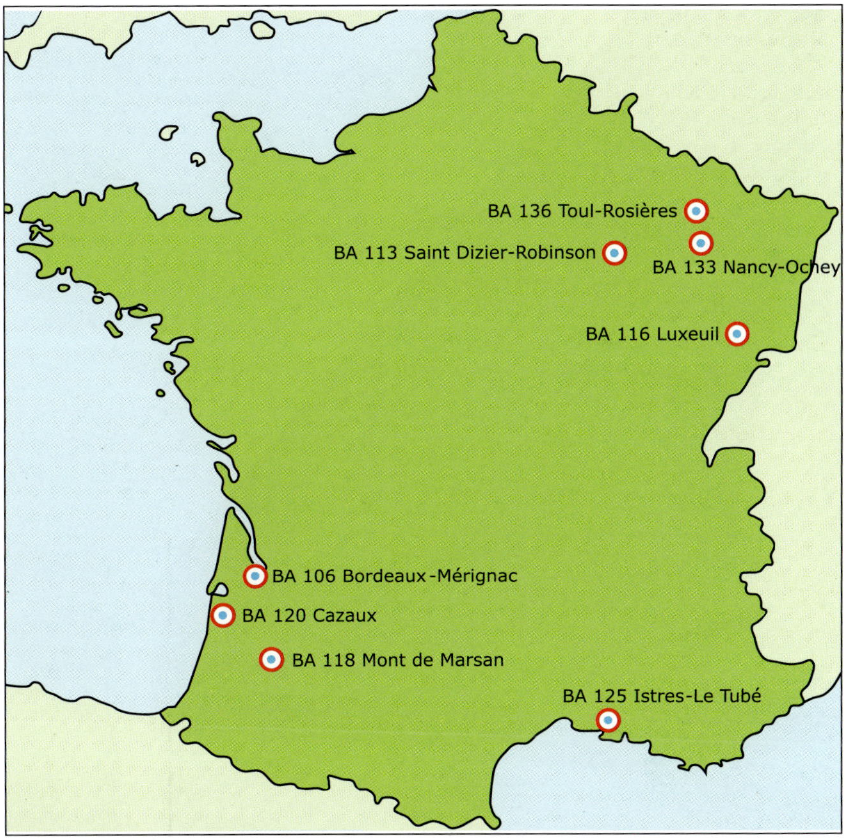

A map of the main operational AdlA Jaguar bases. ***Author***

The Three Escadres

The Jaguar served with the FATac, the Force Aérienne Tactique (Tactical Air Force). The original plan was to build up the fleet at the rate of around 30 aircraft per year. The CEAM at Base Aérienne (BA) 118 Mont de Marsan was the first Jaguar user. Being responsible for service clearance, it received Jaguars A2 and A4 as well as five Jaguar E (including E1 and E2) on which to develop the operational guidelines for the front-line units.

At this point a brief explanation regarding the organisation of AdlA units might be beneficial. The Escadre (Wing) is a formation that assembles various units and personnel dedicated to the same mission – an Escadre de Chasse is a fighter wing (Escadres were disbanded from 1993 and reformed in 2014, nearly a decade after the Jaguar retired). The Escadron (Squadron) is the basic operational unit and is comprised of two or three Escadrilles (Flights). A pilot is assigned to the Escadrille while the aircraft, equipment and other materiel is assigned to the Escadron. On average a fighter squadron – an Escadron de Chasse – would have around 15 aircraft (increased to 20 during the 1990s). The numbering system signifies the Escadron and its parent Escadre, for example '3/7' is the third squadron of the seventh wing. Many of the Jaguar Escadrille were prefixed SPA, which was an honorific title denoting the famous SPAD fighters which they flew when they were formed during the First World War.

The 7ème Escadre de Chasse at BA 133 Nancy-Ochey was selected to be the first operational unit to receive

The insignia of Escadrille SPA 77 'Croix de Jerusalem', of EC 1/7. Usually the triangle was light blue but here has been painted over the grey camouflage paint. The Cross of Jerusalem was chosen by Captain Joseph de l'Hermitte in 1916 as it was the emblem of his tenth-century ancestor Peter the Hermit during the 'Poor People's' crusade in 1096. AdlA Jaguars had their construction/serial number painted on the rudder. *Author's Collection*

The aircraft were assigned to the Escadron, so they sometimes carried the markings of both of its Escadrilles. A19 on its port side featured the 'Casque de Bayard' (Bayard's Helmet) of SPA 15. The knight's helmet with a large plume was selected as the flight's badge by Captain Turin in mid-June 1916. *Author's Collection*

One of EC 3/7's Escadrilles was SPA 38, whose badge features a thistle within a black and red triangular pennant, the unit's moto being 'he who rubs it, stings it'. The badge was selected in 1916 and evokes the thistle emblem of the city of Nancy and the colours of the emblem of the Province of Lorraine. *Author's Collection*

EC 3/7's other Escadrille, 3C1 'Requin' was formed in 1927 as a Aéronavale unit, transferring to the AdlA in September 1936, hence its aquatic name. *Author's Collection*

Jaguar A18 of EC 1/7 assigned to SPA 77 seen at Saint-Dizier on 5 September 1974 with a CEP 52 training round for the AN 52 tactical nuclear bomb. *Author's Collection*

the Jaguar. CEAM visited the unit with one of the early production Jaguar As in October 1972 to give the pilots their first look at the aircraft. The first squadrons to replace their ageing Dassault Mystère IVAs were Escadron de Chasse EC 1/7 'Provence' on 24 May 1973 and EC 3/7 'Languedoc' on 14 March 1974. EC 1/7 was composed of two Escadrilles; SPA 77 'Croix de Jerusalem' (Cross of Jerusalem) and SPA 15 'Casque de Bayard' (Bayard's Helmet). EC 3/7 had Escadrilles SPA 38 'Chardon Lorrain' (Lorraine Thistle) and 3C1 'Requin' (Shark).

The Escadrons began their conversion training at Mont de Marsan in early 1973 and January 1974 respectively. The conversion training was complicated by the differences between the single and two-seat variants, cost-cutting having removed some elements of the avionics from the trainers. On the formation of EC 1/7, the unit had four Jaguar A and two Jaguar E, slowly building up to the authorised strength of 14 Jaguar A and one Jaguar E.

On completion of conversion training, both units moved to their new base at BA 113 Saint-Dizier-Robinson. A ceremony was held there on 19 June 1973 to mark the formal acceptance of the Jaguar into service, with the Minister of Armies, Robert Galley, in attendance. The 7ème Escadre de Chasse at this time was commanded by Commandant Guillou. Both EC 1/7 and 3/7 were assigned to the tactical nuclear strike role armed with the AN 52 bomb. The Jaguar was used for the live trials of the weapon, Opération Maquis. At the end of April 1974, Jaguars A16 and A17 belonging to CEAM were dismantled and flown to Mururoa Atoll in the Pacific in six Transall C-160 transports. Following their arrival the aircraft were reassembled; A17 was assigned to the drop trials with A16 as the reserve aircraft. A test flight was flown on 24 July with an AN 52 bomb casing fitted with the nuclear warhead from a Pluton tactical ballistic missile. The following day at 16:50 Commandant Gautier dropped the weapon, which exploded at an altitude of 02ft (250m), 13.5nm (25km) south-west of Mururoa, attaining a yield of 8kT. Following the success of Opération Maquis the aircraft were dissembled and flown home as cargo.

EC 1/7 was declared operational with the AN 52 on 1 September 1974 and 3/7 followed in July 1975. A nuclear weapons depot was built at Saint-Dizier, which was also home to a maintenance and repair unit for the Jaguar. Regular exercises made it possible to test the level reached by each of the squadrons and at the same time served as a demonstration of the credibility of national deterrence. Delivery of the AN 52 relied on accurate navigation and timing to the second to release their bombs at the right time. Biannual training exercises Poker and Punch involved each aircraft flying independently, with a high-altitude cruise, descending for a low-level penetration over the Massif Central, releasing a CEP 52 practice bomb on the Captieux range and landing either at Cazaux or Mont-de-Marsan.

Jaguar A8 of SPA 15 coded 7-HG parked on the apron at Saint-Dizier in the late 1970s. Today the aircraft is on display at the Musée Chateau de Savigny-lès-Beaune. ***Author's Collection***

The two Escadrons were joined by EC 2/7 'Argonne' on 11 October 1974, under the command of Commandant Norlain. The squadron was the equivalent of the RAF's No. 226 Operational Conversion Unit, being responsible for operational conversion flying training with a secondary ground-attack role. Its two Escadrilles were SPA 31 'Archer Grec' (Greek Archer – sometimes incorrectly referred to as Roman Archer) and SPA 48 'Tête de Coq' (Rooster's Head). When Prime Minister Jacques Chirac visited Saint-Dizier on 19 September 1975, he sat in the cockpit of Jaguar E25, which belonged to the Escadron. Dassault/Dornier Alpha Jet trainers were assigned to the unit in the 1990s to complement the Jaguars as an economy measure.

Jaguar E12 assigned to EC 2/7 'Argonne' in 1976 carried the insignia of both Escadrilles. On the port side was that of SPA 31, which has used the 'Archer Grec' (Greek Archer) since October 1916. ***Author's Collection***

Also dating from October 1916, the 'Tête de Coq' (Rooster's Head) is Escadrille SPA 48's emblem. The unit's commander Capitaine Georges Matton and Lieutenant Armand Galliot de Turenne chose the rooster to represent France. ***Author's Collection***

The Escadre was brought up to full strength on 1 April 1980 when EC 4/7 'Limousin' was formed at Saint-Dizier, this unit also being dedicated to the nuclear strike role with secondary missions of low-altitude air defence and anti-ship strike. The two Escadrille assigned were GC 1/9 'Aigle' (Eagle) and GC 1/9 'Fennec'. The Escadron later moved to BA 125 Istres but its life was short, being disbanded as the Cold War reached its climax and standing down on 31 July 1989. The Escadron was busy though during its short life, being deployed to Africa, participating in North Atlantic Treaty Organisation (NATO) Tactical Leadership Programme exercises and attending the Red Flag air defence exercise at Nellis Air Force Base (AFB), Nevada, in 1984.

Saint-Dizier played host to RAF Jaguars several times in the early years of Jaguar operations; No. 226 Operational Conversion Unit in October 1974 and Nos. 54(F) and 14 Squadrons visiting in April 1975 and August 1978 respectively.

On 22 April 1983 a special parade at Saint-Dizier was held to mark the milestone of 100,000 flying hours and it included a flying display by the Patrouille de France

ABOVE A33 of EC 3/7'Languedoc', Escadrille 3C1 'Requin' being prepared for a sortie. This view shows well the Jaguar's flaps, airbrakes and rugged undercarriage designed for rough short-field performance. *Author's Collection*

LEFT EC 3/7 was assigned to the tactical nuclear strike role. Jaguar A48 here is loaded with a CEP 52 practice weapon, which was aerodynamically identical to the AN 52 bomb. *Author's Collection*

Each Escadron had one two-seater Jaguar E for continuation training. This aircraft is E7 of EC 1/7 based at Saint-Dizier in September 1987. *Terry Panopalis Collection*

in their Alpha Jets. The pilot who had completed the 100,000th flying hour was Lieutenant Colonel Paqueron, who had taken command of 7ème Escadre on 31 August 1982, and he received a commemorative certificate from the FATac commander General Forget.

The second Jaguar wing was the 11ème Escadre de Chasse based at BA 136 Toul-Rosières. EC 3/11 'Corse' was the first squadron to convert from the North American F-100D Super Sabre on 5 January 1975, with the first Jaguar E arriving on 7 February, flown by Commandant Eyraud and Captaine Robert, the commanders of the Escadre and the Escadron respectively. During the previous month the groundcrews had gone to Mont de Marsan for technical training. Pilot conversion got under way from 13 June when four Jaguar E arrived. The two Escadrilles were SPA 69 'Chat' (Cat) and SPA 88 'Serpent'.

The Escadron was assigned to the ground-attack role, with the Escadre earmarked to fulfil overseas deployments to support French allies and interests. The Jaguar's potential for long-distance flights was shown on 19 January 1984 when four armed Jaguars from 3/11 flew a non-stop round-trip reconnaissance mission (Opération Chevense) from Solenzara in Corsica to Beirut with support from the AdlA's C-135F Stratotanker tanker fleet to demonstrate that swift aerial assistance could be brought to bear to support the French units in the United Nations (UN) peacekeeping force should it be needed.

BELOW RIGHT Jaguar E30 illustrates the insignia of both Escadrilles of EC 3/11 'Corse'. SPA 88 'Serpent' adopted the black and yellow snake during the latter part of the First World War. *Author's Collection*

FAR RIGHT SPA 69 'Chat' (Cat) adopted a cat's head in a blue circle as its badge in November 1917 to represent the dangerous game of cat and mouse that the fighter pilots played over the Western Front. *Author's Collection*

EC 3/11 became something of a specialist long-distance unit, flying another record non-stop round-trip flight from Toul-Rosières to the city of Nouadhibou on the West African coast in Mauritania, totalling 5,510nm (10,200km) with two Jaguar Es. During the flight the aircraft were refuelled five times by two C-135Fs, one based in France and the other operating from Dakar in Senegal. Night-time refuelling training began in May 1982 and on 24 September this capability was demonstrated to Prime Minister Pierre Mauroy and Minister of Defense Charles Hernu, who were aboard a Boeing C-135F Stratotanker when three Jaguars refuelled.

The Jaguar training squadron EETIS 68.530 was formed at Toul in October 1975, the ceremony being attended by General Renther, commander of the FATac 1ère RA (Aerial Region) and General Roussel, commander of the technical school at Rochefort. The unit trained pilots and technical support groundcrew and was the only Jaguar training centre. EETIS had one officer and 15 non-commissioned officers. A classroom, life-size models and training benches were available to the instructors to teach around 400 trainees per year. EUOT Jaguar, the operational use team from Saint-Dizier, was attached to the EETIS from June 1984 with three engineering officers, 12 engineering non-commissioned officers and a secretariat.

In June 1977 new silenced engine test cells were completed at Toul, enabling any minor issues to be ironed out before the Adours were installed and test flown. Not long after this Toul also received longer runways and emergency arrester gear.

EC 1/11 'Roussillon' began conversion in October 1975, joining EC 3/11 in the ground-attack role and reaching operational status on 1 March 1976. It was comprised of Escadrilles 5 GC III/6 'Masque de Tragédie' (Mask of Tragedy) and 6 GC III/6 'Masque de Comédie' (Mask of Comedy). The unit received the hundredth production Jaguar A on 22 December 1977, Commandant Dumaz having collected the aircraft from the Toulouse-Colomiers assembly line during a special ceremony. In 1987 the unit became operational with AS.30L and ATLIS. This led to dedicated missile storage and technical support facilities being built at the base. Four of the Escadron's Jaguars visited RAF Lossiemouth, home of the RAF's Jaguar Operational Conversion Unit, in March 1985, sporting the new two-tone desert camouflage.

Two Jaguar Escadrons won the Coupe Comète and Coupe Tactique awards for bombing accuracy, frequently beating the Dassault Mirage squadrons that had formerly done well in these competitions. ATLIS certainly proved its value in increasing accuracy. Seven drop tests of the Matra BGL-400 880lb (400kg) LGB were carried out successfully between July 1988 and February 1989, with two of them made during a Red Flag exercise deployment to Nellis AFB.

Jaguar E18 of EC 1/11 'Roussillon' being prepared at BA 136 Toul-Rosières for its transit flight to Dakar on 11 September 1978. AdlA Jaguars were completed with dark grey and dark green disruptive camouflage with silver-grey undersurfaces. ***Author's Collection***

Jaguars A90 and A86 of EC 2/11 'Vosges' equipped with ventral ferry fuel tanks at Toul-Rosières in September 1978. The red triangles on the tails are the badge of Escadrille SPA 97 'Fanion aux hermines' (Ermine Pennant). ***Author's Collection***

By July 1990 Jaguar A124 had spent all of its service with the 11ème Escadre, and at this time it was assigned to EC 2/11. The aircraft is carrying a Thomson-CSF Barem self-protection radar-jamming pod on the outer underwing hardpoint. ***Terry Panopalis Collection***

EC 2/11 'Vosges' reformed on 3 November 1976 with its first six Jaguars. It became operational in June 1977 and in 1987 took on the electronic warfare and anti-radar role from EC 3/3 'Ardennes' with AS.37 Martel anti-radar ASMs and carrying CT 51, Barracuda and Barax jamming pods. The two Escadrilles were SPA 97 'Fanion aux hermines' (Ermine Pennant) and SPA 91 'Aigle à tête de mort' (Eagle's Head of Death).

General Pironneau visited EC 2/11 on 10 September 1987 during Exercise Punch, the objective of which was to destroy enemy radars to enable the penetration of the AdlA's nuclear strike aircraft. The unit benefitted from the equipment maintenance and repair group GERMAS 15.351, which was co-located at Toul and which maintained and repaired electronic countermeasures equipment for all of the AdlA's squadrons. The secure facility was near 2/11's headquarters, enabling its Jaguars to be equipped and pre-flight tested there.

The Escadron also pioneered the fitting of IRCM to the Jaguar. One of its pilots, Patrick Aranega, had the idea of replacing the braking parachute with a flare dispenser. The manufacturer of such systems, Lacroix, confirmed that 18 40mm cartridges would fit into the space and the groundcrew devised the necessary electrics. Tests in 1979 proved successful and the installation was productionised and fitted more widely, especially to Jaguars serving in Chad.

In late February 1979 Jaguars of the Escadre flew a mock anti-armour mission for the television cameras for a programme aired the following month. Captaine Michel Prunas was killed while flying Jaguar A116 on 30 June 1986 in a midair collision with a Belgian F-16A Fighting Falcon; the Belgian pilot Captaine Cavenas managed to eject safely.

On 29 March 1979 the inaugural Exercise LOG 79 began. This was a logistics exercise, the aim of which was to make all the Jaguars available for operations. BA 136 Toul won the exercise and the associated trophy by achieving a 100% availability rate. Sadly Toul's commandant, Colonel Georges Phelut, was killed in a Jaguar accident near the village of Martincourt during Exercise LOG 81 on 18 March 1981. The Jaguar took a leading part in Exercise Novembre Vert (Green November) in 1982 when FATac squadrons were deployed on to field strips on 20 different types of terrain to prove that its tactical fighters could operate from anywhere in Europe.

A series of high-profile NATO staff officers visited Toul to see the Jaguar in action. Lieutenant General William Eart Brown Jr, USAF, the Commander-in-Chief of Allied Air Forces in Southern Europe, visited the newly built underground headquarters on 8 December 1983 and was shown a quartet of Jaguars on static display with different weapon configurations. General Brown also participated in a mission aboard a Jaguar E. On 9 May 1984 commander

The tail fin of Jaguar A75 of EC 4/11 'Jura' was painted with the insignia of both Escadrilles. On the port side was that of SPA 158 'Serpentaire', a secretary bird, wings outstretched, fighting a serpent. *SDASM Archives*

of the Luftflotten Kommando, Lieutenant General Kuebart, was accompanied by General Forget, commander of the FATac 1st RA. Kuebart was shown the buried headquarters and visited EC 2/11, where he witnessed rearming and refuelling in a chemical warfare environment. On 13 June Air Marshal Sir Patrick Hine, the Air Officer Commanding-in-Chief RAF Germany, arrived, again visiting the command post and seeing operations in a chemical environment and flying a sortie in a Jaguar E. General Rolf Thiemann, commander of the 4th Allied Tactical Air Force (ATAF) visited on 8 February 1988 as part of a wider tour of FATac units and he received a flight aboard a Jaguar E, as did General Fazzino, commander of the 5th ATAF, on 18 April.

Exercise Airex was held during 11–22 March 1985, a multinational exercise involving 140 aircraft from eight NATO air forces. The Escadre's Jaguars were detached to a secondary airstrip at Chambley as well as activation of Toul's command centre, NBC – nuclear, biological, chemical – decontamination facilities and air defences. The exercise involved 785 attack missions, the Jaguars contributing AS.30L precision attacks. Airex was closely followed by the Datex air defence exercise.

In early 1986 EC 2/11 moved into new hardened aircraft shelters (HAS). Plans to provide the other Escadrons with HAS were scuppered by the (then planned) impending retirement of the Jaguar. They received basic 'astroarch' shelters instead, which only offered protection from the weather.

A fourth Escadron was added on 12 December 1978 when EC 4/11 'Jura' was formed at Toul but based at BA 106 Bordeaux-Mérignac (the previous F-100D-equipped incarnation of the unit did not officially disband at Djibouti until 31 December) with SPA 158 'Serpentaire' (Serpentary – also known as secretary bird) and SPA 161 'Sphinx'. The unit had begun re-equipping with the Jaguar at Mérignac in August. By June 1979 most of the pilots were trained in daytime in-flight refuelling and the following month the squadron passed its tactical evaluation and was declared operational (full aircraft strength was finally reached in December).

To starboard was the badge of Escadrille SPA 161 'Sphinx'. *SDASM Archives*

In June 1980 the 11ème Escadre celebrated its 15th anniversary of Jaguar operations and A7 was painted in this very attractive blue colour scheme for the occasion. *Terry Panopalis Collection*

A six-week detachment to Dakar, the capital of Senegal, was made during August 1979 for co-operation training with the Marine Nationale's Breguet Br.1150 Atlantic maritime patrol aircraft. On 20 June 1980 the squadron made a firepower demonstration on the ranges at Pau for a television broadcast.

The 11ème Escadre celebrated the 15th anniversary of Jaguar operations in June 1990, having amassed 35,500 flying hours in overseas deployments. For the occasion Jaguar A7 was painted in a special blue colour scheme.

The third Jaguar wing was the 3ème Escadre de Chasse. EC 3/3 'Ardennes' at BA 133 Nancy-Ochey had previously operated the Dassault Mirage 5F (the Escadre's other Escadrons operated the Mirage IIIE). The Escadron commander, Captaine Dehaeze, began his conversion training at Toul-Rosières, followed by four other pilots between January and March. The squadron received its first Jaguar (A29) on 25 February 1977 and received its full complement of 11 Jaguar A and four Jaguar E by 26 October. The pilots were divided between Saint-Dizier and Toul for training, EC 3/3 finally reforming on 1 June at Nancy. Eight Jaguars led by Commandant Courtet made a flypast parade on 23 June and four days later the unit moved into its renovated facilities and new HAS.

The unit was assigned primarily to the anti-radar role with a secondary attack and medium-altitude fighter role. Commandant Escoffier made the unit's first live AS.37 Martel launch from Jaguar A29 on 4 October. The Martel used three different seeker heads, which covered a frequency range of 1.215–3.7GHz. The drawback of having three different seekers was that the mission planners had to know the frequency of the radar they wished to attack so that the correct seeker could be fitted before the mission. This was impractical for combat sorties where it might not be possible to foresee the possible radars likely to be encountered. In addition, the seekers could not home on to modern frequency-hopping radars. A developed version called ARMAT with a new Electronique Serge Dassault ADAR multi-frequency seeker appeared in the early 1980s for export. The Jaguar was cleared to carry ARMAT but the AdlA did not buy the newer missile; instead it fitted the ADAR seeker into the Martel. From 1978 the unit introduced Phimat chaff and BOZ-103 chaff/flare pods and in 1980 started carrying Barracuda and Barax I- and J-Band jamming pods.

EC 1/11 made a deployment to Nellis AFB in June 1985 for Exercise Red Flag. Jaguar A159 is being rearmed with practice bombs and is carrying a Barem jammer pod. *Terry Panopalis Collection*

EC 3/3 visited RAF Honington in June 1978, where they flew 26 tactical sorties in consort with the Hawker Siddeley Buccaneer S.2B strike aircraft based there. This exchange validated the squadron's ability to operate from a foreign base and was repeated in the following two years. The squadron also deployed to Landivisiau for anti ship training. Having been seconded from 7ème Escadre de Chasse, Commandant Escoffier took command of EC 3/3. The unit was unique within the 3ème Escadre de Chasse in having an aerial refuelling capability. The squadron won the Coupe Comète for bombing accuracy in 1980 and demonstrated operations from roads during Exercise Datex in 1982. Numerous overseas exercises took place; participating in the NATO Tactical Leadership Programme in 1981, attending Red Flag in 1981, 1982, 1984 and 1987 (from 1981, FATac units attended Red Flag every 18 months) as well as the annual Tactical Fighter Meet (deploying at home in 1980 to 1983). The first Red Flag deployment in the spring of 1981 led to several firsts for the Jaguars: a transatlantic crossing, and visiting the capital of Martinique, Fort-de-France, and Pointe-à-Pitre in Guadeloupe, the latter giving rise to an air support exercise for the French Marines based there.

ABOVE A10 of EC 3/3 'Ardennes' outside a hardened aircraft shelter at BA 133 Nancy-Ochey in August 1985 in standard European theatre camouflage. ***Terry Panopalis Collection***

LEFT An AS.37 Martel anti-radar missile loaded on to a Jaguar of EC 3/3 inside a HAS at Nancy-Ochey. The Martel used three different seekers that each covered a pre-selected portion of the electromagnetic spectrum. ***Blue Envoy Collection***

LEFT EC 2/11 in its suppression of enemy air defence role suppression role used the CT 51 radar-jamming pod during the first half of the 1980s. ***Author's Collection***

Jaguar A14 of EC 3/3 is seen at Nancy-Ochey with a single Martel as well as Matra rocket pods beneath the wings. Parked behind is a visiting Dassault Mirage 5 of the Belgian Air Force. ***Terry Panopalis Collection***

A Breguet family outing, the company designed the Br.1150 Atlantic and Br.121 and both were produced by multinational collaborations, SEBCAT and SEPECAT respectively. EC 3/3 practised the anti-shipping role with its Jaguars, with the Atlantics providing navigational and targeting data. ***Author's Collection***

The development of the Jaguar's electronic warfare equipment and its operational doctrine was shaped by the early Red Flag results – the CT 51 ECM pod being an embarrassing failure in 1981. One result was a self-protection manoeuvre, the 'Jink', in which the pilot constantly varied the aircraft's trajectory to thwart small-calibre anti-aircraft artillery (AAA). It was imposed throughout FATac for about a year before being abandoned. Jaguar A68 piloted by Captaine Jean-Marie Monsterlet fatally crashed at Nancy-Ochey during landing on 5 February 1981.

EC 3/3 did not operate the Jaguar for long, with budget issues stemming from the introduction of the Dassault Mirage 2000 resulting in the rationalisation of existing squadrons and equipment. The squadron was reassigned to the Mirage IIIE (to match the Escadre's other Escadrons) and the anti-radar role was passed to EC 2/11 'Vosges' (ironically the Martel was used by the Mirage IIIE between 1991 and February 1994). The Escadron's final Jaguar flight was on 29 May 1987, bringing a decade of Jaguar operations to an end with a total flying time of 35,372 hours 45 minutes and an extensive combat history in Africa.

Another unit to use the Jaguar was the tactical training centre CITac 399 'Aquitaine' formed on 1 July 1987 at Luxeuil BA 116. It used five Jaguar E alongside the Dassault Mystère 20 SNA for combat navigator training. The Jaguars were assigned to low-altitude navigational training.

Mauritania

The North African country of Mauritania was to be the location of the Jaguar's baptism of fire and the first combat for the AdlA since the Algerian War of the early 1960s. The 11ème Escadre de Chasse was tasked with providing support to French interests overseas and EC 3/11 'Corse' undertook several proving deployments, flying three Jaguars to Djibouti in 1975, followed by a further sortie to Senegal and the Ivory Coast in 1976. External operations were designated as an operation exercise (OPEX) and western Africa would become the

Training unit CITac 399 'Aquitaine' operated the Jaguar E from its formation in July 1987 until its disbandment in July 2001. This aircraft is E10. *Terry Panopalis Collection*

setting for many of these during subsequent decades. The situation of Spanish Sahara caused tensions between Morocco and Mauritania as Spain began to decolonise in the mid-1960s. A UN resolution in 1966 had advocated a referendum for the self-determination of Western Sahara. This was opposed by both nations, which coveted the territory for themselves, but was favoured by Libya, which was hoping to gain influence in the region. Local liberation movements formed, becoming the Front pour la Liberation of Saghiet el Amra et Rio de Oro (Polisario) in May 1973. Following the death of the Spanish dictator General Franco and a return to democratic government, Spain began to resolve its lingering colonial legacies and the Madrid Accords set the date of Spanish withdrawal as 28 February 1976 and divided Western Sahara between Morocco and Mauritania. The Polisario began fighting for independence and launched a guerrilla campaign in the southern part of Western Sahara that was focused on the Zouérate–Nouadhibou railway line, a vital route to the Atlantic coast for iron ore mined in Mauritania. The Polisario were well armed and had armoured cars as well as anti-aircraft weapons. Mauritania, whose military forces struggled to deal with Polisario's mobile columns, asked for military support from France in late 1977. The French government agreed on 28 October to send military forces.

The AdlA's contribution to Opération Lamantin (Manatee) was a pair of Breguet Atlantic maritime patrol aircraft, two C-135F tankers and eight Jaguars from EC 3/11 (four from Togo and four from France), which arrived on 22 and 23 November (two more arrived later), all being based at Dakar. A C-160 Transall was used by the Commander as an airborne command post (callsign Rubens Rouge). The French Army deployed four groups of paratroopers (numbering 15 men each) as Postes de Guidage Avancé (PGA – forward air controllers) for the Jaguars. The entire deployment numbered no more than 350 personnel.

The Aéronavale's Breguet Atlantic maritime patrol aircraft provided long-range navigational support and airborne command and control for EC 3/11's Jaguars during Opération Lamantin in Mauritania. *Author's Collection*

A map of Mauritania and the disputed area of Western Sahara. The strategically vital Zouerate-Nouadhibou railway was the Polisario's main objective. The distances involved from the Jaguar's base at Dakar required frequent aerial refuelling during the long sorties. ***Author***

Given the range of the operational area (the Nouadhibou triangle, Zouérate and Atar) from Dakar, the Jaguars had to fly 540–810nm (1,000–1,500km), which involved a mission of four to five hours' duration and refuelling from the tankers up to three times. The Atlantics were used to provide the Jaguars with navigational support. The need for political approval from Mauritania and France for each strike also affected the reaction time. The conditions were difficult with tropical storms, sandstorms and flocks of birds creating hazards during the long flights. Gunnery training sorties were flown over the Bennichab range.

During the morning of 2 December the Bou Lanouar post on the railway was attacked. The Polisario column was kept under observation by an Atlantic and the airborne commander ordered the Jaguars to take off. They flew over the column for more than two hours but no political authority to attack was received and the aircraft returned to base. The Jaguars flew several recce sorties, which allowed the pilots to get to know the nature of the Polisario columns, their composition and weaponry. Remarkably, at this time no ground fire was observed from the columns and they made no attempt to evade the Jaguars. On the 12th an ore train was attacked and this time political authority to attack was given. The column of 50 vehicles was 2.7nm (5km) long, travelling along a relatively narrow passage bordered by small rocks in a flat, sandy area without any natural cover. Strafing attacks using the 30mm cannon proved very effective, knocking out about a quarter of the vehicles. The column was kept under observation all night by an Atlantic and the following morning the column halted after travelling 161nm (300km). The Jaguars took off to attack but no approval was received and they were recalled.

The AdlA had acquired Boeing C-135F tankers for the Dassault Mirage IVA 'Force de Frappe' strategic nuclear bombers in the 1960s, but they were equally important for supporting tactical fighters during OPEX deployments. The short hose seen here was an adapter to enable the probe and drogue method to be used with the standard Boeing Flying Boom system fitted to the C-135Fs. ***Blue Envoy Collection***

Approval was granted later that day, presenting a challenge with just three hours of daylight left and the target now being 728nm (1,350km) away. The first patrol arrived on time over the target at 17:20 and began their attack. The vehicles had been dispersed and hidden under shrubs and in folds in the landscape. Several 9K32 Strela-2 (NATO designation SA-7 *Grail*) shoulder-fired IR-homing surface-to-air missiles (SAMs) – often referred to as man-portable air-defence systems, MANPADS – were fired by the insurgents. The second Jaguar formation attacked between 17:40 and 18:00. By the time the operation was over two-thirds of the column had been destroyed. Some of the pilots had flown for more than eight hours and refuelled six times in the air, the last refuelling being at night.

An attack on the Tmeimichatt post on the 18th by a column, also about fifty vehicles strong, resulted in attacks by three Jaguar patrols, destroying half of the column and with a significant amount of materiel recovered by the Mauritanian army. Only minor damage from ground fire was received.

After these effective attacks the Polisario switched to small-scale raids and a month of relative inactivity followed. The Jaguars focused on armed reconnaissance to monitor the railway and co-operation missions with the Mauritanian Army. The detachment was reinforced by six pilots and 30 groundcrew from EC 3/3 'Ardennes'. Rising levels of attacks saw authorisation being given to Air Brigadier General Maffre to resume missions on 2 May. Operations were flown that day to support a Mauritanian unit and the next day they attacked the retreating Polisario force. The terrain and close proximity of Mauritanian troops made the missions trickier, but they were successful with heavy losses inflicted on the enemy. This was to be the last active intervention by French air forces in Mauritania, although the following day one of EC 3/11's Jaguars was shot down by a SA-7 *Grail*.

Mauritania's President, Mokhtar Ould Daddah, was removed in a coup in July and the country began to step back from the Western Sahara affair. In October a

A line-up of EC 4/11 Jaguars in June 1984 is headed by A107 in desert camouflage of dark brown and sand adopted for deployment to Chad. The aircraft is armed with three bombs on the inner hardpoint and an ECM pod outboard. ***Terry Panopalis Collection***

ceasefire was concluded between Mauritania and the Polisario, who switched their effort against Morocco. Occasionally the ceasefire broke down, as on 12 July 1979 when the Polisario attacked Tichla. The Jaguars were once again called into action, a flight of four aircraft carrying out photo-reconnaissance at very low altitude along the Zouérate–Nouadhibou railway. The flight was supported by an Atlantic, a C-135F tanker as well as a Sud Aviation SA.330 Puma helicopter in the event of a pilot ejection.

Mauritania restored diplomatic relations with Morocco in August 1979 and renounced its claims over Western Sahara, with Moroccan forces leaving the following month. The dispute remains unresolved today, however. Opération Lamantin did not end until May 1980, the deployment being at a reduced level following the ceasefire.

The lessons learned in relation to command and control (especially relating to political clearances), long-distance flying and PGA co-ordination were rapidly put into effect in other interventions. The requirement for additional units to be capable of deployment meant that FATac had to expand air-to-air refuelling training. At the time of Lamantin only one unit and 20 pilots were trained, but soon all Jaguar squadrons began training and the number of qualified pilots rose to over a hundred.

The Jaguar also made a lasting cultural impact in the region, lending its name – thanks to its noisy low flying – to Jakwar, a style of dance music that was created by Jheich ould Abba, a blind musician from Atar in northern Mauritania, who played an amplified tidinit, a traditional five-string lute. Jakwar has since spread across North Africa, a most unlikely legacy for the Jaguar.

Chad

As events in Mauritania were unfolding, unrest in equatorial Africa led to further OPEX. Chad had gained its independence from France in 1960 but soon found itself in a territorial dispute with Libya along its northern border in the Sahara, an area named the Aouzou Strip. Libya occupied and annexed the area in 1972. Following the withdrawal of French military forces in 1977, Libya began supporting the insurgent group Front de Libération Nationale du Tchad (FROLINAT) led by Goukouni Oueddei, which invaded Chad in April 1978. France rushed forces to the Chadian capital N'Djamena in Opération Tacaud and Air Brigadier General Huguet was placed in command of the AdlA forces in the region, which included six Jaguars at Dakar. Huguet secured the transfer of the Jaguars to N'Djamena International Airport. Chadian and French forces stopped the FROLINAT assault on the capital.

Flying conditions were better than those in Mauritania, with only the heat and sandy wind being the main complaints for the pilots and ground personnel. Target designation was sometimes carried out by Aviation Légère de l'Armée de Terre (French Army Light Aviation – ALAT) Cessna O-1E Bird Dog observation aircraft in liaison with the accompanying Breguet Atlantic and a Terminal Guidance Officer (GTO) on the ground. Live cannon fire practice was carried out at the Massaguet range. The detachment also tested the RP 36P camera pod successfully.

FROLINAT captured the town of Ati and on 19 and 31 May Jaguar sorties were flown to support Chadian and French troops fighting to retake it (no fewer than 15 sorties were flown on the 19th). On the 23rd two Jaguars were damaged by small-calibre bullets while attacking a column of vehicles. During a ground-attack

A map of Chad showing the disputed Aouzou Strip and the Libyan airfields that were established above the Red Line and the later 16th Parallel. *Author*

sortie near Jedaa on the 31st, Jaguar A52 was shot down. The pilot ejected and was recovered by an ALAT Puma helicopter. The aircraft wreckage was recovered to determine the cause of the loss, originally thought to have been due to a SA-7 *Grail* but the engine failure may have been due to a lucky hit from shrapnel or possibly a fatigue crack in the afterburner casing. On the same day another three Jaguars arrived from Dakar as reinforcements.On 13 June the Jaguars attacked a concentration of enemy troops at Senatat using 30mm cannon and 275lb (125kg) fragmentation bombs to great effect. A lack of fuel halted operations for two days until N'Djamena could be resupplied. The lack of any Libyan air threat was welcome given the lack of air defence equipment or AAMs for the Jaguars.

Three more Jaguars were lost; A109 crashed near Ati during a reconnaissance mission on 8 August (killing Lieutenant Robert Jacquel), on the 23rd a mid-air collision 216nm (400km) from N'Djamena claimed A111 (the pilot ejecting successfully) but A97 managed to return to base, and on 14 October A106 crashed at N'Djamena.

The aerial attacks broke the back of the FROLINAT offensive and led to the beginning of negotiations. Following the restoration of a ceasefire, the Chadian government requested the French to withdraw. The withdrawal was covered by Jaguars flying patrols over N'Djamena on 15–16 May 1980.

Libya reinvaded in 1981 and was victorious, but the Libyan-imposed puppet government collapsed the following year and in 1983 the French intervened with Opération Manta. President François Mitterrand's chief of private staff, Air Army General Jean Saulnier, proposed a bombing raid against a Libyan airfield in

Jaguar A131 of EC 1/11 'Roussillon' and Escadrille 6 GC III/6 'Masque de Comédie' (Mask of Comedy) is carrying an array of underwing ECM and Phimat chaff dispenser pods during the Chadian OPEX in September 1984. *Terry Panopalis Collection*

A pair of Jaguars from the 11ème Escadre de Chasse, including A129 from EC 1/11 and possibly A104 from EC 2/11 in 1986 in desert camouflage. The badge on the tail fin of A129 is that of Escadrille 'Masque de Comédie'. *Author's Collection*

the Aouzou Strip from Bangui International Airport in the Central African Republic. The plan was for four Jaguars armed with six 881 or 550lb (400 or 250kg) bombs, self-protection pods and a 264gal (1,200L) drop tank to make the raid. But the 2,160nm (4,000km) round trip required tanker support, which was risky given the chances of interception by Libyan fighters at the northernmost refuelling point and this led to Mitterrand rejecting the proposal.

Opération Manta was largely a land campaign but the AdlA was heavily involved in transporting men and equipment in Transall C-160 and Douglas DC-8 transports, along with chartered civil Boeing 747s. For the first time air defence forces were deployed outside of French territory, consisting of surveillance radars, R.440 Crotale SAMs and seven Dassault Mirage F1C interceptors. Between four and eight Jaguars were also deployed, which from January 1984 sported the makeshift defensive IRCM dispenser replacing the braking parachute that EC 2/11 had developed. At Libreville International Airport in Gabon were another four Jaguars with four more at Bangui along with three C-135F Stratotankers and two Atlantic maritime patrol aircraft, which were used to provide long-range reconnaissance and navigational support for the fighters. Numerous logistical problems, especially with the supply of fuel, were encountered and the C-135F and chartered civil aircraft had to empty part of their fuel into the storage tanks at N'Djamena Airport to keep the stocks replenished.

French forces did not intervene in the fighting until 25 January 1984, when they engaged an insurgent column of vehicles near Torodoum, which had attacked Fort Ziguey the previous day, massacring the Chadian soldiers and taking two Médecins Sans Frontières (MSF) humanitarian workers hostage. A pair of Jaguars carried out a recce of the fort in the late afternoon but the photographs proved to be unusable due to the fading light. In the morning a Jaguar escorted by two Mirage F1Cs set off on a reconnaissance patrol, followed by a formation of four Jaguars that spotted the column. At 13:05 another patrol of three Jaguars took off; they photographed the vehicles and ZSU-23-2 AAA as well as the MSF workers' van. A lack of timely permission to attack – communications were routed via the accompanying Atlantic – prevented any offensive action, despite coming under fire from MANPADS, which the aircraft evaded successfully.

On the basis of this intelligence another patrol was readied: Jaguar A101 accompanied by two Mirage F1Cs, which took off at 15:15. Over the enemy column they came under fire from *Grails*, using their cannon in retaliation. They hit several vehicles, including a tanker, which exploded. Another formation of two Jaguars (A81 and A1) and two Mirage F1Cs came under fire from ZSU-23-2 AAA. With orders to avoid hitting the MSF van and the fact that the vehicles were scattered among the trees, the pilots had to make multiple passes to make sure of their targets. A Mirage F1C was hit but returned to N'Djamena safely, but 4/11's Head of Operations, Captaine Michel Croci, in Jaguar A81 was less fortunate. A 23mm shell knocked out the hydraulic systems, which caused the flying controls to seize. Croci ejected too low and was killed. Jaguar A125 was lost on 16 April when Commandant Bernard Voelckel flew his aircraft into a sand dune in the Oum-Chalouba region while on a reconnaissance mission.

The fighting died down and Chad was divided along the 16th Parallel with Libyan occupation to the north of the 'Red Line'. Following negotiations both France and Libya promised to withdraw their forces in 1984. The French left in October but the Libyan forces began building new fortifications and installations in occupied northern Chad. These included five air bases,

The Atlantic was again used to provide long-range navigational and recce support for EC 3/11's Jaguars in Chad. This Atlantic is accompanied by A121 and another of EC 3/11's aircraft over the desert terrain of Chad in 1980. ***Author's Collection***

the most important based being Tanoua in the Aouzou Strip and one at Ouadi Doum that had a 12,470ft (3,800m)-long runway that was capable of operating Libya's Tupolev Tu-22RD *Blinder-C* bombers.

Because of concerns that Libya would not honour its agreement to withdraw, the AdlA undertook a series of reconnaissance flights. On 18 and 24 November 1984 Mirage IVA reconnaissance aircraft based in France flew supersonic, high-altitude sorties over Ouadi-Doum, Faya Largeau and Fada. These were supported by Douglas DC-8 SARIGuE (Système Aéroporté de Recueil d'Information de Guerre Electronique) and Breguet Atlantic electronic intelligence missions to pinpoint radar and SAM sites. Jaguars were used for low-level reconnaissance sorties in Opération Musaraigne (Shrew) in late 1985.

N'Djamena International Airport was the AdA's main operating base in Chad. Here, two Jaguar A's of EC 4/11, Escadrille SPA 161 'Sphinx' are on standby. ***Author's Collection***

Missions Musaraigne III and Musaraigne IV were flown on 7 December. Musaraigne III was carried out by Commandant Chanel and Lieutenant Didier of EC 3/3 'Ardennes'. The Jaguars were configured with Phimat chaff and Barracuda ECM pods on the outboard pylons, two 1,200L tanks inboard and the RP 36P camera pod on the centreline. The braking parachute was replaced with a Lacroix flare dispenser. The four-hour sortie was successful but eventful; one aerial refuelling incident resulted in a torn-off probe and a broken Barracuda pod. Musaraigne IV left from Bangui in the afternoon heat, the aircraft taking off with empty external tanks and topping off from a Transall C-160NG. The two spare Jaguars turned back after another refuelling from a C-135FR 150nm (465km) from Bangui, leaving Captaine Antoine in Jaguar A82 and Captaine Vinson to proceed to the target. They photographed along the Chicha–Yogoun axis on the 16th parallel at an altitude of 15,000ft (4,570m) and obtained coverage of the airfield at Ouadi Doum.Using this intelligence FATac began planning possible attacks on the Libyan-held airfields. A pre-emptive strike was cancelled in December, but a rehearsal was flown against the airfield at Awakaba in the Central African Republic on the 19th. Reinforcements by January 1986 saw 11 Jaguars from EC 2/11 'Vosges' and four Mirage F1C being deployed to Bangui International Airport. The pilots were briefed

Jaguars of the 11ème Escadre de Chasse await their next mission over Chad, alongside a pair of Mirage F1s. The tails carry the insignia of several of the Escadre's Escadrille, including SPA 161 'Sphinx'. ***Terry Panopalis Collection***

on the potential targets and training missions were flown. At around this time a new defensive manoeuvre against SAM batteries was devised by Commandant Amarger; the 'double crank' – which took the 'Jink' as its inspiration – heading towards the target at low altitude, making a 40° turn while dropping chaff, flying straight for 30 seconds and then turning away from the target. The wingman would do the same manoeuvre but in the opposite direction, crossing each other's paths at the start.

On 10 February 1986 Libyan and Chadian insurgent forces launched an offensive into the eastern part of central Chad. The Chadian government requested help from France and Opération Epervier (Sparrowhawk) began. Air Army General Saulnier was now the Chief of Staff and President Mitterrand gave his assent to air strikes.

On 16 February EC 1/11 'Roussillon' launched Opération Trionyx, a raid on Ouadi Doum with a force of 11 Jaguars (a 12th aircraft went unserviceable on take-off). The airfield was protected by two radar sites with a total of five radars and an air defence brigade, including Soviet-supplied 2K12 Kub (SA-6 *Gainful*), 9K33 Osa (SA-8 *Gecko*) and 9K31 Strela-1 (SA-9 *Gaskin*) SAMs, six ZSU-23-4 Shilka self-propelled AA guns and a battery of 14.5mm ZPU-4 quadruple machine gun mounts. The only Libyan aircraft at the airfield were Mil Mi-24 *Hind* attack helicopters and SIAI-Marchetti SF-260 basic trainers. The Jaguars were loaded with two underwing 1200L drop tanks, a Phimat chaff dispenser and a Barracuda ECM pod on the underwing pylons and a Lacroix flare dispenser in the tail cone. Seven of the Jaguars were armed with 18 BAP-100 anti-runway bombs on the centreline hardpoint, the remainder carried 250kg retarded bombs.

The raid was escorted by four Mirage F1Cs and had six C-135F tankers in support, the Jaguars refuelling twice on the inbound leg. The fast low-level ingress caught the defenders by surprise, the attackers making a single pass to maximise the element of surprise. The BAP-100 anti-runway bombs were designed to be dropped at low altitude, a parachute deploying to stabilise them vertically before a rocket fired and forced the bomb into the runway at very high speed, hopefully sinking deeply before exploding. The runway at Ouadi Doum was not concrete, it was a piece of field military engineering using pierced steel planking metal plates placed on the sandy soil compacted with oil.

The BAP-100 were dropped with great accuracy but some drifted on their parachutes to either side of the runway, apparently due to rising vortices of hot air on either side of the metal plates, as well as a batch of defective parachutes. The BAP-100s sank into the sand

Jaguar A110 is carrying a full load of 18 Thomson Brandt BAP-100 anti-runway bombs. Each bomb was parachute retarded before a rocket in the tail ignited to force the bomb through a concrete runway with a delay fuze. It was estimated that 12–18 BAP-100 were required to achieve one cut across a runway. ***Phillipe Ricco***

before exploding, the sandy soil causing a much tighter – but higher – ejection cone of fragments. This caused the only battle damage incurred on the attackers. In the final turn into the attack, the two outside Jaguars in the formation (armed with 250kg bombs) fell behind and took the brunt of the BAP-100 fragments. Jaguar A91 received three shrapnel hits (at the base of the windscreen and the refuelling probe and in the F1 fuel tank behind the cockpit), which required a month-long repair at Bangui, including removing the wing (this would not be A91's last brush with battle damage – see later in this chapter). The runway was out of action for several weeks due to the nature of the metal plating, which required dismantling the track entirely to change a section in the middle.

The following day a Libyan Tupolev Tu-22RD *Blinder-C* bomber attacked N'Djamena International Airport, dropping four bombs in retaliation – the first time the Chadian capital had been bombed since January 1942. Four Jaguars were readied at Bangui to make an attack on the airfield at Faya-Largeau but the mission was cancelled before take-off. On 18 February a Mirage IVA flew a 5,400nm (10,000km) battle damage assessment sortie over Ouadi Doum (this was the longest ever reconnaissance mission carried out by the type). In turn, a Libyan MiG-25R *Foxbat* flew over N'Djamena at high altitude on a reconnaissance flight. In the afternoon the Jaguars carried out an armed recce north-west of N'Djamena.

The Mirage F1Cs were detached to N'Djamena to provide air defence and AdlA Crotale and Army MIM-23B I-HAWK SAMs were also deployed. Aircraft reinforcements arrived too and by 3 March there were ten Jaguars, six Mirage F1Cs, one Atlantic and seven Transall C-160s at N'Djamena, with six Jaguars (including four from EC 3/3 'Ardennes' armed with Martel), another Atlantic and six Transalls at Bangui and two Boeing C-135F tankers at Libreville in Gabon. By the autumn the forces at N'Djamena had been dispersed for safety; a dozen EC 1/11 Jaguars at Libreville with the four EC 3/3 Jaguars at Bangui. This show of strength deterred further Libyan raids and Chad went on the counter-offensive.

To support this operation the AdlA began attacking Libyan radar sites and Ouadi Doum was targeted again on 6 and 7 January 1987 by the Jaguars of EC 3/3 – the anti-radar specialists. Two Mirage F1CRs of Escadron de Reconnaissance 1/33 'Belfort' were the bait, arriving low and fast before climbing. On the 6th no Libyan response was encountered and Commandant André

Jaguar A9 of EC 3/3 Nancy-Ochey in June 1987 following its return from Chad. An AS.37 Martel is under the belly and standard grey-green drop tanks have been fitted. ***Terry Panopalis Collection***

Another Martel-armed Jaguar that served in Chad with EC 2/11 was A113. The temporary paint finish has worn in service, revealing the original grey green underneath. *Terry Panopalis Collection*

Carbon of EC 1/11 devised a backup plan to attack the runway again if it proved impossible to engage the radars. On the following day an Atlantic took off at 09:00 to act as bait, without success until the crew decided on one final attempt and finally a Libyan radar was switched on and the good news was relayed to N'Djamena. At 11:00 two ER 1/33 'Belfort' Mirage F1CRs took off from N'Djamena, while four Jaguars and four escorting Mirage F1Cs headed towards Ouadi Doum on a dogleg flightpath from the east then to the north. The Jaguars were each armed with a single Martel – one of these had its seeker tuned for the P-19 *Flat Face-B* early warning radar and the other three were tuned for the SURN *Straight Flush* fire-control radar for the 2K12 Kub SAM battery. North-west of Faya, the Mirage F1CRs climbed to 6,000ft (1,830m) and were detected by the *Flat Face* radar at Faya-Largeau, which relayed a warning to Ouadi Doum. The Mirages dived back to low level and headed south at high speed (a Libyan fighter chased them for 54nm [100km] but could not catch up).

The Jaguars approached the airfield undetected at low level, flying at 500kts at 200ft (60m), but being pre-warned the defences were on alert and the 2K12 Kub battery turned on its radars, 'painting' one of the Jaguars. The pilot, Lieutenant Guy Wurtz, fired his Martel and destroyed the SURN *Straight Flush* fire-control radar (some accounts incorrectly claim that the airfield's *Flat Face* was destroyed, this was impossible as Wurtz's Martel had a SURN-optimised seeker fitted). The 'double crank' defensive manoeuvre was used during the attack.

Ouadi Doum was captured in March following a ground battle and the Soviet Union demanded that Libya bomb the abandoned materiel to prevent any sensitive equipment falling into the hands of French military intelligence. By August Chadian forces had reached the Aouzou Strip and political approval for further air support missions was withdrawn – although officially unacknowledged Mirage and Jaguar recce sorties were flown north of the 'Red Line', possibly including some ground-attack missions. One such mission in late 1986 by a pair of Jaguars, escorted by two Mirage F1Cs, attacked an insurgent column, destroying eight trucks and two Panhard AML armoured cars with cannon and rocket fire to the north-west of Fada.

The Bangui detachment was marred by the crash of Jaguar A152 into a school following an engine failure shortly after take-off on 27 March 1987. Lieutenant Etcheberry ejected but sadly 21 people were killed on the ground and the Jaguar played no further active role.

EC 3/3 maintained its Martel-armed Jaguars at N'Djamena until 13 April 1987. It had operated the detachment despite only having 14 pilots, leading to three to four two-month detachments per pilot. Negotiations between Chadian and Libyan emissaries took place in Paris during August 1989 under Algerian mediation, leading to the signing of the Algiers Agreement and an end to the fighting. In 1994 the International Court of Justice in The Hague validated Chadian sovereignty over the Aouzou strip.

African OPEX

At the end of 1980 co-operative agreements were signed with several West African Francophone countries to provide detachments of military aircraft. On 23 November EC 4/11 sent four Jaguars to Gabon under the command of Commandant Guevel and on 3 December a second detachment led by Lieutenant-Colonel

Menessier departed for the Ivory Coast, taking part in the 20th anniversary of independence celebrations, overflying the capital Abidjan. In the summer of 1981 EC 3/3 took on the Gabon deployment, flying recce sorties to Zaire and on 6 August reconnoitring the crash zone of two Gabonese Air Force Mirage 5s.

In January 1981 EC 4/11 and 3/3 participated in Opération Barracuda in the Central African Republic. The operation had begun in November 1979 to protect French citizens in the country and to support the government of the newly reinstalled President David Dacko. Opération Barracuda ended in June 1981, although French forces would remain in the country to support the training of the Central African Armed Forces until 1998.

The Republic of Togo, independent of French colonial rule since 1960, had been under the dictatorial rule of General Gnassingbé Eyadéma since 1967. On 23 September 1986 a group of some 70 armed dissidents crossed over the border from Ghana and headed to the capital Lomé in an unsuccessful attempt to overthrow Eyadéma. In response to this Jaguars were flown over Lomé in a demonstration of support for the government to prevent a possible civil war.

Jaguars also participated in exercises during the 1980s in Gabon under Opération Estuaire, in the Ivory Coast with Opération Bandama, Opération Mangrove in Togo and Opération Murene in Senegal. Jaguar A83 from EC 1/11 crashed in Chad during a deployment on 22 August 1993, sadly killing the pilot.

The UN humanitarian mission in Rwanda in response to the genocide of the minority Tutsi population by the Hutu majority ethnic group included the deployment of ten Jaguars, along with Mirage F1s and tanker support, to Kisangani Air Base on 24 June 1994. As part of Opération Turquoise, the Jaguars' main role was to provide reconnaissance and, if required, armed air support. On 1 August, Jaguar A119 struck the foliage on the top of a hill in poor weather at 410kt. The pilot ejected as the aircraft impacted the trees and miraculously escaped unscathed.

Gulf War

Following the Iraqi invasion of Kuwait in August 1990, the 11ème Escadre was placed on standby to deploy to the Gulf on 16 September as part of Opération Daguet (Brocket – a small deer species) – France's participation in the multinational response as part of Operation Desert Shield to protect Saudi Arabia. Although AdlA units began deploying on 2 October, the first eight Jaguars, under the command of Colonel Marc Amberg, did not depart until the 18th, followed by another eight three days later, having been held back for political motives as they were deemed to be 'offensive aircraft'. They were accompanied on the transit flights by Mirage F1CR reconnaissance aircraft, which provided navigational assistance over the long distances.

The Jaguars were based alongside most of the AdlA's combat detachment at Al-Ahsa Airport, south-west of the city of Dhahran in eastern Saudi Arabia. Al-Ahsa was still under construction but offered a 9,840ft (3,000m)-long runway, essential for the heavily laden Jaguars, which would need 7,550ft (2,300m) of it to get airborne – and nearly all of it when the temperatures exceeded 30°C.

A further 12 Jaguars arrived at Al-Ahsa in early January 1991. They were drawn from 11ème Escadre's Escadrons as well as an element from EC 4/11 'Jura' and some 7ème Escadre pilots. A total of 34 Jaguars were deployed but only around 28 were operational at any one time. BA 136 Toul-Rosières sent out 320 tons of equipment, 120 tons of ammunition and 250 drop tanks. EC 4/11's workshops at Bordeaux carried out the majority of the pre-deployment preparations and repainting into desert camouflage.

Other AdlA fighters in the region included 14 Dassault Mirage 2000 and six Mirage F1CR (along with six C-135FR tankers) plus eight Mirage F1C at Doha International Airport in Qatar under Opération Meteil. The French force was located away from the other coalition air forces, partly due to overcrowding and partly due to a desire to avoid coming under American military control.

Given the threat from Iraqi air defences the Jaguars were given a maximised self-defence capability, including a Phimat or BOZ-103 flare/chaff dispenser under the starboard wing and a Barracuda, Barem or Remora jammer pod under the port wing. A 56-cartridge Alkan 5020/5021 conformal flare/chaff launcher was fitted under each wing root and the tail cone held an 18-cartridge Lacroix IRCM dispenser. The centreline pylon was kept free for an ATLIS II laser designator pod or a 1,200L drop tank. The Jaguars had no ability to carry Magic IR-homing AAMs without sacrificing one of the outboard underwing chaff or ECM pods.

Following FATac's realisation how serious the navigational challenges were, a dozen Pronav 100 GPS units were purchased and shipped out at the end of January to enable the pilots to update the navigation computer manually. Following pilot training, the first mission with GPS was flown on 8 February.

Operation Desert Shield gave way to Operation Desert Storm to liberate Kuwait from Iraqi occupation. On 16 January 1991 the Chief of Staff of the Armed Forces, General Maurice Schmitt, passed on President François Mitterrand's authorisation (following a favourable vote of confidence by the Parliament) to Lieutenant General Michel Roquejeoffre, the Commander of the French forces, to take part in offensive operations and place his aircraft under the operational control of Allied Forces Central Europe. General Schmitt also established the missions assigned to the air element:

- ALPHA: on D-Day (beginning of the air offensive), a Jaguar raid on Ahmed Al-Jaber airbase in Kuwait, which was suspected of housing a *Scud* short-range ballistic missile facility. Their potential chemical, biological and nuclear capabilities were a serious hazard to coalition forces and neighbouring nations (the *Scuds* were a mix of Soviet-supplied R-17 (NATO designation SS-1C *Scud-B*) and Iraqi indigenous developments).
- BRAVO: on days D +1 and D +2, attacks focusing on coastal objectives in Kuwait.
- CHARLIE: from day G -4, attacks on objectives located in the planned engagement area of the Daguet Division (the name adopted for the French ground forces).
- DELTA: from G-Day (beginning of the ground offensive), support of coalition troops with priority for the Daguet Division.

Jaguars of the 11ème Escadre on the apron at Al-Ahsa Airport, Dhahran in Saudi Arabia during Opération Daguet. *Author's Collection*

Seen during a combat sortie armed with four bombs, one R.550 Magic AAM and a Barax-NG ECM pod, is A97 of EC 2/7. *Author's Collection*

An old workhorse taxying out for a mission. The first production Jaguar A1 armed with two HE bombs and Barax-NG ECM. *Author's Collection*

The weathered A104 was one of the Operation Daguet aircraft. The markings are those of EC 2/11, Escadrille SPA 91. The CT 51 jamming pod fitted outboard was only used for training by the early 1990s. *Terry Panopalis Collection*

The first combat sortie took place on 17 January, the Mission ALPHA attack on Ahmed Al-Jaber airbase located 32nm (60km) south-west of Kuwait City by 12 Jaguars, mostly from EC 2/11. They were supported by USAF McDonnell Douglas F-4G Phantom 'Wild Weasel' and General Dynamics F-16Cs for the Suppression of Enemy Air Defences (SEAD). The Jaguars attacked from an altitude of 100ft (30m), aiming their Belouga cluster bombs at the suspected hardened *Scud* shelters (the aim being to hamper access to the shelters rather than destroying the missiles and their potentially dangerous chemical warheads) and dropping retarded 550lb (250kg) bombs on the hangars. The pilots fired their 30mm cannon to keep the defenders' heads down and the downward-firing Alkan IRCM launchers sent their flares hurtling towards the ground, bouncing off the sand back into the sky. At an average altitude of just 23ft (7m), four of the aircraft took AAA damage from the defences of an Iraqi divisional command post that was unmarked on the pilots' maps. Lieutenant Christ's Jaguar, callsign 'Jupiter 6', in the first wave was hit by a 7.62mm bullet from an AK-47 that damaged the flying control rods.

The second wave of Jaguars (having accidentally missed the entry point for their attack run) flew into the now alerted defences and encountered a barrage of ZSU 23-4 *Shilka* 23mm cannon fire and 9K32 Strela-2 (SA-7 *Grail*) MANPADS. Captaine Alain Mahagne, 'Jupiter 11', was injured by an AK-47 bullet that passed through the canopy, through his flying helmet and exited via the other side of the canopy; miraculously he escaped with only a scalp injury and managed to fly the aircraft back to Al-Ahsa, collapsing from blood loss and shock following landing. Jaguar A91, piloted by Captaine Jean François Hummel, 'Jupiter 12', was hit by an SA-7 *Grail*. The missile exploded behind the aircraft, knocking out the starboard engine and damaging the rear fuselage. Hummel managed to divert and land at Jubail. 'Jupiter 9', flown by Lieutenant Bonnafoux, was also hit by small arms fire. The port engine oil tank was blown open and the engine seized but Bonnafoux joined formation with the equally one-engine-powered Hummel to land safely at Jubail.

A91 – a veteran of Chad and damaged during the strike on Ouadi Doum – was dismantled and flown back to France in two Transall C-160 transports. Subsequently used as a training aid for combat damage repairs techniques, since 2020 it has been on display at the Musée de l'Air et de l'Espace in Paris, showing its battle scars.

Following the damage to four Jaguars (one write-off and three out of action for 72 hours), General Roquejeoffre asked General Schmitt to pause the

planned raids as he feared that the rate of attrition would deprive the Daguet Division of air cover during the land offensive. However, President Mitterrand refused to ground the aircraft while the rest of the coalition continued flying.

Learning from the previous day's events, the next mission on the 18th was flown at medium altitude to keep out of the reach of AAA. The 12 Jaguars attacked a munitions dump at Ras Al Quilayah, located on the coast 16.5nm (30.5km) outside Kuwait City. Four Jaguars attacked the storage buildings with AS.30L ASMs from an altitude of 4,000ft (1,220m), while the other eight released their 250kg bombs in diving attacks from 15,000ft (4,570m). The facility was attacked again on the following day.

The pilots had dropped their external fuel tanks during the first two missions but they were told to stop jettisoning them because stocks were already running low. Flying at medium altitudes had the bonus of reducing the induced drag caused by the external tanks and improved the range.

Immediately after the first raid on the 17th, the Minister of Defence, Jean-Pierre Chevènement, declared that French missions would be limited to Kuwaiti territory, which provoked a political outcry and public criticism. On 20 January Mitterrand contradicted Chevènement by asserting that military-industrial targets located in Iraq would be attacked. The following day, the Chief of Staff, Admiral Lanxade, transmitted the authorisation to the Joint Allied Headquarters and planning for raids against targets in Iraq began on the 22nd. Poor weather had prevented any further missions over Kuwait until the 22nd, when six Jaguars attacked three Iraqi warships at the Kuwaiti Naval Base with AS.30Ls, causing substantial damage to the vessels. The following day eight aircraft attacked artillery positions with 250kg bombs.

Operations ramped up to two sorties per day from the 24th. Eight Jaguars attacked a Republican Guard artillery position with 250kg bombs, scoring at least one direct hit despite the heavy AAA, although two pilots decided to attack the alternate target. On the following days, ground-attack missions were flown against targets at Tallil, Shaiba and Jalibah, with particular emphasis on attacking Republican Guard positions along the Kuwait–Saudi border. The Jaguars were often accompanied by Mirage F1CRs for navigational support.

Bombing from medium altitude involved a 40° dive with the distance to the target ascertained by the laser rangefinder. The increased altitude, however, exacerbated the obscuring effect of the dust on the ground and reduced the laser's effectiveness. The pilots increased the dive angle to 60° to compensate, entering the dive at 20,000ft (6,095m) at 350kt, releasing at 15,000ft (4,570m) and pulling out at 10,000ft (3,050m) at 550kt (this was within AAA range). The arrival of the GPS receivers during February made it possible to achieve good accuracy with bomb release in horizontal flight at medium altitude.

Jaguar A67 of EC 1/7 shows off the post-Desert Storm desert colour scheme of light brown and sand and an array of conventional HE bombs and Matra rocket pods in 1992. ***Blue Envoy Collection***

On 2 February six Jaguars attacked an ammunition depot. A special mission to destroy vital bridges spanning the Euphrates using AS.30Ls was carried out with several sorties on 10 February. Following this, the missions returned to battlefield targets and another ammunition depot was bombed by six Jaguars on the 15th. In addition to ammunition depots, other targets attacked in this period included command posts, runways, bridges, logistical bases and artillery or armoured positions in the field.

At least one potential chemical weapons storage site was attacked; on return to Al-Ahsa the aircraft were parked in a remote area of the airfield and decontaminated as a precaution by groundcrews in NBC gear. Precautions at the start of the deployment saw the pilots being issued with protective NBC clothing, including a semi-rigid hood over the pilot's helmet and an atropine syringe as a nerve agent antidote. Switching off the air conditioning to the cockpit removed the chance of sucking in potentially lethal particulates, but it meant that the cockpit was like an oven.The final day of operations before the ceasefire took effect was on 28 February, which saw the first (for the Jaguar and the AdlA) – and only – release of two LGBs from the Jaguars. Following the ceasefire, the Jaguars began to return home on 5 March when four Jaguars returned to Toul, accompanied by a C-135F.

The Jaguars during Opération Daguet flew a total of 568 sorties, 1,088 flying hours and conducted 185 air-to-air refuellings. Most of the Jaguars' 140 ground-attack sorties were made in support of Daguet Division operations. The AdlA's aircraft dropped a total of 1,467 bombs (1,434 free-fall and 33 retarded), which outstripped supply, leading the Jaguars to carry retarded bombs stripped of their parachutes as makeshift freefall bombs until the USAF could supply 500lb (227kg) Mk.82 bombs. Jaguars also fired 100mm rockets with good precision and 57 AS.30L missiles were launched.

AdlA Iraq sorties				
Aircraft	Before 17 Jan	17 Jan – 27	Feb 28 Feb – 31 Mar	Total sorties
Jaguar	778	568	197	1,543
Mirage 2000	659	512	284	1,455
Mirage F1CR	398	96	97	591
Total Sorties	1,835	1,176	578	3,589

AdlA Iraq sorties by role			
Sorties 17 Jan – 28 Feb	Jaguar	Mirage 2000	Mirage F1CR
Assault	536	–	48
Escort	–	77	-
Reconnaissance/Assault	–	95	-
Air Combat	–	336	–
Reconnaissance/Search	–	–	21
Photo-Reconnaissance	13	–	25
Other	19	4	2
Total	568	512	96

Following the genocidal attacks on the Kurds by Saddam Hussein's forces after the defeat of Desert Storm, Operation Provide Comfort was launched in April to protect them, backed up by a UN designated 'No-Fly Zone' north of the 36th Parallel under Security Resolution 687. Five Jaguars of EC 3/11 arrived at Incirlik Air Base in Turkey during April 1991 under Opération Aconit to provide an armed reconnaissance force for the northern 'No-Fly Zone'. Two of the aircraft carried the RP 36P reconnaissance pod on the centreline as well as the internal Omera 40 camera. The AdlA detachments at Incirlik rotated, the Jaguars returning in June 1993 before passing the recce role to the Mirage F1CR in March 1994. The Jaguars would play no further part, but the AdlA continued to contribute to Operation Provide Comfort II until December 1996.

In-flight refuelling capability was important in enabling the Jagar to fulfil OPEX across Africa and the Middle East and even to the Caribbean. *Author's Collection*

Peacekeeping

As the 1990s dawned the Cold War came to an end with the collapse of the Communist regimes in the former Soviet Union and its satellite states behind the 'Iron Curtain'. NATO members began to take advantage of the so-called 'Peace Dividend' to divert defence spending into other public budgets. Fears of nuclear war also eased and many tactical and strategic nuclear weapons were dismantled; the nuclear strike role assigned to EC 1/7 and 3/7 was withdrawn in September 1991 (4/7 'Limousin' had already disbanded on 31 July 1989) and the AN 52 nuclear bomb was retired. The two Escadrons were reoriented to the tactical ground-attack role with precision strike using laser-guided weapons and reconnaissance.

The drawdown of the Jaguar force began when EC 4/11 'Jura' was disbanded on 30 June 1992. By this time only 25 of the Jaguar E trainers were still operational. In May 1994 EC 2/7 'Languedoc' attained 75,000 flying hours on Jaguars and had trained almost 750 pilots. The Escadron took on surplus aircraft from the former EC 4/11 to form a third Escadrille on 1 September, SPA 154 'Grue' (Crane), and in October 1995 three Alpha Jets were delivered in an effort to reduce the flying hours on the ageing Jaguar airframes.

EC 1/11 'Roussillon' was disbanded on 31 July 1994 and its aircraft were passed to EC 3/11 'Corse' to form a third Escadrille, while the precision-bombing mission was passed to EC 2/11 'Vosges'. As the 11ème Escadre's units were disbanded, Jaguars were transferred to the 7ème Escadre, whose Escadrons were increased from 15 to 20 aircraft each.

Co-operation with allies was still important. In early February 1993 Jaguars participated in Exercise Northern Banner in the UK, flying offensive support sorties and being refuelled by the RAF's Handley Page Victor K.2 tankers (they would be retired shortly afterwards). In January 1992 a detachment from EC 2/11 visited French Guiana for one month to assist the training of the air defence controllers at the Kourou military control centre.

The break-up of Yugoslavia unleashed a brutal civil war that affected all of the breakaway states. The worst of these conflicts was that between Serbia and Bosnia-Herzegovina, which saw much brutal fighting, including the siege of Sarajevo, and degenerated into genocidal killings. The UN intervened with peacekeeping forces in an attempt to limit the fighting and bring both sides back to the negotiating table. Operation Sky Monitor was set up under UN Security Council Resolution 781 in October 1992 to oversee a specifically military 'No-Fly Zone' to stop Serbian Air Force flights over Bosnia-Herzegovina, which in the event proved powerless to stop infringements by the Serbs. Under Opération Balbuzard (Osprey), EC 1/11 deployed to Solenzara in Corsica on 26 January 1993 on alert to intervene if necessary. The first deployment by the 11ème Escadre to Istrana Air Base in Italy under Opération Crécerelle

occurred on 6 April 1993 and aircraft from EC 3/11 and EC 3/7 were also based at Rivolto. The main task was to provide support to the United Nations Protection Force (UNPROFOR), including targets that threatened the security of UN declared safe areas, with a stand-off precision strike capability with the AS.30L and 1,000lb (550kg) GBU-12B Paveway II LGBs with the ATLIS II pod, as well as reconnaissance.

Six days after the Jaguars arrived at Istrana, Operation Sky Monitor was succeeded by Operation Deny Flight to enforce UN Security Council Resolution 816, which prohibited all Serbian flights by aircraft or helicopters over Bosnia-Herzegovina. The operation ran from 12 April 1993 until 20 December 1995. The first French armed attack was on 21 November 1994, when two Jaguars attacked the Serb-occupied Udbina air base in Croatia, dropping LGBs on the runways and taxiways. By the end of 1994 there were four Jaguars based at Istrana with another four on standby for deployment at Toul-Rosières if required.

Operation Deliberate Force was a sustained air campaign conducted during 30 August to 20 September 1995 in collaboration with UNPROFOR ground operations to degrade the military capability of the Bosnian Serb Army following the Srebrenica and Markale massacres and the shelling of the Sarajevo marketplace on 28 August. The operation involved 400 aircraft, striking 338 targets, dropping 1,026 bombs, of which 708 were precision-guided weapons. The AdlA's contribution included six Jaguars, which conducted 63 strike missions. The only NATO aircraft lost during the operation was a Dassault Mirage 2000N of EC 2/3 'Champagne', which was shot down by a SAM on the first day of operations (the pilot and navigator were captured and finally released on 12 December).

The mission assigned on 6 September was to attack a 460ft (140m)-high communications antenna and associated buildings at Stolyce. Several sorties by other NATO aircraft in the preceding days had already tried – and failed – to destroy it. En route to the target, the Airborne Command and Control Centre tried to re-task the flight with supporting a Dutch Army unit on the ground, but the Jaguars were not well equipped for such a mission and handed it to a nearby flight of RAF GR.1A Jaguars to prosecute while they pressed on to Stolyce. Despite intensive AAA fire and SAMs, two well-aimed Paveway II LGBs brought the tower down.

Following negotiations and the resulting Dayton

ABOVE LEFT A pair of EC 4/7 Jaguars, one of which was A64, were painted in the colours of the tricolour in July 1989 to mark the disbanding of the Escadron. A64 went on to serve with EC 4/11 and EC 3/7. ***Terry Panopalis Collection***

ABOVE RIGHT Escadrille SPA 31 'Archer Grec' turned 80 years old in 1995 and Jaguar E30 was painted in this attractive scheme to commemorate the occasion. ***Terry Panopalis Collection***

Jaguar A29 of EC 2/11 received this special paintwork to celebrate the Jaguar's 20th anniversary in 1993. ***Terry Panopalis Collection***

ABOVE EC 1/7 Jaguar A138 approaching a USAF tanker over the Adriatic Sea during Operation Joint Forge in April 2003. *USAF*

RIGHT In July 1995 A46 was over 20 years old but still going strong, assigned to EC 1/7, Escadrille SPA 77 'Croix de Jerusalem'. An AS.37 Martel is fitted under the fuselage, the Escadron having taken on EC 3/11's air defence suppression role when that unit was disbanded. *Terry Panopalis Collection*

Peace Accords, which were formally signed in Paris on 14 December 1995, Operation Deny Flight ended six days later and from 22 December the AdlA's detachment came under the new Opération Salamandre (Salamander).

War soon returned to the Balkans. Tensions in Kosovo against Serb rule by the Albanian community finally escalated into violence. Attacks by the Kosovo Albanian rebel group, the Kosovo Liberation Army, led to a Serb armed response, which in late February 1998 erupted into an armed conflict. Efforts by NATO to broker peace talks failed and the decision was made to resort to an intensive bombing campaign to degrade Serbia's military capabilities and to force a withdrawal from Kosovo. The campaign, Operation Allied Force, lasted from 24 March to 11 June 1999 and involved up to 1,000 aircraft, including operations from aircraft carriers stationed in the Adriatic and Tomahawk cruise missiles fired from aircraft, ships and submarines. More than 38,000 combat missions were flown.

Six Jaguars from 7ème Escadre were deployed to Istrana as part of France's contribution under Opération Trident. This deployment built on the forces and staff already deployed in-theatre for Opération Salamandre, the number of personnel increasing from 193 to 359. The AdlA's campaign began on 24 March when 13 Mirage 2000s and four Jaguars, reinforced by the aircraft carrier group, began attacks that evening. The Jaguars made their first independent attack on 5 April, a pair each armed with two Paveway IIs with another pair equipped with ATLIS II designator pods. The following day all six Jaguars were in action, bombing several targets in Kosovo during daylight hours (the AdlA's only night-capable LGB strike aircraft was the two-seat Mirage 2000D). The Jaguars were involved in a controversial incident on the 14th when two convoys of refugees were attacked after they were misidentified as Serb military units. A further six Jaguars were deployed to Istrana in May.

The NATO air operation ended on 20 June when the last Serbian forces withdrew from Kosovo, although Jaguars remained in the Balkans to monitor the situation until 2004, with EC 1/7 making the final deployment. The Jaguars had flown 668 flying hours during Opération Trident at the cost of 17.4 million French Francs – or 26,000 Francs per flying hour. The figure was double that of the Mirage 2000's 19,950 Francs per hour, a sign of how the ageing Jaguar was becoming expensive to maintain.

Finale

During the late 1990s the Jaguar force shrank further as preparations began to induct the new Dassault Rafale into service. A display at Saint-Dizier on 4 June 1993 marked the 20th anniversary of the Jaguar in AdlA service. In an accident on 14 December 1994, Colonel Ricour and Lieutenant Colonel Bawejski, the commanders of BA 136 Toul and EC 3/11 'Corse'

In July 2002 the maintenance unit ESTS 2E-007 said goodbye to the Jaguar with this colourful farewell paintwork. *Terry Panopalis Collection*

respectively, had to eject from their Jaguar E, which crashed on to the village of Diane-Capelle in Moselle, making a large crater in the main street, but thankfully causing no casualties on the ground – Ricour and Bawejski were injured.

EC 2/11 'Vosges' was disbanded on 31 July 1996 at Toul and EC 3/11 'Corse' followed on 25 June 1997, Bawejski having made the unit's last Jaguar flight on 30 April. EC 3/11's electronic warfare and anti-radar role passed to EC 1/7 'Provence', so did Escadrille SPA 91. The Martel was finally retired from service in 1998.

The Jaguar force was reduced drastically when both EC 2/7 'Argonne' and 3/7 'Languedoc' were disbanded on 8 June 2001, leaving EC 1/7 as the sole Escadron with a total of 35 Jaguars. The six Jaguar Es assigned to the training unit CITac 339 'Aquitaine' were retired on 10 July and the Jaguar conversion training role was passed to EC 1/7's Escadrille SPA 91, which gained the Jaguar Es and Alpha Jets from EC 2/7. In July 2002 the Saint Dizier maintenance unit ESTS 2E.007 GERMAS was stood down. In 2003 the Jaguar E began to be utilised to tow air-to-air gunnery targets, replacing the Mirage F1Cs previously used.

Jaguar A97 of EC 1/7 crashed near Bar de Luc on 24 February 1999; the pilot ejected successfully. The final Jaguar accident was on 19 November 2001 when E39 crashed. A total of 59 Jaguars were written off in accidents or were combat losses (29.5% of the fleet).

Saint-Dizier held a second major birthday celebration on 24 May 2003 when the 30th anniversary was celebrated. During 2004 EC 1/7 maintained 19 Jaguar A and four Jaguar E and carried out a final peacekeeping deployment to the Balkans. The end though was nearing. At the end of February 2005 the final live firing training took place at BA 120 Cazaux and on 1 July EC 1/7 retired its last six Jaguars. The unit bowed out in style, the ceremony including Jaguar E22 sporting a special paint scheme illustrating the insignia of the

Present at the disbandment of EC 1/7 at BA 113 Saint-Dizier on 1 July 2005 was the last production Jaguar E. Somewhat surprisingly, E40 is today preserved at the Museo Nacional Aeronautico Y del Espacio in Santiago, Chile. *Author's Collection*

E22 received special artwork for the disbandment of EC 1/7 and retirement of the Jaguar. Today E22 resides at the Conservatoire d'Aéronefs non Operationnels Preserves et Exposes at Châteaudun. *Author's Collection*

FAR LEFT **The starboard side of E22's tail fin received a jaguar's head 'bursting' through the skin of the airframe.** ***Author's Collection***

LEFT **The port side was adorned with the head of a panther.** ***Author's Collection***

various units to have operated the Jaguar and with special artwork of a jaguar on the tail fin. Thus the first Jaguar Escadron was also the last and 32 years of operations were brought to an end.

Some 2,000 pilots had flown the Jaguar, which had been maintained by around 10,000 groundcrew during its 32 years of service. Around 760,000 flying hours had been accumulated. Lieutenant Huet became the first pilot to attain 2,000 flying hours on 29 June 1983 during a long-range training mission in Jaguar A48 from Istres to the Balearic Islands for a low-level recce before returning to Saint-Dizier, with aerial refuelling on both the outward and homeward legs.

A small group of pilots achieved 3,000 flying hours. The first was Captaine Hache on 12 January 1989, reaching the milestone while leading an eight-aircraft formation on a training assault mission in the Massif Central in Jaguar A29. Having made his first Jaguar flight on 10 February 1975, Hache was one of the first in-flight refuelling-qualified pilots and took part in Opération Lamantin. He retired from the AdlA with a total of 3,047 hours 45 minutes flying Jaguars. Adjudant Chef (Chief Warrant Officer) Bourdier achieved his 3,000th flying hour on 12 April 1989 and by the time of his last Jaguar flight on 14 September 1990 had amassed the most hours of any AdlA pilot, 3,333 hours 20 minutes. Lieutenant Colonel Dardard's Jaguar career totalled 3,177 hours 20 minutes, which included ten OPEX and 134 combat sorties in Chad, Kuwait/Iraq and the Balkans. Jacques Deltrieu also amassed more than 3,000 hours during 1975 to 1991. Captaine Vincent de Gournay achieved his 3,000th flying hour on 11 July 1997, and his final flight a few weeks later brought his tally to 3,007 hours. Captaine Tani achieved the milestone a few months later, having made both of his first and last flights in Jaguar E28. Captaine Lange achieved 3,000 hours on 18 December 1998 during a 12-aircraft assault mission and he logged a total of 3,018 hours 40 minutes.

Captaine Bonnaffoux was the last pilot to reach the milestone on 9 January 2001 while flying Jaguar E24 on a low-level combat training sortie, including aerial refuelling from a C-135FR – this flight brought E24's total flying time to over 6,000 hours.

The AdlA's Jaguars had deployed in combat across Africa, the Middle East and the Balkans, achieving some notable successes, but also – uniquely of all the air forces operating the Jaguar – had sadly suffered combat losses during these operations. The Jaguars were never extensively upgraded, retaining much of their 1960s-era avionics and the original Adour Mk.102 engines to the end. But they were rugged and maintainable and proved ideal for out-of-area operations in remote regions, despite the lack of hot-and-high performance from the Adours. Although it has often been said that Dassault never supported its stepchild, favouring its own Mirage lineage instead, there is no doubt that the Jaguar played an important role in the AdlA's operations for more than a quarter of a century and had done everything asked of it and more.

Beneath the cockpit of E22 were the insignia of every AdlA unit to have flown the Jaguar. ***Author's Collection***

CHAPTER SIX

Desert Storm

On 2 August 1990 Iraqi forces invaded Kuwait as Iraq's dictator Saddam Hussein attempted to annex Kuwait's oil reserves. This led to a concerted response from the United Nations (UN) and Security Council Resolution 678 called on Iraq to withdraw its troops by 15 January 1991. Failing that, the coalition forces were empowered to use 'all necessary means' to evict the Iraqi forces. The small nation of Kuwait had a relatively small military and was quickly overwhelmed. Fears that Saddam Hussein might go on to attack Saudi Arabia led to Operation Desert Shield, led by the United States, and a coalition of military forces gathered in the region. The government of the United Kingdom was keen to contribute forces and deployments began under Operation Granby. Among the first Royal Air Force assets to arrive in-theatre were 12 Jaguar GR.1As. As it became clear that Saddam was unwilling to leave Kuwait, the coalition began to explore how they might militarily liberate the state. This led to Operation Desert Storm, which began on 16 January 1991. The Jaguar was to play a central role in the air campaign and performed flawlessly, adapting to a new concept of operations at medium altitude and new weapons.

A pair of Jaguars during Operation Granby. The lead aircraft is GR.1A XZ358, which was named 'Diplomatic Service' by its pilot, Flight Lieutenant Roger Crowder, completing 14 missions during the conflict. ***MoD via Terry Panopalis Collection***

Among the first deployment of Jaguars in October 1990 under Operation Desert Shield following the Iraqi invasion of Kuwait to protect Saudi Arabia was GR.1A XZ396. In the background is a McDonnell Douglas F-15E Strike Eagle of 4th Tactical Fighter Wing, USAF. *USAF*

Preparations

Forces from the USA and coalition allies began assembling in the region to protect Saudi Arabia. No fewer than 2,250 aircraft were gathered, 1,800 of them being provided from US forces. The RAF deployed Jaguar GR.1A and Panavia Tornado GR.1 strike aircraft, supported by the Hawker Siddeley Buccaneer S.2B for laser-guided bomb (LGB) designation using AN/AVQ-23E PAVE SPIKE laser designator pods, as well as Tornado F.3 fighters, Hawker Siddeley Nimrod MR.2 maritime reconnaissance aircraft and tanker assets. A dozen Jaguar GR.1As from No. 6 Squadron at Coltishall arrived at the Royal Air Force of Oman's (RAFO) airbase of Thumrait on 12 August. At the time of the invasion four Jaguars had been participating in the Reconnaissance Air Meet RAM 90 competition at Bergstrom Air Force Base in Texas and were quickly flown back to the UK. On 1 October Air Vice Marshal Andrew Wilson was appointed as commander of the British air forces, being relieved by Air Vice Marshal Bill Wratten from 17 November when the second roulement arrived in Bahrain.

The Iraqi Air Force posed a formidable threat for the planners. It possessed at least 500 fighters and 300 ground-attack aircraft and bombers, including: 60 Dassault Mirage F1EQ armed with Matra R.550 Magic infrared (IR)-homing and Super 530F radar-guided air-to-air missiles (AAMs), 220 MiG-21 *Fishbed* interceptors, 55 MiG-23MS *Flogger-E* and 22 MiG-23ML *Flogger-G* equipped with R-23 (NATO designation AA-7 *Apex*) AAMs, around 33 Mach 3-capable MiG-25 *Foxbat* in both interceptor and reconnaissance versions and up to 40 new MiG-29 *Fulcrum-C* fighters. The attack aircraft included 170 of the Sukhoi Su-7, Su-17 and Su-22 *Fitter* family, 36 MiG-23BN *Flogger-H* fighter-bombers and 61 Sukhoi Su-25 *Frogfoot* armoured ground-attack aircraft.

Ground-based air defences included hundreds of batteries of surface-to-air missiles (SAMs) and anti-aircraft artillery (AAA) with a mix of Western and Soviet equipment. Iraq operated at least a dozen SAM systems covering the full range of engagement zones from shoulder-fired man-portable air-defence systems (MANPADS) to high-altitude missiles, including mobile systems to accompany armoured formations. It was hoped that the Soviet-style centralised air defence system with top-down command and control would lead to sluggish reaction times and the reliance on communication links was a weakness that could be capitalised upon by striking these nodes. Much of the Central Tactical Trials Organisation's (CTTO) input into the Jaguar Tactical Manual for Operation Granby was based heavily on the existing standard Warsaw Pact-focused manuals. This was valid given the weapon systems and command structures inherited from Eastern Bloc military advisers and that much of the Jaguar's weaponry had been designed to counter Soviet equipment.

The Jaguar would be operating in its normal Offensive Air Support role. This involved Close Air Support (CAS), Battlefield Air Interdiction (BAI) as well as Air Interdiction and Offensive Counter Air operations against enemy aviation and air defence facilities respectively. CAS would involve engaging enemy armoured and motorised formations. Typical BAI targets included headquarters and command posts, artillery positions and any Nuclear, Biological and Chemical (NBC)-capable weapon systems such as *Scud* short-range ballistic missiles, multiple rocket launchers (MRLs) or long-range artillery.

The BL.755 cluster bomb and 1,000lb (454kg) general-purpose bombs were the most effective weapons for knocking out vehicles and mobile SAM systems. The BL.755 had 147 high-explosive anti-tank bomblets, which were improved to counter the latest Soviet tanks in the upgraded IBL.755 and could penetrate more than 220mm of armour. Even if they missed a tank, each bomblet created 2,200 fragments on exploding that were capable of penetrating 4mm steel plate. The 2.75in (68mm) Matra SNEB rockets could penetrate up to 350mm of armour.

The Jaguar GR.1As selected for deployment were modified in two stages (a third stage was incomplete by the time of the ceasefire) under the Jaguar Fast Track Modifications Programme. Up to 28 aircraft were to be modified to meet the threat levels posed by Iraqi defences. Much of the work was carried out on a Special Trial Fit (STF) basis, with the Jaguar Aircraft Investigation and Development Team doing much of the design work. The Controller Air (CA) Clearance was extended to a maximum ground air temperature of 45°C for the aircraft and its systems (for example, GEC-Marconi tested the Laser Ranger and Marked-Target Seeker (LRMTS) to a maximum temperature of 65°C).

The Stage One modifications were carried out on 12 aircraft during August 1990 at Coltishall shortly before the aircraft flew out to Oman. The modifications were at the minimum level to allow for combat operations and to cope with the hot and dusty conditions. Communications interoperability with the United States Air Force (USAF) required HAVE QUICK radios using a frequency-hopping system to lessen the chances of interception and jamming. To meet the urgent need, AN/ARC-164 RT105 HAVE QUICK II UHF radios were taken out of British Aerospace (BAe) Hawk T.1 trainers and another ten were loaned from the Royal Navy. These were fitted under Modification Mod. 1346 (70 new sets were eventually ordered to equip the Jaguars, 28 Tornado F.3s plus spares and ground-based sets, costing £770,000).

Minor modifications were made to the air conditioning system to reduce canopy fogging and improve ground cooling. The head-up display (HUD) warning panel and G-meter were removed.

The aircraft were painted in 'desert pink' – colloquially known as 'Laura Ashley Pink' – Alkali Removable Temporary Finish (ARTF) paint. The colour scheme was designed by Royal Aircraft Establishment (RAE) expert Philip Barley (the Barley Grey air defence colour scheme adopted in the early 1980s was named after him) and was hastily applied within five hours with the help of visiting Air Cadets at Coltishall. Some Jaguars later sported a false cockpit canopy painted beneath the nose in matt black paint to confuse ground observers and enemy pilots.The Stage 1 effort totalled 2,600 man-hours and had involved the efforts of several units and training schools to collect all of the necessary items. A number of problems arose during the initial roulement due to the hot climate. These included canopy expansion, cockpit misting, low engine thrust, fuel leaks and poor engine starting. All of these problems were resolved in future modifications.

The Stage Two modifications for the second roulement of 12 aircraft (when XX754 was lost in-theatre on 13 November, a replacement 13th aircraft was modified) were conducted between September and November at Coltishall by the groundcrew of No. 54(F) Squadron and the newly formed Jaguar Fast Track Modification Team. To make space for this effort, all routine maintenance was passed to RAF Abingdon. Several aircraft in storage at RAF Shawbury as well as others undergoing maintenance at Coltishall and Abingdon were released for the Fast Track Programme or were used to support the combat work-up flying at Coltishall. The Stage Two aircraft incorporated all the Stage One modifications, fixes for problems encountered in-theatre plus new upgrades. Stage Two was a more considered programme combining several strands: local experience from the RAFO's Jaguar Internationals, a previous Jaguar War Measures Paper that had laid out some wartime improvements and items that were already approved or undergoing trials that were worthwhile fitting if availability allowed. Where necessary, a second line maintenance overhaul was carried out to clear the aircraft for up to 250 flying hours in-theatre.

Compatibility for night vision goggles (NVG) was added. The RAF had begun NVG trials in 1976 and the Jaguar had participated in CTTO's Trial Sure. The use of NVGs was cleared in October 1986 and several GR.1A and T.2A aircraft were fitted with interim NVG-compatible cockpit lighting following trials during 1988–89. (NVGs intensify the visible red and near infrared part of the spectrum and normal cockpit lighting is too bright to allow the NVGs to function properly so is modified to filter out this unwanted light. Anti-collision strobe beacons and navigation lights also cause similar problems.) A limited training

One of the Stage One Jaguars at Coltishall prior to deploying to Oman, resplendent in its Desert Pink colour scheme. An AN/ALQ-101(V)10 ECM pod is fitted to the outboard pylon. *Terry Panopalis Collection*

programme allowed Coltishall to maintain six pilots with NVG expertise (two per squadron). Air Staff Requirement ASR.1011 was issued in 1987 for a definitive cockpit lighting fit, but by 1990 was still at the mock-up stage at Warton. The Stage Two aircraft were fitted with an NVG-compatible windscreen and the interim cockpit lighting.

VHS-C videotape recording of the HUD was fitted under STF/JAG/04/08 to meet the operational and political requirements to record all attacks for evidence of collateral damage. A Vinten HUD Camera System was fitted and eight Ground Replay Systems were purchased to review the tapes. Several missions were often recorded on each videotape, but in February 1991 the detachment had to order a thousand more to cover the rate of usage. A total of 34 systems were bought and 27 aircraft fitted and after Granby this equipment was fitted more widely across the fleet.

Under STF/JAG/07/90 the Marconi ARI.18228 Sky Guardian 200-13PD radar warning receiver (RWR) replaced the older Marconi ARI.18223 (ARI is an airborne radio installation). The units fitted were pre-production models and post-Granby the production 200-15 set was fitted to all Jaguars. Like the older ARI.18223, Sky Guardian scanned three sets of frequency bands within the E to J-Bands (Marconi included optionality for C, D and K-Bands) with a threat priority system to indicate the most dangerous threat, and was a modern crystal video set. The display showed the threat detected, for example '18' being displayed would denote a locked-on 9K33 Osa (NATO designation SA-8 *Gecko*) system guiding a missile. These were backed up by audio tones.The AN/ALE-40 chaff/flare dispensers were modified with a new setting allowing operation as soon as the wheels lifted off the runway to enable use on take-off and the sequencer was modified to allow the firing of three flares at two-second intervals to defeat MANPADS following the results of CTTO trials.

The latest Cossor Mk.12 Identification Friend or Foe (IFF) system was fitted under STF/JAG/11/90 to ensure compatibility with US forces, the important factor being Mode 4 capability that was used by the latest US SAMs and the AIM-120 AMRAAM beyond-visual-range AAM. A new IFF code change panel was designed by BAe and installed.

Once in-theatre, a second V/UHF HAVE QUICK II radio was installed to improve communications with the Airborne Warning and Control System (AWACS) airborne controllers. The original HF radio was retained and this proved very useful as few other coalition aircraft had them and it enabled the pilots to radio

One of the first roulement GR.1As is prepared for a sortie. Efforts were made to reduce the airframe's radar cross section on the Stage Two Jaguars by fitting RAM to the LRMTS nose windows, intakes and leading edges. *USAF*

their reconnaissance reports back to base while in flight. The decision was made to fit the Jaguar International's overwing AAM pylons to provide a self-defence capability of two AIM-9 Sidewinder IR-homing AAMs without reducing the stores capability of the underwing pylons. GR.1A XZ385 was used for the trial installation at Warton in August 1990. The installation took just six days and three weeks of flight trials were flown at the Aeroplane and Armament Experimental Establishment (A&AEE) at Boscombe Down, with operational clearance gained a week later. BAe engineers carried out the delicate task of drilling the holes into the upper wing skins but RAF technicians did much of the electrical work. Rather than the AIM-9G Sidewinder usually assigned to the Jaguar, the improved AIM-9L with increased off-boresight capability for its IR seeker was carried.

A new rocket projectile had been introduced shortly before the deployment to replace the SNEB rocket. The Canadian Bristol Aerospace CRV-7 was based on the standard 2.75in (68mm) folding-fin rocket but its velocity was three times greater than the SNEB for improved accuracy and range. The stand-off range was up to 15,200ft (4,630m). Its improved kinetic performance also increased its lethality to ground targets. The RAF selected the RLU 5002/B (C15)-engined CRV-7 variant with 13lb (5.8kg) RA-79 high-explosive, semi-armour-piercing warheads (which had been designed for the anti-shipping role). They were launched from 19-tube LAU 5003B/A pods as well as the six-round LAU 5002B/A training pod. Initially, only the inner underwing pylons were modified to accept the LAU pods, but all the aircraft were later retrofitted to make the outer pylons compatible.

Shortly before the deployment, the MoD had tasked the CTTO to trial high-angle dive Paveway II LGB deliveries. Clearance was obtained for the Buccaneer, Tornado and Jaguar on the basis of only six weapon drops. As it turned out, the Jaguar was not used for LGB delivery.

Before the Gulf War, the Jaguar's radar cross section (RCS) and IR signature had been measured in trials. The RCS peaks were found to be from the fuselage/wing joints, the LRMTS bay in the nose, the air intakes and the engines. Given the threat environment posed by Iraqi air defence systems, the RAF decided to apply RCS reduction measures as even small changes could make a large difference to detection and lock-on probabilities. The effort began with the Tornado fleet and the same methods were applied to the Jaguar. On 24 August 1990 BAe proposed its package of RCS measures using materials and paints from Plessey and Imperial Chemical Industries. Radar-absorbent material (RAM) tiles would be fitted inside the intakes and RAM paint would be applied on the intake lips (inside and outside), intake diverter and all leading edges (wings, slats, tailplane, tail fin and pylons). RAM foam would be inserted into the resonant cavities – the LRMTS compartment and HF radio aerial bay in the starboard wing – as well as frangible bungs for the cannon ports. Expenditure of £450,000 on RCS reduction was authorised under an Urgent Operational Requirement (UOR).

GR.1A XZ356 was fitted by BAe under STF/JAG/18/90 during late September and used in trials alongside three unmodified Jaguars at Boscombe Down and the Larkhill range on 9 and 10 October. An RCS reduction of 30% was observed, with the best results being obtained in the I-band. A lack of thrust was noted but no other problems were found and XZ356 was deployed to the Gulf. A second aircraft, XX767, was modified but on deployment suffered four cases of engine surging. One case was due to the ingestion of lose intake tiles but the other occasions had no obvious cause and ground testing did not replicate the surging. Rolls-Royce was asked to investigate and they discovered that the rough RAM paint applied to the intake lips was the cause and therefore its application was later discontinued.

Colebrand Defence was asked to apply its adhesive transparent radar reflective film to the canopy of the Tornado F.3 to reduce radar returns from within the cockpit and cut the frontal radar signature. This was achieved within a fortnight with good results and very shortly afterwards the MoD requested that the Jaguar also be fitted. This was accomplished within a week and tested at Coltishall in late January 1991 on XX109. Due to the shape of the canopy, the film had to be fitted on the external surface as well as on the windscreen and quarterlights. XZ369 was fitted two weeks later and the RCS measured both in the air and on the ground. Following this, 40 kits were ordered at a cost of £112,000. Sometimes the adhesive failed and the film came off in flight due to the high temperatures in the Gulf. Colebrand also made sacrificial IR transparent covers for the AIM-9 Sidewinder to prevent sand erosion of the seeker head.

XX719, XZ363 and an unidentified GR.1A at readiness during Operation Desert Shield. The F-15Es behind were a generation ahead in terms of avionics but the Jaguar would prove to be equally potent during Operation Desert Storm. *USAF*

Further modifications were made once the aircraft were in-theatre. BAe and No. 226 Operational Conversion Unit (OCU) had been trialling a modified FH 31F/3 Horizon Gyro Unit with an improved caging rate mechanism successfully over the summer of 1990 and it was decided to fit the modified units to the Granby aircraft. The air conditioning was further modified with a new three-way valve to redirect the air away from the HUD and windscreen to the pilot's feet during high-speed, low-level flying when the temperature was below 25°C.

The AN/ALQ-101(V)8 electronic countermeasures (ECM) and Phimat chaff pods were originally non-jettisonable – because of their high monetary value and the risk of them striking the aircraft following release – but the MoD asked BAe to consider whether it was feasible to do so. The Senior Project Engineer at Warton, N J Knight, felt that without wind tunnel tests – which would take up to six months to complete – that he could only give the theoretical answer that it might be possible at low speed. Regardless of this, the RAF went ahead and activated the jettison for these stores. The Adour Mk.104 was also upgraded, providing an extra 7% thrust in an attempt to offset the loss of performance due to the high temperatures. Climbing above 25,000ft (7,620m) still required use of the Partial Throttle Reheat and any manoeuvring at that altitude led to the aircraft losing height with the occasional pop surge. Engine starting proved to be difficult as the starter motor tended to cut out too soon. A modification to the Microturbo Limited starter control box had been implemented on the Hawk years earlier and Mod. MT180 had been proposed for the Jaguar in April 1980 but was cancelled due to the cost involved. The conditions in the Gulf forced the RAF to rethink the necessity of the modification and Microturbo were contracted in November 1990 to modify 40 control boxes (the modification only took four man-hours to implement). Following Granby this modification was fitted across the fleet.

GR.1A XZ355 of No. 41(F) Squadron getting airborne on another training sortie. The Stage One modified Jaguars lacked the overwing rails for AAMs. *USAF*

Newly arrived GR.1A XX748 shows off the Stage Two modifications, the most obvious being the overwing rails for AIM-9L Sidewinders. An ALQ-101(V)10 pod is fitted to port. XX748 later received the code letter 'U' and flew 36 missions during Operation Granby. ***Author's Collection***

Flight trials were conducted to see whether the Jaguar could be refuelled from a Tornado GR.1 equipped with a Sargent Fletcher buddy refuelling tank. The A&AEE used GR.1A XX979 fitted with camera pods for two test sorties. The Tornado carried the pod on the centreline, the evaluation concluded that refuelling by day was feasible, but that the hose, drogue and tanker lighting were inadequate for night-time use (in the event the few modified Tornadoes with loaned buddy tanks from Germany were not deployed).

The shift from low- to medium-level operations caused some problems with the Marconi FIN 1064 computer's Operational Flight Program (OFP). While the ballistic data was available, accuracy deteriorated above 5,000–10,000ft (1,524–3,050m) because the OFP introduced a delay of up to ten seconds between the pilot initiating weapons release and the actual automated separation in diving attacks, so any manoeuvres made during those seconds affected accuracy (the majority of attacks used automated weapons release). In addition, with no 'time to go' indication on the HUD, several pilots thought that they had a bomb hang-up (indeed software problems did lead to 17 hang-ups). The solution was to add a 'time to go circle' to the HUD to give an exact weapon release time. STF/JAG/06/91 covered the enlargement of the HUD's laser range scale circle to 24,000ft (7,315m) for use with the CRV-7 rocket.

In November a Special Flying Instruction was issued restricting the use of automatic toss attacks above 3,000ft (915m) due to an intermittent fault in the OFP that caused premature release in certain attack modes. BAe were directed to develop new ballistic data and the weapon aiming and navigation software was tested on the avionics rig at Warton. The OFP was also upgraded by GEC-Ferranti to accommodate the CRV-7 and the CBU-87 Combined Effects Munition cluster bomb (revisionary modes were used until these software updates were ready).

One in-theatre modification was to cut off the safety guard over the weapons release switch on the control column after pilots found that their flying glove could get stuck underneath the guard and stop weapons release.Following the shift to medium-altitude operations, a UOR was quickly raised for modifications to the BL.755 cluster bomb. Hunting added a Motorola radar altimeter (as used in the WE.177 nuclear weapon) to ensure that the frangible side-petals did not open before the bomb was close to the ground. This new version, designated RBL.755 ('R' for radar), was not ready before Granby ended, so the US-supplied CBU-87, which had a radar altimeter fuze to deploy its bomblets at an altitude of 1,200ft (365m), was used. Only two CBU-87s could be carried as for safety reasons the rear station on the tandem beam was left empty.

The EMI reconnaissance pod was cleared to an extended maximum ground air temperature of 45°C to give confidence that the air conditioning pack would remain effective. Vinten offered two Series 603 Type 18 Long-Range Oblique Photography (LOROP) pods on free loan in November 1990. These had been developed for the British Army for Britten-Norman Islander aircraft operated over Northern Ireland. There was no time to conduct any training before they were sent to the Middle East. The cameras had 36in (914mm) lenses that gave excellent resolution; from 25,000ft (7,620m) each exposure covered an area of 0.5 × 0.5nm (1 × 1km).

The LOROP pod had several drawbacks, however: a narrow field of view made lining up on the target difficult and there was no data annotation facility for the film. Therefore it was later decided to operationally pair two aircraft, one carrying the LOROP and the other with a standard pod fitted with a F126 camera, to give complementary and correlating images. In contrast to the LOROP, each F126 image from 25,000ft covered an area of 4.8 × 4.8nm (9 × 9km) and was the right scale for a 1:500,000 scale map, which was very handy for target plotting.

The Stage Three programme covered 16 Jaguars, of which eight were Stage 1 aircraft that had returned from the first roulement. The Stage 1 aircraft still required a reasonable amount of work as some of the modifications had been removed for UK operations and they needed second line maintenance, which took up to five weeks. Work began in November and the aim was to have the aircraft ready for another roulement by March 1991. No. 226 OCU was temporarily moved to RAF Wattisham and the Phantom OCU closed to help release the necessary manpower. Stage Three included the Stage Two and in-theatre modifications plus the self-protection suite received further enhancements and a second HAVE QUICK radio was installed – due to lack of space this was mounted with the panel upside down behind the pilot's right shoulder, which made it very awkward to use. Around 20,000 man-hours were

A sortie to practise the switch to low-altitude operations. Three of the Jaguars are carrying four 1,000lb (454kg) HE bombs, and interestingly the rearmost aircraft is carrying a Paveway II laser-guided bomb. Just discernible are the matt black fake cockpits painted on their undersides. *Mike Rondot via Author's Collection*

expended on the programme, which was completed on 14 February. Within a month the second roulement had returned with the end of hostilities and none of the Stage Three aircraft were deployed.

Together the various STFs and modifications had totalled £2.77 million. They proved invaluable and the continued presence of forces in the region meant that the planned removal of these modifications actually became a fleet-wide standard, although it would take until the mid-1990s before an organised upgrade programme got under way.

Planning and training

Following an intensive work-up period at Coltishall – which included four bird strike incidents – the first roulement arrived at Thumrait on 12 August with 12 Jaguar GR.1A, including four in reconnaissance configuration from No. 41(F) Squadron. The pilots were drawn from across the Coltishall squadrons and No. 226 OCU, while the groundcrew and support personnel were mostly drawn from No. 6 Squadron. Officer Commanding (OC) No. 6 Squadron, Wing Commander Jerry Connolly, was the detachment commander. The Jaguar Force already had extensive experience of regular deployments and came prepared with fly-away packs for maintenance support that enabled them to settle in relatively quickly. Connolly sought advice from the RAFO on how best to operate the Jaguar in a desert environment and their assistance was very useful in devising the training programme and handling the shift to medium-altitude operations that came about shortly after. These lessons were passed on to the second roulement.

While practising operational low-level flying (the RAF's term for ultra low-level flying), it was discovered that the aircraft's shadow – which was the same size as the aircraft – often gave away its presence to fighters above, so the altitude was increased slightly to minimise the ground footprint.

In late October the detachment moved to Bahrain International Airport Muharraq (formerly RAF Muharraq), which was closer to the Kuwaiti Theatre of Operations (KTO). The Jaguar had a radius of action from Muharraq of 240nm (440km) with one 264gal (1,200L) drop tank and four bombs without air-to-air refuelling, or 310nm (570km) with two tanks. The Jaguars would be mostly tasked against targets as far north as Kuwait City and as far west as the Iraq–Kuwait–Saudi border area. As it happened, the ability to only carry two CBU-87 cluster bombs reduced drag and fuel consumption and in practice the range achieved was better than forecast.

The second roulement began to arrive at Thumrait on 23 October (seven aircraft) and Muharraq on 2 November 1990 (five aircraft) with the Stage Two Jaguars. The Jaguars, like most of the RAF aircraft deployed to the Gulf, soon sported racy nose art and nicknames, including several characters from the British adult comic *Viz*, which reflected the humour of the pilots and groundcrew.

A total of 158 personnel arrived: 22 pilots drawn from No. 41(F) and the other Coltishall squadrons and the OCU; 11 reconnaissance analysts and 115 engineers and logistics staff mostly from No. 41(F). A 90-day rotation meant that all of the original roulement of pilots were replaced by Christmas. On his arrival on 3 December, Wing Commander Bill Pixton became detachment OC, with Squadron Leader Chris Allam as executive officer and Flight Lieutenant Peter 'Livo' Livesey as operations officer. Flight Lieutenants Pete Tholen and Stevie Thomas were Qualified Weapons Instructors (QWI) and were flight commanders, along with Squadron Leader

Granby aircraft				
Serial No.	Tail Code	Name	Pilots	Sorties
XZ356	N	'Mary Rose'	Wg Cdr Bill Pixton	47
XZ118	Y	'Buster Gonad and his Unfeasibly Large Testicles'	Flt Lts Stevie Thomas & Pete Tholen	38
XX733	R	'Pink Spitfire'	Sqn Ldr Dave Bagshaw & Flt Lt Peter Livesey	39
XZ367	P'	Debbie' later 'White Rose'	Sqn Ldr Mike Gordon, Flt Lt Dave Foote & Fl Off Mal Rainier	40
XZ364	Q	'Saddam'	Sqn Ldr Dick Midwinter & Flt Lt Simon Young	47
XX962	X	'Fat Slags' (with 'St. Georgina' on portside)	Flt Lts Ted Stringer & Dave Foote	37
XZ119	Z	'Katrina Jane'	Flt Lts Dick MacCormac, Toby Craig & Fl Off Mal Rainier	40
XZ375	S	'The Guardian Reader'	Sqn Ldrs Mike Rondot & Mike Seares	17
XX725	T	'Johhny Fartpants'	Flt Lts Steve Shutt & Craig Hill	47
XZ106	O	'Rule Britannia'	Sqn Ldr Chris Allam	35
XZ358	W	'Diplomatic Service'	Flt Lt Roger Crowder	14
XX748	U	No name assigned	Flt Lts Mark Hopkins & Alex Emtage	36

Mike Rondot. Squadron Leader Mike 'Strike' Gordon was responsible for drafting the daily flying programme. The groundcrew was led by Engineering Warrant Officer Mick Cartwright. Once operations began on 16 January, two mission planners and three additional pilots arrived from Coltishall. Accommodation for the detachment was found in the nearby five-star Diplomat Hotel. All the pilots had flown with each other before and knew each other's capabilities well, with their camaraderie helping to keep morale high.

Training missions continued until 15 January. One such mission was Exercise Fish Barrel on the 8th, consisting of 30° dive freefall simulated bombing and level rocket firing on a range north of Dhahran. The following day, eight Jaguars conducted operational low-level flying with USAF McDonnell Douglas F-4G 'Wild Weasel' Suppression of Enemy Air Defences (SEAD) aircraft and US Marine Corps (USMC) McDonnell Douglas F/A-18 Hornets, including aerial refuelling from a No. 55 Squadron Victor K.2 tanker. Low-flying areas in Saudi Arabia were used for low-level evasion training as well as air-to-air refuelling practice. Live firing and weapon trials were conducted at the King Fahad and Faisal ranges, while the Crab Island range in Bahrain was used for CRV-7 training. The detachment also took part in the Royal Navy's self-defence War At Sea Exercises in the Gulf.

Another medium-altitude training sortie accompanied by a Panavia GR.1A peeling away, carrying Skyshadow ECM and BOZ chaff pods but no weapons. *Mike Rondot via Author's Collection*

Operational low-level flying training was a dangerous business. On 12 September, while working up in the UK, Flight Lieutenant Jon Marsden flew into the sea in the Solway Firth in GR.1A XZ387 and on 13 November Flight Lieutenant Keith Collister was killed when he hit an obscured 87ft (26.5m) high sand ridge while flying at 50ft (15m) in XX754 over the Qatari desert.

Another worry for the pilots was the thought of having to eject over enemy territory. They were issued with a Walter PPK pistol for self-protection, but this gave little comfort. Escape and evasion choices were either to sit tight and wait for a search-and-rescue helicopter team or walk to the coast and hope to meet a friendly local – each pilot had a 'goolie chit' promising £15,000 from the British embassy to anyone who helped a downed pilot to reach Saudi Arabia or a neutral country.

The planners considered that it was unlikely that they would encounter a 'heavy' air threat on CAS or BAI missions. The primary threat was MANPADS like the 9K32 Strela-2 (SA-7 *Grail*) and 9K34 Strela-3 (SA-14 *Gremlin*), mobile IR-homing 9K31 Strela-1 (SA-9 *Gaskin*) and 9K35 Strela-10 (SA-13 *Gopher*) SAM systems and AAA ranging from 100mm to 23mm calibre, but even infantry popping off AK-47s were a real threat at low altitude. The KTO was probably the most densely defended area within the Desert Storm theatre. This made carriage of AN/ALQ-101(V)8 ECM, ALE-40 flare dispensers and a Phimat chaff pod vital on all missions. The Phimat pod settings were unchanged from the standard Baltic and Norway threat settings, but the ALQ-101 settings were modified. The pilots were strongly reminded that the best method of threat detection was still the old-fashioned visual lookout using the 'Mark One Eyeball' at all times.

The detachment devised its own concept of operations based on the local situation. Following the ultra-low-level training, it was decided to switch to medium-altitude operations just days before hostilities began. The decision was not taken lightly given that the aircraft, weapons and pilots were all optimised for low-level operations. The decision to change was made because of the large number of fighters countering the Iraqi aerial threat and the fact that the majority of the coalition air forces were operating at medium altitude (the Tornados and French Jaguar As made their first sorties at low level and suffered accordingly from ground defences). The flat terrain offered no terrain masking and target acquisition in relatively featureless areas was difficult at low level. Flight at medium altitude also reduced fuel consumption and improved radio communication with ground units, and it would be above the effective range of light AAA and MANPADS. Attacks using high-angle 30–45° dives would also improve accuracy. The lesson was clear, the Jaguar Force had to be flexible and could not just focus on the operational low-level role. In reality the tactics of the 1960s were outdated as air defence threats had evolved and new stand-off weapons required different delivery methods. It must also be recognised that the RAF lacked a dedicated SEAD force and that it was the availability of American expertise in this area that allowed the shift in operations.

A fully laden Jaguar ready for another interdiction sortie loaded with four 1,000lb (454kg) HE bombs, two Sidewinders, ALQ-101(V)10, Phimat and a fuel tank. The black nose wheel door formed part of the fake cockpit painted underneath to fool enemy AAA gunners. *Crown Copyright via Terry Panopalis*

Operations

Saddam Hussein ignored the deadline of 15 January imposed by Resolution 678 and consequently on 17 January Operation Desert Storm was launched to liberate Kuwait. The first phase of the operation, to last for seven to ten days, was focused on achieving air superiority and damaging strategic sites within Kuwait and Iraq. Phase two was the suppression of Iraqi air defences within the KTO. This would lead into phase three, attacking the Iraqi Army. The coalition commander, General Norman Schwarzkopf Jr (also the commander of United States Central Command), wanted half of the Iraqi armoured vehicles and artillery to be destroyed within three weeks before the ground offensive could be launched. The final phase would be to support the offensive.

From 17 January to 23 February coalition forces flew over 100,000 sorties and dropped 88,500 tons of ordnance. The coalition lost a total of 52 aircraft and helicopters, 44 of them in combat with the majority falling to anti-aircraft fire. In return, the Iraqi Air Force lost 259 aircraft, 105 of them in combat.

All missions were tasked through US Central Command Air Forces (CENTAF) to the UK Jaguar desk at Air Headquarters Riyadh, which was part of the Joint Allied Headquarters. The Air Tasking Order issued each day to the coalition air forces was more than 100 pages long, detailing every sortie throughout the day in minute detail. The commander of the coalition air forces was Lieutenant General Chuck Horner, USAF – who was the Commander of CENTAF and the USAF Ninth Air Force – with the British air commander being Air Vice Marshal Bill Wratten from 17 November for the duration of Desert Storm. Liaison between the Jaguar desk and the detachment at Muharraq worked well and was very successful. The main focus for the Jaguars was to be artillery targets, the Army being concerned about the danger from the Iraqis firing chemical or biological warfare shells on to their positions. The Desired Mean Points of Impact (DMPI) were given for each interdiction target as part of the mission planning. The satellite images supplied by the Joint Air Reconnaissance Intelligence Cell (JARIC) often proved inaccurate and so the Jaguar detachment tended to rely on its own reconnaissance capability to establish the exact DMPIs. The Ground Liaison Officer assigned from the Army's Intelligence Corps was Major Pat King, who had been with No. 41(F) Squadron at Coltishall before the conflict broke out. His role was to brief the pilots on the ground situation and keep the planning staff up to date with latest movements once the ground offensive began.

On take-off the aircraft would identify themselves to the duty Boeing E-3A Sentry AWACS before being passed to the Airborne Command and Control Centre (ABCCC), which was the control authority until the aircraft reached the kill zone containing the target (and sometimes also a Forward Air Controller – FAC). If the target had moved or already been destroyed, the Jaguars would head to an alternate DMPI or a target of opportunity within the kill zone. If an alternate target was in another kill zone the ABCCC had to approve the transfer.

Interdiction targets included missile systems like the Chinese-supplied HY-1 (CSSC-2 *Silkworm*) anti-ship cruise missile, barracks, ammunition storage, electronic equipment, SAM sites, armour and artillery. The latter proved tricky to find; Iraqi soldiers dug far more revetments than they had artillery pieces and MRLs for, so it was difficult for the planners to determine which ones were actually in use. This led to increased use of armed reconnaissance missions to try and identify active sites. The aim of Surface Combat Air Patrol (SUCAP) was to engage the Iraqi Navy before they could attack coalition warships or commercial traffic, such as tankers, in the Persian Gulf. SUCAPs were often controlled from

XZ119 'Katrina Jane' and XX725 'Johnny Fartpants' get airborne from Muharraq fully laden. An engine failure at this moment would have been critical, and the pilot would have had to eject. *MoD via Author's Collection*

the naval task forces in the Gulf. Generally fewer engagements were made than planned because the Iraqi Navy wisely decided to stay in port most of the time. Combat Search and Rescue (CSAR) was similar in scope, with the Jaguars being held on call to provide fire support to helicopter rescue crews rescuing downed coalition aircrew.

Due to co-ordination issues at Air Headquarters, there was no formal tasking for the reconnaissance Jaguars so it was decided to utilise them to support the detachment's own air interdiction role by supplying target intelligence. A pair of aircraft would photograph targets for the following day. This worked well and gradually other coalition units approached the detachment directly for recce support. Eventually things got more organised and from 11 February tasked recce sorties were flown. The detachment felt that the coalition commanders had under-utilised the Jaguar's reconnaissance capability at the strategic level, although they did receive some taskings for the British Army and the USMC. A total of 31 recce sorties were flown, about 5% of all Jaguar sorties.

In the interests of finding a sustainable rate, the detachment was tasked with 18 sorties per day. This allowed each pilot to fly one mission per day with four pilots on 24-hour stand-down (giving every pilot a day off every five days). On average each pilot flew 30 combat missions. From an engineering standpoint, 28 sorties could have been generated daily but the decision to stick to a manageable sortie rate was sensible given that it was unclear how long the conflict would last.

A total of 185 missions and 729 sorties were planned, of which 156 missions and 617 sorties were actually flown. Of these, 113 missions and 440 sorties were successful attacks. A total of 29 missions were aborted before take-off, including 13 due to bad weather, nine were stood down from ground alert with another two cancelled due to debates over the rules of engagement. Another 45 missions (totalling 145 sorties) were cancelled in the air; 16 due to bad weather obscuring the target, five due to smoke obscuring the target, 14 being stood down after not being tasked while on station, two engineering-related aborts, the authority to drop weapons was not given for four missions and nearby friendly forces caused another two aborts. The high number of weather aborts reflected what the pilots' thought was a poor meteorological service during flight planning. Experience gained from exercises such as Red Flag and Maple Flag had proved invaluable in instilling into the pilots' skills such as the importance of time discipline to be over the target at a set time, fitting into multi-aircraft packages, liaising with other air forces and experience of dropping live weapons.

On 16 January the detachment was brought up to full war readiness. The following day they were tasked with their first mission, a CAS sortie in the KTO flown by a formation of four Jaguars, callsign 'Bowler 51', led by Squadron Leader 'Strike' Gordon flying XZ106 'Rule Britannia'. While testing the guns en route to the target, Flight Lieutenant Roger Crowder in the No. 4 position accidentally launched an AIM-9L Sidewinder, narrowly missing Gordon's aircraft. The flight entered the kill zone without achieving contact with the ABCCC and selected a command post as the alternate target, eight 1,000lb bombs being delivered in airburst mode with good results – although one of Flying Officer Malcolm Rainier's bombs detonated prematurely behind his aircraft when the Mk.952 airburst fuze armed itself. Spotting some trucks nearby, Gordon attacked using his ADEN cannon but without effect. He then made another pass, launching a Sidewinder at the trucks, but it failed to lock on and exploded in the desert – perhaps adrenalin overruled caution on this eventful first mission. Another four Jaguars, callsign 'Keeper 85', were maintained on 30-minute ground alert but were stood down after six hours. From this point on, operations at Muharraq were disturbed by *Scud* ballistic missiles on a regular basis, 31 being fired into the eastern sector of the Arabian peninsula. Given the threat of chemical or biological warheads being used, NBC kit had to be donned during the alerts.

On the 18th, the first CAS mission of the day, callsign 'Bowler 51', consisted of four aircraft led by Wing Commander Pixton in XX725 'Johnny Fartpants'. The flight suffered one ground abort and found both the primary and alternate targets obscured by cloud. Instead of returning to base, Pixton contacted the AWACS to see if there was any other business. The flight was vectored on to a USAF Republic A-10A Thunderbolt II ground-attack aircraft serving as a fast FAC that had

Detachment Officer Commanding, Wing Commander Bill Pixton's Jaguar XZ356 'Mary Rose' armed and ready for the next mission under the sun shade. The armament is four 1,000lb (454kg) bombs and two AIM-9L Sidewinders. *MoD via Terry Panopalis Collection*

found a Republican Guard unit. The A-10 marked the target with smoke rockets but came under heavy AAA fire as the Jaguars descended out of the cloud at 10,000ft (3,050m). The Jaguars came under fire and only Pixton dropped his bombs before they exited the area. A second four-ship CAS mission also encountered poor weather and AAA but all aircraft dropped their weapons in the target area.

The 19th was a busy day. The first tasking was an air interdiction mission, callsign 'Keeper 01', against two SA-2 *Guideline* SAM sites in the KTO flown by eight Jaguars led by Flight Lieutenant Stevie Thomas. Very poor weather was encountered and the briefed target location proved to be incorrect. Thomas could not release his bombs but all the other pilots did, 28 1,000lb bombs with Mk.952 airburst fuzes dropped from 9,000ft (2,740m) due to the low cloud base; the HUD video recordings proving the success of the mission. One aircraft suffered minor damage from AAA. Four Jaguars were tasked on a BAI mission against a 155mm GHN-45 howitzer battery. Poor weather made finding the target difficult, the lead dropping his bombs on support vehicles. His wingman did not release but No. 4 managed to with unknown effect. Another four aircraft tasked against an MRL site were also affected by the weather, only the lead and No. 3 bombed the target. No. 2 headed to the alternate, only to encounter even worse weather and he returned to base. Heavy AAA caused minor damage to two aircraft.

On the 20th another eight-ship interdiction mission, 'Keeper 01', was flown but fog obscured both the primary and alternate targets. On leaving the target area the leader of the second formation identified an artillery position and dropped his bombs. The fog prevented a return to Muharraq and instead they diverted to Dhahran. Another three missions were scrubbed due to the weather, as were both missions the following day.

The weather on the 22nd was still poor and two planned interdiction missions were cancelled. The second mission was re-tasked later in the day; seven Jaguars attacked an ammunition depot (one aircraft aborted before take-off), with six releasing their weapons on to the depot, the seventh attacking an alternate target. AAA was encountered and several aircraft were 'painted' by an SNR-75 *Fan Song* acquisition radar belonging to an SA-2 *Guideline* SAM battery. A CSAR mission was tasked over the Gulf, and the CRV-7-armed aircraft flown by Flight Lieutenant Edward Stringer and Flying Officer Nick Collins were held on station with tanker support but were not called into action apart from a low-level pass close to Iranian

Pilots and groundcrews adorned their aircraft throughout the Coalition and the Jaguar detachment was no exception. XZ118 gained a *Viz* comic character, 'Buster Gonad', as its nose art. *Author's Collection*

GR.1A XZ367 was initially named 'Debbie' after the wife of one of the groundcrew. It was later repainted with a white rose. *Author's Collection*

waters to check on a vessel. Another pair were held on 30-minute SUCAP ground alert but were stood down.

The 23rd saw eight Jaguars, callsign 'Keeper 01', tasked for a BAI mission against a 130mm D-30 artillery battery and AAA site. The mission suffered two ground aborts. The target was not located at the briefed location, but an update to the aircraft while en route enabled them to find the target successfully and deliver 24 1,000lb bombs. A formation of six Jaguars attacked an MRL battery, timed for two minutes after an attack on a nearby airfield by the General Dynamics F-16C Fighting Falcons of the USAF's 614th Tactical Fighter Squadron. One of the F-16s, callsign 'Wolf 01', suffered a premature detonation of a 2,000lb (907kg) Mk.84 bomb due to a fault with its FMU-139 fuze. The pilot ejected into the Persian Gulf and was later recovered by US Navy SEALs. Undeterred, the Jaguars pressed home their attack with direct hits, and alternate artillery positions were also hit. Two pairs on SUCAP had uneventful missions, neither being called into action.

The Jaguar detachment was billeted at the Diplomat hotel, which inspired the nose art and name of XZ358 piloted by Flight Lieutenant Roger Crowder. The aircraft flew six recce and eight bombing missions. *Terry Panopalis Collection*

The next day, 24th January, proved to be eventful. The first BAI mission was split into two elements of four aircraft each, one attacking an 130mm M-46 artillery position and the other a 9K52 Luna-M (NATO designation FROG-7) short-range artillery rocket site. The weather was excellent and all four aircraft released on to the artillery position, but one of the second formation suffered a bomb hang-up. Ineffectual carpet AAA was encountered below their height.

Flight Lieutenant Dick McCormac had a narrow escape when he dropped his four 1,000lb bombs with Mk.952 airburst fuzes and one of them prematurely detonated at 10,000ft just ahead of Flight Lieutenant Toby Craig in XZ358 'Diplomatic Service', luckily not damaging either aircraft. After this second fault with the Mk.952 fuze, pilots began factoring in manoeuvres following release to ensure that they remained outside of the bomb's lethal envelope.

Another mission in the KTO saw a six-ship attacking another M-46 position. The smoke from the leader's bombs obscured the target, so his wingman bombed an alternate storage facility target. No. 4 suffered a malfunction with the HUD sight and had to abort his attack.

A pair of Jaguars on SUCAP were vectored on to two inbound Iraqi Mirage F1EQ fighters, but some 13nm (24km) away from the Mirages they lost contact with the E-3 AWACS. They flew through the Mirages, which were engaged by a USAF McDonnell Douglas F-15 Eagle. The F-15 pilot then locked on to the Jaguars but fortunately the AWACS regained contact and got the situation under control. At that point the understandably relieved Jaguar pilots reminded the AWACS controller that their Sidewinders were only meant for self-defence. Another pair of Jaguars on SUCAP made a visual identification of a helicopter and a surface vessel.

On the 25th another eight-ship BAI mission returned empty handed due to the weather, as did a subsequent formation of four aircraft. The SUCAP pair again had reason to grumble about the AWACS controllers when they were called to climb to 44,000ft (13,410m) for visual identification duty – an impossible altitude for the laden Jaguars to reach. They were then vectored on to a barge, releasing four pods of CRV-7 rockets and 480 30mm rounds with confirmed hits. A USMC Grumman A-6E Intruder also attacked, but the barge did not sink and several small craft in the area put up AAA fire. Another pair of Jaguars made a second attack on the barge, again with CRV-7 and cannon hits, but still it would not sink.

The weather on the 26th was much better and good results were obtained. A four-ship interdiction mission bombed a *Silkworm* anti-ship missile site, with good visual and HUD footage for bomb damage assessment (BDA). Five Jaguars attacked an M-46 battery (the sixth suffered a ground abort before take-off), destroying one site and damaging another two. Several other artillery sites were spotted and their co-ordinates were passed back to base. The SUCAP pair were vectored on to a surface vessel, which could not be identified as hostile. A second SUCAP mission was cancelled before take-off.

The following day the weather closed in again. All eight Jaguars of the first mission returned due to thick cloud over the target. A four-ship scored two direct hits on a *Silkworm* site, but the second pair elected to go to the alternate target, an ammunition storage site, which was attacked successfully. Both SUCAP missions were cancelled.

On the 28th an eight-ship interdiction mission attacked a large barracks, divided into two DMPIs. The results were mixed; the smoke from the first eight bombs obscured the target, so the second pair attacked a nearby D-30 artillery position. The second formation attacked their DMPI but four bombs fell short due to an automatic release malfunction. Visual and HUD recordings provided excellent BDA. An air interdiction mission with four Jaguars hit four DMPIs on a large logistics site using CBU-87 cluster bombs for the first time. The first SUCAP mission of the day was vectored on to a burning oil platform for visual reconnaissance. The second SUCAP was vectored to identify a ship close to Kuwait City, but they broke off due to Iraqi Mirage F1 activity in the area. It was on this day that Joint Allied Headquarters declared that air superiority had been won.

Two *Silkworm* sites were attacked by seven Jaguars on the 29th (one aircraft suffered a ground abort). Both sites were attacked successfully with CBU-87s, the second site suffering a direct hit. Light AAA was encountered and one Jaguar had Sky Guardian RWR indications of radar lock-on from a fighter and a missile launch. A formation of four Jaguars led by Wing Commander Pixton attacked another *Silkworm* site, again using CBU-87s. No AAA was encountered and the western half of the site, which included radar and support vehicles, was damaged. The formation was accompanied by XZ106 'Rule Britannia', flown by Squadron Leader David 'Baggers' Bagshaw, equipped with a LOROP pod for its first trial flight.

On the way back to Muharraq the formation spotted four Iraqi Fast Patrol Boats (FPBs), the position being passed to the Type 42 destroyer HMS *Gloucester*. The first SUCAP pair of Jaguars were vectored on to this threat, which turned out to be 15 FPBs. They followed the boats but were not allowed to engage. They were then asked to report on the condition of a partially sunken tanker for the Navy. The second SUCAP pair were scrambled and engaged the FPBs with two pods of CRV-7 each and cannon strafing – Flight Lieutenant Mark 'Hoppy' Hopkins also accidentally fired a Sidewinder during his strafing run. At least one FPB was claimed as destroyed and 12 damaged.

On the 30th an eight-ship BAI mission attacked a 122mm 2S1 Gvozdika self-propelled artillery battery. Target acquisition was difficult due to thick haze and cloud cover but the formation dropped 15 CBU-87s on to the DMPIs, although one aircraft suffered a hang-up and the weather also prevented any BDA. A formation of four Jaguars – accompanied by another equipped with LOROP – was tasked with attacking a command post but the target was completely obscured by smoke and haze and the aircraft returned to base. A pair of Jaguars on SUCAP, callsign 'Longstop 01', flown by Wing Commander Pixton in XX364 'Saddam' and Flight Lieutenant Tholen in XZ356 'Mary Rose', were tasked with observing a burning tanker and then made visual contact on an aerial target, which proved to be a US Navy Lockheed P-3 Orion maritime patrol aircraft.

XX962 was unique in carrying two artworks on the nose. On the starboard side were characters Tracy and Sandra from *Viz*. *Author's Collection*

The port side of XX962 was 'St Georgina', an Arabian woman holding a crusader shield. *Author's Collection*

Groundcrews ponder a fault. The Jaguar proved very reliable throughout Operation Granby, with only 3.6% of missions lost due to unserviceability. *USAF*

Following an aerial refuelling, Pixton and Tholen were vectored on to an Iraqi Project 773K *Polnochny-C*-class landing ship transiting the mouth of the Shatt Al-Arab waterway in an attempt to flee into Iranian waters. Clearance to engage was received and several coalition aircraft, including US Navy A-6E Intruders, attacked the vessel. Pixton and Tholen fired four pods of CRV-7 and 480 30mm rounds in two rocket passes and three or four gun passes each. Some of the rockets probably overshot the ship but it was left burning from end to end and later sank. Pixton spotted life rafts in the water and thought that it was likely that the crew had already abandoned ship. The pair were low on fuel but found the Victor tanker despite low cloud and refuelled before heading home. A second SUCAP mission was uneventful.

The first BAI mission for the 31st had two targets, an ammunition dump and a logistics site. The first four Jaguars dropped a mix of 1,000lb bombs and CBU-87s on to the western side of the large dump while the second four-ship attacked the logistics site. The No. 4 pilot of the second formation received fighter radar lock-on and missile launch indications on the Sky Guardian display and took evasive action while releasing chaff before dropping his bombs on the ammunition dump. Another four Jaguars, with an accompanying LOROP recce aircraft, attacked a *Silkworm* site with seven CBU-87s, the lead aircraft suffering an electrical fault and a hang-up. The formation encountered no enemy defences but were continually locked up by friendly fighters despite the AWACS controller knowing about the formation.

The first SUCAP pair, Flight Lieutenant Simon Young flying XZ119 'Katrina Jane' and Squadron Leader Richard Midwinter in XX748 – callsign 'Batsman 02', were flying top cover for the battleship USS *Missouri*, which was firing 16-inch gun broadsides against shore targets, when they received a CAS task to reconnoitre a road just over the Kuwaiti border for enemy armour. A convoy of trucks was spotted and it was decided to attack using the BL.755 that they had been armed with – the only time they were used during Granby – which required a low-level attack. Most of the bomblets missed, only one truck being hit, but Young destroyed a ZSU-23-4 *Shilka* self-propelled AA vehicle. As Young returned for a second pass he encountered an SA-7 *Grail* and took evasive action, jettisoning all stores – including the ECM and chaff pods. Both aircraft returned safely. The second SUCAP pair were also tasked with CAS, but with sunset already taking place the leader decided not to risk a nocturnal attack and returned to base.

February began with an air interdiction mission against the support area at Ahmed Al-Jaber airbase, 32nm (60km) south-west of Kuwait City (the location of the French Jaguars' eventful baptism of fire the previous month). The formation of eight aircraft was led by Squadron Leader Gordon, callsign 'Keeper 01', flying XZ748. One aircraft suffered a ground abort but the remainder made an attack in ideal weather conditions, releasing 24 1,000lb bombs and four CBU-87s and causing major structural damage to the complex. The formation was also able to confirm the success of an earlier Kuwaiti Air Force McDonnell Douglas A-4KU Skyhawk attack on the airbase's hangars. A formation of three Jaguars attacked a *Silkworm* site with CBU-87s and were accompanied by a LOROP-equipped aircraft for BDA. The difficulty of aiming the LOROP pod was noted during this sortie and the target was marked for re-attack. Both SUCAP pairs were used on convoy search duties but no targets were spotted.

On the 2nd the first BAI mission of the day saw eight Jaguars tasked with hitting an ammunition depot. The aircraft encountered heavy AAA over the target and one aircraft missed the target during evasive manoeuvres, with another suffering a hang-up. Despite these setbacks, a dozen CBU-87s were released over the target area. Four aircraft with an accompanying LOROP Jaguar attacked a *Silkworm* site. Intense AAA again hampered bombing, only No. 4 dropping his weapons but scoring one confirmed direct hit. The first SUCAP pair were quickly tasked with CSAR combat air patrol over a downed USMC A-6 Intruder pilot on Jazirat Miskin Island. In conjunction with another A-6, they released eight 1,000lb bombs with airburst fuzes over a six-gun AAA emplacement. The second SUCAP of the day was cut short when the lead aircraft suffered a bad engine surge.

On the 3rd eight Jaguars attacked a *Silkworm* site on the Kuwaiti coast with two DMPIs with 12 airburst and four impact-fuzed 1,000lb bombs. The second formation had received an updated location of the battery's radar site as they taxied for take-off. The missile and radar sites were destroyed and secondary explosions were seen. Four Jaguars attacked an artillery

battery in hazy conditions, only the lead dropping his weapons and the others bombing the alternate, another *Silkworm* site. No. 4 suffered a hang-up but four airburst and four direct hits from 1,000lb bombs were seen. One aircraft received lock-on indications from a SNR-75 *Fan Song* acquisition radar on the RWR. Both SUCAP missions were recce only and no weapons were released.

The following day smoke and haze hampered the bombing of a barracks and storage complex by four Jaguars but several buildings were seen to be damaged. Another four-ship attacked an Iraqi III Corps command post and despite the thick haze and AAA, including ZSU-23-4 *Shilkas*, all 16 1,000lb bombs impacted within 50ft (15m) of the DMPI. Both SUCAP pairs were not tasked against any vessels.

A radio relay mast and its associated technical building was the main target for the 5th. A formation of five Jaguars attacked with 20 1,000lb bombs with Mk.952 airburst fuzes and the mast was severely damaged (one pilot had technical problems and dropped short). The mast was re-attacked by another four aircraft, but only one pilot managed to cause any damage to what was left of the mast. A four-ship tasked with destroying an artillery battery found the target not where it was supposed to be. Identification of alternate targets in the kill zone proved difficult and only one Jaguar attacked an enemy position. Another formation also failed to find their artillery battery and attacked targets of opportunity instead with their 1,000lb bombs. The detachment now took extra pains to make sure that they had the latest intelligence available when mission planning against highly mobile targets.

Bad weather returned on the 6th and the tasked eight-ship formation returned to base. Another eight Jaguars were tasked against an artillery battery, which was difficult to locate in the thick haze. A total of 32 1,000lb bombs were released, with one aircraft attacking an alternate battery. Several aircraft received RWR warnings of a P-18 *Spoon Rest-D* search radar from a nearby SA-2 *Guideline* site. This would be the last eight-aircraft formation; all following operations would be four-ships with the two pairs split between two and ten minutes apart and attacking from different directions to keep the enemy defences guessing.

The following day two formations of four aircraft each were tasked against artillery positions. The first formation had communication problems with the ABCCC and then found themselves conflicted with USMC F/A-18A Hornets and AV-8B Harrier IIs and only three aircraft bombed their assigned target. The second formation attacked the same battery, two aircraft bombing slightly wide due to aiming problems but No. 4's HUD recording showed that No. 3 made a direct hit. Another battery was attacked at the end of the day by nine Jaguars, but the haze and low position of the sun did not help acquiring the target. Eight aircraft bombed but BDA proved impossible.

Artillery hunting was the task of the day for the 8th. The weather was excellent and the first four Jaguars

Jaguar XZ358 'Diplomatic Service' being readied for a recce sortie with the Vinten LOROP camera pod under the fuselage and AIM-9L Sidewinders on the overwing rails. ***MoD via Terry Panopalis Collection***

Another *Viz* character to appear was 'Johnny Fartpants' on XX725, which is also adorned with its tally of 41 of its 47 missions flown by Flight Lieutenants Steve Shutt and Craig Hill. The lettering inside the bomb outlines how many and what type of ordnance was released. *Terry Panopalis Collection*

bombed successfully. Another four Jaguars released their 1,000lb bombs on the same battery with equally good results. A five-ship encountered communications jamming but found their assigned artillery battery and released 19 1,000lb bombs. A follow-up attack found that smoke and dust from the previous raid made finding the target difficult, so they selected a new DMPI and obtained good results from their bombs.

On the following day a formation of four aircraft released eight CBU-87s on to a logistics site and confirmed intelligence reports that a nearby scrap yard contained military vehicles. A subsequent five-ship formation failed to find its assigned artillery and attacked the scrap yard instead with their ten CBU-87s from 18,000ft (5,490m). Communications jamming was again encountered, as was an attempt at a smokescreen. A four-ship found smoke obscuring its MRL battery target, only two aircraft releasing their CBU-87s (one aircraft had a hang-up) and the third aircraft bombed a *Silkworm* site. Another four Jaguars inbound against MRLs encountered communications jamming, which affected their ability to contact the ABCCC. Cloud hampered the attack and BDA, the aircraft deciding to attack a command post in the same location as the MRL battery. The Jaguar detachment still had plenty of Iraqi artillery to destroy and the task remained unchanged for the 10th. A formation of four Jaguars suffered one ground abort but updated intelligence enabled them to find the target, six CBU-87s scoring four direct hits. The weather was excellent but oil fires had been lit in an attempt to form a smokescreen. Four Jaguars attacked a *Silkworm* site with CBU-87s. Another four were tasked with attacking a second *Silkworm* site but one ground abort and the leader suffering a weapons aiming malfunction meant that only four CBU-87s were released on to the target.

The following day an Astros II MRL battery was attacked and thanks to excellent reconnaissance photography the DMPIs were very accurate, as was the CBU-87 release, with visual sightings and HUD recordings confirming the results. Another Astros II battery was engaged by four Jaguars, the CBU-87s fell short but destroyed the accompanying command and support vehicles. Again oil fires had been used in an attempt to form a smokescreen. Two four-ships were tasked to re-attack the battery but the weather changed and the aircraft headed back to base.

The first reconnaissance mission was flown with a LOROP and F126 pairing, callsign 'Longstop 11', and was the first pairing of Squadron Leader 'Baggers' Bagshaw and Flight Lieutenant 'Livo' Livesey as the detachment's dedicated recce pilots. Livesey, an ex-No. II(AC) Squadron recce pilot, was flying XZ356 'Mary Rose' with the LOROP pod and Bagshaw had the F126 pod. The first target, an artillery position, was obscured by cloud and the second had partial cloud cover and the F126 camera failed. Even so, the results were encouraging enough to prove that the pairing of both cameras would work well.

On the 12th an MRL battery was attacked by four Jaguars using CBU-87s with excellent results despite barrage AAA fire up to 15,000ft (4,570m). Another four-ship attacked an MRL battery. The leader noticed friendly fighters below as he was about to start the attack, breaking off and attacking an AAA site instead. Hang-ups and weapon aiming problems led to six bombs being jettisoned into the sea on the return to base. Another MRL battery was engaged by four Jaguars and despite AAA fire up to 15,000ft the first two aircraft scored direct hits with their 1,000lb bombs and No. 4 dropped two CBU-87s, causing secondary explosions that could be seen 52nm (96.5km) away. No. 3 elected to attack a AAA battery on the coast with his CBU-87s, causing secondary explosions. A formation of four Jaguars re-attacked an MRL battery with eight 1,000lb bombs and four CBU-87s, with direct hits on vehicles and a petrol station. The recce pair of Bagshaw and Livesey covered an artillery position and an MRL battery with both LOROP and F126 and confirmed six new sites for the following day's missions.

The first mission of the 13th was a four-ship air interdiction mission on a communications post near Kuwait International Airport. The formation was locked up by SA-2 *Guideline* battery radars on their run in to the target. Poor weather made target acquisition difficult but all 16 1,000lb bombs were released; BDA was impossible after the attack. A formation of four Jaguars found themselves in excellent weather and they attacked an artillery battery – the leader scoring a direct hit with a manual release. On the way back to base the ABCCC wanted to task them with a CAS mission but a lack of fuel prevented them from accepting the job. An MRL battery was attacked by four Jaguars in good weather but two aircraft failed to achieve a laser lock and only one CBU-87 direct hit was observed. Another formation of four aircraft attacked an artillery battery, excellent reconnaissance photos having enabled them to locate the target quickly. Six CBU-87s were released but one aircraft suffered a hang-up, the pilot not risking a manual release due to the close proximity of civilian housing. Heavy AAA and a possible SA-16 *Gimlet* MANPADS were encountered, but all the aircraft returned safely. The recce pair had an unsuccessful mission when the F126 camera went unserviceable and the LOROP again proved hard to aim.

For the first BAI mission on the 14th, the pilots decided to use a steeper dive angle and all eight CBU-87s impacted on to artillery positions with secondary explosions seen. Several of the flight detected lock-on signals from a nearby *Guideline* battery on egress from the target. The second mission also used the steeper dive with equal success against another artillery battery and secondary explosions were seen within the command post area behind the guns. A four-ship attacked a battery of 152mm D-20 gun-howitzers; four of the eight CBU-87s fell short. Another formation attacked a D-20 battery with more success and passed the co-ordinates of two AAA sites to nearby A-10 Thunderbolts to engage. The recce pair of Bagshaw and Livesey photographed an artillery battery and an Astros II MRL site for the following day's missions.

Wing Commander Bill Pixton's aircraft was XZ356 'Mary Rose', named after his wife. ***Terry Panopalis Collection***

The Astros II battery was engaged by four Jaguars, the eight CBU-87s causing severe damage to the command and control facilities and leaving several vehicles burning. A follow-up attack by another four-ship was interrupted by three F-16s who dropped 12 bombs on to the target. The Jaguars managed to release their CBU-87s on to the battery and nearby artillery. A formation of four Jaguars suffered one ground abort but the remainder arrived at the target, a battery of dug-in 2S1 self-propelled guns, which had already been hit by F/A-18 Hornets. The Jaguars added their six CBU-87s to mop up the stragglers. A follow-up wave of Jaguars found nothing left to attack and went hunting for targets of opportunity – more artillery – with success. The recce pair using LOROP and F126 again produced good imagery of the following day's targets.

By now Saddam's forces had begun setting light to the oil wells, a thick layer of black smoke blanketing southern Kuwait. This made target acquisition impossible and the morning's two missions on the 16th returned empty

Inspired by artwork on Douglas Bader's Hurricane during the Battle of Britain, Squadron Leader Dick Midwinter had Saddam Hussein being kicked by a boot painted on the nose of XZ364. The aircraft released a total of 96 1,000lb bombs, 41 CBU-87 cluster bombs and eight CRV-7 rockets during 47 sorties. ***Author's Collection***

Squadron Leader Dave Bagshaw had flown the Fighter Collection's Spitfire at Duxford, among other warbirds, so 'Pink Spitfire' was a fitting artwork for his mount, XX733, although the artwork was only completed half an hour before the ceasefire. *Terry Panopalis Collection*

handed. Another formation did find their assigned M-46 battery north of the smoke plumes, however, dropping eight CBU-87s with secondary explosions and fires seen. On the way back to base they strafed a barracks – despite heavy AAA – near the coast. A four-ship engaged another M-46 battery in the clear part of Kuwait but the heavy AAA in layers up to 15,000ft encouraged them to head straight home rather than risk loitering to assess what damage their CBU-87s had done.

The detachment was visited by the Joint Commander and Air Officer Commander-in-Chief Strike Command, Air Chief Marshal Sir Patrick Hine, accompanied by the Chief of Staff of Headquarters British Forces Middle East, Air Commodore Ian Macfadyen.

Wing Commander Bill Pixton flew 47 missions in XZ356 'Mary Rose'. The tally shown here comprises 23 interdiction sorties with bomb releases, the CRV-7 rocket attack on the *Polnochny*-class landing ship and six recce missions. *Terry Panopalis Collection*

The following day the smoke and poor weather grounded all missions. On the 18th two four-ships found their primary targets obscured by smoke so they both attacked a large logistics site with CBU-87s and encountered light AAA on the way home. Bagshaw and Livesey flew over northern Kuwait to find targets for the USMC, obtaining good results from the LOROP and F126 combination, and carried out BDA on the logistics site. The site was attacked again by two formations dropping a mix of 1,000lb and CBU-87 bombs, causing more damage to revetted vehicles.

On the 19th the first mission of the day saw four Jaguars attacking an 130mm Type 59-1 artillery battery (a Chinese copy of the M-46). Despite the thick smoke, attacks were made on individual revetted positions but assessment of the damage caused was impossible due to the haze. One aircraft received lock-on warning from the RWR from an SA-6 *Gainful* SAM site. Another formation of four Jaguars found the primary and alternate artillery targets obscured by smoke, so they dropped their CBU-87s on to artillery scrapes that they found. Two other four-ships bombed their alternate artillery positions due to the smoke, CBU-87s again being used. The recce pair had several targets for planning purposes and BDA. They encountered heavy AAA at 12,000ft (3,655ft) and 22,000ft (6,705m) and located a 100mm AAA battery as it fired on them. Having completed their assigned targets, the pair then did a complete sweep of the Kuwait–Saudi border for British Army and USMC planners.The following day, poor weather forced the first mission to go to the alternate, a logistics site, with three aircraft managing to drop their CBU-87s on to several trucks with visual confirmation of the damage caused. Another formation also found their primary obscured so they attacked an alternate artillery battery with eight CBU-87s. Four Jaguars heading for an MRL battery suffered one in-flight technical failure, the aircraft returning to Muharraq with an escort. The remaining pair found the target, their CBU-87s causing possible secondary explosions on the ground. Another formation was tasked on to an MRL battery; No. 3 failed to acquire the target but the other pilots dropped their CBU-87s on to revetted positions. The recce pair were tasked with photographing 19 oil distribution points controlling the fire trenches along the Kuwaiti and Saudi border with Iraq to carry out BDA for previous USAF Lockheed F-117A Nighthawk attacks.

On the 21st poor weather forced the first two missions of the day to return with their weapons. Good target imagery enabled the third formation to find their MRL battery despite the thick smoke; eight CBU-87s were dropped but little effect was seen. The same result was obtained by another four aircraft. The recce pair had several BDA and planning targets but the smoke obscured some of them. They also covered the southern Kuwait–Saudi border defences for the Joint Force Headquarters planning staff.

The following day, the first mission was full of frustrations. The two formations encountered heavy smoke and had communication problems with the USMC control agency due to their short-range equipment and use of secure communications unavailable to the Jaguar. Only one Jaguar received clearance to attack from a FAC, but no weapons were released. A four-ship armed with CBU-87s was re-tasked against an artillery battery in the clearer airspace of northern Kuwait. On leaving the target the leader found an unguided S-75 *Guideline* missile in his twelve o'clock but was able to break away unscathed. Another four Jaguars were tasked against an artillery battery, the first pair dropping their CBU-87s on to the revetments but the second pair electing to attack the alternate position due to the haze. The day's experience confirmed the necessity of good reconnaissance imagery to establish which revetments were actually occupied. Units of Saddam's Republican Guard in western Kuwait were the main targets on the 23rd. Aerial refuelling was required to reach the first target of the day, an artillery battery. On arrival they found Saudi Northrop F-5E Tiger IIs already attacking the target, so they flew on to the alternate, another artillery battery. The 1,000lb bombs caused secondary explosions. The second formation also required refuelling to reach their target, but they were following three B-52H Stratofortresses and witnessed what the leader called an 'awesome sight' as they dropped their payloads. The primary DMPI was obscured by the smoke from the B-52s' attack so another artillery battery was bombed instead. Four Jaguars attacked another Republican Guard artillery battery, two dropping four CBU-87s and two using the new CRV-7 aiming software to release four pods of rockets with excellent results. The final mission of the day saw another four-ship dropping CBU-87s on to yet another artillery position in excellent weather conditions.

Photographed through the rearward-facing periscope aboard the Handley Page Victor K.2 tanker, XZ118 'Buster Gonad' takes on fuel during a SUCAP or CAS mission armed with CRV-7 rocket pods. ***MoD***

The recce pair were tasked into Iraq to cover the ground that would be covered by 1 BR Corps when the ground offensive began. After refuelling they transited via the morning's target to carry out a BDA before crossing over into Iraq. They were locked up by SA-2 *Guideline*, SA-6 *Gauntlet* and SA-8 *Gecko* SAM batteries while over the target but saw no missiles and they returned safely with good imagery.

Aerial refuelling became commonplace as the targets were increasingly located further away from base the Jaguars using the tankers 138 times during Granby. All the pilots were air-to-air refuelling qualified and had practised regularly with the Victor K.2 and BAC VC10 K.2 tankers. Being co-located with the Victor tankers of No. 55 Squadron at Muharraq was beneficial for collaboration and allowed any misunderstandings around procedures to be dealt with quickly. Tanker support was especially vital for SUCAP missions and the longest such mission with tanker support was 5½ hours. Refuelling was conducted in two corridors running south-west–north-east over the Persian Gulf, roughly parallel to the Iraqi coast at an altitude of 25,000–27,000ft (7,620–8,230m).

Given the multinational nature of the operation, it was foreseen that refuelling might involve tankers from other nations, for example the USAF's Boeing KC-135 Stratotanker – if fitted with a boom/drogue adapter – and McDonnell Douglas KC-10A Extender. The A&AEE had investigated compatibility with the KC-135 using a boom/drogue adapter in 1989. The USAF used Boeing's Flying Boom system with a telescoping rigid hose, which connected into a recessed receptacle on the receiving aircraft's fuselage, while the US Navy and most Western air

As tasked missions were progressively located further inside Iraq as the ground offensive rolled on, the Jaguars relied on aerial refuelling. Available RAF tanker assets included the VC10 C.1K tankers of No. 101 Squadron. ***MoD via Terry Panopalis Collection***

forces used a flexible hose and drogue system that connected to an external probe. These systems are incompatible without the adapter that replaces the end of the boom with a short length of hose and a drogue. The A&AEE found that refuelling was possible, but that the Jaguar pilot's workload was demanding and a clumsy hard contact with the solid drogue risked bending the fuel probe. The KC-10 was not assessed in flight trials; being of the same size and layout as the RAF's Lockheed Tristar tankers with a hose drum unit and drogue, it was thought that no problems would occur.

Republican Guard artillery took another beating on the 24th, the day that the coalition's ground offensive began. The Jaguars had problems finding their tankers due to the weather and ended up locating the Victors at 2,000ft (610m). The leader, Flight Lieutenant 'Hoppy' Hopkins in XZ106 'Rule Britannia', callsign 'Keeper 01', experienced a burst refuelling hose seal that sent fuel into the starboard intake and engine, filling the cockpit with acrid blue smoke, and he was forced to turn back for base. Two of the remaining aircraft managed to refuel but the third went outside the allowed Time On Target bracket and had to return to base too. The remaining pair pressed on to the target with good results. Another Republican Guard battery was engaged by four Jaguars, having found their tanker in the difficult conditions. The target was in clear weather and despite the USMC controller not giving clearance to release until two minutes' flying time away from the target, all four aircraft scored direct hits with CRV-7 rockets. Another formation did not attack their primary target due to the close proximity of friendly troops, so they were vectored on to another artillery position further north, the CRV-7 rockets again proving highly effective. A possible IR-homing SAM was sighted over the target. The last four-ship mission of the day met with difficulties, two Jaguars failing to find the tanker and the other pair failing to get clearance to drop their weapons.

The recce pair penetrated into Iraq, again being locked up by SA-2, SA-6 and SA-8 batteries but no missiles were encountered. Unfortunately the F126 camera suffered a technical failure, which made the excellent LOROP imagery unusable.

Bad weather negated all efforts on the 25th. Although four formations found their tankers to refuel, none could find their targets. The thick cloud also prevented the recce pair from photographing their targets.

The following day was no better with two formations returning to base and another two missions scrubbed before take-off. The recce pair decided to descend below the heavy cloud, but coming out of the cloud base at 1,000ft (305m) they immediately came under attack from SA-6 and SA-8 SAMs. Both missiles were evaded successfully, but the pair decided that discretion was the better part of valour and returned home.

The first air interdiction mission of the 27th suffered a ground abort before take-off but the remaining three Jaguars refuelled without problems. On arrival at the target they were informed that CSAR operations were on and were vectored to another kill zone. They found the area blanketed with cloud and could not release any weapons. The second formation experienced severe problems with the aerial refuelling and were also called on to CSAR tasks, but again the weather thwarted any weapons release. A third formation also returned home without sighting any targets.

The recce pair flew into Iraq but cloud prevented them taking any imagery. On the way home Bagshaw checked whether the water towers in Kuwait City were still intact, making a visual sighting and aiming the LOROP camera in a 90° bank to take a photograph. A final four-ship tanked successfully but were then tasked with reconnoitring a target for the USMC. The lead aircraft found a target but the close proximity of friendly troops prevented any weapons release. This proved to be the final Jaguar mission of the war as the ceasefire took effect and all offensive air operations stopped from 03:00 on the 28th.

By 14 March the detachment was back at Coltishall. Flight Lieutenant Pete Tholen had an eventful flight home when one of the Adours surged over Cairo; he continued without touching the throttle, wisely as it turned out. As he taxied in at Coltishall the engine failed.

The detachment had accumulated 887 flying hours in 618 sorties, the total flying achievement while in the theatre of operations was 3,921.5 flying hours in 2,883 sorties. For their efforts during the campaign and bravery under fire while on operations, Wing Commander Pixton, Squadron Leader Mike Gordon and Flying Officer Malcolm Rainier were awarded the Distinguished Flying Cross and Flight Lieutenants Craig Hill, Peter Tholen and Stevie Thomas were Mentioned in Despatches.

XW725 'Johnny Fartpants' at Coltishall in July 1991 following its return from the Gulf. Apart from the addition of the squadron code letters 'GU' to the tail fin, it remains in stock Granby condition. *Terry Panopalis Collection*

Jaguar XZ119 'Katrina Jane' returns home safely to Coltishall in early March 1991 having flown 40 missions. *Terry Panopalis Collection*

Granby sorties				
	Total	Successful combat missions	Air aborted missions	Ground aborted missions
Missions planned	185	113	43	29
Equivalent no. of sorties	729	482	145	102
Missions flown	156	113	43	0
Successful sorties flown	617	440	0	0

The Jaguars had dropped 741 1,000lb bombs – totalling 63% of all weapons dropped from the type. Initially, the delivery profile was a 30° dive, entering at 23,000ft (7,010m) with target acquisition at 17,000–18,000ft (5,180–5,485m), weapon release at 15,000ft (4,570m) and pull-out at 12,000ft (3,660m). As experience grew and AAA defences got tougher the angle was steepened to 45–60° with target acquisition at 32,000ft (9,750m), release at 22,000ft (6,705m) and recovery at 15,000ft. Release was usually automated, when a stick of four bombs would hopefully straddle the target.

The main problem encountered was that the detachment had a limited supply of Mk.960 multi-function bomb fuzes (MFBF) and Mk.114 freefall bomb tails. The Mk.960 in the nose was usually paired with a Mk.947 tail impact fuze, but after two weeks this was changed to using just the Mk.947 or a Mk.952 air-burst fuze to conserve stocks. The Mk.952 fuze sometimes detonated prematurely if it sensed another weapon nearby. This happened on at least two occasions, luckily not damaging either Jaguar. After another fortnight stocks were so low that the armourers had to resort to basic pistols and delayed arming devices. To overcome the shortage of Mk.114 freefall tails, the Battle Damage Repair team – having little actual damage to repair – modified Mk.117 retarded tails for freefall use.

Initially, the CBU-87 cluster bomb used the weapons computer's revisionary aiming mode (based on 540lb (245kg) bomb ballistics with a fudge factor added), which consequently tended to drop short. With practice – and software upgrades that arrived in the last week of the campaign – it became a potent weapon with 387 dropped.

No LGBs were dropped by Jaguars. Despite the existing close Jaguar and Buccaneer co-operation, the decision was made to use the Tornado GR.1, although some practise sorties were flown with the Buccaneers when they arrived at Muharraq. After the war the CTTO mused how successful the Jaguar might have been given that they would have delivered their LGBs in the high-angle dives that Paveway was designed for.

A total of 32 pods of CRV-7 rockets were fired, totalling 608 projectiles. The CRV-7 was optimised for anti-ship missions and was first used in the SUCAP role, being fired against Iraqi naval vessels five times. The first four rockets fired missed their target, but this was due to not accounting for the different trajectories of the live rounds from practise ones – only 12 practise

Granby weapons		
Weapon	Number delivered	Reported hang-ups
1,000lb	741	11
CBU-87	387	6
CRV-7	32	0
BL.755	8	0
Total number	1,172	17
30mm rounds	9,500	0

Had Operation Granby carried on into the spring, No. 41(F) Squadron would have deployed GR.1A XZ113 with the Stage Three modifications. The aircraft took part in Operation Warden over northern Iraq in 1992 instead. XZ113 is carrying the standard Jaguar reconnaissance pod under the fuselage. ***Terry Panopalis Collection***

XZ733 was another Stage Three aircraft that was not deployed. By April 1991 the overwing AAM rails had been removed and the temporary ARTF paint was wearing off (surprisingly looking scruffier than those Jaguars that returned from Granby). *Terry Panopalis Collection*

rounds had been available per pilot for practise shoots. After three weeks the updated weapon aiming program and extended-range laser aiming circle were available. The accuracy of the CRV-7 was such that it was said to be possible to select and destroy individual guns within an artillery battery.

The 30mm ADEN cannon was also used against enemy shipping, as well as for suppressing ground fire, and was credited with contributing to the sinking of the *Polnochny*-class landing ship. A total of around 9,500 rounds were fired.

No AIM-9L Sidewinders had been fired at enemy aircraft (at least two pairs of Jaguars flown by Wing Commander Pixton and Flight Lieutenant Tholen and Flying Officer Malcolm Rainier and Flight Lieutenant Roger Crowder were vectored on to Iraqi Mirages but failed to make contact), although two had been accidentally fired and one intentionally launched against a ground target without success.

The success of BDA was mixed, with the poor weather and smoke often hampering visual assessment during the sorties. Review of the HUD videotapes suggested that 77% of the missions were successful, but there was little concrete data on how effective the Jaguar's weapons had been in destroying their targets. For example, one *Silkworm* missile site on the Kuwaiti coast was attacked at least a dozen times because it was impossible to get detailed enough images to determine whether the site had been knocked out. Post-war analysis indicated that many of the Jaguar's targets were more severely damaged than the pilots thought at the time.

The Jaguar maintained its record for reliability. There were eight ground aborts due to technical reasons and 13 air aborts due to malfunctions, which was only 3.6% of the missions flown. The 115 engineers and technicians kept the aircraft serviceable in the heat and dust, coming up with solutions to problems as they arose. The dust caused problems, scouring the LRMTS window and affecting laser lock-on until the transparencies were replaced, although the Adour seemed to tolerate the dusty conditions without problems.

The detachment were short of armourers, but this problem was overcome by re-tasking other groundcrew. It was commented that 115 was a small number of support personnel given the task at hand, when a Bardufoss deployment would usually include 340 groundcrew. There were only three cases of battle damage and only two of these required repair; a damaged slat jack shroud and one small 2cm hole in the skin plating.

Warden

Following the Gulf War, the UN imposed 'No-Fly Zones' over northern and southern Iraq in an attempt to protect the Kurds and the Shi'ite Muslims in the Euphrates delta from Saddam's revenge for perceived disloyalty to his rule. In the north, the UK-led Operation Provide Comfort – also known as Operation Haven – began in April 1991 to protect the Kurds and was backed up by a UN designated 'No-Fly Zone' north of the 36th Parallel under Security Resolution 687. The 'No-Fly Zone' was maintained under Operation Provide Comfort II (July 1991–December 1996) and Operation Northern Watch until the events of Operation Enduring Freedom in March 2003, which saw Saddam Hussein finally toppled from power. Jaguar deployments under Operations

XZ355 had been one of the aircraft that missed the Gulf War but was subsequently deployed on peacekeeping missions over northern Iraq, including in April 2002 with No. 41 Squadron. It is carrying a Vinten LOROP camera pod, as is the No. 6 Squadron Jaguar behind. *US DoD via Terry Panopalis Collection*

Jaguars continued to fly over Iraq for another decade. GR.3s and GR.3As of Nos. 6, 41(F) and 54(F) Squadrons flying a patrol during Operation Northern Watch in September 2002 to maintain the UN No-Fly Zone over northern Iraq. *USAF*

Resinate and Resinate North were part of this effort during 2001–02. The coalition forces maintained around 45 aircraft at Incirlik Air Base (AB) in southern Turkey, with RAF and USAF detachments flying patrols over Iraq for 18 days per month on average.

The Jaguar Force was rotated to Incirlik under Operation Warden from September 1991. No. 54(F) Squadron was the first to deploy with eight aircraft and flew nearly 900 sorties over northern Iraq in 11 months. No. 41(F) contributed LOROP-equipped Jaguars to provide reconnaissance capability. The Jaguar deployment between September 1991 and April 1993 amassed 2,786 sorties and 6,358 flying hours.

The second deployment of four Jaguars – which relieved the Tornados – from 1 October 1998 to 28 February 2003 totalled 2,030 sorties and 4,640 flying hours. As part of this deployment, No. 54(F) returned to Incirlik in January 1999. The Jaguars did not take part in Operation Desert Fox, a series of aerial attacks on Iraq in December 1998. Patrols during Warden were not without danger as coalition aircraft came under AAA fire on a daily basis, Saddam Hussein having offered a bounty to his soldiers if they shot down an aircraft. Squadron Leader Jex Milne, from No. 54 Squadron, was awarded the Distinguished Flying Cross in November 2001 for his actions during seven operational sorties over northern Iraq.

CHAPTER SEVEN

Peacekeeping and retirement

The 1990s would be busy for the Jaguar. Beyond the events of Operation Granby, routine operations continued at RAF Coltishall and RAF Lossiemouth. As the break-up of Yugoslavia led to civil war in 1991, the international community deployed peacekeeping forces and 'No-Fly Zones' with mixed success. The Jaguar was called upon to contribute and evolved with new weapons and sensors during six years of operations, including two periods of combat against Serb armed forces. The Jaguar received further upgrades, with the aircraft reaching the peak of its capabilities by the end of the decade, but the end of its RAF service life was approaching as its successor, the Eurofighter Typhoon, finally entered service.

1990s operations

Following the end of the Cold War, the *Options for Change* defence review was announced in July 1990. Unlike previous reviews, which had been a response to financial pressures, *Options for Change* was responding to the

The Jaguar GR.1A entered the post-Cold War era little modified since the early 1980s. By the end of the 1990s the type's capabilities had been drastically improved. This is XZ709 of No. 6 Squadron in 1993 with overwing rails for a pair of AIM-9L Sidewinders air-to-air missiles. ***Terry Panopalis Collection***

Following the Gulf War, peacekeeping deployments under Operation Warden lasted from 1991 until 2003 to enforce the United Nations designated 'No-Fly Zone' over Northern Iraq. GR.1A XZ363 is pictured in July 1992 on one of these deployments. The aircraft served with No. 41(F) Squadron from August 1977 until its accidental loss in Alaska in July 2001 during Exercise Cope Thunder. *Terry Panopalis Collection*

Jaguar GR.1A XZ113 of No. 41(F) Squadron in desert camouflage for Operation Warden. *Blue Envoy Collection*

To celebrate its 75th birthday in 1991, No. 41(F) Squadron gave XZ398 a colourful dorsal and tail fin decoration. ***Terry Panopalis Collection***

changing strategic environment in the post-Cold War era, although the resulting savings from the so-called 'peace dividend' were certainly a welcome bonus.

Options for Change threatened the disbandment of the Jaguar Force and a concerted campaign was made to save it. It was pointed out that the Jaguar squadrons consistently exceeded North Atlantic Treaty Organisation (NATO) generation and readiness requirements. The excellent operational record in the Gulf was maintained during Operation Warden, with more than 3,000 missions flown by that time. The Jaguar was cost-effective to operate; a squadron cost £30 million annually compared to £40 million for a Tornado or Harrier squadron. There was a sufficient pool of airframes and wings to manage the fatigue life until the planned out of service date sometime during 2003–05 and new undercarriage legs had already been funded. In addition, the Jaguar Force was maintaining a cadre of single-seat pilots until Eurofighter arrived in service, a cadre that the Harrier force could not sustain alone. Although saved, the Jaguar Force by 1992 had fallen to 65 GR.1A and 18 T.2A aircraft with a peacetime aircrew/aircraft ratio of 1.33:1. Nos. 6, 54(F) and 41(F) Squadrons with 12 GR.1As remained at Coltishall; No. 6 specialised in night attack, No. 54(F) was dedicated to delivering LGBs and No. 41(F) remained dedicated to tactical reconnaissance. All three squadrons remained assigned to Supreme Allied Commander Europe's Strategic Reserve (Air), with wartime deployment to Tirstrup and Bardufoss. National emergency contingency plans now included Maritime Counter-Terrorism Patrol. All pilots were trained in day and night aerial refuelling and transatlantic flights often staged through the Azores with tanker support, known as 'Leopard Trails' by the Victor K.2 tanker crews of No. 55 Squadron.

The squadrons participated in many overseas exercises during the decade. Six No. 41(F) Squadron GR.1As took part in NATO exercise Strong Resolve in Norway in 20 February–10 March 1995. In August the squadron deployed ten GR.1As for exercise Air Warrior 95-11 at Nellis AFB. Nine Jaguars from Nos. 41(F) and 54(F) Squadrons deployed to Bardufoss on 5 March 1996 for Exercise Battle Griffin, which included live weapons training with 1,000lb bombs and CRV-7 rockets. On 24 July, No. 54 lost GR.1A XZ362 during dissimilar aerial combat against a USAF F-16C during exercise Cope Thunder near Eielson AFB, Alaska. The pilot ejected safely. On 29 November ten GR.1As and two T.2As deployed to Egypt – the first time that RAF aircraft had visited the country since 1956 – as the guests of No. 222 Tactical Fighter Brigade equipped with F-4E Phantoms. Around 90 sorties were flown during the two-week deployment. During this time No. 54(F) Squadron visited Thumrait in Oman, flying co-operative sorties with Omani Jaguars using TIALD. No. 41(F) Squadron deployed to Bardufoss again in November 1997 for Exercise Snow Goose and later that month nine Jaguars returned to Thumrait for exercises. In October 1999 the squadron deployed six Jaguars to Mirosławiec airbase to participate in Exercise Jade Fusion alongside Polish Air Force Sukhoi Su-22 *Fitters*.

The Jaguar's armament continued to be revised. From 31 March 1992, the low-drag US Mk.82 bomb replaced the older 540lb (245kg) weapon. By April 1993

No. 54(F) Squadron celebrated its 75th birthday in 1991 and XZ112 received this colourful scheme, including blue and yellow chequerboard drop tanks. ***Terry Panopalis Collection***

No. 41 (F) Squadron trialled two winter camouflage schemes for use in Norway in February 1990. GR.1A XZ115 was painted in overall light grey. The Alkali Removable Temporary Finish soon ablated in use, hence the scruffy appearance here. ***Author's Collection***

The second aircraft in the trial, XZ355, received a disruptive patten, with white replacing the normal green. ***Author's Collection***

the Carrier Bomb Light Series (CBLS) 100 Mk.4 had been cleared for new 6.6lb (3kg) and 31lb (14kg) practice bombs, being complemented by the new CBLS Mk.5 that used compressed nitrogen instead of explosive release units, which was safer and left no corrosive combustion product deposits on the airframe. There were sufficient six-round LAU 5002B/A training pods for the CRV-7 rockets by February 1994 to deliver some to No. 16(R) Squadron, enabling the OCU to familiarise student pilots with the CRV-7 head-up display (HUD) aiming symbology and maintain a cadre of QWIs proficient in all ground-attack weapon delivery modes. This also allowed all Jaguars to be of a common standard and allowed aircraft to rotate between Lossiemouth and Coltishall for fatigue management.

Progress on getting a Night Vision Goggle (NVG)-compatible cockpit was mixed. Air Staff Requirement ASR.1011 was finally issued as SR(A).1011 for a limited night attack and reconnaissance capability from 1993 with 39 GR.1A and 2 T.2A modified aircraft – plus the two GR.1A and T.2A NVG trials aircraft. Then cost-saving measures included the removal of the NVG modification to save £3.9 million. The Director of Air Plans, Air Commodore John Day, supported a case by Air Commodore Roderick Goodall, the Director Air Offensive, to retain a limited NVG cadre capability for the cost of £260,000, the benefits far outweighing the modest cost involved. Goodall's plan was to rationalise the NVG fit across eight GR.1A and eight T.2A, sufficient to enable each squadron to maintain two NVG-qualified pilots.

During the summer of 1992 there were doubts whether the Eurofighter project would continue and thoughts turned to whether the Jaguar's life could be extended. One option was life extension to 6,600 hours along with recovering 14 of the ground instructional airframes.

Certainly the Jaguars were seeing punishing use; on 9 October 1992 GR.1A XZ366 flew through a flock of ten seagulls, sustaining Category 2 damage to the starboard front fuselage and the starboard Adour. The pilot, Flight Lieutenant Gosling, managed to divert to RAF Marham safely.

Stealth became an increasing concern and the radar cross-section reduction methods applied to the Granby aircraft were more thoroughly researched and applied. The use of radar-absorbent material (RAM) tiles inside the intake ducts was reserved for wartime due to the maintenance costs and effort required.

A 17% reduction in thrust was noted during Operation Granby due to the high ambient temperatures. About 7% of this loss was recovered by increasing the Adour's Turbine Exhaust Temperature (TET) by 50°C, the trade-off being an inspection of the turbine blades every 35 hours. Rolls-Royce tested a series of improvements to give a 90°C TET increase, which required a new anti-screech fuel shield to prevent a catastrophic jet pipe burn through. Not ready in time for Granby, these modifications were issued in 1992.

The Jaguars were getting fresh coats of paint too. Two snow camouflage schemes for use by No. 41 (F) Squadron in Norway were trialled In February 1990. Until this point white distemper had been applied during deployments to Bardufoss but it was decided to find an operationally – and scientifically – effective solution to aid camouflage in the air against a snowy landscape (on the ground the aircraft would be inside a Hardened Aircraft Shelter (HAS) anyway). The trial used Alkali Removable Temporary Finish (ARTF) paint, which would last up to three months. GR.1A XZ115 was painted in overall light grey and GR.1A XZ355 received a disruptive patten with white replacing the normal green. They were flown over a mix of rock, snow and light vegetation. The light grey was not effective against the landscape or water (though it was against the sky), the disruptive scheme was better but not much more effective than the normal green/dark grey scheme. The Royal Aircraft Establishment (RAE) argued that Medium Sea Grey would offer the best compromise to avoid the necessity of repainting aircraft on a temporary basis. The BAe Harrier GR.7 had already adopted all-over NATO Green paint and the Jaguar moved to a light grey air defence colour scheme with toned down pink/light blue national insignia.

The uniform grey was less successful over Norway's winter terrain. ***Author's Collection***

Bosnia – Deny Flight

The break-up of Yugoslavia unleashed a series of civil wars, the worst of which was that between Serbia and Bosnia-Herzegovina, which degenerated into genocide. Operation Deny Flight was set up to enforce United Nations Security Council Resolution 816, which prohibited Serbian flights (by fixed or rotary-winged aircraft) over

The first operational use of the new Arctic camouflage was on No. 41(F) Squadron's XZ363 in September 1993. ***Terry Panopalis Collection***

Mobility remained vital for the Jaguar Force in the post-Cold War era for both training exercises and deployments to trouble spots in the Middle East. This pilot's eye view shows a GR.1A of No. 54(F) Squadron taking on fuel from Lockheed Tristar ZD950. Note the fuel streaming from the dump vent at the base of the tail. ***Blue Envoy Collection***

OPPOSITE TOP Two Jaguars of No. 54(F) Squadron on deployment at Gioia del Colle in March 1994 equipped with AIM-9L Sidewinders and ALQ-101 ECM pods. ***Terry Panopalis Collection***

OPPOSITE CENTRE Two Jaguars, including XZ104 from No. 41(F) Squadron, at readiness at Gioia del Colle in September 1993. XZ104 is fully armed with a pair of 1,000lb (454kg) bombs, two AIM-9L Sidewinders plus an AN/ALQ-101(V)10 ECM pod. ***Terry Panopalis Collection***

OPPOSITE BOTTOM GR.1A XZ373 of No. 54(F) Squadron on deployment to Gioia del Colle in September 1993. All Jaguars deployed had the Stage Three Granby modifications for combat operations. ***Terry Panopalis Collection***

Bosnia and to provide air support for UN troops, including targets that threatened the security of UN declared safe areas. Operation Deny Flight ran from 12 April 1993 until 20 December 1995.

The first Jaguar deployment began on 16 July 1993 when 12 aircraft of No. 6 Squadron deployed to Gioia del Colle in Italy, refuelling en route near Dover from a pair of Victor K.2s and from a No. 216 Squadron Lockheed Tristar K.1 operating from Milan. The GR.1As were equipped to full Granby standard and were painted in grey air defence colours with all squadron markings removed. The British Army loaned three Vinten Series 603 Type 18 Long-Range Oblique Photography (LOROP) reconnaissance pods to the RAF for the deployment (they were retained in-theatre when the Harrier Force took over the deployment in July 1995).

Operations were assigned by the 5th Allied Tactical Air Force (5ATAF) Combined Air Operations Centre (COAC). The Jaguars flew standing Combat Air Patrols (CAP) over Bosnia, ready to respond to calls for air support from NATO troops and also to deter Serbian aggression by their presence – making mock attacks to keep Serb artillery quiet. Recce sorties using the LOROP pod were sometimes accompanied by an armed pair flying top cover. GR.1A XZ373 was lost on 26 June 1995 over the Adriatic due to an engine failure during an air combat manoeuvring exercise, the USAF exchange pilot ejecting safely.

The first mission to drop live weapons was on 22 September 1994, with three Jaguars flown by No. 41(F) Squadron pilots destroying a Serb T-55 tank that had pinned down a French armoured personnel carrier using unguided 1,000lb (454kg) bombs. In retaliation the Serbs closed Sarajevo airport for two and a half weeks. Two No. 54(F) Squadron Jaguars dropped 1,000lb bombs on the Krajina Serb airfield at Udbina on 21 November 1995, being followed by a recce pair to make a bomb damage assessment (BDA).

The Jaguar's lack of a self-designation capability for precision-guided munitions was found to be a handicap. A study was made into the most cost-effective way of obtaining this capability and it was decided to integrate the GEC-Marconi Thermal Imaging Airborne Laser Designator (TIALD) 200 Series pod on to ten GR.1As and two T.2As. TIALD used a stabilised sensor ball containing a thermal imager, video auto tracker and a Ferranti laser designator/tracker that could be used for range finding or target designating for laser-guided bombs (LGBs). The Series 200 pod had been specially designed for single-pilot operation in the Jaguar and proved to have smoother target tracking than the Tornado's pods.

Earlier, in 1992, the Defence Research Agency (DRA) – the semi-privatised successor to the RAE – had conducted a Technology Demonstration Programme to determine the feasibility of using the TIALD pod on

GH
XX974

FM
XZ104

GF
XZ373

XZ118 of No. 41(F) Squadron in full Bosnia deployment standard including low-visibility paint and markings, AN/ALQ-101 ECM and AIM-9L Sidewinders in January 1995. The aircraft is carrying a single 1,000lb (453kg) bomb on the centreline. ***Terry Panopalis Collection***

single-seat aircraft. Jaguar T.2A XX833 (with the moniker 'Night Cat') had been modified and over 80 sorties were flown, proving the soundness of the concept.

Urgent Operational Requirement UOR(A) 41/94 was approved in June 1994, along with £11 million in funding. Reducing the pilot's workload while maintaining situational awareness was important and led to plans to introduce new cockpit displays and hands on throttle and stick (HOTAS) controls. An autopilot to reduce pilot workload was considered, but not fitted. GPS was integrated into the Inertial Navigation System (INS) and a MIL-STD 1553B digital databus was added. All conversions – redesignated as GR.1B and T.2B – were completed within 16 months at the Major Servicing Unit at RAF St Athan (BAe were not involved) and XX833 was also brought up to full standard.

A BAC VC10 K.2 of No. 101 Squadron refuelling two No. 226 OCU Jaguars. All Jaguar pilots were trained in aerial refuelling. ***Blue Envoy Collection***

Operationally, the GR.1B aircraft were flown with a single 1,000lb Paveway II LGB and a TIALD pod under the wings as an asymmetric load with a centreline fuel tank. The aircraft could also be flown in a 'spiking' configuration to designate targets for other aircraft with TIALD on the centreline and two underwing fuel tanks for increased endurance. The first GR.1Bs arrived at Gioia del Colle in June 1995. During July, a Jaguar nearly used TIALD and Paveway in anger, but the aircraft – part of a multinational NATO mission – was recalled after take-off.On 27 July the Harrier Force took over the deployment, but two GR.1Bs were retained on standby at Coltishall in case they were needed to designate targets for the Harriers. Since 1993 the Jaguars had flown 3,130 sorties and 5,127 flying hours.

Deliberate Force

Operation Deliberate Force was a sustained air campaign conducted from 30 August to 20 September 1995 in collaboration with United Nations Protection Force (UNPROFOR) ground operations to degrade the military capability of the Bosnian Serb Army following the Srebrenica and Markale massacres and the shelling of the Sarajevo marketplace on 28 August. The operation involved 400 aircraft striking 338 targets, using 1,026 bombs, 708 of which were LGBs.

The RAF's contribution was Operation Vulcan and involved the Harrier GR.7s of No. IV(AC) Squadron supported by two Jaguar GR.1Bs from No. 6 Squadron; XX725 flown by Squadron Leader Alex Muskett and XX962 by Flight Lieutenant Simon Blake. The first combined sortie of four Harriers and both Jaguars was part of Strike Package Bravo at 12:30 on 30 August, hitting an ammunition depot at Hadzici with Paveways. The final mission that day was Strike Package Delta,

including two Harriers and a Jaguar, against an ammunition storage complex near Pale. The following day a mission was flown to the ammunition storage area at Ustikolina, but low cloud prevented weapons release.

A pause in operations until 6 September for negotiations was followed by attacks on the 7th on a range of communications, ammunition and electronic warfare sites. Poor weather affected the missions on subsequent days to some degree, the 14th being another temporary halt.

The Jaguars flew 28 TIALD sorties (and four without TIALD). During the 25 combined missions the Harrier GR.7s released 48 Paveway IIs on to 19 targets, with the Jaguars providing target designation (they also designated for some freefall bomb attacks). The result was 41 direct hits (85%) with four near misses within 20ft (6m). This impressive performance was not bettered in subsequent RAF deployments and was better than that obtained by the F-117A Nighthawk and General Dynamics F-111F during Desert Storm. This success rate had been achieved despite the pilots only having one week's training.

Success was aided by the fact that all drops were in daylight and mostly in the absence of air defences, which lessened the need for evasive tactics and allowed several runs by the Harriers before weapons release. In recognition of these efforts, in March 2020 Queen Elizabeth II approved the battle honour 'Bosnia 1995' for both squadrons.

The canopy of XZ114 belonging to No. 41(F) Squadron has been left open in March 1994 to reduce the temperature inside the cockpit. Full reheated thrust from the Adours was required to get airborne to cope with even moderately warm springtime temperatures, while an engine failure in the summertime would result in a crash. Note the overwing missile rail still painted in desert pink. ***Terry Panopalis Collection***

Ready to go. Jaguar XZ362 in full deployment standard at Coltishall in February 1995 with a pair of Sidewinders and a Phimat chaff dispenser pod. Two 1,000lb (454kg) practice bombs are on the centreline. ***Terry Panopalis Collection***

A BAC VC10 C.1K of No. 101 Squadron refuelling a formation of Jaguars on an overseas deployment. *Blue Envoy Collection*

Some issues had been identified, however. The radios had poor reception, the Sky Guardian 200 RWR gave many false indications that increased the pilot's workload (and stress levels) and the Adour's lack of thrust forced the accompanying Harriers to operate at a lower altitude than they desired, which increased fuel consumption. The Jaguars often had to use reheat, which not only consumed fuel but provided a good target for infrared (IR)-homing missiles. Another handicap was that the Harrier GR.7 was night capable, but the Jaguar GR.1B was not, which prevented nocturnal TIALD missions. An upgrade to provide NVG compatibility for four of the GR.1B aircraft was in hand, but not ready in time.

Following the negotiations and the resulting Dayton Peace Accords, which were formally signed in Paris on 14 December 1995, the NATO Implementation Force (IFOR) took over responsibility for policing in Bosnia-Herzegovina. No. 6 Squadron deployed a pair of Jaguars, along with four pilots and 28 groundcrew, in 23–30 April 1996. A total of 14 sorties were flown with the Harriers of No. 1(F) Squadron over five days. On one sortie a Jaguar had to return due to an AN/ALE-40 flare dispenser failure. The TIALD performed well, although a ban on activating lasers over Bosnia prevented any realistic training.

No. 41(F) Squadron deployed two TIALD-equipped GR.1Bs flown by Wing Commander Harper, the Squadron Officer Commanding (OC), and Flight Lieutenant Herbert, along with 24 support personnel to Gioia del Colle between 23 and 27 September for Operation Decisive Edge to provide laser designation capability for the Harriers. Poor weather prevented any laser training on the Glamoc range.

Six mixed formation sorties were flown over Bosnia, three of them with tanker support. The aircraft flew without any 30mm ammunition, but AIM-9L Sidewinders were carried. Communications and airspace clearance support from the Boeing E-3 AWACS was still vital, although a more structured airways system now existed over the region, controlled from Zagreb by NATO controllers. There was still a threat from MANPADS up to 15,000ft (4,570m) and the pilots in their post-deployment report highlighted the need for more powerful engines for operations above 20,000ft (3,050m). Following the deployment the Jaguars headed directly to Decimomannu in Sardinia for weapons training.

Jaguar 96 & 97

The introduction of TIALD capability was followed by a more structured two-phase upgrade programme. This was described by the Ministry of Defence (MoD) as a 'spend-to-save' measure to reduce temporary upgrade and running costs until the Eurofighter entered service. The interim standard was known as Jaguar 96 and saw the aircraft receive a MIL-STD 1553B databus and an improved navigation/attack system – the GPS-interfaced FIN1064G INS – and a BASE Terprom terrain reference navigation system, which provided a passive terrain warning/avoidance capability as well as passive weapons aiming. The cockpit was modernised with a Smiths flat multi-function display for the moving map and TIALD imagery (only four Jaguar 96 converted from GR.1B aircraft were TIALD compatible), GEC-Marconi FD4500 wide-angle HUD and HOTAS controls (the top of the control stick was from the Tornado F.3 and the hand controller from the Harrier GR.3). Two colour video recorders for HUD and TIALD imagery were also fitted. Aircraft destined for No. 41(F) Squadron retained the capability to carry the Vinten Series 603 Type 18 pod. The converted aircraft were redesignated as GR.3, XX738 being the first to be completed in January 1996.

The Jaguar 97 programme made further enhancements, adding TIALD and Vinten 601 GP1 VICON reconnaissance pod capability for all aircraft. The cockpit was further improved with a multifunctional colour LCD display screen, a new mission planning system, NVG compatibility and a GEC-Marconi Helmet Mounted Sight System (HMSS) (initially only 20 headsets were bought).

The HMSS allowed the pilot to generate co-ordinates for a point of reference on the ground, which removed the need to bring the aircraft to bear to generate accurate co-ordinates for either a strike or recce target. The pilot could also receive co-ordinates from a ground-based Forward Air Controller (FAC), with the helmet providing steering cues to guide their eyes on to the target for a quicker response time.The overwing air-to-air missile (AAM) pylons were replaced by new Common Rail Launchers that featured BOL chaff dispensers in the rear and were compatible with the new highly agile AIM-132 ASRAAM IR-homing AAM. Another new weapon was the 2,000lb (907kg) Paveway III LGB. The Jaguars were also fitted with the

A line-up of No. 41(F) Squadron Jaguars awaiting their next sortie at Eielson AFB, Alaska, in 1996. Some of the Jaguars have been repainted in the then new low-visibility air defence grey camouflage. *USAF*

Photo Reconnaissance Intel Strike Module – Improved Data Modem (PRISM-IDM) – to capture, receive and transmit frames of video imagery over a digital communications system, as well as other information such as FAC target co-ordinates. This allowed the pilots to receive target information while in the air and BDA images could be transmitted back to base before the aircraft returned. The upgraded aircraft were delivered as GR.3A and T.4A. A total of 64 single-seat and 17 two-seaters were upgraded under both programmes.

Jaguar GR.1B XX725 from No. 6 Squadron was used for TIALD trials at the Naval Air Warfare Center Weapons Division at China Lake, California, in November 1996. *US Navy via Terry Panopalis Collection*

The long-serving first production Jaguar S, XX108, was used for trials with Paveway LGBs and TIALD and is seen here carrying an inert Paveway and TIALD targeting pod inboard and AN/ALQ-101(V)10 ECM and chaff pods outboard. ***Blue Envoy Collection***

The continual calls for more power finally bore fruit with another 'spend-to-save' upgrade. From 2001 the engines were upgraded to Adour Mk.106 standard, which provided 25% more thrust. The Mk.106 married the cold section of the Adour Mk.871 (as fitted to the US Navy's McDonnell Douglas T-45A Goshawk variant of the Hawk) with the Mk.811's afterburner plus digital engine controls to reduce fuel consumption. One visible difference was that the Mk.106's hotter afterburner exhaust plume was blue rather than yellow.

The venerable first production GR.1 XX108 was fitted with a Mk.106 on the portside and flown on 7 June 2000 by BAe test pilot Gordon McClymont in a 55-minute sortie. This was followed by a test programme of 50 flights. Rolls-Royce were contracted to convert 122 Mk.104 engines to re-engine 62 Jaguars, the company's East Kilbride factory being responsible for upgrading the engines and the Defence Aviation Repair Agency at St Athan carrying out the installation.

The cost of the engine upgrade programme was £100 million, but it was estimated that the saving on running costs would amount to £40 million. XX108 was delivered by McClymont to St Athan on its final flight on 28 May 2002. On 8 May 2003 an in-flight problem led to a temporary grounding for all re-engined Jaguars until the 27th while the issue was sorted.

The small number of TIALD pods across the RAF (just 23 in total for the Tornado, Harrier and Jaguar) was too low to sustain a realistic training programme. The Jaguar Force was better off as it had its own 200 Series pods to enable it to train at a reasonable level, but this training was later severely curtailed when these pods were recalled for updating to 400 Series standard, which became eligible for transfer to the Harriers and

Tornados. The Jaguar was the first aircraft to get a desktop, computer-based, synthetic training package for TIALD, which was later rolled out to the Harrier and Tornado during the early 2000s.

The Jaguar Replacement Reconnaissance Pod programme was launched to replace the VICON Type 18 and Vinten was awarded the contract. This entered service as the Digital Joint Reconnaissance Pod (DJRP) in August 2000, subsequently being fitted to other RAF combat aircraft. The pod was 2.3m (7ft 8in) long, 46cm (18in) in diameter and weighed 595lb (270kg). It offered medium- and low-level reconnaissance modes. A Super Vigil IR sensor was common to both modes and offered horizon-to-horizon coverage. In the medium-altitude mode, one Vinten 8042 electro-optical sensor was mounted in the nose of the pod, was capable of rotating 180° from horizon to horizon and provided a stand-off capability. In low-level mode one camera was normally mounted on each side of the pod.The DJRP was designed to be fully automated, with the Jaguar Mission Planner providing the co-ordinates of pre-planned targets and with a manual control for targets of opportunity. The sensors fed digital data to two recording modules for data storage, which was either downloaded after the flight, or could be transmitted to Networked Imagery Exploitation System (NIES) consoles for interpretation via a datalink. The DJRP was used in Operation Telic in March 2003 and in Afghanistan (although in both cases not aboard Jaguars) and was exported to South Africa for their Saab Gripen fighters.

Deliberate Guard

The Jaguar Force returned to Gioia del Colle in February 1997. The deployment was renamed Operation Deliberate Guard as the mission was revised to support SFOR (Stabilisation Force) personnel in Bosnia as well as the continued enforcement of the 'No-Fly Zone'. The detachment was commanded by Group Captain R J Horwood between 15 November 1996 and 28 April 1997, and Wing Commander A D Stevenson from 19 August to 20 December, when Wing Commander W G Evans took over for the remainder of the deployment. The detachment numbered six Jaguars with two TIALD pods. The number of personnel deployed was around 190. The mission task was eight sorties per day: three for Close Air Support (CAS), three for recce and two training flights.

The venerable XX108 was also used as the testbed for the improved Adour Mk.106, the new engine being installed on the port side. Two dummy 1,000lb (454kg) bombs have been fitted to provide a representative load for performance testing. ***Terry Panopalis Collection***

Bosnia Operations				
	CAS	Recce	Training	Total
3 Feb-27 Mar 97				
Tasked	116	100	38	254
Flown	104	88	33	225
Hours	189	192	41	422
30 May-23 Jul 97				
Tasked	150	140	21	311
Flown	122	124	19	265
Aborted	24	12	0	36
19 Nov-7 Jan 98				
Tasked	110	66	62	238
Flown	66	30	42 1	38
Ground Alert	22	2	4	28
Aborted	18	32	16	66

A Jaguar of No. 41(F) preparing to take off on a reconnaissance sortie during Operation Northern Watch in February 1999 with a Vinten VICON reconnaissance pod and AIM-9L Sidewinders. *USAF*

The first deployment was by No. 41(F) Squadron between 3 February and 27 March. It had been hoped to deploy with Jaguar 96-standard aircraft but delays to the upgrade programme meant that this was not possible.

Delays in receiving clearance and documentation for the new Vinten 601 GP1 VICON reconnaissance pod caused some pre-deployment worries and removed any chance to train on them, operational flying using the pods commencing on 10 February. The VICON pod contained a 17.7in (450mm) focal length camera and a 3in (76mm) panoramic camera that provided better image quality and twice the field of view compared with the previous Vinten 603 pod. The panoramic camera was also very useful for low-level photography and as a mapping camera. Jaguar XZ112 arrived at Gioia del Colle on 17 February with the first of the new pods. Visual aiming worked well but was reliant on the Garmin GPS mounted on the cockpit coaming to ensure that the pilot was on track (in the north-eastern area of Bosnia the GPS signal would often unlock).

CAS sorties were flown with full electronic countermeasure (ECM) fit and one 1,000lb bomb at 10,000–20,000ft (6,100–3,050m), sometimes operating as low as 5,000ft (1,525m). Due to the Adour's poor performance, however, frequent use of reheat was required to maintain height. Aerial refuelling from Tristar K.1 tankers based at Palermo increased endurance by up to 20 minutes. The tanker support, as ever, was excellent but using the single-point K.1 meant that the lead aircraft used up ten minutes of fuel waiting for the wingman to refuel, with the problem even worse for a four-ship formation. The detachment advised using BAC VC10 K.2 three-point tankers instead, but they were unavailable. Serviceability was excellent with 70% availability, and the standard daily tasking was easily achieved. Only nine sorties were aborted due to technical issues (the regulations stated that both aircraft had to return to base if one went unserviceable in the air for safety). There were delays in getting spares, however, and two aircraft suffered so badly from fuel leaks that they could not be fitted with recce pods due to a risk of damage to them from fuel contamination. The aircraft were eventually fixed, but a third leaking Jaguar was left behind. Jaguar XZ360 suffered a loss of fuel content gauge indications after an aerial refuelling on 26 February, causing a diversion to Dubrovnik. The problem reoccurred on a subsequent flight and was traced to chafed and arcing cable in the port wing leading edge. XZ355 suffered two air conditioning failures that both necessitated a return to Coltishall to rectify (it turned out to be a canopy lock microswitch problem), and on 20 March XZ113 aborted due to a nozzle position indication fault.

No. 54(F) Squadron deployed during 24 March to 29 May 1997 under Wing Commander B R Armstrong with six Jaguar GR.1B and a further six Jaguars held at Coltishall as a reinforcement package on 72 hours' notice to deploy. Four of the Jaguars were swapped for upgraded Jaguar 96 GR.3 aircraft during the deployment, three of them being reconnaissance capable (the detachment only had three VICON pods).

The advantages of the HOTAS controls to reduce pilot workload while improving tactical awareness and flight safety were soon demonstrated and the clarity of the new HUD was praised, as were the improved radio channel switches and VICON pod controls. At that time, TIALD clearance had not been obtained for the GR.3. The Special Trials Fit (STF) to jettison the AN/ALQ-101(V)10 ECM and Phimat chaff pods had been withdrawn, but after much complaint this was restored on 2 May.

Overall aircraft availability was 99%, with only 13 air aborts for technical reasons. There were few major faults; XZ109 requiring a nose undercarriage leg replacement (being flown back to Coltishall for the work), the brakes

Jaguar XX965 of No. 226 OCU carrying a single inert training Paveway LGB on the ventral hardpoint and an ALQ-101 ECM pod outboard. *Blue Envoy Collection*

failed while taxying on XZ363 and XZ115 suffered a cracked fuel manifold pipe on one of its Adours.

One problem was the lack of Tactical Air Control Party (TACP) authority to make dummy diving attacks on targets. While this avoided any inadvertent weapons release (a US Navy F/A 18 Hornet pilot had done this), it denied the chance to practise medium-level attacks.

During this period three VICON pods replaced the older LOROP pods (which were retained in reserve) and quickly demonstrated their superior imagery. Initially the recce tasking was devoted to strategic mapping, despite the Jaguar being a tactical platform and the Canberra PR.9s of No. 39 Squadron flying monthly mapping sorties over the area. Most of the recce targets were Dayton Agreement Sites, a mix of open and enclosed stores of heavy weapons and SAMs that were created by the Agreement and inspected by IFOR monitors. A number of suspected mass grave sites were also monitored, as were other military and command installations, military units and infrastructure.

Battlefield Air Interdiction (BAI) missions were also key. The squadron was involved in planning an Exercise Griffin training mission to attack 17 targets, which involved the simulated delivery of freefall 'dumb' bombs from medium altitude on to a large target (clearance for TIALD designation of LGBs for the Harrier Force had been withdrawn at this time).

No. 6 Squadron took its turn during 30 May to 23 July and all six Jaguars were GR.3s. A further six Jaguars were held at Coltishall as a reinforcement package. While the Jaguar 96 upgrade was a success, it was found that the Sky Guardian RWR needed tweaking for the local range of electromagnetic emissions encountered.

The squadron requested that the TACPs should use more accurate eight-figure target co-ordinates, a reflection of the increased accuracy attained by the Jaguar 96; this was implemented and NATO TACPs also began using them. The restriction on diving attack practice was gradually lifted by the TACPs.

The COAC considered the Jaguar's VICON pod to be one of the most reliable reconnaissance assets that it possessed in-theatre due to its ability to gain accurate information and return it in a timely fashion. The squadron was very pleased with the exceptional results obtained with the pod with 100% coverage of targets (weather permitting) – although they complained that tasking to reconnoitre a single target was an inefficient use of the aircraft.

Coltishall-based Jaguars retained their disruptive camouflage. This pair of 54(F) Squadron aircraft are on a training sortie in August 1995. *Terry Panopalis Collection*

GR.1A XZ394 of No. 54(F) Squadron and T.2A XX845 of No. 6 Squadron on a training sortie from Coltishall in August 1995. ***Terry Panopalis Collection***

The Jaguar's lack of thrust at high ambient temperatures remained its Achilles heel. An engine failure on take-off would result in the pilot having to abandon the aircraft. One solution was to programme Tristar tanker support for afternoon missions to allow take-offs with a reduced fuel load and topping off from the tanker once airborne. Tristar flying hours were limited, however, and there were still no VC10 tankers available. Clearance for trials to refuel from French Boeing KC-135FR Stratotankers had been obtained, but a proposal to delegate operational clearance to experienced qualified pilots was rejected by the Air Staff and it was discovered that the French had no drogue-equipped KC-135s available anyway.

No. 41(F) Squadron was deployed during 24 July to 24 September. A surge period of 12 sorties per day was maintained, with an eighth pilot sent from the UK during 12–18 September and 1–3 October to cover periods of heightened tension during the Serbian elections. By now TIALD was cleared for the GR.3 and the pilots agreed that its integration was much better than it had been on the GR.1B. The squadron's Reconnaissance Information Centre (RIC) was also deployed from Coltishall to support the detachment.

A Jaguar of No. 54(F) Squadron receiving fuel from an aerial tanker during an Operation Northern Watch mission over Iraq on 19 September 2002. ***USAF***

No. 54(F) Squadron took its turn during 25 September to 19 November. The squadron was praised for planning and leading one of the best BAI missions flown – BAI 97-15 on 4 November involving eight multinational sections – as well as paving the way to use the Glamoc range for training with lasers (TIALD and LRMTS).

In October the STF to jettison the ALQ-101 and Phimat pods was removed as the temporary clearance had finally expired, though the squadron warned that the capability would be required again in the following spring due to the high ambient temperatures (in the event the detachment would end before that happened).

No. 6 Squadron took up the deployment under the command of Wing Commander M J Roche from 19 November 1997 to 7 January 1998. One new piece of kit trialled by the pilots was a new Pro Boot that provided improved warmth and comfort compared to the standard-issue flying boots. The winter weather hampered operations, some flights being scrubbed en route, and the COAC also restricted weekend flying. The squadron was tasked with two CAS missions per day on average. Practice dive attacks on targets were flown on the majority of missions – with TACP clearance – to keep the Serbs' heads down.

The VICON pod gave excellent results, although there were complaints about the slow uploading of mission briefing data – an issue that the Jaguar 97 upgrade solved with its increased data transfer capability.

Ready Force Practice (RFP) was flown on average once a day, which gave continuation training on TIALD when the weather allowed, including flights over the Glamoc range. Winter conditions meant increased use of braking parachutes and led to extra parachutes being supplied from the UK.One unwelcome intrusion was pressure from the MoD and COAC to co-operate with laser designation training for Harrier GR.7s deployed aboard the carrier HMS *Invincible* – but which were not part of Deliberate Guard – at short notice during December. This task involved nine mixed Sea Harrier FA.2 and Jaguar recce and CAS sorties, and top cover had to be flown for the GR.7s as they were unable to land back aboard the carriers with external stores.

No. 6 Squadron was replaced by No. 41(F) between 6 January and 18 February 1998. This period was marked by the relocation of the Tristar tankers from Palmero to Brindisi. The RIC still lacked a LOCE (Linked OPS-INTEL Centre Europe) terminal – which cost £10,000 – which meant that distributing information between 5ATAF COAC and the UK was made more difficult.

While TIALD proved mostly reliable, a lack of contractor support in-theatre did cause some issues, for example when a fuel leak led to contamination of one pod. The squadron also suffered from sight-line failures in the TIALD pods, with the fault noticeable to the pilot in the display image. The engineers concluded that high airspeeds caused the problem, and a more powerful ball-drive motor for the sensor ball later solved the issue.

Operation Dynamic Strike was flown on 3 April 1998, supporting the deployment of a USMC Marine Expeditionary Unit. Four practise missions were flown beforehand, but the results were mixed due to inappropriate TACP close control as well as the poor weather. Reconnaissance was also sapping morale as repetitive tasking against low-priority targets taxed both the pilots and the photo interpreters, and it was not clear to the detachment that their imagery was being used wisely by the COAC. The repetitive nature of the flying tasks led to pilot complacency creeping in despite the crews being aware of this danger. Despite this, the morale of the pilots and groundcrews remained high. Five years of very successful deployments were ended on 7 April 1998.

Retirement

During the Labour government's Strategic Defence Review of 1997, the Secretary of State for Defence, George Robertson's aide, Bernard Gray, had argued strongly for the disbandment of the Jaguar Force and the closure of Coltishall for the considerable savings that this would achieve. The new Chief of the Air Staff, Air Chief Marshal Sir Richard Johns, fought against this. At that time the Jaguar 96 and 97 upgrades were in full swing and the RAF was still heavily committed to Operations Warden, Southern Watch and Deliberate Guard. It could therefore not afford to disband three squadrons and transferring these tasks on to the Tornados and Harriers was unsustainable. The Eurofighter (soon to be named Typhoon) was still half a decade away from service. So strongly did Air Chief Marshal Johns feel about this that he secretly wrote a letter of resignation should the Review include the disbandment of the Jaguar Force. Thankfully wiser counsel prevailed and the Jaguar continued in service.

Medium-altitude operations became the norm for Jaguar pilots post-1990. This December 2002 image shows GR.3 XZ109 of No. 6 Squadron. Three months later it was upgraded to GR.3A standard. ***Terry Panopalis Collection***

Ironically, just as the Jaguar reached the peak of its technological and combat effectiveness, its contribution to combat operations declined. The Jaguar did not take part in NATO Operation Allied Force, between March and June 1999 in response to Serbian repression of the Albanian population of Kosovo, who were seeking independence, although No. 41(F) Squadron did deploy its RIC to Gioia del Colle to support the Harrier Force detachment led by No. 1(F) Squadron.

The Operation Warden detachment at Incirlik Air Base from No. 6 Squadron was planned to be involved in Operation Telic in March 2003, but Turkey's decision not to get involved and refusal to give diplomatic clearance for flights from Turkish airspace meant that the eight Jaguars could not take part. Attempts to deploy the Jaguars to airfields south of Iraq were frustrated by lack of airfield space and it was decided that the Harrier GR.7 fitted with the DJRP (at that stage it was not fully cleared for service) could handle the tactical reconnaissance mission instead. No. 41(F) once again deployed its RIC, along with five DJRPs and NIES to support the Harriers.

The Jaguar Force did not contribute to subsequent deployments in Iraq and Afghanistan, despite its capabilities and the fact that out of the RAF's fighter fleet, the Jaguar was the only one with a reliably working cannon (cannon

A Jaguar of No. 16(R) Squadron takes off from Coltishall on another training sortie in November 2002. *MoD/ OGL 2002*

by this time being appreciated as one of the more accurate precision weapons against enemy personnel). The Jaguar also had a lower cost per flight hour compared with the Harrier and Tornado and could have given much-needed relief to the demanding Joint Force Harrier deployments to areas such as Kandahar, which were stretching Harrier resources to the limit, but it was not to be.

Eight Jaguars visited the Bulgarian Graf Ignatievo airbase, near Plovdiv, for two weeks in August 2002 Exercise Lone Cat, flying sorties with their Bulgarian hosts and familiarising them with NATO procedures and tactics.

One highlight was a flypast over Norwich and Coltishall on 19 September 2003 to mark the Jaguar's 30th anniversary of RAF service. The formation was comprised of GR.3As: XX729, XZ115, XX112, XX117, XZ104, XZ398, XZ357, XZ360, XZ400, XZ106, XX720, XX748 and XZ394 plus T.4s XX845, XX846 and XX150. In addition, T.4s XX841 and XX139 and GR.3 XX766 (with special markings '30 Years Jaguar' were air spares and photo ships.

The Strike Attack Operational Evaluation Unit (SAOEU) at RAF Coningsby began flying the Jaguar in 2004. This unit was part of the Air Warfare Centre and undertook trials of weapons, systems and tactics for all of the RAF's front-line attack aircraft. This encompassed tactical advice on the use of existing equipment and employment of current doctrine, and the evaluation of new equipment for its operational utility and suitability.

As the twenty-first century dawned, the retirement of the Jaguar loomed closer as replacement by the Typhoon became a reality. The MoD announced in 2004 that the Jaguar Force would be retired during 2009 and Coltishall would be closed.

In early 2004, No. 6 Squadron visited the Romanian Air Force's Mihail Kogălniceanu airbase for NATO co-operation exercises – Romania having joined the alliance that year. They flew training exercises alongside the upgraded MiG-21 Lancer A, which were optimised for the ground-attack role.During August–November 2005 No. 41(F) Squadron had a busy time: there was the joint RAF/USAF Exercise Excalibur at the Wainfleet and Holbeach ranges on 17–18 August (Flight Lieutenant Alex 'Tenno' Tennant winning the 10° Low Altitude High Drag Bomb competition and Flight Lieutenant Mike 'Sooty' Sutton, coming second in the 45° degree High Altitude Release Bomb competition), an Annual Practice

In April 2002 GR.3A XZ103 was given an experimental camouflage scheme combining the air defence grey and desert pink. *D Hedge via Terry Panopalis Collection*

Jaguar XX729 was upgraded to GR.3A standard and was one of the last aircraft to serve with No. 6 Squadron. *MoD*

Camp in Cyprus until 2 September, then an exchange visit to Base Aérienne (BA) 133 Nancy-Ochey until 7 October and finally Exercise Uhlan Barbara in Poland during 10–21 November.

The Jaguar's draw-down proceeded as planned, Nos 54(F) and 16(R) Squadrons disbanding on 11 March 2005, with No. 41(F) following in March 2006. The SAOEU also stopped flying the Jaguar and received the now vacant No. 41 Squadron numberplate, being renamed the Fast Jet & Weapons Operational Evaluation Unit.

By this time the decision had been made to move No. 6 Squadron to Coningsby to permit Coltishall to close earlier; the base has since gained a new life as a prison and solar farm. In 2021 the RAF Coltishall Heritage

Jaguars wore winter camouflage throughout their RAF service. GR.3A XX720 of No. 54(F) Squadron is seen here in February 2005. *Terry Panopalis Collection*

In March 2005 Coltishall celebrated its 65th anniversary and GR.3A XZ112 of No. 41(F) Squadron received special tail markings to mark the occasion. Only a month later the airfield was closed. *Terry Panopalis Collection*

To commemorate No. 54(F) Squadron's standing down on 11 March 2005, XZ112 received fresh special tail artwork featuring the colours of the squadron along with the lion rampant, which features the arms of France and Flanders, commemorating the unit's First World War service on the Western Front. *D Hedge via Terry Panopalis Collection*

Centre opened to the public, located in the former Guardroom; it received Jaguar XZ384 in July 2024 for preservation and display. The squadron had 14 GR.3A and two T.4s along with 21 pilots, with a high proportion of first tourists. The squadron moved at the beginning of April, not long after participating at Red Flag. At the same time it was announced that the retirement date would be brought forward to October 2007 as clearance for the Typhoon in the air-to-ground role was imminent. During this time the squadron attended various Tactical Leadership Programme exercises as well as a month-long deployment to the United Arab Emirates in early 2007 and other deployments to Oman and Cyprus.

Unexpectedly the disbandment date was again brought forward and the OC, Wing Commander John Sullivan, was notified on 24 April 2007 that his unit was to cease operations six days later before disbanding at the end of May. The squadron during those six days managed to deploy ten Jaguars to Lossiemouth for a farewell visit and flew 12 aircraft in a 'Big 6' formation on the 30th to mark the end of RAF Jaguar operations.

Some limited continuation flying continued while the pilots awaited transfer to Typhoon squadrons. The squadron formally disbanded on 31 May, ending a record 93 years of uninterrupted service that included operations from 91 airfields across three continents. GR.3A XX725 was given a desert pink scheme to honour the use in Operation Granby at the disbandment parade with a formation flypast. GR.3A XX119 emerged with an eye-catching 'spotty Jaguar' paint scheme at the end of June as a fitting end to the type's career.

The remaining aircraft were delivered in batches to the Defence College of Aeronautical Engineering at RAF Cosford for ground instructional use from April. XX119, flown by Wing Commander John Sullivan, was among the last to arrive on 2 July, accompanied by T.4 XX835 and XX725 flown by Flight Lieutenant Matt D'Aubyn, No. 6's youngest pilot and newest qualified Jaguar pilot. Rotary Hydraulic Arrestor Gear was temporarily fitted to Cosford's short 3,890ft (1,185m) runway for these delivery flights, but no mishaps occurred. Some of the aircraft were maintained in taxying condition at Cosford for a while and trials work with an improved Adour intended for the Indian Air Force Jaguar fleet was conducted on XX119.

During 2023 some of the Cosford Jaguars were retired from being ground instructional airframes and several have been donated to museums (see Appendix 2 for details). In December 2023 XX119 – still in its fantastic colours – was moved to Lossiemouth for preservation with No. 6 Squadron.

'Spotty Jag' bows out. The 12th Jaguar GR.1 built, XX119 received this striking colour scheme to ensure that the type left RAF service with style. ***MoD/OGL 2007***

The end of the road. XX119 sits in a hangar at Cosford in September 2008 in its splendid colours with the tail fin adorned with the badges of all the RAF's Jaguar squadrons. In December 2023 it returned to the Jaguar's spiritual home of Lossiemouth with ex-Jaguar squadron No. 6, which now flies Eurofighter Typhoons (although it was Coltishall-based for most of its long career, XX119 never actually served with No. 6 Squadron). ***Terry Panopalis Collection***

CHAPTER EIGHT

The Jaguar goes to sea

The Jaguar Marine was a naval aircraft carrier-based development to meet the needs of the French Marine Nationale to replace its Dassault Étendard IVM attack aircraft. While the Jaguar proved adaptable to meet the tough demands of the marine environment and operation aboard aircraft carriers, its lack of engine thrust was an Achilles heel and structural problems and the request to fit a new wing inflated the development costs to a point where it was unfeasible to continue the project. Prototype M05 was diverted to other aerodynamic trials work and ultimately the Marine Nationale would acquire the Dassault Super Étendard instead.

Jaguar Marine

The Marine Nationale had been one of the pioneering navies to operate seaplanes from its warships as early as 1913. It became the fourth navy in the world to operate an aircraft carrier when the *Béarn* was completed in May 1927 (converted from an unfinished battleship). The Second World War prevented the planned expansion of France's carrier fleet, but in the early post-war years both the United Kingdom and the United States gifted new ships as France's recovering economy could not afford to fund new construction. France's early attempts at building its own carrier-based aircraft for the Aéronavale – fighters such as the Arsenal VB.10 and

On approach to land aboard *Clemenceau* in July 1970. *Dassault via Author's Collection*

VG.90, SNCASO SO.8000 Narval, Nord 2200 and the Nord 1500 Noréclair bomber – ended in failure due to one technical reason or another. France opted to licence-build the de Havilland DH.112 Sea Venom FAW.20 fighter as the SNCASE Aquilon in single- and two-seat versions, both equipped with American radars.

The acquisition of jet-powered aircraft demanded modern carriers and in 1954 and 1955 two new ships were approved. The *Clemenceau* was laid down in November 1955 and commissioned on 22 November 1961, being followed by her sistership *Foch* on 15 July 1963. They had a displacement of 22,000 tons and a flightdeck 843ft 10in (257m) long, were equipped with two British BS.5 steam catapults and Mark 13 arresting gear and could accommodate up to 40 aircraft. The 164ft (50m)-long BS.5 catapults could launch a 33,000lb (15,000kg) aircraft at 110kt with an acceleration force of 3.6g – later increased to 125kt at 4.4g with a slightly lighter 30,900lb (14,000kg) aircraft. They were the first modern carriers in Europe to be built from the keel up. A larger third carrier, the 35,000-ton PA 58 project, proved too expensive and was cancelled in the early 1960s.

As early as 1952 the Marine Nationale had wanted to order prototypes of the new Dassault Aviation Mystère IVM single-seat day fighter, but this project was soon cancelled by the Air Ministry. Then it was proposed to navalise a prototype of the Mystère XXII powered by two Turbomeca Gabizo turbojets, but again cancellation befell the programme. A navalised prototype of the Breguet Br.1100, the Br.1100M powered by two Gabizos, was completed and flown – but only once – on 15 November 1957. Concerns about growing weight led to its cancellation before the flight testing programme could begin. Finally, in October 1956 the Marine Nationale ordered a navalised Mystère XXIV, Dassault redesigning it with a 9,700lbf (43.16kN) thrust SNECMA ATAR 08B turbojet, a larger wing with lift-increasing flaps and folding outer sections, fuselage area ruling to cut transonic drag and a modified Messier undercarriage with stronger shock absorbers and a longer nose leg to attain the correct angle of attack (AoA) for catapult launches. On 31 May 1957 five Étendard IVM pre-series aircraft were ordered, the first flying on 28 May 1958 from Melun Villaroche with test pilot Jean Michel Saget at the controls. Production totalled 69 Étendard IVM fighters and 21 Étendard IVP reconnaissance aircraft, with the first delivery in December 1961.

By 1964 the Aéronavale was looking at a successor and attention turned to the SEPECAT Jaguar to fulfil this need. The British Royal Navy had also been interested in providing the capability for the Jaguar B trainer to land aboard a carrier, so the basic groundwork already existed to further extend this maritime capability and as the Jaguar was still in the development phase any necessary design changes could be incorporated easily. The Étendard IVM replacement was to be an attack aircraft, armed with either a single 25kT AN 52 nuclear bomb or anti-ship guided missiles. A slightly larger airframe and more advanced avionics to improve navigational accuracy were wanted but the aircraft did not need to be supersonic. It had to be capable of operation from the two *Clemenceau*-class carriers.

Prototype Jaguar Marine M05 on static display surrounded by an array of weaponry including HE bombs, BL.755 cluster bombs, Matra rocket pods, AS.37 Martel and AIM-9 Sidewinder missiles. ***Blue Envoy Collection***

In 1962 the requirement for a supersonic all-weather interceptor had been met by buying the American Ling Temco Vought (LTV) F-8E(FN) Crusader, which opened the door to another potential foreign purchase if a French land based aircraft could not be adapted successfully.

The fifth prototype was allocated as the Jaguar Marine airframe, designated M05. The Royal Aircraft Establishment (RAE) at Farnborough investigated the take-off performance using a steam catapult, covering not just the *Clemenceau* class but also the British carriers HMS *Eagle* and HMS *Hermes* in case of future use from those ships (although by this time the Royal Navy had withdrawn from the Jaguar programme). The RAE used the early design data available from Breguet and the British Aircraft Corporation (BAC), looking at the use of 20° and 40° flap angles with launching weights of 22,000lb (9,980kg) clean with a full fuel load and 29,000lb (13,155kg) at maximum weight. The RAE recommended launching with 40° of flap and initial 10° AoA (Breguet had proposed 7.5°) with a 25kt headwind over the deck to allow a maximum-weight take-off; the longer catapults aboard the British ships imposed fewer weight penalties.

The technical requirements were issued in May 1967 and Breguet began work on modifying the airframe. The fuselage was reinforced to withstand a maximum catapult stress of 5.5g – the requirement for take-off a linear acceleration of 1.5kt/sec with a loss of

M05 on RAE Bedford's BXS.4 steam catapult in April 1970 to determine the minimum catapulting speed and the correct flap settings for take-off. *Author's Collection*

height of no more than 5ft (1.5m) at up to maximum take-off weight with engines at full reheated thrust. The lower fuselage structure was strengthened and catapult strop anchor points were added. The airframe also needed suitable anti-corrosion treatment given the heavily salt-laden operating environment. The existing airfield emergency arrester hook was replaced by a stronger carrier-capable hook rated to brake a 22,045lb (10,000kg) aircraft at 5g and the braking parachute was removed.

The maximum vertical speed on landing was to be 18ft/sec (5.5m/sec), with an approach speed of at least 130kt. The undercarriage was accordingly redesigned with single-wheel main legs with long shock absorbers which were vertically oriented when extended and a new longer twin-wheel nose leg for the correct nose-up attitude for catapult launching. Stronger undercarriage attachment points to the spars were also provided. A fuel dumping system was fitted to ensure that the aircraft could rapidly attain landing weight in the event of an emergency requiring a sooner than planned landing back aboard the carrier. The standard inflight refuelling probe was retained and a 'buddy' refuelling pod could be carried ventrally. The RB.172 Adour Mk.101 engines were initially unmodified, however, later in the trials programme Mk.102 engines with partial throttle reheat (PTR) were fitted. Maximum speed was to be Mach 1.6 at 36,000ft (10,970m) with a combat radius of 270nm (500km).

Serviceability had to meet the same standards as the land-based Jaguars with the ability to operate five one-hour sorties daily. The provision for armament was identical to that of the Jaguar A. In the anti-ship role up to three Nord AS.30 or one Matra/Hawker Siddeley Dynamics AS.37 Martel air-to-surface missile could be carried.

The Système de Navigation et d'Attaque (SNA) navigation/attack system was fitted with an inertial navigation system coupled with a Doppler radar to measure drift and a radar altimeter. A Thomson-CSF TAV-38 laser rangefinder fitted below the nose cone (also added to the production Jaguar A). A vertical OMERA camera was fitted for reconnaissance. In the cockpit, the ejection seat was updated to a 'zero-zero'-capable Martin-Baker Mk.9B for improved safety. Even the cockpit windscreen washers were modified, using jets of water mixed with de-icing fluid to clear away salt water deposits during low-altitude flying. In total, the changes added around 1,540lb (700kg) to the aircraft's empty weight, which was now 14,574lb (6,611kg).

Flight trials begin

Prototype Jaguar M05 (registered F-ZWRJ) made its first flight on 14 November 1969 at the Centre d'Essais en Vol (CEV) at Melun Villaroche with Breguet test pilot Jacques Jesberger at the controls. Jesberger was a former Aéronavale pilot who had transferred to the CEV in 1957 as a test pilot before joining Breguet in 1962. During the flight, Jesberger observed that the main undercarriage doors were suffering from vibration when the undercarriage was extended, especially at angles of attack greater than 11°.

Breguet's Chief Test Pilot, Bernard Witt, flew the aircraft on 18 and 20 November and noted the same severe lateral instability that dogged the other early aircraft. Witt ferried the aircraft to Istres on 21 November, where it joined the other prototypes. At this point the aircraft was modified with the twin ventral strakes and wing fences as applied to the other prototypes to cure the instability. Focus then switched to curing the vibration issue, more tests being carried out after the twelfth flight and the cause being traced to the turbulent airflow from the nosewheel door, which was then removed. The nose pitot probe was also shortened. To improve the low-speed flying characteristics, the flaps were altered with two deflection settings; 40° for the inboard flaps and 34° outboard.

During December only two flights were made, Jesberger taking the Jaguar M aloft on the 10th and on Christmas Eve. Flying resumed in early 1970, initially focused on the low-speed handling, with Jesberger amassing 23 flights.

The test pilot team was soon expanded. BAC's senior experimental test pilot Paul Millett made his first flight in M05 on 6 February. Millett was an experienced naval pilot, having served in the Fleet Air Arm with operational service over Korea totalling 175 sorties and more than 200 deck landings. He was awarded a Distinguished Service Cross for saving his observer's life following a ditching. He flew several carrier approach sorties as second pilot to Jesberger, but ultimately he was not selected to join the seagoing trials. Lieutenant de Vaisseau Daniel Pierre, a naval pilot from the CEV, joined the team on 15 April.

At this stage the trials programme began focusing on simulated deck landings – Appontages Simulés Sur Porte-avions (ASSP) (an airfield dummy deck landing in British parlance) – in preparation for the catapult launch trials, which would be carried out at RAE Bedford. The ASSP sorties were carried out at the Aéronavale station at Nîmes-Garons, using the mirror approach sight to conduct realistic deck-landing conditions on its 8,015ft (2,440m)-long runway. During these trials the quality of the damping, the structural stresses and the throttle response of the engines was measured and the best speeds and AoA to adopt for take-off were assessed. During one of these flights M05 ingested a bird into one of the intakes. The aircraft was able to make a successful single-engine landing and the Adour was returned to Rolls-Royce Turbomeca Limited (RRTM) for repair.

Bedford trials

The catapult launching trials were carried out at RAE Bedford, which was the major naval aircraft experimental site in Europe. The RAE had moved its Naval Air Department from Farnborough to Thurleigh airfield during 1955–58. Runway 07/25 was converted into the Arrested Landing Deck experimental area. To the north, two catapult sites were built parallel with each other on the same orientation as the runway, each with a 2,500ft (760m) paved runway at the end of the steam catapult. A safety barrier was erected 350ft (107m) from the end of the runway. The first catapult site to be completed was a BXS.4 steam catapult mounted 6ft (1.8m) above the ground and used for evaluating aircraft and proof-testing airborne stores and equipment. It was capable of accelerating an aircraft weighing 30,000lb (13,600kg) to 155kt within 200ft (62m) with a maximum force of 6g. A second site completed in 1960 had a BXS.5 steam catapult mounted flush with the ground and was intended for catapult component trials but was also capable of launching aircraft, which it did for the first time in April 1964. It was capable of accelerating an aircraft weighing 30,000lb to 190kt within 200ft with a maximum force of 8.8g.

The Arrested Landing Deck runway could accommodate up to three arrester systems at any one time, including rotary hydraulic gear and the new Direct Acting Arrester Gear, which used a piston and water spray for the braking action (it had been developed for the cancelled British CVA-01 carrier programme). There was also a V/STOL test pit for the Hawker Siddeley P.1127 and Harrier test programmes. Even though the site was slowly winding down as the UK had decided to pay off its aircraft carriers by the end of the decade, the facilities were unique in Europe.

The Jaguar's arrival at Bedford was delayed by industrial action by RAE personnel, Bernard Sigaud, Breguet's director of test operations refusing to let his team leave until the strike had ended. On 20 April 1970 Jesberger ferried M05 from Istres to Bedford, the flight taking two hours. Catapulting tests used the raised BXS.4 catapult, the aim being to find the VMC

M05 emerges from *Clemenceau*'s hangar to prepare for another test flight. *Dassault via Author's Collection*

(Minimum Catapulting Speed) in all configurations and to determine the correct flap configuration.

Jesberger flew 'free stick' launches, letting the aircraft choose by itself the optimal aerodynamic attitude just after launch, a method that was common to all carrier-based aircraft fitted with mechanical flight controls. Camera pods were fitted on the outer wing hardpoints but no other external stores were fitted, the airframe remaining in a clean configuration. A total of nine catapult launches and 38 arrested landings were made by Jesberger and Daniel Pierre before another bout of industrial action saw M05 being flown back to Istres on 4 May.

M05 has caught the arrester wire aboard *Clemenceau*. The undercarriage was redesigned and strengthened by Messier to cope with the stresses of landing aboard aircraft carriers. *Terry Panopalis Collection*

At Istres, the Marine Nationale's Jaguar M project officer, Capitaine de Corvette Yves Goupil, was checked out on M05 on 28 May. He had been the first Aéronavale pilot to qualify on the F-8E(FN) and had been commander of the F-8 unit Flotille 14F. A three-day intensive series of ASSPs from 27 May at Istres evaluated the final configuration of the high-lift condition – new flap settings of 45° for the inner flaps and 25° for the outer flaps.

Goupil and Jesberger also flew tests to determine the handling during inflight refuelling, making dummy air-to-air refuellings from an Étendard IVM fitted with a 'buddy' tanking pod. The first attempt did not go well. It proved very difficult to disengage from the drogue and the resulting forceful attempt to break contact nearly destroyed the refuelling hose. Following inspection on the ground, the starboard engine's compressor blades were found to have been damaged by metal debris from the drogue and the engine had to be replaced.

On 8 June Jesberger flew M05 back to Bedford for a second round of tests. Over ten days Jesberger, Pierre and Goupil made 15 catapult launches and 37 arrested landings, the aircraft returning to Istres on 18 June. Back at Istres another series of ASSP flown during 27 June to 7 July finalised the clearance to enable the carrier trials to begin.

The Jaguar goes to sea

The carrier *Clemenceau* was assigned for the trials. The ship was sailing 25nm (46km) off Lorient near the island of Île-de-Groix in the Bay of Biscay. The naval air station at Lann-Bihoué was denoted as the emergency landing airfield should the aircraft be unable to land safely on the carrier. A group of engineers from Breguet, along with military observers from the United Kingdom and France, boarded the ship. The engineers took great care to take enough catalysts – the 2in (5cm)-diameter platinum-rhodium gauzes used to spontaneously ignite the fuel in the afterburners – with them as they were prone to fail. Even the other prototypes at Istres were robbed of catalysts to ensure that they would not run out aboard ship. Jesberger, Pierre and Goupil arrived at Lann-Bihoué, where they each flew another 30-minute ASSP sortie to make sure that they were ready for the task ahead.

Yves Goupil took off from Lann-Bihoué on 8 July to conduct the first landing aboard the *Clemenceau*. The mirror landing sight developed an electrical fault at the critical point, however, and Goupil had to return to the airfield. After refuelling, he set off again, rendezvousing with the carrier, simulating two landings and conducting two touch-and-go landings – with the arrester hook safely in the up position to avoid any accidents – before finally making an arrested landing. An elated Goupil told the ship's captain, 'Captain, that's it, the Tiger has swallowed the Jaguar' – 'Tiger' being the famous nickname of former Prime Minister Georges Clemenceau. Two days later Daniel Pierre made the first catapult launch from the ship. A total of 12 test flights were made aboard the carrier before the trial period came to an end on 13 July. A total of 173 ASSP had been conducted during this phase of the trials campaign.

The aircraft was flown in clean condition for all of the flights, the take-off weight being 21,160lb (9,600kg) and the landing weight 19,400lb (8,800kg). For ASSP approaches, the AoA was between 12 and 13.5° and was judged to be 'very comfortable'. It provided a minimum guaranteed performance of 136–139kt, and tests at 14–15° AoA revealed no problems other than reduced visibility for the pilot.

One issue that was quickly identified was jet exhaust blast damage to the ship's deck due to the inclination of the jet pipes on take-off, the tail being angled downwards at 6–7° as the aircraft was held in the correct take-off attitude. The 200°C jet efflux from the afterburners was very close to the deck and powerful enough to blow away a couple of plates – the existing water-cooled blast shields fitted to the deck having remained retracted due to the close proximity of the exhausts (they had been developed by Breguet in 1967 to allow the ship to operate the Crusader). Given the lack of dry thrust from the two Adours, reheat had to be used for catapult take-offs to ensure the necessary degree of safety. The solution to this problem was to provide more engine power or upgrade the steam catapults (implementing both solutions was soon advised). On 15 July M05 was flown back to Istres for modifications.

M05 gets airborne from *Clemenceau* during the first carrier trials in July 1970. The bridle has just been released and the Jaguar will begin to climb away. *Dassault via Author's Collection*

The aircraft was flown to the UK the following September to participate in the Society of British Aircraft Constructors Show at Farnborough, being displayed with dummy weapons under the wings to give an impression of the type's military capability. On the 9th, Paul Millett suffered engine trouble during his display in prototype S06 and M05 was selected as the backup aircraft to fill the display slot. The aircraft was run up but sadly ill luck struck again and an engine malfunction resulted in an aborted take-off run, with M05 remaining grounded for the remainder of the event.

Back in France, on 15 October Jesberger and Goupil conducted another two air-to-air refuelling test sorties. During the winter of 1970–71 the aircraft underwent further modifications. The vertical tail fin was made taller to increase the area. A small 'step' in the upper

M05 landing back aboard *Clemenceau* in July 1970. The picture shows well the revised undercarriage with single mainwheels and a longer nosewheel leg. *Dassault via Terry Panopalis Collection*

Preparations to launch. The bridle is being attached from M05's fuselage attachment points to the steam catapult shuttle aboard *Clemenceau* during the October 1971 carrier trials. The aircraft is loaded with six dummy bombs and a centreline fuel tank. ***Terry Panopalis Collection***

surface of the elevators was also smoothed out. The step had been designed to ease the load on the servo operating the elevator at high supersonic speeds, but this had been found to be redundant, partly due to the fact that high supersonic speeds were not attained given the lack of thrust from the Adours. Following its maintenance and upgrades, M05 again enjoyed the limelight at the Paris Air Show at Le Bourget on 5 and 6 June 1971.

The test pilot team was also refreshed. Goupil was posted as First Officer aboard the patrol boat *L'Opiniatre* and was replaced by Capitaine de Frégate Pierre Thireaut, and Lieutenant de Vaisseau François Champion replaced Daniel Pierre, who had been posted away from the CEV.

M05 returned to RAE Bedford for further catapult trials on 24 June, this time to clear the various external loads of missiles, bombs and fuel tanks and operations at loaded weights. Jesberger, Thireaut and Champion

Ready for another catapult launch in October 1971. Note the badge of the Royal Aircraft Establishment mounted on the intake splitter plate. ***Terry Panopalis Collection***

completed a total of 27 catapult launches and 90 arrested landings. On 15 July Champion flew M05 back to Istres, the aircraft being adorned with an improvised tricolour paintjob and the title '14 July 1789' on the nose to celebrate Bastille Day. The bored groundcrew had applied this while waiting for a replacement alternator to arrive at Bedford before the aircraft could be flown home. Champion bravely flew the less than neat-looking Jaguar back home but quickly taxied into the hangar to head off any potential official reprimands!

Setbacks

The clearances received at Bedford to operate at higher weights cleared the way for the next stage of the carrier trials programme. The *Clemenceau* was again earmarked. The ship's landing signals officer carried out a flight in M05 on 18 October 1971 to gauge the stability of the aircraft on approach. M05 was landed aboard the *Clemenceau* off Fos-sur-Mer on the Mediterranean coast near Marseille on 20 October.

The maximum take-off weight was now 30,270lb (13,730kg) when loaded with six dummy bombs and a ventral drop tank and the landing weight was 20,830lb (9,450kg). One complication was that even though the aircraft could be catapulted with a full load of dummy bombs, it was not allowed to land back aboard with them in order to meet the landing weight. So the pilot either had to jettison the expensive dummy stores into the sea or fly to Istres for them to be removed before returning to the carrier. Despite this, 216 ASSPs and 21 landings in 25 sorties were achieved by Jesberger, Thireaut and Champion.

The deck scorching issue had been mitigated by changing the settings of the blast shields to deflect the efflux to one side. The tests revealed that acceleration during catapulting was significantly slower than at Bedford, but the minimum speed performance results were better due to the different airflow around the bows of the carrier and a faster AoA response due to the new elevator servo control.

The pilots found another problem, however, stemming from the Adour's lack of thrust. If one engine failed, a safe go-around could not be guaranteed due to insufficient power. The pilot had to engage afterburner on the good engine but that caused an over-powered asymmetric load that was difficult to control. On one flight, the pilot just managed to avoid hitting the water before managing to gain height and land successfully at the second attempt. The solution would not appear until April 1972 when RRTM offered to install the improved Adour Mk.102 with PTR to modulate the reheat control, along with the use of two catalysts, and a 5% increase in thrust.

Then another serious problem emerged, one that would ultimately contribute to the demise of the Jaguar M. During a routine pre-flight inspection at Istres ten days after the aircraft's return from the *Clemenceau*, two cracks were found in the engine mountings. The aircraft had by now accumulated 200 flight hours. The stress of catapult launches with accelerations of 5.5g when fully loaded had taken their toll on the airframe. Jacques Desmazures, the engineering project manager, subsequently suggested that a production defect in the engine mounting bolts may have been the cause of the cracks. Either way, the aircraft was grounded immediately and repairs at Cazaux lasted until March 1972, Jensberger performing the check flight on the 8th.

By this time the Jaguar M was no longer a Breguet product, the company having been subsumed as part of Avions Marcel Dassault-Breguet Aviation (AMD-BA) on 14 December 1971. The test programme resumed at Cazaux, with the focus switching to assessing the SNA navigation system and the fire-control system, including the laser rangefinder. Dummy weapons were often carried on these flights, but no live weapons were carried or released from the aircraft. These avionics trials were continued at Landivisiau during 4–14 June before M05 returned to Istres on the 30th. The Adour Mk.102 was not ready for installation until

Given the landing weight restrictions aboard ship, M05 had to land ashore when carrying dummy bombs in order to have them removed before returning to the *Clemenceau*. The load here consists of six dummy 880lb (400kg) bombs, two each on the inner underwing hardpoints and singles outboard as well as a fuel tank beneath the fuselage. *Terry Panopalis Collection*

M05 touches down aboard *Clemenceau*, having caught the arrester wire. The stresses of carrier landings eventually took their toll, leading to cracking in the engine mountings. They were repairable but became a convenient reason to cancel the expensive development programme. *Dassault via Author's Collection*

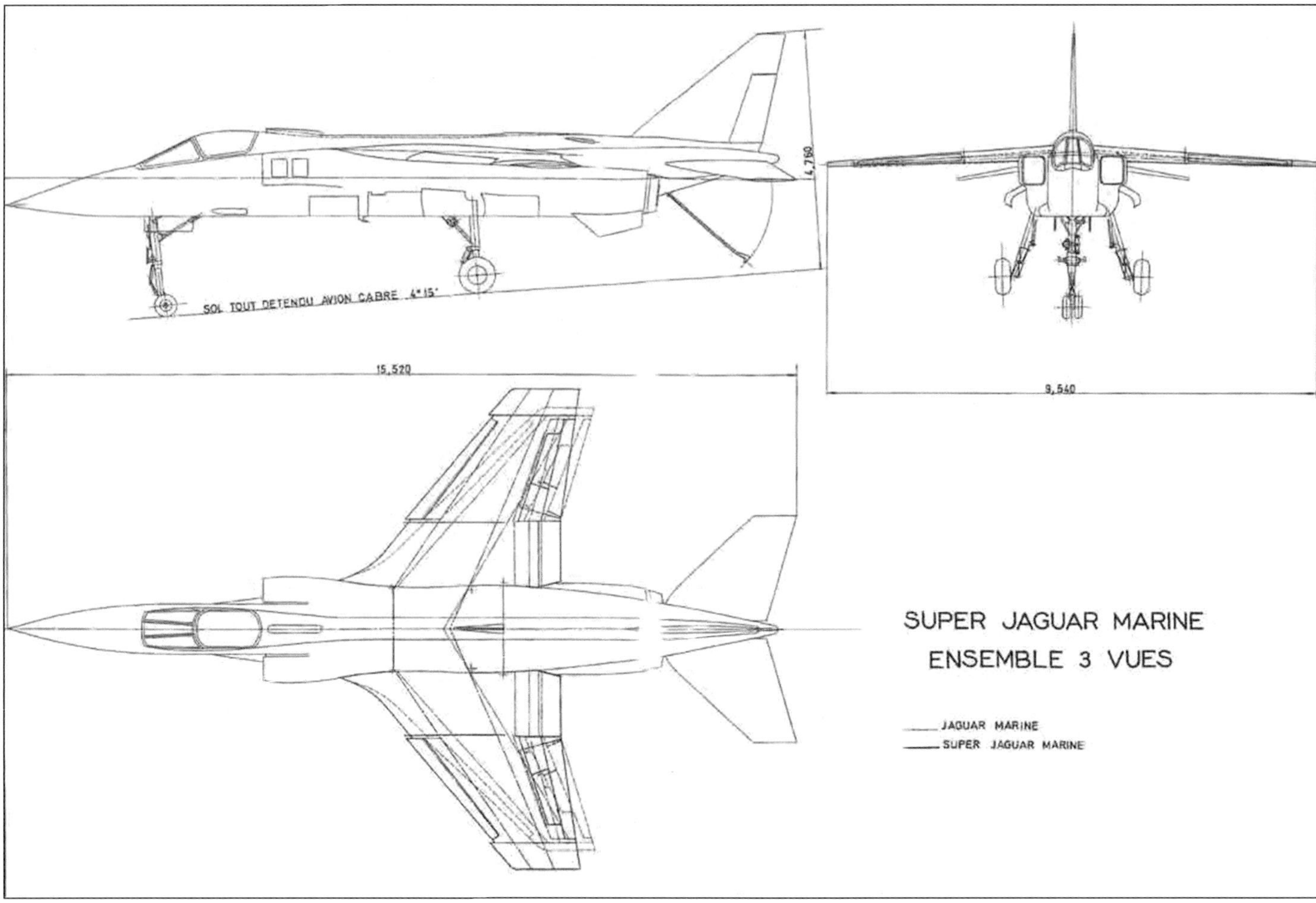

A general arrangement drawing showing the planned enlarged wing compared with the original. Work to fit the new wing was begun but never completed. With the larger wing and Adour Mk.102 engines the M05 would have become the Super Jaguar Marine. ***Dassault via Author's Collection***

clearance flight tests on Jaguar E02 had been completed; it was not fitted until early October. ASSPs were flown at Istres to determine what improvements the smoother application of full power using PTR offered.The M05 was also planned to receive another major upgrade. Breguet's chief aerodynamicist, Joseph Czinczenheim, had designed a larger wing to cure the deficiencies observed during the carrier trials. The addition of wing area and other design changes would enable the approach speed on landing to be lowered and also reduce the induced drag during approach. The result was dubbed the Super Jaguar Marine. BAC was happy to give its approval for Dassault to carry out this redesign – being a national development the UK was not liable for any of the costs. Marcel Dassault wanted the new wing to be fitted before the next round of carrier trials scheduled for 1973 and M05 returned to the Cazaux factory, but by then the writing was on the wall and the work was never carried out.

Cancellation and aftermath

The Marine Nationale had originally estimated a need for 50 aircraft, including ten Jaguar E two-seat trainers, but by 1966 the number of Jaguar Ms had risen to 86 and the number of trainers to 20. Costs began to grow as development proceeded with the improvements required to the avionics and the Adour. The lack of engine power had revealed several issues on take-off and the landing approach, and safe operation was not completely assured. The option of lengthening the steam catapults on the aircraft carriers as an additional safeguard (as well as better water cooling for the blast deflectors) would be very expensive. In addition, the inclusion of a new wing was further eroding commonality with the other Jaguar variants and increasing production costs. It was estimated that only 75 aircraft could be afforded, although this was still a cheaper option than developing a new aircraft. The five months of structural repairs that delayed the trials programme did not help matters either.

Judging by informal reports of political gossip submitted by the British Embassy in Paris, the Marine Nationale had always been lukewarm about accepting the Jaguar and by January 1972 rumours had surfaced that the McDonnell Douglas A-4M Skyhawk or new-build Étendards might be purchased instead. In November a member of the Assemblée Nationale, Joël Le Theule, during a debate on the defence budget, judged that the Jaguar M; 'brings together all the inconveniences; cost, delay, insecurity'. Faced with political opposition, the programme was cancelled in January 1973. With hindsight, it can only be surmised whether the new wing together with the Adour Mk.102 engines would have overcome the shortcomings and single-engine safety concerns revealed during the carrier trials.

The competition from foreign aircraft was becoming stronger, especially following the purchase of the F-8. By the summer of 1972 proposals had been put forward to purchase A-4M Skyhawks or the LTV A-7 Corsair II. The newly formed Aérospatiale (formed from the merger of Nord and Sud Aviation in 1970) acquired an A-7 production licence from LTV and, coincidently, Switzerland at this time was looking at the A-7G to re-equip its de Havilland DH.112 Venom squadrons. Political gossip in Paris was that a French A-4M purchase would scupper any chance of selling the Dassault Mirage 5 to the Swiss. Two US Marine Corps A-4Ms were flown across the Atlantic from Naval Air Station Patuxent River to Landivisiau in September 1972, where they flew a week of ASSPs before conducting carrier compatibility trials aboard the *Foch* totalling 17 catapult take-offs and landings. These sorties were flown at increasing weights until the final sorties were conducted at the maximum weight limit of the catapult.

There have been claims that Dassault were never completely supportive of the Breguet-designed Jaguar. Indeed, in May 1970 Dassault had proposed a navalised version of the Mirage G1 variable-geometry fighter and in September 1971 a navalised Mirage F1 multi-role fighter, the F1M, with an enlarged wing of 296.8ft^2 (27.6m^2) area, strengthened undercarriage and an arrester hook. The aircraft retained the standard Thomson-CSF Cyrano IV radar so that it could be used as an interceptor as well as a nuclear strike aircraft. An early-production Armée de l'Air F1C was made available to the Aéronavale in November 1971 for trials. The pilots rated the aircraft as being superior to the F-8E(FN) and the groundcrew found that the accessibility for maintenance was better than that of the Étendard IVM. Despite these recommendations, the proposal went no further; at that time the Jaguar M was still in contention and development of the F1M would not have been a cheaper option.

When it became clear that the Jaguar M was becoming unpopular in political circles during 1972, Dassault offered to reopen the Étendard production line. Originally it was intended to replace the ATAR 8 with the 8,550lbf (38kN) Pratt & Whitney J52 turbojet, but politically and fiscally the import of foreign engines was seen as undesirable and choice shifted to the 11,025lbf (49kN) ATAR 8K-50 without reheat. The aircraft evolved into the Super Étendard. Fitting the 8K-50's larger diameter exhaust pipe required changes to the rear fuselage. The wings were modified and the nose was enlarged to fit a Thomson-CSF Agave multi-mode radar that allowed the use of the new AM.39 Exocet anti-ship missile (which had entered development in 1974) and the cockpit and avionics were modernised. The Super Étendard became the favoured choice and an order was placed.

The Dassault Super Étendard was selected to fulfil the Marine Nationale's requirements following the cancellation of the Jaguar Marine. Prototype 01 seen here was modified from an Étendard IVM and made its first flight on 28 October 1974. ***Author's Collection***

The two prototypes were modified Étendard IVMs, the first making its maiden flight on 28 October 1974, followed by the first new-build production aircraft on 24 November 1977. The original plan was for 100 aircraft but only 71 were bought; just like the Jaguar M, as development costs grew, the order shrank to compensate. Deliveries began in June 1978 with the first squadron, Flottille 11F, becoming operational in February 1979. Ironically, the Étendard family outlived the Jaguar in French service; modernised from 1990 as the Super Étendard Modernisé, they were not retired until July 2016, seeing combat over Serbia in 1999, Afghanistan during 2001–11 and Libya in 2011.

Argentina ordered 14 in 1979, and the first four newly delivered aircraft armed with the Exocet saw action during the Falklands/Malvinas conflict in 1982, sinking the guided-missile destroyer HMS *Sheffield* on their second mission and then the container ship *Atlantic Conveyor*. Five Super Étendards were loaned to Iraq in 1983 while the country was waiting for deliveries of its Agave-equipped and Exocet-capable Mirage F1EQ-5s. The loan was politically controversial, Iraq using them to carry out 34 attacks on Iranian merchant shipping in the Persian Gulf during 1984.

Following the cancellation of the Jaguar Marine programme, M05 was assigned to spinning trials as part of the wider Jaguar development programme (for details see Chapter 2) and made its final flight on 12 December 1975. Following retirement the aircraft was transported to the School of Air Force Mechanics at Rochefort, before finally joining the collection of the nearby Musée de l'Aéronautique Navale, where it still resides on display today as a reminder to what might have been for the French Navy.

CHAPTER NINE

Jaguar International

The Jaguar soon caught the attention of several air forces following its public unveiling at the 25th Paris Salon de l'Aéronautique at Le Bourget, Paris, in June 1966. By mid-January 1967, SEPECAT had given briefings to staff officers of the Federal German Luftwaffe, the Royal Australian Air Force, and the Japan Air Self-Defense Force, and interest had been received from air forces of Switzerland, Spain, Denmark and South Africa.

Under the Memorandum of Understanding (MoU), export deals had to be approved by the French and British governments. Both partners would take a share of the profits and the lead nation would depend on whether the French or British variants were offered. In practice the British Aircraft Corporation (BAC) took the lead while Dassault focused on its successful Mirage family for orders. The British Ministry of Defence's (MoD) Defence Sales organisation, the Foreign and Commonwealth Office (FCO) and the Treasury were all involved in supporting BAC's efforts and the Royal Air Force was often involved in providing flying training packages.

On 28 August 1974 BAC announced the first export sales to two undisclosed customers – later revealed to be Ecuador and Oman – for the Jaguar International, an export version of the Jaguar S and B variants with more powerful engines. This chapter outlines the use of the Jaguar in three of the four nations that acquired Jaguars – Ecuador, Oman and Nigeria (India is covered in the next chapter) – and looks at the 'ones that got away', the prospective customers who, for one reason or another, decided not to place an order.

For the 1976 SBAC Show at Farnborough, the newly completed GR.1 XZ362 masqueraded as a Jaguar International, complete with overwing AAM rails. The dummy payload includes six BL.755 cluster bombs, 2.75in (68mm) SNEB rocket launchers and Matra R.550 Magic IR-homing AAMs. ***Terry Panopalis Collection***

The first production Jaguar GR.1, XX108, became the prototype Jaguar International. It was displayed at Farnborough in September 1974 surrounded by a wide array of potential weapons and stores including bombs, rocket pods, drop tanks and a reconnaissance pod. *Blue Envoy Collection*

Going international

A few days after BAC's announcement on 28 August 1974, the first production Jaguar GR.1, serial XX108, was displayed at the Society of British Aircraft Constructors (SBAC) Show at Farnborough with a mock Thomson-CSF Agave radar nose and an array of weaponry to launch the Jaguar International. XX108 was retained by BAC to become the Jaguar International prototype, later receiving improved Rolls-Royce Turbomeca Limited (RRTM) RT.172-26 (Mk.804) Adour engines. BAC test pilots Eric Bucklow, Reg Stock and Roy Kenward were assigned to the engine handling and supersonic performance trials. The prototype S07, XW563, also took part in the development programme and Jaguar T.2 XX846 became the Jaguar International trainer prototype in September 1975. XX108, now fitted with further upgraded RT.172-58 (Mk.811) engines and overwing pylons for Matra R.550 Magic infrared (IR)-homing air-to-air missiles (AAMs), was displayed at Farnborough in 1979 by Jerry Lee and Chris Yeo. This included take-offs and landings on the grass beside the runway, with Yeo unfortunately suffering a collapse of the nose leg on the final day.

Both the British and French defence ministers expressed their concern in 1976 at the lack of export orders, which were vital to maintain the Jaguar production lines as deliveries to the RAF and Armeé de l'Air wound down – Warton's Jaguar workforce declining from 1,000 to 300. British Aerospace (BAe) had to keep Warton in work until Panavia Tornado production began and once the Jaguar line shut, reopening it would be cost prohibitive. Two dozen aircraft to Oman and Ecuador seemed a poor return given SEPECAT's original plans for up to 200 export aircraft. The securing of contracts for India and Nigeria within the next few years redressed the balance, but the Jaguar was never a serious competitor on the fighter market. It was not an air defence aircraft and was an expensive ground-attack aircraft in what was a crowded market. French officials responsible for defence exports at the Direction of International Affairs (DAI) felt that the Jaguar was reliant on dedicated air superiority fighters in order to operate, which reduced its potential market in Europe, let alone to foreign air forces who often had to rely on a single type of fighter. Thus Dassault was given more or less a free hand to push its Mirages, which had air-to-air capability, and had no incentive to market the Jaguar. With full technical details in their possession, Dassault could emphasise any shortcomings and development problems while minimising those of the Mirage F1, the Jaguar's major rival. As soon as the F1 prototype had been ordered back in 1967, the President of Breguet, General (retired) Henri Ziegler, had warned BAC that it would be a major competitor. A total of 192 Jaguars were exported to four nations, in contrast to 457 Mirage F1s to 10 clients.

There was little attempt to sell surplus Jaguars in the mid-1980s when RAF Germany re-equipped its Jaguar squadrons with the Panavia Tornado, which

Jaguar International XX108 is here loaded with six dummy BL.755 cluster bombs, two dummy Matra Magic R.550 AAMs and a centreline fuel tank. *BAE Systems via Author's Collection*

may have been a missed opportunity. As the fleet of Jaguars was further reduced following the 'Peace Dividend' at the end of the Cold War, the MoD began looking at selling surplus airframes in order to recoup the sales receipts into funding Jaguar upgrades. Apart from attrition replacements offered to Ecuador and Oman, little came of this initiative.

Ecuador

Ecuador was one of the first Latin American nations to take an interest in the Jaguar. The Fuerza Aérea Ecuatoriana (FAE) approached SEPECAT in 1972 with the need for eight or ten aircraft to replace their obsolete Gloster Meteor FR.9 fighters. They quickly signed a letter of intent with BAC for eight Jaguar S fighters and two Jaguar B trainers, with the type seeing off competition from the Mirage, Northrop F-5E Flying Tiger II and the Hawker Siddeley Harrier. The order was potentially worth £20 million and was achieved in spite of the USA having keenly priced the F-5E at $1.5 million each (plus delivery within six months) as well as rumours that Dassault were pushing their Mirage F1 as a direct competitor. Some sense of the importance of the order is illustrated by an exceptional move from the British Treasury, which offered to match the financial terms offered by any competitor. BAC quoted a delivery time of 28 months, but it was hoped to divert RAF production aircraft in order to secure delivery before the end of 1974. The RAF were, however, reluctant to release any aircraft given the production difficulties at that time. In addition, BAC hoped the RAF would provide pilot conversion training at No. 226 Operational Conversion Unit (OCU) at RAF Lossiemouth, a task that the RAF claimed it would be unable to fulfil until at least 1977. A frustrated Assistant Chief of the Air Staff (Policy), Air Vice-Marshal Peter de L. Le Cheminant, suggested that SEPECAT should be working harder to increase production and forming their own training organisation if they were so keen to secure sales. When the Commander-in-Chief of the FAE, Brigadier General Jorge Izurieta Iturralde, arrived at the Farnborough Show that September, the unwelcome news was broken to him, although he did get to fly in the Jaguar.

BAC still had hopes of an imminent order. Because of Ecuador's economic situation, BAC offered an alternative proposal for an initial buy of six Jaguar S and two Jaguar B with the first delivery 24 months following contract signature, with an option for another four Jaguar S at a later date. There were rumours that the French government had become aware of the offer and proposed releasing the Jaguar A and E to Ecuador. When BAC complained, the French claimed that Ecuador had approached them directly but that they had not made any formal proposal in response. Despite these political issues, in April 1974 the Ecuadorian government signed a firm order for 12 Jaguar Internationals, ten single-seat ES and a pair of EB trainers, with a financial agreement to fund the purchase. BAC announced the order – anonymously – on 28 August, just ahead of the Farnborough Show.

The Jaguar International ES was of similar standard to the RAF's GR.1, including the laser ranger and marked-target seeker (LRMTS) and ARI.18223 radar warning receiver (RWR). The FAE's Jaguars were the first fighters in Latin America to have a head-up display. The armament included several French items: 30mm DEFA 553 cannon, Matra R.550 Magic IR-homing AAMs (overwing pylons were retro-fitted from 1994), Matra Durandal anti-runway bombs, 550lb (250kg) and 880lb (400kg) SAMP retarded bombs and Matra rocket pods. British BL.755 cluster bombs and American Mk.117, Mk.81 and Mk.82 general-purpose bombs were also carried, including Chilean-manufactured versions. The engines were the upgraded RT.172-26 Adour Mk.804 rated at 5,320lbf (23.7kN) dry and 8,040lbf (35.7kN) reheated. This produced a 27% thrust increase at sea level at speeds between Mach 0.8 and 0.9, 10% more at take-off and 30% more during manoeuvring combat. The Jaguars adopted a similar camouflage pattern to the RAF's, which blended in well with the local rainforest terrain.

Two FAE pilots joined the Tactical Weapons Unit (TWU) lead-in course in September 1975, flying Hawker Hunters, before progressing to No. 226 OCU's No. 11 course in March 1976. They were followed in 1977 by four more pilots. Following graduation, two of the pilots delivered the final pair of FAE Jaguars from Warton. The pilots returned to Lossiemouth for check rides and emergency procedure refreshers using the simulator every 18 months throughout the Jaguar's Ecuadorian service life. BAC appointed one of their pilots, Alexander 'Sandy' Aitken, as the in-country Jaguar Training Pilot/Instructor in 1977 and he

The first production Jaguar International EB trainer, FAE-283 of Esc 2111, at Taura Air Base during the joint US–Ecuadorian Exercise Blue Horizon 86 on 22 August 1986. ***USAF***

The second production Jaguar International ES, serial FAE-302 of Escuadrón de Combate Esc 2111 'Águilas', in the circuit to land. ***BAE Systems via Author's Collection***

Ecuadorian Jaguars					
FAE Serial	**Type**	**C/N**	**First Flight**	**Delivery Date**	**UK B Cond Serial**
FAE-283	EB	EB1	19/08/1976	04/01/1977	G-27-266
FAE-289	ES	ES1	28/09/1976	04/01/1977	G-27-268
FAE-302	ES	ES2	14/12/1976	31/05/1977	G-27-269
FAE-305	EB	EB2	07/01//1977	31/05/1977	G-27-267
FAE-309	ES	ES3	08/02/1977	18/04/1977	G-27-270
FAE-318	ES	ES4	25/02/1977	18/04/1977	G-27-261
FAE-327	ES	ES5	01/04/1977	16/08/1977	G-27-272
FAE-329	ES	ES6	26/04/1977	16/08/1977	G-27-273
FAE-339	ES	ES7	05/07/1977	05/09/1977	G-27-274
FAE-340	ES	ES8	04/08/1977	05/09/1977	G-27-275
FAE-348	ES	ES9	19/09/1977	24/10/1977	G-27-276
FAE-349	ES	ES10	27/09/1977	24/10/1977	G-27-277

remained in-post until 1981, the FAE awarding him the status of Honorary Chief Pilot when he left. He was replaced by Alan Dachtler, who had been a member of the first Jaguar conversion course at Lossiemouth in 1974, serving as a Qualified Flying Instructor (QFI) at No. 226 OCU before he retired from the RAF and joined BAe. While in Ecuador in 1982, Dachtler completed his 2,000th flying hour on Jaguars. Weapons practice took place at the range at Las Playas, south-west of Guayaquil, which included a copy of the Peruvian Talara Air Base marked out on the ground.

The first Ecuadorian aircraft, Jaguar EB serial FAE-283, made its maiden flight at Warton on 19 August 1976 with test pilots Tim Ferguson and Jim Evans aboard. Deliveries began on 4 January 1977 when FAE-283 and the first production Jaguar ES, FAE-289, left Warton flown by Ferguson with Roy Kenward as navigator and Peter Ginger respectively. Following their transatlantic flight, both aircraft arrived on the 14th to a reception hosted by the President of Ecuador. The aircraft had performed well, the fuel consumption being within 44lb (20kg) of the brochure figures. The ferry flights took up to ten days and transited via Toulouse, Morocco, Senegal, Liberia, Wideawake Airfield on Ascension Island, Recife, Belem and Trinidad. Further pairs followed from April and included: Jaguar EB FAE-305 flown by Ferguson and ES FAE-302 flown by Allan Love departing Warton on 31 May; two Jaguar ES, FAE-327 and FAE-329, flown by Eric Bucklow and John Cockburn – who narrowly avoided being caught up in an armed insurrection during the transit stop in Liberia – during 16–25 August; Jaguar ES FAE-339 and FAE-340 flown by Dave Eagles and Reg Stock in September; the last two aircraft departed Warton on 24 October and arrived on 9 November, one of them being ES FAE-349 flown by Love.

The importance of airfield performance in the high terrain of the Andes led to BAC conducting tests at Latacunga, an airstrip at an altitude of 9,140ft (2,785m) above sea level. The Jaguar proved able to take off with a full payload and make single-engine landings safely. Ecuador became interested in buying a second batch of up to 24 aircraft in 1976 but eventually opted for the Israeli IAI Kfir C2 (an improved copy of the Dassault Mirage IIICJ). However, a US embargo on the General Electric J79 turbofan delayed delivery in 1982 and the FAE purchased 16 Mirage F1JA fighters instead, which were delivered in 1978.

The Jaguar entered service with Escuadrón de Combate (Esc) 2111 of Ala de Combate 21 at Base Aérea Taura, the only FAE unit to fly the type. The unit had been formed as Escuadrón Táctico 13 with Gloster

A pair of Ecuadorian Jaguar ES taking off from Warton before delivery. The camouflage was identical to the RAF's Dark Sea Grey and Dark Green, but with Light Aircraft Grey undersurfaces. ***BAE Systems via Author's Collection***

Meteor FR.9s in January 1957, being renumbered as Esc 2111 in 1966 and renamed in 1981 from 'Águilas' (Eagles) to 'Jaguares'. On average, the unit had ten pilots on its roster.

The Jaguar saw some limited active use early on in its career. The Falso Paquisha War of January–February 1981 was a flaring up of the long-running border dispute with Peru over control of a strip of territory on the eastern side of the Andean Cordillera del Cóndor mountain range. The Ecuadorian Army seized three border surveillance posts along the Comaina River from the Peruvian Army, who counter-attacked and retook the posts. The Jaguars did not take part in the ground support operations but on 31 January were used to escort a helicopter that attacked the PV-22 post, which had been recaptured by Peruvian troops the previous day. The squadron also flew a reconnaissance mission over Peruvian territory.

The Jaguar gave the FAE an important deep penetration attack capability and operations were optimised for attacks at very low altitude; 250ft (76m) at 420kt, descending to 200ft (60m) at 540kt over the border region and also able to fly at 200ft over the sea. The usual formation consisted of two pairs, widely separated to make them harder to spot, and the standard turn was made at 60° pulling 2g, to avoid losing or gaining altitude to remain hidden against the landscape below. Radio silence was also paramount. The pilots appreciated the weapon aiming and navigational accuracy of NAVWASS (the stipulated Time on Target allowed a delay of only three seconds), although a lack of Night Vision Goggle (NVG) capability prevented any nocturnal missions.

By the 1990s the FAE was conducting dissimilar combat training with mixed Jaguar, Mirage F1JA and Kfir C2 formations, and they began to fly in combined formations – the Mirage using its radar to detect aerial targets, the Kfirs supplying electronic warfare data from their superior Elta RWR and sharing the data between each other. Esc 2111 conducted training with the Army's anti-aircraft artillery and Russian 9K33 Osa (NATO designation SA-8 *Gecko*) mobile surface-to-air missile (SAM) system. Annual exercises were also held with the United States Air Force (USAF), including mock combat against General Dynamics F-16 Fighting Falcons, with the Jaguar more than holding its own at low altitude and either evading combat or using the Magic AAMs in self-defence if required. Other exercises with the US Navy saw the Jaguar leading attacks

The FAE routinely flew mixed formations of Jaguars, IAI Kfir C2s and Dassault Mirage F1JAs, which combined the technical strengths of each aircraft in targeting, electronic warfare and radar capability respectively. ***USAF***

Jaguars FAE-309, FAE-327 and a third unidentified ES taxi out for another mission during the joint US–Ecuadorian Exercise Blue Horizon 86. ***US DoD via Terry Panopalis Collection***

The Ecuadorian Jaguars were the first to be fitted with the upgraded RT.172-26 Adour Mk.804 rated at 8,040lbf (35.7kN) reheated. *US DoD via Terry Panopalis Collection*

against aircraft carriers, although with less success in the face of the naval SAM defences.

Three Jaguars were lost in accidents early in the type's career, prompting the arrival of BAe test pilot Reg Stock and Tony Randall, the head of the Technical Support Unit, at the FAE's request in 1981 to provide advice on improving the training programme (Stock had conducted conversion training in Ecuador for BAC Strikemaster pilots during 1973). Following the loss of FAE-289 in a fatal crash following engine failure on 29 March 1990, BAe secured two RAF GR.1s as replacements, XX121 and XX722 being taken from store and reconditioned at Warton. A third aircraft, XX744, was inspected and an option for a further three aircraft was considered but by July 1993 the deal had fallen through. The surviving aircraft in FAE service were upgraded to GR.1A standard in 1994 with the Ferranti FIN 1064 navigation/attack system and overwing AAM missile pylons.

The border dispute with Peru again flared up into active hostilities in 1995; the month-long Cenepa War during January–February saw heavy air activity from both air forces but the four to six serviceable Jaguars were held back in reserve in case of a wider conflict with the Peruvians. By 2000 Esc 2111 had just six active

The second production OB 203 for Oman was displayed at the Paris Air Show in 1977 by BAC test pilots Peter Ginger and Jerry Lee, temporarily registered as G-BETB for the event. *Author's Collection*

aircraft: ES FAE-302, FAE-309, FAE-327, FAE-329 (FAE-339 and FAE-348 were in storage) and the twin-seaters FAE-283 and FAE-305. The Jaguar was withdrawn from front-line service in 2002 and Esc 2111 was disbanded.

The aircraft remained in storage until they were officially declared withdrawn in 2006. Four of the aircraft are currently serving as decoys at Taura but FAE-302 is preserved at the FAE Academy at Salinas and FAE-327 was donated to the Museo Aéreo de la Fuerza Aérea Ecuatoriana in Quito.

Oman

The Sultan of Oman's Air Force (SOAF) – from 1990 the Royal Air Force of Oman (RAFO) – had been a user of the Hunter FGA.9 during the latter stages of the Dhofar War in the mid-1970s for close support sorties and the Jaguar was seen as an ideal replacement. The SOAF purchased a complete Integrated Air Defence System from BAC comprising ground-based radars, 12 Rapier SAM launchers, a communications system and the Jaguar. The order for ten single-seat Jaguar OS and a pair of two-seat Jaguar OB was announced – anonymously – on 28 August 1974 was worth £36 million (the entire deal was worth £200 million).

The Jaguar Internationals were equipped with LRMTS and Marconi 920ATC NAVWASS with the upgraded 920M GT computer with 32,000 word storage, and were powered by Adour Mk.804 engines. The first aircraft was flown by BAC's Deputy Chief Test Pilot Tim Ferguson on 2 September 1975, Ferguson making two flights that day. He was complimentary about the additional performance that the Mk.804 engines provided, especially the improvement in acceleration.

Eager to demonstrate their new aircraft, the Omani government requested that BAC send a Jaguar to their annual National Day celebrations. BAC elected to send Jaguar International demonstrator T.2 XX846 on a month-long sales tour in the Middle East. Peter Ginger left Warton on 13 November 1975 accompanied by a support crew in a BAC 1-11 airliner operated by the SOAF. The flight to Seeb in Oman staged through Rome, RAF Akrotiri in Cyprus and Tehran. During the 15,000-mile (24,100km) tour the aircraft visited 11 countries. Ginger flew 53 sorties, including 11 demonstration flights plus 24 with foreign representatives aboard in the back seat. Air displays were flown at Seeb, Thumrait and Salalah in Oman as well as Abu Dhabi, Dubai, Dhahran and Riyadh in Saudi Arabia, Doha in Qatar, Kuwait, Tehran and Ankara. Several evaluation sorties had also been flown with guest pilots, who praised the Jaguar's NAVWASS system, manoeuvrability, rate of climb, smooth ride in high-speed, low-level flight, excellent visibility from the cockpit on the ground and the short take-off and landing performance. The flight home, with Roy Kenward as navigator, staged through Tehran, Ankara, Akrotiri, Brindisi and Istres before landing back at Warton on 13 December. Despite only being installed a couple of weeks before setting off, the RT.172-26 Adour engines performed flawlessly in the hot conditions.

Omani Jaguars				
SOAF serial	Type	First flight	Delivery date	UK B Cond serial
201	OB	04/11/1976	07/03/1977	G-27-278
202	OS	27/01/1977	07/03/1977	G-27-280
203	OB	06/04/1977	27/06/1977	G-27-279
204	OS	18/05/1977	27/06/1977	G-27-281
205	OS	18/08/1977	26/09/1977	G-27-282
206	OS	19/08/1977	26/09/1977	G-27-283
207	OS	07/10/1977	07/11/1977	G-27-284
208	OS	14/10/1977	07/11/1977	G-27-285
209	OS	16/12/1977	06/02/1978	G-27-286
210	OS	12/01/1978	06/02/1978	G-27-287
211	OS	08/03/1978	08/05/1978	G-27-288
212	OS	31/03/1978	08/05/1978	G-27-289
213	OB	05/11/1982	23/05/1983	G-27-375
214	OB	26/11/1982	25/07/1983	G-27-376
215	OS	15/09/1982	23/05/1983	G-27-377
216	OS	02/11/1982	23/05/1983	G-27-378
217	OS	07/01/1983	25/07/1983	G-27-379
218	OS	12/05/1983	25/07/1983	G-27-380
219	OS	26/04/1983	19/09/1983	G-27-381
220	OS	18/05/1983	19/09/1983	G-27-382
221	OS	01/06/1983	19/09/1983	G-27-383
222	OS	15/06/1983	24/11/1983	G-27-384
223	OS	07/07/1983	24/11/1983	G-27-385
224	OS	15/07/1983	24/11/1983	G-27-386
200	T.2	-	??/01/1982	G-27-332 Ex-RAF XX138, Ex-IAF JI001
225	GR.1	-	04/11/1984	Ex-RAF XX740, Ex-IAF JI017
226	GR.1A	-	11/08/1998	Ex-RAF XX719

The maiden flight of the first OB, serial 201, at Warton on 4 November 1976 proved to be highly eventful. Piloted by Eric Bucklow with Vic Mallings in the back seat, Bucklow turned the aircraft inverted at 5,000ft (1,525m) to check for any foreign objects or debris that may have been left over from manufacture. On re-righting and levelling off he found that he could not move the control stick backwards, maintaining level flight required sufficient engine power but the flaps could not be lowered to slow down because an uncontrolled pitch down could occur. Facing a flapless landing, Bucklow diverted to Boscombe Down with its longer runway. Then the port reheat fire warning light came on, so he shut the engine down. Facing a flapless one-engined landing, Bucklow decided to invert the aircraft again in an attempt to dislodge whatever was

ABOVE A two-seat OB leads a pair flying over the desert terrain of Oman. Each aircraft carries six 1,000lb (454kg) bombs and two AIM-9J Sidewinder AAMs. *Blue Envoy Collection*

Jaguar International OB 203/G-BETB on the flightline at Le Bourget. All Omani Jaguars were finished in sand and stone disruptive camouflage. *Terry Panopalis Collection*

jamming the controls. This worked and normal control was regained. Bucklow reversed course back to Warton only to find during the approach that the flaps would not lower. He made a perfect single-engine flapless landing at Warton, with three separate faults – including a loose rivet and false fire alarm – having conspired to make the flight more exciting than planned.

The first delivery flight of one Jaguar OB and one OS left Warton on 7 March 1977. The second production OB 203 was demonstrated at the Paris Air Show by Peter Ginger and Jerry Lee in June and later that month Ginger delivered the second production OS 204 to Oman. Tim Ferguson delivered OS5 207 on 7 November, staying on to fly Jaguars 204 and 205 for displays at the National Day on the 18th. On 31 March 1978 Bucklow, as Senior Production Test Pilot, made his 100th Jaguar first flight in OS10 212 covering the entire flight envelope, including maximum speed and maximum permissible 'g' in the one flight. All deliveries were completed by April 1978.

The Jaguars entered service with No. 8 Squadron at Thumrait, which later moved to Al Masirah. The squadron operated in both strike and air defence roles, although its air defence capability was weak without a radar. The aircraft had IR-homing AAMs on the outer underwing pylons – Matra R.550 Magic for the first batch of aircraft and AIM-9P Sidewinder for the second batch – an adequate armament given the local aerial threats. The Jaguar was operated without external fuel tanks, unless specific tasking requirements called for them, which aided in extending the fatigue life of the aircraft. The dry hot weather also helped aircraft serviceability. The aircraft were painted in disruptive sand and stone desert camouflage. Experiments with the Hunters later gave rise to a dark matt grey colour scheme for air defence.

The RAF was instrumental in pilot training. Two Jaguar pilots were loaned to the SOAF to form the nucleus of the conversion team and contract officers with considerable fighter experience made up the bulk of the initial pilots. Pre-flying conversion comprised the full No. 226 OCU ground school before returning to Oman for the initial dual checks and conversion flying. The foundations laid were followed for all subsequent Omani pilot conversions. Providing loan QFIs and Qualified Weapon Instructors was sometimes a challenge; by 1978 the MoD had increased the rate of loan service pay to improve the attractiveness of the posting (a flight lieutenant's pay increased from £1,555 to £2,590). Two trawls for volunteers in 1992 and 1993 had no success, which led the MoD to shorten the posting to six months but with a full year's loan service payment. The shortage of Omani pilots meant that loaned and ex-RAF pilots remained important in maintaining sufficient manpower well into the 1990s.

Operational training covered all possible commitments and concentrated on achieving a high level of proficiency. Given the possibility of being diverted from a training sortie to an operational task, the Jaguars were flown with loaded cannon and live AAMs, with ready-use ordnance held prepared on the airfield. Training was therefore realistic and engendered a high degree of weapons awareness to the pilots and groundcrews. Air defence training sorties were also flown to train the ground radar operators and controllers, and pilots would often engage in 'free play' with US Navy aircraft from aircraft carriers stationed in the Persian Gulf. Air combat training was conducted close to the airfield, but the lack of restrictions on supersonic flight overland was especially useful. Tactical strike training sorties were flown over varied types of terrain and often included live ordnance release on a range.

When they were still in service, a formation of four Hunters would often accompany the Jaguars, flown in a 'fluid 4' with the Hunters trailing 1.7nm (3.2km) behind with an average altitude of 100ft (30m). Successful penetration of Airborne Early Warning (AEW)-controlled Combat Air Patrols (CAPs) were made. The Jaguars also undertook impressive firepower demonstrations where four Jaguars would drop their 16 880lb (400kg) SAMP retarded bombs simultaneously with another four dropping 16 400kg freefall bombs.

The Jaguar pilots worked closely with the laser designator-equipped forward air controllers (FAC). With language barriers between Baluchi-speaking Army personnel and Omani pilots communicating in a third language (English), communication was aided by personal call signs for clear identification and minimal radio chatter in order to pinpoint the target exactly with the laser designator for, hopefully, a successful first-pass attack. This FAC co-operation also assisted night

Although not an interceptor, this photograph from 1987 shows that the Omani Jaguar OS, while reliant on intercept control from the ground, was capable of intercepting aerial targets, in this case a Soviet Navy Ilyushin Il-38 *May* maritime patrol aircraft, probably operating from Aden in the then People's Democratic Republic of Yemen. *US Navy*

Two-seat OB 214 and single-seat OS 217 during a training sortie in 2006. *Terry Panopalis Collection*

Jaguar OS 221 taxying at its home base of Thumrait during Exercise Magic Carpet 2005. *MoD/Open Government Licence*

operations, with Jaguars dropping Lepus flares to illuminate a target of interest or even bombing blind.

A second order for ten Jaguar OS and two OB aircraft was received in 1980 – along with 12 Blindfire fire-control radars for the Rapiers – worth £147 million, the Jaguars costing £44.3 million plus 307.6 million French Francs – FF). These aircraft had Adour Mk.811-26 engines. The pair of OB trainers had fixed nose aerial refuelling probes like those of the French Jaguar E. Eric Bucklow flew the last Omani Jaguar, OS 224, on 15 July 1983, his 109th Jaguar first flight and the 275th first flight of a British-built Jaguar. In 1982 one T.2 trainer was acquired from BAe as an attrition replacement for No. 8 Squadron; serial 200 having formerly been XX138 in RAF service and having previously been loaned to the Indian Air Force. Another attrition replacement, received in 1984 for No. 20 Squadron, was GR.1 XX740, also previously loaned to India. In 1986 Ferranti was contracted to upgrade both batches of Jaguars with the GEC-Marconi FIN1064 nav/attack system as well as receiving overwing pylons for the AAMs. The modification work was carried out at Warton, with the final upgraded aircraft being redelivered in October 1989.

The second batch of aircraft equipped No. 20 Squadron at Al Masirah and the unit was fully equipped by the end of 1983. In the late 1980s both squadrons relocated from Al Masirah to Thumrait. In August 1990, during the build-up of coalition forces for Operation Desert Storm, the RAF's Jaguar detachment arrived at Thumrait and benefitted greatly from the RAFO's experience of using the type in the desert. The Omani Jaguars participated in work-up exercises with the RAF, USAF, US Navy and US Marine Corps, including simulated attacks against US Navy carrier groups in the Gulf, but, in the event, played no part in Operation Desert Storm, although they did fly some CAPs to deter Yemen from supporting Iraq.

Several Jaguars were lost in accidents. On 26 February 1979 OS 212 crashed after a 500lb (226kg) bomb prematurely detonated shortly after release. The pilot, Flight Lieutenant Rick Lea, ejected successfully but was severely burned. Jaguar OB 201 crashed north of Thumrait during an air combat training sortie on 1 March 1981, with both pilots – Flight Lieutenant Prest and Flight Officer Steve Waring – ejecting safely. OS 218 was just over a year old when it crashed near the Sultan's Palace in Salalah, Dhofar, on 21 June 1984. The pilot had come out of cloud inverted, probably due to disorientation. Jaguar OS 208 blew up in mid-air on 12 December 1985 in similar circumstances to those of 212, when a 1,000lb (454kg) bomb exploded prematurely, Flight Lieutenant T A F 'Paddy' Mullen being literally blown out of the cockpit and his ejection seat initiating in mid-air! The year1991 proved to be an unlucky one with three aircraft lost: OS 216 crashed on 29 January, 205 on 27 October near Masirah and 207 of No. 20 squadron crashed west of the Jebel range on 17 December following a bird strike, the pilot ejecting safely.

Given the scale of attrition to the fleet, the SOAF looked at obtaining more replacement aircraft as the two ex-RAF Jaguars acquired in the early 1980s had only partially made up the losses. Enquiries to the British Embassy in Muscat and directly to BAe drew a blank, which surprised the SOAF given the large numbers of Jaguars that the RAF had retired in the 1980s. The MoD offered a package of GR.1A airframes and equipment for £1.95 million in the spring of 1993, but this did not materialise and not until August 1998 did a single GR.1A arrive, the former XX719.

In September 1997 a contract worth £40 million was signed to upgrade the surviving 16 Jaguar OS and three OBs to Jaguar 97 standard, including the purchase of GEC-Marconi TIALD 200 Series laser designation pods and the upgrading of the Adours. BAe's Jaguar Project Pilot, Gordon McClymont, made the maiden flights of all the upgraded Jaguars at Thumrait. He was also involved in live weapon integration trials, including the first live release of a 1,000lb laser-guided bomb in front of an audience including the Chief of the SOAF. The upgrade programme was completed by the end of 2000.

It was planned to operate the Jaguar until 2012, but it was given a reprieve until 6 August 2014, when No. 8 Squadron made a final disbandment flypast with its last four operational Jaguars. The Jaguars had been replaced by the Lockheed Martin F-16C and the Eurofighter Typhoon.

Nigeria

Nigeria was looking at the Jaguar as early as 1976. Nigeria's military government wanted to ensure that the nation was well armed before handing over to a civilian government and in 1979 its 4th National Development Plan for the Armed Forces identified the need to replace the Nigerian Air Force's (NAF) sole fighter squadron's MiG-21MF *Fishbed-J* aircraft acquired from the Soviet Union in 1975. A requirement was defined for up to 32 Jaguars.

An MoU was signed in 1982, the aircraft and the support and training package being worth £200 million. A formal order was placed in June 1983 for 13 single-seat Jaguar SN and five two-seat Jaguar BN with an option for a further 18 aircraft. The Maritime Strike Version with Thomson-CSF Agave radar and BAe Dynamics P3T Sea Eagle anti-ship missiles was offered to Nigeria and six of these were part of the option, which was later cancelled due to budget cuts. A military coup in December 1983 did not affect the order, although it did disrupt the payments to BAe and by autumn 1984 the full amount of the agreed downpayment had still not been paid.

The Jaguar Internationals were equipped with RT.172-58 Mk.811 Adours rated at 5,520lbf (24.6kN) dry and 9,270lbf (41.23kN) reheated. The first aircraft was

This is the first production Jaguar SN, serial NAF705, on a test flight before delivery to Nigeria, wearing its B-Conditions registration G-27-392. *BAE Systems via Author's Collection*

completed in May 1984, but the early production examples were retained at Warton for the initial conversion training.

The first aircraft to arrive at Makurdi in August 1984 were BN4 serial NAF703 flown by Deputy Chief Test Pilot Chris Yeo with Roy Kenward as navigator and SN1 NAF705 flown by Sandy Aitken. BN1 NAF700 arrived on 20 September flown by Eric Bucklow and Jim Stuttard and BN4 NAF703 on 30 October. SN6 NAF710 had been displayed at the SBAC Show at Farnborough in September 1984 before delivery marked as G-27-397. Dave Eagles delivered SN8 NAF712 in April 1985 and the last pair, SNs NAF716 and 717, arrived on 25 June 1985. These were the last Warton-built Jaguars, the production line closing for good.

Part of the Jaguar package was the provision of conversion training for the first batch of NAF pilots. The original plan to send the pilots to No. 226 OCU at Lossiemouth proved too expensive, so BAe devised a low-altitude training programme for 11 pilots using the early production Nigerian Jaguars at Warton, with access to RAF low-flying training areas.

The syllabus consisted of five phases: consolidation and solo, instrument flying, weapons aiming and introduction to heavy weights, formation flying and low-level flying (BAe had to cover any indemnity for potential nuisance or damage caused by low flying). The syllabus totalled 31 flying hours, more than half of which would be flown solo. The three pilots selected for instructor duties would also receive QFI conversion training. The 11 pilots would be split into three courses. The BAe pilot in charge was Jerry Lee, with Chris Yeo as deputy. Ground school training, including simulator flights, was provided by the RAF at Lossiemouth. Further training would take place in Nigeria under the supervision of two BAe contract pilots. The NAF

Nigerian Jaguars

NAF serial	Type	First flight	Delivery date	UK B Cond serial
NAF700	BN	13/10/1983	18/09/1984	G-27-387
NAF701	BN	02/11/1983	25/09/1984	G-27-388
NAF702	BN	22/11/1983	30/10/1984	G-27-389
NAF703	BN	01/03/1984	20/08/1984	G-27-390
NAF704	BN	18/04/1984	11/12/1984	G-27-391
NAF705	SN	21/12/1984	20/08/1984	G-27-392
NAF706	SN	10/01/1984	28/08/1984	G-27-393
NAF707	SN	03/02/1984	28/08/1984	G-27-394
NAF708	SN	28/03/1984	18/09/1984	G-27-395
NAF709	SN	11/05/1984	25/09/1984	G-27-396
NAF710	SN	18/06/1984	30/10/1984	G-27-397
NAF711	SN	18/07/1984	11/12/1984	G-27-398
NAF712	SN	07/08/1984	10/04/1985	G-27-399
NAF713	SN	14/12/1984	10/04/1985	G-27-400
NAF714	SN	14/12/1984	04/06/1985	G-27-401
NAF715	SN	12/03/1985	04/06/1985	G-27-402
NAF716	SN	11/03/1985	25/06/1985	G-27-403
NAF717	SN	01/05/1985	25/06/1985	G-27-404

The second production Jaguar BN, serial NAF701, at Warton before delivery in 1984. ***Terry Panopalis Collection***

candidates had to have 1,000 flying hours' experience, including some MiG-21 or instructor time. Five of the 11 pilots selected were of low average standard, however, but given the limited number of pilots available, releasing a larger number of more skilled pilots would have brought the NAF's MiG 21 and Dassault/Dornier Alpha Jet operations to a halt and BAe had to accept the outcome. Following the initial three courses held at Warton, there were two intermediate/advanced flying training courses, each for six pilots, using the BAe Hawk in 1984.

BAe also assessed the engineering support that would be required. Based on the potential total fleet of 36 Jaguars, they estimated that a single base would require 310 technicians and 27 managers to support a monthly flying task of 20 hours per aircraft – the RAF Engineering team calculated that 400–420 personnel was a more likely figure. Either way, the NAF was short of trained manpower. BAe undertook the conversion training of 50 personnel, with some of them getting on-the-job training at the Jaguar Aircraft Servicing School at Lossiemouth. The RAF also provided basic training for 124 men to mechanic level and to progress 227 mechanics to technician level. It was planned that many of the mechanics would return to Lossiemouth after just a year to be trained as technicians, which was ambitious and risky given the short time to gain hands-on experience. The NAF Director of Engineering, Group Captain Imam, refused to allow the RAF to fail any trainees and so any deficiencies had to be made good back in Nigeria with further training provided by BAe and the NAF. BAe offered to send a servicing team of 46 personnel to assist with setting up and initial operation, but this was politically unacceptable to the NAF and arbitrarily cut to just 20.

A visit by RAF engineers to Lagos to see the NAF groundcrews in action did not inspire confidence given the NAF's low serviceability rates across its fleets and the potentially large orders for new aircraft types that could syphon away trained Jaguar personnel. The Makurdi airfield was assessed as having an unreliable power supply with frequent power cuts and surges that would cause problems with the delicate servicing equipment and flight simulators. Makurdi only had one hangar, which could accommodate up to 18 Jaguars, and outside storage in hot humid conditions would cause serviceability problems. Sadly most of these doubts were proved right.

The Jaguars were based at Makurdi with the 64th Air Defence Group, originally part of Strike Command, but when that formation was disbanded they passed to Tactical Command. The aircraft were armed with Matra R.550 Magic AAMs, Matra 440lb and 880lb (200kg and 400kg) freefall and retarded bombs, Durandal anti-runway bombs, BL.755 cluster bombs and British practice bombs and 2.75in (68mm) Matra SNEB rocket pods.

During their brief operational life, two pilots were sadly killed in flying accidents; Flight Lieutenant Shaman

The sixth production SN, NAF710, was displayed at the Farnborough Show in September 1984 before its delivery. The dummy BAe ALARM anti-radar missile on the outer underwing pylon is an interesting addition. Other weapons include Martel, Sea Eagle and ASRAAM, which was then in early development. *Blue Envoy Collection*

SN6 NAF710 carried the B-Conditions markings G-27-397 for its appearance at Farnborough. The overwing missile pylon is clearly visible here, although BAe declined to show off the feature by fitting a dummy AAM to it. *Blue Envoy Collection*

The fourth production two-seat BN for the Nigerian Air Force, serial NAF703. The Nigerian Jaguars had a camouflage scheme of dark green, mid-green and sand. *Author's Collection*

Musa in 1984 flying NAF714 and Squadron Leader Garba in 1990. Two-seat Jaguar BN NAF702 ran out of fuel and belly landed in open country during the NAF's 25th Anniversary celebrations at Kaduna in April 1985.

In 1991 the NAF withdrew the Jaguar from service as an economy measure, although by then the BAe support contract had expired and was not renewed, leaving the NAF reliant on spares from Hindustan Aeronautics Limited. Only ten Jaguar SN and four Jaguar BN remained and most had clocked up few flying hours, the highest-timed airframe being BN NAF703 with 150 hours 54 minutes.

The retirement was perhaps inevitable given the NAF's poor resourcing and eclectic mix of aircraft. Politically, the sales agreement had been shackling too. In addition to the usual no re-export clause preventing them being transferred or sold to a third party without British and French approval, the Jaguars were supplied as defensive aircraft and the British government threatened that if they were ever used offensively the support contract would be terminated. The NAF was also unable to obtain advanced strike weapons or tanker aircraft to improve the strike capabilities of the Jaguar.

In 1993 there was a BAe proposal to refurbish 15 of the aircraft for Chile but nothing came of this (see later in this chapter). BAe inspected the airframes stored at Makurdi and found them possible to salvage but offered a much lower price than Nigeria had paid for them. No deal was possible so they remained stored outdoors.

On 20 June 2012 the NAF put up a large inventory of surplus aircraft for sale, including the Jaguars, but there were no takers. There were rumours of a refurbishment programme in 2014 but little, if any, work was done. Things took a bizarre twist; one aircraft was listed on eBay in 2012 with a starting bid for $900,000 and a scammer tried to sell them all to the high-end pawnbroker presenter of the British television series *Posh Pawn*. In 2024 the aircraft were again listed online for sale. At least 11 airframes remain at Makurdi (in 2014 the confirmed airframes were NAF700, 702, 703, 705, 708 to 712, 716 and 717).

The ones that got away

Not every sales campaign ends in success. Sometimes British and French political sensitivities, local politics or difficulties obtaining credit made a deal impossible. Competition from other countries and manufacturers was strong, with offers of lower prices or quicker delivery, and some potential purchasers were merely window shopping without intending to buy. Sales campaigns were not trivial affairs and were carefully planned, budgeted and focused on the most important regions.

These tours would often involve MoD Defence Sales and the RAF. For example, in March 1975 BAC asked the RAF to support two tours to Buenos Aires and Kuwait, including providing Handley Page Victor tankers, three Lockheed C-130K Hercules and a Bristol Britannia. The RAF was not keen given the costs involved; tanker support to Buenos Aires would cost £300,000–500,000 depending on whether two or four Jaguars were sent, or £150,000–230,000 to Kuwait. On top of this were spares and transport costs.

There was resistance from Dassault in selling Jaguars at the expense of its own Mirages. While Dassault and the French government denied this, BAC and embassy staff amassed evidence of competing deals from diplomatic sources and it is possible that some buyers may have played up these rumours in an attempt to lower the price.

New partners?

The first country outside the original partnership to see details about the Jaguar was the USA.

In September 1965, the RAF's Assistant Chief of the Air Staff (Operational Requirements), Air Vice-Marshal Reginald Emson, visited the Department of Defense in Washington and raised the topic of the Jaguar. At that time the USAF was undertaking its F-X program for a cheap tactical fighter for close air support and the Jaguar fell within the scope of some of the parametric studies. The USAF became interested in seeing if the requirements could be harmonised to form a tri-national development programme. Emson was torn between causing massive disruption to the programme – SEPECAT had not yet been formed – and the potential that US interest could bring. Interest in the Jaguar faded away as F-X became an air superiority fighter – the McDonnell Douglas F-15 Eagle – and a variant of the US Navy's Ling Temco Vought (LTV) A-7 Corsair II fulfilled the ground-attack role.

The Federal Republic of Germany's Luftwaffe wanted to replace its Fiat G.91 light fighters and received a briefing on the Jaguar in early January 1967. Following the briefing, the Inspector-General of the Luftwaffe, Lieutenant General Johannes Steinhoff, included the Jaguar as a contender in his report to the Minister of Defence, making a personal presentation to the Minister on 3 April.

By the summer, talks had progressed to a stage where Germany was potentially a third SEPECAT production partner (this option was restricted to North Atlantic Treaty Organisation [NATO] countries), although the UK's Ministry of Aviation (MoA) worried about the risk of disrupting the existing production plans. A meeting held in Bonn on 5 July between the Jaguar Management Committee and Luftwaffe staff officers was followed by another in Paris during the 20th–21st involving Breguet, BAC, Rolls-Royce and Turbomeca and their German industrial counterparts for initial discussions. The German airframe consortium would consist of Vereinigte Flugtechnische Werke (VFW), Hamburger Flugzeugwerk, Dornier and Messerschmitt with MAN-Turbo and Klöckner Humboldt Deutz forming the engine consortium. Further meetings were held in Paris on 28 July and 5 August to see whether the industrial consortiums were practical and if the Jaguar met the Luftwaffe's requirements.

The Luftwaffe's requirements and concept of operations most closely matched the Jaguar S and Jaguar B. The Jaguar could not meet all of the performance requirements and meeting the specified 4,000ft (1,220m) take-off distance from a runway at an altitude of 2,000ft (610m) required the provision of rocket-assisted take-off (RATO). Luckily SEPECAT had already studied the feasibility of adding RATO using two 2,500lbf (11.1kN) rocket boosters faired into the lower fuselage, but with the penalty of 20% less range at low altitude.

The Luftwaffe also wanted a terrain-following radar and different armament; a 20mm M61 Vulcan rotary cannon and two additional dedicated hardpoints for AIM-9 Sidewinders. SEPECAT was asked to consider the structural and weight penalties of adding RATO, a Ferranti lightweight radar and wing tip AAM rails to the Jaguar S and the provision of additional radios in the Jaguar B for a secondary tactical reconnaissance role. The British MoD felt that the German changes would enhance the Jaguar's capability and Group Captain R A Watts of the Operational Requirements Branch felt that the RAF should reconsider its earlier rejection of the Sidewinder.

The attractiveness of the Jaguar S and the closeness of both nations' training philosophies saw the German Ministry of Defence seeking the MoD's willingness to host flying and ground technical training. Discussions in Bonn during January 1968 revealed that the German armed forces were undergoing a major review and consideration of a Jaguar purchase had been deferred. In the end, no Jaguar purchase was forthcoming, but Germany did join the Multi-Role Combat Aircraft (MRCA) programme shortly afterwards, which would result in the Panavia Tornado.

Belgium's interest also came early in the programme. The Belgian Air Force had a requirement for 100 Jaguars (88 Jaguar A and 12 Jaguar E) with deliveries from the end of 1975. Belgium wanted to assemble its own aircraft to support its own aviation industry. Talks in 1967 stumbled on the high price and the Belgian Air Staff at that time favoured the Northrop F-5 Freedom Fighter, although the USAF's LTV A-7D Corsair II was also a strong contender.

The Jaguar Management Committee set up a tripartite Production Working Group in 1968 to study the possibility of integrated production involving Belgium. No problems were foreseen in terms of capability, production costs or

By the time that the prototype Jaguar International, XX108, got airborne at Farnborough in September 1974 the Jaguar had received orders from Ecuador and Oman, while India and Kuwait were in the midst of negotiations and Turkey was about to take interest. The Jaguar was, however, losing the NATO Eurogroup contest and Brazil, Egypt, Libya, Qatar and Saudi Arabia had walked away for a variety of political and economic reasons. *Terry Panopalis Collection*

labour productivity in Belgium, and the French and British governments were agreeable to the idea – in marked contrast to the earlier discussions with Germany – as long as their aircraft were not delayed or made more expensive. Belgium would become involved in production from 1969, some six years before it received its own Jaguars. Breguet and BAC would give 7.75% and 4.75%, respectively, of their production shares to Avions Fairey and SABCA, with Rolls-Royce and Turbomeca giving up a 21.8% and 20.8% stake in Adour production, respectively, to Fabrique Nationale. Belgium would contribute £1 million/12 million FF to the tooling costs and pay a 12.5% stake of the research and development costs already incurred by Britain and France, totalling around £4.2 million/50 million FF plus 8.4 million FF annually until 1973 as well as licensing fees (the two nations gaining the value of one-third of the production costs). The value of the Belgian production line would be around £8 million/92 million FF. If the Belgian government failed to confirm its Jaguar order, it would have to repay 12% of the value of any production contracts already fulfilled as compensation. The British MoD was against expanding the FRUGAL integrated supply support agreement to Belgium but was willing to let other users become customers of the system, with SEPECAT being responsible for increasing the production of spares to cover any additional needs. Despite the success of the talks, no official order materialised.

Eurogroup: Starfighter replacement

Belgium's interest returned with the advent of the Lockheed F-104G Replacement programme in late 1973. This effort became the Eurogroup as the NATO members Belgium, the Netherlands, Norway and Denmark sought to replace their Starfighters. Of this group, the Belgians and the Dutch were the key decision-makers (Belgium's requirement alone was for 108 aircraft). BAC offered the Jaguar S and B against stiff opposition from the Northrop P.530 Cobra, Saab Viggen and the Dassault F1 International powered by the new SNECMA M53 turbofan (Dassault hoping that Belgian and Dutch contributions would pay for half of the development costs). Belgium insisted on local production worth 50% by value.

In December 1973 BAC offered to spread the offset value over 100 production aircraft plus another 20 export aircraft but the additional tooling and high proportion of work transfer increased the risk of higher costs. Following discussions with Belgium's Ministry of Economic Affairs and Fairey, SABCA and Fabrique Nationale, a smaller offset manufacture share was considered acceptable. BAC lobbied all four nations but the Jaguar could not meet all of their requirements; it had the advantage of a lower price tag, an important factor if the Eurogroup wanted one-for-one replacements for their F-104Gs. The Royal Netherlands Air Force had asked the Supreme

Allied Commander Europe (SACEUR), General Andrew Goodpaster, which role was most important to NATO. Goodpaster responded that they should be concentrating on, 'conventional offensive air operations with the capability for limited air superiority and a limited nuclear capability'. The Dutch chose to interpret this as needing a high level of interceptor capability, much to the chagrin of BAC given that the Jaguar could fulfil everything else on SACEUR's list. The MoD Defence Sales organisation felt that the Jaguar had a good chance given that a handful of the projected MRCA Air Defence Variant or the Mirage F1 could handle the air superiority role. BAC tried to interest Dassault in a two-aircraft solution pairing the Mirage F1 with Jaguar, but Dassault had little interest in this.

A Belgian evaluation team travelled to Warton in February 1974 to assess the Jaguar, including flights in prototype B08 and the sixth production Jaguar B, XX141. They also visited the Jaguar Conversion Team at Lossiemouth on 26–27 February to discuss the aircraft and its operations. BAC's Military Aircraft Sales Manager, Jeffery Quill, offered an 80% offset with joint production (using transferred tooling) from the 330th Jaguar onwards, including assembly of the final 70 French Jaguar As and a share of future export orders. Also included was involvement in FRUGAL and spares production. SABCA and Avions Fairey would get a manufacturing package covering the wing, tail fin and rudder, tailplanes, air intakes, weapon pylons and final assembly. There was also the possibility of future MRCA work.

But Dassault's lobbying paid off and by the spring the Belgian government was keen to secure the Mirage. Despite this, Northrop announced an MoU in May with the Belgian Aerospace Manufacturers Group (GEBCOMA) to take part in the production of 100–120 P.530s as well as participation in the General Electric J101 engine programme.

The Royal Netherlands Air Force evaluated the P.530, Mirage F1 and the Viggen, favouring the P.530, while the Mirage F1 was politically unacceptable to the Dutch. BAC pulled out all the stops, briefing a Dutch Parliamentary Committee in March – pointing out Jaguar's cheaper unit cost of £1.8 million (rising to £2.5 million before the end of the year) – and hosting them at Warton a month later, closely followed by a team of Dutch journalists. But the Chief of the Air Staff, General Knoop, who favoured the P.530, tried to persuade BAC not to demonstrate the Jaguar to the Committee and made efforts to brief against the Jaguar. By October Dassault was mired in alleged bribery of Dutch politicians, which further harmed the Mirage F1's prospects there.

BAC offered Norway a Jaguar with higher-rated Adours, but by May it seemed that the Working Party had decided against the Jaguar and Denmark seemed uninterested. The Danish briefing finally took place in August and at Farnborough a month later, Major General Bordersen, the Commander of the Royal Danish Air Force's Tactical Command, flew in the Jaguar. Bordersen favoured an American replacement but BAC hoped that the flight might change his opinion. The Royal Danish Navy was also interested in BAC's assurance that the Jaguar could carry Aérospatiale AM.39 Exocet or Messerschmitt-Bölkow-Blohm AS.34 Kormoran anti-ship missiles.

One problem was the USA's unwillingness to sanction the integration of its tactical nuclear weapons on to non-US aircraft and it was felt that the Jaguar might not be immune to this embargo. The Americans favoured all four NATO members operating the same aircraft to improve compatibility and interoperability, with the unspoken suggestion that an aircraft operated by the USAF would be even more favourable. At that time the Lightweight Fighter (LWF) competition between the General Dynamics YF-16 and the Northrop YF-17 (developed from the P.530 Cobra) was not yet decided, but the Eurogroup agreed that they would consider the winner. By October General Dynamics were lining up 350 production slots for the four nations with European industry building 10% of USAF aircraft, 40% of their own aircraft and 15% of another 500 export aircraft, which would keep 10,000 workers busy for many years.

The British Minister of Defence – and Chairman of Eurogroup – Roy Mason, declined to back the two-aircraft solution or intervene in favour of the Jaguar; he felt that the four countries had to make their own decision. MoD Defence Sales knew by December that it was flogging a dead horse and ceased its efforts to support BAC's lobbying. In hindsight it is amazing that BAC persisted against such long odds for so long, although the estimated £150 million value to British industry was obviously an attractive prize.

On 13 January 1975, the US Secretary of the Air Force, John McLucas, announced the YF-16 as the LWF winner and at the Paris Air Show on 7 June the European Participation Group signed for 348 F-16As (116 for Belgium, 58 for Denmark, 102 for the Netherlands and 72 for Norway) – what was termed at the time as 'the arms deal of the century'. Two European production lines were set up at Fokker's Schiphol-Oost site and at SABCA's Gosselies factory along with subassembly and component manufacturing work in Norway and Denmark. Deliveries to Belgium and the Netherlands began in January and June 1979 respectively, with Norway and Denmark receiving their first F-16s the following year.

Europe

Beyond the Eurogroup, other European nations showed interest in the Jaguar. Spain asked for information in 1966, but this was a politically sensitive issue for the UK, given General Franco's fascist regime and continuing disagreements over the status of Gibraltar. France was less inhibited and, fearing that the French might go it alone, the British government agreed to release technical information up to the security classification of 'Confidential'. Spain did not show any subsequent intent to buy and eventually bought the Mirage F1 in large numbers in the mid-1970s.

Interest was shown by the Hellenic Air Force in November 1971 for 20 Jaguars to replace their North American F-86 Sabres. Although BAC submitted a proposal, they opted for the McDonnell Douglas F-4E Phantom II instead (finally retired in early 2024). BAC kept up hopes for an order in subsequent years but Greece acquired 40 Mirage F1CG interceptors.

The Turkish Air Force indicated a need for 20 ground-attack aircraft plus four trainers in December 1974 and approached BAC for a quotation. MoD Defence Sales were sceptical given that previous efforts to sell arms to Turkey had failed due to a lack of credit and because the USA already had an extensive military aid programme in place. This time, however, Turkey was offering a cash deal (the MoD supposed from Libyan or Saudi coffers) and US aid had been suspended following the invasion of Cyprus earlier in the year. The RAF grudgingly accepted a BAC proposal to divert two Jaguar B in the spring of 1976 and ten Jaguar S during 1977. By early 1975 the post-Cyprus embargoes were breaking down, with the Germans and French already resuming supply of military equipment, so MoD Defence Sales and the FCO saw no reason to prevent a deal. Another sales team visited Turkey in the autumn of 1977 to offer prices for 40 Jaguars plus an option for another 40 with deliveries extending to 1986. The Export Credits Guarantee Department (ECGD) were prepared to offer credit, but no order materialised.

The Força Aérea Portuguesa asked BAC for financial proposals for 24 Jaguars in 1976. BAC and the British government felt that Portugal's reliance on US defence aid funding would make a purchase unlikely. Indeed, in 1982 they purchased the first of an eventual three batches of refurbished LTV A-7A Corsair II airframes as the A-7P.

Middle East

The Middle East was the main geographical area for potential sales. The region was a network of complicated Cold War geopolitics and rivalries that created political headaches that severely limited the options open to BAC. The re-export contractual clause, preventing the aircraft being transferred or sold to a third party without British and French governmental approval, was standard practice but was a sensitive issue in the region.

Egypt was keen to obtain the Jaguar, expressing its interest in 1972. President Anwar Sadat met with Sir Arnold Hall, the Chairman of Hawker Siddeley, in Cairo for discussions during Hall's visit to the Middle East in February 1972, at the request of Kamal Adham, an emissary of King Faisal of Saudi Arabia. Hall was also shown around the Helwan aircraft factory by the Commander of the Egyptian Air Force (EAF), General Bagdidi. Sadat informed Hall that he was anxious to obtain a fighter-bomber as a deterrent against Israeli air strikes against important infrastructure assets, such as the Aswan High Dam, by threatening retaliatory deep strikes against Israel. The Soviets had refused his request for such aircraft but he hoped that Britain would provide them. Sadat wanted a modern aircraft that could be manufactured in Egypt with funding from Saudi Arabia, Libya and Kuwait to expand their aviation industry to match Israel's burgeoning equivalent. Hall felt that Sadat had the Buccaneer or Jaguar in mind, although the Harrier was mentioned, and Hall considered that the forthcoming Hawk trainer/light strike aircraft might also be suitable.

Hall alerted Prime Minister Edward Heath about his discussions, which led to the FCO and the MoD becoming involved in assessing the situation. Any sale of Buccaneer or Jaguar was politically problematic, with the Harrier and Hawk less so, although they were hardly the deterrent that Sadat was seeking.

Separately, Sadat's Minister of Defence, General Sadiq, informally approached the British Ambassador and BAC regarding interest in the Jaguar, suggesting an interim buy of 15 aircraft until licence-production agreements could be reached. The Vice Chief of the Air Staff (VCAS), Air Chief Marshal Sir Denis Smallwood, emphasised the potential manning and serviceability problems.

Even though the EAF's Soviet-supplied Sukhoi Su-7 *Fitter* fighters and Tupolev Tu-16 *Badger* bombers were acquired for offensive roles, the MoD concluded that they were employed defensively and that 15 Jaguars would make a minor addition to 'the small EAF offensive capability'. As part of the Egyptian discussions, Libya also enquired about the supply of 60 to 80 Jaguars for its air force. Any potential transfer of Libyan Jaguars to the EAF would significantly change the balance of power in the region with political repercussions. There were also security concerns and BAC would have to offer lower-capability avionics. The Vice Chief of the Naval Staff, Vice Admiral Sir Terence Lewin, concluded that while seeking to reverse Egypt's dependence on the USSR was a valid strategic and political aim, the sale of Jaguar would not present 'a suitable opportunity for this'.

The EAF expressed firmer interest in March 1972 for 12 single-seat and three two-seat Jaguars for delivery later that year. This was unrealistic; the first Jaguars could not be ready until 1976 and the RAF would be unable to provide any training assistance before then. Diverting Jaguar A production was a possibility, but French approval was not forthcoming. There matters rested until a French offer to sell Jaguars to Iraq in 1975 reopened the debate and in November President Sadat visited London for talks. However, the potential sale immediately drew private and public criticism from Israel. Delegations from the Arab Organisation for Industrialisation visited the UK several times from August 1976, but they decided that licence-manufacture of a 20% share of the airframe was not economically viable and by this time the EAF was critical of the Jaguar's lack of air-to-air capability.

The EAF went on to seek American fighters, while Libya purchased the Mirage F1AD attack aircraft – a specialised version without radar – as well as F1ED radar-equipped fighters and the two-seat F1BD conversion trainer. Despite this, BAe was still receiving requests in late-1977 from Libya for 60 aircraft worth around £500 million. The FCO vetoed any deal, however.

Saudi Arabia had agreed the Saudi Arabian Air Defence Scheme with BAC in 1966, which included Lightning F.55 fighters and training aircraft. By 1972 they had a strong interest in the Jaguar, wanting to buy 30. A draft MoU with a forecast delivery lead time of 30 months was sent for consideration in February 1973. It was clear that some additional tropicalisation would be required, adding up to six months to the lead time. The Saudis were unwilling to accept the re-export clause and even attempted to sweeten the deal by offering to fund five BAC/ Aérospatiale Concordes for an Arab consortium if they could be allowed to resell the Jaguars to Egypt.

The British and French governments remained firm, so the Saudis began to cast their net wider in the hopes of securing a more relaxed deal. Dassault offered the Mirage F1 and the Americans upgraded their Northrop F-5E Tiger II offer in May 1973 to the F-4E Phantom with no resale clauses, but without success. The Saudis issued a letter of intent to buy 38 Mirage IIIE fighters in October, but again re-export clause issues scuppered the deal. The fighter eventually ordered in 1974 was the F-5E. In their export growth plans of September 1975, BAC were keen to offer the Saudis licence production but the government encouraged the company to drop the idea.

The prototype S06 had been demonstrated to the Shah of Iran on 20 June 1972 by BAC Chief Test Pilot Paul Millett at Boscombe Down. Efforts by MoD Defence Sales to sell Jaguar to Iran may have resumed in early 1977, but without success.

Following a British MoD survey of his nation's defence needs – which recommended purchasing a squadron of Jaguars – the Amir of the Kingdom of Qatar, Khalifa bin Hamad Al Thani, informed the visiting Minister of State for Defence, Lord Balniel, in September 1972 that he wished to purchase up to a dozen Jaguars. Despite the unwillingness to sell to Egypt and Saudi Arabia at this time, the British government eagerly gave their approval and the French concurred – as long as there was a re-export clause. BAC proposed a unit price of £1.55 million, but the need to maintain the RAF order meant that it would be 1975 before any deliveries or RAF conversion training could begin. Despite the Amir's keenness to conclude a deal and Peter Ginger's successful display of T.2 XX846 in December, no deal was agreed. A decade later, 12 Mirage F1EDA fighters and a pair of F1DDA trainers were acquired.

Another head of state showed his interest – and became the first Royal personage to pilot the Jaguar – when King Hussein of Jordan and his Aide de Camp Major Bader Zaza flew familiarisation sorties in a Jaguar T.2 at RAF Coningsby on 30 January 1974 under the guidance of Wing Commander John Walker and Squadron Leader Fowler of the Jaguar Conversion Team. After the flight, King Hussein expressed his enthusiasm for the Jaguar, but no order materialised – Jordan would later become a Mirage F1 customer following its failure to acquire the F-16.

Having recently bought Lightnings, BAC had good contacts in Kuwait and they held discussions regarding the Jaguar in 1972, a technical sales manager being sent out in January 1973. A delegation from the Kuwaiti Air Force (KAF) visited Warton in August, where BAC test pilot Peter Ginger – who had previous contacts with the Kuwaitis – briefed them and both KAF pilots in the party (Major Abdul Latif Du'Eij and Captain Abdul Mohammed Shaya) made flights in a T.2. They had also evaluated the F-5E Tiger II, A-7 Corsair II and the Mirage F1. Both the British and French governments gave their approval to the potential deal, with the usual re-export clause, which would also include the AJ.68 Martel TV-guided air-to-surface missile.

Finally, after ministerial wrangling, an MoD/BAC team visited Kuwait in May 1974 and the Minister of DAI, De l'Estoile, also promoted the Jaguar against any possible American competitors. Despite this, Dassault offered a fixed-price deal for the radar-less Mirage F1A attack variant in direct competition, although they claimed that this was at the request of the Kuwaitis. To make matters worse, Dassault refused to supply BAC with a fixed-price quotation for their share of the Jaguar work.

BAC offered a lower price in order to match the F-5E and A-7 and hoped for an order of 30 Jaguar S and six Jaguar B worth £100 million. Also included was a package of basic and advanced training in the UK for up to 30 students annually for three years, with the best eight pilots progressing to the TWU and the remainder returning to Kuwait for their advanced training with locally available RAF instructors. In November 1974 Kuwait decided to purchase the McDonnell Douglas A-4 Skyhawk, claiming that it could buy three Skyhawks for the price of one Jaguar. Later, the KAF would also acquire 18 Mirage F1CK

The rivals square up. No. 226 OCU displayed GR.1 XX752 at the International Air Tattoo at Greenham Common in July 1983. Parked alongside were a pair of Jordanian Dassault F1EJ multi-role fighters. *Terry Panopalis Collection*

interceptors and two F1BK trainers, followed later by nine improved F1CK-2 and four F1BK-2.

Dassault offered Iraq a package deal of F1 Mirage and Jaguar A fighters in 1975. The British government, despite its restrictive list of weapons that could be exported to Iraq, gave its approval in an attempt to move Iraq away from the Eastern Bloc in the interests of maintaining a balance of power between the Arab nations and Israel and hopefully easing Iraqi tensions with Iran and Kuwait (the latter being a key local British ally). Negotiations went well but the Iraqi Air Force showed more interest in the F1, of which they ordered 16 F1EQ and 16 F1EQ-2 fighters and four F1BQ trainers (ultimately they would order 110 of various models including the attack F1EQ-4 version – not all were delivered due to arms embargoes during the 1980s).

Iraq did not rule out a subsequent purchase of Jaguar, indeed local BAe contacts indicated that the Iraqi Air Force wanted 30 Jaguar S for the attack role (plus ten Jaguar B trainers). There was some disagreement regarding this between the partners; Dassault had originally refused to offer the Jaguar S as part of its package, claiming that the Iraqis had no interest in it, but BAe's contacts told a different story.

The FCO were disinclined to do business without firm proof of Iraq's intent to buy (the industrial benefits of a large order would enable the FCO to 'rationalise their views', as one memo put it), but the Iraqis would not place an official order until British governmental approval was secured. This conundrum prevented any progress and given Dassault's apparent duplicity, any French government authorisation may have been difficult to achieve. MoD Defence Sales was even thinking of ways to sell the Jaguar to Iran by early 1977, such was the tangled web of Arab defence sales. By the early 1980s Iraq wanted more advanced aircraft like the Tornado and Mirage 4000 or BAe's private venture P.110 multirole fighter.

Sudan had a desire to purchase 12 Jaguars and requested information from BAC in early 1976. This purchase would have been funded by Saudi Arabia, who questioned Sudan's need for such aircraft. A BAC sales team dutifully gave a presentation but, unsurprisingly, nothing happened thereafter.

The Emirate of Abu Dhabi, part of the United Arab Emirates (UAE), considered buying 17 Jaguars instead of a second batch of Mirage IIIs, but eventually ordered more Mirages (the Abu Dhabi Air Force commander and many of the pilots were ex-Pakistan Air Force (PAF) personnel who favoured the Mirage that they were acquainted with). Sheikh Mohammed Bin Rashed had flown in the back seat of T.2 XX846 during its sales tour

Omani Jaguar OS 204, shown here in April 2006, is representative of how other Middle Eastern export Jaguars would have looked had any of the myriad negotiations resulted in orders. ***Terry Panopalis Collection***

to the region in November 1975 and was impressed by its handling and the navigational accuracy of NAVWASS. The Agave radar-equipped variant was mentioned by BAC, but at that stage was still a feasibility study rather than a funded development.

When the UAE ordered Hawk trainers in 1980, there were hints of a possible revival of interest in Jaguar and BAe was keen to offer a Hawk/Jaguar/Tornado package to head off Dassault's Alpha Jet and Mirage series, but this last effort also failed. Years of intensive sales effort and politicking ultimately resulted in failure, which is surprising given the scale of British arms and military aircraft sales in the region since 1945.

East Asia

A group of officers from the Royal Malaysian Air Force, headed by the Chief of Air Staff Air Commodore Suleiman, visited the UK in late March 1969 to evaluate several potential new aircraft. The group received briefings on the Jaguar, Harrier, air defence radars, as well as maintenance and pilot training in the UK for whichever new aircraft was chosen. The presentations on the Jaguar and Harrier covered the performance and operational concepts of both types. The group visited RAF Wattisham to examine the BAC Lightning, Air Commodore Suleiman being given a flight in a two-seat Lightning T.5, before heading to Hawker Siddeley's Dunsfold factory to examine the Harrier and refurbished Hunters. The small but efficient Royal Malaysian Air Force could not afford new equipment, however. A brief resurgence of interest in late 1971 to replace their F-86 Sabres saw BAC making a proposal to supply 16 Jaguars at reduced price in the face of competition from the Northrop F-5E.

In early 1968 a delegation from the Japanese Defence Agency visited several overseas manufacturers, including SEPECAT in connection with the Japan Air Self-Defense Force's second F-X contest for a new interceptor. The Jaguar, however, was quickly ruled out. In March 1969 the Defence Agency announced plans to buy 31 supersonic trainers to fulfil an interim requirement before the Mitsubishi T-2A entered service in 1974. The T-2A was remarkably similar in design to the Jaguar B and was also powered by the Adour – a licence-built version by Ishikawajima-Harima Heavy Industries, the TF40-IHI-801A. SEPECAT offered to lease 30 Jaguar trainers for the period 1971–74 but the discussions failed to reach an agreement.

The Pakistan Air Force (PAF) had sought details on the Jaguar in 1966 but no sales progress was made. Another approach was made following the Indo-Pakistan War in 1971, but the British government was unwilling to authorise a sale in the interests of preserving the balance of power in the region. BAC made a presentation to the PAF in 1976 in response to interest for 80–100 aircraft. BAC gauged that the interest was not genuine and was an attempt to pressurise the US government to approve the PAF's previous order for 110 LTV A-7 Corsair IIs, which had been part funded by Saudi Arabia. The newly inaugurated President Jimmy Carter had vetoed the sale in an attempt to pressure Pakistan to abandon its plans to buy a nuclear reprocessing plant from France. Carter offered 100 F-5Es, but these were rejected and US-Pakistani relations soured. Britain offered to sell Jaguars to India and Pakistan in an attempt at even-handedness, but this idea foundered. Even if it had wanted to buy, Pakistan lacked the money and the ECGD was reluctant to give credit. Eventually the PAF ordered the Dassault Mirage 5.

Australia and Africa

Despite SEPECAT having briefed the Royal Australian Air Force in 1966, it was a decade before a formal Request for Proposals was received for the Tactical Fighter Force Requirement, which envisioned a two-aircraft fighter fleet. BAe concluded that the Tornado would be the better choice in the face of strong US competition from the General Dynamics YF-16 and Northrop YF-17, the latter finally being selected in its developed form as the McDonnell Douglas F/A-18A Hornet.

Other than Nigeria, the only other African nation to show interest in the Jaguar was South Africa. A request for information had been made in 1966 but the UK would not sanction any sale given the arms embargoes in place due to Apartheid rule. The British government was worried that France might make a deal independently or supply Mirages instead. This eventually happened, the South African Air Force receiving 32 radar-less Mirage F1AZ attack aircraft in November 1975, followed by 16 radar-equipped F1CZ fighters.

Latin America

Following Ecuador's purchase, BAC was keen to exploit interest in Latin America. A 1975 sales tour received interest from the air forces of Argentina, Bolivia and Venezuela. Nothing came of these overtures, however, as Argentina and Venezuela were already operating the Mirage III and V, while Bolivia had neither the money nor military resources to operate the Jaguar.

The Brazilian Air Force proposed sending an evaluation team to visit BAC in 1973. BAC quoted a price of £84 million for 40 aircraft but Brazil bought the Northrop F-5E instead, which they are still flying today in heavily upgraded form as the F-5EM.

Venezuela rekindled its interest with an evaluation flight using T.2 XX838 at Warton in May 1978, and in July 1981 a delegation headed by Dr Aguilar, Head of the Venezuelan Senate Defence Committee, visited BAe's Dunsfold factory for a presentation on the Jaguar and Tornado. Production test pilot Sandy Aitken performed the briefing in Spanish and Keith Hartley gave a flying demonstration in the Jaguar. In May 1982 the Venezuelan Air Force became one of the first export buyers of the F-16A with US funding under the Peace Delta programme, with deliveries beginning the following year.

BAe failed to interest Chile in the Jaguar in 1980. Another offer was made in 1993 to sell Jaguars (plus English Electric Canberra PR.7 reconnaissance aircraft) to replace the Fuerza Aérea de Chile's (FACh) ageing Hunters. BAe offered 15 refurbished Nigerian airframes with delivery within three years and five RAF aircraft for immediate delivery for £62 million. The refurbished airframes would have a three-year warranty from BAe, although at this stage the survey of the airframes languishing in Nigeria had not yet been completed to determine what level of work was required to get them airworthy. A FACh team visited BAe and Coltishall for detailed briefings. Belgium, however, made a cheaper offer of Mirage IIIs with immediate availability. The RAF could not give up any more front-line aircraft (though they did offer to loan a couple more) but the MoD emphasised the Jaguar's cheaper running costs to the Chilean Minister of Defence, Perez Yoma. Many FACh staff officers preferred the Jaguar, but a group led by the Chief of Staff General Vega wanted the Mirage. Given the risks over whether the Nigerian airframes were salvageable, the deal did not look attractive and the proposal went no further.

CHAPTER TEN

Shamsher

The Indian Air Force (IAF) was the third largest operator of the SEPECAT Jaguar and (as of 2024) they are the last in front-line service. The IAF was interested in the Jaguar as soon as it was officially unveiled, but politics and financial issues would delay its acquisition until the early 1980s. India became a third production site, with Hindustan Aeronautics Limited (HAL) at Bangalore (since 2005 officially named Bengaluru) initially assembling British-made kits before moving to constructing the entire airframe locally and with greater amounts of indigenous avionics. The HAL-built aircraft have been referred to as the Shamsher – Sword of Justice – since the 1980s. Continually upgraded, the aircraft are likely to remain in IAF service until at least 2035.

Procurement

IAF interest in the Jaguar began in November 1966 when a SEPECAT team visited the HAL factory at Bangalore and gave general presentations to government and IAF officials in New Delhi. At that time, security classifications prevented more than a cursory overview of the aircraft's performance and capabilities. The UK was keen to actively promote defence sales to India and Pakistan and preferred that such deals be made on a commercial basis, partly to avoid either country increasing its debt burden on defence spending.

A more direct approach in September 1967 was a memorandum to the British High Commissioner, John Freeman, by Wing Commander (Retired) A R Hindley, the manager of Greaves Cotton & Company

Two of the RAF loaned Jaguars, T.2 XX138 and GR.1 XX116, in Indian Air Force service as serials JI001 and JI008 respectively. ***BAE Systems via Author's Collection***

Limited's aviation division based in Bangalore (they were agents for British aeroengine and accessory component manufacturers in India). Hindley called on Britain to negotiate the sale and licence manufacture of the Jaguar and to offer collaboration on a larger variable-geometry wing aircraft to replace the IAF's English Electric Canberras. Freeman passed on Hindley's suggestion to the relevant Ministries in London, but Assistant Secretary Ronald Jardine at the Ministry of Technology (Mintech) did not take kindly to Hindley's privateering as a private citizen, especially as the British Aircraft Corporation's (BAC) representative in India, a Mr Mollan, had already been trying to drum up interest in the Jaguar. Even so, all this activity convinced Mintech that there was an opportunity to make a sale and authorised further presentations to the Indian government.

In early 1968 the IAF identified a requirement for up to 317 attack aircraft between 1971 and 1982, either the HAL HF.24 Marut, then in development, or the Jaguar built under licence. BAC's Military Aircraft Sales Manager Jeffrey Quill and Breguet's Paul Jaillard gave a presentation in New Delhi in April 1968, with air advisers, attachés and ministry representatives – including Jardine – from Britain and France in attendance, to gauge the seriousness of the IAF's interest. Some classified information was specially downgraded to allow it to be shared. The Managing Director of HAL, Air Marshal Lal, was certainly impressed by the Jaguar's performance and capability compared to the Marut, whose development was stalled due to a lack of powerful enough engines – a pair of 4,850lbf (21.57kN) Bristol Siddeley Orpheus 703 turbojets – and was technologically at least a decade behind in terms of design and avionics.

India wanted to develop its own Advanced Strike Aircraft (ASA) programme in collaboration with foreign companies and BAC hoped that a Jaguar order might obtain them a sponsorship position. Rolls-Royce was also keen on getting their new RB.199 turbofan project into the ASA. The IAF were, however, hesitant to be the Jaguar's export launch customer given their experiences with the Folland Gnat, which had suffered a high accident rate in service, and they still had hopes that the Marut could be further developed.

Jeffrey Quill returned to New Delhi in 1970, accompanied by Deputy Chief Test Pilot Jimmy Dell. The presentation was well attended by senior IAF staff officers but again they seemed uninterested, reportedly being more enthusiastic to hear Quill's tales of his wartime Spitfire test flying. Serious interest began when the prototypes S06 and B08 were flown during an IAF evaluation visit to Warton in June 1972.

By the following November the Indian government had informed BAC that credit would be necessary to fund the purchase and the Export Credits Guarantee Department (ECGD) was called upon to help India finance the deal. The main problem was the size of the order; 100 aircraft would require ECGD cover over a ten-year period for £192 million, but a smaller – and more likely – order of 30 aircraft would only amount to £58 million.

The Jaguar was facing a strong competitor financially, not from the Soviets offering cut-price MiGs or Sukhois, but the Dassault Mirage F1, with suspicions that Dassault were offering subsidised prices with a fixed rate of cost escalation of 4% per annum, in contrast to BAC's rate of 10–12% due to spiralling inflation and Dassault's own 12% charge on Jaguar components for the RAF's Jaguars. Dassault were prepared to offer a cash deal, telling the Indians that buying a smaller number of superior Mirage F1s would require less cash. BAC also claimed that it had evidence – from a sensitive source – that a ten-year credit deal had been offered, but this could not be revealed to the French government, who denied that such a deal was offered. Despite official complaints, the French government seemed unable, or unwilling, to rein in Dassault's competition.

There was also competition from the SAAB Viggen, although the Viggen's use of a Pratt & Whitney JT8D turbofan with a Volvo-designed afterburner and thrust reverser risked an American embargo.

The RAF mandated that the Navigation/Weapon Aiming Sub-System (NAVWASS) and the Marconi passive radar warning (RWR) system could not be made available before 1975. BAC argued that NAVWASS was the unique selling point on which to beat the Mirage F1, but security restrictions hampered disclosure of its performance and the IAF were apprehensive about its ability to maintain inertial systems on forward airfields. India's own efforts had focused on Doppler ground-drift radar systems and the Assistant Chief of Air Staff Plans, Air Marshal Idris Hasan Latif, enquired whether a Doppler radar could replace the Elliott E3R inertial platform.

On 6 September 1973 the IAF Chief of Air Staff, Air Chief Marshal O P Mehra, visited RAF Lossiemouth and the newly formed Jaguar Conversion Team. Wing Commander John Walker gave a presentation and Mehra was given the opportunity to inspect a static Jaguar while test pilot Paul Millett gave an impressive flying display in Jaguar T.2 XX137. Mehra wrote to his RAF counterpart in early 1974 asking for details of the Weapons System Accuracy Measurement trials then under way but the reply was non-committal given the security implications. Throughout these discussions, the RAF made it clear that they supported the IAF deal as long as their deliveries were unaffected and that they would not be involved in the training programme.

By May 1973 the IAF evaluation team had also flown Dassault's various Mirages and had recommended that

The acquisition of the Jaguar turned into a decade-long series of negotiations with several stumbling blocks along the way. Even so, the end result was a boost to not only the Indian Air Force's capabilities, but also those of India's aviation industry. ***Author's Collection***

the Jaguar should be purchased. The total requirement was now for 87 aircraft (12 to be two-seaters) with an initial purchase of 30 and the remainer to be assembled or manufactured in India. BAC offered a first delivery 24 months after contract signature.

Credit remained a thorny issue and in March 1975 the British government withdrew its offer of credit (perhaps as much as £350 million) but was prepared to offer a cash purchase for a smaller number of aircraft. This seemed a precipitous move given that India had never defaulted on payments for any defence contract placed with British firms. A worried Allen Greenwood, BAC's Deputy Chairman, proposed to BC Vallieres, the President of Avions Marcel Dassault-Breguet Aviation, that they should offer a genuine Anglo-French government credit guarantee to secure a Jaguar order for the benefit of both companies. Vallieres was receptive as 80% credit for the Mirage F1 was on equally shaky ground and further Soviet penetration into Indian aerospace would harm his company's future prospects.

Pressure was growing to reverse the decision due to the economic value of the order for British industry and the potential 1,500 redundancies at Warton. The Labour Member of Parliament (MP) Kenneth Warren, as Chairman of the All Party Aviation meeting of Trade Union shop stewards, wrote to the Secretary of State for Defence Roy Mason to push for credit to be given. The Foreign Secretary, James Callaghan, was chided over lunch by his old wartime Commanding Officer, Major General CMF Deakin, now at Engineering and Industrial Exports Limited, over the lack of a deal. In a Foreign and Commonwealth Office (FCO) file in the National Archives there is even a letter from a chicken farmer, a constituent of MP Walter Clegg, bemoaning (among other agricultural policy issues) the lack of credit to fund the Jaguar purchase to secure British aviation jobs and consequently making India dependent on the Soviet Union, imploring his MP to 'strive to kick some sense into them'.

Callaghan agreed to a sale on 5 June and reopened access to credit. An IAF technical commission rated the Jaguar first, Viggen second and the Mirage F1 third, and confirmed an intent to order 24 aircraft. The ECGD initially offered £24.5 million of credit, which only covered the cost of 12 aircraft once the ground equipment and spares were factored in. Eventually the government was persuaded to raise this to £49 million and France contributed £34 million of credit, with India paying the remaining 30% in cash.

New complications arose following the detonation of India's first nuclear weapon on 18 May 1974. The fact that the Jaguar was capable of carrying nuclear weapons now raised worries in the FCO's Arms Control and Disarmament Department about breaching the Non-Proliferation Treaty. The credit issue, to some extent, was a useful smokescreen for the government's fears over the nuclear issues and potential diplomatic damage to Anglo-Pakistani relations. The Non-Proliferation Treaty Review Conference sat in May 1975 and the fears of international criticism failed to materialise, which reassured the FCO that the deal could go ahead but it warned that if India declared a nuclear weapon capability and an intent to deploy nuclear-armed forces then the government would have no choice but to cancel the deal.

There were concerns that France might offer the Jaguar A in that scenario but it was unclear whether the UK government would actually use its veto given the industrial implications. President Carter's Administration in Washington was eager to prevent the proliferation of advanced military aircraft in South East Asia and to deter Pakistan from seeking its own nuclear weapons in response. The MoD and FCO were unmoved by these arguments; if India wanted modern aircraft it would obtain them from wherever it could. Prime Minister Harold Wilson and Foreign Secretary Callaghan did not waiver in their decision and a visit by Wilson to New Delhi in 1977 reaffirmed the deal, as did Callaghan's visit – as Wilson's successor as Prime Minister – in January 1978.

Progress on the renamed Deep Penetration Strike Aircraft (DPSA) was slow. The IAF received financial approval in November 1977 for 150 aircraft to equip five squadrons, 40 to be purchased and the remainder licence-built by HAL with an option for a further 20 aircraft. Licence production was vital, preserving 3,000 jobs at HAL and ensuring that it remained at the forefront of aviation technology and manufacturing capability. Initially it was desired that the first six or eight aircraft would come equipped with Thomson-CSF Agave radar.

In March 1978 an Indian team led by the Defence Secretary, Govind Narain, visited the UK, France and Sweden. On the 17th the Secretary of State for Defence, Fred Mulley, approved the release of 16 RAF Jaguars (12 GR.1 – later increased to 14 – and four T.2) to the newly nationalised British Aerospace (BAe) to allow rapid delivery. There was also a training agreement for 12 pilots covering 35 flying hours each plus five hours' instructor training for the best three pilots. Six of the pilots would be attached to RAF squadrons for a familiarisation period of three months and BAe would train the IAF technicians. This was an offer that was unmatched by Dassault or SAAB.

The IAF also wanted to purchase quantities of BL.755 cluster bombs, 1,000lb (454kg) freefall and retarded bombs, 550lb (250kg) low-drag bombs, Matra Durandal anti-runway bombs, 2.75in (68mm) SNEB rockets, practice bombs, fuel-air explosives and napalm containers.

The Indian government finally announced on 6 October 1978 that the Jaguar had been selected and the contract was signed in April 1979 for 40 aircraft plus licence production of another 120. The cost of licence production was estimated at £500 million, with the value being worth £350 million and £220 million to the UK and France respectively. BAe Warton's Divisional Managing Director, Ivan Yates, appointed Wing Commander (Retired) Alan Keys – who had made no fewer than 24 Jaguar promotional visits to India – as Executive Director India based in New Delhi to co-operate with the Indian government. A support organisation was created at Warton under its Commercial Director (and SEPECAT Director), Richard Evans, who also became Director-in-Charge (India) in 1979 responsible for helping HAL set up its production line.

Production

The 18 RAF Jaguars were designated as Batch One aircraft and were on loan until the HAL production line was capable of producing locally assembled aircraft. The aircraft were overhauled by BAe before delivery and more powerful RT.172-26 Adour Mk.804E engines were fitted. The 40 Batch Two Jaguar Internationals built by BAe were basically equivalent to the GR.1 and had the Adour Mk.804E. The 35 single-seaters were designated Jaguar IS (assigned serials JS101–135) and the five trainers the IB (JT051–055). BAe's Jaguar Project Pilot, Keith Hartley, made the maiden flight of JS101 at Warton on 17 February 1981. Production was delayed by issues affecting Dassault's production line.

Deliveries began when JT051 arrived on 5 March 1981 and production continued at the rate of three aircraft per month until August 1982, the last aircraft (JS135) leaving Warton on 6 November. JS135 had been exhibited at the 1982 Society of British Aerospace Companies Show at Farnborough as G-27-367 in early September. All the delivery flights were made by IAF pilots.

The 45 Batch Three aircraft were assembled by HAL from BAe-supplied kits, gradually switching over to HAL-produced components, and comprised 35 IS and ten IB aircraft. The first shipment of materials was in May 1981 and the first aircraft flew at Bangalore on 31 March 1982. These aircraft had the more powerful RT.172-58 Adour Mk.811 rated at 5,520lbf (24.6kN) dry and 9,270lbf (41.23kN) reheated.

There were teething troubles in setting up the HAL production line, the Indian company being dissatisfied with BAe's efforts. There were problems with the documentation of tooling, the testing equipment and other materials, and there were discrepancies in the paperwork for the final assembly process sheets and the requirements of castings and forgings and test equipment. This was BAe's first licence-production agreement and the process was new to them, but personnel problems did not help. Liaison with Rolls-

Indian production		
Serial range	**Type**	**Quantity**
JI001-JI018	RAF loan aircraft	18 (returned)
JS101-JS135	BAe manufactured IS	35
JS136-JS204	HAL manufactured IS	79
JT051-JT053	BAe manufactured IB	3
JT054-JT065	HAL manufactured IB	12
JT066-JT082	HAL manufactured IB Night Attack	17
JM251 -JM262	HAL manufactured IM	12

This is one of the HAL-built Jaguar IS DARIN aircraft – also known as Shamsher – featuring the overwing rails for Matra R.550 Magic AAMs, but otherwise externally little different from the BAe-manufactured Jaguar International IS. ***Author's Collection***

Royce went much more smoothly. HAL were worried as any delays in production would cause serious headaches on the shopfloor (none of their workers could be discharged), and they knew that maintenance problems with the avionics and fuel system had been due to the insufficient numbers of British technicians. BAe set up a new office in New Delhi in 1979 and retired test pilot Peter Ginger was appointed as Operations Manager. In 1980 the Chairman of BAe, Sir Frederick Page, flew out to personally address the issues and Ginger was promoted to General Manager.

In July 1980 there was a scare that the Indian government might cancel licence production and buy a second batch of 40 Jaguars from BAe instead. There was also a debate whether the Dassault Mirage 2000 or the Mikoyan-Gurevich MiG-23BN *Flogger-H* should replace the Jaguar on the production line. BAC and the FCO suspected that Dassault had been attempting to derail the Jaguar deal to clear the way for the Mirage 2000. They appeared to be offering two squadrons of second-hand Mirage F1s and local production of the Mirage 2000 if the Jaguar production contract was cancelled. The IAF was not overly impressed by this offer and there were doubts that HAL could manufacture the Mirage 2000 without gaining experience on the Jaguar first – some IAF staff officers even doubted whether HAL had the ability to build the Jaguar. There was certainly a press campaign in favour of cancellation; the newspaper *Surya India* alleging excessive prices and arguing that the MiG-23BN was a much better deal, *India Today* dispassionately noted the excessive cost of home production and the ongoing political tug-of-war over the Jaguar, while the *Hindustan Times* and *Tribune* both defended the Jaguar. The latter put the teething troubles down to the rapidly expanding IAF logistics and maintenance branches and pointed out that the cancellation penalties would be equally expensive. Prime Minister Mrs Indira Ghandhi opposed any cancellation. Her younger son, Sanjay Gandhi, decided to scrutinise the deal for suspected corruption and was convinced that the IAF had been influenced by the previous government to opt for the Jaguar. He had no constitutional authority but was invited by the IAF to examine the records and was surprised to find that the air force had in fact always been steadfast in its intention to buy the Jaguar. Sanjay Gandhi was killed in a flying accident on 23 June 1980 and there the matter rested. Dassault's efforts had backfired, leading to increasing official pressure on BAe, who drastically improved their performance.

Although initially impressed with NAVWASS, like the RAF, the IAF became aware of its limitations and poor reliability and sought an improved system (in 1975 the Aircraft and Systems Testing Establishment (ASTE) in Bangalore had tested NAVWASS on an HF-24 Marut and rejected it). The IAF was offered the export standard Ferranti Type 1024E inertial navigation system (INS) but this did not match the capability of the RAF's FIN 1064 upgrade. In response, the Defence Research and Development Organisation (DRDO) created the Inertial Nav-Attack System Integration Organisation, which co-operated with the French company SAGEM to develop the Display Attack Ranging Inertial Navigation (DARIN) avionics suite (initially called INDRA – Inertial Nav Digital Ranging & Attack – but the similarity to the name of Prime Minister Indira Gandhi saw this being changed). SAGEM built a static integration rig at Pontoise for testing, which was later moved to Bangalore. There was also co-operation with BAe over the necessary structural modifications and GEC-Marconi.

The avionics comprised a wide field-of-view Smiths Type 1301 head-up display and weapon-aiming computer (HUDWAC), GEC-Ferranti COMED 2045 combined map and electronic display, SAGEM ULISS 82 INS and a Crouzet air data system. If the ULISS went unserviceable the HUDWAC was able to take over. The Ferranti LRMTS was retained. A MIL-STD-1553B digital databus was fitted, allowing for the fitting of a wide range of new weapons and systems in future upgrades (it would be another decade before the RAF Jaguars received the MIL-STD-553B). DARIN also included a range of Indian-developed avionics; the Identification Friend or Foe (IFF) system, automatic direction finder, radar altimeter, V/UHF and HF/SSB radio equipment. The avionics bay cooling was also redesigned and improved. Overwing missile pylons were also fitted for Matra R.550 Magic infrared (IR)-homing air-to-air missiles (AAMs).

In August 1982 the Indian government approved HAL's proposal to establish an avionics division in Korwa, in the state of Uttar Pradesh, to produce the DARIN avionics, as well as those for the MiG-27ML Bahadur (*Flogger-J*), which HAL was beginning to licence manufacture at its factory in Nasik.

Two Jaguar IS (JS102 and JS103) were delivered to ASTE to act as DARIN prototypes and the first flight with the new avionics took place on 17 December 1982. Navigation accuracy trials revealed a better performance than the specified 1nm (1.8km) per hour drift. Weapon-aiming accuracy trials were carried out at the Indian Space Research Organisation's Sri Harikota Air Range before live releases were made at the desert range in Rajasthan. DARIN received initial operational capability status in 1984 and full operational capability was declared a year later.

BAe's Deputy Chief Test Pilot, Chris Yeo, flew a demonstration of the Jaguar Low-Light TV System (LLTV) in 1983 and that was the first overseas demonstration of the equipment.

Technology transfer was progressive over seven phases; from six locally assembled kits of fully equipped major assemblies in Phase One to Phase Seven (the 46th airframe onwards) with the import of complex components only, such as integrally milled wing panels, with the remainder being produced from locally sourced materials. The first completely Indian-built Jaguar was delivered in January 1988. It was estimated that the average cost per aircraft, including the engines, equipment and avionics, was lower than if the aircraft had been purchased flyaway from abroad. The Adour Mk.811 was also subject to licence-production agreements, with HAL manufacturing several components. During the mid-1980s, the DARIN Jaguars gained a new name, Shamsher or Sword of Justice, although the name Jaguar remained in common usage and endures today.

Eight of the Batch Three aircraft were completed as the maritime anti-ship Jaguar IM with the Thomson-CSF Agave radar and a ventral hardpoint for the BAe P3T Sea Eagle anti-ship missile. The I-band Agave provided a detection range of around 70nm (130km) against a large surface vessel and 10–15nm (18–28km) against a fighter-sized aerial target. The first Jaguar IM flew in 1985 and was delivered in January 1986, all eight being completed by mid-1993. The aircraft were finished in a unique disruptive camouflage scheme using two shades of grey-blue.

Plans to build another batch of 56 aircraft was cancelled in favour of assembling 31 Jaguar IS kits ordered from BAe in August 1982. In January 1988 another batch of 15 aircraft were approved but were cancelled the following year and were eventually re-ordered in 1993; four of them being of IM standard fitted with an Israeli Elta EL/M-2032 multi-mode X-band radar under the DARIN II programme.

A further batch of 17 Jaguar IB were ordered in 1999 as night attack aircraft with the weapons system officer in the rear cockpit. The aircraft were equipped with the Israeli Rafael Litening targeting pod containing a camera, forward-looking infrared (FLIR) and a laser

Based on the maritime attack version of the Jaguar International, the Jaguar IM featured a Thomson-CSF Agave multi-mode radar in the nose. This is the fifth production Jaguar IM, serial JM255. ***SDASM Archives***

The first pair of loaned Jaguars on their delivery flight to India in July 1979. The aircraft are Jaguar T.2 serial JI001 (ex-XX138) and GR.1 JI003 (ex-XX117). ***Terry Panopalis Collection***

GR.1 JI004 (ex-XX117) arrived in India on 14 October 1979. This backdrop is the rather chillier Cumbrian landscape during testing before the ferry flight. The standard RAF camouflage was retained. *BAE Systems via Author's Collection*

designator, and the Rafael RecceLite reconnaissance pod could also be carried. Problems with the integration of the avionics delayed delivery by two years to 2003. The final order was placed on 31 March 2006 for another 20 Jaguar IS to full DARIN II standard. There seem to have been some production issues; it was reported in January 2006 that the IAF refused to fly two newly built Jaguars and refused to accept a further five due to manufacturing defects and all were returned to HAL for repair.

The final aircraft was delivered in 2008, ending 26 years of production. The total number of Jaguars, from all manufacturing sources (excluding the original loan aircraft) was 124 Jaguar IS, 15 IB, 17 IB Night Attack and 12 IM, with HAL manufacturing 128 of them.

Operational service

The first four IAF pilots to undergo training (Wing Commander D R Nadkarni, Squadron Leaders Mike McMahon and J S Sisodia and Flight Lieutenant S C S Adhikari), arrived at No. 226 Operational Conversion Unit (OCU) at Lossiemouth on 26 February 1979. Following completion of the Jaguar course, they were posted to No. 54(F) Squadron at RAF Coltishall to gain 25 flying hours of operational experience.

They were followed by two batches each of four pilots in April and August, four of them (including Squadron Leaders S P Tyagi and D D S Kumar) also going to No. 41(F) Squadron to take the reconnaissance course. These 12 pilots on their return formed the nucleus of the first Jaguar unit, No. 14 'Bulls' Squadron, and many went on to attain high rank during their careers, two of them serving as Chief of the Air Staff. Some of these pilots became qualified flying instructors (QFIs) during their time in the UK and began conversion training for other IAF pilots at Ambala Air Force Station (AFS). Groundcrew were also sent to the UK for training. The IAF set up the Jaguar ground school with appropriate facilities and simulators at Ambala.

The Bulls were – and still are – based at Ambala as part of Western Air Command. Ambala is located in the northern part of the state of Haryana and is one of the most strategically important IAF bases, around 136 miles (220km) from the border with Pakistan. No. 14 Squadron had been previously equipped with the Hawker Hunter F.56 between November 1959 and January 1979, seeing combat during September 1965 and in December 1971.

No. 14 Squadron was initially equipped with the 18 loaned RAF Jaguars, the first pair – Jaguar T.2 IAF serial JI001 (ex-XX138) and GR.1 JI003 (ex-XX117) – being officially handed over on 19 July and arriving at Jamnagar in India on the 27th following their lengthy ferry flight exactly on time at 11:00. JI001 had been flown by BAC Deputy Chief Test Pilot Tim Ferguson and Wing Commander Nadkarni and JI003 by Project Test Pilot Chris Yeo.

The second pair arrived on 14 October, T.2 JI002 (ex-XX143) flown by Squadron Leader Mike McMahon and Paul Millett and GR.1 JI004 (ex-XX117) flown by Wing Commander Nadkarni. The first ferry flights from Warton to Ambala were conducted via Toulouse,

Brindisi, Luqa, Akrotiri and Seeb in Oman, arriving in Jamnagar before onward transfer to Ambala. Briefly Baghdad was used as a stopover but the outbreak of the Iran-Iraq War saw subsequent flights transiting via Luxor in Egypt. Quite often Grumman F-14A Tomcats of the US Navy operating in the Indian Ocean would tail the Jaguars.

As mentioned earlier, there were some technical issues. The IAF had expected a defect rate of one per 20 flying hours but actual experience was much worse at one defect per hour and during 600 flying hours since August 1979 there were 56 groundings, 20% due to the NAVWASS system. This had knock-on effects for mission planning. The spares supply pack that came with the interim aircraft should have contained 14,600 items but only had 11,000, with 900 of those of partial quantity. Maintenance records, manuals and publications were sometimes lacking and BAe staff seemed unable to provide prompt information. This experience was contrasted with the Soviet teams, who stayed for two years after delivery with full documentation and knew all the answers.

The armament situation was equally dire; the Carrier Bomb Light Series (CBLS) used for practice bombs supplied by the RAF via BAe were missing parts, the weapon pylons had no testing equipment, while the ADEN cannon had been supplied with defective components and they could not be harmonised due to a lack of bore sighting equipment. Up to April 1980 not a single round of ammunition had been fired or a bomb dropped. Even after Sir Freddie Page's visit, problems persisted with missing parts. Part of the problem was that under the terms of the contract, the interim RAF-loaned aircraft spares were 'supplied as available' and were treated separately by BAe from the new-build direct supply aircraft following from Warton. The IAF were unaware of this – although they pointed out that BAe had contracted to supply the interim aircraft to secure the Jaguar order so they had a duty to meet the terms and provide serviceable aircraft. Inadequate facilities and personnel at Ambala and lengthy customs clearance were further problems and the aircraft may have not been flown often enough to keep them serviceable. The haste of the operation did not help but things gradually improved as both sides learned from experience.

No. 14 Squadron became operational in June 1980, although the full declaration of combat readiness was not achieved until September. Once the serviceability issues settled down, as many as six sorties were flown by some aircraft between dawn and dusk during operational training exercises. The pilots were very happy with the handling and low-level performance of the Jaguar, with a smooth ride even during hot summers with strong thermals. The early NAVWASS-equipped aircraft provided a welcome introduction to

RAF Loans

IAF serial	Type	C/N	RAF serial	Handover date	UK B Cond serial	Return Date
JI001	T.2	B3	XX138	19/07/1979	G-27-320	To Oman 01/1982
JI002	T.2	B8	XX143	14/10/1979	G-27-321	09/09/1982
JI003	GR.1	S17	XX720	19/07/1979	G-27-319	24/02/1982
JI004	GR.1	S10	XX117	14/10/1979	G-27-317	24/02/1984
JI005	GR.1	S8	XX115	11/12/1979	G-27-316	23/07/1982
JI006	GR.1	S162	XZ397	11/12/1979	G-27-322	W/o 16/04/1981
JI007	GR.1	S163	XZ398	14/08/1980	G-27-323	??/04/1984
JI008	GR.1	S9	XX116	11/12/1979	G-27-315	19/09/1984
JI009	GR.1	S25	XX728	29/04/1980	G-27-324	23/07/1982
JI010	GR.1	S22	XX725	13/02/1980	G-27-325	19/04/1984
JI011	GR.1	S6	XX111	13/02/1980	G-27-314	W/o 10/05/1982
JI012	GR.1	S26	XX729	29/04/1980	G-27-326	25/05/1982
JI013	GR.1	S33	XX736	13/02/1980	G-27-327	24/02/1984
JI014	GR.1	S31	XX734	14/08/1980	G-27-328	11/02/1982
JI015	GR.1	S34	XX737	14/08/1980	G-27-330	25/05/1982
JI016	GR.1	S35	XX738	13/02/1980	G-27-329	19/04/1984
JI017	GR.1	S37	XX740	23/04/1980	G-27-331	19/05/1984
JI018	GR.1	S11	XX118 2	9/04/1980	G-27-318	25/04/1982

The Himalayas form an impressive backdrop to a Jaguar IS cruising at medium altitude. The Jaguar is also known as Shamsher (Sword of Justice) in Indian service. ***Terry Panopalis Collection***

Jaguar IS JS141 of No. 14 'Bulls' Squadron receiving fuel from an IAF Ilyushin IL-78 *Midas* aerial refuelling tanker during Exercise Cope Thunder 04-01. *US DoD via Terry Panopalis Collection*

modern avionics and when it worked it gave excellent results. Pilots favoured the part throttle reheat feature of the Adour but, like all their brethren, they bemoaned the lack of power at high altitude.

The squadron began to demonstrate the Jaguar's weapon accuracy. Following ADEN cannon firing trials, work began to obtain clearances for the bombs, the first being the freefall and retarded 1,000lb bombs, the BL.755 and then the Matra Durandal anti-runway, rocket-powered bomb. The Durandal deployed a parachute to retard the fall to the optimum attitude before the rocket fired to penetrate up to 15in (40cm) of concrete to explode beneath the runway, making a large crater. The Jaguar could carry between six and 11 Durandals. Firing trials with the SNEB rocket pods followed and excellent accuracy was obtained with the Thomson-CSF Atlis laser pod, mirroring the Armeé de l'Air's experience.

From March 1981, the unit began receiving the UK-built Batch Two Jaguars to replace the loaned aircraft. By the end of the year there were 17 Jaguars at Ambala (12 IS and five IB) for the two squadrons based there. Two of the loaned Jaguars were lost in accidents; JI006 (ex-XZ397) on 16 April 1981, when Flight Lieutenant S Adhikari hit a vulture during a low-level training flight, and JI011 (ex-XX111) on 10 May 1982, when Flight Lieutenant R K Srivastava flew into a hill and was killed. Another pair were retained by HAL until 1984 for trials work; one being JI007 (ex-XZ398) used on Matra Magic integration and DARIN trials. The remaining aircraft were returned to the UK during 1982–84.

On 4 June 1981, Air Chief Marshal Idris Hasan Latif, now the Chief of Air Staff, visited the Armeé de l'Air airbase BA 136 Toul-Rosières, which was home to the Jaguar-equipped 11ème Escadre de Chasse. The visit included a tour the Jaguar maintenance facilities, and a static presentation of the Jaguar equipped with various weapons was followed by an aerial demonstration. The squadron, at the time of writing in 2024, is still operating the Jaguar.

The second squadron to form was an ex-Canberra B(I).58 unit, No. 5 'Tuskers', which was reformed at Ambala AFS in March 1981 from a cadre of No. 14 Squadron pilots. The unit was equipped with the UK-built Batch Two Jaguars and became operational in August 1981. In July 1988 the squadron participated in Operation Pawan, the Indian Peacekeeping Force operation in Sri Lanka, flying long-range reconnaissance missions during the civil war there. These operations continued until 1990. The Tuskers began receiving upgraded DARIN II Jaguars in December 2005. As of 2024, No. 14 Squadron is still operating its upgraded aircraft.

No. 27 'Flaming Arrows' Squadron was the first to form on the HAL-built Batch Three DARIN aircraft after retiring its Hunter F.56s. Initial conversion took place at HAL's factory at Bangalore in January 1985 before moving to its new home, Gorakhpur AFS in the state of Uttar Pradesh, in June. The Flaming Arrows won several trophies in various exercises and gunnery meets and on 13 November 1996 was awarded the President Colour for its contributions both in war and peace. In March 2003, the squadron was the first to carry out air-to-air refuelling with the Ilyushin Il-78 *Midas* aerial refuelling tanker (at the time a pair of these were on loan from Russia), demonstrating a new long-range penetration capability in IAF service. As of 2024 the squadron is still operating the Jaguar.

The next squadron to form was No. 16 'Cobras', converting from the Canberra B(I).58 at Gorakhpur during October to December 1986. The squadron is still operating the Jaguar. The maritime strike Jaguar IM was operated from 1987 by 'A' Flight of No. 6 Squadron 'Dragons' based at Pune AFS, as part of the 2nd Wing of the South Western Air Command. All eight aircraft were delivered by mid-1993. 'B' Flight continued to fly the Canberra B(I).58 until December 1992, when it was re-equipped with Jaguar IS aircraft. The squadron retains a mix of Jaguar IS and IM aircraft and in late 2007 moved to Jamnagar AFS, located on the Gulf of Kutch in the state of Gujarat.

The last IAF squadron to form on the Jaguar was No. 224 'Warlords'. The squadron had been formed on 4 July 1983 with the Mikoyan-Gurevich MiG-23MF *Flogger-G* at Adampur AFS in the air defence role. On 31 March 2007 the squadron was disbanded, having accumulated 32,581 flying hours on its MiGs. The Warlords were reformed at Jamnagar on 31 March 2008, receiving a batch of new-build Jaguar IS DARIN II aircraft. As of 2024, the squadron is still operating its DARIN II aircraft. Although the majority of the squadrons are still operating the Jaguar after 40 years of use, attrition remains a problem. For example, during the period 2000–10 alone at least 13 Jaguars were lost in crashes due to various reasons, including poor weather, technical malfunctions and pilot error.

Shortages of spares has also affected aircraft serviceability and availability. With many of the original suppliers now out of business or no longer producing old items, the only option is to purchase surplus aircraft for cannibalisation. In 2018 India purchased 31 Jaguar A and E airframes from France and a pair of airframes each from the UK and Oman. This package included Adour engines and several hundred types of critically needed spares. In June 2024 the IAF were looking to purchase five stored ex-RAF GR.1 and four T.2 airframes from Jet Art Aviation in the UK as well as around 150 types of spare parts. As part of its commitment to keep the Jaguar in service, the IAF purchased two Fixed-Base Full Mission Simulators for Jamnagar and Gorakhpur from HAL in 2022 and agreed a five-year maintenance contract.

The Jaguar saw active service during the Kargil conflict against Pakistan in 1999 along the disputed Line of Control in Kashmir. Operation Safed Sagar (White Ocean) covered the IAF's provision of air support to the Indian Army during engagements against regular and irregular troops of the Pakistani Army from vacated Indian positions in the Kargil sector. It was the first large-scale use of airpower in this region since the Indo-Pakistani War of 1971. No. 27 'Flaming Arrows' Squadron were the main Jaguar unit involved, along with a detachment from No. 5 'Tuskers' at Halwara. The Jaguars were quickly modified to carry laser-guided bombs (LGBs) and GPS-guided bombs. The air support operations began on 26 May and during June the Jaguars conducted ground-attack sorties in conjunction with MiG-27ML Bahadurs. At the end of June the focus of the air operations was striking Pakistani-occupied positions on the heavily defended 'Tiger Hill', including nine LGB drops, one of which was conducted by a two-seat Jaguar IB (the remainder were dropped from Dassault Mirage 2000H fighters).

No. 27 Squadron was also the first IAF unit to be deployed for Operation Parakram, another military stand-off with Pakistan in Kashmir, on 16 December 2001.

The provision of aerial refuelling tanker support has enabled the IAF to participate in a growing number of international exercises and has enabled the Jaguars to travel much further than before. Following its earlier loaned aircraft, the IAF ordered six new-build Il-78MKI *Midas* tankers in 2002 fitted with Cobham Mk.32B air refuelling pods with drogues that allow the aircraft to refuel both Western and Russian-built aircraft. They

A Jaguar IS releases a stick of 1,000lb (454kg) bombs following the release of flares to attract any IR-homing SAMs during Exercise Vayu Shakti 2019. *Indian Air Force/Government Open Data License – India*

Jaguar IS JS141 carrying a CBLS pod holding four practice bombs on the ventral hardpoint. ***USAF***

were delivered during 2003 and 2004 and are operated by No. 78 'Battle Cry' Squadron based at Agra AFS.

In June 2004 a group of ten fighters, including six Jaguars, left India for Alaska for Exercise Cope Thunder 04-01 with tanker support from a pair of Il-78MKI tankers. The flight from Ambala AFS to Eielson Air Force Base (AFB) staged through Qatar, Egypt, the Azores, Newfoundland and Edmonton – something never before attempted by the IAF. The selected Jaguar pilots and the six Jaguar IS (JS141, 144, 150, 154, 170 and 177) were pooled from the four squadrons based at Ambala and Gorakhpur (Nos. 5, 14, 16 and 27); flying without any squadron markings. Group Captain S J Nenodkar was selected to lead the Jaguar flight. Air Chief Marshal Krishnaswamy and Air Officer Commanding in-Chief, Western Air Command, Air Marshal S P Tyagi (a graduate of No. 2 Jaguar course) were also present.

The exercise began on 15 July and involved aircraft from the USA, Canada, UK, Germany, Singapore, Japan, Malaysia and Sri Lanka. During the training missions the Jaguar's low-level capabilities came into their own, the Alaskan hills providing helpful terrain masking that enabled them to penetrate the 'enemy' air defences and make successful attacks. The pilots also had to

Among the array of international fighters on the flightline at Eielson AFB, Alaska, during Exercise Cope Thunder 04-01 was Jaguar IS JS170. ***USAF***

adapt to an unusual natural element during their operations, the 'Midnight Sun' that never sets in the Arctic latitudes in summer. Following this successful deployment, the group began their return flight on 6 August. After their return, Ambala hosted a special ceremony on 11 September to celebrate the Jaguar's silver jubilee in Indian service.

Other international exercises include Exercise Malabar 07-2 in the Bay of Bengal in September 2007, which saw the Jaguar IMs of No. 6 Squadron supporting the Indian Navy's aircraft carrier INS *Viraat* (R22) and its BAe Sea Harrier FRS.1 fighters alongside Boeing F/A-18E and F/A-18F Super Hornets of the US Navy. Between 22 and 29 October 2009 the Jaguars exercised with the Jaguars and General Dynamics F-16C Fighting Falcons of the Royal Air Force of Oman in Exercise Eastern Bridge. No. 6 Squadron was hosted at Thumrait, the home of Oman's Jaguars.

In 2016 the Jaguars returned to Alaska for Exercise Red Flag Alaska 16-1, an advanced aerial combat training exercise at Eielson AFB between 28 April and 14 May. The IAF contingent was led by Group Captain Assudani. This time the Sukhoi Su-30MKI provided the centrepiece of the IAF's combat capability but the four examples were accompanied by four DARIN II Jaguars in the strike role. The contingent were again supported by a pair of Il-78MKI tankers. The IAF was flying as part of the 'Blue Force' alongside US Air Force (USAF) and US Navy squadrons and later had the chance to fly as part of the 'Red Force' alongside the 18th Squadron USAF Aggressors. The Jaguars also got a chance to release practice bombs over the JPARC air-to-ground range. Despite the sub-zero temperatures, no major serviceability issues were encountered.

During 2004, a bilateral exercise series with the USAF began, being hosted at Gwalior AFS in the state of Madhya Pradesh. Following a gap from 2018, in 2023 Exercise Cope India took place at Kalaikunda AFS in the state of West Bengal between 13 and 24 April. The exercise was co-ordinated by the IAF's Tactics and Combat Development Establishment. The IAF fighter element included the Su-30MKI-3, the newly delivered Dassault Rafale, HAL Tejas Mk.1 as well as the venerable Jaguar. The USAF deployed Boeing B-1B Lancer bombers and Boeing F-15E Strike Eagles as well as a range of transport aircraft. Personnel from the Japan Air Self-Defense Force also observed the exercise. Given their age, it is unlikely that the Jaguars will make many more overseas deployments.

DARIN II & III

By the 1990s there was a clear need to refurbish the 40 UK-built Batch Two Jaguars equipped with the increasingly obsolete NAVWASS and lacking any precision-guided munitions (PGM) capability. Upgrading the Jaguar has been hampered by technological delays and budget issues as the IAF struggles to update its various combat aircraft fleets, fund purchases of new aircraft from foreign suppliers, as well as build up the capability of its home industry to develop projects like the Tejas Light Combat Aircraft and the planned Advanced Medium Combat Aircraft fifth-generation, stealth, multi-role combat aircraft for the 2040s.

The DARIN II modernisation project was launched in the 1990s, receiving final approval to proceed in June 2003 with the aim to extend the Jaguar's operational life by another two decades. The avionics were upgraded with a SAEGEM Sigma 95 navigation system with a ring-laser gyro INS integrated with GPS to provide position accuracy within 330ft (100m) and the DRDO's Defence Avionics Research Establishment developed a new mission computer, two of which were installed. The cockpit was modernised with an Elbit wide-angle HUD, an LCD multifunction display and an autopilot. The starboard ADEN cannon was replaced by an Elta EL/L-8222 radar jammer, while other defensive equipment included an Israel Aerospace Industries (IAI) Malat chaff dispenser (built under licence in India) and the Indian Tarang Mk.1 RWR. The LRMTS was replaced with a new Thales electro-optical sensor, the nose cone 'chisel' windows being replaced by a single, downwards-facing window. It is believed that a range of low-cost radar cross-section reduction measures were trialled (such as engine intake mesh screens) and possibly adopted as upgrade kits. DARIN II also covered the replacement of the Jaguar IM's Agave radar by the Elta EL/M-2032 multi-mode radar during 1998–2002. Thomson-CSF Caiman radar-jamming pods were delivered and it is possible that a couple of Basilisk pods, surplus from the French Jaguar A fleet, were also acquired.

Only the final production batches of Jaguars received the complete DARIN II fit. Many existing airframes received a mix of DARIN II features depending on which items were available at the time of their scheduled major overhauls. This led to a fleet that has widely different standards of avionics.

Air-to-air refuelling has become important and one of the two-seater IB night attack aircraft (JT068) belonging to No. 224 'Warlords' Squadron was modified in 2008 with a fixed 'L'-shape refuelling probe on the nose. Clearly there is a desire to provide the squadron's DARIN II Jaguars with a strategic penetration capability.

The additional capabilities brought with it new weapons; the Raytheon GBU-16/B Paveway III LGB, the Textron CBU-105 Sensor Fuzed Weapon (an anti-armour cluster PGM) in 2010 and the AIM-132 ASRAAM IR-homing AAM in 2014. The DRDO's Armament Research & Development Establishment developed a new 1,100lb (500kg) Preformed Fragmentation Bomb with a proximity fuze, which on detonation produces 10,300 steel fragments that can penetrate up to 0.5in (12mm) of steel plate. India has also developed a family of dumb and smart High Speed Low Drag (HSLD)

Since 2015 the Jaguar IM maritime attack aircraft of No. 6 'Dragons' Squadron have been armed with the AGM-84 Block II Harpoon anti-ship missile. This aircraft is seen on manoeuvres in February 2024. *Indian Air Force/Government Open Data License – India*

bombs that will arm all of the IAF's combat aircraft, including the Jaguar. The Aeronautical Development Establishment and the Instruments Research and Development Establishment developed the 990lb (450kg) Sudarshan LGB, which was tested aboard a Jaguar in 2010 and entered service in 2013. In May 2016 a DARIN II Jaguar was used for the initial trials of the DRDO Smart Anti-Airfield Weapon (SAAW), a stand-off PGM with a range of 54nm (100km) and a weight of 276lb (125kg). The high-explosive warhead can pierce hardened structures such as concrete runways and aircraft shelters. A Jaguar was used for three live warhead tests at the Chandan range in the state of Rajasthan in August 2018. Production has now begun for the Su-30MKI and Dassault Rafale; whether the Jaguar will also receive SAAW is unclear, but certainly the weapon can be integrated with the aircraft.

A replacement for the ageing BAe Sea Eagle anti-ship missile for the Jaguar IM was announced in 2006, but funding issues delayed the procurement. The Jaguar IM finally received the AGM-84 Block II Harpoon, the first test firing taking place on 22 May 2015 and the 200nm (370km)-long test sortie also including an aerial refuelling.

The DARIN III programme was announced in July 2008 with the aim to enter service by December 2012. That timeline proved too ambitious; the prototypes did not fly until 2012 and according to press reports from *India Today*, the aircraft 'could not meet expectations'. HAL estimated in 2013 that upgrading all 125 Jaguars would take until 2019 and the programme was subsequently reduced to 68 aircraft. The first upgraded two-seat Jaguar IBs achieved initial operational capability in November 2016.

The cockpit was upgraded with three MFD-55 active matrix LCD multifunction displays, a new digital HUD, Elbit Display and Sight Helmet (DASH) – helmet-mounted sights being vital to allow full utilisation of ASRAAM – and hands on throttle and stick (HOTAS) controls. The avionics are upgraded with indigenous mission computers and digital flight data and video recorders. The navigation system, radar altimeter, autopilot and IFF system are all updated. The sensors are upgraded with an Elta EL/M-2032 multi-mode pulse-Doppler radar and a Litening-3SU laser designation pod. The provision of radar includes converting the Jaguar IS with the nose section of the Jaguar IM and upgrading the air conditioning system for improved avionics cooling. The self-defence equipment was largely that of the DARIN II upgrade but with better integration with the Combat Aircraft Systems Development and Integration Centre's D-JAG integrated electronic warfare system, and MILDS-F missile warning was added.

It was recognised that the DARIN III upgrade would add a considerable amount of weight to the airframe and so a separate project was begun in 2009 to replace the Adour Mk.811 with the Honeywell F125IN low-bypass, two-spool turbofan to improve performance, particularly at altitudes above 30,000ft (9,145m). Honeywell estimated that the new engine would increase the dry thrust by 9% and 12% in afterburner compared with the Adour and in high ambient temperatures the thrust would be 25% greater with consequent improvements in climbing performance and single-engine safety.

The F125 was a reheated version of the F124, which was derived from the civil TFE731 engine in the late 1970s. It had a three-stage fan and a five-stage turbine as well as full authority digital electronic control (FADEC). Maximum reheated thrust was rated at 9,850lbf (43.8kN). The F125IN was specially tailored for installation in the Jaguar's engine bays and offered improved reliability with the time between overhaul increased to 2,000 hours and offering 30% growth potential. It was planned that more than 25% of the components would be manufactured in India and all installation and certification would also take place in India.

The engine was demonstrated to HAL and Honeywell acquired two retired RAF aircraft (one of them being GR.1A XX737) for installation trials. The project was abandoned due to spiralling costs in August 2019; 280 engines would have cost $2.4 billion.

The Adour has received several indigenous updates as the result of local industrial research. The DSRO's Defence Metallurgical Research Laboratory (DMRL) has developed technologies for the production and thermo-mechanical processing of high-temperature titanium alloys such as isothermal forging technology, which has been used to manufacture components such as discs and shafts for the Adour. Vacuum investment casting technology has also been used to develop high-pressure turbine blades for the Adour. Much of this technology is also feeding into the Gas Turbine Research Establishment's GTX-35VS Kaveri turbofan programme, which has been running since 1986, but as yet is still not ready for production.

The DARIN III upgrade has itself been upgraded. In 2015 the Israeli electronics company Elta signed a contract to supply the Elta EL/M-2052 multi-mode active electronically scanned array (AESA) radar for the Jaguar and the Tejas. The radar has air-to-air, air-to-ground and air-to-sea modes with multiple target tracking capability as well as moving target indication and mapping functionality. Using a modular design, it is compact enough to fit into small nose cones like those of the Jaguar. On 11 August 2017, the Chairman of HAL, T Suvarna Raju, announced that a Jaguar would soon fly with an AESA radar but it is thought that this did not happen at that time. As part of the technology transfer agreement with IAI for licence production of 54 EL/M-2052 radars, the first production version was to be ready by March 2021 as part of the new DARIN III UPG standard. This involves rebuilding the nose of the Jaguar IS to a standard similar to that of the IM, although heat dissipation was an issue that needed to be overcome. During the Aero India 2019 exhibition in Bengaluru, HAL displayed their latest proposal, Jaguar MAX (Mothership for Augmented Xploitation) – also called DARIN III+. This includes many of the DARIN III UPG features but adds an AESA-based wide-band jammer, combined IFF interrogator transponder, a flight management system, an L-band long-range datalink and an INS that is compatible with GPS, the Russian GLONASS and the Indian GPS-aided GEO augmented navigation (GAGAN) system. The cockpit is further upgraded with a configurable display using larger displays and a voice command system. The option for modernised engines would seem mandatory given the increased weight and drag. The aircraft can be configured with laser, synthetic aperture radar (SAR) or electro-optical pods – a radar targeting pod can be fitted to the two-seat IB Night Attack – to meet various mission requirements.

The weapons include a range of new indigenous programmes: one 2,200lb (1,000kg) DRSO Gaurav gliding PGM or the new-generation LGB (NG-LGB), five multi-warhead anti-armour PGMs, 16 DRDO SAAW, one Naval Anti-Ship Missile-Medium Range (NASM-MR), four Astra Mk.1 beyond visual-range AAMs, five medium-range cruise missiles or 12 swarming UAVs. Jaguar MAX is probably one upgrade proposal too far but would have provided the pinnacle of the Jaguar's capability with a full range of twenty-first-century weapon and sensor capabilities that usually belong to the latest combat aircraft, let alone one designed 60 years ago. The planned replacement for the Jaguar is the HAL Tejas Mark 2, also known as the Medium Weight Fighter, which will also replace the IAF's Mirage 2000 and MiG-29 *Fulcrums* sometime after 2027 and the IAF plans to phase out the Jaguar during 2027–35. It seems likely that the Jaguar will reach over 55 years in Indian service, something unforeseen back in 1966. The IAF have proved that the Jaguar, with the right upgrades, can still provide a credible strike platform.

A pair of Jaguar IM from No. 6 Squadron overflying the aircraft carrier INS *Viraat* (R22) alongside two of *Viraat*'s BAe Sea Harrier FRS.1 fighters operated by INAS 300 'The White Tigers' Squadron and US Navy Boeing F/A-18F and F/A-18E Super Hornets of VFA-102 and VFA-2 during Exercise MALABAR 07-2 in the Bay of Bengal. *US Navy*

CHAPTER ELEVEN

Jaguar ACT

At the time that the Jaguar was being designed, electronic fly-by-wire (FBW) flight controls were still in their infancy. As development continued, a new field opened up in aeronautical design, Active Control Technology (ACT) – the computerised control of the control surfaces to expand the manoeuvrability and handling of aircraft beyond that which the human brain can control. ACT enables the design of intentionally unstable aircraft, which offers improved performance and allows a smaller and lighter airframe as less time and energy is required to initiate manoeuvres; the aircraft turning faster and tighter during combat and reducing fuel consumption. With an ACT system, small control forces have to be exercised continuously at many times a second to keep the aircraft flying straight and level. Any momentary loss of control through a system failure would lead to a crash, the control task being too much for a human pilot to maintain for any length of time and so much so that providing a manual backup is pointless.

Development of a Jaguar successor under the Air Staff Targets AST.396 and AST.403 during the 1970s and 1980s created the demand for a flying testbed to prove the application of FBW and ACT. Warton proposed converting one Jaguar into an ACT research aircraft, and the result was the world's first aircraft to fly with a fully digital, totally autonomous ACT system.

The Jaguar ACT XX765 flying along the Blackpool promenade in 1983 in the attractive 'Raspberry Ripple' colour scheme of the RAE. ***BAE Systems via Author's Collection***

Hawker Hunter T.12 XE531 on a test sortie in 1978. The aircraft was the RAE's principal fly-by-wire research aircraft and Jaguar ACT was to be the next stage of technical development. *Terry Panopalis Collection*

FBW history

Early research into FBW resulted in the start of development of multiple-redundant flight control systems such as Autoland for the Hawker Siddeley Trident airliner by 1958 and Manoeuvre Demand Control had been trialled in the delta-winged Avro 707C research aircraft. These early systems were complicated analogue electronic devices and not until the emergence of solid-state digital electronics during the 1970s did enough computing power and reliability become available to realise the development of ACT. Although British industry were major suppliers of FBW equipment for Concorde, Panavia Tornado and the Boeing YC-14 STOL transport, the prime development contracts had gone to European partners. The Royal Aircraft Establishment (RAE) began fitting two-seat Hawker Hunter T.12 XE531 with a full-authority quadruplex ACT system in 1968. XE531 made its first post-conversion flight in 1973 and in 1978 became a joint project with Hawker Siddeley Aviation (HSA) in order to maximise its potential given the scarcity of available resources.

In October 1974 the British Aircraft Corporation (BAC) and HSA were contracted by the Ministry of Defence Procurement Executive – MoD(PE) – to carry out feasibility studies into an FBW research programme using the Jaguar or the Buccaneer respectively and Smiths Industries carried out a feasibility study for the avionics. These studies were submitted in September 1975 and BAC's Jaguar proposal was selected. The three essential reasons for the Jaguar programme – at least from the RAE's point of view – were: to establish the capability of applying full-time active control systems to future combat aircraft; to ensure that the procedures and techniques developed were applicable in the next generation of combat aircraft; to ensure that the equipment supplied for the rig and aircraft was capable of incorporating different system concepts and more advanced control policies that would emerge from parallel studies, like those under way for AST.403.

BAC wanted to gain confidence in the airworthiness of full-time FBW and both rig testing and flight testing were essential to prove the systems. The system was treated in all airworthiness aspects as though it was intended for production. It was intended that the flight control system (FCS) would not impose any reduction in the flight envelope limits of the Jaguar. Potential future flight tests were identified for alternative motivator research, task-oriented control laws, direct force control and gust alleviation techniques. The FCS processor system was to be designed for significant expansion to allow for a range of alternative control law designs and additional sensors. The software

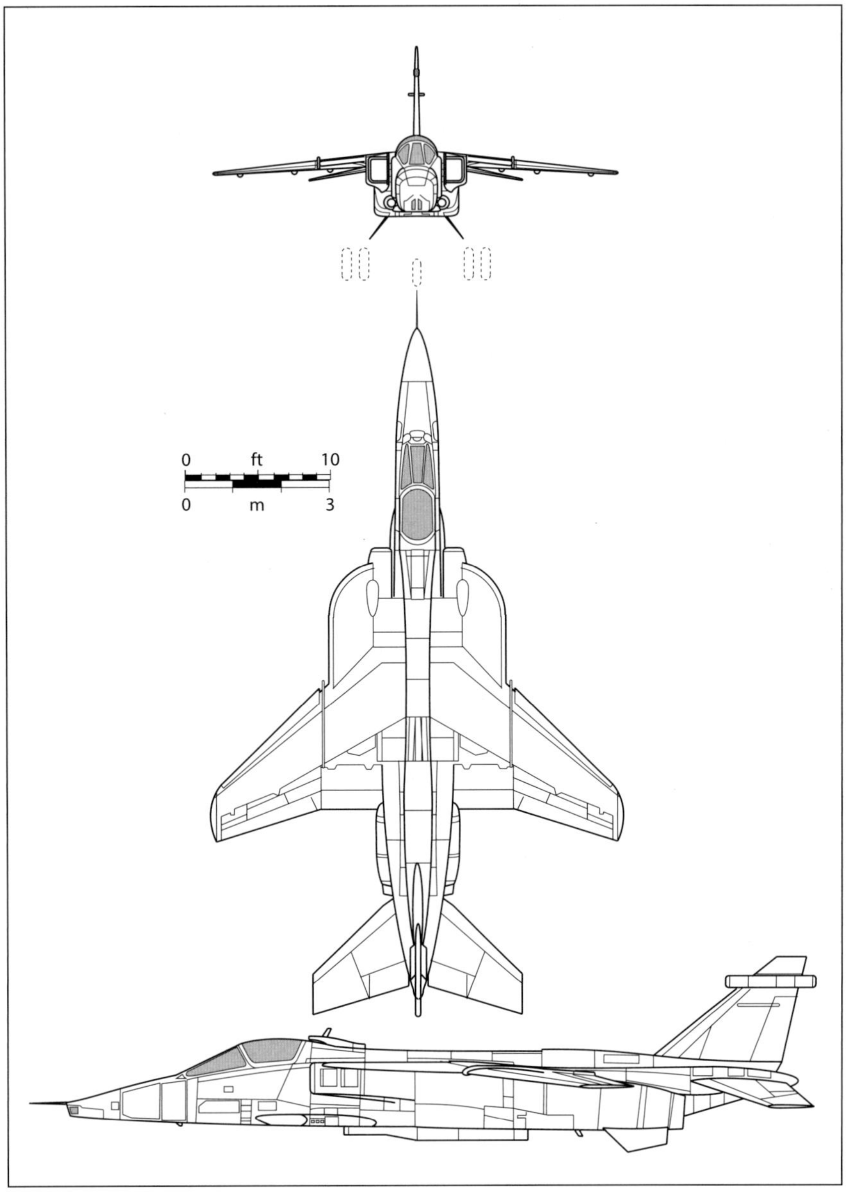

A general arrangement drawing of the Jaguar ACT in its final configuration with the leading edge strakes fitted. *Chris Gibson*

would be modular to ease reprogramming. The main powered flying controls were unaltered from the standard Jaguar, which was recognised as being a limitation if trials of direct lift or direct side force controls were desired in the future.

David Parry was appointed as Jaguar Fly-By-Wire Project and Technical Manager and a team was set up at Warton, initially in the Jaguar Projects Office but later moving to Hangar 7 where the ground rig was located.BAC selected two sub-contractors to develop the FCS following a round of competitive tendering. Marconi Avionics would develop the high-speed digital computer and the software, while Dowty-Boulton Paul would supply the servo actuator systems. Dowty-Boulton Paul was working on 'voting' actuator systems in which functioning servo valves could 'out vote' faulty valves to ensure that the control commands were carried out safely.

In 1977 BAC and HSA were nationalised and merged as British Aerospace (BAe). Early FBW co-operation soon faltered as the teams began competing for resources and vying for future implementation in the next generation of combat aircraft then being designed. Warton was managing the Jaguar FBW programme, hoping to feed the experience into its AST.403 designs, while Brough and Kingston were sharing the Hunter FBW and ACT (a proposed combined Hunter–Hawk programme lost out to Jaguar). Kingston also proposed the Harrier V/STOL Displays and Advanced Control programme to feed into its next-generation supersonic V/STOL studies such as the P.1216.

The Jaguar ACT had to be made aerodynamically unstable. Flight control would be ensured by the world's first fully digital, totally autonomous active FCS, without any manual backup in the event of a system failure. This required exceptional levels of reliability backed up by redundancy to ensure a total system loss probability of one chance in ten million per flying hour. The control-configured aircraft would operate a continual loop, receiving a stream of inputs from the air data sensors and control surfaces and automatically applying corrective movements to the control surfaces via the FBW system without lag. The pilot was out of the control loop beyond moving the stick and rudder pedals to instruct the aircraft where to go; the actual movements of the control surfaces were under computer control, with some element of haptic feedback to the pilot. The system also imposed safety limits so that the airframe's structural limits could not be exceeded no matter how vigorously the pilot moved the controls – what is termed 'carefree handling'.

Simulations of the Jaguar utilising the new PDP 11/55 computer were the starting point for establishing the requirements for the sensors, actuators and digital processors. Initially a monitored triplex system was preferred but quadruplex sensors were eventually selected. Other alternatives that were assessed included fibre-optic data transfer, optical readout sensors and multiple-surface redundancy. A powered flying controls rig was built at Warton on which to conduct the integration and testing. Electromagnetic interference and lightning strike tests were carried using Hunter XE351 to determine the safety factors of the system. By September 1980 there were signs of cost overruns and a long-term flying programme seemed unlikely given the available Flight Systems Research Area budget, with the Air Staff unlikely to fund more than 40% of the costs. The RAE was keen to push ahead and get the Jaguar ACT to flight status, as it did not believe that relying on static rigs would be sufficient given the overseas competition in the field. Nigel Hughes, Head of the RAE's Flight Systems Department, commented that, 'The achievement of safe flight with the highly unstable aircraft (i.e. with strakes fitted) in my view wins a number of political Brownie points, but is not as essential as the achievement of stand-alone digital flight control.' Mr J Gibson at Warton argued that after its planned test flying programme, the Jaguar ACT would remain a very powerful tool for flight dynamic research (although admitting that XE531 was likely to have already covered all the relevant flight dynamic research points by that time).

There were internal pressures within BAe; Brough believed that Warton wanted to kill off the Hunter FBW programme, which the company was funding to the tune of £300,000 per year. The Hunter had achieved good results and had offered good value for money. Any rivalry stopped when XE351 was lost on 17 March 1982 when the newly installed 11th stage compressor disc of its Rolls-Royce Avon engine disintegrated following take-off from Farnborough. Flight Lieutenant Rod Sears and John Leng ejected safely, although Leng was injured when he landed in burning fuel.

Creating the Jaguar ACT

Jaguar GR.1 XX765 was selected for conversion and loaned to BAe by the MoD(PE). Delivered to the RAF in June 1975, it had served with squadrons based at RAF Coltishall, Brüggen and Lossiemouth. The aircraft was delivered to Warton from RAF Abingdon by BAe test pilot Eric Bucklow on 4 August 1978. The existing flight control rods and actuators were removed, along with the HF radio in case of electromagnetic interference. The ADEN cannon were removed and the ammunition bays converted to house the additional avionics. The aircraft was also repainted in the RAE's attractive 'Raspberry Ripple' white, red and blue colour scheme.

The aircraft was made aerodynamically unstable – a standard Jaguar was never less than +2% stable. Initially ballast was carried aft in the fuselage to prove the operation of the FCS before the aerodynamic solution was fitted. The rear ballast was progressively increased to around 560lb (255kg) to move the centre of gravity (cg) behind the centre of lift (centre of pressure) to create an instability of -4% static mean chord – while avoiding tipping the aircraft on to its tail when parked on the ground. The aerodynamic solution was to fit two large strakes – effectively leading-edge extensions (LERX) – to the wing roots to shift the centre of lift forwards, which together with the ballast would create an instability of around -10% in the pitch axis (in theory up to -14% was possible). With the strakes fitted the aircraft would be a control configured vehicle – an unstable aircraft that could only be controlled by the flight control computers (FCCs).

The airframe was used for several tests before the avionics were installed. Artificial stability is reliant on structure-mounted sensors, so the natural structural resonance of the airframe had to be fully understood. It was suspended in a rig and excited by hydraulic rams across a wide range of frequencies. Having identified several natural resonant frequencies, suitable notch filters

A close-up of the strake. The ADEN cannon were removed, the firing ports faired over and the ammunition bay repurposed to house the additional avionics required. ***Author***

XX765 gets airborne for the first time in Phase One configuration from Warton on 20 October 1981. ***BAE Systems via Terry Panopalis Collection***

were then designed to suppress these inputs to the FCCs.

The FCS was composed of two major elements, the executive system and the ancillaries. The executive continuously monitored and controlled the aircraft throughout the flight. It was comprised of the computing system, the associated input sensors and the flight control surface actuators.

The ancillaries consisted of the computer status controls and displays and all other systems associated with the FCS, including the electrical and hydraulic supplies, flight test instruments and the spin recovery system.

The spin recovery equipment for the high-incidence trials included additional instruments, canopy fragilisation and a spin recovery parachute. The flight test instrumentation included in-flight telemetry and crash recording equipment.

The core of the executive was the four interchangeable FCCs located in the former ammunition bays. The FCCs implemented the aircraft control laws for the control surface movements. The data inputs came from a variety of analogue, discrete and digital signals, the FCCs carrying out the necessary signal filtering and analogue/digital conversion. A digital datalink ensured that all four FCCs received the same data and digital links were also provided to a pair of actuator drive and monitor computers (ADMCs). The ADMCs monitored the output of the FCCs and consolidated the control surface position demands into a further two output channels (making a total of six). The ADMCs continuously monitored the FCC outputs to screen for any failures, which would be disregarded by the system. The FCCs and ADMCs were 16-bit computers with a 16kb program store and a 6kb data store. They were supplied with DC electric power from three busbars, each computer being connected to two separate busbars for redundancy and each busbar having its own backup battery supply.

The software was built up gradually in a modular fashion with simple documentation to ensure that all the engineers could understand it. A diagnostic display unit was fitted in the port undercarriage bay that allowed the groundcrew to check any failures, which were shown as a series of four-digit codes.

The pilot interacted with the executive using the normal cockpit controls and any system failures would be signalled on the central warning panel. A training switch could be used to simulate failures of the incidence/sideslip and pitot/static sensors.

The input sensors included the driving sensors: the control position pick-offs (on the control stick, rudder pedals and trim controls; the aircraft pitch, yaw and roll rate gyros; the angle-of-attack and sideslip probes. These quadruplex sensors provided data that was used to directly compute the required control surface movements. The scheduling and switching sensors included: pitot/static pressure transducers; undercarriage selection and weight-on-undercarriage switches; and flap and airbrake position transducers. These provided additional information to vary the control laws, for example preventing inadvertent selection of ground modes during flight. FFC4 interfaced with the autopilot, which received its information from the normal NAVWASS system, including the air data computer and horizontal situation indicator, and shared this data with the other FCCs via the datalink.

The minimum control stick deflection of 0.4in (1cm) per 'g' of the standard Jaguar was retained, with a feel gradient of 5lb/in (2.5kg/cm) and a stick force of 2lb/g (0.9kg/g). Combined with a very tight pitch rate demand, this gave excellent handling, both in pitch tracking and in high-speed, low-level flight in turbulence. The control surface position demands from the FCCs and ADMCs were sent to five Dowty powered flying control units (PFCUs) which moved the tailerons, spoilers and rudder. The PFCUs were powered by the normal duplex hydraulic system. The six computer channels were split into two groups of three, which enabled the system to withstand failures in two of the six computer channels, or one computer and one hydraulic channel.

Safety was paramount and the lessons learned during development were applied directly as the basis of the active controls chapter of the international standard DEF STAN 00 970. The safety requirements were: the ability to give handling qualities at least as good as a standard Jaguar; the ability to control a longitudinal aerodynamically unstable aircraft configuration; the ability to prevent departure (stall) or loss of control (spin); the probability of aircraft loss as a result of electronic failures of computers, sensors or actuation was not to exceed one chance in ten million per flight hour. Lightning strike testing was carried out in co-operation with the Lightning Studies Unit at Culham Laboratories, working up to 80kA strikes to clear the aircraft to fly in areas of potential lightning activity.

The static rig at Warton was used to test the system using a computer model of the Jaguar's aerodynamics and could be reconfigured rapidly to trial new developments and changes to the software and hardware. Loading actuators were used to assess the aerodynamic loading effects. The data acquisition system allowed a large amount of data to be analysed quickly.

Electromagnetic interference testing was conducted at Marconi and once the system was installed into XX765 full testing was carried out to ensure that there was no interference from the fuel, engine, electrical and radio systems along with the central warning system and stores jettison system. The flight-qualified computers were delivered by Marconi to Warton for installation in March 1981.

Flight test programme

The objective was to demonstrate the system and build confidence with a relatively limited flight programme. Originally it was planned that the flying programme would last into 1983 with potential continuation to 1987 to support the development of any AST.403 prototypes. The flight test programme was divided into three phases. The initial Phase I flight trials were performed without any external modifications and used fixed gain control laws to provide a stable condition to prove the system to provide flight clearance. For Phase II the fully scheduled control laws would be introduced for more carefree handling and Phase III would be the full demonstration of controlling an aerodynamically unstable aircraft.

Chris Yeo, as BAe's Senior Experimental Test Pilot and Jaguar Project Pilot, was assigned as the FBW Project Pilot. Yeo took XX765 up for the first flight on 20 October 1981, its handling being assessed up to Mach 1.26. The aircraft proved very easy to fly with general handling being as good as, if not better, than a standard Jaguar. Yeo described the sortie as an 'effortless and easy flight'. There was no sign of pilot-induced oscillation or over-control and the aircraft generally conformed to the computer predictions. Later a damper was added to the lateral control circuit to avoid any unintentional pilot-induced oscillations due to the absence of mechanical linkages, which would usually impart damping in the system due to the inertia within the mechanics. Flight testing progressed to proving the stall departure and spin prevention systems before the rear ballast was fitted to begin the unstable flying portion of the programme. Yeo was joined by Peter Orme, who was heavily involved in the Experimental Aircraft Programme (EAP) and its predecessors (P.110, Agile Combat Aircraft and the

Chris Yeo banks XX765 with the flaps and undercarriage lowered during an early test flight. At this stage there was little external clue to the extent of the modifications made. ***Terry Panopalis Collection***

XX765 in concert with the Tornado ADV F.2 prototype ZA254 refuelling from a Handley Page Victor K.2 tanker of No. 55 Squadron. *BAE Systems via Blue Envoy Collection*

The ACT takes off at Warton displaying the Phase Three leading edge strakes. *BAE Systems via Author's Collection*

XX765 leaves vortex condensation trails as it flies over the Lancashire countryside, the fligh control system continuously converting the pilot's control inputs into digital signals to the actuators for the control surfaces. Without the computers the aircraft would become instantly uncontrollable. *BAE Systems via Terry Panopalis Collection*

European Combat Aircraft).

The first flight of Phase II took place in August 1983 with Orme as the pilot, involving several test manoeuvres and a ground-attack dive on to a simulated target at Warton. Orme flew the next two flights before Yeo made his first flight with the new configuration. The rear ballast was increased progressively. Aggressive flight manoeuvring revealed no tendency to depart from controlled flight and any oscillations induced by the pilot or turbulence were suppressed quickly by the FCS. Serviceability was excellent and 22 flights were made in the clean unstable configuration. XX765 had amassed a total of 50 flights by March 1984.

Now the wing root strakes were fitted and the FCS was updated with new control laws. The combination of the strakes and ballast enabled longitudinal instabilities of -10 to -12% static mean chord to be assessed – a condition that no human could control without the computers.

Yeo made the first flight of Phase III on 15 March 1984, flying a 75-minute sortie. After landing, Yeo confirmed that the handling performance had been markedly improved, especially at low speed during take-off and landing, with less drag and a significantly

XX765 in trail with a Victor K.2 tanker. The ACT was flown with the strakes and underwing fuel tanks as confidence in the FBW system increased. The aim was to achieve carefree handling even when underwing stores were carried. ***BAE Systems via Author's Collection***

improved rate of turn. The control responses were better than predicted. Yeo flew the aircraft at maximum instability with two underwing fuel tanks inboard for the first time on 11 July. The flight was again a success. The aircraft appeared at the 1984 Society of British Aircraft Constructors Show at Farnborough, where Yeo and Orme flew several displays – Orme showing off the aircraft's ability to do level slow rolls, something very difficult to do in a standard Jaguar. Shortly after Farnborough, on 26 September, the RAE Active Control Technology Test Pilot, Squadron Leader Jon Pierce, flew the last two sorties.

This brought the ACT flights to a total of 96 (including 45 by Yeo and 44 by Orme), totalling 79

XX765 during its display at the 1984 SBAC Farnborough Show. The additional wing area provided by the strakes is evident in this view. ***Terry Panopalis Collection***

The 1984 Farnborough Show was the only chance the ACT had to demonstrate its value in public. A couple of weeks later the trials programme was over and XX765 never flew again. *Terry Panopalis Collection*

hours 31 minutes. Also in 1984, Yeo received recognition for his work as part of the Jaguar ACT team, being awarded the Queen's Commendation for Valuable Service in the Air in the Queen's Birthday Honours List.

The programme had been completely successful. All the objectives had been achieved and the success gave BAe great confidence in its ability to design a modern FBW FCS and implement it effectively. The work carried out fed directly into the EAP technology demonstrator, which was an aerodynamically unstable design from its inception, and whose FCS had begun development in 1981. The EAP made its maiden flight on 8 August 1986 at Warton. The subsequent success of the EAP kept the European Fighter Aircraft programme alive and several aspects of EAP's technology – including the FCS – can be found within the Eurofighter Typhoon today.

Retirement

Once its flying days were over, the MoD declined to take XX765 back. BAe acquired the aircraft in June 1986 for electromagnetic compatibility ground testing. Once this work was completed, it was left on the south side of the Warton airfield, where it was eventually used to test two competing brands of paint stripping chemicals, losing its 'Raspberry Ripple' scheme in the process. It was painted in olive drab in 1990 ahead of its donation to Loughborough University as a teaching training aid on 16 January 1991. In May 1996 the Royal Air Force Museum offered Loughborough the opportunity to swap XX765 for the EAP demonstrator and it arrived at Cosford in July 1996, being repainted in its 'Raspberry Ripple' colours for display. It was joined by the EAP when it arrived from Loughborough in 2012. At the time of writing the aircraft seems to have an uncertain future, in 2023 the RAF Museum announced it was seeking to divest XX765 from its collection, before putting the aircraft back on display in June 2024.

CHAPTER TWELVE

Drawing board projects

There were many design studies conducted to improve on the Jaguar. The most ambitious developments were designed to meet the RAF's Air Staff Target AST.396 for a successor to the type. These studies covered an array of designs divided into three groups, including provision for vertical/short take-off and landing (V/STOL) capability and naval versions for use aboard the Royal Navy's aircraft carriers and new, larger wings – including the variable-geometry (VG) wing from the Panavia Tornado – as well as a range of new engines. The succeeding AST.403 saw the Jaguar further developed with a larger wing. These designs were rejected in favour of fresh-sheet designs that would ultimately lead to the Eurofighter Typhoon. The Big Wing Jaguar was the final attempt to fit an enlarged wing to improve the turning capabilities, allied with increased engine thrust and improved avionics. All of these projects remained on the drawing board but they offer a tantalising glimpse at how adaptable the Jaguar's basic design was and how far that development could go before the results were effectively new designs.

AST.396

Work on various staff studies leading to AST.396 for a successor to the Jaguar and Hawker Siddeley Harrier had begun around 1969. AST.396 was endorsed by the Operational Requirements Committee in May 1971 to enable Hawker Siddeley Aviation (HSA) and the British Aircraft Corporation (BAC) to begin parametric design studies to study the aircraft, Rolls-Royce the engines and Marconi-Elliott Avionic Systems Limited the avionics. The new aircraft would be a battlefield air

Extensive efforts were made by the design team at Warton to improve upon the baseline Jaguar and to further develop the airframe to find a successor. This is GR.1 XX969 of No. 31 Squadron based at RAF Brüggen. ***Terry Panopalis Collection***

support/short-range interdiction and reconnaissance aircraft with a night and all-weather capability to enter service in the early 1980s and was intended for operation in the NATO Central Region. The option for a two-seat aircraft due to pilot workload was open. The main requirements were:

- Sustained speed of Mach 0.9 (450kt) at low altitude with a Mach 1.1 supersonic dash.
- 165nm (305.5km) radius of action lo-lo or 240nm (445km) hi-lo to attack targets 60nm (111km) beyond the Forward Edge of the Battle Area (FEBA).
- High manoeuvrability with a turning capability of 7.5g at Mach 0.8 while carrying six bombs.
- Specific excess power (SEP) of 900–1,000ft/sec (274–305m/sec) for combat against modern Warsaw Pact fighters.
- Operations from dispersed sites.
- Short take-off and landing (STOL) to enable operations from damaged runways; at a take-off weight of 45,000lb (20,410kg) the aircraft should clear a 50ft (15m)-high obstacle in within 1,200ft (365m), possibility of vertical landing – STOVL (V/STOL was preferred but was recognised as being expensive and technically complicated).
- Weapon payload of 6,000lb (2,720kg), sufficient for three attacks with weapons delivered in pairs; main weapon was the BL.755 cluster bomb with provision for a WE.177 nuclear bomb, a reconnaissance pod, short-range air-to-air missiles (AAMs) and one or two cannon.
- A fire-control system for high-speed, low-level, first-pass attacks using low-light TV (LLTV) and forward-looking infrared (FLIR) technology coupled with laser range finding and inertial navigation. No search radar or automatic flight control system.
- The cockpit would have a head-up display (HUD), combined projected map/head-down display and hands on throttle and stick (HOTAS) controls.

The Defence Operational Analysis Establishment (DOAE) visited RAF Germany (RAFG) in late 1971 to gather information. From their discussions it was clear that STOL capability was important; a field airstrip 1,200ft (365m)-long was much more difficult to spot from the air than a 4,000ft (1,220m)-long strip. Industry studies indicated that a non-thrust-vectoring aircraft would require at least 3,000ft (915m) of runway. The Air Staff wanted analysis on the use of helmet-mounted sights and helmet imaging and pointing sights, and AST.604 was issued for FLIR development and AST.610 for the LLTV.

At Warton, Ivan Yates and his design team began work on a wide variety of design studies over a period of six years. Early work began in March 1971 with developments of the Jaguar under the designation P.63 alongside new designs labelled P.64. The formal issue of AST.396 (Issue 1) led to the P.69 studies in January 1972, the P.70 STOVL designs of May 1971 and the P.71 with lift engines in September 1971 using a mix of Jaguar and new components. Delta-wing designs – including at least one Jaguar development – and lightweight fighters were the P.72 and P.73 studies, while the P.74 covered the Jaguar with new engines from March 1973.

The P.69 series covered relatively simple modifications to the Jaguar for a cost-effective solution, even if not all of the requirements were fully met. STOL capability would be provided by additional engine thrust. There was strong commonality with the Jaguar S and the Laser Ranger and Marked-Target Seeker (LRMTS) chisel nose was retained. BAC also hoped that converting existing Jaguars into prototypes would reduce the airframe development costs, a key factor given the expensive avionics.

The first study was EAG.8438 (note that EAG numbers refer to technical drawings produced by Warton – either a specific drawing or a block of drawings – rather than to a particular project. The numbers are sequential and the system continues in use today). This had Adour Stage 2 engines rated at 9,430lbf (41.9kN) reheated with additional acoustic vibration and temperature protection fitted to the tail cone and the tailplane, and an additional third auxiliary intake door on the sides of the intakes to cater for the increased airflow required. To improve control authority, the vertical fin and tailplanes and were enlarged, the latter receiving more powerful hydraulic jacks. The longer nose leg of the carrier-based Jaguar M was fitted to increase the angle of incidence on the ground to aid short take-offs and a larger braking parachute was fitted for short landings. The suggested weapon load was a pair of AIM-9 Sidewinder AAMs outboard with triple BL.755s or Matra rocket/fuel pods inboard and another two BL.755s on the centreline.

EAG.8439 added a 7in (18cm) fuselage plug behind the cockpit and a 12in (30cm) plug aft for the Stage 2 engine's larger afterburner. The main undercarriage was strengthened and the wing was modified with combat slats and combat flaps outboard. The estimated take-off weight was 31,870lb (14,420kg). EAG.8440 featured a 31in (80cm)-long extension ahead of the cockpit to accommodate a pair of retractable foreplanes to maintain lift at high angles of attack to improve the take-off distance.

The next study, EAG.8441, took a different approach, being fitted with booster rockets offering 10,000lbf (44.4kN) for post-attack egress boost. The threat from air defences during the pull-out following the attack was heightened as the aircraft lost momentum, with acceleration vital in getting out of the effective zone of anti-aircraft artillery and surface-to-air missiles (SAMs)

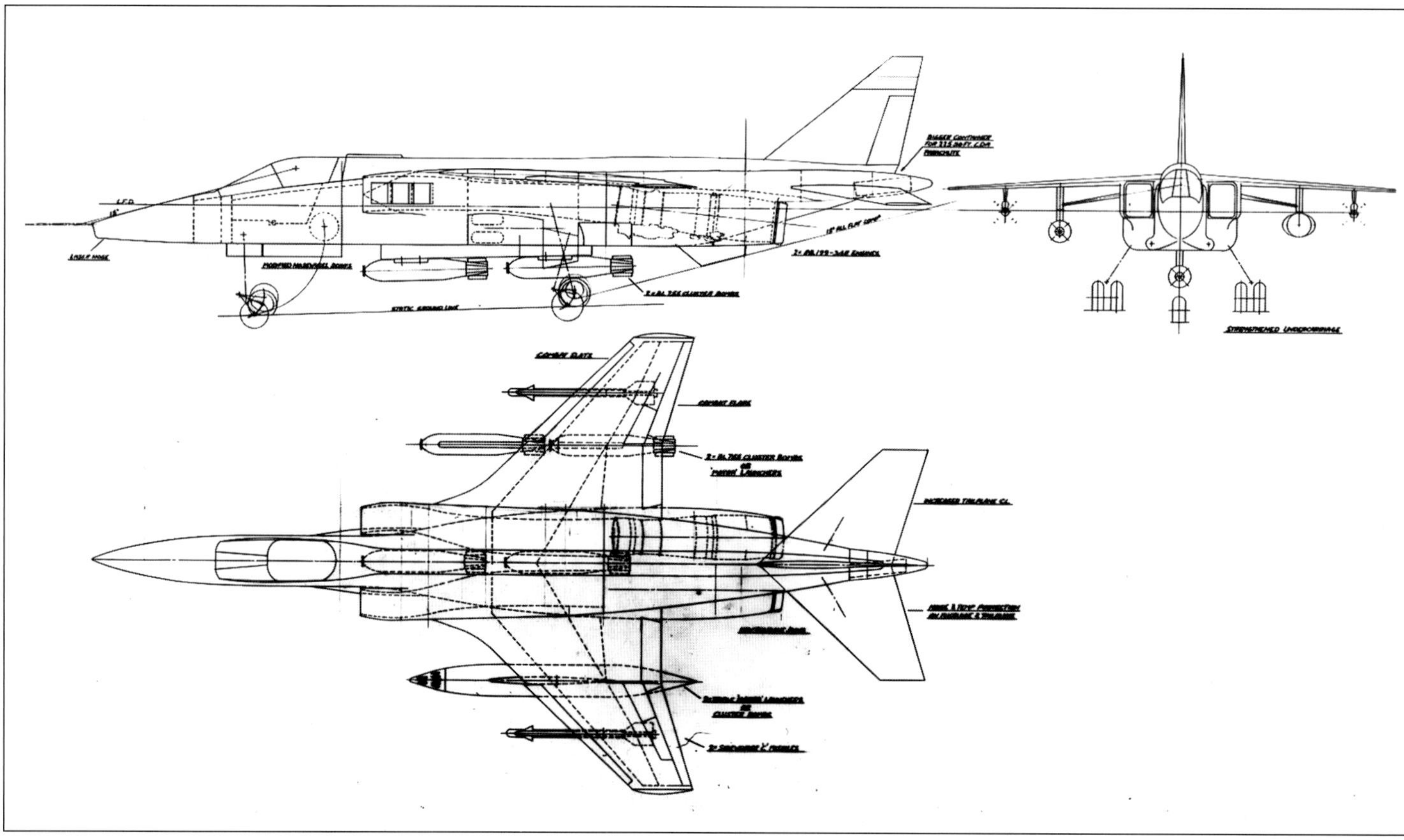

Drawing EAG.8442 was one of the P.69 STOL designs to meet AST.396 with two Rolls-Royce/ Turbo Union RB.199-34R engines as used by the Panavia Tornado. ***North West Heritage Group via Chris Gibson***

as quickly as possible. The rockets were fitted in a retractable housing forward of the jet tailpipes; either two Rocketdyne Mk.25 solid rocket motors or one high-test peroxide (HTP) and kerosene-fuelled Bristol Siddeley BS.605 (as used on South Africa's Hawker Siddeley Buccaneer S.50s) with a large ventral tank fairing containing the HTP. With the HTP tank occupying the ventral hardpoint, two wing tip rails for Sidewinders were added to free the four underwing pylons for offensive weaponry. A later iteration added revised wings of 5% thickness/chord (t/c) ratio with a straight trailing edge. The estimated gross weight was 36,400lb (16,510kg) including 8,690lb (3,940kg) of fuel.

EAG.8442 was a version of EAG.4838 powered by a pair of Rolls-Royce/Turbo Union RB.199-34R turbofans rated at 8,100lbf (36kN) dry or 15,950lbf (71kN) reheated as used in the Tornado. EAG.8448 was a further development of EAG.4839 with a new high-lift wing featuring wing root strakes/leading edge extensions (LERX), six trailing edge blown flaps and two spoilers. The revised leading-edge slats formed a dog-tooth discontinuity in the wing, again improving lift.

Warton considered that thrust vectoring was the simplest solution to achieve STOVL, but at the cost of drag and fuel consumption. The engine would be either be a Rolls-Royce Pegasus 15-03 with four thrust-vectoring nozzles with plenum chamber burning (PCB) for additional thrust to enable supersonic performance, or the new RB.422-04 with PCB rated at between 25,580–26,860lbf (113.7–119.4kN) dry and 38,100–40,000lbf (169.4–177.9kN) reheated. The use of PCB meant that the forward nozzles were integral with the engine, so to allow the engine to be 'dropped out' for maintenance the structure below the nozzles had to be removable as well. This left a relatively small area available for load carrying unless suitable load-carrying cowl doors were used. Extensive use of carbon fibre composites and fly-by-wire (FBW) flight controls was foreseen.

A total of nine options were looked at for P.70, three twin-boom designs and the remainder with modified Jaguar fuselages combining a pair of lift engines behind the cockpit and translating nozzles for the main engines to provide vectored thrust.

The first detailed P.70 design, EAG.8404 of May 1971, married a Jaguar S forward fuselage and empennage with a new centre and aft fuselage. The use of a conventional rear fuselage and the thrust-vectoring Pegasus required a layout like that of the Harrier. The intakes were enlarged for the increased airflow required. The undercarriage was also modified an comprised the longer Jaguar M nose leg with a single twin-wheel unit behind the aft nozzles and two outrigger legs mounted in fairings ahead of the nozzles. The wings were modified with a t/c ratio of 7%. The armament comprised two 30mm ADEN cannon under the intakes, four BL.755s carried abreast under the forward fuselage and four underwing pylons.

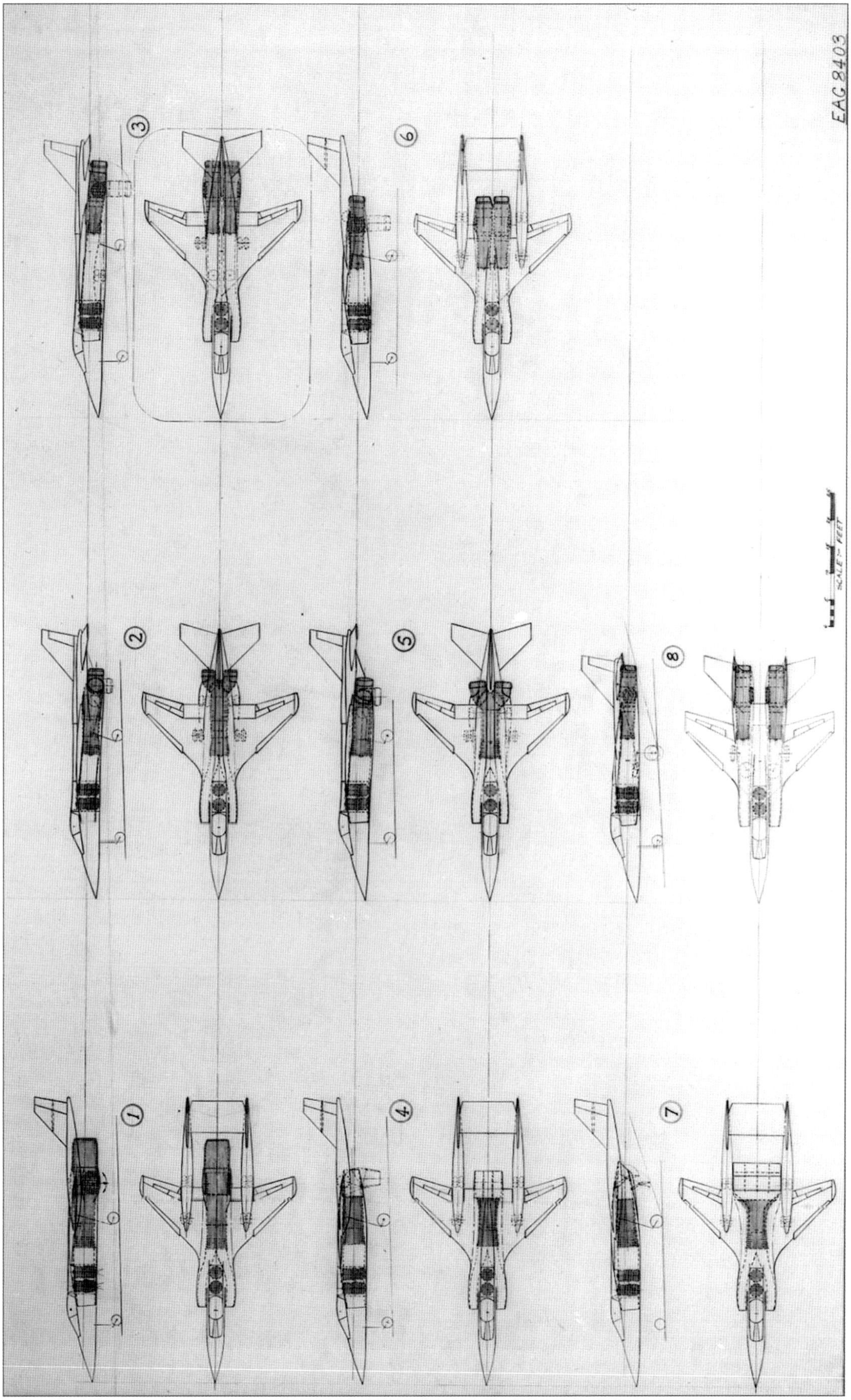

Drawing EAG.8403 covered a range of V/STOL concepts based on the Jaguar with lift engines and thrust vectoring to meet AST.396. ***North West Heritage Group via Chris Gibson***

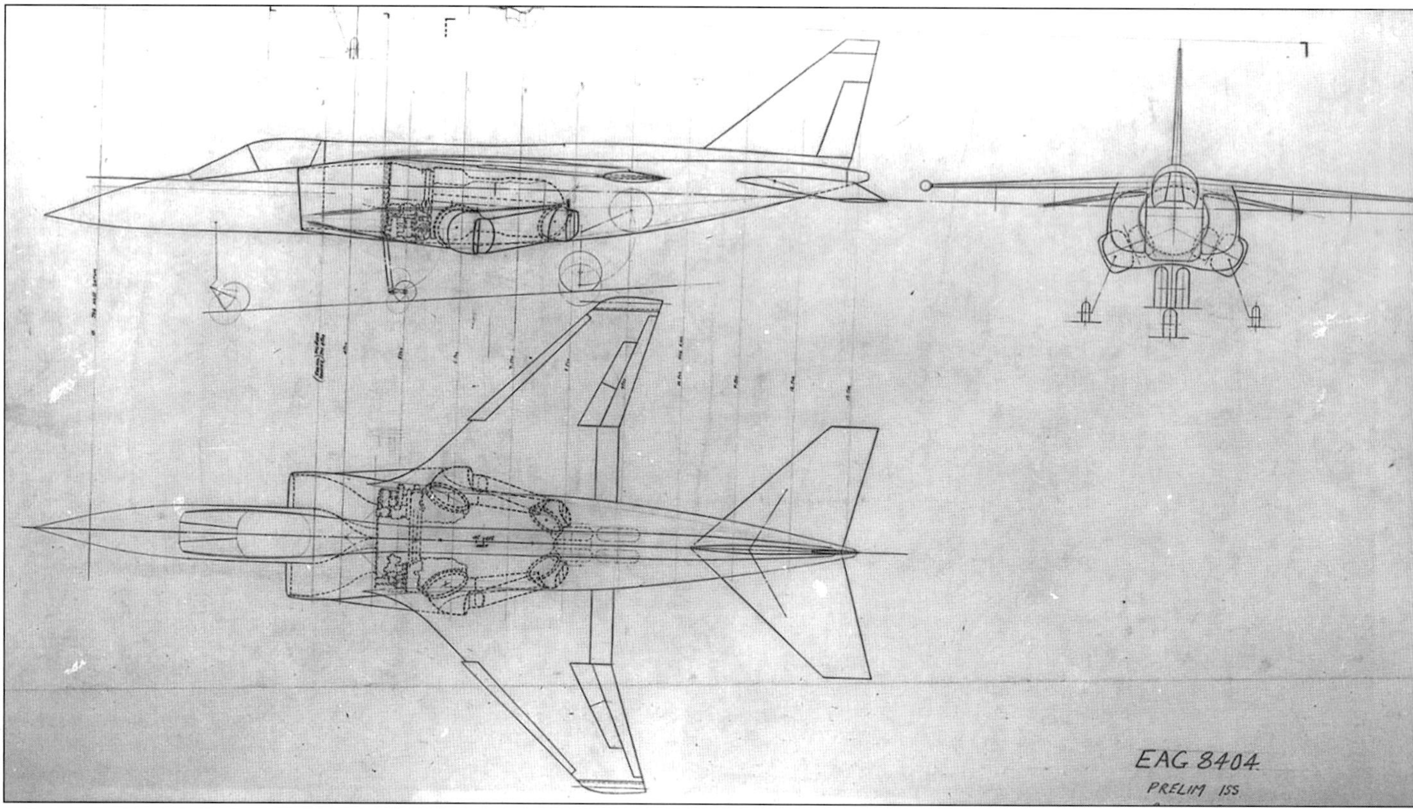

EAG.8404 was the preliminary version of the P.70 with a layout similar to the Hawker Siddeley Harrier. ***North West Heritage Group via Chris Gibson***

Development of the basic design continued into early 1972; 8404C(1) had a higher-rated Pegasus 16-13 and an all-up weight (AUW) of 49,000lb (22,225kg), and 8404C(11) had a Pegasus 15-03 and an AUW of 47,000lb (21,320kg). Take-off run clearing a 50ft obstacle could be accomplished within 1,500ft (460m). The 8404D was the 1980s technology version using the RB.22-04 with an AUW of 34,000lb (15,420kg).

EAG.8472 was a version for the Royal Navy capable of carrying two Matra/Hawker Siddeley Dynamics Martel air-to-surface missiles (ASMs) under the wings. A 27in (69cm)-diameter radar was fitted in a longer nose cone and the engine would be the RB.422 with 75% scaled PCB.

EAG.8436 had a twin-boom configuration to allow the rear translating nozzles to be closer together, providing better management of the structural loads, with the wing box taking the engine loads. There were two hardpoints under the outer wings for single BL.755s, two hardpoints beneath the intakes carrying a pair of BL.755s each and wing tip rails for Sidewinders. The cannon were moved to the forward end of the area-ruled tail booms, which also carried the main undercarriage units and fuel tanks. Between the booms was a single all-moving tailplane.

Following the P.70, work on the STOVL configurations progressed to the P.71 in September 1971 with separate lift engines and propulsive engines fitted with thrust-diverting cascades aft. This basic layout had been proven in several V/STOL designs around the world. Although the operating economics of carrying 'dead weight' lift engines in normal flight was an insurmountable drawback, Warton preferred this solution over thrust vectoring. The lift engines were either the Rolls-Royce/Allison XJ.99 rated at 9,000lbf (40kN) or new designs then on Rolls-Royce's drawing boards; the 10,780lbf (48kN) RB.227-01 and the 15,500lbf (69kN) RB.228-02. The propulsive engines were either the RB.199-42R, General Electric YJ101 or the Pratt & Whitney F100. Nozzle location was important to avoid hot air reingestion (which reduced engine power and lift) and heating effects on the airframe and undercarriage. Thrust balancing was also vital to minimise pitching, vibration and ground erosion, and the P.71 was designed with all these issues in mind. A low-speed reaction control system was required, using bleed air tapped from the lift engines. The location of the lift engines meant that the air conditioning heat exchangers had to be moved elsewhere in the aircraft.

The datum design was EAG.8413, a Jaguar S with a 30in (76cm) fuselage plug aft of the cockpit for two XJ.99 lift engines, which were inclined by 15° and fitted with blade deflectors. The Adours were replaced by a pair of RB.199-34R, the intakes being enlarged by 50% and thrust-diverting cascades fitted on the rear lower fuselage for vertical thrust. It shared the nose, wing and empennage of the P.70 EAG.8404 and had the Jaguar M nose wheel leg. The gross weight was estimated as 37,750lb (17,120kg). In an effort to lighten the design, the RB.199s were replaced with RB.231s or F100s, again fitted with cascades. Development continued into

1972; 8413A had an AUW of 48,000lb (21,770kg) for a combat speed of Mach 0.8 or 39,000lb (17,690kg) to attain Mach 1.1.

The 8413B with RB.228-02 lift engines and RB.231-02 turbofans had an AUW of 35,000lb (15,875kg) or 33,000lb (14,970kg) depending on whether the structure was of light alloy or composites. Design 8413C coupled the RB.228-02 with a pair of RB.199-42R and had an AUW of 35,000–37,000lb (15,875–16,780kg) depending on the extent of composites used.

The next study was EAG.8447 with a single F100 with twin cascades and one XJ.99 or RB.227 lift engine. The rear fuselage was redesigned for a tail pipe jet exhaust with the tailplanes moved lower and their anhedral reduced. The leading-edge slats were extended to almost cover the full span. The structure and systems were altered to reduce weight to 26,980lb (12,200kg). A ventral pack could carry two BL.755s side-by-side. A second option fitted two lift engines by moving the ADEN cannon and some of the avionics into a larger ventral pack, which could alternatively carry four BL.755s in tandem pairs.

EAG.8461 had a smaller wing with a straight trailing edge and extended leading-edge slats and the fuselage was shortened by 36in (90cm). It was powered by one RB.228-02 lift engine with a central blade deflector and a single RB.199-42R rated at 9,700lbf (43.1kN) dry and 17,000lbf (75.6kN) reheated and equipped with two cascades. Once the load-carrying access doors were removed the entire engine and cascades could be removed. A belly pack could carry a pair of BL.755s side-by-side. The estimated gross weight was 25,325lb (11,490kg). A take-off run to clear a 50ft obstacle could be accomplished within 2,750ft (840m) at a weight of 22,400lb (10,160kg).

The 8461B replaced the RB.199 with the RB.231-02 and had an AUW of 28,000lb (12,700kg) with a reduced weapon load and avionics; at 26,300lb (11,930kg) a take-off distance of 1,500ft (460m) clearing a 50ft obstacle was possible.

EAG.8464 married a Jaguar forward fuselage, wings (with revised section) and empennage to a new mid and aft fuselage with two XJ.99s behind the cockpit and one F100 with cascades. EAG.8477 was another version on the same theme with a pair of lift engines and a pair of RB.231s. It also featured an active control system with control valves in the nose, tail cone and mid-wing blisters on the upper and lower surfaces using air tapped from the main engines. The nose depicted was that of the Jaguar A with no sensors, presumably as a prototype testbed. A later set of drawings labelled EAG.8496 covered more detail on the avionics and air conditioning system, fuel system, engine installation and the thrust control system.

Although AST.396 was focused on the RAF's needs, the P.70 and P.71 (as well as other suitable new V/STOL designs from BAC and HSA) were considered as potential replacements for the Royal Navy's McDonnell Douglas F-4K Phantom FG.1s and Buccaneer S.2s (the order for the

Drawing EAG.8447 was one of the P.71 series powered by a single Pratt & Whitney F100 turbofan with two cascades, which diverted the exhaust downwards for vertical thrust, and one Rolls-Royce XJ.99 or RB.227 lift engine behind the cockpit. ***North West Heritage Group via Chris Gibson***

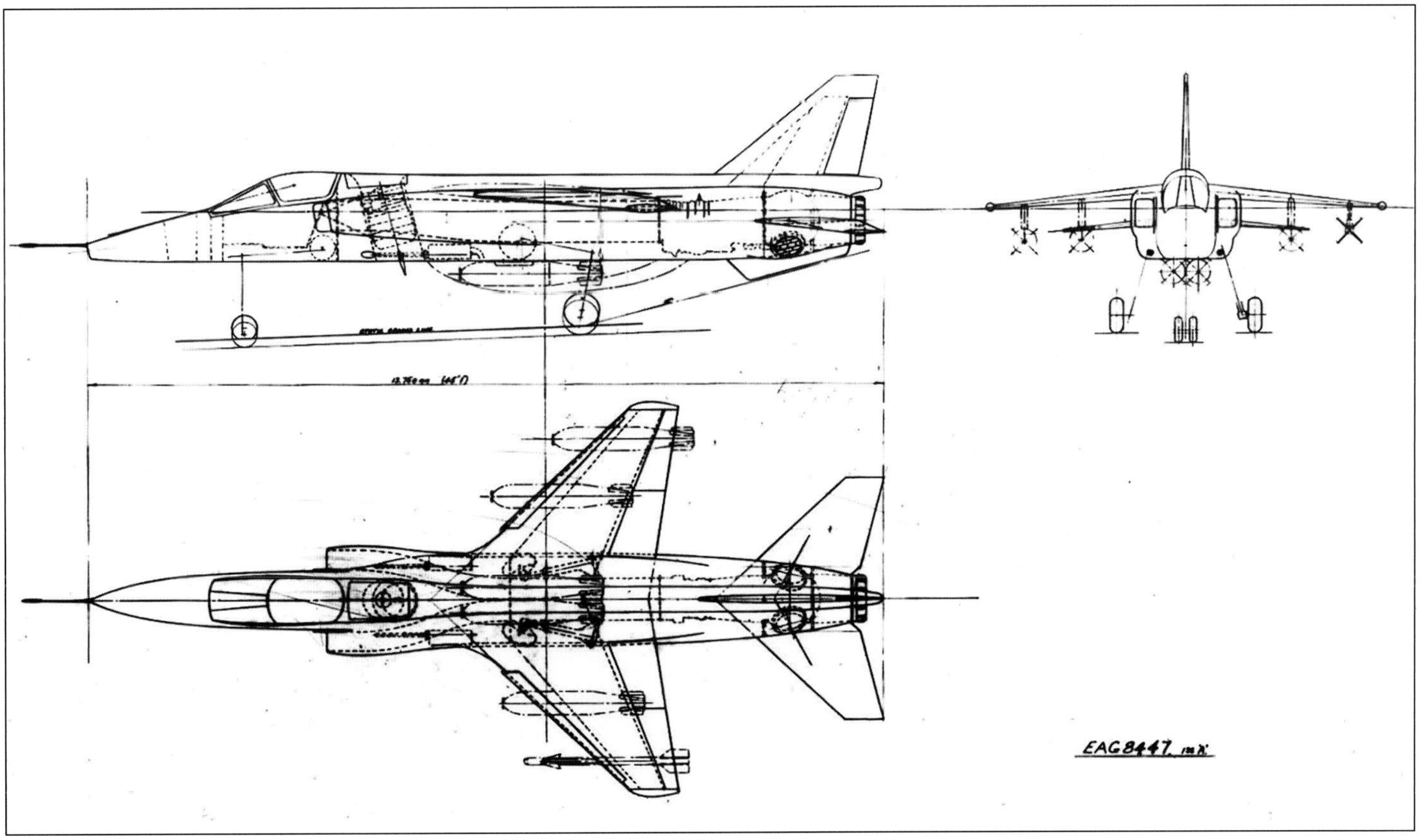

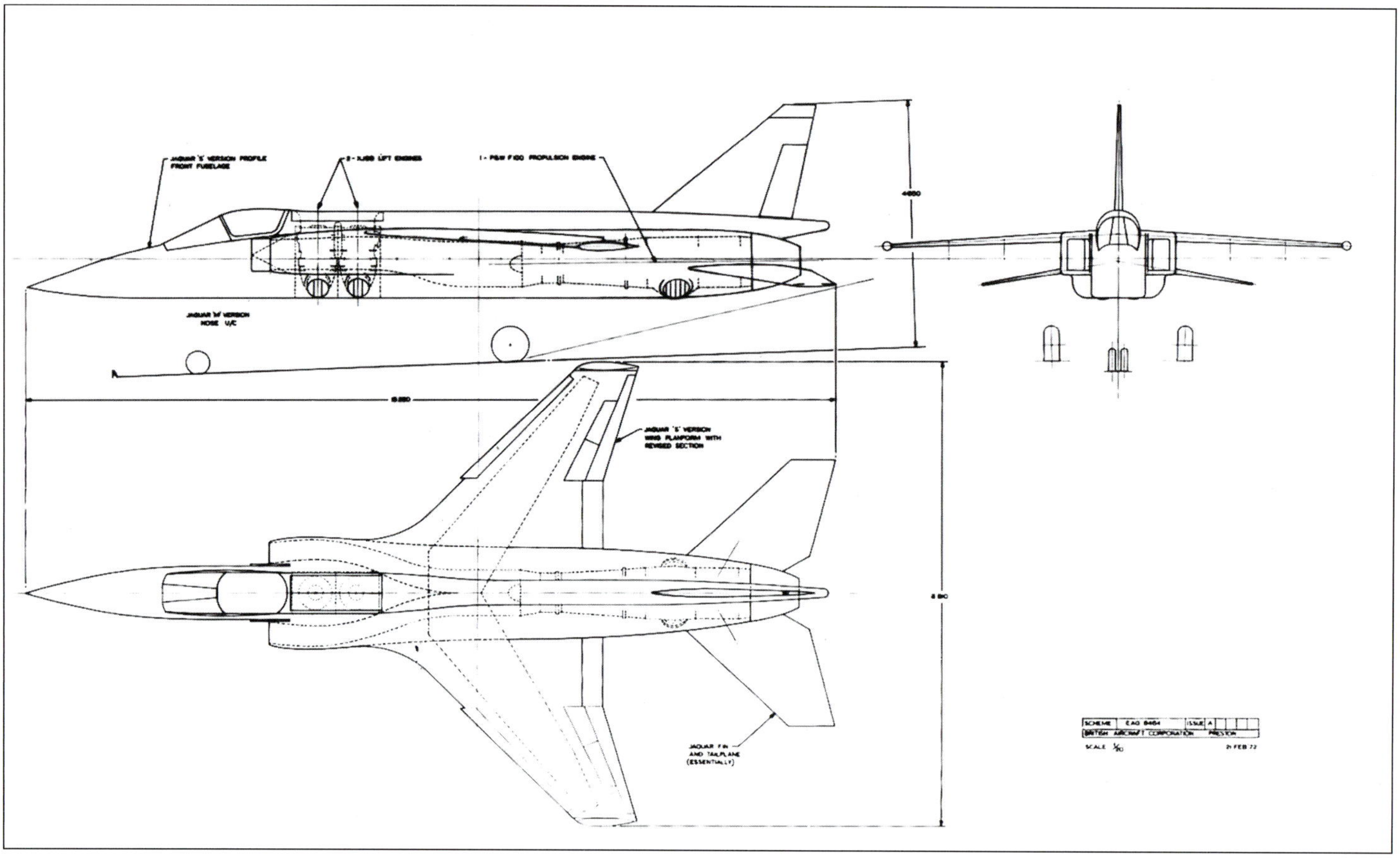

ABOVE EAG.8464 was similar to EAG.8447 but with two lift engines behind the cockpit and a revised rear fuselage. *North West Heritage Group via Chris Gibson*

What-if? A Sea Jaguar FRS.3 of No. 800 Naval Air Squadron climbs to make an attack on enemy ships using AJ.68 TV-guided Martel missiles. In reality, EAG.8469 was a navalised EAG.8413 with radar, two XJ.99 lift engines and two RB.199-42Rs fitted with cascades. *Luca Landino*

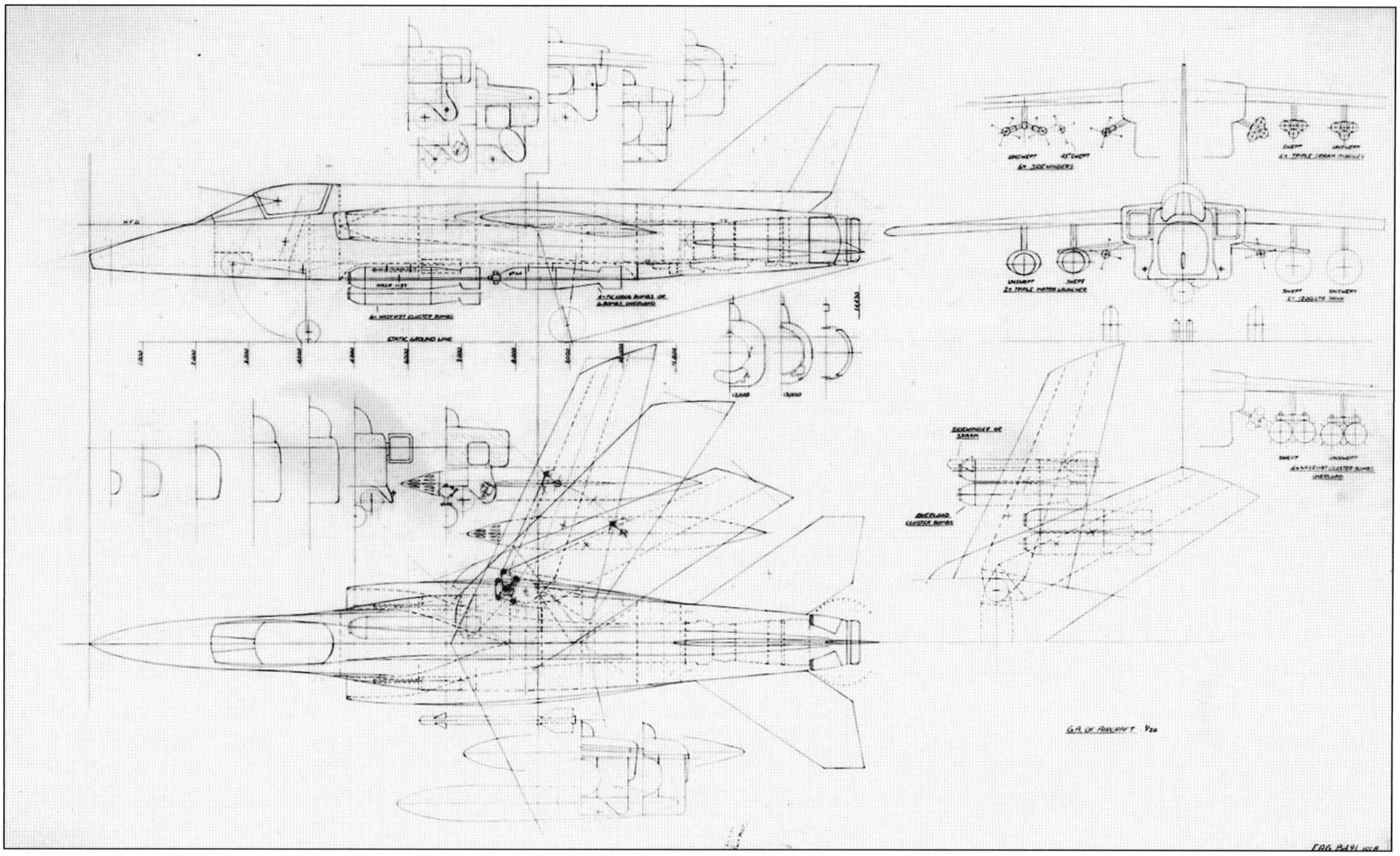

EAG.8491 married the Jaguar's fuselage with the Tornado's variable-geometry wings and was powered by a single RB.199-42R. The weapons layout is interesting with semi-recessed BL.755 cluster bombs beneath the fuselage and two pylons under the intakes and wings for AIM-9 Sidewinder or future SRAAM AAMs. ***North West Heritage Group via Chris Gibson***

Invincible-class V/STOL carriers and the development of the Sea Harrier were still a year and two years away respectively). A variant of EAG.8447 was offered with a search radar in a 13in (34cm) longer nose. EAG.8469 was a navalised EAG.8413 with radar and capable of carrying two AJ.68 Martel ASMs with the required TV-guidance datalink pods on the outboard pylons. Two XJ.99 lift engines were fitted along with two RB.199-42Rs with cascades. EAG.8471 was a navalised EAG.8461 with a 24in (61cm) diameter radar. The small 22ft 11in (6.98m) span wing did not require folding aboard ship and could carry two ASMs like the AGM-84A Harpoon along with a pair of Sidewinders.

The P.72 series were tailless delta-wing designs and among them the EAG.8479 of late 1971 was a Jaguar with a new centre and rear fuselage and a 24ft (7.32m)-span delta wing. A XJ.99 lift engine was mounted behind the cockpit and the single turbofan had twin cascades.

Work began on the P.74 series of Jaguars with new engines around March 1973; at least two studies were looked at in September, EAG.8489 and 8490. The first was powered by a pair of RB.231-05s, a proposed small military turbofan engine with a thrust rating of 10,900lbf (48.4kN) dry and 15,600lbf (69.3kN) reheated; the second had two Adour Mk.802s.

There were two further designs with more radical changes. EAG.8491 was a Jaguar S with new centre and aft fuselage with VG wings from the Tornado and powered by a single RB.199-42R. The new tail exhaust was fitted with retractable bucket-type thrust reversers. The weapons layout was completely new; four or six bombs semi-recessed into the lower fuselage in two tandem pairs or two triples, two pylons under the intakes for either a pair of Sidewinders or six SRAAMs and two rotating hardpoints under the outer wing, each capable of carrying a pair of BL.755s or Sidewinders or three SRAAMs (SRAAM was a new-generation, highly agile, infrared (IR)-homing AAM being developed by HSA as Taildog). The pair of ADEN cannon were retained.

EAG.8493 was a further development that lacked the underwing pylons. The cannon were moved forwards into new fuselage bulges below the cockpit to free up space for six BL.755s in a semi-recessed belly space that extended as far aft as the tailplanes. It is likely that these two designs were connected to the P.76 series of modified Tornados.

A report on the AST.396 (Issue 1) pre-feasibility studies was released in September 1973. The BAC datum designs included some of the P.70 and P.71 designs; EAG.8404C(11), 8413B and 8461B. The use of carbon fibre composites to give comparatively small savings in AUW for the same performance only achieved small cost savings. The conclusion was that more advanced structures would be better used to obtain improved performance by increasing payload or fuel, rather than focusing on costs. The EAG.8404C, 8413B and 8472 were all considered suitable for naval use.

AST396 options						
	P.70 EAG.8404	**P.71 EAG.8436**	**P.71 EAG.8447**	**P.71 EAG.8464**	**P.71 EAG.8471**	**P.72 EAG.8479**
Span	29ft 6in (8.99m)	29ft 2in (8.89m)	25ft 2.5in (7.68m)	28ft 9in (8.81m)	22ft 11in (6.98m)	24ft 0in (7.32m)
Length	51ft 6in (15.70m)	51ft 0in (15.40m)	45ft 7in (13.90m) RAF, 46ft 8.5in (14.24m) RN	50ft 1in (15.28m)	43ft 7in (13.29m)	42ft 2in (12.85m)
Wing area	–	–	–	–	–	320ft² (29.8m²)
t/c ratio	7%	7%	7%	–	7%	7%
Gross weight	37,100lb (16,830kg)	36,000lb (16,330kg)	–	–	26,000lb (11,795kg)	–
Powerplant	One RR Pegasus 15-03 with PCB	One RR Pegasus 15-03 with PCB	One GE YJ101, two RR/Allison XJ.99 or RR RB.227-02	One P&W F100, two RR/Allison XJ.99 or RR RB.227-02	One RR RB.199-42R, one RB.228	One RR RB.199, one RR/Allison XJ.99
Maximum speed/ height	Mach 1+	Mach 1+	Mach 1+	Mach 1+	Mach 1+	Mach 1+
Armament	Six bombs or other stores, two 30mm ADEN cannon	Six bombs or other stores, two 30mm ADEN cannon	Six bombs or other stores, two Sidewinder, two 30mm ADEN cannon	Six bombs or other stores, two Sidewinder, two 30mm ADEN cannon	Six bombs, two Martel or Harpoon ASMs, two 30mm ADEN cannon	Six bombs or other stores, two 30mm ADEN cannon

The release of the amended AST.396 (Issue 2) in early 1973 saw work on the vectored thrust and direct lift solutions cease and development effort went into modifying the wings and fuselage. The work was divided into three phases. Phase One designs retained either the standard chisel nose or a spherical nose turret for the LLTV/FLIR with LRMTS and a terrain-following radar (TFR) mounted below. Phase Two aircraft had one of the sensor noses from a series that Warton had designed to cater for the wide range of possibilities given that the equipment was still very much in early development, with the ball turret diameters of 26in (66cm), 22in (56cm) or 16in (40cm). The single-seat Jaguars received Nose 'D' and two-seaters the similarly configured Nose 'X'. The Marconi ARI.18223 radar warning receiver (RWR) was also included. Many of the designs also featured two air conditioning packs to cope with the additional avionics, with the second pack located in the rear section of the dorsal spine.

Phase Three studies focused on the two-seat Jaguar B airframe with a simplified nose sensor turret, with the TFR moved to a pod under the port wing (balanced to starboard by an electronic countermeasures (ECM) pod). Helmet sights were included for the pilot and the navigator/weapon systems operator.Some of the Phase Three work was probably linked to the belated issuing of AST.396 (Issue 3) in 1975, just before the requirements were superseded by AST.403. BAC assigned several designations to these designs; P.77 from April 1973, P.78 with new wings from June and the P.79, which married Jaguar wings with heavily modified fuselages, in December.

The P.77 series probably began with EAG.8517 with a 24in (61cm) plug behind the cockpit and a 21in (53cm) plug behind the engine exhausts as well as four additional longitudinal strips to widen and deepen the centre fuselage – the first of the 'wide body' Jaguars. The central wing box also received a plug to extend the span and a third auxiliary intake door was provided for the intakes for the two RB.199-34Rs. No sensors were shown in the nose other than an F.95 camera, suggesting a tactical reconnaissance role.

EAG.8522 had a new rear fuselage featuring a higher-mounted tailplane and powered by one RB.199-34R with thrust reversers. This was further modified for Phase Two with Nose 'D', the high-lift wing from EAG.8448 with blown flaps but with a much larger LERX and slats added to the tailplanes. EAG.8530 was a Jaguar B with a pair of RB.199-34Rs and an estimated AUW of 29,260lb (13,270kg), which was further modified for Phase Three with the new nose sensor ball and podded TFR pod. One option was the addition of two conformal fuel tanks under the wing roots (no flight refuelling probe was fitted).

EAG.8540 was a Jaguar S with a new wing with a straight trailing edge and a centre fuselage plug to accommodate the wider wing chord. EAG.8545 reverted back to the P.71 layout with a XJ.99 lift engine aft of the cockpit and the Adours replaced by General Electric YJ101s.

EAG.8546 had Nose 'D' and the modified high-lift wing and slatted tailplanes from EAG.8522B. It had larger intakes with three auxiliary inlet doors for a pair of Adour RT.172-19s, which had an upgraded low-pressure (LP) compressor with estimated thrust ratings of 6,020lbf (26.7kN) dry and 9,405lbf (41.8kN) reheated. EAG.8549 was a Jaguar B with a 1m (3ft) mid-fuselage plug for a wider chord wing and two RT.172-19 engines.

Work progressed to the P.78 series, most of which had the Phase Two avionics. EAG.8551 began as a

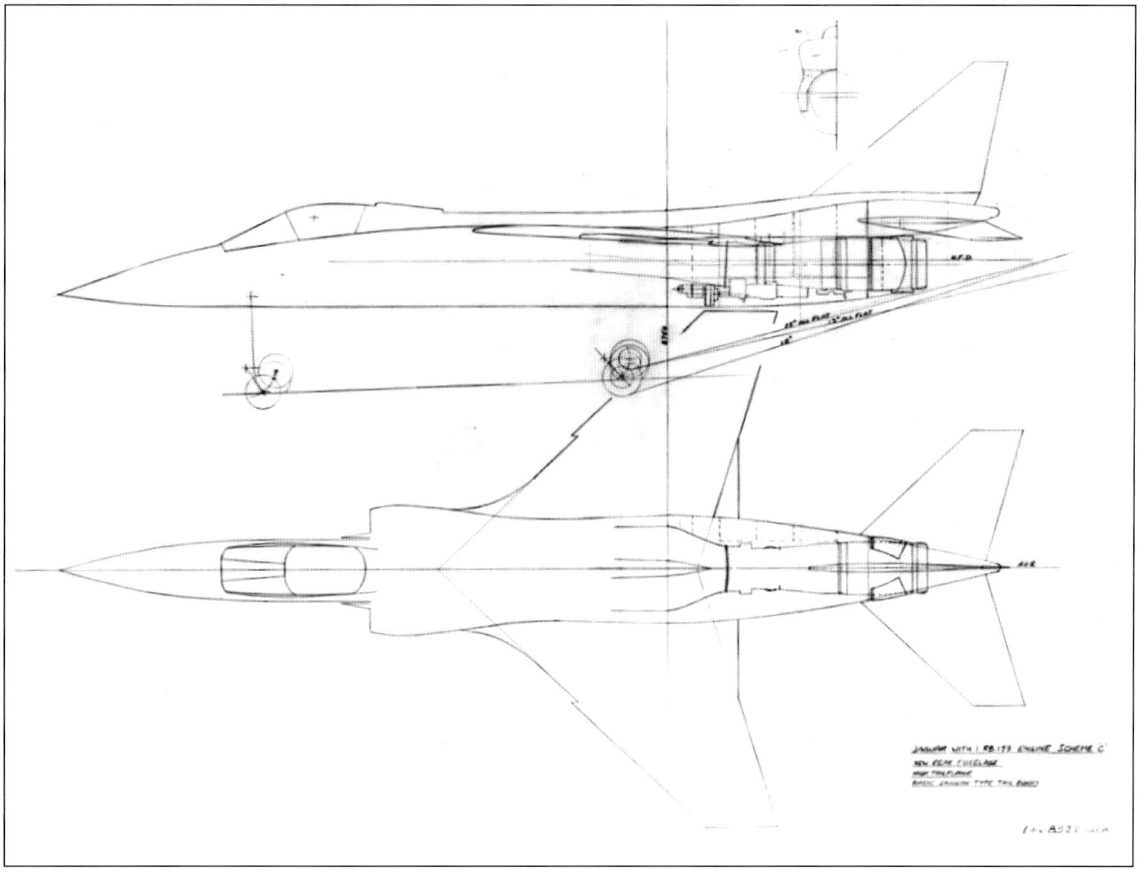

The Working Party on Battlefield Support Aircraft in April 1976 considered that the EAG.8522 powered by one RB.199-34R was the most feasible lightweight low-cost design offered. ***North West Heritage Group via Chris Gibson***

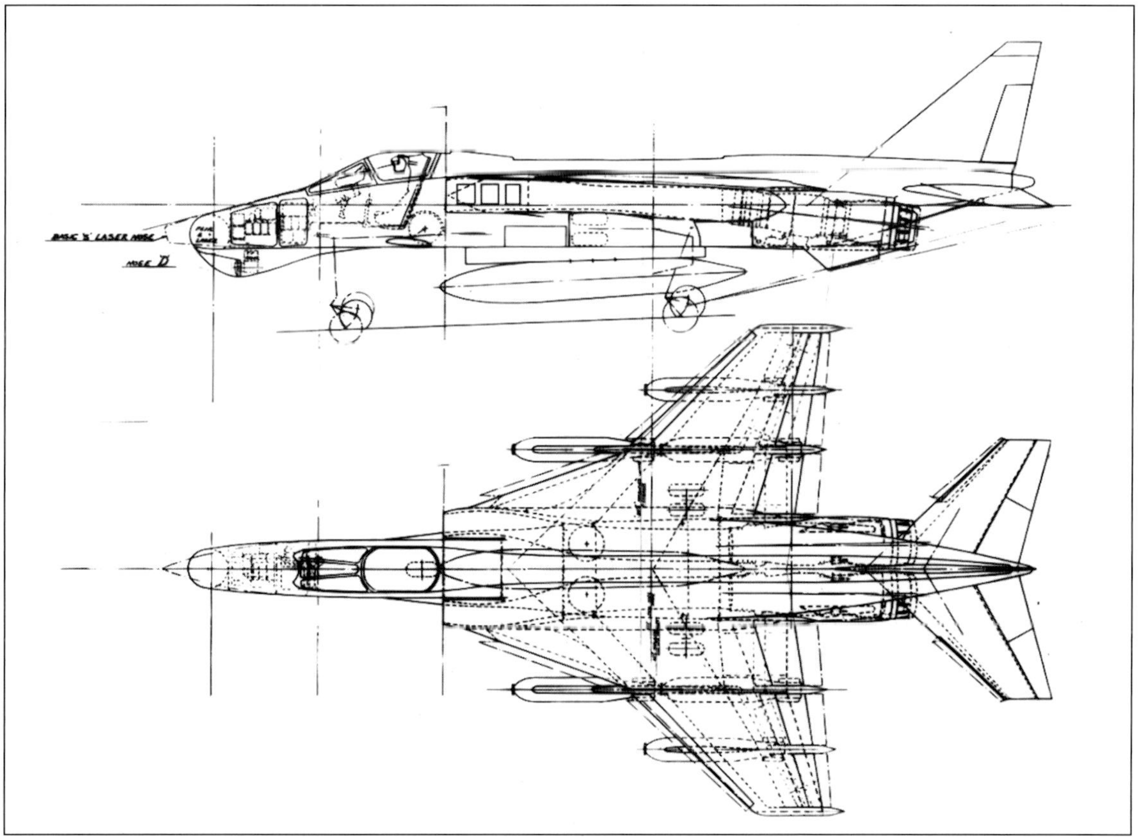

Notable features of the EAG.8546 include the Nose 'D' AST.396 visual target acquisition avionics, a new high-lift wing, slatted tailplanes and larger intakes with three auxiliary inlet doors for two uprated Adour RT.172-19 engines. ***North West Heritage Group via Chris Gibson***

Had the EAG.8551B been selected to fulfil AST.396 it could well have served during Operation Granby in the Gulf in 1991. These aircraft are armed with the BAe Sabre, a laser-guided development of the Rapier SAM for the anti-armour role to fulfil AST.1227. *Luca Landino*

EAG.8552 was based on the EAG.8551B but using the wide-body fuselage, allowing two pairs of BL.755s to be carried ventrally. The engine was an RB.199. *North West Heritage Group via Chris Gibson*

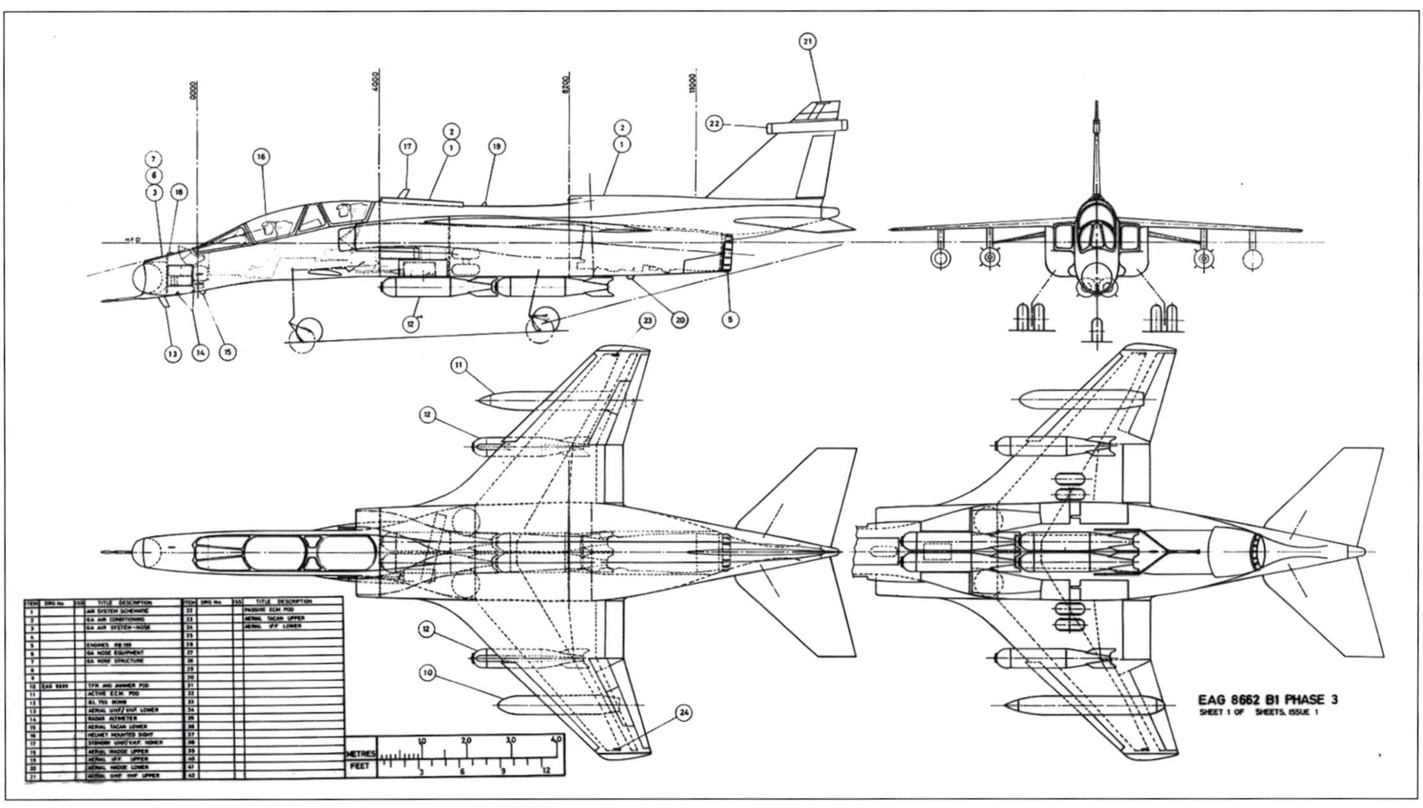

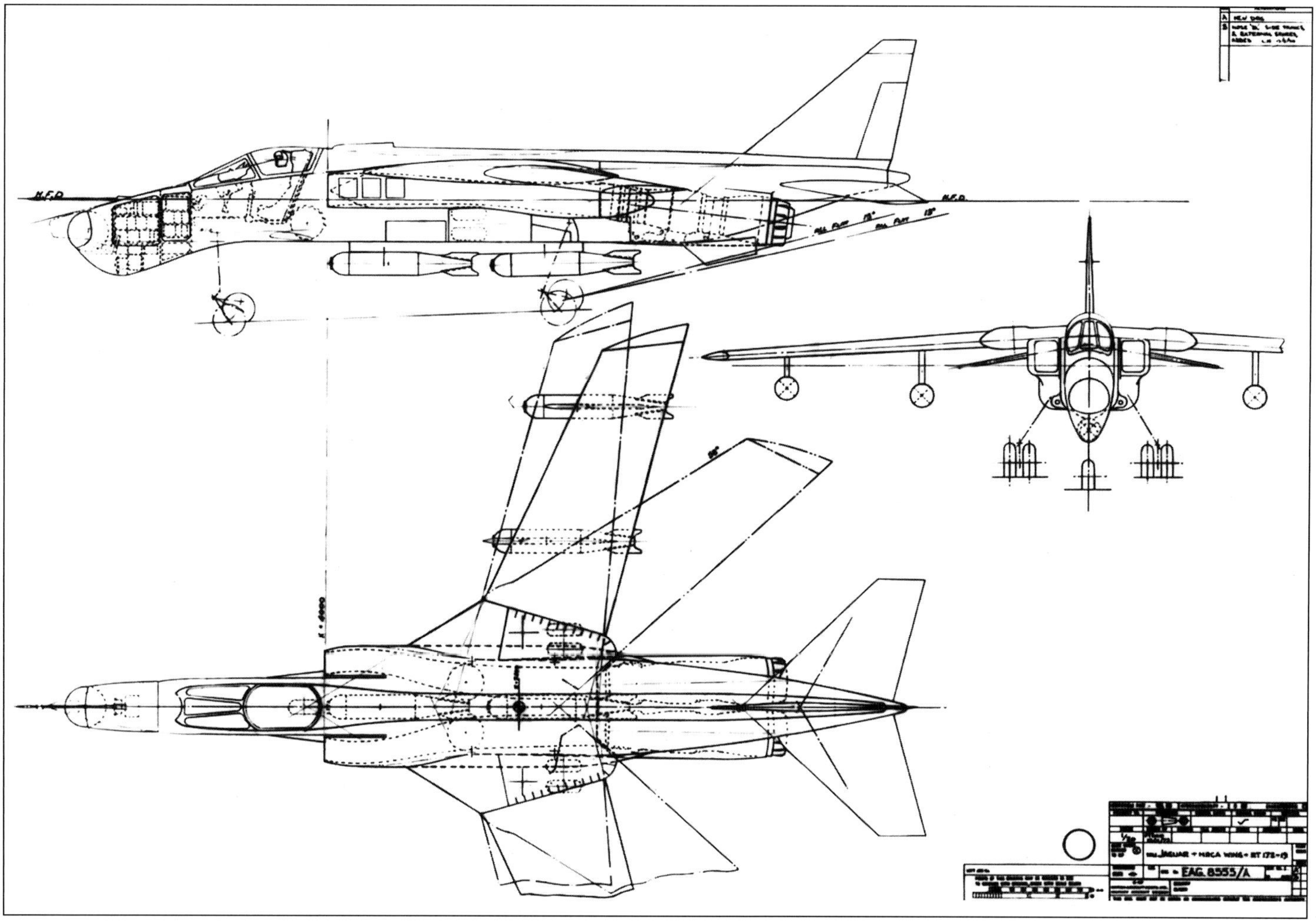

The EAG.8555 revisited using the Tornado's wings and was powered by two Adour RT.172-19s. ***North West Heritage Group via Chris Gibson***

Jaguar S with a new larger wing with an area of 301ft^2 (28m^2), a t/c ratio of 7% and 32.5° leading edge sweep with six underwing hardpoints. A larger tailplane was fitted, as were larger intakes for two RT.172-19s. Nose 'D' soon replaced the chisel nose of the preliminary design. The two-seat EAG.8551B had a revised rear fuselage. Later 8551 received a new wing with six trailing edge flaps, extended span spoilers, four leading-edge slats, a large LERX with slats, a 10% t/c ratio and a straight trailing edge while still retaining six underwing hardpoints.

EAG.8552 was a Jaguar B development with a standard Jaguar wing married to the wide-body fuselage for one RB.199 and allowing for two pairs of BL.755s to be carried ventrally. It was one of the designs that went forward to Phase 3. The single-seat EAG.8553 had the 10% t/c wing and a rear fuselage similar to that of EAG.8522 for one RB.199.

The next development used the VG wings from the Tornado. The first of these was EAG.8555, a Jaguar S powered by two RT.172-19s developed during July–November 1973. The wings retained their two swivelling pylons outboard so that six BL.755s could be carried along with a single fuel drop tank in maximum load. The nose section was altered a few times, 8551A gaining the Phase Two Nose 'D'. EAG.8593 of November 1973 was similar except for being powered by one RB.199 with the rear fuselage of EAG.8553.

The wide-body family continued with EAG.8662 powered by one RB.199; the aim seems to have been to trade width for length to reduce weight. The sensor noses 'D' and 'X' were also shortened. The wider fuselage allowed for two tandem pairs of BL.755 beneath the fuselage. Only the port ADEN cannon was fitted in the single-seater 8662A and the two-seat 8662B, while the two-seat 8662B1 had no cannon and lacked a TFR.

EAG.8666 was a thinner version of EAG.8662 with a revised rear fuselage with a tail jet exhaust and a repositioned tailplane of new design. The wing was enlarged with 7% t/c ratio and six hardpoints. Nose 'D' was fitted to the single-seat 8666A (the preliminary design featured the chisel nose with another sensor faired in ahead of the nose undercarriage bay). The 8666B was a two-seat version.

The EAG.8668 was perhaps one of the ugliest Jaguars. It was a Jaguar S with a much wider and deeper fuselage with large lateral intakes feeding a single RB.431

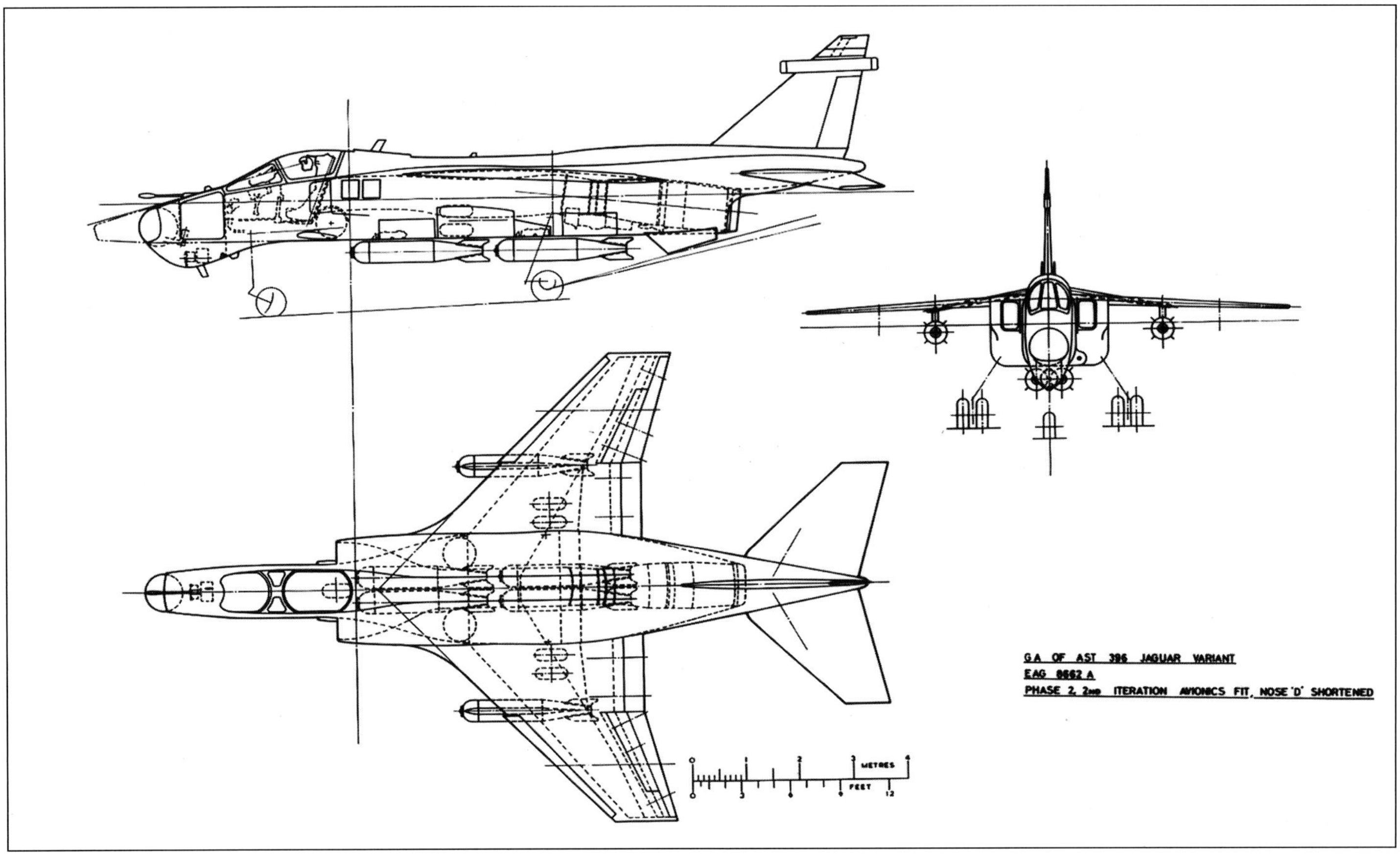
G.A. OF AST 396 JAGUAR VARIANT
EAG 8662 A
PHASE 2, 2ND ITERATION AVIONICS FIT, NOSE 'D' SHORTENED
METRES
FEET

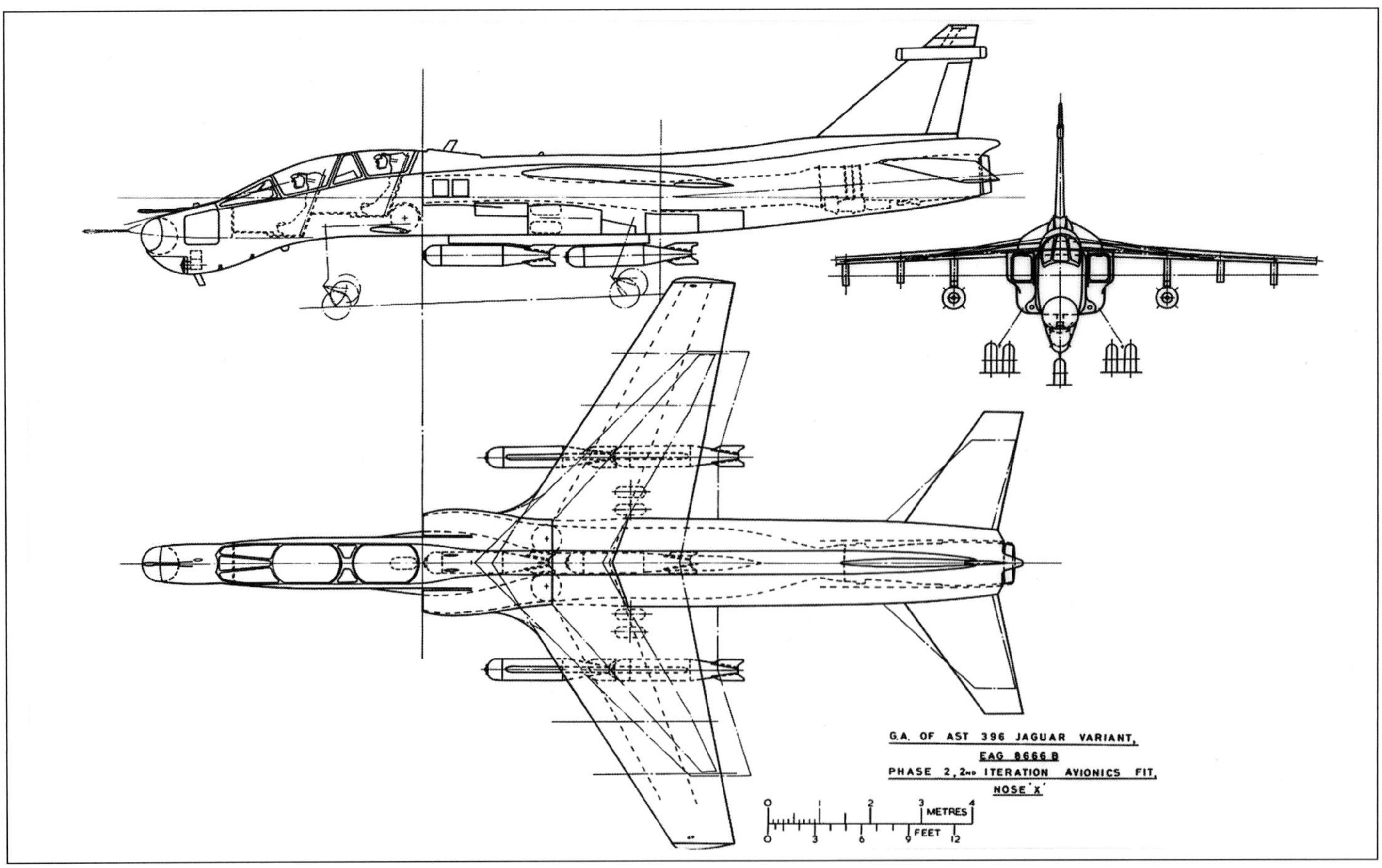
G.A. OF AST 396 JAGUAR VARIANT,
EAG 8666 B
PHASE 2, 2ND ITERATION AVIONICS FIT,
NOSE 'X'
METRES
FEET

TOP LEFT **Drawing EAG.8662 shows one of the wide-body Jaguars with a single RB.199 turbofan.** *North West Heritage Group via Chris Gibson*

BELOW LEFT **Reverting to the standard-width fuselage, the EAG.8666 had a new rear fuselage, the two-seat 8666B looking very elongated. The plan view shows the comparison of the enlarged wing with the original.** *North West Heritage Group via Chris Gibson*

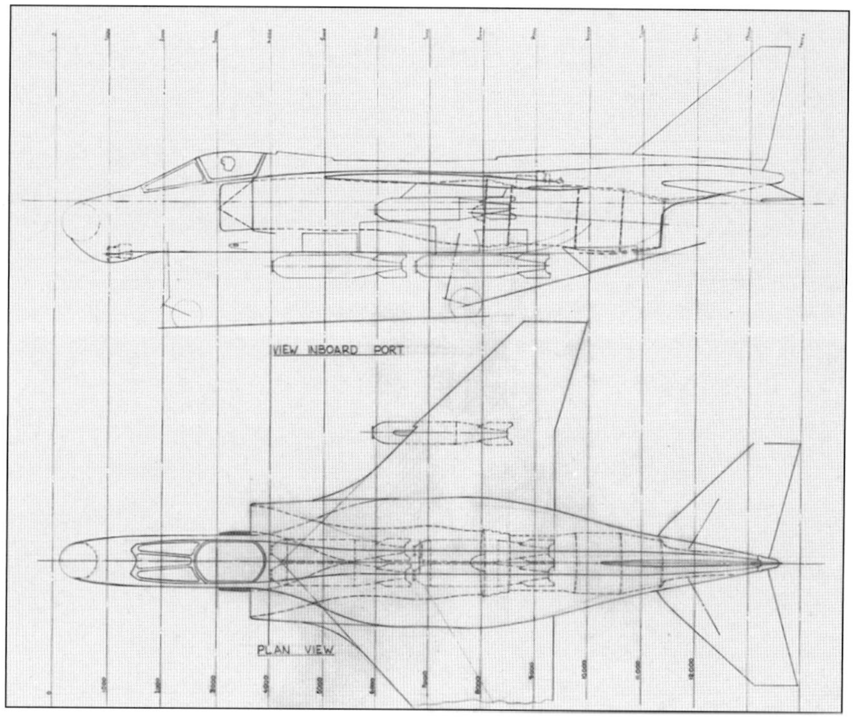

RIGHT **Jaguar Max. The EAG.8668 had a much wider and deeper fuselage for a Rolls-Royce RB.431 turbofan, a 'straight-through' development of the Pegasus rated at 28,030lbf (124.6kN) reheated.** *North West Heritage Group via Chris Gibson*

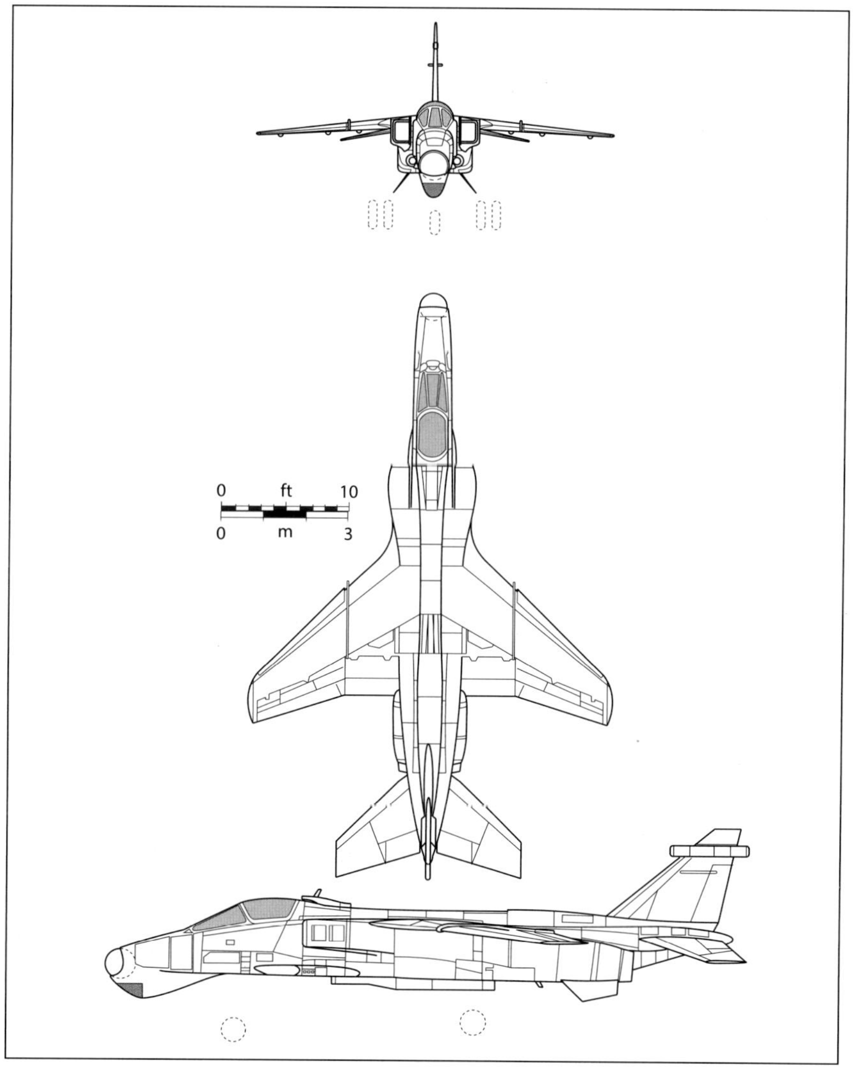

BEOW RIGHT **The EAG.8669 could be easily mistaken for a standard Jaguar except for its bulbous nose. Actually it had the wide body fuselage to accommodate two RB.199-34Rs or General Electric YJ101 engines.** *Chris Gibson*

turbofan – a 'straight-through' development of the Pegasus rated at 15,850lbf (70.5kN) dry and 28,030lbf (124.6kN) reheated. Nose 'D' was modified to fit the deeper fuselage contours. Only the portside ADEN was fitted. Four BL.755 were carried ventrally and the wing had four hardpoints.

The EAG.8669 series (including the single-seat 8669A and two-seat 8669B) were wide boded with larger intakes for two RB.199-34Rs or two General Electric YJ101s rated at 9,500lbf (42.2kN) dry or 14,300lbf (63.6kN) reheated (as used on the Northrop YF-17). They had the revised wing and a stronger undercarriage, the gross weight with RB.199 being 35,476lb (16,090kg) including 10,180lb (4,620kg) of fuel. Most of the iterations had only the port cannon, but the initial studies retained a pair.

The two-seater was taken forward for Phase Three, reverting to a single ventral tandem beam for the BL.755. The final set of designs included the Phase Three EAG.8665B, an improved two-seat EAG.8662B but with the Tornado's VG wings that were modified with a new centre section.

The heavily modified P.79 designs looked quite different. EAG.8870 was a two-seater and its only obvious Jaguar heritage was the cockpit area. The Tornado's VG wings received redesigned wing root gloves and the fuselage had new faired-in lateral intakes feeding a single RB.199-34R. A completely new empennage and undercarriage was fitted, the latter having single mainwheels. Two sensor fits were proposed; the strike aircraft had a modified AST.396 set-up with a sensor ball in the nose with a large protruding chin pod, either for a visual sensor or TFR, while the battlefield fighter variant had a 26in (66cm) diameter radar developed from the Thomson-CSF Cyrano IV (which was fitted to the Mirage F1).

The EAG.8874 was described as a low-cost version of EAG.8665B with a much shorter fuselage of around 51ft 6in

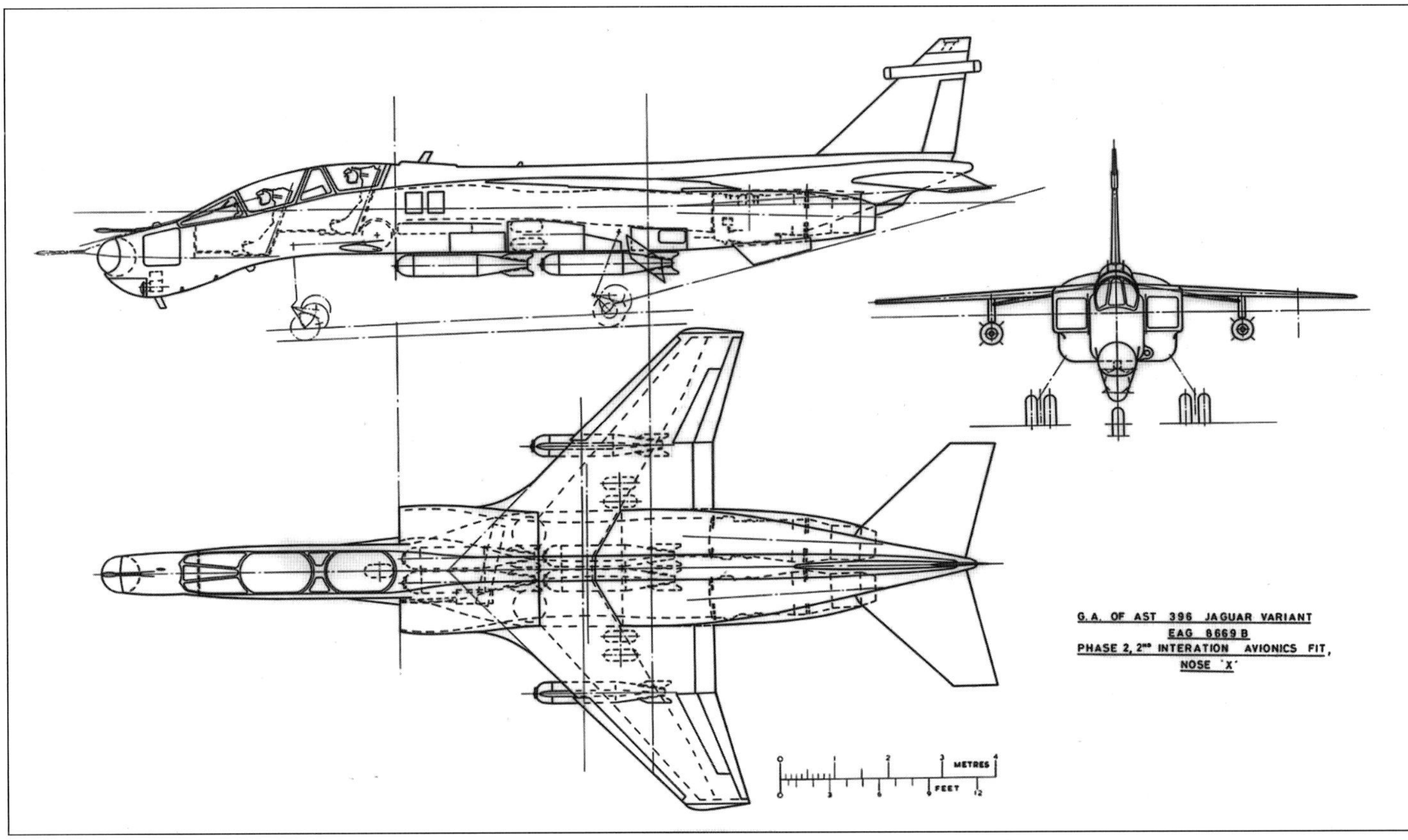

ABOVE The two-seat version of the EAG.8669. *North West Heritage Group via Chris Gibson*

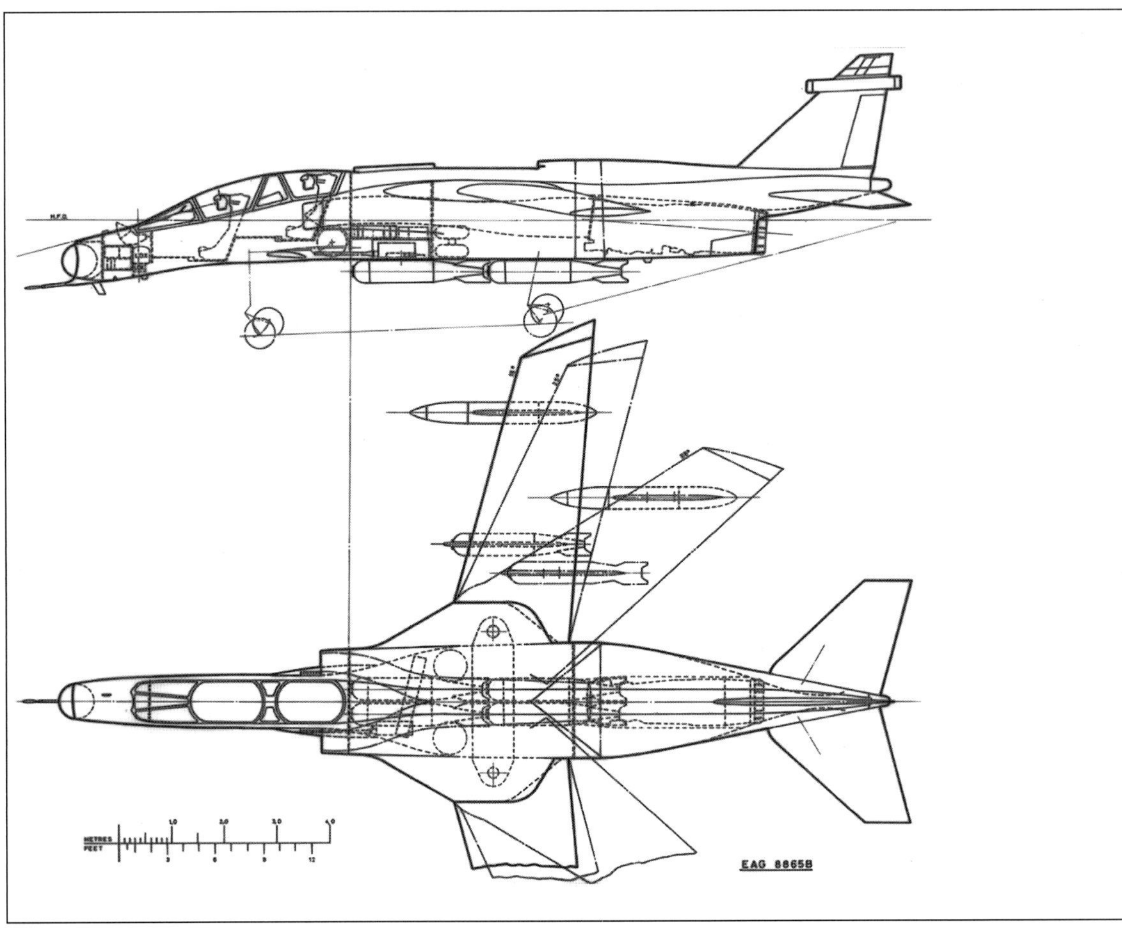

This is the Phase Three iteration of EAG.8865 with simplified avionics including a terrain-following radar pod under the starboard wing. The Tornado's wings would have received a new wing glove. *North West Heritage Group via Chris Gibson*

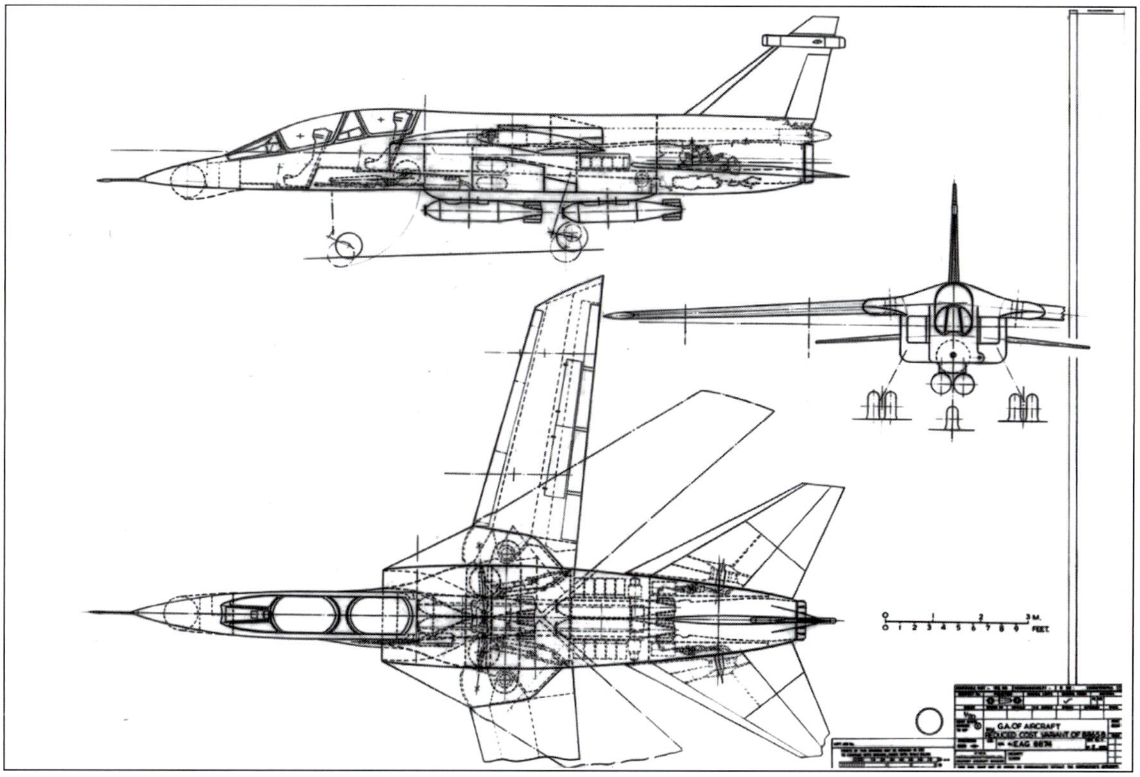

EAG.8874 was a reduced-price version of the EAG.8665B. *North West Heritage Group via Chris Gibson*

(15.7m) with a new tail jet exhaust and a low-mounted tailplane. The FLIR/laser ball turret was recessed into the nose, which gave a reduced field of vision (a pointed nose cone was fitted). No TFR was included and only one cannon. Four BL.755s were carried in tandem pairs ventrally and the Tornado wings retained their four pylons.

Following the release of AST.396 (Issue 3), work from the summer of 1975 concentrated on the P.86 requiring long-term developments and the P.87 covering the short and medium-term developments. EAG.8903, a single-seater with the Tornado wings, reverted to the chisel nose with a new, shorter, rear fuselage modelled on that of EAG.8874. A single RB.199-34R was fitted and two additional pylons were fitted above the inner wing glove for Sidewinders. EAG.8904 had an enlarged Jaguar wing with large LERX. EAG.8905 reverted to a standard-length Jaguar S fuselage but used the Tornado's VG wing with a new centre section and had enlarged intakes for two RB.199-34Rs. EAG.8906 had the modified wings of EAG.8904.

In November 1975 the DOAE released its final report into the cost-effectiveness of the take-off performance and basing policy. It was concluded that the concept of dispersed site operations would result in a lower level of battlefield support being generated over five days compared with main base operations. Forward operations of eight sorties per day with six aircraft per site would be reduced in effectiveness after five days due to attrition. When operating from a main base, there was no compelling case for a take-off performance better than 2,625ft (800m). Even so, RAFG argued strongly for vertical landing for greater flexibility and they considered landing on repaired runways was hazardous. There were a large number of available runways; the 2nd Allied Tactical Air Force had 27 main airbases with eight located within 107nm (200km) of the Inner German Border, of which the AST.396 aircraft could use 11 and four respectively.

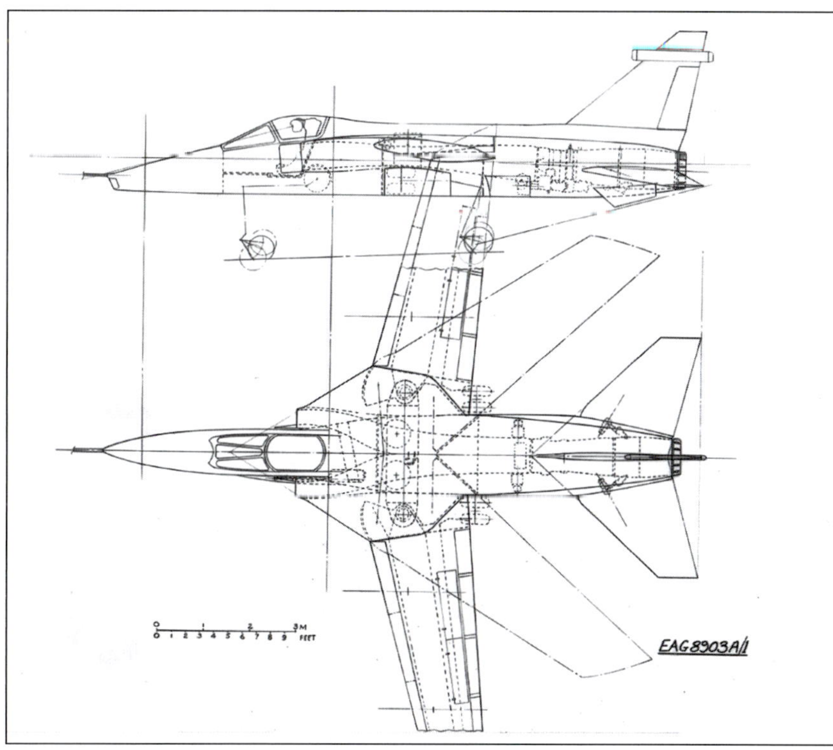

Warton's *Flogger*. Among the last of the AST.396 design studies, EAG.8903A with the Tornado's wings and single RB.199-34R resembles the Mikoyan-Gurevich MiG-27 ground-attack fighter. *North West Heritage Group via Chris Gibson*

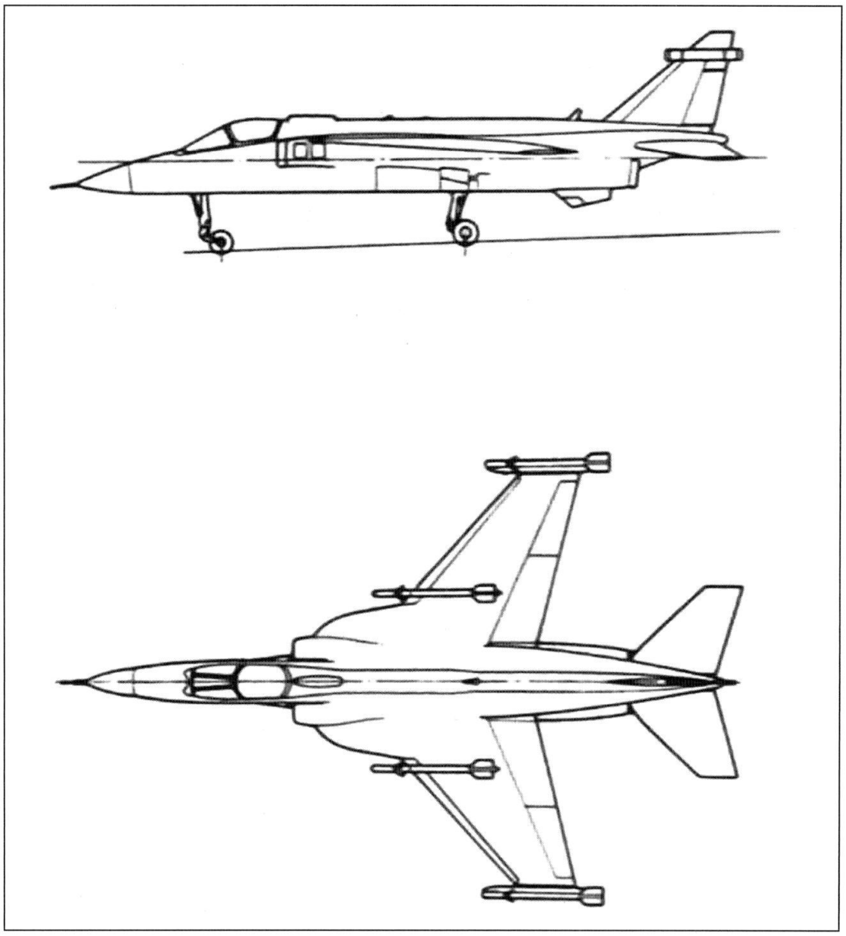

A plan drawing of the P.97 Super Jaguar studied as part of BAC's AST.403 submission. Noteworthy are the wing tip and overwing rails for AIM-9 Sidewinders for an increased self-defence capability and a multi-mode radar in the nose. *Author's Collection*

A total of 27 designs were submitted by BAC and HSA, covering developments of existing aircraft from Buccaneer to Hawk and fresh-sheet designs. In April 1976 the Working Party on Battlefield Support Aircraft released its official report and concluded that it would be possible to meet AST.396 by further developing an existing aircraft. The report favoured a lightweight and low-cost solution like the EAG.8522. But the avionics were a major obstacle given that the current technology could not offer good enough visual resolution with wide angles of view. In addition, the lack of air combat capability was becoming worrying to the Air Staff. The outcome was the cancellation of AST.396.

AST.403: Super Jaguar

In early 1975 work began on a modified set of requirements. Air superiority became the primary element, with ground attack – with emphasis on attacking vehicles – and reconnaissance as the other roles. The planned date of CA Release to Service was 1987. The first issue of AST.403 was released on 8 July 1975 and the Operational Requirements Committee gave its formal endorsement on 29 April 1976. At this point AST.396 was withdrawn.

Work on the Phase I studies lasted from May 1976 to June 1978. At a meeting at the Ministry of Defence (MoD) on 26 August 1976, the Controller Aircraft, Air Chief Marshal Sir Douglas Lowe, and the Vice Chief of the Air Staff, Air Marshal Sir David Evans, confirmed to representatives from the major companies involved that they desired to buy British rather than buying American competitors like the General Dynamics F-16A. Within a year, however, there was increasing political pressure to make the aircraft a collaborative European venture. The main requirements were:

- An air combat profile including seven 360° turns pulling 8g at Mach 0.9 at 5,000ft (1,525m).
- SEP to accelerate from Mach 0.9 to Mach 1.5 at 20,000ft (6,100m) within 70 seconds.
- Minimum speed of Mach 1.1 at sea level and Mach 1.6 at the tropopause.
- Radius of action of 240nm (445km) at low level at Mach 0.8 minimum penetration speed.
- Normal operation from paved surfaces but with an undercarriage capable of dispersed operations from roads; low approach and landing speeds. STOVL or STOL capability still desirable.
- Air combat role armament of four short-range AAMs (SRAAM such as Taildog), two XJ521 Skyflash medium-range AAMs (an improved semi-active licence-built AIM-7F Sparrow) and one cannon.
- Attack role armament of 6,000lb payload including BL.755 and the future AST.1227 anti-armour weapon.
- An advanced multi-mode radar and navigation/ attack system.

Warton's design team under the leadership of Ivan Yates offered an extensive set of studies: the VG-winged P.91 and P.92 with one or two engines respectively, the tailless delta P.93, the fixed wing P.95 and P.96 with one or two engines respectively, the P.97 Super Jaguar and single-seat developments of the Tornado. The P.97 was not part of the study contract but BAC felt that the development might be attractive to the RAF.

The P.97 featured a new carbon fibre wing with LERX with an improved section, wing tip and overwing pylons for four Sidewinders or SRAAM in addition to the four underwing hardpoints. The wing area was increased from 258.3ft^2 (24m^2) to 323ft^2 (30m^2). The leading edge sweep was 42° and the thickness-chord ratio was 5%. The wing spar attachment points and fuselage cut-out for the wing were unchanged from the standard Jaguar. It had moving leading edge surfaces and the trailing edge had four plain flaps that were flaperons, combining the functions of take-off/ landing flaps, combat flaps and ailerons. An FBW flight control system was used. The LRMTS was replaced with a Westinghouse WX160 radar and a single 27mm Mauser BK27 cannon replaced the pair of 30mm ADEN.

The engines were a pair of RB.409-07R turbofans, a smaller 'cropped fan' version of the RB.199, retaining the

P.97 'Super Jaguar'	
Span	32ft 10in (10m) (without missiles)
Length	52ft 10in (16.09m)
Wing area	312ft² (29.02m²)
Leading edge sweep	42°
t/c	5%
Aspect ratio	3.3
Empty weight	17,900lb (8,119kg)
Fuel weight	7,600lb (3,447kg)
Gross weight	29,700lb (13,472kg
Take-off weight	27,000lb (12,246kg)
Powerplant	Two RB.409-07R 5,965lbf (26.5kN) dry, 10,150lbf (45.1kN) with reheat
Maximum speed/height	Mach 1.26 at sea level, Mach 1.86 at 36,090ft (11,000m)
Subsonic sustained turn rate	21°/sec at sea level
Subsonic SEP	915ft/sec (278m/sec)
Take-off roll (ISA + 15°C)	1,080ft (330m)
Landing roll (ISA + 15°C)	1,480ft (450m)
Armament	Four AAM, six bombs, one 27mm Mauser BK-27 cannon

intermediate and high-pressure (HP) spools and operating at a lower temperature. The RB.409 was tailored as an Adour replacement for the Jaguar with thrust ratings of 5,965lbf (26.5kN) dry and 10,150lbf (45.1kN) reheated (an alternative was a pair of Adour 63s).

Maximum speed at sea level was estimated at Mach 1.26 with Mach 1.86 at 36,090ft (11,000m). The P.97 met the fighter mission radius and had a 25nm (46km) surplus for the offensive support mission. The increased wing area and thrust improved the subsonic sustained turn rate from 10°/sec at sea level to 21°/sec and the subsonic SEP was 915ft/sec (278m/sec) – the MoD reviewers estimated that the acceleration time from Mach 0.9 to Mach 1.5 would be 56 seconds. The take-off and landing roll was 1,080ft (330m) and 1,475ft (450m) respectively. BAC felt that the performance was broadly comparable to the F-16A.

The estimated cost for development and production tooling for 300 aircraft was £1,120 million – half the price of the P.96F. BAC hoped to reduce the prototypes required by fitting the new wing to the fly-by-wire Advanced Control Technology demonstrator (XX765) once its research tasks were completed and using standard Jaguars as a flying testbed for the RB.409-07R (only one would be fitted) and avionics and weapons clearance. The plan was to fly the three development aircraft during 1980–81, being joined by two early production aircraft by early 1982. Production of long-lead items would begin in 1980–81, airframe manufacture in mid-1982 with service deliveries from April 1985, obtaining initial operational capability by the end of the year.

A total of 28 designs from BAC and HSA were submitted in June 1977. By the following February the choice had narrowed to six designs, one of them being the P.97. It failed, however, to be taken to Phase II. Although it was cheaper, it offered poor cost-effectiveness given its inferior performance in comparison with new designs and Warton concentrated on the improved twin-engined P.96F.

Not long after this, AST.403 (Revise 1) increased the performance requirements and the P.96 was superseded by further design studies. AST.403 was effectively cancelled as part of Secretary of Defence John Nott's Defence White Paper *The Way Forward* in June 1981 and superseded on 1 May 1984 by ASR.414 for an Agile Combat Aircraft. Thus began the long road to Typhoon.

Big Wing Jaguar

Air Vice-Marshal David Craig, the Assistant Chief of the Air Staff (Operations), had invited British Aerospace (BAe) and Rolls-Royce to carry out studies during 1977 on potential improvements to the Jaguar covering the avionics, handling and performance. Several reports were submitted and on 14 July 1978 at the MoD's Main Building a presentation was held by Alan Constantine from Warton's design team, who presented the latest designs for the Big Wing Jaguar, while Geoff Barlow from Derby discussed the Adour's development potential.

The developments fell into two groups. The Performance Group included fitting a duplex high-incidence roll damper, scheduled combat slats with 23°

A model of the Big Wing Jaguar, the most obvious feature being the wing tip rails for AIM-9 Sidewinders. ***Author's Collection***

Adour choices for Big Wing Jaguar					
	Mk 104	RT.172-58	RT.172-58C	RT.172-63	RT.172-69
Max dry thrust	4,390lbf (19.52kN)	4,710lbf (20.9kN)	5,260lbf (23.39kN)	5,540lbf (24.64kN)	5,390lbf (23.97kN)
Max reheat thrust	7,900lbf (35.14kN)	8,400lbf (37.36kN)	8,470lbf (37.67kN)	10,100lbf (44.49kN)	9,200lbf (40.92kN)

deflection, limited 20–12° deflection combat flaps, stronger spoilers and the RT.172-58 Adour. Other options included the RT.172-26, -52 or -53; the -52 had a three-stage LP and a seven-stage HP compressor for 30% more thrust and 10% lower specific fuel consumption, while the 53 had a five-stage HP compressor for 20% more thrust and slightly worse fuel consumption. Other options for improving the wings included fitting LERX or wing tip extensions. The development price tag was £4–5 million (excluding the RT.172-58), adding £70,000 to the production cost.

The Extended Operational Capability Group offered the Thomson-CSF Agave multi-mode radar, overwing AAM missile pylons, ECM and chaff dispenser pods, helmet-mounted sights and a Ferranti Type 105D laser rangefinder located beneath the Agave radome (omitted on the air combat-oriented version). The inclusion of an alternative Thomson-CSF TAV-38 laser rangefinder and AS.37 Martel ASMs hints that BAe may have been hoping to entice the Armeé de l'Air to upgrade their Jaguars.

Fitting a radar would include either a Raster HUD or a combined map/radar display, and the additional 'black boxes' would be fitted into the starboard cannon ammunition bay. Prototype B08 (XW586) was used for Agave-NAVWASS integration trials, mounting the radar scanner and electronics into a modified centreline fuel tank. The Maritime Strike Version lacked the ECM pod and helmet sights; the RAF were uninterested, but the Indian Air Force later acquired this version as the Jaguar IM and it was ordered – but later cancelled – by the Nigerian Air Force.

The MoD was interested in the Performance Group items plus the ECM and helmet sights. The latter two items were already being funded, but the rest of the package would cost around £4–5 million to develop and add £250,000 to the production cost. BAe were also offering new-generation VHF/UHF radios, improved audio warning, a reshaped rear fairing to improve supersonic performance and cockpit noise reduction, all of which would add another £50,000, plus development costs.

The feasibility study for the new wing began in January 1978 under MoD contract and called for improved high-incidence handling and combat manoeuvrability, increased carriage of defensive and offensive weapons

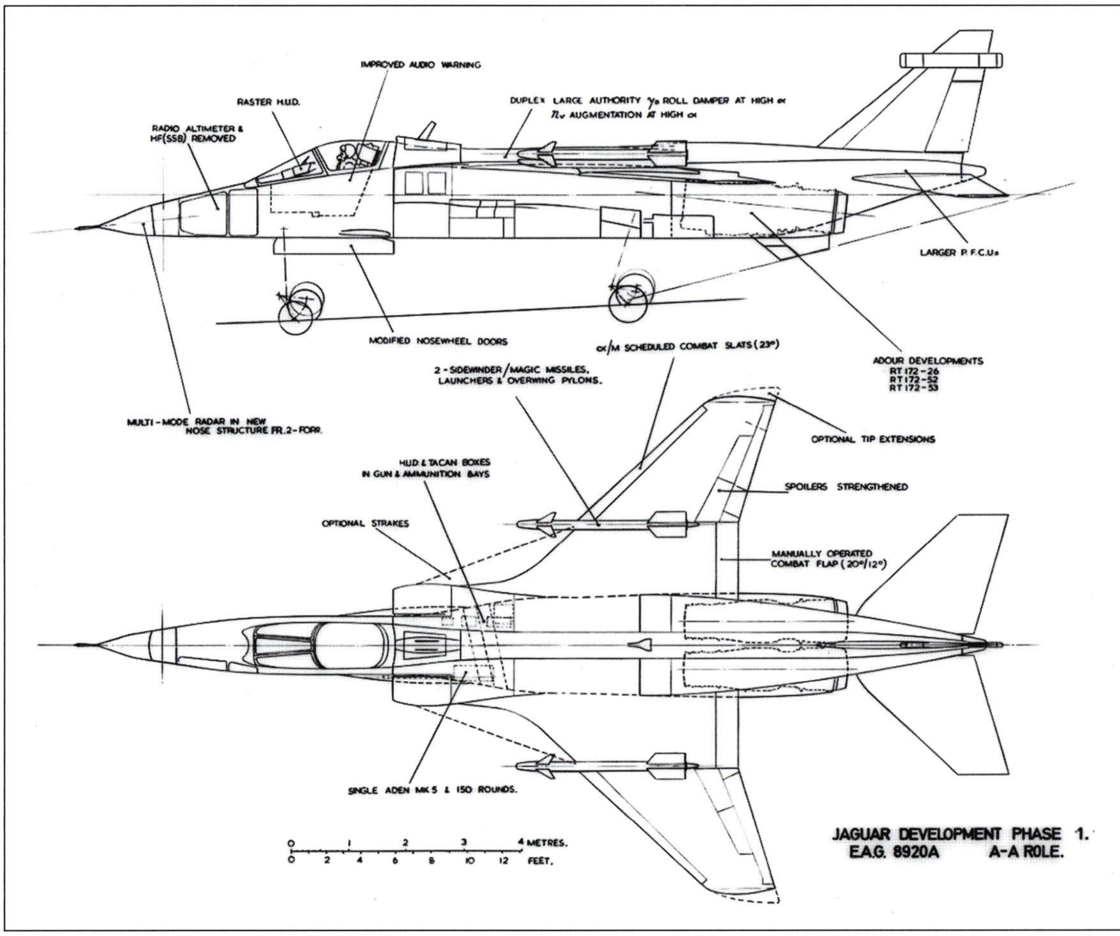

The set of EAG 8920 drawings covered the Phase One developments. This plan drawing covers the changes for the air-to-air role – the new wing, overwing rails and radar (at the cost of one 30mm ADEN cannon). ***North West Heritage Group via Chris Gibson***

Jaguar International prototype XX979 was fitted with a dummy Agave radar nose for the 1981 Paris Air Show. The aircraft was surrounded by a wide array of ordnance, including the range of bombs from the French manufacturer SAMP, a Paveway laser-guided bomb, rocket pods and under the starboard wing are a dummy AIM-9 Sidewinder and AGM-84 Harpoon anti-ship missile. ***Terry Panopalis Collection***

and increased internal fuel capacity. BAe considered this to be a more cost-effective solution than upgrading the Adour.

The new wing was based on work by the UK Combat Wing Design Steering Group and had 10% greater area; 290.6ft^2 (27m^2) compared with 258.3ft^2 (24m^2) (this was smaller than the P.97 wing). It had a new wing section and variable-camber control using full-span, hinged, leading-edge slats and trailing edge flaperons extending from the root to three-quarters span to provide good subsonic performance and supersonic efficiency. There were four underwing pylons, separate outboard ECM and chaff dispenser pods as well as two overwing and wing tip rails for AIM-9 Sidewinder AAMs. Fuel capacity would be 656lb (298kg). The sustained turn rate would be increased by 3°/sec and with the Adour RT.172-58 the take-off roll would be reduced by 245–900ft (75–275m) depending on the flap settings.

At this stage the materials had not been decided, the wing could be either constructed entirely from carbon fibre composites, all metal or a mix of both materials. The all-metal wing would be based on the existing structure but with a multi-spar torsion box. BAe were planning to construct a Jaguar wing set out of carbon fibre as part of an experimental programme,

A top-view plan of the proposed new wing and weapon stations. ***BAE Systems via Author's Collection***

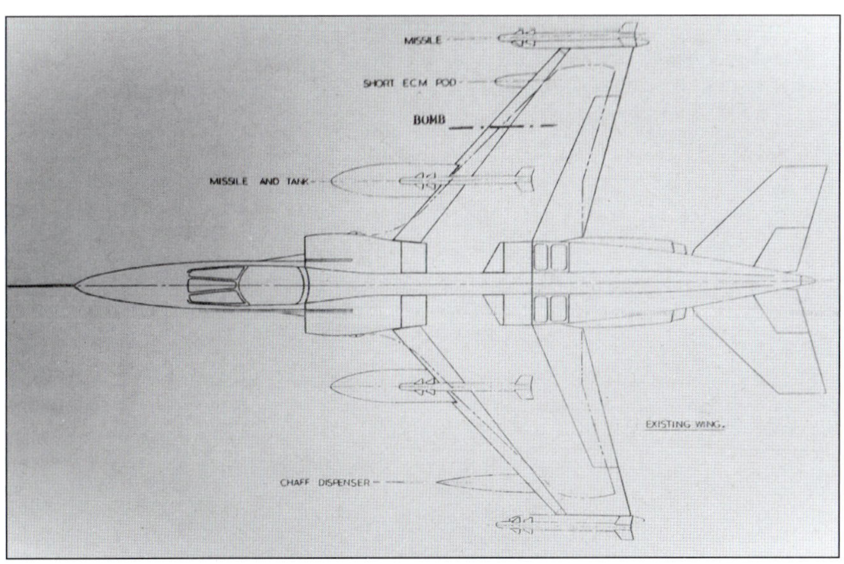

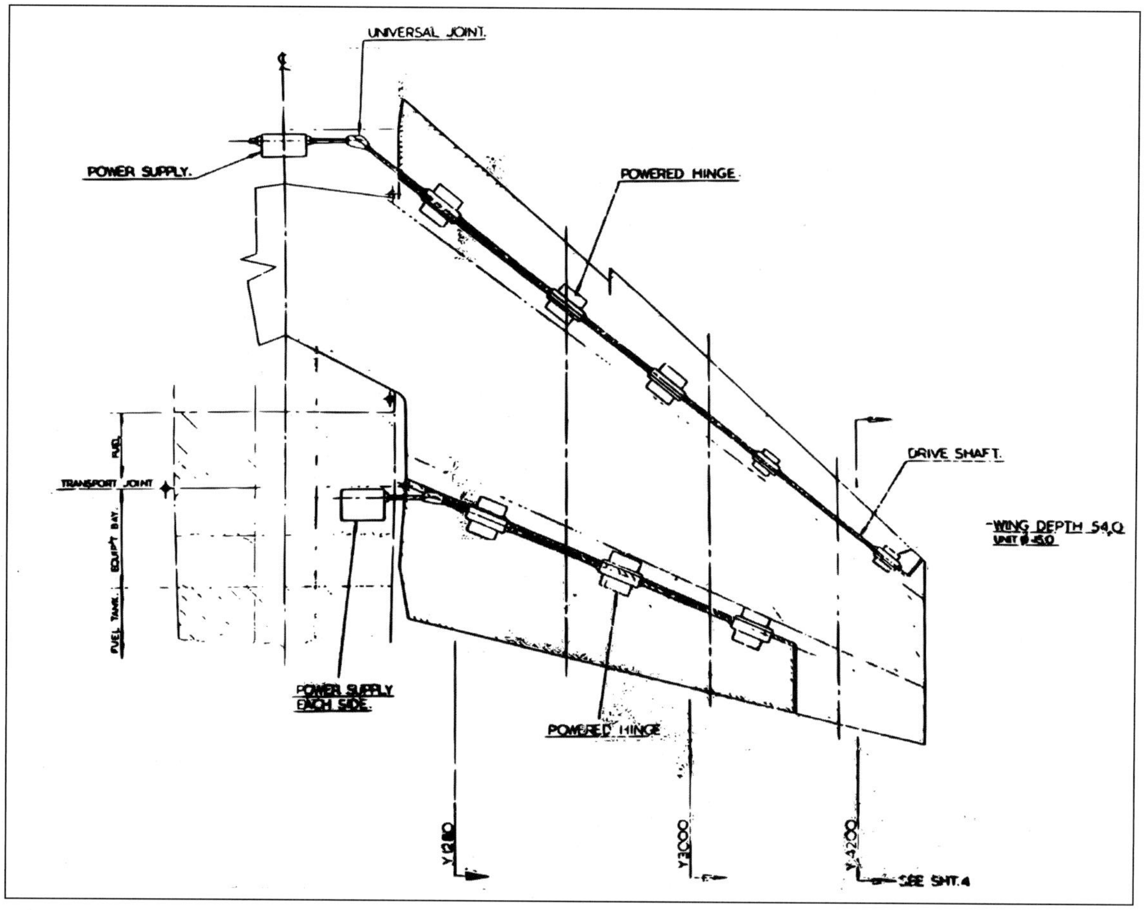

A plan of the leading edge and trailing edge control surfaces on the enlarged wing. ***BAE Systems via Author's Collection***

but the larger wing was a feasibility study only and not a firm RAF requirement at this stage. The wing could take six years to develop; BAe presented no cost estimates but it was clear it would be an expensive project.

Following the July 1978 presentation, BAe were asked to examine the possibility of modifying the existing wing as a cheaper solution. BAe came back with a proposal to cut the existing wings just inboard of No. 6 rib and fit a new one-piece centre section to

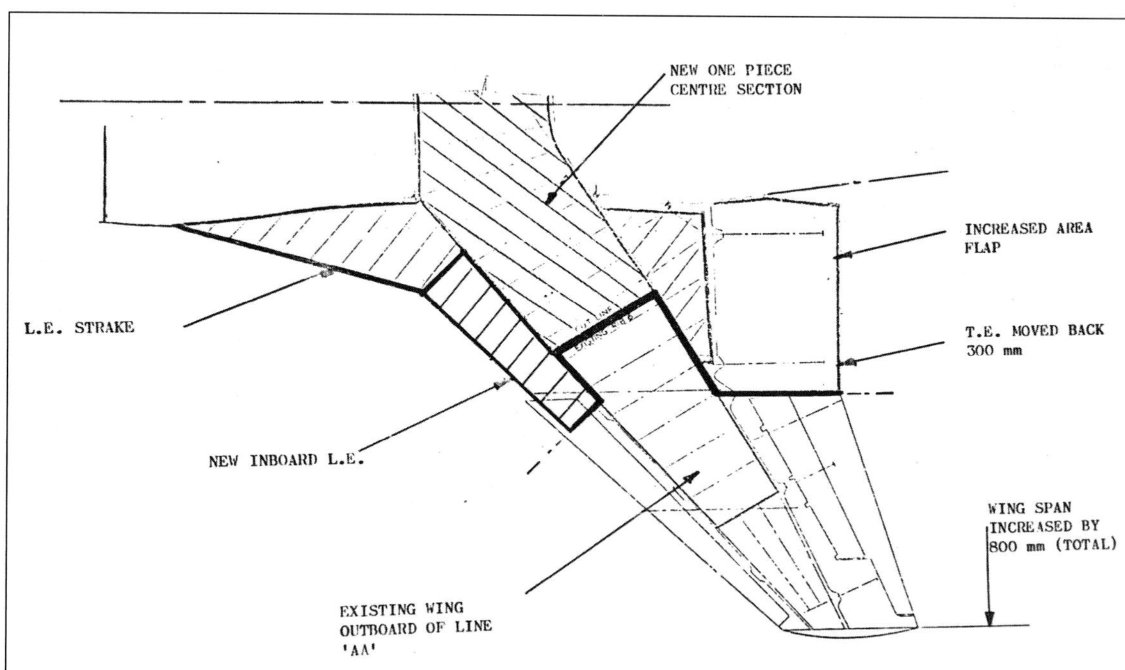

The expense of the new wing led to proposals to modify the existing wing but the more urgent need to rectify fatigue issues ruled out more extensive modifications. ***BAE Systems via Author's Collection***

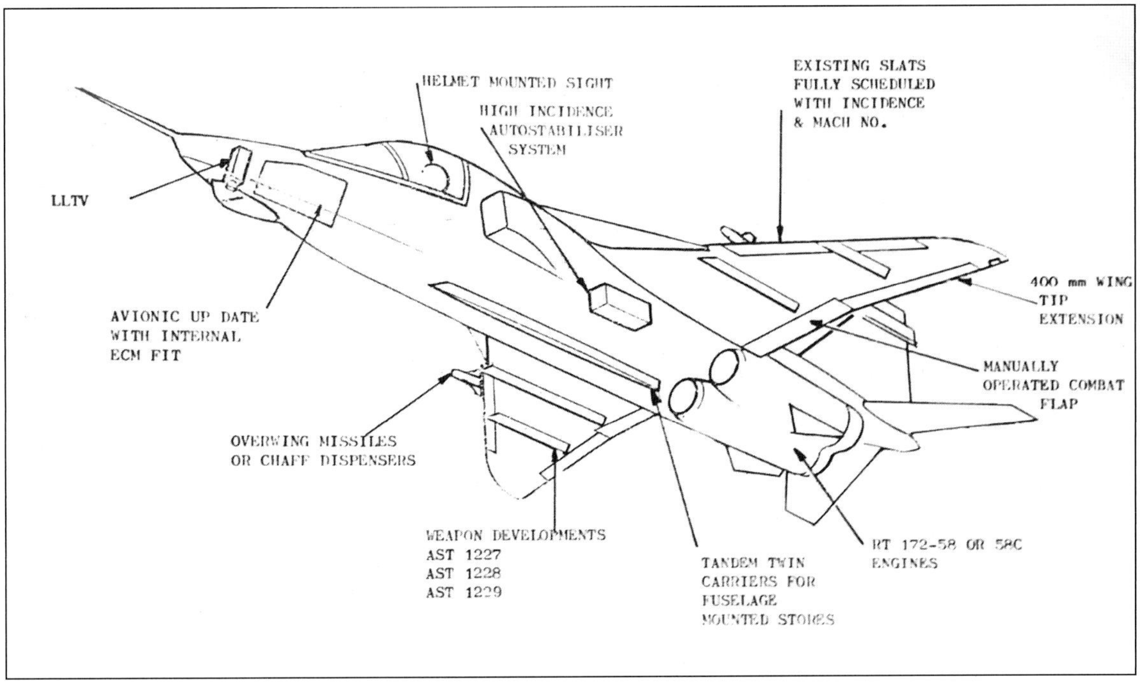

This diagram shows the improvements proposed in 1978 that Warton thought could be in service on upgraded Jaguars in 1982. It would be nearer two decades before some of these items found their way on to the Jaguar. ***BAE Systems via Author's Collection***

extend the span by 2ft 6in (80cm). All existing flaps, spoilers and slats would be retained but strengthened. A new large inboard flap would be added along with leading edge strakes to increase the wing area. The existing underwing pylons were retained but new overwing pylons would be located 15in (40cm) further outboard. The sustained turn rate would be increased by 1°/sec and take-off roll would be reduced by 620ft (190m) with the RT.172-58.

It was noted that both proposals required an increased-capacity hydraulic pump, which may have also required a new engine gearbox casing and a new hydraulic system heat exchanger. Development costs were estimated at £32 million plus production costs of £132 million, although sufficient spare wings existed to enable a modification pool to be set up.

The urgent need to carry out wing reinforcement of the existing wing centre sections to extend the fatigue life pre-empted the efforts to develop a new or modified wing. The cost and a declining number of in-service aircraft made the wing improvement programme cost prohibitive and it remained a paper study.

Upgrade options to provide a night attack capability using LLTV or FLIR were also open. LLTV for target search and designation was being developed under AST.610, endorsed in September 1975. The Royal Aircraft Establishment (RAE) tested the prototype equipment in Hawker Hunter T.7 WV383 in 1976, their test pilot Roger Searle flying the trials with a safety pilot in the left-hand seat. The LLTV in the nose projected its image on a small black and white display located on the right-hand side of the cockpit. Searle flew the first night-time test, having to descend to 200ft (61m) before a 'flyable' visible image appeared on the screen. A 1979 symposium of Jaguar pilots was divided in its opinion of its usefulness but they recommended pursuing the technology. B08 was used in related trials in the spring of 1977 with an ISOCON camera in a pod under the port wing, with the image being projected on to the HUD. The results were disappointing, however, due to poor picture quality. With costs rising close to £1 million, LLTV was ruled out for the Jaguar, although testing continued. BAe assigned Jaguar Project Pilot Chris Yeo as their LLTV Project Pilot and in January 1982 B08 was modified at Warton with a combined HUD/LLTV display for RAE trials (the delivery to Farnborough by Keith Hartley and John Scutt was its 718th flight).

In 1978, AST.1006 was raised to cover feasibility studies into using electro-optical equipment to improve target acquisition and weapon aiming, which included trials using B08 with a modified AN/AVQ-23E PAVE SPIKE laser designator, borrowed free of charge from the USAF. The French also offered the use of a Jaguar A with a Thomson-CSF ATLIS I laser designator pod, which at the cost of just £150,000 was a bargain the MoD could not pass up.

AST.1230 had been formulated for helmet-mounted sights for the Jaguar. The intent was to allow the pilot to communicate sightlines to the NAVWASS over the full range of head movement, allowing him to feed navigational fixes and the co-ordinates of targets of opportunity into the system without having to overfly them.

BAe had already flown flight trials of Honeywell Modified Visual Target Acquisition System (MOVTAS) equipment in a Jaguar T.2 during 1975–76 with satisfactory results. This was in parallel to the RAE's Helmet Sighting and Pointing Systems with Electro-Optical Seekers (HIPSEOS) programme run between 1974 and 1976 using English Electric Canberra B(I).6 WT308 to determine if single-seat fighter pilots could lock on to and track targets using a MOVTAS helmet sight and a TV tracker. MOVTAS used two IR scanners in the cockpit and four helmet-mounted photo-transistors to determine the location of the pilot's head, with the weapon aiming and cueing marks shown on a display attached to the helmet. Following the potential shown by MOVTAS and HIPSEOS, it was envisioned that future developments might add aiming functionality for laser designators, radar and AAMs. It was hoped to begin full development in 1979 at a total cost of £1.7 million with the aim of an in-service date of 1981 (in reality the technology took another decade to enter service).

AST.611 was issued in 1975 for an integrated threat warning system that would include a rearward-looking Doppler missile approach warning radar and a laser warning receiver (LWR) for the AST.403 aircraft and Jaguar, Harrier and Tornado. Progress was slow; the Jaguar never received missile approach warning radar (Harrier GR.5 and Tornado GR.4 did in the late 1980s) and development of the LWR was not completed the early 1990s.

ASR.633 for a new RWR and ECM for Jaguar was released in 1985. Plessey and Elettronica bid jointly, but this was overtaken by other developments in the 1990s.

When ASR.1217 was raised for a runway-cratering weapon – resulting in the JP.233 sub-munition dispenser – it was intended for carriage by Tornado, Buccaneer and Jaguar. The latter two would have used two underwing pods, one carrying the SG.357 runway-cratering munitions and the other HB.876 area denial mines. BAe was contracted to undertake wind tunnel work but it was clear that the weight and drag would cause insurmountable problems given the lack of engine thrust, so the Jaguar was removed from ASR.1217 in August 1980.

AST.1227 was issued in 1975 for an anti-armour weapon with all-weather capability and a high single-shot kill probability against main battle tanks for the AST.403 aircraft as well as the Jaguar and Harrier. The wide choice of weapon design studies was narrowed down to the BAe Sabre (a Rapier SAM with semi-active laser guidance using the Thomson-CSF/Martin Marietta ATLIS 2 laser designator pod) and the Hunting Engineering VJ.291, a winged stand-off cluster bomb with dual-purpose bomblet/minelets. ASR.1229 was later raised to cover the PAVE SPIKE laser designator for the weapon.

The Jaguar could carry the PAVE SPIKE and AN/ALQ-101(V)10 ECM pods outboard with up to ten AST.1227 weapons on the inner pylons fitted with multiple racks and a ventral fuel tank, or alternatively two fuel tanks and ECM and chaff pods underwing, six AST.1227 missiles on the two overwing pylons and PAVE SPIKE on the centreline.

Ultimately, the guided missiles needed far more technical development and were split off into AST.1238, with VJ.291 cancelled in December 1980. AST.1227 (First Revise) was issued in 1981 for an interim low-cost weapon and off-the-shelf solutions included the AGM-65D Maverick ASM with an imaging infrared seeker or the BL.755 with improved bomblets, the latter being selected in 1982 as the IBL.755 (the existing BL.755s being upgraded). The AST.1238 weapon emerged as the MBDA Brimstone in 2005, but by then the Jaguar's operational life was nearly over.Another new weapon that never materialised was the BAe Dynamics ALARM anti-radiation missile for suppression of enemy air defences (SEAD). It was designed to destroy radars, loitering over the battlefield beneath a parachute, homing on to the emission source and then making a rocket-powered vertical attack to destroy the radar. Developed to AST.1228 issued in 1978, ALARM entered service in 1990 on the Tornado GR.1 (also used on Tornado F.3 fighters from 2003).

Battlefield interdiction planning for the NATO Central Region earmarked the Jaguar and Buccaneer for ALARM. In the nuclear strike role the Jaguar would carry four on the inner underwing hardpoints to suppress enemy defences during its penetration. For the close support role, modified inner underwing pylons would each take a pair of BL.755s and one ALARM. Planning envisioned four daily sorties over the FEBA to destroy Warsaw Pact air defences, requiring 100 missiles to sanitise each battlefield corridor. The cost of the programme proved prohibitive and once the Cold War ended the Jaguar's planned SEAD role was abandoned.

Rolls-Royce's Assistant Project Manager (Jaguar) D W Haworth in late 1978 offered a '1982 Development Package' – the RT.172-58C, -63 and -69. The -58C had a digital fuel control system and improved HP compressor blades, but the unchanged LP compressor created a mismatch that limited increase in reheat static thrust to only 70lbf (0.3kN) and unreheated at Mach 0.7 the increase was 570lbf (2.5kN). The -69 had a new three-stage LP compressor and turbine blades manufactured with a directionally solidified cast process. The engine was larger but still fit within the Jaguar's engine bay. The -63 represented the limit of Adour development with all the features of the -69 plus RB.199 afterburner technology to enable cold stream burning at the exhaust cone. It would still fit in the Jaguar but new engine doors would be required.

Against these official proposals the RAF's Air Engineering Branch felt that a Mk.104 with a rematched LP compressor would give similar performance to the -58 (Mk.811) for less cost. The Air Engineering Branch analysed the options; it was the attack speed

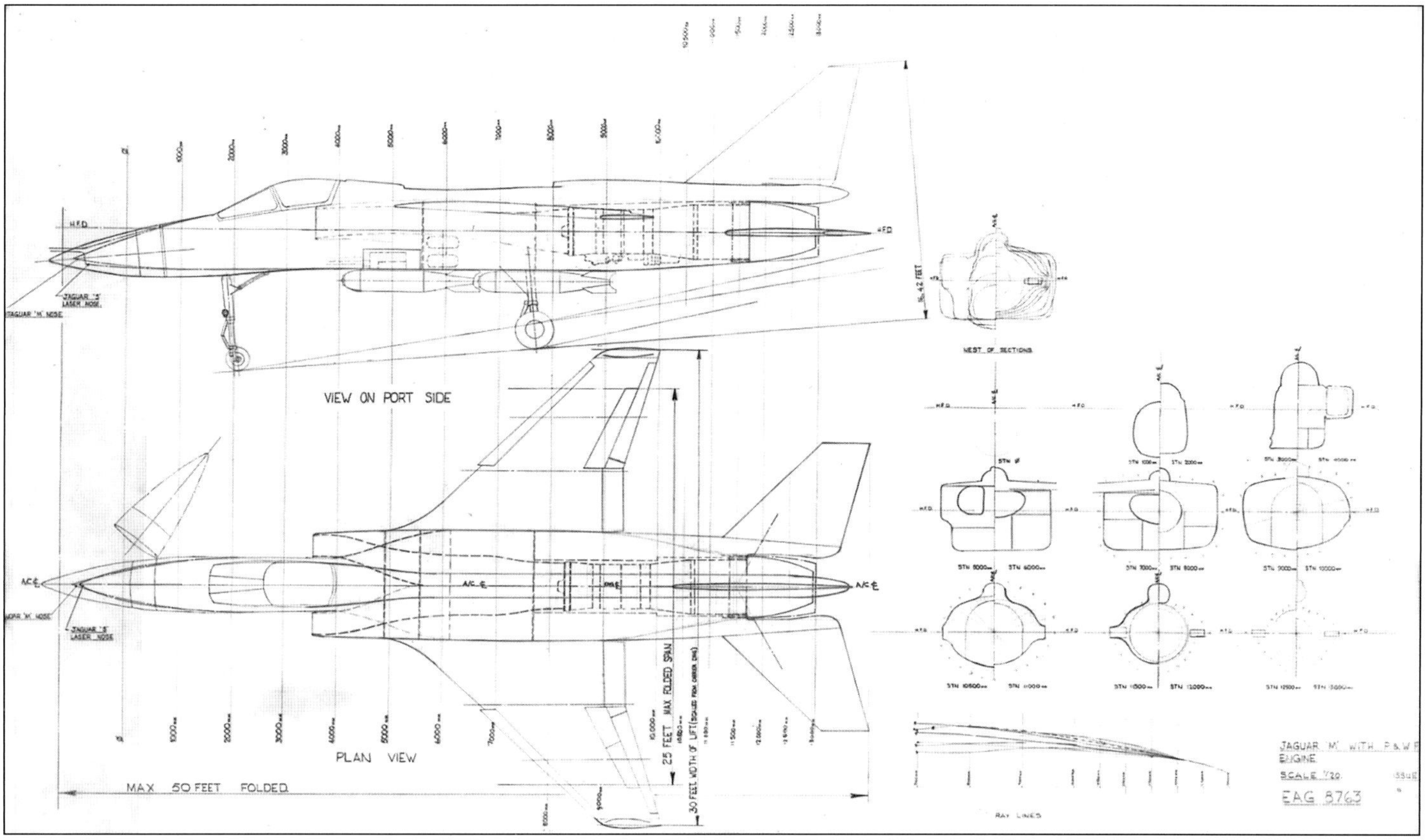

This intriguing study is the French carrier-borne Jaguar M revised for a Pratt & Whitney F100 turbofan with afterburner. Presumably the EAG.8763 study was offered to the Royal Navy in the early 1970s. ***North West Heritage Group via Chris Gibson***

requirement of 550kt at sea level with a full war load that led to the need for increased engine power and expensive high-risk engine development programmes. Discarding this requirement and focusing on the take-off distance and sustained turning requirements would enable use of a modified Mk.104 alongside the modified wing, which would cost £91.15 million. From this point on the Big Wing Jaguar was discarded in favour of more modest upgrades – the GR.1A and T.2A.

Other designs

The EAG.8763 of 1974 was a Jaguar M powered by a single Pratt & Whitney F100 turbofan with a new rear fuselage and empennage and options for either the standard Jaguar M or the Jaguar S nose cones. Reference to a 30ft (9.1m)-wide aircraft carrier lift suggests that carriage aboard HMS *Ark Royal* was contemplated despite its impending retirement a few years later (its lifts were around 34ft (10.3m) wide).

Other studies concentrated on increasing the weapons payload of the Jaguar. For example, EAG.8933 of 1974 showed a GR.1 with a ventral pallet for four BL.755s or one 264gal (1,200L) drop tank and triple bomb carriers for the inboard underwing pylons, which gave a total of twelve bombs if another pair were carried on the outboard pylons.

Within the same series of studies an anti-ship role was looked at; EAG.8934 featuring AM.39 Exocet missiles on either the ventral and/or both inboard pylons and EAG.8935 with the AGM-84A Harpoon (the electronics for the latter required removal of the starboard ADEN cannon to make the necessary space). At the time the RAF had no dedicated anti-ship missile and it would be a decade before the BAe Dynamics P3T Sea Eagle entered service on the Buccaneer S.2B. Both of these studies retained the normal LRMTS-equipped nose – presumably target designation would be via another aircraft, most probably Hawker Siddeley Nimrod MR.1 maritime patrol aircraft.

APPENDIX ONE

Prototype production

This is a listing of the prototype Jaguars, including a concise history of each aircraft. Changes in serial numbers and applications of static ground instruction airframe serials are highlighted in bold text.

In these entries the following abbreviations may be found:

- A&AEE – Aeroplane & Armament Experimental Establishment
- BAC – British Aircraft Corporation
- CEV – Centre d'Essais en Vol (Flight Test Centre)
- ff – first flown
- GIA – ground instructional airframe
- RAE – Royal Aircraft Establishment
- Wfu – withdrawn from use

Two production orders covered eight aircraft: two Jaguar E, two Jaguar A, one Jaguar M, two Jaguar S and one Jaguar B, construction numbers (c/n) E01, E02, A03, A05, M05, S06, S07, B08.

E01 F-ZWRD, ff 08.09.1968. Prototype for aerodynamic, handling, flutter and general systems tests, coded 'B'; rolled out at Villacoublay for ground and taxying tests 17.04.1968; transported to Istres-Le Tubé, taxying tests 05.08.1968; crashed near Istres due to engine failure 26.03.1970, Commandant Brossier ejected safely.

E02 F-ZWRC, ff 11.02.1969. Prototype for engine, flight performance, spinning and flutter tests, coded 'C'; structural repairs 17.04.1969, flying resumed 31.05.1969; to Rolls-Royce and BAC, Warton 09.09.1971; structural repairs 31.12.1971, flying resumed 24.03.1972; intake modifications 05.1973, flying resumed 10.08.1972; spinning trials programme 12.1973; wfu, transported to France 29.05.1980 as a GIA; preserved at Conservatoire de l'Air et de l'Espace d'Aquitaine, Bordeaux, spuriously marked as E1 '7-JH'.

A03 F-ZWRD, ff 29.03.1969. Prototype for navigation/attack system development, store clearance carriage and weapons firing tests, coded 'D'; landing accident due to engine stall at Istres-Le Tubé 08.05.1969, repaired; landing accident due to engine failure at Istres 14.02.1972 and wfu.

A04 F-ZWRE, ff 27.05.1969. Prototype for single-seater version aerodynamics and handling, stores clearance and weapons firing tests, coded 'E'; official initial release trials 12.1971; fuel tank repairs 15.03.1973, flying resumed 05.1973, to CEV, Melun-Villaroche; wfu; to Musée Air and Space, Île-de-France, by 09.1979; to Musée de l'Air, Le Bourget, Paris; preserved at Musée Aeroscopia, Toulouse-Blagnac, since 2014.

M05 F-ZWRJ, ff 14.11.1969. Prototype for naval version, carrier handling and clearance tests, coded 'J'; to Nîmes-Garons 04.1970; to RAE Bedford 20.04 to 04.05.1970 and 08.06 to 18.06.1970; *Clemenceau* carrier trials 08.07 to 13.07.1970; to RAE Bedford 24.06 to 15.07.1971; *Clemenceau* carrier trials 20.10.1971; structural repairs 11.1971, flying resumed 08.03.1972; to Cazaux; to Landivisiau 04.06 to 14.06.1972; new engines 10.1972; grounded for new wings, never fitted, Jaguar M cancelled 01.1973; to CEV, Melun-Villaroche for spinning tests 10.01.1974; to Istres-Le Tubé 13.06.1974, final flight 12.12.1975; GIA at School of Air Force Mechanics, Rochefort; preserved at Musée de Tradition de l'Aeronautique Navale, Rochefort.

S06 XW560, ff 18.08.1969. Prototype for navigation/attack system development, weapons and in-flight refuelling tests; to A&AEE 07.1972; destroyed by fire following engine failure during ground testing 11.08.1972; nose section preserved on display at the Boscombe Down Aviation Collection.

S07 XW563, ff 12.06.1970. Prototype for avionics and stores carriage tests, first Jaguar with full Navigation/Weapon Aiming Sub-System (NAVWASS); to A&AEE 07.1972; nuclear bomb modifications 10.1973, flying resumed 01.1974; to BAC 02.1975; wfu Boscombe Down 06.1977; to Brüggen as GIA **8563M**, later gate guardian marked as 'XX822' 'AA'; to Coltishall 08.08.2001; preserved at Norwich County Hall, Norfolk, since 27.02.2007.

B08 XW566, ff 30.08,1971. Prototype for two-seat cockpit tests and avionics development; to A&AEE 12.09.1974; to CEV; to A&AEE, modifications 01.1974, final flight 17.06.1985; to RAE Farnborough as GIA; preserved at the Farnborough Air Sciences Trust, Farnborough.

APPENDIX TWO

RAF production

This is a listing of all Jaguars ordered for the RAF, including a concise history of each aircraft. Changes in serial numbers and applications of B-Condition and static ground instruction airframe serials are highlighted in bold text.

In these entries the following abbreviations may be found:

- ff – first flown
- Fg Off – Flying Officer
- Flt Lt – Flight Lieutenant
- GIA – ground instructional airframe
- Gp Capt – Group Captain
- Sqn – Squadron
- Sqn Ldr – Squadron Leader
- Wfu – withdrawn from use
- Wg Cdr – Wing Commander

Two-letter squadron codes were allocated, with the initial letter as follows:

- No. II(AC) – individual letters
- No. 6 – E
- No. 14 – A
- No. 16(R) – P
- No. 17 – B
- No. 20 – C
- No. 31 – D
- No. 41(F) – initially individual letters, then F
- No. 54(F) – G
- No. 226 OCU – individual numbers and letters

First production order

the first production order covered 30 aircraft: 15 Jaguar GR.1, construction numbers (c/n) S1–S15 and 15 T.2, c/n B1–B15.

S1 XX108, ff 01.10.1972. Retained by BAC as part of trials fleet; upgrade as Jaguar International prototype with Adour Mk.804 then Mk.811; displayed SBAC Farnborough 09.1978 as **G-27-313**; nosewheel collapse 1979 Paris Salon; GR.1B upgrade St Athan mid-1996; Adour Mk.106 flight trials Warton from 07.06.2000; wfu St Athan for spares recovery 28.05.2002; preserved at Imperial War Museum Duxford, extant on display (IWM seeking to divest).

S2 XX109, ff 16.11.1972. First aircraft with full NAVWASS and LRMTS; delivered A&AEE for stress monitoring and WSAM trials 01.05.1973; GIA **8918M** 17.10.86, to Coltishall as Weapon Load Trainer and AEDIT development aircraft 21.10.86, desert pink camouflage paint test 09.1990, static display at Coltishall for Jaguar 30th anniversary 09.2003; City of Norwich Aviation Museum 01.09.2004, extant on display.

S3 XX110, ff 01.03.1973. Delivered A&AEE for WSAM trials 03.1973; No. 6 Sqn coded 'EP' 04.1976; No. 2 SoTT Cosford as GIA **8955M** 24.07.1985; preserved as gate guardian at Cosford.

S4 XX111, ff 19.04.1973. Delivered Jaguar Conversion Team 30.5.1973; stored 06.05.1977; BAe Warton as **G-27-314** 16.10.79, Jaguar International upgrade and loan to Indian Air Force, delivered 12.02.1980 as **JI011**; crashed in India 10.05.1982, Flt Lt R K Srivastava killed.

S5 XX112, ff 02.05.1973. Delivered A&AEE for WSAM trials 17.09.73; No. 6 Sqn 18.10.1979, GR.1A upgrade early 1985, Phase 1 upgrade for first Operation Granby roulement 08.1990, GR.3 upgrade by 1998 and GR.3A upgrade 2003; stored DARA St Athan 19.10.2006 to 27.11.2006; DCAE Cosford 13.07.2007, extant as GIA.

S6 XX113, ff 31.05.1973. Delivered A&AEE for WSAM trials 18.10.1973; No. 226 OCU 22.12.1975; crashed 17.07.1981 near Malvern due to a jammed control system during a test flight from Abingdon, pilot ejected safely.

S7 XX114, ff 05.07.1973. Delivered No. 226 OCU coded '02' 13.09.1973; crashed on take-off due to a bird strike at Lossiemouth 19.09.1983, Fg Off Iain McLean ejected safely.

S8 XX115, ff 16.08.1973. First aircraft with ARI.18223 RWR; delivered 13.09.1973; stored 01.1978 to 07.1979; BAe Warton 10.07.1979 as **G-27-316**, Jaguar International upgrade and loan to Indian Air Force, delivered 11.12.1979 as **JI005**; returned to UK 23.07.1982, stored; No. 2 SoTT Cosford as GIA **8821M** 08.1984.

S9 XX116, ff 10.09.1973. Delivered 02.10.1973; stored 02.1978 to 08.1979; BAe Warton 07.1979 as **G-27-315**, Jaguar International upgrade and loan to Indian Air Force, delivered as **JI008**; returned to UK 19.09.1984, stored Warton; GR.1A upgrade, No. 6 Sqn coded 'EE'; No. 226 OCU '02'; second Jaguar 97 trials aircraft 01.1999, BAE Systems

Warton 09.2001; QinetiQ Boscombe Down 11.2001; wfu St Athan 03.2005; FCSTE Manston 26.09.2005 for fire training; sold to Jet Art Aviation 2020, restoration in all-black 'The Saint' colours completed for a new private owner in Chippenham, Suffolk 07.2024.

S10 XX117, ff 08.10.1973. Delivered 31.10.1973; No. 226 OCU coded '06'; stored 03.1977; BAe Warton 07.1979 as **G-27-317**, Jaguar International upgrade and loan to Indian Air Force, delivered 14.10.1979 as **JI004**; returned to UK 24.02.1984; GR.1A upgrade Warton, GR.3 upgrade; SAOEU Boscombe Down, GR.3A upgrade 2001; No. 16(R) Sqn coded 'A'; No. 6 Sqn; wfu St Athan 07.2005; No. 2 SoTT Cosford as GIA 20.09.2005, extant as GIA.

S11 XX118, ff 24.10.1973. Delivered No. 226 OCU 19.11.1973; No. 6 Sqn; stored 01.1978; BAe Warton 13.02.1980 as **G-27-318**, Jaguar International upgrade and loan to Indian Air Force, delivered 11.12.1979 as **JI018**; returned to UK 25.04.1982; Abingdon as GIA **8815M**; No. 1 SoTT Halton 23.08.1983; returned Abingdon, fuselage dumped by 02.1992.

S12 XX119, ff 05.11.1973. Delivered No. 54 Sqn 17.12.1973; A&AEE; No. 226 OCU, GR.3A upgrade 1998, GR.3A upgrade by 2000; No. 54 Sqn coded 'GD', Operation Resinate deployment 10.2002; No. 16(R) Sqn; DERA; received special 'spotty Jaguar' colour scheme for Jaguar retirement ceremony 29.07.2007; DCAE Cosford 02.07.2007 as GIA **8898M**, Adour trials work for Indian Air Force; Lossiemouth 12.2023 as No. 6 Sqn gate guardian.

S13 XX120, ff 23.11.1973. Delivered No. 54 Sqn 31.01.1974; crashed into the Kattegat off Samsoe Island, Denmark, during Exercise Teamwork 76, Flt Lt Paul Samuel West killed.

S14 XX121, ff 21.12.1973. First aircraft with refuelling probe; delivered No. 226 OCU 01.02.1974; No. 54 Sqn; No. 6 Sqn coded 'EQ'; stored Shawbury 12.11.1984; earmarked for sale to Fuerza Aérea Ecuatoriana as an attrition replacement but deal cancelled; sold to Park Aviation Supply, Charlwood, in 1994 for disposal, to Aerospace Logistics, Charlwood; stored at Jet Art Aviation since 2015.

S15 XX122, ff 11.01.1974. Delivered No. 54 Sqn; crashed into the Wash off Heacham 02.04.1982, the low-altitude audio warning had been set to 0ft due to a calibration error during servicing, Capt Thor Bjørnstad (Royal Norwegian Air Force) killed.

B1 XX136, ff 28.03.1973. Delivered A&AEE 01.07.1973; crashed near Wimborne St Giles, Dorset, after getting into a flat spin 22.11.1974, Wg Cdr C C Rustin and Flt Lt C J Cruickshanks ejected safely.

B2 XX137, ff 26.06.1973. Delivered Jaguar Conversion Team coded 'A' 04.10.1973, No. 226 OCU; crashed into the Moray Firth 06.02.1976 after running out of fuel, Flt Lt A. I. Aitken and Flt Lt R K Jackson ejected safely; wreckage recovered 10.02.1976; target P&EE Shoeburyness.

B3 XX138, ff 10.10.1973. Delivered Jaguar Conversion Team 25.10.1973, No. 226 OCU; BAe Warton 18.12.1978 as **G-27-321**, Jaguar International upgrade and loan to Indian Air Force, delivered 23.07.1979 as **JI001**; BAe as **G-27-332**, sold to Sultan of Oman's Air Force as an attrition replacement in 1982 as serial **200**, overhauled Abingdon 09.83 to 12.83, extant stored at Thumrait.

B4 XX139, ff 05.12.1973. Delivered 10.12.1973; No. 226 OCU coded 'C', T.2A upgrade mid-1985, T.4 upgrade by 2000; No. 16(R) Sqn coded 'T' (later 'PT'); wfu St Athan 12.04.2005; sold to Everett Aero, Sproughton 27.10.2005 for disposal, extant on site.

B5 XX140, ff 21.12.1973. Delivered No. 54 Sqn 29.01.1974; No. 226 OCU; stored Shawbury 04.07.1985; No. 2 SoTT Cosford as GIA **9008M**; sold to Park Aviation Supply, Faygate, for disposal by 05.1999; nose section preserved by a private owner at Selby, North Yorkshire.

B6 XX141, ff 25.01.1974. Delivered Jaguar Conversion Team 13.03.1974, No. 226 OCU, coded 'E' by 11.1981, T.2A upgrade by 02.1985; No. 16(R) Sqn; No. 6 Sqn; wfu post-1996; Aircraft Maintenance Instruction Flight Cranwell as GIA **9297M**, extant as GIA.

B7 XX142, ff 29.03.1974. Delivered Jaguar Conversion Team coded 'G' 08.05.1974, No. 226 OCU; crashed into the Moray Firth 10nm north of Lossiemouth after loss of control while flying inverted 22.06.1979, Capt Rasmussen (Royal Danish Air Force) and instructor Flt Lt John Skinner killed.

B8 XX143, ff 14.03.1974. Delivered 18.04.1974; bird strike 29.05.1975, repairs taking almost two years; BAe Warton 21.12.1978 as **G-27-321**, Jaguar International upgrade and loan to Indian Air Force, delivered 14.10.79 as **JI002**; returned to UK 09.09.1982; T.2A upgrade; No. 226 OCU; No. 54 Sqn, T.2B upgrade St Athan in 1993 abandoned due to insufficient remaining airframe fatigue life; No. 16(R) Sqn; crashed into the Moray Firth after the student pilot shut down the wrong engine after engine fire 18.09.1996, both pilots ejected safely.

B9 XX144, ff 11.06.1974. Delivered Jaguar Conversion Team 11.07.1974, No. 226 OCU; No. 54 Sqn 02.11.1976; No. 6 Sqn 02.1981, T.2A upgrade in mid-1985; No. 226 OCU/No. 16(R) Sqn coded 'U'; wfu Shawbury 2000; sold to Everett Aero, Sproughton, in 2005 for disposal, extant on site.

B10 XX145, ff 24.05.1974. Delivered Jaguar Conversion Team 14.07.1974, No. 226 OCU; ETPS early 1980s; wfu mid-2006; Boscombe Down Aviation Collection at Old Sarum, Wiltshire 24.08.2023, extant on display.

B11 XX146, ff 25.05.1974. Delivered 10.07.1974; engine failure on take-off from Coltishall 30.08.1984, T.2A upgrade; No. 16(R) Sqn coded 'J' by 03.1993, T.4 upgrade by 2000; wfu St Athan 07.03.2005; sold to Everett Aero, Sproughton, on 06.12.2005 for disposal, Bradwell Bay Military & Science Museum 05.2017; Solway Aviation Museum, Carlisle Airport 07.2022, extant on display.

B12 XX147, ff 02.07.1974. Delivered Jaguar Conversion Team 20.08.1974, No. 226 OCU; No. 2 Sqn in 1976; No. 17 Sqn coded 'BY'; crashed due to a bird strike at Sudlohn Borken, West Germany 26.03.1979, Flt. Lt M Brooks and Flt Lt W Kirkpatrick ejected safely.

The brand-new Jaguar T.2 XX145 of No. 226 OCU at Saint-Dizier on 2 October 1974. *Author's Collection*

B13 XX148, ff 13.08.1974. Delivered Jaguar Conversion Team coded 'M' 13.09.1974, No. 226 OCU; crashed near Whittingham, Northumberland 29.07.1977, Flt Lt Hinchcliffe and Fg Off R F Graham killed.

B14 XX149, ff 27.08.1974. Delivered Jaguar Conversion Team coded 'N' 20.09.1974, No. 226 OCU; crashed into a mountain at Cullen, Banff 27.04.1978, Flt Lt C Everitt and Flt Lt J Rigby initiated ejection just before impact but were killed.

B15 XX150, ff 30.09.1974. Delivered No. 6 Sqn 23.10.1974; No. 20 Sqn; No. 14 Sqn; No. 31 Sqn, T.2A upgrade; stored Shawbury 11.1985 to 06.1989; No. 226 OCU, T.4 upgrade, loan to DERA, returned No. 16(R) Sqn coded 'PW'; No. 41 Sqn 03.2005; wfu St Athan 09.01.2006; sold to Everett Aero, Bentwaters 09.08.2006 for disposal; sold to Honeywell for F125IN installation trials for Indian Air Force; Pima Air & Space Museum 14.10.2021, extant on display.

Second production order

The second order covered 81 aircraft: 61 Jaguar GR.1, c/n S16–S76 and 20 T.2, c/n B16–B35.

S16 XX719, ff 31.01.1974. Delivered No. 226 OCU 04.03.1974; No. 54 Sqn; No. 6 Sqn, GR.1A upgrade, Phase 1 upgrade for first Operation Granby roulement 08.1990; sold to the Royal Air Force of Oman as an attrition replacement, delivered 10.08.1998 as serial **226**, stored at Thumrait.

S17 XX720, ff 16.04.1974. Delivered A&AEE 08.05.1974, aerial refuelling, hot-weather trials in USA and cold weather trials in Canada 1975; BAe Warton 22.05.1979 as **G-27-319**, Jaguar International upgrade and loan to Indian Air Force, delivered 23.07.1979 as **JI003**; returned to UK 24.02.1982, GR.1A upgrade Warton; No. 54 Sqn; No. 6 Sqn coded 'EN'; stored mid-1992 to late 1995; GR.1B upgrade, No. 54 Sqn 'GB'; No. 41 Sqn, GR.3 upgrade then GR.3A upgrade 2001; wfu 04.2006 St Athan; sold to Everett Aero, Bentwaters 26.01.2007 for disposal; sold to a private owner in Kent in 2019.

S18 XX721, ff 06.03.1974. Delivered No. 54 Sqn 28.02.1974; crashed 8nm south of Hahn Air Base, West Germany, following double engine flameout 12.06.1983, Capt. Nils Halvgaard (Royal Danish Air Force) ejected but seriously injured.

S19 XX722, ff 28.02.1974. Delivered No. 54 Sqn coded 'GF' 20.03.1974; No. 6 Sqn; stored Shawbury 22.02.1985; BAe Warton 07.1993 for possible sale to Fuerza Aérea Ecuatoriana but deal fell through, returned to Shawbury; DARA St Athan 25.06.1997 as Battle Damage Repair Training airframe; Aircraft Recovery and Transportation Flight; sold 05.01.2006 for scrapping, nose section extant preserved at St Athan.

S20 XX723, ff 19.03.1974. Delivered 198.04.1974; No. 54 Sqn coded 'GG', GR.1A upgrade then GR.1B upgrade, GR.3A upgrade late 1999; loan to DERA 11.999, returned to No. 54 Sqn 'GQ'; No. 41 Sqn 11.03.2005; No. 6 Sqn 'FF' 01.04.2006; stored Shawbury 14.12.2005; DCAE Cosford 24.04.2007, extant as GIA.

S21 XX724, ff 26.04.1974. Delivered A&AEE 29.05.1974, used for aerial refuelling trials; No. 54 Sqn coded 'GA'; stored Shawbury 27.02.1989; overhauled before issue to No. 54 Sqn 'GC' 26.04.2001, GR.3A upgrade St Athan 03.2003; No. 6 Sqn 03.2005; DCAE Cosford 13.06.2007, extant as GIA.

S22 XX725, ff 08.05.1974. Delivered No. 54 Sqn 30.05.1974; BAe Warton 22.05.1979 as **G-27-325**, Jaguar International upgrade and loan to Indian Air Force, delivered 13.02.1980 as **JI010**; returned to UK 19.04.1984, GR.1A upgrade; No. 6 Sqn coded 'EL' 12.08.1985, Phase 2 upgrade for second Operation Granby roulement 23.10.1990, coded 'T' and named 'Johnny Fartpants', flew 47 missions; 6 Sqn 'GU' by 07.1991; GR.1B upgrade, Operation Deliberate Force deployment 09.1995, flew 7 lasing missions, GR.3A upgrade 1999; SAOEU; No. 54 Sqn 'GU'; No. 41 Sqn; No. 6 Sqn 'FE', received 'Flying Canopeners' nose art and recoded 'T' 29.06.2007; DCAE Cosford 02.07.2007, extant as GIA 'KC-F' commemorating Line Training Flight 238 Sqn's Second World War role.

S23 XX726, ff 07.05.1974. First aircraft with definitive LRMTS nose; delivered No. 6 Sqn 30.05.1974; stored from 1985; No. 1 SoTT Halton as GIA **8947M**; No. 2 SoTT Cosford, extant as GIA.

S24 XX727, ff 14.05.1974. Delivered No. 54 Sqn coded 'GC' 16.07.1974; No. 6 Sqn; stored from 1984; No. 2 SoTT Cosford as GIA **8951M** in 1988; preserved at South Wales Aviation Museum, extant on display.

S25 XX728, ff 29.05.1974. Delivered No. 226 OCU; No. 6 Sqn; BAe Warton as **G-27-324**, Jaguar International upgrade and loan to Indian Air Force, delivered 29.04.1980 as **JI009**; returned to UK 23.07.1982 and stored; No. 6 Sqn 11.07.1983, GR.1A upgrade; mid-air collision with GR.1 XX731 at Hartside Pass, Cumbria 07.10.1985, Fg Off Friday ejected safely.

S26 XX729, ff 03.06.1974. Delivered No. 226 OCU 08.07.1974; No. 6 Sqn; BAe Warton 22.05.1979 as **G-27-326**, Jaguar International upgrade and loan to Indian Air Force, delivered 19.08.1980 as **JI012**; returned to UK 25.05.1982 and stored; No. 54 Sqn 25.07.1983; No. 6 Sqn in 1984, GR.1A upgrade 1987; No. 226 OCU; No. 54 Sqn coded 'GC'; No. 6 Sqn, GR.1B upgrade 1995, loan to SAOEU, GR.3 upgrade by 1999 then GR.3A upgrade 2002; No. 41 Sqn coded 'EL', Operation Resinate deployment 10.2002; DCAE Cosford 18.05.2007, extant as GIA.

S27 XX730, ff 13.06.1974. Delivered No. 226 OCU 30.09.1974; No. 6 Sqn, loan to No. 54 Sqn for Exercise Red Flag 1980; stored Shawbury from 1985; No. 2 SoTT Cosford as GIA **8952M**; sold to Polish Aviation Museum, Krakow 03.2010, extant on display.

S28 XX731, ff 29.05.1974. Delivered No. 54 Sqn 16.08.1974; No. 6 Sqn, GR.1A upgrade; mid-air collision with GR.1 XX728 at Hartside Pass, Cumbria 07.10.1985, Flt Lt Leonard Stovin killed.

S29 XX732, ff 08.07.1974. Delivered No. 54 Sqn 19.07.1974; No. 6 Sqn 10.1983, GR.1A upgrade; No. 226 OCU coded '03' 08.11.1985; crashed 9.5nm south-west of Hawick 27.11.1986, Capt. David Bateau (USAF) killed.

S30 XX733, ff 17.107.1974. Delivered No. 6 Sqn 21.08.1974; A&AEE; No. 54 Sqn, GR.1A upgrade, Phase 2 upgrade for second Operation Granby roulement 23.10.1990, coded 'R' and named 'Pink Spitfire', flew 39 missions; 41 Sqn 'ER' by 07.1991, participated in Operations Grapple and Warden, GR.1B upgrade 1995; crashed at Coltishall when the pilot failed to engage reheat on take-off and the struck the barrier 23.01.1996, Flt Lt Gregory Mark Noble killed.

S31 XX734, ff 05.08.1974. Delivered No. 6 Sqn 22.08.1974; BAe Warton as **G-27-328**, Jaguar International upgrade and loan to Indian Air Force, delivered 14.08.1980 as **JI014**; returned to UK 11.02.1982; stored Shawbury; Coltishall as GIA **8816M** for Battle Damage Repair Training 11.1984; sold to Park Aviation, Charlwood, for disposal; Boscombe Down Aviation Collection, extant on display.

S32 XX735, ff 15.08.1974. Delivered No. 6 Sqn 13.09.1974; crashed near Eggebeck, West Germany, during Exercise Teamwork 76 15.09.1976, Flt Lt Geoff Sheppard killed.

S33 XX736, ff 27.08.1974. Delivered 30.09.1974; BAe Warton as **G-27-327**, Jaguar International upgrade and loan to Indian Air Force, delivered 13.02.1980 as **JI013**; returned to UK 24.02.1984 and stored; Coltishall as GIA **9110M** for Battle Damage Repair Training 1992; nose and tail transferred to BAE Systems Brough for fatigue testing in late 1996; nose section preserved at South Yorkshire Aircraft Museum at Doncaster, won Grand Champion Award at Newark Cockpit-Fest 2023.

S34 XX737, ff 27.08.1974. Delivered 27.09.1974; BAe Warton as **G-27-330**, Jaguar International upgrade and loan to Indian Air Force, delivered 14.08.1980 as **JI015**; returned to UK 25.08.1982, GR.1A upgrade; No. 54 Sqn; stored Shawbury 05.1989 to 11.1994; No. 6 Sqn coded 'EE', GR.3 upgrade mid-1997 then GR.3A upgrade 2001; wfu St Athan for spares recovery 15.12.2005; sold to Everett Aero, Bentwaters 21.07.2006 for disposal; sold to Honeywell for F125IN installation trials for Indian Air Force; Pima Air & Space Museum 14.10.2021; extant on display.

S35 XX738, ff 09.09.1974. Delivered 27.09.1975; BAe Warton as **G-27-329**, Jaguar International upgrade and loan to Indian Air Force, delivered 13.02.1980 as **JI016**; returned to UK 19.04.1984, GR.1A upgrade; No. 54 Sqn; stored Shawbury 11.1990 to 12.1993; GR.1B upgrade; No. 6 Sqn 12.12.1994; No. 54 Sqn 02.1995, loan to SAOEU 09.1996 to 03.1997, GR.3 upgrade then GR.3A upgrade, Operation Resinate deployment 10.2002 coded 'GG'; No. 6 Sqn 'ED' 10.2005; DCAE Cosford 18.05.2007, extant as GIA.

S36 XX739, ff 17.09.1974. Delivered No. 6 Sqn 23.10.1974, later operated by Gibraltar Detachment; stored Shawbury from 10.1985; No. 1 SoTT Halton in 12.1986 as GIA **8902M**; No. 2 SoTT Cosford; sold to Delta Force Paintball, Hockley Heath, Solihull 05.2018, extant.

S37 XX740, ff 25.09.1974. Delivered 23.10.1974; BAe Warton as **G-27-331**, converted to Jaguar International standard for loan to Indian Air Force, delivered 13.02.1980 as **JI017**; returned to UK 19.05.1984; sold to Sultan of Oman's Air Force as an attrition replacement as serial **225**, delivery 04.11.1986, currently stored at Thumrait.

XX733 with No. 54 Squadron at the time of Operation Granby. It was Squadron Leader Dave Bagshaw's aircraft, nicknamed 'Pink Spitfire', and is seen here at Coltishall in May 1991. *Terry Panopalis Collection*

S38 XX741, ff 04.10.1974. Delivered No. 226 OCU 18.11.1974; No. 54 Sqn; No. 6 Sqn, Phase 1 upgrade for first Operation Granby roulement 08.1990; stored Shawbury from 08.1994; sold to Everett Aero, Sproughton, 18.11.2005 for disposal; preserved in taxiable condition at Bentwaters Cold War Museum.

S39 XX742, ff 21.10.1974. Delivered A&AEE 15.11.1974 for engine stall trials; No. 226 OCU; No. 6 Sqn 05.01.1976; crashed into North Sea 35nm off Bacton due to an uncommanded flight control manoeuvre 19.04.1983, Fg Off J L Jackson ejected but seriously injured.

S40 XX743, ff 20.10.1974. Delivered No. 6 Sqn coded 'EG' 26.11.1974; stored Shawbury 05.02.1985; No. 1 SoTT Halton as GIA **8949M**; No. 2 SoTT Cosford 09.1994; preserved at Morayvia Sci-Tech Experience Project at Kinloss, extant on display.

S41 XX744, ff 07.11.1974. Delivered A&AEE 05.12.1974; to No. 17 Sqn; No. 14 Sqn; No. 6 Sqn; No. 31 Sqn coded 'DG'; No. 17 Sqn 09.1983; No. 31 Sqn 'DJ' 01.1984; stored Shawbury 02.1985; BAe Warton 07.1993 for possible sale to Fuerza Aérea Ecuatoriana but deal fell through, returned to Shawbury; Coltishall as GIA **9251M** 05.1998; sold to Everett Aero, Sproughton, for disposal by 07.2002; extant at Mayhem Paintball, Abridge, Essex.

S42 XX745, ff 05.11.1974. Delivered No. 226 OCU 16.12.1974; No. 20 Sqn 10.1976; No. 6 Sqn 03.1979, GR.1A upgrade Abingdon 1984; No. 54 Sqn; No. 226 OCU 12.1986; No. 6 Sqn 08.1988; No. 16(R) Sqn coded 'D'; No. 54 Sqn 'GV'; damaged in a mid-air collision with XX832 07.2000; stored Shawbury 11.2000; used as a spares source Boscombe Down, stripped to nose section; No. 1350 Sqn ATC Fareham; sold to a private owner 03.2022.

S43 XX746, ff 04.12.1974. Delivered No. 226 OCU 20.12.1974; No. 31 Sqn; No. 6 Sqn; No. 17 Sqn; No. 14 Sqn coded 'AB'; No. 226 OCU 11.1985; stored Shawbury; No. 1 SoTT Halton 08.1986 as GIA **8895M**; No. 2 SoTT Cosford, wfu and stored 2023.

S44 XX747, ff 04.12.1974. Delivered No. 226 OCU 20.12.1974; No. 54 Sqn 02.1980; No. 17 Sqn 01.1983; No. 31 Sqn 09.1983; No. 20 Sqn 11.1983; No. 6 Sqn by 08.1984, part of the Gibraltar Detachment until 10.1985; No. 1 SoTT Halton as GIA **8903M**; Airframe Technology Flight Cranwell; Boscombe Down 2014; sold to Jet Art Aviation 03.2019 and restored, current status unknown.

S45 XX748, ff 24.12.1974. Delivered No. 226 OCU coded '20' 05.02.1975; No. 14 Sqn 08.1983; No. 54 Sqn 10.1985; stored Shawbury; GR.1A and Phase 2 upgrade for second Operation Granby roulement 02.11.1990, coded 'U', flew 36 missions; GR.1B upgrade, GR.3 upgrade 07.2000, then GR.3A upgrade; No. 54 Sqn 'GK', Operation Resinate deployment 10.2002; No. 6 Sqn 'EG' 03.2005; DCAE Cosford 18.05.2007, extant as GIA.

S46 XX749, ff 14.01.1975. Delivered No. 226 OCU 17.02.1975; nosewheel collapse 04.1975, grounded until 06.1976 for repair; mid-air collision with XX755, crashed near Lumsden, Aberdeenshire 10.12.1979, Flt Lt Nicholas James Brown killed.

S47 XX750, ff 16.01.1975. Delivered No. 226 OCU coded '22' 17.02.1975; No. 14 Sqn 1983; struck the ground during a Red Flag deployment at Nellis range, Nevada 07.02.1984, Flt Lt Jackson killed.

S48 XX751, ff 27.01.1975. Delivered No. 14 Sqn 14.04.1975; No. 226 OCU; stored Abingdon; No. 2 SoTT Cosford 03.1988 as GIA **8937M**; sold to a private owner in Surrey; extant on display at the Iron Curtain Museum, Guildford, from 04.05.2024.

S49 XX752, ff 07.02.1975. Delivered No. 54 Sqn 04.03.1975; No. 226 OCU coded '06', GR.1A upgrade; No. 54 Sqn 'GF'; stored Shawbury 12.1988 to 10.1990; No. 6 Sqn by 06.1991, GR.3A upgrade St Athan by 2000; No. 16(R) Sqn 'D' 03.2000; No. 41 Sqn 'FC' 12.2001; No. 6 Sqn 'EK' 03.2005; wfu St Athan 01.08.2006; DCAE Cosford 13.06.2007, extant as GIA.

S50 XX753, ff 24.02.1975. Delivered No. 6 Sqn 18.03.1975; No. 226 OCU coded '05', loan to No. 54 Sqn 02.1980 for Red Flag deployment; stored Shawbury by 11.1990; nose section to RAF Exhibition Flight as **9087M**; extant on display at Newark Air Museum.

S51 XX754, ff 12.03.1975. Delivered No. 226 OCU 22.04.1975, loan to No. 54 Sqn for Red Flag deployment 02.1980, coded '23' by 05.1981, GR.1A upgrade 01.1987; No. 6 Sqn by 06.1990, Phase 2 upgrade for second Operation Granby roulement 02.11.1990, impacted sand dune in Qatar during low-altitude training flight, Flt Lt Keith Collister killed.

S52 XX755, ff 12.03.1975. Delivered 14.04.1975; No. 14 Sqn; No. 226 OCU; mid-air collision with XX749, crashed near Lumsden, Aberdeenshire 10.12.1979, pilot ejected safely.

S53 XX756, ff 21.03.1975. First aircraft delivered directly to Germany for No. 14 Sqn 23.04.1975; No. 226 OCU coded '07' 10.1975; No. 20 Sqn; No. 14 Sqn coded 'AM'; No. 2 SoTT Cosford by 10.1986 as GIA **8899M**, extant as GIA.

S54 XX757, ff 03.04.1975. Delivered No. 14 Sqn 06.05.1975; No. 226 OCU; No. 20 Sqn; stored Shawbury 07.1984; No. 1 SoTT Halton by 03.1988 as GIA **8948M**; No. 2 SoTT Cosford; Brazilian Air Force Aerospace Museum, Rio de Janeiro, in 2012, extant on display.

S55 XX758, ff 11.04.1975. Delivered No. 14 Sqn 02.05.1975; No. 226 OCU coded '18' 10.1975; flew into ground in a snowstorm 12nm north-west of Dingwall, Scotland 18.11.1981, Fg Off A Crowther killed.

S56 XX759, ff 18.04.1975. Delivered No. 14 Sqn 01.05.1975; No. 226 OCU 10.1975; crashed near Selkirk, Scotland 01.11.1978, Cesar Raul Aguirre (Fuerza Aérea Ecuatoriana) killed.

S57 XX760, ff 30.04.1975. Delivered No. 14 Sqn coded 'AL' 22.05.1975; No. 226 OCU 11.1975; No. 14 Sqn coded 'AA' 12.1976; crashed due to uncontained engine failure 1.7nm north of Rogart, Scotland 13.09.1982, Flt Lt D Steve Griggs ejected safely (this was Griggs' second Jaguar ejection – see XX963).

S58 XX761, ff 24.04.1975. Delivered No. 14 Sqn 04.06.1975; No. 226 OCU 11.1975; written off after engine explosion and ground fire 06.06.1978, retained at Lossiemouth as GIA **8600M**; front fuselage preserved on display at Boscombe Down Aviation Collection.

S59 XX762, ff 14.05.1975. Delivered No. 14 Sqn 04.06.1975 coded 'H'; No. 226 OCU 1976; crashed 2,000ft (610m) up Beinn a'Chleigh mountain near Dalmally, Argyle 23.11.1979, Flt Lt Alan Graham Proctor ejected but died from head trauma and hypothermia.

S60 XX763, ff 12.05.1975. Delivered No. 226 OCU 26.06.1975; stored Shawbury by 04.1985; No. 4 SoTT St Athan as GIA **9009M**; sold to a private owner at Winterpick Industrial Estate, Blackstone, West Sussex; Bournemouth Air Museum from 09.2009, extant on display.

S61 XX764, ff 07.06.1975. Delivered No. 14 Sqn 04.07.1975 coded 'J'; No. 226 OCU 11.1975; stored Shawbury 09.1984; No. 4 SoTT St Athan by 07.1989 as GIA **9010M**; sold to a private owner at Enstone, Oxfordshire, extant under restoration.

S62 XX765, ff 13.06.1975. Delivered No. 14 Sqn 02.07.1975, loan to No. 17 Sqn; No. 226 OCU 03.12.1975; stored Abingdon 06.1976; BAe 04.08.1978 for conversion into Active Control Technology testbed, ff 20.10.1981; donated to Loughborough University as a teaching aid 16.01.1991; Royal Air Force Museum Cosford since 07.1996 (returned to display 06.2024).

S63 XX766, ff 14.06.1975. Delivered No. 14 Sqn 08.07.1975; No. 226 OCU coded '14' 12.1975; SBAC Farnborough as 'Jaguar International' 09.1978; GR.1A upgrade Abingdon 01.1984; No. 54 Sqn 'GP'; No. 6 Sqn 'EC' 02.1989, Phase 3 upgrade for Operation Granby by 14.02.1991 but not deployed, recoded 'EA' 1992, GR.3A upgrade 2001; No. 16(R) Sqn 'PE' 05.2001, received special '30 Years Jaguar' markings 19.09.2003; DCAE Cosford 31.01.2006, extant as GIA.

S64 XX767, ff 25.06.1975. Delivered No. 14 Sqn 18.05.1975; No. 226 OCU; No. 14 Sqn; No. 31 Sqn; No. 17 Sqn, GR.1A upgrade; No. 54 Sqn 09.1986, Phase 3 upgrade for Operation Granby by 14.02.1991 but not deployed, GR.1B upgrade 1995, GR.3 upgrade 2000, Operation Resinate deployment 10.2002 coded 'GE'; No. 41 Sqn 'FK' 03.2005; wfu Shawbury 11.04.2006; DCAE Cosford 20.03.2007, extant as GIA 'Z'.

S65 XX768, ff 02.07.1975. Delivered No. 14 Sqn 12.08.1975; No. 17 Sqn coded 'BA'; crashed due to engine failure and fire near Heinsberg-Rauderath, West Germany 29.09.1982, Wg Cdr Lovett ejected safely.

S66 XX817, ff 10.07.1975. Delivered No. 17 Sqn 20.08.1975; crashed due to inflight fire caused by fuel leak 6nm from Brüggen 17.07.1980, Flt Lt J Wittingham ejected safely.

S67 XX818, ff 10.07.1975. Delivered No. 17 Sqn 15.08.1975; No. 20 Sqn coded 'CC'; No. 31 Sqn 'DE'; stored Shawbury 11.1984; No. 1 SoTT Halton 03.1988 as GIA **8945M**; No. 2 SoTT Cosford; wfu Shawbury; Waddington 10.2019 for fire training.

Two groundcrew take the opportunity of a siesta beside GR.1 XX752 during a visit by No. 54(F) Squadron to Escadron de Chasse 3/7 'Languedoc' at BA 113 Saint-Dizier-Robinson in May 1975. ***Author's Collection***

S68 XX819, ff 05.08.1975. Delivered No. 17 Sqn 20.08.1975; No. 20 Sqn, loan to No. 226 OCU 02.1982; stored Shawbury 05.1984; No. 2 SoTT Cosford 01.2000 as GIA **8923M**; wfu and stored 2023.

S69 XX820, ff 13.08.1975. Delivered No. 17 Sqn 03.09.1975; No. 20 Sqn; crashed on approach to **Brüggen** following engine failure caused by ingesting an auxiliary intake door hinge bolt 11.06.1982, Flt Lt Colin Turner ejected safely.

S70 XX821, ff 14.08.1975. Delivered No. 17 Sqn 01.09.1975; No. 14 Sqn; No. 41 Sqn coded 'P'; stored Shawbury; Servicing Instructional Flight Cranwell 07.1986 as GIA **8896M**, extant as GIA.

S71 XX822, ff 29.08.1975. Delivered No. 14 Sqn 22.09.1975; crashed 13nm west of Aldorn, West Germany 02.07.1976, Flt Lt T M Bushnell killed (first RAF Jaguar fatality).

S72 XX823, ff 22.08.1975. Delivered No. 17 Sqn 15.09.1975; crashed into a hill near Cagliari, Sardinia 25.07.1978, Flt Lt Roger John West killed.

S73 XX824, ff 02.09.1975. Delivered No. 14 Sqn 23.09.1975; No. 17 Sqn coded 'BH'; stored Shawbury 11.1985; No. 1 SoTT Halton by 01.1990 as GIA **9019M**; No. 2 SoTT Cosford; extant on display at Royal Air Force Museum Hendon.

S74 XX825, ff 14.09.1975. Delivered No. 14 Sqn 16.10.1975; No. 31 Sqn; No. 17 Sqn; stored Shawbury; No. 1 SoTT Halton as GIA **9020M**; No. 2 SoTT Cosford, wfu and stored 2023.

S75 XX826, ff 12.09.1976. Delivered No. 14 Sqn coded 'AD' 02.10.1975; No. 20 Sqn; No. II(AC) Sqn; stored Shawbury 03.1985; No. 2 SoTT Cosford as GIA **9021M**; sold to Everett Aero, Sproughton 01.109.2006 for disposal; sold to a private owner in Welshpool; nose section extant at Atlantic Air Adventure, Shannon, Eire.

S76 XX827, ff 22.09.1975. Delivered No. 14 Sqn 06.10.1975; No. 20 Sqn 03.1977; No. 17 Sqn coded 'BM' by 09.1978; crashed during a Red Flag deployment at Nellis range, Nevada 12.02.1981, Flt Lt David Plumbe killed.

B16 XX828, ff 07.10.1974. Delivered No. 226 OCU coded 'P' 07.11.1974; crashed following a bird strike and double engine failure 4nm north of Forfar, Scotland 01.06.1981, Flt Lt Dave Webb and Flt Lt I P Kenvyn ejected safely.

B17 XX829, ff 28.11.1974. Delivered No. 54 Sqn coded 'GT' 23.12.1974; No. 6 Sqn 'ER' by 01.1985, T.2A upgrade, loan to No. 226 OCU, returned recoded 'ET' 10.1989; No. 16(R) Sqn 03.1994; No. 54 Sqn 05.1994; wfu Shawbury 06.03.2001; sold to Everett Aero, Sproughton, for disposal; extant on display at Newark Air Museum.

B18 XX830, ff 25.11.1974. Delivered No. 226 OCU 20.12.1974; ETPS 1986; stored St Athan 11.1996, moved to Shawbury 02.1999; fuselage to BAe Warton for T.2A development work; Coltishall 07.2000 as GIA **9293M**; nose section extant on display at City of Norwich Aviation Museum, the remainder of the airframe was scrapped at Bruntingthorpe.

B19 XX831, ff 10.12.1974. Delivered A&AEE for engine flameout tests; No. 226 OCU coded 'W' 21.03.1975; crashed due to a flying control restriction at Lossiemouth 30.04.1975, pilot ejected safely.

B20 XX832, ff 16.12.1974. Delivered No. 226 OCU 03.02.1975; stored Shawbury 01.1991; No. 16(R) Sqn 05.1995, T.2A upgrade; No. 6 Sqn coded 'EZ' by 09.1999; damaged in a mid-air collision with XX745 07.2000; sold to Everett Aero, Bentwaters, for disposal; sold to a private owner at Chino, California, by 05.2015. Still extant at Chino in No. 6 Sqn markings 02.2024.

B21 XX833, ff 17.01.1975. Delivered No. 226 OCU 20.02.1975; No. 20 Sqn 1977; No. 14 Sqn coded 'AY' 1984, T.2A upgrade; RAE, DRA Experimental Flying Squadron 1992, TIALD testbed named 'Night Cat', QinetiQ 07.2001; made last UK Jaguar flight 20.12.2007, extant as GIA.

B22 XX834, ff 05.02.1975. Delivered No. 226 OCU 17.03.1975; No. 14 Sqn; No. II(AC) Sqn; return to No. 14 Sqn; struck power line cables and crashed near Wildbad-Kreuth, West Germany 07.09.1988, Flt Lt Sheridan Paul Nelson killed, rear-seater 1st Lt Jerry Black (USAF) ejected safely.

B23 XX835, ff 14.02.1975. Delivered No. 226 OCU 17.03.1975; RAE 09.1986, T.2B upgrade; No. 54 Sqn 1995; No. 6 Sqn; No. 41 Sqn, T.4 upgrade; No. 6 Sqn coded 'EX', received special tail fin markings for the RAF's 100th anniversary (port) and Cosford's 80th anniversary (starboard) in 2018, recoded 'P'; DCAE Cosford 02.07.2007, extant as GIA.

B24 XX836, ff 08.03.1975. Delivered No. 54 Sqn 12.03.1975; No. 14 Sqn 07.04.1975; No. 17 Sqn, T.2A upgrade Abingdon 10.1985; No. 6 Sqn coded 'ER'; stored Shawbury 1989; sold to Everett Aero for disposal 05.2005, extant on site.

B25 XX837, ff 21.03.1975. Delivered No. 226 OCU 23.05.1975; stored 1986; No. 1 SoTT Halton 1989 as GIA **8978M**; No. 2 SoTT Cosford, extant as GIA.

B26 XX838, ff 05.04.1975. Delivered No. 226 OCU 29.04.1975; stored Shawbury 09.1991 to 06.1998, T.4 upgrade St Athan; No. 16(R) Sqn coded 'R' 05.1999; No. 41 Sqn 03.2005; wfu St Athan 29.11.2005; sold to Everett Aero, Bentwaters, for disposal in 2006, extant on site.

B27 XX839, ff 18.04.1975. Delivered No. 226 OCU 22.05.1975; No. 54 Sqn by 04.1995, wfu due to structural issues 10.1995; CTTS St Athan as GIA **9256M**; sold to Cronifer Metals, Chesterfield, for scrapping 05.2002.

B28 XX840, ff 17.05.1975. Delivered No. 17 Sqn 12.06.1975; No. 20 Sqn 09.1989; stored St Athan 10.990 to 09.1998, T.4 upgrade; No. 16(R) Sqn coded 'PS' 05.1999; No. 6 Sqn 03.2006; stored St Athan 29.03.2006; No. 6 Sqn 'EY' 09.05.2006; DCAE Cosford 13.06.2007, extant as GIA.

B29 XX841, ff 16.05.1975. Delivery delayed by loan to BAC for display at 1975 Paris Salon; No. 226 OCU 27.06.1975; No. 41 Sqn by 04.1985; stored 05.1986; ETPS early 1990; No. 6 Sqn 06.1992, T.4 upgrade St Athan 10.1999; No. 226 OCU coded 'T', No. 16(R) Sqn coded 'PQ'; No. 6 Sqn 'EW' 03.2006; wfu Shawbury 15.08.2006; sold to Everett Aero, Bentwaters, for disposal 24.07.2007; sold to a succession of private owners, currently at North Weald.

B30 XX842, ff 04.06.1975. Delivered No. 226 OCU 30.06.1975; No. 54 Sqn 07.1975; No. 41 Sqn 09.1976, T.2A upgrade; No. II(AC) Sqn late 1986; No. 6 Sqn 10.1988, loan to ETPS and RAE 1989–90; stored Shawbury 08.1994; No. 41 Sqn coded 'FV' 07.1996, T.4 upgrade 10.2000, loan to BAE Systems for Adour Mk.106 upgrade trials; No. 16(R) Sqn 31.10.2002; No. 41 Sqn 'FX' 03.2005; wfu St Athan 02.2006; sold to Everett Aero, Bentwaters, for disposal 10.08.2006, extant on site.

B31 XX843, ff 24.06.1975. Delivered No. 226 OCU 08.07.1975; No. II(AC) Sqn by 05.1976, T.2A upgrade 1985; No. 54 Sqn coded 'GT' 08.1987; mid-air collision with Cessna 152 G-BMHI over Carno, near Newtown, Powys 29.08.1991, both pilots ejected but back-seater Wg Cdr J Marden was killed, as was the Cessna pilot.

B32 XX844, ff 05.08.1975. Delivered No. 31 Sqn 27.08.1975; No. 17 Sqn; No. 226 OCU, loan to A&AEE 07.1987; No. 2 SoTT Cosford 1990 as GIA **9023M**; scrapped St Athan 01.1998.

B33 XX845, ff 12.08.1975. Delivered No. 17 Sqn 27.08.1975; No. 20 Sqn; No. II(AC) Sqn; No. 17 Sqn; No. 14 Sqn coded 'AZ'; No. 226 OCU, T.2A upgrade; No. 41 Sqn 02.1989; No. 226 OCU 09.1993; No. 6 Sqn 'ET' 06.1994, T.4 upgrade St Athan, recoded 'EV' 03.2005; wfu St Athan 01.06.2005; DCAE Cosford 17.10.2005; currently stored dismantled at the South Wales Aviation Museum.

B34 XX846, ff 21.08.1975. Retained by BAC for sales tour to Middle East 11.1975 to 12.1975; delivered No. 226 OCU coded 'A' 14.03.1976, T.2A upgrade 09.1987, loan to RAE 11.1987; No. 41 Sqn 08.1988, loan to ETPS 02.1989, stored Shawbury later that year; No. 226 OCU 05.1992; No. 41 Sqn 07.1993; No. 16(R) Sqn 'V' (later 'PV') 02.1995; wfu 08.2004 as spares source, left Coltishall 20.02.2006.

B35 XX847, ff 23.10.1975. Delivered No. 226 OCU 16.03.1976; No. II(AC) Sqn 06.1976; No. 14 Sqn; No. 20 Sqn; No. 31 Sqn, returned to UK 10.1984; No. 226 OCU by 03.1985; stored Shawbury 07.1986 to 05.1990; T.2A upgrade, No. 41 Sqn by 04.1991; stored St Athan 12.1995; T.4 upgrade 2002, No. 16(R) Sqn coded 'PY' 10.2002; No. 6 Sqn 'EZ' 03.2005; DCAE Cosford 18.05.2007, extant as GIA.

B36 XX915, ff 22.06.1976. Delivered ETPS 20.07.1976; crashed near CDRE Porton Down, Wiltshire due to an engine fire 17.01.1984, Sqn Ldr Tim Allen ejected safely.

B37 XX916, ff 02.12.1976. Delivered ETPS 18.07.1977; crashed into the Bristol Channel off Hartland Point due to a bird strike 24.07.1981, both crew ejected but the back-seater Flt Lt S Sparks drowned.

Third production order

The third production order covered 45 aircraft, all Jaguar GR.1, c/n S77–S121.

S77 XX955, ff 18.09.1975. Delivered No. 14 Sqn 06.10.1976; No. 17 Sqn by 10.1983; No. 14 Sqn coded 'AN' by 10.1984; No. 54 Sqn 10.1985, GR.1A upgrade Abingdon 11.1986; stored Shawbury 05.1998; extant on display at Hermeskeil Museum, Germany, since 05.2005.

XX965 in June 1990 during its time with No. 226 OCU. ***Terry Panopalis Collection***

S78 XX956, ff 26.09.1975. Delivered No. 17 Sqn 22.10.1976; No. 14 Sqn 10.1978; No. 17 Sqn by 03.1979; No. 31 Sqn 08.1984; No. 17 Sqn by 10.1984; stored Shawbury 02.1985; No. 1 SoTT Halton as GIA **8950M** early 1988; No. 2 SoTT Cosford; static display at Gibraltar 2009 to 2020, returned in a dismantled state to Boscombe Down by 10.2021, remains sold to Spey Bay Salvage, Moray.

S79 XX957, ff 03.10.1975. Delivered No. 14 Sqn 24.10.1975; No. 20 Sqn by 03.1977; crashed on approach to Brüggen after a lightning strike caused both engines to flameout 21.10.1981, pilot ejected but injured.

S80 XX958, ff 07.10.1975. Delivered No. 14 Sqn 24.10.1975; No. 17 Sqn by 12.1983; stored Shawbury 03.1985; No. 2 SoTT Cosford as GIA **9022M** by 03.1990, extant as GIA.

S81 XX959, ff 14.10.1975. Delivered No. 14 Sqn 04.11.1975; No. 20 Sqn coded 'CN' by 06.1977, displayed 1981 Paris Salon, recoded 'CJ' 07.1981; stored Shawbury 04.07.1984; No. 2 SoTT Cosford as GIA **8953M** early 1988; wfu and stored 2023.

S82 XX960, ff 18.10.1975. Delivered No. 14 Sqn 03.11.1975 coded 'AK'; struck a TV transmitter mast at Iserlohn, W. Germany 18.07.1979, Flt Lt G A Wardell ejected safely.

S83 XX961, ff 20.10.1975. Delivered No. 17 Sqn 10.11.1975; mid-air collision with XX964 near Brüggen 25.05.1980, Flt Lt J Cathie killed.

S84 XX962, ff 30.10.1975. Delivered No. 17 Sqn; No. 6 Sqn coded 'EK' 08.1986, Phase 2 upgrade for second Operation Granby roulement 02.11.1990, coded 'X' and named 'Fat Slags' (with 'St. Georgina' on portside), flew 37 missions, returned to Coltishall 13.03.1991; GR.1B upgrade Boscombe Down 02.1995, Operation Deliberate Force deployment 09.1995, flew 5 lasing missions; stored Coltishall mid-1996; Aircraft Maintenance Instruction Flight Cranwell as GIA **9275M**; No. 1 SoTT Cosford 07.2002; Pembrey ranges as a target 2009, scrapped 2019 but nose section preserved at Coningsby.

S85 XX963, ff 18.11.1975. Delivered No. 14 Sqn coded 'AL' 02.12.1975; accidently shot down near Wesel, West Germany, by a live AIM-9L Sidewinder fired by No. 92 Sqn Phantom FGR.2 XV422 during a combat exercise 25.05.1982, Flt Lt Steve Griggs ejected safely.

S86 XX964, ff 11.11.1975. Delivered No. 17 Sqn 27.11.1975; mid-air collision with XX961 near Brüggen 25.05.1980, pilot ejected safely.

S87 XX965, ff 06.11.1975. Delivered No. 14 Sqn 21.11.1975, GR.1A upgrade 1983; No. 54 Sqn 08.1984; No. 226 OCU 03.1986 coded 'C', later recoded '07'; stored Coltishall 01.1996; Aircraft Maintenance Instruction Flight Cranwell as GIA **9254M**, extant as GIA.

S88 XX966, ff 19.11.1975. Delivered No. 17 Sqn 02.12.1975; No. 20 Sqn by 09.1978, GR.1A upgrade; No. 54 Sqn 08.1984; No. 6 Sqn by 04.1985; stored Shawbury 09.1985; No. 1 SoTT Halton 12.1986 as GIA **8904M**; No. 2 SoTT Cosford; Pembrey ranges as a target 05.2009.

S89 XX967, ff 24.11.1975. Delivered No. 31 Sqn coded 'DA' 15.01.1976; No. 14 Sqn by 10.1983 'AC'; stored Shawbury by 11.1985; No. 2 SoTT Cosford 07.1989 as GIA **9006M**; Gatwick Aviation Museum 18.04.2024 for restoration and display.

S90 XX968, ff 24.11.1975. Delivered No. 31 Sqn coded 'DB' 19.12.1975; No. 14 Sqn 'AJ' 12.1983; stored Shawbury 11.1987; No. 2 SoTT Cosford 07.1989 as GIA **9007M**, extant as GIA.

S91 XX969, ff 01.12.1975. Delivered No. 31 Sqn coded 'DC' 06.01.1976; No. 226 OCU 11.1983; stored Shawbury by 11.1985; No. 2 SoTT Cosford 08.1996 as GIA **8897M**, extant as GIA.

S92 XX970, ff 08.12.1975. Delivered No. 31 Sqn 06.01.1976; No. 17 Sqn by 01.1984; No. 226 OCU 04.1985; No. 6 Sqn 01.1986, Phase 1 upgrade for first Operation Granby roulement 08.1990, Phase 3 upgrade for Bosnia UN peacekeeping deployment 06.1993 coded 'EH', GR.1B upgrade St Athan 10.1995 to 01.1996, GR.3A upgrade 01.2002; DCAE Cosford 13.06.2007, extant as GIA.

S93 XX971, ff 11.12.1975. Delivered No. 31 Sqn coded 'DE' 06.01.1976; crashed on take-off at CFB Lahr, West Germany 21.03.1978, Flt Lt P A New ejected safely.

S94 XX972, ff 12.12.1975. Delivered No. 31 Sqn 06.01.1976; crashed near Barnard's Castle, Northumberland, during Exercise Osex 4 06.08.1981, Sqn Ldr Roger Martin Matthews killed.

S95 XX973, ff 05.01.1976. Delivered No. 31 Sqn 15.01.1976; crashed 3.5nm south-west of Gutersloh 14.04.1981 due to an unrecoverable spin during an air combat exercise, Sqn Ldr David Milne-Smith ejected safely.

S96 XX974, ff 09.01.1978. Delivered No. 31 Sqn 28.01.1976; No. 6 Sqn coded 'EG' 10.1984, GR.1A upgrade 04.1987, Phase 1 upgrade for first Operation Granby roulement 08.1990; No. 54 Sqn 'GH', Phase 3 upgrade for Bosnia UN peacekeeping deployments 06.1993 and 06.1994; No. 16(R) Sqn 'B', GR.3A upgrade 11.2001; No. 41 Sqn 'FE' 03.2003; wfu St Athan for spares recovery 16.12.2004; sold to Everett Aero, Sproughton 25.10.2005 for disposal; sold to a private owner at Baarlo, Netherlands 08.2006.

S97 XX975, ff 12.01.1976. Delivered A&AEE for UHF radio trials 30.01.1976; No. 31 Sqn 28.05.1976; No. 17 Sqn; No. 226 OCU; stored Shawbury 03.1986; No. 1 SoTT Halton 12.1986 as GIA **8905M**; No. 2 SoTT Cosford, wfu and stored 2023. Sold to Montrose Air Station Heritage Centre 07.2024.

S98 XX976, ff 13.01.1976. Delivered No. 31 Sqn 28.01.1976; No. 17 Sqn 06.1984; stored Shawbury 03.1985; No. 1 SoTT Halton 12.1986 as GIA **8906M**; No. 2 SoTT Cosford, wfu and stored 2023.

S99 XX977, ff 20.03.1976. Delivered No. 31 Sqn 20.02.1976, damaged by bird strike 04.1978, in-flight emergency after clipping a tower at Charwelton, near Northampton, 1984; stored Shawbury 12.1984; Abingdon as Battle Damage Repair Training airframe 12.1984 as **9132M**; St Athan; sold to Everett Aero, Sproughton 01.11.2005 for disposal, nose section preserved by a private owner at Boronia, Victoria, Australia, the fuselage is extant at Sproughton.

S100 XX978, ff 22.01.1976. Delivered No. 31 Sqn coded 'DM' 25.02.1976; struck a house and crashed near Verden, West Germany 14.06.1977, Fg Off Timothy Valentine Penn killed.

S101 XX979, ff 27.01.1976. Delivered A&AEE Boscombe Down 11.02.1976, A&AEE Farnborough 08.1980, displayed 1981 Paris Salon as Jaguar International coded '244'; GR.1A upgrade; stored St Athan 09.1999; Coltishall as a ground procedures trainer **9306M** 19.02.2002, spares recovery by 09.2005 before disposal; cockpit is preserved at the RAF Air Defence Radar Museum, Neatishead, Norfolk.

S102 XZ101, ff 04.02.1976. Delivered No. II(AC) Sqn 26.02.1976 coded 'S'; No. 17 Sqn 08.1982, GR.1A upgrade; No. II (AC) Sqn 08.1984; first GR.1A operated by No. 41 Sqn 07.05.1986; No. 226 OCU early 1993; Boscombe Down as GIA **9282M** 06.1996.

S103 XZ102, ff 11.02.1976. Delivered No. II(AC) Sqn 05.03.1976; crashed 5nm north-east of Laarbruch 14.12.1976, Flt Lt William Langworthy ejected safely.

S104 XZ103, ff 16.02.1976. Delivered No. II(AC) Sqn 27.02.1976, GR.1A upgrade late 1984; stored Shawbury 11.1990 to 06.1992; No. 41 Sqn coded 'P', recoded 'FP', GR.3 upgrade St Athan 05.1998 to 08.1998, suffered a multiple bird strike over Hepburn with emergency landing at Newcastle Airport 16.11.1998, repaired St Athan and GR.3A upgrade by 01.2000, No. 41 Sqn display aircraft 2005; No. 6 Sqn 'EF' 03.2006; DCAE Cosford 13.06.2007, extant as GIA.

S105 XZ104, ff 25.02.1976. Delivered No. II(AC) Sqn coded 'N' 11.03.1976; No. 6 Sqn 01.1989; No. 41 Sqn 'FM', reserve aircraft for Operation Granby, Bosnia UN peacekeeping deployment, GR.3 upgrade, loan to SAOEU 08.1996; stored St Athan 11.07.2005; DCAE Cosford 27.10.2005, extant as GIA.

S106 XZ105, ff 13.02.1976. Delivered No. II(AC) Sqn coded 'Y' 05.03.1976; mid-air collision with XZ110 near CFB Goose Bay, Canada 16.06.1983, pilot ejected safely.

S107 XZ106, ff 23.02.1976. Delivered No. II(AC) Sqn 15.03.1976, GR.1A upgrade by 08.1984; stored Shawbury 01.1989 to 08.1990; Phase 2 upgrade for second Operation Granby roulement 06.12.1990, coded 'O' and named 'Rule Britannia', flew 35 missions, returned to Coltishall 13.03.1991; No. 41 Sqn, Operation Warden deployment 04.09.1991, loan to SAOEU 11.1995, GR.1B upgrade, GR.3A upgrade St Athan during 2002, recoded 'FR' by 2000; wfu St Athan for spares recovery 03.05.2005; Sold to Everett Aero, Bentwaters 02.08.2006 for disposal; extant on display at RAF Manston History Museum.

In the summer of 1988 GR.1 XZ104 received the squadron badge on the tail fin and '1912–1988' titling on the RWR housing to mark the impending disbandment of No. II(AC) Squadron later that year. *Terry Panopalis Collection*

S108 XZ107, ff 05.03.1976. Delivered No. II(AC) Sqn coded 'R' 18.03.1976; No. 6 Sqn by 12.1982; No. 41 Sqn 'H' by 11.1983, GR.1A upgrade, GR.3 upgrade mid-1997 then GR.3A upgrade 2003; recoded 'FH'; wfu St Athan for spares recovery 04.01.2006; sold to Everett Aero, Bentwaters 02.08.2006 for disposal, extant on site.

S109 XZ108, ff 03.03.1976. Delivered No. II(AC) Sqn 09.06.1976; GR.1A upgrade by 08.1984; No. 54 Sqn 05.01.1989; mid-air collision with Tornado GR.1A ZA394 over Northumberland 09.01.1990 losing 1m (3ft) of the wingspan (the Tornado crashed), repaired; No. 16(R) Sqn 02.1994; No. 54 Sqn coded 'GL' 08.1996, GR.3 upgrade St Athan 01.1998; crashed into the North Sea off Norfolk after the pilot lost control during air combat manoeuvring 03.09.1998, pilot ejected safely.

S110 XZ109, ff 16.03.1976. Delivered No. II(AC) Sqn coded 'O' 02.04.1976, GR.1A upgrade 10.1984; No. 54 Sqn 13.04.1989, Operation Warden deployment 09.09.1991; No. 6 Sqn 'EN' by 03.1993, Bosnia UN peacekeeping deployments, GR.3 upgrade late 1998, GR.3A upgrade 03.2003; stored Shawbury 07.03.2007; DCAE Cosford by 29.08.2007, extant as GIA.

S111 XZ110, ff 22.03.1976. Delivered No. II(AC) Sqn 05.04.1976; mid-air collision with XZ105 at CFB Goose Bay 16.06.1983, pilot ejected safely.

S112 XZ111, ff 22.03.1976. Delivered No. II(AC) Sqn 07.04.1976 coded 'A'; No. 6 Sqn 01.1989, GR.1A upgrade; stored Shawbury 09.1993 to 10.1995; No. 54 Sqn 'GO'; crashed 4nm north-east of Dumfries due to a bird strike 27.10.2000, Flt Lt Clarke (RNZAF) ejected safely but injured.

S113 XZ112, ff 22.03.1976. Delivered No. II(AC) Sqn 12.04.1976, GR.1A upgrade 11.1982; stored Shawbury 01.1989 to 02.1991; Phase 3 upgrade for Operation Granby by 14.02.1991 for No. 54 Sqn coded 'GA' but not deployed, Bosnia UN peacekeeping deployments 1993 and 1994, GR.3 upgrade 10.1999, GR.3A upgrade 01.2001; No. 41 Sqn 'EA' 03.2005, received special 'Coltishall 65th Anniversary' markings; wfu Shawbury 12.04.2006; DCAE Cosford 25.04.2007, extant as GIA.

S114 XZ113, ff 02.04.1976. Delivered No. 41 Sqn 27.04.1976, GR.1A upgrade 02.1985; No. 54 Sqn 01.1989; No. 41 Sqn 'FD' by 08.1989, Phase 3 upgrade for second Operation Granby by 14.02.1991 but not deployed, Bosnia UN peacekeeping deployments 1993, GR.3 upgrade mid-1998, GR.3A upgrade early 2003, loan to SAOEU 08.2003; wfu St Athan for spares recovery 15.03.2006; sold to Everett Aero, Bentwaters 04.08.2006 for disposal; extant on display at Morayvia Sci-Tech Experience Project, Kinloss.

A Jaguar changes its spots. GR.1 XZ114 displays Arctic camouflage in August 1987, unusually, the camouflage has also been applied inside the engine intakes. ***Terry Panopalis Collection***

S115 XZ114, ff 08.04.1976. Delivered No. 41 Sqn coded 'B' 06.05.1976, GR.1A upgrade; stored Shawbury 12.1994 to 10.04.03' GR.3A upgrade St Athan, No. 41 Sqn 'FB' 05.05. 2004; No. 6 Sqn 'EO' 03.2005; wfu Shawbury 11.04.2006; DCAE Cosford 03.04.2007, extant as GIA.

S116 XZ115, ff 30.04.1976. Delivered No. 41 Sqn 04.06.1976, GR.1A upgrade 06.1986; stored Shawbury 08.1994 to 12.1995; GR.1B upgrade, No. 41 Sqn coded 'C', loan to SAOEU 01.1997 to 12.2001, on return recoded 'FC'; No. 16(R) Sqn 'PD' 12.2001, GR.3A upgrade 12.2004; No. 6 Sqn 'ER' 03.2005; wfu Shawbury 10.07.2006; DCAE Cosford 24.10.2006, extant as GIA.

S117 XZ116, ff 22.04.1976. Delivered No. 41 Sqn coded 'D' 28.05.1976, GR.1A upgrade 11.1986; head-on mid-air collision with Tornado GR.1 ZA493 in Barrowdale Valley, Cumbria, 17.06.1987 crashing 5nm south of Keswick, pilot Flt Lt Andrew Mannheim killed.

S118 XZ117, ff 29.04.1976. Delivered No. 41 Sqn coded 'E' 28.05.1976, GR.1A upgrade 01.1987; No. 54 Sqn 04.1991 'GG'; stored Shawbury 12.07.1994; GR.3 upgrade St Athan 1996, No. 6 Sqn 'EP', GR.3A upgrade 2001, loan to QinetiQ 07.2002; No. 41 Sqn 'FB' 03.2005; No. 6 Sqn 03.2006; QinetiQ 01.2007; DCAE Cosford 07.2007, extant as GIA.

S119 XZ118, ff 12.05.1976. Delivered No. 41 Sqn coded 'F' 04.06.1976, GR.1A upgrade 10.1986, Phase 2 upgrade for second Operation Granby roulement 02.11.1990, coded 'Y' and named 'Buster Gonad and his Unfeasibly Large Testicles', flew 38 missions, returned to Coltishall 13.03.1991, Operation Warden deployment 04.09.1991, Bosnia UN peacekeeping deployments 'FF', GR.3 upgrade late 1998, GR.3A upgrade 04.2004; wfu St Athan for spares recovery 29.09.2005; fuselage sold to Everett Aero, Bentwaters by 03.2006 for disposal; displayed upside down and stripped back to polished metal as a modern art piece by Fiona Banner at the Tate Britain 2010 to 2011, was scrapped after the exhibition.

S120 XZ119, ff 18.05.1976. Delivered No. 41 Sqn coded 'G' 28.05.1976, GR.1A upgrade, Phase 2 upgrade for second Operation Granby roulement 23.10.1990, coded 'Z' and named 'Katrina Jane', flew 40 missions, returned to Coltishall 12.03.1991, Operation Warden deployment 04.09.1991; wfu Coltishall 06.1996; Aircraft Maintenance Instruction Flight Cranwell as GIA **9266M**; extant on display at the National Museum of Flight at East Fortune, East Lothian.

S121 XZ120, ff 19.05.1976. Delivered No. II(AC) Sqn 15.06.1976; crashed into the North Sea off Nordholm, Denmark 25.02.1977, Flt Lt Douglas Graham Stein killed.

Fourth production order

The fourth production order covered 44 aircraft, all Jaguar GR.1, c/n S122–S165.

S122 XZ355, ff 10.06.1976. Delivered No. 41 Sqn 08.07.1976; No. 54 Sqn 04.1982; No. 41 Sqn 03.1984 coded 'J', GR.1A upgrade 08.1986, Phase 1 upgrade for first Operation Granby roulement 08.1990, Phase 3 upgrade for Operation Warden deployment 04.09.1991, loan to A&AEE Boscombe Down 07.1996, GR.3 upgrade 10.1998, GR.3A upgrade 08.2001; No. 41 Sqn 'FJ'; wfu St Athan for spares recovery 16.03.2006; fuselage sold to Everett Aero, Bentwaters 10.08.2006 for disposal; sold to a private owner in Greece by 2009.

S123 XZ356, ff 07.06.1976. Delivered No. 41 Sqn 09.07.1976, damaged by bird strike 1978; stored Abingdon; No. 17 Sqn 10.1980 coded 'BP'; No. 14 Sqn 04.1985, GR.1A upgrade; No. 41 Sqn 'R' 02.1986, Phase 2 upgrade for second Operation Granby roulement 02.11.1990, coded 'N' and named 'Mary Rose', flew 33 missions; No. 6 Sqn 'EP', Bosnia UN peacekeeping deployments; stored Shawbury 08.1997 to 09.03.2001, GR.3A upgrade St Athan; No. 54 Sqn 'GF' 30.05.2002, one-month loan to SAOEU; No. 41 Sqn 'FU' 03.2005; wfu St Athan for spares recovery 02.2006; fuselage sold to Everett Aero, Bentwaters 21.07.2006 for disposal; sold to a private owner at Welshpool 05.2011.

S124 XZ357, ff 17.06.1976. Delivered No. 41 Sqn coded 'A', first GR.1 to receive Adour Mk.104 in 1978, GR.1A upgrade 1986, recoded 'K', upgraded as spare aircraft for Operation Granby, GR.3 upgrade 02.1999, GR.3A upgrade St Athan 09.2001; wfu St Athan for spares recovery 28.10.2004; fuselage sold to Everett Aero, Sproughton 27.10.2005 for disposal; sold to private owners in the Netherlands in 2006 and 2019.

S125 XZ358, ff 25.06.1978. Delivered No. 41 Sqn 02.11.1976, coded 'L', GR.1A upgrade 1986, Phase 2 upgrade for second Operation Granby roulement 23.10.1990, coded 'W' and named 'Diplomatic Service', flew 14 missions, returned to Coltishall 13.03.1991, Operation Warden deployment 04.09.1991; wfu Coltishall 07.1996; Aircraft Maintenance Instruction Flight Cranwell 10.1996 as GIA **9262M**, extant as GIA.

S126 XZ359, ff 08.07.1976. Delivered No. 41 Sqn coded 'M' 25.08.1976, GR.1A upgrade 07.1986; struck cliffs and crashed at St Abbs Head, Northumberland 16.04.1989, Sqn Ldr Paul Victor Lloyd killed.

S127 XZ360, ff 14.09.1976. Delivered Abingdon for storage 14.09.1976; No. 41 Sqn 29.04.1977, GR.1A upgrade 07.1986, Phase 3 upgrade for Bosnia UN peacekeeping deployment 1993, GR.3 upgrade 09.1998, GR.3A upgrade 02.2003; wfu St Athan for spares recovery 08.11.2005; sold to Everett Aero, Bentwaters in 2006 for disposal; Teesside International Airport 08.2019 for fire training.

XZ357 of No. 41(F) Squadron during the late 1990s in the all-grey air defence colour scheme. ***Terry Panopalis Collection***

S128 XZ361, ff 04.08.1976. Delivered Abingdon for storage 02.09.1976; No. II(AC) Sqn 03.1977, GR.1A upgrade 02.1985; stored Shawbury 01.1989; No. 41 Sqn coded 'FT' 09.1992, GR.3 upgrade 2000; stored Shawbury 0.62002; sold to Everett Aero, Sproughton 15.12.2005 for disposal; sold to CoTech in Kempston for spares recovery 2019; Jet Art Aviation for restoration, extant on display at the Estonian Aviation Museum.

S129 XZ362, ff 19.08.1976. Retained by BAC for SBAC Farnborough display marked as Jaguar International; delivered 27.09.1976; No. II(AC) Sqn; No. 41 Sqn coded 'E' 05.1990; No. 54 Sqn 'GC' 04.1993, Phase 3 upgrade Bosnia UN peacekeeping deployment; crashed in Alaska 24.07.1996 during Exercise Cope Thunder, pilot ejected safely.

S130 XZ363, ff 25.08.1976. Delivered Abingdon for storage 14.09.1976; No. 41 Sqn 08.1977, GR.1A upgrade 10.1986, coded 'FO' by 07.1992; stored Shawbury 10.1995, GR.1B upgrade St Athan 1996, loan to A&AEE Boscombe Down, GR.3 upgrade on return; crashed in Alaska 25.07.2001 during Exercise Cope Thunder, Flt Lt Jason Hayes killed.

S131 XZ364, ff 03.09.1976. Delivered Abingdon for storage 27.09.1976; No. II(AC) Sqn by 08.1980, GR.1A upgrade 02.1985; No. 54 Sqn 01.1989, Phase 2 upgrade for second Operation Granby roulement 23.10.1990, coded 'Q' and named 'Saddam', flew 47 missions, GR.1B upgrade 1996, recoded 'GJ', GR.3 upgrade 05.1999 then GR.3A upgrade, received special 'Coltishall 60th Anniversary' markings; No. 41 Sqn 'FS' 03.2005; wfu St Athan 28.11.2005; sold to Everett Aero, Sproughton 01.2007 for disposal; nose section sold to a private owner 2008 and rest of airframe scrapped; nose section sold to Jet Art Aviation 2018.

S132 XZ365, ff 19.09.1976. Delivered Abingdon for storage 01.10.1976; No. 41 Sqn coded 'J' by 09.1977, GR.1A upgrade 03.1984; No. 54 Sqn in 03.1984; No. II(AC) Sqn 08.1984; crashed near Meschede, east of Dortmund, West Germany 09.07.1985, Fg Off I J Baston ejected safely.

S133 XZ366, ff 20.09.1976. Delivered Abingdon for storage 06.10.1976; No. II(AC) Sqn 1978, GR.1A upgrade 07.1984; stored Shawbury 01.1989; No. 41 Sqn coded 'S' 06.1992, Phase 3 upgrade for Bosnia UN peacekeeping deployment 1995, GR.3 upgrade 03.1999, GR.3A upgrade 12.2000; No. 41 Sqn 'FC' 03.2005; wfu St Athan for spares recovery 04.11.2005; sold to Everett Aero, Bentwaters in 2006 for disposal, extant on site.

S134 XZ367, ff 06.10.1976. Delivered Abingdon for storage 01.11.1976; No. II(AC) Sqn by 05.1977; stored Abingdon 01.1978 to 06.1980; No. 226 OCU coded '25' 06.1981, GR.1A upgrade 10.1985; No. II(AC) Sqn; No. 54 Sqn 01.1989, Phase 2 upgrade for second Operation Granby roulement 23.10.1990, coded 'P' and named 'Debbie', later 'White Rose', flew 40 missions, returned to Coltishall 13.03.1991, was the last Jaguar overhauled at Abingdon 06.1991; No. 54 Sqn 'GP' by 01.1992, Phase 3 upgrade for Bosnia UN peacekeeping deployment 1993, GR.3A upgrade 03.2000, aircraft was over-stressed during Operation Warden; stored Shawbury 09.2000; Coltishall as weapons loading trainer 02.10.2002, received No. 6 Sqn 90th anniversary markings; sold to Everett Aero, Bentwaters 01.09.2006 for disposal, received tail fin from XX725 on repurchase by MoD for DCAE Cosford 04.2010, extant as GIA.

S135 XZ368, ff 01.10.1976. Delivered No. 14 Sqn 01.11.1976; No. 6 Sqn coded 'AG' 06.1979; No. 14 Sqn 02.1984; No. 2 SoTT Cosford 10.1986 as GIA **8900M**, extant as GIA.

S136 XZ369, ff 11.10.1976. Delivered No. 14 Sqn coded 'AP' 01.11.1976; No. 17 Sqn by 10.1983; stored Shawbury 03.1985, GR.1A upgrade 1987; No. 6 Sqn, Phase 3 upgrade for Bosnia UN peacekeeping deployment 1993 and 1995 coded 'EF', GR.1B upgrade 10.1995, GR.3 upgrade 1997 then GR.3A upgrade 09.2000, Operation Resinate deployment 10.2002, recoded 'EU' 03.2005; wfu St Athan 01.12.2005; DCAE Cosford 03.2006; extant on display at East Midlands Aeropark.

S137 XZ370, ff 20.10.1976. Delivered No. 14 Sqn 04.11.1976; No. 17 Sqn coded 'BN' by 1980, later recoded 'BJ'; stored Shawbury 03.1985; No. 2 SoTT Cosford 01.2000 as GIA **9004M**; wfu and stored 2023.

S138 XZ371, ff 03.11.1976. Delivered No. 17 Sqn coded 'BB' 01.12.1976; No. 14 Sqn 08.1984; stored Shawbury 12.1985; No. 2 SoTT Cosford 01.2000 as GIA **8907M**, extant as GIA.

S139 XZ372, ff 10.11.1976. Delivered No. 14 Sqn 01.12.1976 coded 'AQ', recoded 'AK' by 08.1981; No. 20 Sqn by 10.1983; No. 226 OCU 01.1984, GR.1A upgrade 09.1985; No. 6 Sqn 'ED'; stored Shawbury 1996 to 2000; GR.3A upgrade, No. 6 Sqn 'ED' 30.11.2000; wfu St Athan for spares recovery 05.07.2005; fuselage sold to Everett Aero, Bentwaters 02.08.2006 for disposal; Aberdeen Airport for fire training 2011.

S140 XZ373, ff 19.11.1976. Delivered No. 17 Sqn 01.12.1976; No. 20 Sqn by 11.1983, GR.1A upgrade 09.1984; No. 6 Sqn 01.1985; No. 54 Sqn coded 'GF' 06.1988, Phase 3 upgrade for Bosnia UN peacekeeping deployment, coded 'GF'; crashed into the Adriatic Sea during an air combat manoeuvring training mission 26.06.1995, Capt. R L Paradis (USAF) ejected safely.

S141 XZ374, ff 09.12.1976. Delivered No. 20 Sqn 05.01.1977 coded 'CA'; No. 14 Sqn by 10.1983; stored Shawbury 08.1985; No. 2 SoTT Cosford as GIA **9005M**, extant as Spadeadam gate guardian.

S142 XZ375, ff 16.12.1975. Delivered No. 20 Sqn 25.01.1977; No. 14 Sqn coded 'AX' by 10.1983, GR.1A upgrade 02.1986; No. 54 Sqn 'GB'; stored Abingdon 09.1987 to 10.1990; Phase 2 upgrade for second Operation Granby roulement 23.10.1990, coded 'S' and named 'Guardian Reader', flew 17 missions, returned to Coltishall 13.03.1991, Operation Warden deployment 09.09.1991, GR.1B upgrade St Athan 08.1995; DARA civilian technical training school St Athan as GIA **9255M**; Coltishall 02.2002 as Battle Damage Repair Training airframe; nose section preserved at the City of Norwich Aviation Museum, remainder of airframe scrapped.

S143 XZ376, ff 13.01.1977. Delivered No. 14 Sqn 08.03.1977; No. 17 Sqn coded 'BE' 09.1978; crashed on the Tain range, Scotland, after loss of control during practice toss bombing 07.03.1983, Flt Lt B R Iddon ejected but seriously injured.

A worn-looking GR.1A XZ377 in October 1994 in the markings of No. 6 Squadron and the traditional camouflage scheme worn from 1973 into the late 1990s. *Terry Panopalis Collection*

S144 XZ377, ff 21.01.1977. Delivered No. 20 Sqn 15.02.1977; No. 31 Sqn by 03.1984; No. II(AC) Sqn 11.1984, GR.1A upgrade 03.1985; No. 226 OCU; No. 54 Sqn 02.1987; No. 6 Sqn coded 'EB', upgraded as spare aircraft for Operation Granby; No. 16(R) Sqn 04.1997, GR.3 upgrade; No. 6 Sqn 'EG', GR.3A upgrade 2004, recoded 'EP'; wfu St Athan for spares recovery 16.03.2006; DCAE Cosford 06.2007, extant as GIA 'P'.

S145 XZ378, ff 01.02.1977. Delivered No. 20 Sqn 25.02.1977; No. 31 Sqn by 12.1983; No. 17 Sqn by 06.1984; No. 41 Sqn, GR.1A upgrade 07.1985; No. 6 Sqn coded 'EP'; stored Shawbury 10.1990; sold to a private owner at Topsham, Exeter 14.11.2005.

S146 XZ381, ff 16.02.1977. Delivered No. 20 Sqn 17.03.1977; No. 17 Sqn coded 'BL' by 01.1984; stored Shawbury 03.1985; GR.1A upgrade 03.1989, No. 54 Sqn, Phase 3 upgrade for Operation Warden deployment 09.09.1991; No. 6 Sqn 'EC' by 03.1993; TIALD trials Boscombe Down, GR.1B upgrade by 01.1996, GR.3 upgrade 08.1999; No. 16(R) Sqn; crashed in the Moray Firth after a double hydraulic failure 20.10.1999, pilot Lossiemouth Station OC Gp Capt Alan Hudson ejected safely.

S147 XZ382, ff 10.03.1977. Delivered No. 17 Sqn coded 'AE' 06.04.1977; No. 14 Sqn coded 'AE' by 09.1978; stored Abingdon 1981, St Athan by 05.1983 then Shawbury by 11.1985; No. 1 SoTT Halton 12.1986 as GIA **8908M**; Coltishall as Battle Damage Repair Training airframe 10.1992 to 05.1998; sold to a private owner at Bruntingthorpe for preservation.

S148 XZ383, ff 11.03.1977. Delivered No. 17 Sqn 19.04.1977; No. 14 Sqn coded 'AF' by 11.1983; No. 2 SoTT Cosford 27.10.1986 as GIA **8901M**; extant on display at Yorkshire Air Museum, Elvington.

S149 XZ384, ff 18.03.1977. Delivered No. 20 Sqn coded 'CM' 06.04.1977; No. 31 Sqn 07.1984; No. 17 Sqn 10.1984; stored Shawbury in 1985; No. 2 SoTT Cosford 03.1988 as GIA **8954M**, wfu 2023, sold to RAF Coltishall Heritage Centre, arrived onsite 20.07.2024.

S150 XZ385, ff 23.03.1977. Delivered No. 14 Sqn coded 'AG' 21.04.1977; No. 17 Sqn 'BE' by 06.1983; stored Abingdon early 1985; No. 41 Sqn 04.1985, joined Gibraltar Detachment; No. 6 Sqn by 09.1985, GR.1A upgrade 07.1986; No. 54 Sqn, loan to A&AEE Boscombe Down 09.1990 for overwing AAM rail trials; No. 16(R) Sqn by 09.1993 coded 'F', GR.3 upgrade 08.2000 then GR.3A upgrade; No. 16(R) 'PC' Sqn 01.12.2003; No. 41 Sqn 'FT'; wfu St Athan by 03.2006; sold to Everett Aero for disposal; sold to Jet Art Aviation 07.2019, nose section only restored and sold to a private owner in Staffordshire 08.2020.

S151 XZ386, ff 19.04.1977. Delivered No. 14 Sqn 16.05.1977; No. 31 Sqn by 12.1983; No. II(AC) Sqn 04.1985, joined Gibraltar Detachment; No. 6 Sqn 10.1985, GR.1A upgrade 12.1985, to No. 226 OCU coded '05' 02.1986; crashed into a hillside near Aberedu, Powys 24.06.1987, Flt Lt Ian David Hill killed.

S152 XZ387, ff 06.05.1977. Delivered No. 31 Sqn coded 'DN' 26.05.1977, GR.1A upgrade; No. 6 Sqn; No. 54 Sqn 03.1990; crashed into the Solway Firth 4nm off Southerness Point 12.09.1990, Flt Lt J Marsden killed.

S153 XZ388, ff 12.05.1977. Delivered No. 17 Sqn coded 'BK' 05.06.1977; No. 14 Sqn 'AH'; crashed near Celle, West Germany 01.04.1985, Fg Off G Brough knocked unconscious during ejection.

S154 XZ389, ff 07.05.1977. Delivered No. 20 Sqn coded 'CN' 24.06.1977; No. 31 Sqn 10.1983; No. 17 Sqn 10.1984, stored Shawbury 02.1985; No. 1 SoTT Halton by 03.1988 as GIA **8946M**; No. 2 SoTT Cosford; extant on display at the Ulster Aviation Collection at Long Kesh, Lisburn, Northern Ireland, since 11.2023.

S155 XZ390, ff 09.06.1977. Delivered No. 31 Sqn coded 'DM' 05.07.1977; No. 20 Sqn 'CL'; No. II(AC) Sqn by 07.1984; stored Shawbury 04.1985; No. 2 SoTT Cosford as GIA **9003M**, extant as GIA.

S156 XZ391, ff 23.06.1977. Delivered No. 31 Sqn 15.07.1977 coded 'DF', GR.1A upgrade 03.1984; No. 54 Sqn; stored Shawbury 02.1990, overhauled St Athan 02.1991; No. 226 OCU 11.1991; No. 54 Sqn by 06.1992, Phase 3 upgrade for Bosnia UN peacekeeping deployments 1993 and 1994; No. 16(R) Sqn 07.1996, GR.3 upgrade 1999; No. 6 Sqn 'EB' 04.1999, GR.3A upgrade 2001, recoded 'ET' 03.2005; wfu Shawbury 12.04.2006; DCAE Cosford 06.03.2007, extant as GIA.

S157 XZ392, ff 13.07.1977. Delivered No. 31 Sqn 17.08.1977 coded 'DE'; No. 20 Sqn by 11.1983; No. 54 Sqn by 10.1984, GR.1A upgrade 06.1987; stored Shawbury 10.1990; GR.3A upgrade 10.2000; No. 16(R) Sqn 'FP' 02.2002; No. 6 Sqn 'EM' 03.2005; stored St Athan 27.09.2006; DCAE Cosford 13.06.2007, extant as GIA.

S158 XZ393, ff 12.08.1977. Delivered No. 20 Sqn 01.09.1977; No. 17 Sqn by 06.1980; No. 226 OCU, GR.1A upgrade 02.1984; No 54 Sqn; mid-air collision with Tornado GR.1 ZA408, crashed into the North Sea off Cromer 12.07.1984, pilot ejected safely.

S159 XZ394, ff 02.09.1977. Delivered No. 20 Sqn coded 'CQ' 26.09.1977; No. 17 Sqn; stored Shawbury 03.1985, GR.1A upgrade early 1987; No. 6 Sqn; No. 54 Sqn 'GN' by 03.1990, Phase 3 upgrade for Bosnia UN peacekeeping deployments 1993 and 1994, GR.3 upgrade 10.1998, GR.3A upgrade 11.2001; No. 41 Sqn 'FG' 03.2005; wfu St Athan for spares recovery 15.03.2006; sold to Everett Aero, Bentwaters 09.08.2006 for disposal; extant at RAF Sculthorpe Heritage Centre, displayed in nearby Tattersett village in 'The Saint' display colours of XX116.

S160 XZ395, ff 08.09.1977. Stored Warton until issued to No. 54 Sqn 30.01.1979; No. 6 Sqn 05.1984, GR.1A upgrade 08.1984; No. 54 Sqn; crashed into the North Sea 26nm north of Coltishall after loss of control due to excessive rudder movement 22.08.1984, Sqn Ldr John Froud ejected safely.

S161 XZ396, ff 19.12.1977. Stored Warton until issued to No. 6 Sqn coded 'EM' 23.02.1979; No. 226 OCU by 05.1984, GR.1A upgrade; No. 6 Sqn 02.1985, Phase 1 upgrade for second Operation Granby roulement 08.1990, Phase 3 upgrade for Bosnia UN peacekeeping deployments 1993 and 1994, GR.3 upgrade St Athan 21.02.2002; No. 6 Sqn 'EQ'; wfu St Athan for spares recovery 04.11.2005; sold to Everett Aero, Bentwaters in 2006 for disposal. Extant on display at the Pima Air & Space Museum since 2014.

S162 XZ397, ff 27.10.1977. Stored Warton, upgrade to Jaguar International standard as **G-27-322** for loan to Indian Air Force, delivered 11.12.1979 as **JI006**; crashed in India due to a bird strike 16.04.1981, Flt Lt S Adhikari ejected safely.

S163 XZ398, ff 16.11.1977. Stored Warton, upgrade to Jaguar International standard as **G-27-323** for loan to Indian Air Force, delivered 14.08.1980 as **JI007**; returned to UK 04.1984, stored Warton; GR.1A upgrade, No. 6 Sqn 02.1985; No. 41 Sqn 08.1987; No. 54 Sqn 06.1989; No. 41 Sqn coded 'FA' in early 1991, GR.3 upgrade 12.1999, GR.3A upgrade 04.2004; No. 6 Sqn 'EQ' 03.2005; DCAE Cosford 18.05.2007, extant as GIA.

S164 XZ399, ff 23.11.1977. Stored Warton until issued to No. 6 Sqn 17.05.1979 coded 'EL'; No. 14 Sqn 01.1983; No. 6 Sqn 02.1984; No. 226 OCU 05.1984, GR.1A upgrade 10.1985; No. 6 Sqn; No. 226 OCU '03' 10.1987; No. 6 Sqn by 06.1993; Jaguar 97 trials aircraft 02.1999 (ff 04.08.1999), GR.3A upgrade **GR.3A** 11.2000; No. 6 Sqn 'EJ'; DCAE Cosford 13.06.2007, extant as GIA.

S165 XZ400, ff 16.02.1978. Stored Warton until issued to No. 54 Sqn coded 'GP' 29.06.1979, was the second GR.1A upgrade completed 12.1983; No. 6 Sqn 'EG' by 1990; stored Shawbury 06.1992; overhauled and issued No. 54 Sqn 'GR' 03.1997; GR.3 upgrade 05.2000; Adour Mk.106 trials, returned Coltishall 24.01.2002; wfu St Athan for spares recovery 06.07.2005; sold to Everett Aero in 2006 for disposal; sold to Jet Art Aviation for restoration 07.2019.

ETPS aircraft

An order for one Jaguar T.2A, c/n B38.

B38 ZB615, ff 23.09.1982. Delivered RAE Farnborough 1983; wfu 11.2005; Cranwell by 09.2003; DCAE Cosford, extant as GIA.

Armée de l'Air production

This is a listing of all Jaguars ordered for the Armée de l'Air, including a concise history of each aircraft.

In these entries the following abbreviations may be found:

EC – Escadron de Chasse
ff – first flown
GIA – ground instructional airframe
Wfu – withdrawn from use

Squadron codes were allocated as follows:

EC 1/7 'Provence' – 7-Hx
EC 2/7 'Argonne' – 7-Px
EC 3/7 'Languedoc' – 7-Ix
EC 4/7 'Limousin' – 7-Nx
EC 1/11 'Roussillon' – 11-Ex
EC 2/11 'Vosges' – 11-Mx
EC 3/11 'Corsica' – 11-Rx
EC 4/11 'Jura' – 11-Yx
EC 3/3 'Ardennes' – 3-Xx

Jaguar A

Production of the single-seat Jaguar A totalled 160 aircraft, construction numbers A1–A160, which were marked on the rudder as the serial number.

A1 ff 20.04.1972, AdA acceptance 05.1972, joined flight test programme; EC 3/3 coded '3-XJ' 02.1983, deployed to Chad 01.1984; EC 4/11 '11-YQ' 07.1987; EC 1/11 '11-EQ' 03.1988, recoded '11-RW' 1990, Operation Daguet deployment 10.1990 to 03.1991; EC 4/11 '11-YP' 05.1992; EC 3/7 '7-IA' 1993; EC 1/7 '7-HL' 08.1996; EC 2/7 '7-PF' 05.1997; wfu 02.1998; extant on display at Musée de l'Air et de l'Espace, Le Bourget, Paris since 2007.

A2 CEAM coded '118-AE' for operational trials 1972; EC 3/3 '3-XN' by 06.1985, recoded '3-XC' by 05.1987; EC 2/11 '11-MD' by 04.1988; wfu and stored Châteaudun 10.1996; sold to Indian Air Force for spares recovery 08.2018.

A3 Joined flight test programme, CEAM, transferred CEV; GIA Cazaux, scrapped by 2023.

A4 CEAM coded '118-AG' for operational trials 1972, TAV-38 laser rangefinder trials, ATLIS designation pod trials 1976; EC 1/7 '7-HK' 01.1988; CEV trials; wfu 2009, extant on display at Ailes Anciennes Toulouse, Blagnac.

A5 EC 1/7 coded '7-HD' 05.1973; EC 2/7 '7-PZ' 1975, stored 11.1976, returned recoded '7-PK' 05.1978, recoded '7-PQ' 06.1982 and '7-PM' 06.1983; EC 3/3 '3-XP' 1987; EC 2/7 '7-PF' 02.1988, stored 06.1989; EC 3/7 '7-IE' 03.1993; EC 2/7 '7-PN' 03.1994; dumped Saint-Dizier by 06.2022.

A6 Delivered EC 1/7 coded '7-HB' 1973; EC 3/3 '3-XA' by 06.1978, recoded '3-XH' by 05.1982 then '3-XL'; crashed at Meurthe-et-Moselle 27.07.1983, Lieutenant G Ribiere ejected safely.

A7 EC 3/3 coded '3-XB' by 1986; EC 2/7 '7-PR', recoded '7-PG' by 06.1992; aircraft scrapped.

A8 Delivered EC 1/7 coded '7-HG' 01.1973; EC 2/7 '7-PW' 08.1975; stored 06.1979; EC 3/3 '3-XC' 01.1979, recoded '3-XL' 09.1983; stored 01.1986; EC 1/11 '11-EB' 06.1988; stored 01.1990; EC 3/11 '11-RB' 05.1991; EC 3/7 '7-IE' 05.1992; extant on display at Musée Chateau de Savigny-lès-Beaune, coded '11-EB'.

A9 EC 2/7 coded '7-PV' 08.1975; stored 06.1980; EC 3/3 '3-XK' 05.1981; stored 01.1983; EC 3/11 '11-RI' 12.1983; EC 3/3 '3-XD' 06.1985, stored 01.1986, returned recoded '3-XF' 05.1987; EC 2/11 '11-MS' 06.1987; EC 2/7 '7-PD' 04.1990, recoded '7-PB' 05.1992; wfu and stored Châteaudun 09.1993.

A10 EC 3/7 coded '7-IE' 06.1974; EC 2/7 '7-PU' 06.1975, recoded '7-PD' 07.1977; EC 3/3 '3-XE' 01.1979, stored 10.1981, returned recoded '3-XH' 06.1984; EC 1/11 '11-EC' 05.1988; EC 4/11 '11-YH' 05.1988; crashed near Temblecourt 04.02.1991, pilot Ducas ejected safely.

A11 EC 1/7 coded '7-HL' by 06.1974; EC 3/3 '3-XA'; wfu and stored Châteaudun.

A12 EC 2/11 coded '11-MO' 09.1981; EC 3/3 '3-XI' 06.1982; EC 2/7 '7-PC' 06.1983, displayed 1983 Paris Salon; EC 3/3 '3-XI' 06.1985; EC 4/11 '11-YH' 05.1986; EC 3/11 '11-RB' 08.1987, recoded '11-RA' 05.1989, Operation Daguet deployment 10.1990 to 03.1991; EC 1/11 '11-EB' 05.1991; EC 3/7 '7-IF' 09.1992; crashed during a bombing training sortie 23.02.1994, pilot killed.

The sixth production Jaguar A, A6, at BA 113 Saint-Dizier-Robinson on 5 September 1974 in the markings of Escadron de Chasse 1/7 'Provence', Escadrille SPA 77 'Croix de Jerusalem' (Cross of Jerusalem). *Author's Collection*

Jaguar A8 in the markings of EC 3/3 Ardennes' in June 1984. The wild boar's head on the tail fin was the Escadron's insignia, having had pet boars as squadron mascots since 1915. *Terry Panopalis Collection*

A13 EC 1/7 coded '7-HV' by 1993; wfu and stored Châteaudun.

A14 EC 3/3 coded '3-XF' 06.1983; EC 2/11 '11-MG' 1987; EC 2/7 '7-PG' 05.1988; stored 07.1990; EC 2/11 '11-MA' 06.1993; EC 2/7 '7-PO' 07.1995; wfu 09.2000, scrapped by 07.2021.

A15 Delivered EC 1/7 coded '7-HP' by 09.1974; EC 3/7 '7-IE' 03.1983, stored 07.1987, returned recoded '7-IG' 06.1989 and '7-IJ' 04.1992; EC 1/11 '11-EA' 11.1992; EC 2/11 '11-MS' 02.1994; EC 2/7 '7-PC' 07.1994; EC 1/7 '7-HG' 12.1994; wfu and stored 01.1997; gate guardian at CEV 03.2008; extant on display at Musée de l'Épopée de l'Industrie et de l'Aéronautique, Albert, since 06.2013.

A16 First aircraft with AN 52 nuclear bomb capability; CEAM for Opération Maquis nuclear bomb trial 04.1974 to 07.1074; EC 1/7 by 1978; EC 3/7 '7-IL'; EC 4/7 coded '7-NG' by 07.1985; wfu and stored Châteaudun.

A17 Delivered EC 1/7 coded '7-HD' 01.1973; CEAM for Opération Maquis nuclear bomb trial 04.1974 to 07.1974, was drop trial aircraft; EC 1/7 '7-HO' 01.1976; EC 3/11 '11-RK' 06.1978; EC 2/7 '7-IH' 10.1982; stored 04.1983; EC 1/7 '7-HC' 08.1985; EC 2/7 '7-PG' 07.1986; EC 1/7 '7-HE' 10.1986, stored 10.1988, returned recoded '7-HF' 01.1990; EC 2/7 '7-PJ' 05.1994; EC 2/11 '11-MW'; wfu and stored Châteaudun; nose section preserved at Vraux, rest of airframe sold to Indian Air Force for spares recovery 08.2018.

A18 EC 1/7 coded '7-HC' by 09.1974; crashed near Troyes 14.02.1977, Capitaine Boullier killed.

A19 EC 1/7 coded '7-HE' 1974; aircraft scrapped.

A20 EC 1/7 coded '7-HF' 1974, displayed 1975 Paris Salon, recoded '7-HE' by 06.1986; EC 4/7 '7-NN' by 08.1986; crashed following engine failure during combat training at Cadenet 30.01.1987, Aspirant Patrick Pascal killed.

A21 EC 1/7 coded '7-HG' 06.1974; EC 3/11 '11-RA' 01.1979.; EC 3/7 '7-IN' 08.1981, recoded '7-IK' 01.1982 and '7-IA' 06.1984; wfu and stored 05.1992; extant on display at Musée du Chateau de Savigny-lès-Beaune since 05.1996, coded '11-YA'.

A22 EC 1/7 coded '7-HH' by 06.1974; EC 1/7 '7-HC' by 05.1987; extant on display at Pôle aéronautique d'Avord, coded '11-RL'.

A23 EC 2/7 coded '7-PG' by 06.1986; EC 1/7 '7-HK' by 06.1992; wfu and stored Châteaudun.

A24 EC 1/7 coded '7-H' 20.06.1976, recoded '7-HH' by 06.1984; dumped Saint-Dizier by 06.2022.

A25 EC 2/7 coded '7-IB' by 1986; extant on display at Saint-Yan Airport, Saône-et-Loire.

A26 EC 3/7 coded '7-II' 11.1975; stored 06.1978; EC 1/7 '7-HI' 09.1980, stored 06.1981, returned recoded '7-HJ' 10.1982, stored 03.1985, returned recoded '7-HQ' 1986; stored 05.1987; EC 2/11 '11-MC' 05.1990; EC 1/7 '7-HM' 1991, recoded '7-HC' 09.1992; EC 1/11 '11-EB' 03.1993; EC 2/11 '11-MH' 1995; EC 2/7 '7-PJ' 08.1996; EC 1/7 '7-HO'; EC 3/7 '7-IB', extant at Nancy-Ochey.

A27 EC 1/7 coded '7-HM' by 1975, displayed 1979 Paris Salon coded '190'; EC 2/7 '7-PE' by 10.1982; EC 3/3 '3-XP' early 1980s; aircraft scrapped.

A28 EC 3/3 coded '3-XE'; EC 4/7 '7-NK' by 05.1986; EC 2/11 '11-MF' by 1987; wfu and stored Châteaudun.

A29 EC 1/7 coded '7-H' by 09.1974; EC 3/3 '3-XF' 25.02.1977; EC 1/7 '7-HA' by 05.1987; EC 2/11 '11-MB' by 1993, received special 20th Jaguar anniversary paint scheme 1993; wfu and stored Châteaudun.

A30 EC 3/3 coded '3-XP' by 09.1981; EC 4/11 by 1982; crashed at Gironde near Bordeaux, hitting a car on impact 26.04.1982, Aspirant Wurtz ejected safely but the woman in the car was killed.

A31 EC 1/7 coded '7-HE' by 09.1981; EC 2/7 '7-PW' by 1995; crashed at Vitry-le-Francois 12.01.1995, the ejection failed and Lieutenant Delion was killed.

A32 EC 3/7 coded '7-IL' by 1975, aircraft scrapped.

A33 EC 3/7 by 1977; EC 1/7 coded '7-HL'; wfu and stored Châteaudun; sold to Indian Air Force for spares recovery 08.2018.

A34 EC 1/7 coded '7-HM' by 06.1978; EC 2/7 '7-PC'; dumped Saint-Dizier by 06.2022.

A35 EC 1/7 coded '7-HG' by 11.1988; EC 3/7 '7-IH' by 1991, recoded '7-IF' by 06.1992; wfu and stored Châteaudun.

A36 EC 2/7 coded '7-II' by 09.1983; preserved at Musée du Chateau de Savigny-lès-Beaune; being converted into an art installation by Dan Gerbo in Dornach for the Contemporary Art Museum, Mühlhausen 2023.

A37 EC 1/7 coded '7-HB' by 06.1982; EC 3/7 '7-IP' by 07.1985; EC 1/7 '7-HB' by 1990, later recoded '7-HI'; wfu and stored Châteaudun.

A38 EC 3/7 coded '7-IL' by 05.1987; Operation Daguet deployment 10.1990 to 03.1991; wfu and stored Châteaudun; sold to Indian Air Force for spares recovery 08.2018.

A39 EC 1/7 coded '7-HD' by 06.1978; EC 1/11 '11-EI' by 06.1982; nose section preserved at Base Museum Mont de Marsan.

A40 EC 1/7 coded '7-HD' by 1977; wfu and stored Châteaudun; sold to Indian Air Force for spares recovery 08.2018.

A41 EC 3/7 coded '7-IP' 11.1975; stored 06.1981; EC 1/7 '7-HP' 06.1981; stored 04.1983; EC 1/11 '11-EG' 02.1984; EC 4/7 '7-ND' 08.1984; EC 2/7 '7-PR' 09.1989; stored 07.1990; EC 1/7 '7-HM' in 06.1992, recoded '7-HE' 07.1994; EC 3/11 '11-RN' 06.1996; EC 3/7 '7-IG' 06.1997; wfu and stored 06.1999; sold to Sirpa Air 11.05.2011, extant coded '7-DE'.

Seen here just rolling out on to the taxiway for a weapons training sortie armed with 3.9in (100mm) rocket projectiles is A56 with EC 1/7, Escadrille SPA 77 in September 1982. ***Terry Panopalis Collection***

A42 EC 1/7 by 1982; crashed in Aquitaine 01.07.1982, pilot ejected safely.

A43 Delivered EC 3/7 coded '7-IQ' 12.1975; EC 2/7 '7-PB' 04.1978; EC 1/7 '7-HK' by 09.1982, stored 04.1983, returned recoded '7-HD' 07.1984; EC 4/7 '7-NF' 10.1988; stored 08.1989; EC 1/7 '7-HJ' 08.1991; EC 1/11 '11-EC' 11.1992; EC 3/7 '7-IH' 03.1995; EC 1/7 '7-HF' 08.1996; wfu and stored at Conservatoire d'Aéronefs non Operationnels Preserves et Exposes (CANOPEE) Châteaudun 07.1998; sold to Indian Air Force for spares recovery 08.2018.

A44 EC 2/11 coded '11-MC' by 1996; crashed into a field near Paris 03.06.1996, pilot ejected safely.

A45 EC 3/7 coded '7-IB' by 1979; undercarriage and flaps damaged during landing attempt at Neuberg, West Germany, and Lieutenant Alain Roux decided to abandon aircraft 12.07.1979.

A46 EC 2/7 coded '7-IL' by 05.1982, recoded '7-IM' by 09.1984; EC 1/7 '7-HP', recoded '7-HZ' by 07.1995; wfu and stored Châteaudun.

A47 EC 3/7 coded '7-IB' 06.1976; EC 1/7 '7-HP' by 03.1984, recoded '7-HC' 03.1992; EC 3/7 '7-IG' 02.1994; stored 05.1995; EC 1/7 '7-HJ' 08.1996; stored 04.1997; EC 2/7 '7-PJ' 03.1998; EC 3/7 coded '7-IC', recoded '7-IE'; extant Nancy-Ochey.

A48 EC 3/11 coded '11-RK' by 05.1976; EC 4/7 '7-NM' by 07.1985; EC 2/7 '7-PC' in early 1990s, received special 20th Jaguar anniversary markings 1993 coded '7-EC'; extant on display at Aéroscopia, Blagnac.

A49 EC 3/11 coded '11-RM' by 05.1976; EC 3/3 '3-XA' by 07.1983; wfu and stored Châteaudun; extant as EC 2/4 gate guardian Saint-Dizier.

A50 Delivered EC 3/11 coded '11-RN' 02.1976; stored 07.1979; EC 1/11 '11-EC' 02.1981; EC 4/11 '11-YM' 07.1983; stored 04.1990; EC 2/11 '11-MC' 05.1991; stored 1992; EC 3/7 '7-IE' 05.1994; stored 09.1996; EC 1/7 '7-HP' 05.1997, recoded '7-HL' 06.1999; wfu and stored Châteaudun.

A51 EC 3/11 coded '11-RO' by 11.1976; written off 16.06.1981.

A52 EC 3/11 coded '11-RQ' by 11.1976, deployed to Chad 04.1978, shot down near Jedaa, Chad 31.05.1978, pilot ejected safely.

A53 Delivered EC 3/11 coded '11-RS' 02.1976; EC 1/7 '7-HC' 01.1982; EC 2/7 '7-PG' 07.1985; stored 01.1986; EC 1/7 '7-HK' 07.1988; stored 07.1989; EC 3/7 '7-IE' 02.1991; EC 3/11 '11-RB' 07.1992; stored 06.1993; EC 2/7 '7-PW' 08.1994; EC 3/7 '7-IP' 11.1994; EC 1/7 '7-HD' 10.1996; EC 2/7 '7-PB' 02.1999; wfu and stored Châteaudun 06.2000; sold to Indian Air Force for spares recovery 08.2018.

A54 Delivered EC 3/11 coded '11-RT' 05.1976; EC 3/7 '7-IQ' 1982; EC 1/7 '7-HM' 07.1984, stored 07.1987, returned recoded '7-HB' 07.1990; EC 1/11 '11-EF' 06.1993; EC 3/11 '11-RF' 06.1994; EC 2/11 '11-MN' 07.1995; EC 3/3 '3-XI'; wfu and stored Châteaudun.

A55 Delivered EC 3/11 coded '11-RV' 05.1976, recoded '11-RH' 08.1977; EC 3/3 '3-XO' 01.1979; EC 3/7 '7-IC' 01.1983; EC 1/7 '7-HN' 05.1984; EC 4/7 '7-NN' 02.1987; EC 3/7 '7-IL' 05.1990; stored 05.1991; EC 1/7 '7-HB' 03.1993; EC 2/7 '7-PA' 07.1994, stored 02.1998, returned with same code 04.1999; wfu and stored Châteaudun 06.2000; nose section preserved at Espaces Aéro Lyon Corbas.

A56 EC 1/7 coded '7-HI' by 10.1982, recoded '7-HD' by 1989; crashed at Écriennes 06.11.1989.

A57 Delivered EC 1/11 coded '11-EC' 05.1976; EC 3/3 '3-XM' 1977; EC 1/11 '11-EB' by 07.1983; EC 4/7 '7-NB' by 1984; crashed at Montaren-et-Saint-Médiers 11.05.1984, Capitaine Léopold Eyharts ejected safely.

A58 Delivered EC 3/11 coded '11-EF' 07.1976; EC 2/7 '7-PH' 10.1977; EC 3/7 '7-II' 1978, recoded '7-ID' 08.1983; EC 4/7 '7-NM' 02.1985; EC 3/11 '11-RH' 07.1990; stored 05.1991; EC 1/7 '7-HL' 03.1993, stored 04.1996, returned recoded '7-HE' 08.1997; EC 3/7 '7-IR', Operation Daguet deployment 10.1990 to 03.1991; nose section preserved coded '11-RS' (starboard) and '3-XG' (port), remainder of airframe scrapped by 07.2021.

A59 Delivered EC 1/11 coded '11-EG' 06.1976; EC 2/7 '7-PS' with EC 3/7 Escadrille markings 07.1978; EC 3/7 '7-IC' 06.1980; EC 4/11 '11-YG' 06.1983; EC 1/7 '7-HB' 12.1984; stored 01.1988; EC 3/7 '7-IO' 06.1989; EC 3/11 '11-RH' 03.1993, recoded '11-RG' by 07.1993; EC 3/7 '7-IH' 09.1993; wfu and stored Gergy 01.1995; extant at Chalon-sur-Saône.

A60 EC 3/11 by 05.1976; EC 1/7 coded '7-HO' by 10.1982; crashed 05.10.1987, the pilot ejected safely.

A61 EC 4/7 coded '7-IF' by 1986; EC 3/11 '11-RG' by 09.1994; wfu and stored.

A62 EC 3/3 coded '3-XI' by 06.1978; crashed near Nancy during low-level flying 20.06.1979, Sous-Lieutenant Philippe Georges killed.

A63 EC 4/11 by 1981; crashed on take-off at Toul-Rosières 18.03.1981, Colonel Georges Phélut killed.

A64 Delivered EC 3/3 coded '3-XK' 06.1976; EC 1/11 '11-ER' 09.1976, recoded '11-EE' 07.1980; EC 3/11 '11-RO' by 06.1983; 3/3 '3-XB' 06.1985; EC 4/7 '7-NE' 08.1987; stored 07.1989; EC 4/11 '11-YI' 03.1991; EC 3/7 '7-IS' by 09.1992, recoded '7-IK'.

A65 EC 2/7 coded '7-IO' by 05.1987; crashed after take-off from N'Djamena, Chad, due to a bird strike 12.06.1992, the pilot ejected safely.

A66 Delivered EC 1/11 coded '11-EV' 07.1976; EC 3/11 '11-RT' 07.1983; EC 4/7 '7-NC' 09.1985; EC 3/7 '7-IM' 12.1989; stored 03.1990; EC 2/11 '11-ME' 05.1992; EC 3/7 '7-IB' 03.1993; EC 3/3 '3-XM'; wfu and stored Châteaudun; sold to Indian Air Force for spares recovery 08.2018.

A67 Delivered EC 1/11 coded '11-EB' 07.1976; EC 3/3 '3-XM' 06.1978, recoded '3-XN' 09.1979 and '3-XD' 06.1983; EC 4/7 '7-NB' 06.1983; EC 3/11 '11-RR' 09.1989; EC 3/7 '7-IT' 10.1989; stored 1990; EC 1/7 '7-HQ' 05.1992; EC 2/7 '7-PT' 12.1994; EC 2/7 '7-PT' 12.1994, stored 05.1997, returned recoded '7-PV' 05.1999, received special paint scheme for the unit disbandment 06.08.2001; wfu and stored Châteaudun; nose section preserved by Sirpa Air, remainder of airframe sold to Indian Air Force for spares recovery 08.2018.

A68 EC 3/11 coded '11-RJ' by 11.1976; EC 4/7 '7-NB' by 09.1982; EC 3/3 by 1981; crashed during landing at Nancy-Ochey 05.02.1981, Capitaine Jean-Marie Monsterlet killed.

A69 EC 3/11 coded '11-RX' by 11.1976; EC 3/7 '7-IN' by 1984; mid-air collision with Mirage IIIE No. 443 during a night-time exercise near Villemoyenne 20.05.1984, Sous-Lieutenant Pernod ejected but injured.

A70 EC 3/7 coded '7-II' by 10.1982; EC 4/7 '7-NI' by 07.1985; wfu and stored Châteaudun.

A71 EC 2/11 coded '11-MB' by 11.1976; crashed near Villers-sous-Preny 14.11.1977, Capitaine Amarger ejected safely.

A72 EC 1/11 coded '11-ET' 06.1977; EC 3/7 '7-IE' 06.1978; stored 06.1982; EC 3/11 '11-RW' 06.1984, recoded '11-RY', deployed to Chad; EC 1/7 '7-HJ' 07.1985; stored 07.1990; EC 2/7 '7-PD' 05.1992; wfu and stored 01.1993; extant on display at Musée Chateau de Savigny-lès-Beaune since 06.1996, coded '7-HJ'.

A73 Delivered EC 1/11 coded '11-FB' 06.1976, stored 07.1977, returned recoded '11-EF' 03.1980; stored 09.1980; EC 3/3 '3-XP' 06.1983; EC 2/7 '7-PB' 06.1985; stored 02.1987; EC 4/7 '7-NJ' 04.1988, recoded '7-NC' 07.1989; EC 1/7 '7-HR' 12.1989, stored 07.1990, returned recoded '7-HR' 03.1992; wfu and stored Châteaudun 04.1994; sold to Indian Air Force for spares recovery 08.2018.

A74 EC 4/7 coded '7-NA' by 06.1986; EC 3/7 by 05.1990; wfu and stored Châteaudun.

A75 EC 3/7 coded '7-IJ'; EC 1/11 '11-EH' by 07.1983; EC 4/11 '11-YH' by 07.1985; wfu and stored.

A76 EC 3/11 coded '11-ER' 07.1977; stored 1979; EC 3/3 '3-XB' 10.1981; stored 06.1982; EC 1/7 '7-HL' 1985; stored 1990; EC 4/11 '11-YR' 07.1992; EC 1/7 '7-HI' 04.1993; EC 3/7 '7-IB'; wfu and stored Châteaudun.

A77 EC 2/7 by 1982; crashed due to engine failure at Éclaron-Braucourt-Sainte-Livière 07.07.1982, Capitaine Jean Rault killed.

A78 EC 3/11 coded '11-RA' by 1976; EC 1/7 '7-HM' by 1984; flew into ground at Berzème during low-level flying 28.03.1984, Lieutenant Xavier Frey killed.

A79 EC 4/7 coded '7-NP' by 08.1986; wfu and stored Châteaudun.

A80 EC 1/11 coded '11-EM' 10.1977, recoded '11-EH' 12.1979; EC 2/7 '7-PG' 11.1982; EC 1/7 '7-HD' 06.1984; EC 3/7 '7-IN' by 07.1986; EC 1/11 '11-EJ'; EC 1/7 '7-HM' 04.1990, recoded '7-HN' 05.1992, received special EC 1/7 60th and SPA 15 80th anniversary markings 10.10.1992; wfu and stored 05.1993, scrapped.

A81 EC 2/11 coded '11-MA' by 09.1978, deployed to Chad 01.1984, shot down 25.01.1984, Capitaine Michel Croci killed.

A82 EC 2/11 coded '11-MB' by 08.1977; EC 3/11 '11-RB' by 06.1982; EC 3/3 by 1985, deployed to Chad late 1985; EC 4/11 '11-YB' by 07.1985, deployed to Chad; EC 1/7 '7-HM' late 1980s; wfu and stored Châteaudun.

A83 EC 3/11 coded '11-MC' by 06.1982, heavy landing and nosewheel collapse 15.11.1982; CEAM '118-AH' by 08.1985; EC 4/11 '11-YL' by 03.1987; EC 1/11 by 1993; crashed near Biltine, Chad 22.08.1993, pilot killed.

A84 EC 2/11 coded '11-MD' 09.1978; stored 12.1981; EC 4/11 '11-YJ' 04.1984, Operation Daguet deployment 10.1990 to 03.1991; EC 3/11 '11-RQ' 10.1991; stored 03.1992; EC 2/11 11.1994; EC 1/7 '7-HA' 08.1996; EC 2/7 '7-PY' 06.1997; wfu and stored Châteaudun 06.2000; sold to Indian Air Force for spares recovery 08.2018.

A85 EC 2/11 coded '11-MO' by 09.1978, recoded '11-MG' by 1986; crashed at Villars-sous-Dampjoux 03.01.1986, Capitaine Olivier ejected safely.

A86 Delivered EC 2/11 coded '11-MG' 07.1976; stored 04.1982; EC 3/11 '11-RT' 01.1988; stored 05.1991; EC 1/7 '7-HA' 01.1994; stored 04.1994; EC 2/11 '11-MS' 01.1996; stored 06.1996; EC 2/7 '7-PF' 03.1998; EC 2/11 '11-MF'; scrapped by 07.2021.

A87 EC 2/11 coded '11-MH' 09.1978, stored 07.1982, returned recoded '11-MG' 08.1983; EC 3/11 '11-RX' 02.1985; stored 01.1990; EC 1/11 '11-EM' 07.1991; EC 3/7 '7-IN' 05.1993; EC 1/7 '7-HN' 10.1995; EC 2/7 05.1997, recoded '7-PT' 09.1997, '7-PF' 06.1998 and '7-PY' 09.2000; extant at Conservatoire d'Aéronefs non Operationnels Preserves et Exposes (CANOPEE) Châteaudun.

A88 EC 2/11 coded '11-MG' by 1977, displayed 1977 Pairs Salon; EC 3/7; wfu and stored Châteaudun.

A89 EC 2/11 coded '11-MM' by 03.1987, EC 3/11 '11-RE'; Operation Daguet deployment 10.1990 to 03.1991; extant at Camp Drachenbronn, Alsace.

A90 EC 2/11 coded '11-MP' 01.1979; stored 08.1980; CEAM '118-AI' by 07.1981; EC 4/11 '11-YI' 01.1983; stored 10.1985; EC 2/11 '11-MR' 01.1987, recoded '11-MV' then '11-MB' 07.1989, Operation Daguet deployment 10.1990 to 03.1991; EC 1/7 '7-HE' 09.1992; stored 04.1994; EC 2/11 '11-MI' 07.1995; stored 04.1996; EC 1/7 '7-HN' 12.1997; wfu and stored Châteaudun 01.2001; sold to Indian Air Force for spares recovery 08.2018.

A91 Delivered EC 2/11 coded '11-MQ' 04.1977; stored 01.1979; EC 3/11 '11-RI' 01.1982, stored 10.1984, returned recoded '11-RJ' 06.1985; EC 4/11 '11-YG' 10.1985, Operation Daguet deployment 10.1990; damaged by a SAM during attack on Ahmed Al Jaber airbase, Kuwait 17.01.1991; assigned as GIA combat damage repair training; extant on display at Musée de l'Air et de l'Espace, Le Bourget, Paris, since 2020.

A92 EC 2/11 coded '11-MT'; EC 3/11 '11-RS' by mid-1980s, deployed to Chad; stored Saint-Dizier coded '7-PT' but dumped by 06.2022.

A93 EC 2/11 coded '11-MU' 01.1979, recoded '11-MV' 08.1985, '11-MR' 01.1987, '11-MV' 05.1990 and '11-MS' 02.1992; EC 1/7 '7-HP' 09.1992; EC 2/11 '11-ME' 06.1994; EC 3/7 '7-IO' 09.1979; stored 09.1998; EC 2/7 '7-PN' 03.1999; EC 2/11 '11-MT'; wfu and stored.

A94 EC 1/11 coded '11-EF' by 09.1978, recoded '11-ED' by 06.1982; EC 2/11 '11-MD' by 1984, Operation Daguet deployment 10.1990 to 03.1991; wfu and stored Châteaudun by 10.2003.

A95 EC 1/11 coded '11-ED' by 09.1981, recoded '11-EC' by 07.1983; EC 2/11 '11-MQ'; EC 3/11 by 1990, Operation Daguet deployment 10.1990 to 03.1991; EC 2/7 by 1992; crashed 1nm short of the runway at Saint-Dizier 15.09.1992, the pilot ejected safely.

A96 EC 3/11 coded '11-RQ' 07.1983; EC 2/11 '11-MW' 06.1985; EC 3/11 '11-RC' 12.1986, stored 06.1988, returned recoded '11-RA' 06.1990, recoded '11-RQ' 01.1991; EC 4/11 '11-YH' 06.1992, received special markings for EC 4/11 disbandment; EC 2/11 '11-MD' 09.1992; stored 06.1993; EC 3/11 '11-RQ' 06.1994; EC 1/7 '7-HA' 02.1996; EC 3/7 '7-IO' 06.1996; stored 09.1996; EC 1/7 '7-HB' 11.1998, recoded '7-HD' 04.1999; EC 1/11 '11-EH'; wfu and stored Châteaudun; nose section extant at Évreux-Fauville.

A97 EC 1/1 coded '11-ED' by 1978, mid-air collision with A111 215nm from N'Djamena, Chad 23.08.1978, aircraft returned safely; EC 3/11 '11-RH' by 05.1983; EC 4/11 '11-YD' by 07.1985; EC 2/7 '7-HI' (note this is an EC 1/7 code) by 1990, Operation Daguet deployment 10.1990 to 03.1991; EC 1/7 '7-HR' by 1999; crashed near Bar-le-Duc 24.02.1999, pilot ejected safely.

A98 EC 2/11 coded '11-MT' by 09.1982, Operation Daguet deployment 10.1990 to 03.1991; wfu and stored Châteaudun.

A99 EC 1/11 coded '11-EU' 01.1981, recoded '11-EV' 01.1982; EC 2/11 '11-MK' 01.1985, recoded '11-MQ' 09.1985; EC 1/11 '11-EI' 04.1987, Operation Daguet deployment 10.1990 to 03.1991; stored 05.1991; EC 2/11 '11-MQ' 01.1996; EC 3/11 '11-RJ' 10.1996; EC 1/7 '7-HI' 06.2000; EC 3/7 '7-IR'; EC 1/7 '7-HC' 07.2002; nose section extant at Base Museum Mont de Marsan.

A100 EC 11/1 coded 11-ED 05.1979; stored Châteaudun by 05.1981; EC 2/11 coded 11-MP 04.1986; EC 1/11 coded 11-ER 01.02.1990, Operation Daguet deployment 10.1990 to 03.1991, recoded 11-EE 05.1992; EC 1/7 coded 7-HK 03.1994, recoded 7-HR 06.1999; wfu and stored Châteaudun; sold to Indian Air Force for spares recovery 08.2018.

A107 of EC 4/11 'Jura', SPA 158 'Serpentaire' (Serpentary) is seen here in May 1985 in the two-tone desert camouflage developed for OPEX deployments to Chad. ***Terry Panopalis Collection***

A101 EC 11/11 coded '11-EJ' by 09.1978; EC 2/11 '11-MF' by 1984, deployed to Chad 01.1984; EC 4/7 '7-NR' 01.1986, deployed to Chad early 1986; EC 3/11 '11-RK' 12.1986; EC 2/11 '11-MP' 01.1989; EC 1/11 '11-ED' 01.1991; EC 2/11 '11-MH' 05.1993; EC 1/7 '7-HB' 05.1997, stored 09.1998, returned 09.2000; wfu and stored.

A102 EC 4/11 coded '11-YK' by 1983; crashed at Saint-Porchaire 16.08.1983, Aspirant S Maurin ejected safely.

A103 EC 1/11 coded '11-EB' 08.1986; EC 2/11 '11-MA' 02.1988, Operation Daguet deployment 10.1990 to 03.1991, stored 05.1991, returned recoded '11-MB' 03.1995; EC 3/11 '11-RI' 02.1996; EC 3/7 coded '7-IE' 09.1998; wfu and stored Châteaudun 09.1999; sold to Indian Air Force for spares recovery 08.2018.

A104 EC 3/11 coded '11-RT' 01.1982; EC 1/11 '11-EV' 01.1984; EC 2/11 '11-MP' 06.1985, recoded '11-MT' 09.1985 and '11-MO' 07.1987; EC 1/11 '11-EK' 06.1989, Operation Daguet deployment 10.1990 to 03.1991, recoded '11-EC' 03.1991; EC 2/11 '11-MT' 06.1991; EC 3/7 '7-IL' 09.1992, recoded '7-IT' 09.1996; EC 1/7 '7-HM' 02.2000; EC 1/11 '11-EI' 2001; wfu and stored Châteaudun; sold to Indian Air Force for spares recovery 08.2018. preserved IAF Maintenance Command HQ, Nagpur, in 2022.

A105 EC 1/11 coded '11-EV' by 05.1981; crashed near Bapaume, Pas-de-Calais 05.04.1983, Général Jacques Boichot killed. [Note: since 07.2022 one of the Jaguars sold to the Indian Air Force for spares recovery has been preserved at Sainik School Chandrapur spuriously marked as A105.]

A106 Crashed at N'Djamena, Chad 14.10.1978, Capitaine Serge Linemann killed.

A107 EC 4/11 coded 11-YC by 05.1985, deployed to Chad; EC 2/11 coded 11-MV by 1990, Operation Daguet deployment 10.1990 to 03.1991; airframe minus nose section extant at Saint-Dizier.

A108 EC 3/11 coded '11-RW'; EC 1/11 '11-ES' 10.1981; EC 2/11 '11-MP' 01.1991, Operation Daguet deployment to 03.1991, recoded '11-MT' 02.1994; EC 3/11 '11-RF' 02.1996; EC 1/7 '7-HQ' 09.1998; wfu and stored Châteaudun 09.2000; sold to Indian Air Force for spares recovery 08.2018.

A109 EC 3/11 by 1978; crashed near Ati, Chad 08.08.1978 during a recce mission, Lieutenant Robert Jacquel killed.

A110 CEAM coded '118-AG' by 07.1981; EC 1/11 '11-EJ' by 1988; mid-air collision with another Jaguar near Puiseaux 07.06.1988, the pilot was killed.

A111 EC 3/11 by 1978; mid-air collision with A97 215nm from N'Djamena, Chad 23.08.1978, Lieutenant J Francois ejected safely.

A112 EC 3/11 coded '11-RV' 06.1982, stored 1983, returned recoded '11-RM' 03.1985; EC 4/11 '11-YV' 07.1985; EC 2/11 '11-MO' 06.1988, Operation Daguet deployment 10.1990 to 03.1991; EC 1/11 '11-EK' 08.1991, recoded '11-EG' 12.1991; EC 2/11 '11-ME' 1993, recoded '11-MA' 07.1995; EC 3/7 '7-II' 09.1996; EC 1/7 '7-HS' 11.1998; EC 4/11 '11-YK' 2001; wfu and stored.

A113 EC 4/11 coded '11-YA' 12.1978; EC 2/11 '11-MW' 01.1982; EC 1/11 '11-EX' 07.1987; EC 3/11 '11-RB' 06.1994; EC 3/7 '7-IR' 01.1997, recoded '7-II' 04.1998; EC 3/11 '11-RQ'; extant as gate guardian at Saint-Dizier, coded 7-HJ.

A114 EC 4/11 coded '11-YB' by 09.1980; crashed 10.02.1982, Commandant B Lissonde of EC 4/7 killed.

A115 EC 4/11 coded '11-YC' 02.1981; EC 1/11 '11-ES' 06.1982; EC 3/11 '11-RH' 05.1985; EC 4/11 '11-YA' 07.1987; EC 3/11 '11-RL' 02.1991, Operation Daguet deployment to 03.1991; EC 1/7 '7-HC' 06.1993, recoded '7-HF' 05.1994, stored 03.1995, returned recoded '7-HT' 05.1997 and '7-HO' 09.2000; wfu and stored Châteaudun 05.2005; sold to Indian Air Force for spares recovery 08.2018.

A116 EC 1/11 coded '11-EJ' by 1986; EC 2/11 '11-MW' by 06.1986; mid-air collision with Belgian Air Force F-16A (serial 'FA-79') over Petit-Han, Belgium 30.06.1986, Capitaine Michel Prunas killed (the Belgian F-16 pilot Capitaine Cavenas ejected safely).

A117 EC 4/11 coded '11-YE' 09.1980; EC 2/11 '11-MH' 01.1985; EC 4/11 '11-YE' 01.1986; EC 2/11 '11-MH' 01.1991, Operation Daguet deployment to 03.1991; EC 1/7 '7-HO' 03.1994, stored 05.1995, returned recoded '7-HA' 04.1999; wfu and stored Châteaudun 10.2000.

A118 EC 4/11 coded '11-YF' by 09.1980; wfu and stored Châteaudun.

A119 EC 4/11 coded '11-YG' by 1978; EC 2/11 '11-MN'; EC 3/7 by 1990, Operation Daguet deployment 10.1990 to 03.1991, Operation Turquoise deployment Rwanda; flew into trees on high ground in the Democratic Republic of Congo 01.08.1994, pilot ejected safely.

A120 EC 1/11 coded '11-ER' 05.1982; EC 2/11 '11-MM' 07.1983m recoded '11-MG' 09.1986 then '11-MR' 04.1990; EC 3/7 '7-IN' 1997, recoded '7-IJ' 04.1999; EC 1/7 '7-HL' by 2001; extant at Conservatoire d'Aéronefs non Operationnels Preserves et Exposes (CANOPEE) Châteaudun since 2013.

A121 EC 3/3 coded '3-XJ' by 1979, deployed to Chad 1980; EC 3/11 '11-RW' by 06.1982; EC 1/11 '11-EA' by 07.1983; crashed 02.11.1987.

A122 EC 2/11 coded '11-ME' 07.1981; EC 3/11 '11-RN' 01.1982, recoded '11-RJ' 05.1983; EC 2/11 '11-MO' 01.1986; EC 3/11 '11-RA' 07.1986; EC 4/11 '11-YA' 01.1987; EC 1/11 '11-EA' 06.1989, Operation Daguet deployment 10.1990 to 03.1991, recoded '11-EQ' 03.1991; EC 1/7 '7-HG' 03.1993; EC 2/11 '11-ME' 01.1996; EC 3/11 '11-RL' 10.1996; EC 3/7 '7-IL' 04.1998, recoded '7-IM' 01.2000; GIA Saint-Dizier 05.2003; extant at Saint-Dizier, coded '7-HA'.

A123 EC 2/11 coded '11-MQ' by 05.1981; EC 3/11 '11-RO' by 06.1982; Operation Daguet deployment 10.1990 to 03.1991; extant as gate guardian at Salon-de-Provence, coded '7-IO'.

A124 EC 4/11 coded '11-YL' 01.1979, recoded '11-YK' 02.1984 and '11-YE' 01.1987; EC 2/11 06.1987; EC 4/11 '11-YB' 05.1991; EC 1/7 '7-HN' 03.1994; EC 3/7 '7-IM' 02.1996, stored 09.1996, returned recoded '7-IN' 01.1999; wfu 09.2000; extant as gate guardian at Saint-Dizier, coded '11-RJ' and '11-YD'.

A125 EC 2/11 coded 11-MD by 07.1983, deployed to Chad 01.1984; aircraft flew into a sand dune in the Oum-Chalouba region during a recce sortie 16.04.1984, Commandant Bernard-León Voelckel killed.

A126 To EC 3/11 coded '11-RB' by 07.1983; wfu and stored Châteaudun.

A127 EC 4/11 coded '11-YI' 1979; stored 02.1981; EC 3/11 '11-RM' 05.1984, recoded '11-RK'; EC 1/11 '11-EJ' 06.1986, recoded '11-EH' 05.1988 and '11-EW' 04.1990, Operation Daguet deployment 10.1990 to 03.1991, recoded '11-EH' 05.1991; EC 2/11 '11-MM' 09.1992; EC 1/7 '7-HA' 11.1994; EC 3/7 '7-IP' 11.1996; wfu 09.2000; extant at Saint-Dizier.

A128 EC 4/11 coded '11-YJ' 01.1979; EC 3/11 '11-RI' 06.1985; EC 2/11 '11-MF' 08.1986, stored 10.1990, returned recoded '11-MD' 05.1993 then '11-MB' 01.1996; EC 3/7 '7-IT' 07.1996, recoded '7-IU' then '7-IC' 03.1998; GIA Cazaux 06.2014; extant as gate guardian at Cazaux.

A129 EC 1/11 coded '11-ER' by 1980; EC 3/11 '11-MK' by 1986, deployed to Chad 1986; wfu and stored.

A130 EC 2/11 coded '11-MK' 07.1981; EC 1/11 '11-EK' 01.1984; EC 2/11 '11-MC' 08.1984; EC 1/11 '11-EN', Operation Daguet deployment 10.1990 to 03.1991; EC 4/11 '11-YK' 05.1992; EC 1/7 '7-HJ' 03.1993; EC 3/11 '11-RN' 02.1996; EC 1/7 '7-HU' 05.1997; EC 2/7 '7-PW' 09.2000; extant at Toul-Rosières, coded '11-ED'.

A131 First Jaguar with ATLIS designation pod capability; EC 4/7 coded' 7-NR' 1980, recoded '7-NA' 06.1982; EC 1/11 '11-EE' 09.1984; EC 3/11 '11-RO' 05.1992; EC 3/7 '7-IC' 11.1996, recoded '7-IR' by 1993; EC 1/7 '7-HF' 09.2000, participated in EC 1/7 closing ceremony 01.07.2005, final AdA Jaguar flight to Tours, wfu and stored 11.07.2005; extant as gate guardian at Tours since 2012, coded '11-EE'.

A132 EC 1/7 coded '7-HL' 01.1980; EC 4/7 '7-NE' 06.1980; EC 2/11 '11-MO' 06.1982; EC 1/11 '11-EA'; EC 2/11 '11-MD' by 1985; crashed at Soulanges 13.02.1985.

A133 EC 1/11 coded '11-EG' by 07.1983, recoded '11-EF' mid-1980s, deployed to Chad; EC 3/7 '7-IK' by 1993; EC 3/11 '11-RZ' by 09.1994; extant on display at Le Tube Airport, Istres, coded '7-HB'.

A134 EC 4/7 coded '7-NJ' 1980; EC 1/11 1982; crashed near Marne, 25.06.1982, Capitaine Bellaton killed.

A135 EC 4/7 coded '7-NC' 06.1980; EC 1/11 '11-ES' 06.1984; EC 3/11 '11-RA' 06.1986, recoded '11-RJ' by 1990, Operation Daguet deployment 10.1990; EC 1/11 '11-EJ' 01.1991; EC 3/11 '11-RU' 02.1996; EC 1/7 '7-HL' 09.1997; EC 3/7 '7-IU' 01.1999; wfu 09.2000; extant as gate guardian at Cazaux.

A136 EC 1/11 by 1985; mid-air collision with A156 near Massif des Écrins, Valjouffrey 17.10.1985, Aspirant Stephen Delattre killed.

A137 EC 4/7 coded '7-NK' 08.1982; EC 3/11 '11-RO' 06.1984; EC 1/11 '11-ES' 10.985, recoded '11-EG' 1986; 11-ES' 1987 and '11-EJ' 1988, Operation Daguet deployment 10.1990 to 03.1991, recoded '11-EM' 12.1991; EC 2/11 '11-MM' 06.1994; EC 3/7 '7-IA' 09.1996; EC 1/7 '7-HG' 03.1998, recoded '7-HQ' 11.2000; nose section extant on display at Musée de l'Aviation Clément Ader, Lyon Airport.

A138 EC 4/7 coded '7-NG' by 08.1982; EC 4/11 '11-YE' 06.1984, recoded '11-YF' 07.1987; EC 3/11 '11-RF' 1990, recoded '11-RX' 10.1990; EC 1/7 '7-HV' 06.1997; received special colour scheme for 28th anniversary of ESTS 2E.007 summer 2001; wfu and stored Châteaudun 10.2002; sold to Indian Air Force for spares recovery 08.2018.

A139 EC 4/7 coded '7-NF' by 08.1982; EC 2/11 '11-MO' 06.1984; stored 01.1985; EC 1/11 '11-EL' 01.1986; EC 3/11 '11-RW' 07.1987; stored 08.1988; EC 1/11 '11-EV' 01.1990, Operation Daguet deployment 10.1990 to 03.1991; EC 3/11 '11-RC' 06.1991; stored 02.1996; EC 3/7 '7-IE' 05.1997; stored 02.1998; EC 1/7 '7-HU' 10.1999, participated in EC 1/7 closing ceremony 01.07.2005; wfu and stored 06.07.2005; 18 Regiment de Transmission 10.2009; extant at Evreux-Fauville 03.2010.

A140 EC 4/7 coded '7-NH' 12.1982; EC 4/11 '11-YK' 1986; EC 1/11 '11-EE' 1987, recoded '11-EL' 10.1988, stored 05.1991, returned recoded '11-EN' 06.1992; EC 2/11 '11-MV' 06.1994; EC 3/11 '11-RR' 06.1996; EC 3/7 '7-IU' 09.1997, recoded '7-HI' 11.1998; wfu and stored 01.1999; extant at Base Museum Mont de Marsan.

A141 EC 4/7 coded '7-NI' by 08.1982; EC 3/11 '11-RN' 05.1986; EC 4/11 '11-YO' 09.1987; stored 05.1991; EC 1/11 '11-EO' 01.1993; EC 2/11 '11-MK' 06.1994; EC 3/11 '11-RT' 10.1996; EC 1/7 '7-HW' 09.1997; stored 06.1998; EC 3/7 '7-IB' 02.000; extant on display at Espaces Aéro Lyon Corbas, coded '7-HE'.

A142 EC 4/7 coded '7-NM' by 08.1982, recoded '7-NL' by 05.1986; EC 3/11 coded '11-RO' 05.1986, deployed to Chad, recoded '11-RQ' 08.1988; EC 4/11 '11-YP' 05.1991; crashed 28.05.1991, Sous-Lieutenant Guillomon ejected safely.

A143 EC 2/11 coded '11-MH' by 07.1983; crashed at Damblain 10.01.1984.

A144 EC 1/11 coded '11-EL' by 06.1981; EC 3/11 '11-RN' 05.1983, recoded '11-RW' 02.1986 and '11-RM' 09.1987; stored 05.1988; EC 4/11 '11-YE' 10.1989; stored 05.1991; EC 3/11 '11-RW' 03.1992; EC 2/11 '11-MG' 07.1994; EC 3/7 '7-IF' 06.1996; wfu and stored Châteaudun 09.2000; sold to Indian Air Force for spares recovery 08.2018.

A145 EC 3/11 coded '11-RG'; EC 3/7 coded '7-IQ' by 06.1996; EC 1/7 '7-HG' by 2005, participated in EC 1/7 closing ceremony 01.07.2005; wfu and stored Châteaudun 06.07.2005; sold to Indian Air Force for spares recovery 08.2018.

A146 EC 3/11 by 1988; crashed 18.04.1988.

A147 EC 1/11 coded '11-EF' by 07.1983, recoded '11-EB' by 1984; crashed shortly after take-off from Toul-Rosières 05.12.1984.

A148 CEAM coded '118-AI' 1980 to 1981; EC 4/11 '11-YL' 08.1985; EC 3/11 '11-RB' 09.1986; EC 4/11 '11-YN' 09.1987, recoded '11-YD' 03.1988, Operation Daguet deployment 10.1990 to 03.1991; stored 07.1991; EC 1/11 '11-EQ' 09.1992; EC 2/11 '11-MZ' 05.1994, stored 07.1994, returned recoded '11-MF' 01.1996; EC 3/7 '7-IL' 05.1996, stored 05.1997, returned recoded '7-IK' 01.1999; wfu and stored Châteaudun 06.2002.

A149 EC 4/11 coded '11-YB' 07.1983; EC 1/11 '11-EK' 01.1986; stored 07.1988; EC 3/11 '11-RK' 02.1990, Operation Daguet deployment 10.1990 to 03.1991; EC 1/7 '7-HG' 05.1997, recoded '7-HP' 09.1998; wfu and stored 10.2000; extant on display at Musée Aéronautique d'Orange.

A150 Operation Daguet deployment 10.1990 to 03.1991; EC 3/7 coded '7-IT' by 1993; wfu and stored Châteaudun; sold to Indian Air Force for spares recovery 08.2018.

A151 EC 4/7 coded '7-NE' 06.1981, displayed 1981 Paris Salon; EC 1/11 '11-EA' 1986; EC 4/11 '11-YD' 08.1986; EC 1/11 '11-EU' 05.1988; EC 3/11 '11-RP' 03.1992; EC 1/11 '11-ER' 07.1992; EC 2/11 '11-ML' 12.1994; EC 3/11 '11-RS' 12.1995; EC 1/7 '7-HH' 08.1997, participated in EC 1/7 closing ceremony 01.07.2005; extant on display at Pôle aéronautique d'Avord, coded '7-HJ'.

A152 CEAM 1980; EC 3/11 coded '11-RG' by 06.1982; EC 3/3 by 1986, deployed to Central African Republic 1986; crashed into a school in Bangui shortly after take-off 27.03.1986, Lieutenant M Etcheberry ejected safely but at least 31 fatalities on the ground.

A153 EC 2/11 coded '11-MB' by 09.1981; EC 1/11 '11-EX' 01.1986; EC 2/11 '11-MR'; EC 3/11 '11-RB' 07.1988, recoded '11-RA' by 1990, Operation Daguet deployment 10.1990 to 03.1991, stored 02.1994, returned recoded '11-RO' 02.1996; EC 1/7 '7-HA' 06.1997; EC 3/7 '7-ID' 07.1998; stored 09.2000; EC 1/7 '7-HK' 07.2003; airframe minus nose section extant at Saint-Dizier.

A154 EC 2/11 coded '11-MP' 01.1982; EC 3/11 '11-RT' 1987; EC 4/11 '11-YN' 03.1988; EC 3/11 '11-RE' 1990; EC 4/11 '11-YM' 01.1990; stored 06.1991; EC 3/11 '11-RP' 02.1994; EC 2/11 '11-MU' 1996; EC 3/7 '7-IN' 06.1996, stored 09.1996, returned recoded '7-IS' 10.1999; wfu 09.2000; stored Conservatoire d'Aéronefs non Operationnels Preserves et Exposes (CANOPEE) Châteaudun; sold to Indian Air Force for spares recovery 08.2018.

A155 EC 1/11 coded '11-EH' by 1981; crashed 14.09.1982.

For the disbandment ceremony of EC 1/7 at Saint-Dizier on 1 July 2005, A153 was surrounded by ordnance – including a CEP 52 practice nuclear weapon, AS.37 Martel, R.550 Magic, various bombs and rocket pods – carried by the Jaguar during its service. ***Author's Collection***

A156 EC 4/7 coded '7-NB' 1980; EC 1/11 by 1985; mid-air collision with A156 near Massif des Écrins, Valjouffrey 17.10.1985, Capitaine Bernard Boudigue killed.

A157 EC 4/11 coded '11-YI' 06.1982; EC 1/11 '11-EN' by 05.1987; EC 2/11 '11-MQ' 1986; EC 4/11 '11-YK' early 1991, Operation Daguet deployment to 03.1991; stored 05.1991; EC 1/11 '11-ES' 07.1992; stored 02.1994; EC 2/11 '11-MW' 1995; EC 3/7 '7-IK' 07.1996; EC 1/7 '7-HK' 11.1998, stored 04.1999, returned recoded '7-HH' 03.2000; wfu and stored 10.2003; extant on display at Musée Européen de l'Aviation de Chasse, Montélimar, since 10.2012.

A158 EC 2/11 coded '11-MW' by 06.1982; EC 1/11 '11-EU' 04.1985, recoded '11-EG' 10.1985; EC 3/11 '11-RI' 1988, recoded '11-RM' 05.1989; EC 3/11 '11-EV' 11.1989; EC 3/11 '11-RM' 07.1990, Operation Daguet deployment 10.1990 to 03.1991; EC 3/7 '7-IA' 04.1998; wfu and stored Châteaudun 09.2000; sold to Indian Air Force for spares recovery 08.2018.

A159 EC 3/11 coded '11-RS' by 06.1982; EC 1/11 '11-EV' by 08.1985; wfu and stored.

A160 CEAM EC 5/330 1988; EC 4/11 coded '11-YA' 05.1991; EC 3/11 '11-RT' 03.1992; EC 3/7 '7-IV' 08.1996, stored 06.1998, returned recoded '7-IH' 07.1999; EC 1/7 '7-HS' 06.2003; wfu and stored Châteaudun; sold to Indian Air Force for spares recovery 08.2018; preserved No. 3 Airmen Selection Centre, Chakeri, using parts of A90 by 08.2022.

Jaguar E

Production of the two-seat Jaguar E totalled 40 aircraft, construction numbers E1–E40, which were marked on the rudder as the serial number.

E1 ff 02.11.1970, AdA acceptance 12.1971, joined flight test programme with CEAM; extant at Conservatoire l'Air et l'Espace d'Aquitane (CAEA), Bordeaux-Merignac Airport.

E2 CEAM coded '118-AA' (starboard) and '118-AC' (port) for operational trials 1972; EC 3/3 '3-XU' by 06.1985; wfu and stored Châteaudun; sold to Indian Air Force for spares recovery 08.2018.

E3 Retained by Dassault for SBAC Farnborough display 09.1972, AdA acceptance 29.09.1972; CEAM 06.1973 coded '118-AI', recoded '118-AD' by 10.1978; EC 1/7 '7-HL' 07.1984; EC 4/7 '7-NN' by 03.1985; EC 2/7 '7-PN' 01.1986, stored 08.1988, returned recoded '7-PL' 07.1990; CITac 339 '339-WI' 10.1990; EAA 07.1992; EC 3/7 '7-IC' 10.1993; stored 05.1995; CITac 339 '339-WF' 04.1996; EC 1/7 '7-HL' 05.2000; CITac 339 and EAA coded '339-WF' 06.07.2001; extant on display at Musée de l'Air et de l'Espace, Le Bourget, Paris, since 09.2007.

E4 EC 1/11 coded '11-EM' by 1983; EC 1/7 '7-HK' by 05.1987; EC 2/7 '7-PA' by 11.1990, recoded '7-PG' by 1998; wfu and stored Châteaudun by 09.2004.

E5 EC 4/7 coded '7-NA' 1980; EC 3/11 '11-RY' by 05.1985; scrapped by 07.2021.

E6 EC 1/7 coded '7-HR'; EC 2/11 '11-ME' by mid-1980s; dumped at Saint-Dizier by 06.2022.

E7 Delivered EC 1/7 coded '7-HA' 06.1973, recoded '7-HE'; EC 2/7 '7-PA' by 10.1974, stored 05.1980, returned recoded '7-PI' by 10.1982 then '7-PN' 07.1990; stored 09.1993; CITac 339 '339-WH' 07.1994; EC 2/7 '7-PL' 07.1997; wfu, GIA Saint Agnant with fictional code '11-EC' 05.2001 (briefly restored to taxying condition 2011); extant on display at Musée Aéronautique d'Orange since 07.2013.

E8 EC 1/7 coded '7-HC' by 09.1974; EC 2/7 '7-PB' 1974; CEAM '118-AB' by 07.1981; wfu and stored Châteaudun.

E9 EC 2/7 coded '7-PC' 12.1975; stored 01.1977; EC 1/7 '7-HE' 10.1982; EC 2/7 '7-PH' 02.1983; stored 01.1985; EC 2/7 '7-PQ' 10.1988, stored 01.1991, returned recoded '7-PL' 03.1996 then '7-PD' 03.1998; EC 3/7 '7-IC'; wfu and stored Châteaudun.

E10 EC 1/7 coded '7-HH' 1973; EC 2/7 '7-PD' 11.1975; stored 01.1976; EC 3/3 '3-XG' 01.1984, recoded '3-XP'; EC 4/11 '11-YY' 01.1987; EC 3/7 '7-IC' 08.1996; CITac 339 '339-WF'; EC 1/7 '7-HH'; EC 2/7 '7-PI' by 08.2005; extant on display at Musée Chateau de Savigny-lès-Beaune since 08.2008.

E11 EC 2/7 coded '7-PE' by 1975, recoded '7-PM' by 10.1982 and '7-PE' by 07.1994; wfu and stored Châteaudun.

E12 EC 2/7 coded '7-PF' 11.1975, stored 06.1980, returned recoded '7-PA' 01.1983; stored 01.1984; EC 3/7 '7-IJ' 03.1986; stored 10.1986; EC 4/7 '7-NK' 08.1988; EC 2/7 '7-PB' 07.1989; stored 05.1990; EC 2/7 '7-PR' 05.1994; stored 05.1995; EC 2/11 '11-ML' 03.1996; EC 2/7 '7-PI' 06.1996; EC 1/7 '7-HE', recoded '7-HM' and '7-HN'; CITac 339 '339-WI' 07.2001, received special artwork for disbandment of CITac 339 07.10.2001; extant at Conservatoire d'Aéronefs non Operationnels Preserves et Exposes (CANOPEE) Châteaudun.

E13 EC 1/7 coded '7-HN' by 1974; EC 2/7 '7-PM' by 09.1975, recoded '7-PD' by 10.1982; wfu and stored Châteaudun.

E14 Aircraft abandoned due to electric failure and missed approach at Saint-Dizier 21.07.1978, Lieutenant Sable and Adjudant Grandclement ejected safely.

E15 Delivered EC 3/7 coded '7-IA' 12.1973; EC 2/11 '11-MT' 11.1976; EC 3/3 '3-XO' 1979; EC 3/7 '7-IF' 1983; EC 4/11 '11-YZ' 1985; CITac 339; EC 2/7 '7-PF' 06.1992, stored 1994, returned recoded '7-PP' 06.1996; EC 3/11 '11-RW'; EC 2/7 '7-PE', recoded '7-PJ' and '7-PZ'; wfu and stored; nose section extant.

E16 EC 2/11 coded '11-MV' by 11.1976; EC 3/3 '3-XP'; EC 2/7 '7-PI'; EC 2/11 '11-MS' by 1995; crashed into a forest at Chalon-sur-Saône 27.03.1995, both pilots killed.

Jaguar E15 in the markings of EC 2/7 'Argonne', SPA 48 'Tête de Coq' (Rooster's Head). ***Terry Panopalis Collection***

E17 EC 1/11 coded '11-EO' by 05.1976; EC 2/11 '11-MB' by 11.1976; EC 2/7 '7-PC' with EC 1/7 Escadrille markings by 10.1982; EC 2/7 '7-PN' by 1991; crashed following a bird strike near Saint-Dizier 14.03.1991, Sous-Lieutenant Moutoussamy ejected safely.

E18 Delivered EC 3/7 coded '7-ID' 01.1973; stored 06.1974; EC 1/11 '11-EN' 06.1976, recoded '11-ET' by 1978; EC 4/4 '11-YY' 01.1982; stored 07.1983; EC 2/11 '11-ME' 01.1984; EC 4/7 '7-NG' 01.1986; EC 2/7 '7-PI' 07.1990; stored 02.1993; EC 2/11 '11-MD' 05.1995; EC 3/11 '11-RW' 10.1996; EC 2/7 '7-PJ' 05.1997; EC 3/3 '3-XO'; CITac 339 '339-WL' by 2001; wfu and gate guardian at Saint Agnant, Rochefort 05.2001.

E19 EC 3/7 coded '7-IF' by 06.1974; EC 2/7 '7-PI' by 1977; CITac 339 '339-WH' by 08.1989; EC 1/11; EC 2/7 '7-PN' by 07.1996; wfu and stored.

E20 EC 2/7 coded '7-PO' 01.1979; EC 3/7 '7-IJ' 06.1980; EC 3/11 '11-RV' 07.1985; stored 01.1986; EC 1/11 '11-EV' 06.1989; EC 3/11 '11-RI' 02.1992; stored 02.1994; EC 2/7 '7-PR' 07.1995; stored 05.1997; EC 2/7 '7-PM' 03.1999; EC 1/7 '7-HO'; EC 3/7 '7-IG'; wfu and stored Châteaudun.

E21 EC 3/7 coded '7-IK' by 06.1974; EC 2/7 '7-PJ' 10.1974, displayed 1975 Paris Salon; EC 2/11 '11-MW' by 09.1978; EC 4/11 '11-YY'; stored Châteaudun by 05.1981; EC 2/7 '7-PM' by 07.1996; wfu and stored Châteaudun.

E22 EC 3/7 coded '7-IL' 1976; EC 2/11 '11-ME' 1979; EC 4/11 '11-YY' 1986; EC 2/7 '7-PC' by 05.1987, stored 03.1992, returned recoded '7-PI' 05.1993, stored 05.1995, returned recoded '7-PU' 09.1999; stored 05.2000; EC 1/7 '7-HB' 06.2005, received special paint scheme for EC 1/7 closing ceremony 01.07.2005; wfu and stored 06.07.2005; extant at Conservatoire d'Aéronefs non Operationnels Preserves et Exposes (CANOPEE) Châteaudun.

E23 EC 2/7 coded '7-PC' by 11.1974 (at one point had EC 2/7 Escadrille markings and EC 3/7 code '7-IN'); EC 1/11 '11-EI' by 05.1984; CITac 339 '339-WG' by 2001; extant at Merignac-Bordeaux Airport.

E24 EC 3/7 coded '7-IJ' by 10.1982; EC 2/7 '7-PH' by 05.1998; stored at Conservatoire d'Aéronefs non Operationnels Preserves et Exposes (CANOPEE) Châteaudun 2005; sold to Indian Air Force for spares recovery 08.2018.

E25 EC 2/7 coded '7-PL' 04.1977; stored 1981; EC 3/7 '7-IK' 08.1983; EC 2/7 '7-PE' 1986; EC 3/7 '7-IL' 10.1986; stored 1987; CITac 339 '339-WG' 1990; EC 3/7 '7-PK' 1992, stored 07.1996, returned recoded '7-PR' 04.1999; wfu and stored Châteaudun.

E26 Crashed 14nm north-east of Reims 26.03.1975, both pilots killed.

E27 EC 1/11 coded '11-EL' by 11.1976; CITac 339 '339-WI'; crashed at Diane-Capelle 14.09.1994, Lieutenants Ricour and Bawejski ejected safely.

E28 EC 1/11 coded '11-EP' by 08.1977; EC 3/7 '7-IB'; EC 1/11 '11-EI' 01.1979; EC 4/7 '7-NO' 01.1982; EC 2/7 '7-PJ' 07,1985, recoded '7-PK' 01.1986; stored 01.1987; EC 3/7 '7-IJ' 10.1989; EC 2/7 '7-PM' 07.1990, recoded '7-PR' 01.1992; stored 05.1995; EC 2/11 '11-MK' 03.1996; EC 2/7 '7-PS' 07.1996, recoded '7-PS' by 05.2000; wfu and stored Saint Agnant 06.2000; GIA Rochefort 07.2000, wfu 2006; extant on display at Musée Européen de l'Aviation de Chasse, Montélimar, since 30.04.2010.

E29 EC 3/11 coded '11-RA' by 11.1976; EC 1/11 '11-EA' by 09.1978; EC 2/7 '7-PA' by 05.1982; CITac 339 '339-WJ' by 1998; wfu, GIA Séchault.

E30 EC 3/11 coded '11-RC' by 11.1976; stored Châteaudun by 05.1981; EC 2/7 '7-PL' 06.1982, recoded '7-PU' 01.1985; EC 1/11 '11-EH' 01.1987; EC 2/7 '7-PO' 05.1989, stored 02.1992, returned recoded '7-PD' 01.1994, stored 04.1994, returned recoded '7-PK' 10.1996, received special 80th anniversary of SPA 31 and SPA 48 markings; stored 06.1999; CITac 339 '339-WN' 07.2001; EC 1/7 '7-HW' by 08.2002; wfu and stored Saint Agnant 05.2003; GIA Rochefort; displayed at Musée de l'Aviation Clément Ader, Lyon Airport 06.2010; extant at Saint-Yan Airport, Saône-et-Loire since 07.2013.

E31 EC 3/11 coded '11-RF' by 11.1976; EC 2/7 '7-PF' by 10.1982, EC 1/7 '7-HK' by 06.1987; EC 2/7 '7-PE' 1989; crashed near Saint-Eulien 23.10.1989, the pilot ejected safely.

E32 EC 4/11 coded '11-YZ'; EC 3/11 '11-RG' 09.1978; EC 2/7 '7-PO' 01.1985; EC 4/7 '7-NE' 09.1985; stored 01.1987; EC 2/7 '7-PO' 09.1993, recoded '7-PF' 07.1995, stored 08.1996, returned recoded '7-PD' 10.1999; EC 1/7 '7-HW' 07.2004; wfu and stored Châteaudun; sold to Indian Air Force for spares recovery 08.2018.

E33 EC 3/11 coded '11-RH' by 11.1976; CEV by 1987; crashed near les Baux-de-Provence during a test sortie from Istres 20.08.1987, Monsieur F Jouslin and Commandant B Berthaud ejected safely.

E34 Crashed 02.07.1975.

E35 EC 3/11 coded '11-RI' 11.1976; EC 2/7 '7-PH' 01.1982; EC 3/11 '11-RC' 04.1982; stored 06.1982; EC 1/7 '7-HI' 07.1984; EC 2/7 '7-PF' 08.1987, stored 08.1987, returned recoded '7-PK' 09.1989, stored 07.1990, returned recoded '7-PM' 07.1994 then '7-PU' 03.1999; EC 2/11 '11-MW'; EC 3/11 '11-RV'; EC 2/7 '7-PR'; CITac 339 '339-WK' 07.2001; EC 1/7 '7-HY' 06.2003; wfu and stored Saint Agnant 09.2005; extant on display at Musée de l'Épopée de l'Industrie et de l'Aéronautique, Albert, since 06.2013.

E36 EC 2/7 coded '7-PO' 06.1980; EC 4/11 '11-YZ' 07.1983; EC 2/7 '7-PL' 08.1985; stored 07.1987; EC 1/7 '7-HB' 12.1988; EC 2/7 '7-PP' 05.1990, stored 05.1992, returned recoded '7-PM' 1998 then '7-PK' 09.1999; EC 1/7 '7-HR' by 2003; wfu and stored; extant as gate guardian Saint-Dizier since 06.2011.

E37 EC 3/11 coded '11-RD' 11.1976; EC 2/11 '11-M' (starboard) and '11-ME' (port) 06.1978; EC 2/7 '7-PH' 01.1980, recoded '7-PQ' 04.1984; stored 08.1987; EC 2/11 '11-MK' 05.1988; EC 2/7 '7-PM' 05.1989; EC 3/7 '7-IG' 05.1990; stored 02.1991; EC 2/7 '7-PP' 10.1993, stored 05.1995, returned recoded '7-PQ' 06.1996, stored 05.1998, returned recoded '7-PM' 09.2000 then '7-PJ'; EC 1/7 '7-HZ' 2003, received special 30th anniversary colour scheme 24.05.2003; extant on display at Espaces Aéro Lyon Corbas since 07.2010.

The last production Jaguar E, E40, on the last operational day, 1 July 2005. The aircraft has been on display at the Museo Nacional Aeronautico Y del Espacio in Santiago, Chile, since early 2012, an unusual resting place given that Chile never operated the Jaguar, but proving that the Jaguar has international appeal and is not forgotten. ***Author's Collection***

E38 EC 2/7 coded '7-PI' 06.1980; EC 1/7 '7-HK' 06.1982; EC 3/3 coded '3-XG' 01.1985; EC 4/7 '7-NN' 01.1986; EC 2/7 '7-PM' 08.1986, stored 01.1989, returned recoded '7-PP' 04.1990; EC 2/11 '11-MK' 07.1990; EC 2/7 '7-PM' 04.1992; crashed near Bar-le-Duc 16.09.1993, Lieutenant O Nemes ejected safely.

E39 EC 4/7 coded '7-NO' by 08.1982; EC 4/11 '11-YX' by 05.1987; EC 2/7 '7-PH' by 05.1992; EC 1/7 '7-HJ' by 2001; crashed near Saint-Dizier 19.11.2001, both pilots ejected safely (this was the final AdA Jaguar crash).

E40 EC 2/7 coded '7-PN' 06.1980; EC 4/11 '11-YY' 01.1985; stored 01.1986; EC 1/11 '11-EG' 06.1987; EC 2/7 '7-PH' 07.1990, stored 01.1991, returned 05.1993, stored 09.1993, returned recoded '7-PG' 01.1994, stored 03.1995, returned recoded '7-PI' 02.1998; stored 09.2000; EC 1/7 '7-HX' 07.2001, participated in EC 1/7 closing ceremony 01.07.2005; wfu and stored Saint Agnant 11.06.2005; extant on display at Museo Nacional Aeronautico Y del Espacio, Santiago, Chile, since 02.2012.

APPENDIX FOUR

Ecuadorian production

This is a listing of all Jaguars ordered for the Fuerza Aérea Ecuatoriana (FAE), including a concise history of each aircraft. Changes in serial numbers and applications of B-Condition markings for delivery flights are highlighted in bold text.

In these entries the following abbreviations may be found:

Esc – Escuadrón de Combate
ff – first flown
Wfu – withdrawn from use

EB1/PS841/168 FAE-283, ff 19.08.1976. Delivery 04.01.1977 as **G-27-266**; to Esc 2111; wfu 2002, extant as decoy airframe at Taura.

EB2/PS842/183 FAE-305, ff 07.01.1977. Delivery 31.05.1977 as **G-27-267**; to Esc 2111; wfu 2002, extant in store at Taura.

ES1/PS901/172 FAE 289, ff 28.09.1976. Delivery 04.01.1977 as **G-27-268**; to Esc 2111; crashed near Guayaquil due to bird strike and engine failure 30.03.1990, pilot killed.

ES2/PS1002/181 FAE-302, ff 14.12.1976. Delivery 31.05.1977 as **G-27-269**; to Esc 2111; wfu 2002; preserved at FAE Academy, Salinas.

ES3/PS1003/188 FAE-309, ff 08.02.1977. Delivery 18.04.1977 as **G-27-270**; to Esc 2111; wfu 2002; extant as decoy airframe at Taura.

ES4/PS1004/191 FAE-318, ff 25.02.1977. Delivery 18.04.1977 as **G-27-261**; to Esc 2111; written off 16.08.1988.

ES5/PS1005/197 FAE-327, ff 01.04.1977. Delivery 16.08.1977 as **G-27-272**; to Esc 2111; wfu 2002; persevered at Museo Aéreo de la Fuerza Aérea Ecuatoriana, Quito.

ES6/PS1006/199 FAE-329, ff 26.04.1977. Delivery 16.08.1977 as **G-27-273**; to Esc 2111; wfu 2002; extant as decoy airframe at Taura.

ES7/PS1007/206 FAE-339, ff 05.07.1977. Delivery 05.09.1977 as **G-27-274**; to Esc 2111; wfu, stored by 2000; extant in store at Taura.

ES8/PS1008/207 FAE-340, ff 04.08.1977. Delivery 05.09.1977 as **G-27-275**; to Esc 2111; written off 22.10.1989.

ES9/PS1009/214 FAE-348, ff 19.09.1977. Delivery 24.10.1977 as **G-27-276**; to Esc 2111; wfu by 2000; extant as decoy airframe at Taura.

ES10/PS1010/215 FAE-349, ff 27.09.1977. Delivery 24.10.1977 as **G-27-277**; to Esc 2111; crashed into mountain 16.09.1981.

APPENDIX FIVE

Omani production

This is a listing of all Jaguars ordered for the Sultan of Oman's Air Force, including a concise history of each aircraft. Changes in serial numbers and applications of B-Condition markings for delivery flights are highlighted in bold text.

In these entries the following abbreviations may be found:

AFTC – Air Force Technical College
ff – first flown
GIA – Ground Instructional Airframe
Wfu – withdrawn from use

B(O)1/PS861/177 Serial 201, ff 04.11.1976. Delivery 07.03.1977 as **G-27-278**; to No. 8 Sqn; crashed near Thumrait 01.03.1981, both pilots ejected safely.

S(O)1/PS1051/189 Serial 202, ff 27.01.1977. Delivery 07.03.1977 as **G-27-280**; to No. 8 Sqn; wfu 2010.

B(O)2/PS882/195 Serial 203, ff 06.04.1977. Registered to BAC as **G-BETB** 26.04.1977, displayed Paris Air Show 06.1977; delivery 27.06.1977 as **G-27-279**; to No. 8 Sqn; wfu 2013; preserved at Sultan's Armed Forces Museum, Bait-al-Falaj.

S(O)2/PS1052/202 Serial 204, ff 18.05.1977. Registered to BAC as **G-BEET**, displayed Paris Air Show 06.1977; delivery 27.06.1977 as **G-27-281**; to No. 8 Sqn; midair collision with '204' 11.09.2013 (Captain Alazhar al-Shraiqi killed, the other pilot was injured).

S(O)3/PS1053/210 Serial 205, ff 18.08.1977. Delivery 26.09.1977 as **G-27-282**; to No. 8 Sqn; crashed near Masirah 27.10.1991.

S(O)4/PS1054/211 Serial 206, ff 19.08.1977. Delivery 26.09.1977 as **G-27-283**; to No. 8 Sqn; wfu 2009, to Seeb AFTC as GIA.

S(O)5/PS1055/218 Serial 207, ff 07.10.1977. Delivery 07.11.1977 as **G-27-284**; to No. 8 Sqn; crashed west of Jebel range following a bird strike 17.12.1991, pilot ejected safely.

S(O)6/PS1056/219 Serial 208, ff 14.10.1977. Delivery 07.11.1977 as **G-27-285**; to No. 8 Sqn; crashed following premature bomb detonation 12.12.1985, pilot ejected safely.

S(O)7/PS1057/223 Serial 209, ff 16.12.1977. Delivery 06.02.1978 as **G-27-286**; to No. 8 Sqn; wfu 2010, stored at Thumrait.

S(O)8/PS1058/224 Serial 210, ff 12.01.1978. Delivery 06.02.1978 as **G-27-287**; to No. 8 Sqn; wfu 2010, stored at Thumrait.

S(O)9/PS1059/225 Serial 211, ff 08.03.1978. Delivery 08.05.1978 as **G-27-288**; to No. 8 Sqn; wfu 2013; to Seeb AFTC as GIA 08.2014.

S(O)10/PS1060/226 Serial 212, ff 21.03.1978. Delivery 08.05.1978 as **G-27-289**; to No. 8 Sqn; crashed following premature bomb detonation 26.02.1979, pilot ejected but injured.

B(O)3/PS863/230 Serial 213, ff 05.11.1982. Delivery 23.05.1983 as **G-27-375**; to No. 20 Sqn; wfu 2013; to Seeb AFTC as GIA 08.2014.

B(O)4/PS864/231 Serial 214, ff 26.11.1982. Delivery 25.07.1983 as **G-27-376**; to No. 20 Sqn; crashed 10.03.2013, scrapped at Thumrait 08.2014.

S(O)11/PS1061/232 Serial 215, ff 15.09.1982. Delivery 23.05.1983 as **G-27-377**; to No. 20 Sqn; midair collision with '223' 03.11.2007, made successful emergency landing at Thumrait; wfu; to Seeb AFTC as GIA 08.2014.

S(O)12/PS1062/237 Serial 216, ff 02.11.1982. Delivery 23.05.1983 as **G-27-378**; to No. 20 Sqn; crashed near Thumrait 29.01.1991.

S(O)13/PS1063/217 Serial 217, ff 07.01.1983. Delivery 25.07.1983 as **G-27-379**; to No. 20 Sqn; midair collision with '204' 11.09.2013(Captain Alazhar al-Shraiqi killed, the other pilot was injured).

S(O)14/PS1064/239 Serial 218, ff 12.05.1983. Delivery 25.07.1983 as **G-27-380**; to No. 20 Sqn; crashed near the Sultan's Palace in Salalah, Dhofar, 21.06.1984.

S(O)15/PS1065/244 Serial 219, ff 26.04.1983. Delivery 19.09.1983 as **G-27-381**; to No. 20 Sqn; wfu; to Seeb AFTC as GIA 08.2014.

S(O)16/PS1066/245 Serial 220, ff 18.05. 1983. Delivery 19.09.1983 as **G-27-382**; to No. 20 Sqn; wfu 12.2012, stored at Thumrait.

S(O)17/PS1067/250 Serial 221, ff 01.06.1983. Delivery 19.09.1983 as **G-27-383**; to No. 20 Sqn; crashed near Masirah 22.06.2010, pilot ejected safely.

S(O)18/PS1068/251 Serial 222, ff 15.06.1983. Delivery 24.11.1983 as **G-27-384**; to No. 20 Sqn; wfu 2013; to Seeb AFTC as GIA 08.2014; preserved at Adam.

S(O)19/PS1069/252 Serial 223, ff 07.07.1983. Delivery 24.11.1983 as **G-27-385**; to No. 20 Sqn; midair collision with '215' 03.11.2007, pilot ejected safely.

S(O)20/PS1070/256 Serial 224, ff 15.07.1983. Delivery 24.11.1983 as **G-27-386**; to No. 20 Sqn; wfu 2014, stored at Thumrait.

Attrition replacements

B3/PS803 Serial 200, ff 10.10.1973, ex-RAF **XX138**, ex-Indian Air Force **JI001**. Returned to UK, to BAe as **G-27-332**; sold to Sultan of Oman's Air Force as an attrition replacement in 1982, overhauled Abingdon 09.83 to 12.83; extant stored at Thumrait.

S37/PS637 Serial 225, ff 25.09.1974, ex-RAF **XX740**, ex-Indian Air Force **JI017**. Returned to UK 19.05.1984; sold to Sultan of Oman's Air Force as an attrition replacement, delivery 04.11.1986; wfu 2008, stored at Thumrait.

S16 Serial 226, ff 31.01.1974, ex-RAF **XX719**. Sold to the Royal Air Force of Oman as an attrition replacement, delivery 10.08.1998; wfu 01.05.2010, stored at Thumrait.

APPENDIX SIX

Indian production

This is a listing of all Jaguars ordered for the Indian Air Force, including a concise history of each aircraft. Specific movements are difficult to trace and many accident losses have been unidentified, so where possible a last in service or proven extant date is provided; the unidentified crashes are also listed. Changes in serial numbers and applications of B-Condition markings for delivery flights are highlighted in bold text.

In these entries the following abbreviations may be found:

- AFS – Air Force Station
- ASTE – Aircraft and Systems Testing Establishment
- ff – first flown
- Fg Off – Flying Officer
- Flt Lt – Flight Lieutenant
- HAL – Hindustan Aeronautics Limited
- Sqn Ldr – Squadron Leader
- TPS – Test Pilot School
- Wfu – withdrawn from use
- Wg Cdr – Wing Commander

Batch one

The first batch covered 18 aircraft on loan from the RAF and later returned to the UK: 16 Jaguar GR.1 and two T.2.

B3/PS803 JI001, ex-**XX138**. Delivery 19.07.1979 as **G-27-320**; to No. 18 Sqn; sold by BAe directly to the Sultan of Oman's Air Force as an attrition replacement 01.1982.

B8/PS808 JI002, ex-**XX143**. Delivery 14.10.1979 as **G-27-321**; to No. 18 Sqn; returned to UK 09.09.1982.

S17/PS617 JI003, ex-**XX720**. Delivery 19.07.1979 as **G-27-319**; to No. 18 Sqn; returned to UK 24.02.1982.

S10/PS610 JI004, ex-**XX117**. Delivery 14.10.1979 as **G-27-317**; to No. 18 Sqn; returned to UK 24.02.1982.

S8/PS608 JI005, ex-**XX115**. Delivery 11.12.1979 as **G-27-316**; to No. 18 Sqn; returned to UK 23.07.1982.

S162/PS609 JI006, ex-**XZ397**. Delivery 11.12.1979 as **G-27-322**; to No. 18 Sqn; crashed due to bird strike 16.04.1981, Flt Lt S Adhikari ejected safely.

S163/PS763 JI007, ex-**XZ398**. Delivery 11.12.1979 as **G-27-323**; to No. 18 Sqn; to HAL for DARIN development work; returned to UK 04.1984.

S9/PSPS609 JI008, ex **XX116**. Delivery 11.12.1979 as **G-27-315**; to No. 18 Sqn; to HAL for DARIN development work; returned to UK 19.09.1984.

S25/PS625 JI009, ex-**XX728**. Delivery 29.04.1980 as **G-27-324**; to No. 18 Sqn; returned to UK 23.07.1982.

S22/PS622 JI010, ex-**XX725**. Delivery 13.02.1980 as **G-27-325**; to No. 18 Sqn; returned to UK 19.04.1982.

S6/PS606 JI011, ex-**XX729**. Delivery 13.02.1980 as **G-27-314**; to No. 18 Sqn; crashed into high ground 10.05.1982, pilot Flt Lt R K Srivastava killed.

S26/PS626 JI012, ex-**XX729**. Delivery 29.04.1980 as **G-27-326**; to No. 18 Sqn; returned to UK 25.05.1982.

S33/PS633 JI013, ex-**XX736**. Delivery 12.02.1980 as **G-27-327**; to No. 18 Sqn; returned to UK 24.02.1982.

S31/PS631 JI014, ex-**XX734**. Delivery 14.08.1980 as **G-27-328**; to No. 18 Sqn; returned to UK 11.02.1982.

S34/PS634 JI015, ex-**XX737**. Delivery 14.08.1980 as **G-27-330**; to No. 18 Sqn; returned to UK 25.05.1982.

S35/PS635 JI016, ex-**XX738**. Delivery 12.02.1980 as **G-27-329**; to No. 18 Sqn; returned to UK 19.04.1984.

S37/PS637 JI017, ex-**XX740**. Delivery 23.04.1980 as **G-27-331**; to No. 18 Sqn; returned to UK 19.05.1985.

S11/611 JI018, ex-**XX118**. Delivery 29.04.1980 as **G-27-318**; to No. 18 Sqn; returned to UK 25.04.1982.

Batch two

The second batch covered 40 Jaguar International aircraft built by BAe: 35 Jaguar IS, five Jaguar IB.

B(I)1/PS0881 JT051. Delivery as **G-27-368**; to No. 5 Sqn; to No. 7 Wing; in service 01.2023.

B(I)2/PS0882 JT052. Delivery as **G-27-369**; to No. 5 Sqn 02.1980; in service 03.2024.

B(I)3/PS0883 JT053. Delivery as **G-27-370**; to No. 5 Sqn; extant 01.2015.

B(I)4/PS0884 JT054. Delivery as **G-27-371**; to No. 5 Sqn; extant 01.2015.

B(I)5/PS0885 JT055. Delivery as **G-27-372**; to ASTE; crashed 03.10.2016.

S(I)1/PS1101 JS101, ff 17.02.1981. Delivery 01.07.1981 as **G-27-333**; to No. 7 Wing; extant 01.2011.

S(I)2/PS1102 JS102. Delivery 01.07.1981 as **G-27-334**; to ASTE, converted to DARIN prototype, flown 17.12.1982; to 5 Sqn; to 14 Sqn; in service 01.2024.

S(I)3/PS1103 JS103. Delivery 16.09.1981 as **G-27-335**; to ASTE, converted to DARIN prototype; to 7 Wing; in service 01.2023.

S(I)4/PS1104 JS104. Delivery 16.09.1981 as **G-27-336**; crashed 01.06.1984.

S(I)5/PS1105 JS105. Delivery 14.10.1981 as **G-27-337**; no further details known.

S(I)6/PS1106 JS106. Delivery 14.10.1981 as **G-27-338**; no further details known.

S(I)7/PS1107 JS107. Delivery 17.10.1981 as **G-27-339**; to No. 7 Wing; extant 02.2009.

S(I)8/PS1108 JS108. Delivery 17.12.1981 as **G-27-340**; to No. 14 Sqn; in service 01.2024.

S(I)9/PS1109 JS109. Delivery 17.12.1981 as **G-27-341**; to No. 7 Wing; overhaul by HAL; in service 01.2023.

S(I)10/PS1110 JS110. Delivery 17.12.1981 as **G-27-342**; to No. 7 Wing; in service 01.2023.

S(I)11/PS1111 JS111. Delivery 30.01.1982 as **G-27-343**; no further details known.

S(I)12/PS1112 JS112. Delivery 30.01.1982 as **G-27-344**; to No. 7 Wing; extant 12.2018.

S(I)13/PS1113 JS113. Delivery 30.01.1982 as **G-27-345**; no further details known.

S(I)14/PS1114 JS114. Delivery 18.03.1982 as **G-27-346**; to No. 7 Wing; crashed 11.04.1984.

S(I)15/PS1115 JS115. Delivery 18.03.1982 as **G-27-347**; to TPS by 2012; to ASTE by 04.2023.

S(I)16/PS1116 JS116. Delivery 18.03.1982 as **G-27-348**; to ASTE; displayed at Aero India 02. 2015.

S(I)17/PS1117 JS117. Delivery18.03.1982 as **G-27-349**; to ASTE by 04.2023.

S(I)18/PS1118 JS118. Delivery 22.04.1982 as **G-27-350**; no further details known.

S(I)19/PS1119 JS119. Delivery 22.04.1982 as **G-27-351**; to No. 5 Sqn; extant 02.2001.

S(I)20/PS1120 JS120. Delivery 22.04.1982 as **G-27-352**; to No. 14 Sqn; crashed at Naraingarh near Ambala AFS due to double hydraulic failure 22.11.1993, Fg Off Puneet Pareek ejected safely.

S(I)21/PS1121 JS121. Delivery 22.04.1982 as **G-27-353**; to No. 14 Sqn.

S(I)22/PS1122 JS122. Delivery 14.06.1982 as **G-27-354**; crashed 07.08.1984.

S(I)23/PS1123 JS123. Delivery 14.06.1982 as **G-27-355**; to No. 5 Sqn; extant 02.2001.

S(I)24/PS1124 JS124. Delivery 14.06.1982 as **G-27-356**; to No. 7 Wing; to No. 14 Sqn; active 01.2024.

S(I)25/PS1125 JS125. Delivery 14.06.1982 as **G-27-357**; no further details known.

S(I)26/PS1126 JS126. Delivery 09.08.1982 as **G-27-358**; to No. 14 Sqn; active 01.2024.

S(I)27/PS1127 JS127. Delivery 09.08.1982 as **G-27-359**; no further details known.

S(I)28/PS1128 JS128. Delivery 09.08.1982 as **G-27-360**; to No. 7 Wing; to No. 14 Sqn; active 01.2024.

S(I)29/PS1129 JS129. Delivery 09.08.1982 as **G-27-361**; to No. 5 Sqn; to No. 7 Wing; active 01.2023.

S(I)30/PS1130 JS130. Delivery 24.09.1982 as **G-27-362**; to No. 7 Wing; active 01.2023.

S(I)31/PS1131 JS131. Delivery 24.09.1982 as **G-27-363**; to No. 5 Sqn; extant 12.2018.

S(I)32/PS1132 JS132. Delivery 24.09.1982 as **G-27-364**; to No. 7 Wing; extant 02.2011.

S(I)33/PS1133 JS133. Delivery 06.11.1982 as **G-27-365**; to No. 14 Sqn; in service 01.2024.

S(I)34/PS1134 JS134. Delivery 24.09.1982 as **G-27-366**; to No. 5 Sqn; in service 01.2023.

S(I)35/PS1135 JS.135. Displayed SBAC Show Farnborough 09.1982; delivery 06.11.1982 as **G-27-362**; to No.5 Sqn; in service 01.2023.

Batch three

The third batch covered Jaguar International aircraft kits built by BAe and assembled by HAL, gradually switching over to HAL-produced components: 35 Jaguar IS, ten Jaguar IB.

B(I)6 JT056. To TPS; to ASTE by 04.2023.

B(I)7 JT057. To No. 5 Sqn; to No. 27 Sqn.

B(I)8 JT058. To No. 224 Sqn; extant 02.2013.

B(I)9 JT059. To No. 27 Sqn; DARIN I upgrade; extant 10.2017.

B(I)10 JT060. Crashed near Bamraulli AFS 16.06.2015, both pilots ejected safely.

B(I)11 JT061. To HAL.

B(I)12 JT062. No details known.

B(I)13 JT063. To No. 17 Wing; extant 11.2011.

B(I)14 JT064. No details known.

B(I)15 JT065. To No. 6 Sqn; extant 10.2001.

S(I)36 JS136, ff 31.03.1982. To No. 14 Sqn; in service 01.2024.

S(I)37 JS137. To No. 14 Sqn.

S(I)38 JS138. To No. 14 Sqn.

S(I)39 JS139. To No. 14 Sqn; crashed on take-off at Ambala AFS 09.05.2002, Fg Off S Palarwal killed.

S(I)40 JS140. No details known.

S(I)41 JS141. To No. 7 Wing; participated in Exercise Cooperative Cope Thunder 2004 deployment to Elmendorf AFB, Alaska, 23.06.2004 to 06.08.2004.

S(I)42 JS142. No details known.

S(I)43 JS143. No details known.

S(I)44 JS144. To No. 7 Wing; participated in Exercise Cooperative Cope Thunder 2004 deployment to Elmendorf AFB, Alaska, 23.06.2004 to 06.08.2004.

S(I)45 JS145. No details known.

S(I)46 JS146. To No. 7 Wing; extant 04.2017.

S(I)47 JS147. Extant 02.2013.

S(I)48 JS148. To No. 6 Sqn. Crashed near Ambala AFS due to fire shortly after take-off 07.05.2004, Sqn Ldr Tamaskar ejected with minor injuries.

S(I)49 JS149. Extant 03.2001.

S(I)50 JS150. To No. 7 Wing; to No. 33 Wing; participated in Exercise Cooperative Cope Thunder 2004 deployment to Elmendorf AFB, Alaska, 23.06.2004 to 06.08.2004.

S(I)51 JS151. To No. 6 Sqn; extant 02.2021

S(I)52 JS152. No details known.

S(I)53 JS153. Extant 02.2003.

S(I)54 JS154. To No. 6 Sqn; participated in Exercise Cooperative Cope Thunder 2004 deployment to Elmendorf AFB, Alaska, 23.06.2004 to 06.08.2004; extant 02.2007.

S(I)55 JS155. No details known.

S(I)56 JS156. To No. 6 Sqn; extant 02.2003.

S(I)57 JS157. To No. 7 Wing; extant 10.2021.

S(I)58 JS158. To No. 16 Sqn; extant 02.2005.

S(I)59 JS159. To No. 6 Sqn; to No. 33 Wing; in service 02.2023.

S(I)60 JS160. No details known.

S(I)61 JS161. To No. 16 Sqn; crashed on approach to Gorakhpur AFS 25.06.1995, braking parachute inadvertently deployed, Flt Lt Chauhan ejected safely but two people killed on the ground.

S(I)62 JS162. To No. 16 Sqn; extant 02.2005.

S(I)63 JS163. Extant 02.2019.

S(I)64 JS164. To No. 33 Wing; in service 02.2022.

S(I)65 JS165. No details known.

S(I)66 JS166. Crashed due to electrical failure and engine flame out near Uttarlai AFS 26.02.1997, Flt Lt Puneet K Pareek ejected safely.

S(I)67 JS167. To No. 16 or No. 27 Sqn; crashed at Kurmi Village near Gorakhpur AFS due to engine fire 13.08.1996, Flt Lt Navneet Raina ejected safely.

S(I)68 JS168. DARIN I upgrade; to No. 27 Sqn; extant 10.2017.

S(I)69 JS169. To No. 16 Sqn 12.1998.

Batch four

This covers production by HAL from HAL-built components: 24 Jaguar IS, eight Jaguar IM.

M(I)1 JM251, ff 11.1985; to No. 6 Sqn.

M(I)2 JM252. To No. 6 Sqn; in service 02.2022.

M(I)3 JM253. To No. 6 Sqn, coded '14'; crashed on take-off Pune AFS 16.02.1999, Flt Lt Agarwal ejected safely but injured.

M(I)4 JM254. To No. 6 Sqn; in service 02.2022.

M(I)5 JM255. To No. 6 Sqn; to HAL, DARIN III upgrade; extant 02.2017.

M(I)6 JM256. To No. 6 Sqn; in service 02.2022.

M(I)7 JM257, ff 12.1993. To No. 6 Sqn; extant 02.2003.

M(I)8 JM258, ff 12.1993. To No. 6 Sqn; extant 10.2013.

S(I)70 JS170, ff 1988. Participated in Exercise Cooperative Cope Thunder 2004 deployment to Elmendorf AFB, Alaska, 23.06.2004 to 06.08.2004; extant 02.2011.

S(I)71 JS171. DARIN I upgrade; to No. 27 Sqn; extant 10.2017.

S(I)72 JS172. To No. 17 Wing; extant 10.2009.

S(I)73 JS173. To No. 6 Sqn; extant 02.2009.

S(I)74 JS174. Extant 02.2013.

S(I)75 JS175. To No. 5 Sqn; extant 09.2003.

S(I)76 JS176. No details known.

S(I)77 JS177. Participated in Exercise Cooperative Cope Thunder 2004 deployment to Elmendorf AFB, Alaska, 23.06.2004 to 06.08.2004.

S(I)78 JS178. To No. 6 Sqn; extant 02.2009.

S(I)79 JS179. Extant 02.2013.

S(I)80 JS180. No details known.

S(I)81 JS181. No details known.

S(I)82 JS182. No details known. To No. 33 Wing; overhaul by HAL; in service 02.2022.

S(I)83 JS183. Extant 02.2011.

S(I)84 JS184. Extant 10.2018.

S(I)85 JS185. No details known. To No. 14 Sqn; extant 02.2003.

S(I)86 JS186. To No. 6 Sqn; in service 02.2023.

S(I)87 JS187. To No. 6 Sqn; extant 02.2009.

S(I)88 JS188. No details known.

S(I)89 JS189. No details known.

S(I)90 JS190. To No. 16 Sqn 12.1998.

S(I)91 JS191. No details known.

S(I)92 JS192. No details known.

S(I)93 JS193. To No. 17 Wing; to No. 6 Sqn; in service 02.2023.

S(I)94 JS194. No details known.

Batch five

This covers production by HAL from HAL-built components: 11 Jaguar IS, four Jaguar IM.

M(I)9 JM259, ff 12.1993. To No. 6 Sqn; extant 02.2013.

M(I)10 JM260. To No. 6 Sqn; in service 02.2022.

M(I)11 JM261. To No. 6 Sqn; extant 12.2017.

M(I)12 JM262. To No. 6 Sqn; in service 02.2022.

S(I)95 JS195. To No. 6 Sqn; in service 02.2023.

S(I)96 JS196. To No. 16 Sqn; extant 12.1998.

S(I)97 JS197. To No. 16 Sqn; to No. 27 Sqn; crashed 04.11.2011.

S(I)98 JS198. To No. 27 Sqn; crashed 28.01.2019.

S(I)99 JS199. To No. 16 Sqn 12.1998.

S(I)100 JS200. No details known.

S(I)101 JS201. No details known.

S(I)102 JS202. To No. 16 Sqn; crashed near Devri Village, Uttar Pradesh 11.05.2005, Flt Lt Ajit Singh killed.

Jaguar JS207 was the second aircraft of the final batch of Jaguars built by HAL and is of DARIN II standard. JS207 was operated by No. 14 'Bulls' Squadron. *Author's Collection*

S(I)103 JS203. To No. 6 Sqn 02.1999; extant 02.2007.

S(I)104 JS204. No details known.

S(I)105 JS205. Delivered 09.1999; to No. 224 Sqn by 02.2013; extant 03.2016.

Batch six

This covers production by HAL of 17 Jaguar IB (Night Attack) from HAL-built components.

B(I)16 JT066. To ASTE; to No. 7 Wing 2002; in service 01.2023.

B(I)17 JT067. To No. 5 Sqn; crashed near Bholasar Village, Rajasthan, at night due to technical failure 22.01.2014, both crew ejected safely.

B(I)18 JT068. To No. 224 Sqn; flight refuelling probe modification 2008; extant 02.2013.

B(I)19 JT069. To No. 6 Sqn; extant 02.2005.

B(I)20 JT070. To No. 224 Sqn; extant 02.2013.

B(I)21 JT071. To No. 6 Sqn; extant 02.2007.

B(I)22 JT072. To No. 6 Sqn; extant 02.2007.

B(I)23 JT073. Extant 03.2016.

B(I)24 JT074. To No. 16 Sqn; extant 11.2006.

B(I)25 JT075. To No. 14 Sqn; extant 10.2007.

B(I)26 JT076. To No. 33 Wing; in service 02.2022.

B(I)27 JT077. To No.14 Sqn; extant 10.2007.

B(I)28 JT078. No details known.

B(I)29 JT079. No details known.

B(I)30 JT080. To No.14 Sqn; in service 01.2022.

B(I)31 JT081. To No.14 Sqn.

B(I)32 JT082. To No.14 Sqn; extant 02.2010.

Batch seven

This covers production of 20 Jaguar IS by HAL from HAL-built components.

S(I)106//JQ082 JS206. Extant 02.2019.

S(I)107//JQ083 JS207. To No. 14 Sqn; extant 10.2015.

S(I)108//JQ084 JS208. To No. 14 Sqn; in service 01.2024.
S(I)109/JQ085 JS209. Crashed 13.09.2016.

S(I)110/JQ086 JS210. To No. 14 Sqn; extant 05.2016.

S(I)111/JQ087 JS211. No details known.

S(I)112/JQ088 JS212. To No. 14 Sqn; in service 01.2024.

S(I)113/JQ089 JS213. Extant 10.2010.

S(I)114/JQ090 JS214. To No. 33 Wing 2008; DARIN II upgrade; extant 08.2017.

S(I)115/JQ091 JS215. No details known.

S(I)116/JQ092 JS216. Extant 2013.

S(I)117//JQ093 JS217. To No. 224 Sqn; extant 02.2013.

S(I)118/JQ094 JS218. Built 10.2007.

S(I)119/JQ095 JS219. To No. 33 Wing; crashed 05.06.2018.

S(I)120/JQ096 JS220. No details known.

S(I)121/JQ097 JS221. To No. 14 Sqn; extant 05.2016.

S(I)122/JQ098 JS222. To No. 14 Sqn; extant 05.2016.

S(I)123/JQ099 JS223. Extant 03.2010.

S(I)124/JQ100 JS224. To No. 224 Sqn; extant 02.2013.

S(I)125/JQ101 JS225. To No. 14 Sqn; in service 01.2022.

Unidentified accident losses

Many Jaguars have been lost in accidents and a surprising number have never been accurately identified to a specific aircraft. This list covers the known accidents in descending order by date.

S(I)? Crashed near Hissar 19.10.1983, Flt Lt A K Bugnait ejected safely.
S(I)? Crashed 01.06.1984, Sqn Ldr G Singh ejected safely.
S(I)? Crashed near Jaitsar Village, Jaipur 28.02.1985, Sqn Ldr G Singh ejected safely.
S(I)? Crashed 17.10.1985, Flt Lt J S Walia ejected safely.
S(I)? Crashed 27.05.1986, Flt Lt A C Bharali ejected safely.
S(I)? JS1?? of ASTE, crashed Coonoor near Bangalore 30.08.1987, Wg Cdr Ashok Yadav killed.
S(I)? JS1?? of ASTE, crashed at Barur, Tamil Nadu 06.06.1989, Sqn Ldr Karve and one person on the ground killed.
S(I)? JS1?? of No. 16 Squadron, midair collision with another Jaguar 01.08.1990, pilot ejected safely.
S(I)? JS1?? of No. 16 Squadron, midair collision with another Jaguar 01.08.1990, pilot ejected safely.
S(I)? JS1?? of No. 16 Squadron, crashed Gorakhpur AFS 25.08.1991, Fg Off Rana killed.
B(I)? JT??? (previously incorrectly attributed as JT051) of No. 16 Sqn, crashed on take-off at Gorakhpur AFS due to an unauthorised carboard box on the rear seat jamming the controls 01.06.1994, pilot did not eject but survived.
S(I)? Crashed on take-off Ambala AFS 22.03.1995, pilot ejected safely.
S(I)? JS1?? of No. 14 Sqn dived into ground during low-altitude flight in Rajasthan 17.10.1995, Fg Off R Singh killed.
S(I)? JS1?? of No. 14 Sqn crashed during an exercise in the Punbjab 30.06.1999, Flt Lt Modak ejected safely.
S(I)? JS1?? of No. 16 Sqn crashed on take-off Gorakhpur AFS 20.09.1999, pilot ejected safely.
S(I)? JS1?? crashed near Chiduapur, Gorakhpur district, during a training sortie 07.11.1999, the pilot ejected safely.
S(I)? JS1?? of No. 5 Sqn crashed due to loss of control near Bulahedi 25.10.2001, Flt Lt Romesh Sharma ejected safely.
S(I)? JS1?? of No. 14 Sqn crashed in Anand Vihar Colony, Dilipgarh village, Ambala 05.11.2002, Flt Lt Vipin Rehani ejected safely but six people killed on the ground.
S(I)? JS1?? of No. 5 Sqn crashed Mahajan Firing Range 28.01.2003, Wg Cdr P K Mukhopadhyay killed.
S(I)? JS1?? caught fire on take-off and crashed Ambala AFS 22.07.2003, Flt Lt S Kanvinde rescued from the cockpit.
S(I)? JS1?? of No.6 Sqn crashed Chandhan Firing Range 26.02.2004, Wg Cdr Ravi Khanna ejected but killed as parachute did not open in time.
S(I)? JS1?? of No.5 Sqn midair collision with another Jaguar in cloud 02.04.2004, Lt Mayak Aggarwal ejected safely
S(I)? JS1?? of No.5 Sqn midair collision with another Jaguar in cloud 02.04.2004, Flt Lt Gagan Oberoi killed.
S(I)? JS1?? crashed due to double engine failure during attempted emergency landing Gwalior AFS 07.10.2005, Sqn Ldr Vishal Gupta ejected safely.
S(I)? JS1?? destroyed by premature detonation of weaponry over Pokhran Firing Range 18.01.2007, Flt Lt Ronald Kevin Serrao killed.
S(I)? JS1?? crashed on take-off Jamnagar AFS 26.10.2007, Sqn Ldr Sangwan ejected safely.
S(I)? JS19? crashed near Dilahi Firozpur village, Uttar Pradesh 04.08.2011, pilot and one person on the ground killed.
S(I)? Crashed near Sikkim 30.11.2012, pilot ejected safely.
S(I)? Crashed near Bibber village, Gujarat, due to technical failure 01.08.2014, pilot ejected safely.
S(I)? Crashed near Bibber village, Gujarat 01.10.2014, pilot ejected safely.
S(I)? Crashed near Ambala AFS due to technical failure 05.03.2015, pilot ejected safely.
S(I)? Aircraft of No. 7 Wing caught fire during taxying Ambala AFS 13.09.2016, aircraft destroyed.
B(I)? Crashed near Pokhran due to technical failure 03.10.2016, both pilots ejected safely.
S(I)? Crashed near Mundra, Gujrat during a training sortie 04.06.2018, Air Cmdre Sanjay Chauhan killed.
S(I)? Crashed near Kushinagar, Uttar Pradesh 28.01.2019, pilot ejected safely.

APPENDIX SEVEN

Nigerian production

This is a listing of all Jaguars ordered for the Nigerian Air Force, including a concise history of each aircraft. Changes in serial numbers and applications of B-Condition markings for delivery flights are highlighted in bold text.

In these entries the following abbreviations may be found:

ff – first flown
Wfu – withdrawn from use

B(N)01/PS865 NAF700, ff 13.10.1983. Delivery 18.09.1984 as **G-27-387**; wfu 1991; extant at Makurdi 2014.

B(N)02/PS866 NAF701, ff 02.11.1983. Delivery 25.09.1984 as **G-27-388**; crashed 22.03.1989, pilot killed.

B(N)03/PS867 NAF702, ff 22.11.1983. Delivery 30.10.1984 as **G-27-389**; ran out of fuel and belly landed near Kaduna 26.01.1985, wfu; extant at Makurdi 2014.

B(N)04/PS868 NAF703, ff 01.01.1984. Delivery 20.08.1984 as **G-27-390**; wfu 1991; extant at Makurdi 2014.

B(N)05/PS869 NAF704, ff 18.01.1984. Delivery 11.12.1984 as **G-27-391**; wfu 1991.

S(N)01/PS1071 NAF705, ff 21.12.1984. Delivery 20.08.1984 as **G-27-392**; wfu 1991; extant at Makurdi 2014.

S(N)02/PS1072 NAF706, ff 10.01.1984. Delivery 28.08.1984 as **G-27-393**; wfu 1991.

S(N)03/PS1073 NAF707, ff 03.02.1984. Delivery 28.08.1984 as **G-27-394**; wfu 1991.

S(N)04/PS1074 NAF708, ff 28.03.1984. Delivery 18.09.1984 as **G-27-395**; wfu 1991; extant at Makurdi 2014.

S(N)05/PS1075 NAF709, ff 11.05.1984. Delivery 25.09.1984 as **G-27-396**; wfu 1991; extant at Makurdi 2014.

S(N)06/PS1076 NAF710, ff 18.06.1984. Displayed at SBAC Show Farnborough 09.1984; delivery 18.09.1984 as **G-27-397**; wfu 1991; extant at Makurdi 2014.

S(N)07/PS1077 NAF711, ff 18.07.1984. Delivery 11.12.1984 as **G-27-398**; wfu 1991; extant at Makurdi 2014.

S(N)08/PS1078 NAF712, ff 07.08.1984. Delivery 10.04.1985 as **G-27-399**; wfu 1991; extant at Makurdi 2014.

S(N)09/PS1079 NAF713, ff 07.08.1984. Delivery 10.04.1985 as **G-27-400**; wfu 1991.

S(N)10/PS1080 NAF714, ff 14.12.1984. Delivery 04.06.1985 as **G-27-401**; crashed 07.1985, Lieutenant Shaman Musa killed.

S(N)11/PS1081 NAF715, ff 12.03.1985. Delivery 04.06.1985 as **G-27-402**; wfu 1991.

S(N)12/PS1082 NAF716, ff 11.03.1985. Delivery 25.06.1985 as **G-27-403**; wfu 1991; extant at Makurdi 2014.

S(N)13/PS1083 NAF717, ff 01.05.1985. Delivery 25.06.1985 as **G-27-400**; wfu 1991; extant at Makurdi 2014.

Second Jaguar S prototype S07 XW563 on an armament carriage test flight with paired Matra SNEB rocket pods outboard.
Terry Panopalis Collection

Glossary

AAA – Anti-aircraft artillery
A&AEE – Aeroplane and Armament Experimental Establishment
AAM – Air-to-air missile
ABCCC – Airborne Command and Control Centre
ACAS(OR) – Assistant Chief of the Air Staff (Operational Requirements)
ACMI – Air Combat Manoeuvring Instrumentation
ACT – Active Control Technology
AdlA – Armeé de l'Air
ADEN – Armament Development Enfield
AE – Aircraft establishment (unit strength)
AESA – Active Electronically Scanned Array
AEW – Airborne early warning
AFB – Air Force Base (USAF)
AFS – Air Force Station (Indian AF)
AFVG – Anglo-French Variable Geometry Aircraft
AoA – Angle of attack
APC – Annual Practice Camp
ARI – Airborne Radio Installation
ARTF – Alkali Removable Temporary Finish
ASM – Air-to-surface missile
ASR – Air Staff Requirement
AST – Air Staff Target
ATAF – Allied Tactical Air Force
ATLIS – Automatic Tracking Laser Illumination System
ATREL – Air Transportable Reconnaissance Exploitation Laboratory
AUW – All-up weight
AWACS – Airborne Warning and Control System

BA – Base Aérienne (Air Base)
BAC – British Aircraft Corporation
BAe – British Aerospace
BAI – Battlefield Air Interdiction
BDA – Bomb Damage Assessment

CAP – Combat air patrol
CAS – Chief of the Air Staff
CAS – Close air support
CBLS – Carrier Bomb Light Series
CEAM – Centre d'Expériences Aériennes Militaires (Centre for Military Aerial Experimentation)
CEV – Centre d'Essais en Vol (Flight Test Centre)
CFB – Canadian Forces Base
CFS – Central Flying School
COAC – Combined Air Operations Centre
COIN – Counter-insurgency
CSAR – Combat Search and Rescue
CTTO – Central Trials and Tactics Organisation

DARA – Defence Aviation Repair Agency
DARIN – Display Attack Ranging Inertial Navigation
DCAS – Deputy Chief of the Air Staff
DEFA – Direction des Études et Fabrications d'Armement (Directorate of Armament Studies and Manufacturing)
DJRP – Digital Joint Reconnaissance Pod
DMA – Ministerial Delegation for Armament
DOAE – Defence Operational Analysis Establishment
DTCA – Direction Technique des Constructions Aéronautique (Technical Directorate of Aeronautical Construction)

EASAMS – Elliott Automation Space and Advanced Military Systems Limited
ECAP – Ecole/Appui
ECAT – Ecole de Combat et Appui Tactique
ECM – Electronic countermeasures
EPNER – Ecole du Personnel Navigant d'Essais et de Réception (Test and Reception Flight Personnel School)
ETPS – Empire Test Pilots' School

FAC – Forward air controller
FAE – Fuerza Aérea Ecuatoriana
FBW – Fly-by-wire
FCO – Foreign and Commonwealth Office
FEBA – Forward Edge of the Battle Area
FLIR – Forward-looking infrared
FPB – Fast Patrol Boat

GPS – Global positioning system

HAL – Hindustan Aeronautics Limited
HAS – Hardened aircraft shelter
HDD – Head-down display
HMS – His/Her Majesty's Ship
HMSS – Helmet-mounted sight system
HOTAS – Hands on throttle and stick
HUD – Head-up display

IAF – Indian Air Force
IAM – Institute of Aviation Medicine
ILS – Instrument landing system
INS – Inertial navigation system
IRCM – Infrared countermeasures

JCT – Jaguar Conversion Team

KTO – Kuwaiti Theatre of Operations

LGB – Laser-guided bomb
LLTV – Low-light television
LOROP – Long-range oblique photography
LRMTS – Laser Ranger and Marked Target Seeker

MANPADs – Man-portable air defence systems
MAREL – Mobile Air Reconnaissance Exploitation Laboratory
MoA – Ministry of Aviation (UK)
MoD – Ministry of Defence (UK)
MoD(PE) – Ministry of Defence (Procurement Executive)
MoU – Memorandum of understanding
MRCA – Multi-Role Combat Aircraft
MRL – Multiple rocket launcher

NASR – Naval Air Staff Requirement
NATO – North Atlantic Treaty Organisation
NAVWASS – Navigation/Weapon Aiming Sub-System
NBC – Nuclear Biological Chemical

OC – Officer Commanding
OCU – Operational Conversion Unit
ONERA – Office Nationale d'Etude et de Recherches Aéronautiques (National Agency for Aerospace Studies and Research)

PTR – Part throttle reheat

QFI – Qualified Flying Instructor
QRA – Quick reaction alert
QWI – Qualified Weapons Instructor

RAE – Royal Aircraft Establishment
RAF – Royal Air Force
RAFG – Royal Air Force Germany
RAFO – Royal Air Force of Oman
RAM – Radar-absorbent material
RCS – Radar cross section
RIC – Reconnaissance Information Centre
RRE – Radar Research Establishment
RRTM – Rolls-Royce Turbomeca Limited
RWR – Radar warning receiver

SACEUR – Supreme Allied Commander Europe
SAM – Surface-to-air missile
SAP – Simulated Attack Profile
SBAC – Society of British Aircraft Constructors
SEAD – Suppression of Enemy Air Defences
SEPECAT – Société Européenne de Production de l'Avion Ecole de Combat et Appui Tactique
STAé – Service Technique de l'Aéronautique (Technical Department of Aeronautics)
STF – Special Trial Fit

TACAN – Tactical Air Navigation
TACEVAL – Tactical Evaluation
TGT – Turbine Gas Temperature
TIALD – Thermal Imaging Airborne Laser Designator
TWU – Tactical Weapons Unit

UE – Unit Establishment
UN – United Nations
UOR – Urgent Operational Requirement
USA – United States of America
USAF – United States Air Force

VCAS – Vice Chief of the Air Staff
VG – Variable geometry (wings)
V/STOL – Vertical/short take-off and landing

WSAM – Weapons System Accuracy Measurement

Two-seat Jaguar E9 of EC 1/7 'Provence', SPA 77 'Croix de Jerusalem' awaits its next training sortie at Base Aérienne 113 Saint-Dizier-Robinson. ***Author's Collection***

Bibliography and sources

During the research for this book a great deal of primary source material was consulted, including documents held by the National Archives at Kew and individuals as noted in the acknowledgments. There is not space here to list every file but the following File Divisions were consulted at Kew:

AIR 2, 8, 10, 20, 29, 41, 58, 64 and 77
AVIA 6, 18, 65 and 69
DEFE 5, 24, 56, 58, 71, 72
DSIR 23
FCO 8, 25, 37, 46

Good secondary sources are important starting points for further research and for cross-checking other sources. Listed here are the most important ones that were consulted:

Askley, Glenn, *Sepecat Jaguar in Action*, Squadron/Signal Publications, No. 179

Burt, Danny, *Desert Cats: The RAF's Jaguar Force in the First Gulf War*, Air World, 2023

Buttler, Tony, *British Secret Projects, Vol.1: Jet Fighters since 1950*, Midland Publishing, 2000

Buttler, Tony, *British Secret Projects, Vol.2: Jet Bombers since 1949*, Midland Publishing, 2000

Carbonel, Jean-Christophe, *French Secret Projects, Vol.2: Cold War Bombers, Patrol and Assault Aircraft*, Crécy Publishing, 2017

Chesneau, Roger and Rimell, Ray, *Aeroguide No. 2: Jaguar*, Linewrights Ltd, 1983

Craig, Malcolm M, *'I think we cannot refuse the order': Britain, America, nuclear non-proliferation, and the Indian Jaguar deal, 1974–1978*, in *Cold War History*, Vol. 16, No. 1, 2016

Flintham, Vic, *Aircraft in British Military Service*, Airlife Publishing, 1998

Gardner, Charles, *British Aircraft Corporation: A History*, Anchor Press, 1981

Gibson, Chris, *Typhoon to Typhoon: RAF Air Support Projects and Weapons Since 1945*, Hikoki Publications/Crécy Publishing, 2019

Gunston, Bill, *Attack Aircraft of the West*, Ian Allan, 1974

Longworth, James H, *Test Flying in Lancashire from Samlesbury and Warton Aerodromes, Vols 1, 2 & 3: From the 1960s into the 1980s*, BAE Systems Heritage, 2012–2014

Michell, Simon (Ed.), *Jane's Civil and Military Aircraft Upgrades 1993–94 (1st Ed.)*, Jane's Information Group, 1992

Petit, Martin H et al, *British Military Aircraft Serials and Markings*, British Aviation Research Group, 1980

Royal Air Force Historical Society, *The Jaguar in RAF Service*, 2023

Revell, Doug, *Under B-Conditions: British Manufacturers' Trials Aircraft Since 1929*, Air-Britain, 2020

Ritchie, Dr Nick and Walker, Dr John, *Irreversibility and Nuclear Disarmament: The Case of Denuclearising the Royal Air Force*, University of York IND Research Report No. 3, 2023

Sturtivant, Ray and Hamlin, John, *Flying Training and Support Units since 1912*, Air-Britain, 2007

Taylor, Michael (Ed.), *Brassey's World Aircraft & Systems Directory 1996/97 (1st Ed.)*, Brassey's Publishing, 1996

Various issues of the following journals, periodicals and magazines were also consulted:

Aeroplane Monthly
Air-Britain publications *Aeromilitaria*, *Air Digest* and *Aviation World*
Air Historical Branch (RAF) Narratives
Air International
Aviation Historian
Flight/ Flight International
Jane's International Defence Review
Royal Air Force Historical Society Journal
Le Trait D'Union

A pair of No.54(F) Squadron Jaguar GR.3As taxi to the runway at RAF Coltishall to begin another sortie. The L-shaped outline of the retractable refuelling probe can be seen on the side of the nose. *MoD/Open Government Licence 2003*

Jaguar A11 of EC 3/3 'Ardennes' sits at readiness on the apron at Base Aérienne133 Nancy-Ochey in July 1986. The ground power trolley is a reminder that the Jaguar lacked an internal auxiliary power unit with which to start its Adours. *Terry Panopalis Collection*

Index

Avionics

Companies

Engines and motors

General

Organisations

People

Places

Requirements

Ships

Units

Weapons

Train to fight. This No.54(F) Squadron Jaguar GR.3A is equipped with CBLS pods outboard, holding a pair of 28lb (12.7kg) training bombs. *MoD/Open Government Licence 2003*